Handbook of Rational—Emotive Therapy
Volume 2

Albert Ellis, Ph.D., the founder of rational-emotive therapy (RET) and cognitive behavior therapy (CBT), is Executive Director of the Institute for Rational–Emotive Therapy in New York City. He is the author of more than 500 articles and 49 books, including *Reason and Emotion in Psychotherapy, A New Guide to Rational Living, A Guide to Personal Happiness,* and *Overcoming Resistance: Helping Difficult Clients with Rational–Emotive Therapy.*

Russell M. Grieger, Ph.D., holds appointments at the University of Virginia as both Adjunct Associate Professor in the Institute of Clinical Psychology and Clinical Associate Professor of Behavioral Medicine and Psychiatry in the Department of Psychiatry. In addition, he is a clinical psychologist in private practice, a Fellow of the Institute for Rational–Emotive Therapy in New York, Executive Director of the Mid–Atlantic Institute for Rational–Emotive Therapy in Charlottesville, Virginia, a member of RET's International Standards and Training Committee, and co-editor of the *Journal of Rational–Emotive Therapy.* Active as a teacher, lecturer, and workshop leader, Dr. Grieger has published three texts and many articles on RET.

Handbook of Rational-Emotive Therapy
Volume 2

Albert Ellis and Russell M. Grieger
with contributors

Springer Publishing Company/New York

Springer Publishing Company, Inc.
536 Broadway
New York, NY 10012

86 87 88 89 90 / 5 4 3 2 1

Library of Congress Cataloging-in-Publication Data
(Revised for vol. 2)

Handbook of rational-emotive therapy.

   Includes bibliographies.
   1.   Rational-emotive psychotherapy—Collective works.
2.   Psychotherapy—Handbooks.   I.   Ellis, Albert.
II.   Grieger, Russell.   [DNLM: WM420 H2324]
RC489.R3H36   616.8'914   77-21410
ISBN 0-8261-2200-0 (v. 1)
ISBN 0-8261-2201-9 (v. 1 : pbk.)
ISBN 0-8261-2202-7 (v. 2)
ISBN 0-8261-2203-5 (v. 2 : soft)

Printed in the United States of America

Contents

Part Two

The Dynamics of Emotional Disturbance

Part Three

Primary Techniques and Basic Processes

Appendixes

A

B

C

Contributors

BARRY A. BASS, PH.D.
Associate Professor of Psychology
Towson State University
Towson, Maryland

IRVING BEIMAN, PH.D.
Department of Psychology
University of Georgia
Athens, Georgia

MICHAEL E. BERNARD, PH.D.
Senior Lecturer
Department of Education
University of Melbourne
Parkville, Victoria
Australia

JOHN BOYD, PH.D.
Clinical Psychologist in Private
Practice
Charlottesville, Virginia

WINDY DRYDEN, PH.D.
Department of Psychology
Goldsmiths' College
University of London
London, England

ALBERT ELLIS, PH.D.
Executive Director
Institute for Rational–Emotive
Therapy
New York, New York

WILLIAM L. GOLDEN, PH.D.
Psychologist in Private Practice
New York, New York

RUSSELL M. GRIEGER, PH.D.
Clinical Psychologist in Private
Practice
and Executive Director
Mid–Atlantic Institute for
Rational–Emotive Therapy
Charlottesville, Virginia

THOMAS H. HARRELL, PH.D.
School of Psychology
Florida Institute of Technology
Gainesville, Florida

MARIE R. JOYCE, M.ED.
Consultant Psychologist
Penleigh and Essendon Grammar
School
Parkville, Victoria
Australia

KAREN LAPOINTE, PH.D.
Department of Psychology
University of Georgia
Athens, Georgia

TERRANCE E. MCGOVERN, M.A.
Counseling Psychologist
Chicago Institute for Rational Living
Chicago, Illinois

ix

THOMAS J. NARDI, PH.D.
Clinical Psychologist in Private
Practice
New York, New York

MANUEL SILVERMAN, PH.D.
Associate Professor of Guidance and
Counseling
Loyola University
Chicago, Illinois

SUSAN WALEN, PH.D.
Associate Professor of Psychology
Towson State University
Towson, Maryland

RICHARD L. WESSLER, PH.D.
Professor of Psychology
Pace University
Pleasantville, New York
and Clinical Psychologist
Multimodal Therapy Institute
New York, New York

JANET WOLFE, PH.D.
Associate Executive Director
and Director of Clinical Services
Institute for Rational–Emotive
Therapy
New York, New York

NINA WOULFF, PH.D.
Director, Dartmouth Branch
Atlantic Child Guidance Center
and Instructor, Division of Family
Medicine and Department of
Psychiatry
Dalhousie University
Halifax, Nova Scotia

Preface

We frankly expected Volume One of our *Handbook of Rational–Emotive Therapy* to be a success when it was published in 1977, but we were delighted when it soon became even more popular than we had hoped. It now has gone through several reprintings, continues to sell well every year, and is one of the most quoted books in the field of psychotherapy.

Meanwhile, partly aided by the popularity of Volume One, RET has become even more widely known among professionals and the public. In its general or nonspecialized form it is now known by many names, including cognitive behavior therapy (CBT), cognitive therapy, social learning therapy, rational behavior therapy, self-instructional training, cognitive restructuring, semantic therapy, and multimodal therapy. Under these names and under the name of RET, general or nonspecialized rational–emotive therapy is easily one of the most popular of all modern psychotherapies. Specialized or elegant RET, which overlaps with but is also significantly different from the other cognitive behavior therapies, is also quite popular and is practiced by thousands of therapists all over the world.

Indeed, generalized RET has become so popular in recent years that it has been increasingly incorporated into the practice of a wide variety of therapists, including many who officially call themselves psychoanalysts, Gestalt therapists, systems therapists, hypnotherapists, eclectic therapists, and stress-management trainers. If this present trend continues, we can predict that by the end of this century some of the main aspects of RET, and especially its pioneering emphasis on the disputing of irrational beliefs and the teaching of rational coping statements, will be routinely employed by the vast majority of professional counselors and therapists.

The last decade has seen the publication of dozens of books on RET and CBT. Some of the most notable of those specifically concerned with RET have been James A. Bard, *Rational Emotive Therapy in Practice;* Michael E. Bernard and Marie R. Joyce, *Rational–Emotive Therapy with Children and Adolescents;* Albert Ellis and Michael E. Bernard, *Rational–Emotive Approaches to the Problems of Childhood;* Albert Ellis and Michael E. Bernard, *Clinical Applications of Rational–Emotive Therapy;* Albert Ellis, *Overcoming Resistance;* Albert Ellis and John M. Whiteley, *Theoretical and Empirical Foundations of Rational–Emotive Therapy;* Russell Grieger and John Boyd, *Rational–Emotive Therapy: A Skills Based Approach;* Russell Grieger and Ingrid Z. Grieger, *Cognition and Emotional Disturbance;* Ruth Wessler and Richard Wessler, *The Principles and Practice of Rational–Emotive Therapy;* and Susan R. Walen, Ramond

DiGiuseppe, and Richard L. Wessler, *A Practitioner's Guide to Rational–Emotive Therapy*.

The clinical and research literature on rational–emotive therapy (RET) and on cognitive behavior therapy (CBT) is now immense, with new articles and studies appearing at the rate of hundreds every year. Several professional journals are wholly devoted to papers on RET and CBT, including *Cognitive Therapy and Research, Cognitive Behaviorist,* the *British Journal of Cognitive Therapy,* and the *Journal of Rational–Emotive Therapy.* Many other journals also continually publish relevant papers and studies on RET and CBT, including *Behavior Therapy, Behavior Therapy and Research,* the *Journal of Consulting and Clinical Psychology,* the *Journal of Clinical Psychology,* and *Psychological Reports.*

As noted in Volume One, research in RET and CBT was already extensive in 1977. Since that time it has become even more widespread, and literally scores of new studies have appeared, some of which are reviewed in the chapter by McGovern and Silverman in this volume. The vast majority of the studies of RET and CBT published during the last decade have once again shown that when these therapies are used with anxious, depressed, hostile, or otherwise emotionally disturbed individuals, and when control groups are treated with other types of therapy or put on a waiting list, the subjects using RET and CBT make more significant improvement than those in the control group.

As a result of these research studies, as well as the success that many clinicians have had with RET and CBT, psychologists, counselors, psychiatrists, and other mental health professionals have increasingly acknowledged their effectiveness. For example, Darrell Smith (1982) studied 800 clinical and counseling psychologists who were members of the American Psychological Association and found that more of his respondents (15%) favored RET and other modes of cognitive behavior therapy than favored psychoanalysis or any other kind of treatment method. He also found that the three most influential psychotherapists were Carl Rogers, Albert Ellis, and Sigmund Freud and that "cognitive behavioral and/or rational therapy was the predominant representation among the 10 most influential therapists (Ellis, Lazarus, Beck, Meichenbaum). These findings suggest quite clearly that cognitive behavior therapy is one of the major trends in counseling and psychotherapy" (Smith, 1982, p. 807).

Heesacker, Heppner, and Rogers (1982) made a frequency analysis of approximately 14,000 references cited in three major counseling psychology journals for the past two years and found that, of those works published after 1957, Ellis was easily the most frequently cited contributor, with other cognitive behaviorists (Meichenbaum, Bandura, Mahoney, and Thoresen) also being in the top 10 contributors. Sprenkle, Keeney, and Sutton (1982) surveyed 600 therapists who were clinical members of the American Association of Marital and Family Therapists and found that the theorists who influenced them the most were, in descending order, Virginia Satir, Sigmund Freud, Carl Rogers, and Albert Ellis. These three surveys show the great influence of RET and CBT on American therapists in recent years.

Finally, innumerable self-help books and popular articles have been published during the last decade that have incorporated major RET techniques, especially the active discovery, analysis, and disputing of important irrational beliefs. Some of these self-help publications have been immensely popular. Best-selling books that largely consist of RET-oriented theory and practice include R. E. Alberti and M. L. Emmons, *Your Perfect Right;* David Burns, *Feeling Good;* Wayne Dyer, *Your Erroneous Zones;* Albert Ellis, *How to Live with a Neurotic;* Albert Ellis and Robert A. Harper, *A New Guide to Rational Living;* Albert Ellis and William Knaus, *Overcoming Procrastination;* Stephen Johnson, *First Person Singular;* Paul Hauck, *Overcoming Depression;* Patricia Jakubowski and Arthur Lange; *The Assertive Option;* Maxie C. Maultsby, Jr., *Help Yourself to Happiness;* Arnold A. Lazarus and Allen Fay, *I Can If I Want To;* and John Powell, *Fully Human, Fully Alive.*

Because of the new developments in RET and CBT, and because of their growing popularity among professionals and among members of the public, we think it most suitable to update the theory and practice of RET by adding this second volume of the *Handbook of Rational–Emotive Therapy.* The present volume includes a good many of the important papers and chapters on RET that have appeared since 1977. While we have had to be selective in what we have included because of space limitations, we nevertheless think that readers of this volume will readily see that RET and CBT are still notably advancing in theory, in techniques, in research studies, and in influence. We also hope that those who peruse Volume Two will have ample opportunity to keep up with this fascinating, scientific, and highly important area of modern psychotherapy.

ALBERT ELLIS, PH.D.
Institute for Rational–Emotive Therapy
45 East 65th Street
New York, New York 10021

RUSSELL M. GRIEGER, PH.D.
University of Virginia
and Private Practice
2120 Ivy Road, Suite B
Charlottesville, Virginia 22903

References

Heesacker, M., Heppner, P. P., & Rogers, M. E. (1982). Classics and emerging classics in counseling psychology. *Journal of Counseling Psychology, 29,* 400–405.

Smith, D. (1982). Trends in counseling and psychotherapy. *American Psychologist, 37,* 802–809.

Sprenkle, D. H., Keeney, B. P., & Sutton, P. M. (1982). Theorists who influence clinical members of AAMFT: A research note. *Journal of Marital and Family Therapy, 8,* 367–369.

Part One

Theoretical and Conceptual Foundations of Rational–Emotive Therapy

1

What Is Rational–Emotive Therapy (RET)?*

Albert Ellis and Michael E. Bernard

We shall try to outline, in this introductory chapter, an up-to-date version of the origins and history of RET, including its values and goals, its theory of personality and personality change, and its main differences with other theories and practices of cognitive behavior therapy (CBT), as the therapies of Albert Bandura (1977), Aaron Beck (1976), William Glasser (1965), Marvin Goldfried and Gerald Davision (1976), Harold Greenwald (1973), George Kelly (1955), Arnold Lazarus (1971, 1981), Richard Lazarus (1966), Michael Mahoney (1977), Maxie C. Maultsby, Jr. (1975, 1983), Donald Meichenbaum (1977), and Victor Raimy (1975). RET constantly changes and develops (as many chapters in this book will show). Here, in an introductory overview, is what it is like almost 30 years after Albert Ellis (1957a, 1957b, 1958, 1962, 1975a) first started to practice it in 1955.

ORIGINS AND HISTORY

The earliest beginnings of rational–emotive therapy (RET) can be traced to Albert Ellis' personal life as a child and adolescent in the 1920s and 1930s, when he began coping with severe physical problems (acute nephritis) and personality problems (shyness in general and fear of public speaking and of encountering females in particular). Although he had no intention of being a psychologist or

*This chapter originally appeared in A. Ellis and M. E. Bernard (Eds.), *Clinical applications of rational–emotive therapy* (New York: Plenum, 1985).

3

psychotherapist at this time, Ellis became vitally interested in the philosophy of happiness and read hundreds of books and articles on philosophy, psychology, and many related fields, particularly the writings of Epictetus, Marcus Aurelius, Ralph Waldo Emerson, Emile Coué, John Dewey, Sigmund Freud, Bertrand Russell, and John B. Watson. Ellis began to work determinedly on himself to overcome what he conceived of as his needless emotional problems. Especially from the age of 19 onward (in 1932), he adopted a cognitive-philosophic approach combined with *in vivo* desensitization and active-directive homework assignments. Eventually he completely overcame his public speaking and social anxiety difficulties (Ellis, 1972c).

In 1939, Ellis started to do research on sex, love, marriage, and family problems, mainly because he was interested in writing in those areas. As a side-effect, he discovered that he could effectively counsel his friends and relatives who were anxious and depressed in those areas. He subsequently received his M.A. in clinical psychology from Columbia University in 1943 and his Ph.D. in 1947, and he began to practice formal psychotherapy and sex and marital therapy in 1943. Although he had some doubts about the unscientific manner in which psychoanalysis was usually practiced, he still believed that it was a deeper form of therapy and therefore started his personal analysis and training analysis in 1947, with a training analyst from the Karen Horney Institute. He practiced classical analysis and psychoanalytically oriented therapy until 1953, when he became increasingly disillusioned with its theory and its efficacy and began to call himself a "psychotherapist" rather than a "psychoanalyst." Up to this time, he had tried in vain to reformulate psychoanalysis in scientific terms (Ellis, 1949a, 1949b, 1950, 1956b), but he then abandoned it, concluding that it often does more harm than good (Ellis, 1962, 1968; Ellis & Harper, 1961a).

At first, rational–emotive therapy was called "rational therapy" (RT) because Ellis emphasized its cognitive and philosophic aspects and wanted to differentiate it clearly from the other therapies of the 1950s (Ellis, 1957b, 1958, 1975a). Many people, however, identified RT with eighteenth-century rationalism, to which it actually was opposed. It always had very strong evocative-emotive and behavioral components and from the start favored activity homework assignments, *in vivo* desensitization, and skills training (Ellis, 1956a, 1962). It was also highly confrontive, quite unlike classical analysis and Rogerian client-centered therapy. So Ellis, in collaboration with his first associate in this new mode of treatment, Dr. Robert A. Harper, decided in the early 1960s to change its name to rational–emotive therapy (RET).

From the beginning, RET was highly philosophical and disputational, because Ellis at the age of 16 took as his main interest and hobby the pursuit of philosophy and held that if people acquired a sane philosophy of life they would rarely be "emotionally disturbed." RET was influenced by the writings of many philosophers, especially Epictetus, Marcus Aurelius, Baruch Sprinoza, John

Dewey, Bertrand Russell, A. J. Ayer, Hans Reichenbach, and Karl Popper. Psychologically, it incorporated some of the views of important cognitive therapists, such as Adler (1927, 1929), Coué (1923), Dubois (1907), Frankl (1959), Herzberg (1945), Horney (1939), Johnson (1946), Kelly (1955), Low (1952), and Rotter (1954), although Ellis did not read some of these cognitivists (such as Dubois, Frankl, Kelly and Low) until after he had already originated the basic theory and practice of RET.

 RET was the first major school of psychotherapy to wed philosophical disputation and cognitive restructuring to both behavior therapy and experiential therapy. At first it employed a few basic behavioral methods, such as assigning activity homework, encouraging *in vivo* desensitization, using reinforcement methods, and doing skills training (Ellis, 1956a, 1962; Ellis & Harper, 1961a, 1961b). Later on, as the behavior therapy movement developed, RET adopted (at least at certain times) almost the whole range of behavioral techniques and became the pioneering form of cognitive behavior therapy (CBT). Bandura (1969), Beck (1967), and R. Lazarus (1966) seem to have developed their own forms of cognitive behavior therapy independently of RET, but they did so about a decade after Ellis originated RET in 1955 and gave his first paper on it at the American Psychological Association annual convention in Chicago in 1956 (Ellis, 1965b). Other pioneers in cognitive behavior modification—such as Glasser (1965), Goldfried & Davison (1976), Greenwald (1973), A. Lazarus (1971, 1981), Mahoney (1977), Masters & Rimm (1974), Maultsby (1975, 1983), Meichenbaum (1977), Raimy (1975), and—seem to have been largely influenced by Ellis. Their first experiments tended to validate the hypotheses of cognitive therapy by using RET-type cognitive restructuring. Hans Eysenck (1964) included RET as a form of behavior therapy in one of his early influential books; and other authorities on behavior therapy, such as Cyril Franks, Alan Kazdin, Leonard Krasner, and G. Terence Wilson, have generally acknowledged RET as the pioneering form of cognitive behavior therapy (CBT).

 RET also was unique in being highly experiential (and experimental) from the start and became even more so when, in the early 1960s, some of the encounter methods originated by Perls (1969), Schutz (1967), and others were incorporated. Since that time, experiential exercises particular to RET have been invented, such as its famous shame-attacking exercise (Ellis, 1969, 1971b; Ellis & Abrahms, 1978). Just as RET has adopted certain experiential methods, so also has the experiential movement been influenced by RET and adopted some of its basic cognitive behavioral orientation (S. Emery, 1978; Erhard, 1976; Goulding & Goulding, 1979).

 For a good many years, Ellis was remarkably alone in writing major treatises on RET, but in recent years a good number of other authors have published clinical texts applying RET to various kinds of emotional problems. These RET texts have included books by Bard (1980), Bernard and Joyce (1983), Church (1975), Diekstra and Dassen (1976), Ellis and Abrahms (1978), Ellis and

Bernard (1983), Ellis and Grieger (1977), Grieger and Boyd (1980), Grieger and Grieger (1982), Hauck (1972, 1980), Lange and Jakubowski (1976), Lembo (1976), Maultsby (1983), Morris and Kanitz (1975), D. Schwartz (1981), Tosi (1974), Walen, DiGiuseppe, and Wessler (1980), Wessler and Wessler (1980), and Wolfe and Brand (1977).

RET has always specialized in self-help procedures, and Ellis pioneered in this respect by publishing a good many popular books on rational–emotive procedures that have been designed for self-actualization purposes. These books have included *How to Live with a "Neurotic"* (Ellis, 1975a), *Sex without Guilt* (Ellis, 1965), *The Art and Science of Love* (Ellis, 1965a), *A Guide to Rational Living* (Ellis & Harper, 1961a), *A Guide to Successful Marriage* (Ellis & Harper, 1961b), *Sex and the Liberated Man* (Ellis, 1976c), *Overcoming Procrastination* (Ellis & Knaus, 1977), *The Intelligent Woman's Guide to Dating and Mating* (Ellis, 1979b), and *A Guide to Personal Happiness* (Ellis & Becker, 1982).

In addition to these, many other popular books have been written to help members of the public benefit from RET, including those by Bedford (1980), Blazier (1975), Burns (1980), Butler (1981), G. Emery (1982), Garcia and Blythe (1977), Goodman and Maultsby (1974), Grossack (1974, 1976), Hauck (1973, 1974, 1975, 1976, 1979, 1981, 1983), Jakubowski and Lange (1978), S. Johnson (1977), Knaus (1982), Kranzler (1974), Lazarus and Fay (1975), Lembo (1974, 1977), Little (1977), Losoncy (1980), Maleske (1976), Maultsby (1975, 1978), Maultsby and Hendricks (1974), McMullen and Casey (1975), Miller (1983), Nash (1981), Powell (1976), Silverstein (1977), Thoresen (1975), and Young (1974).

Furthermore, RET has been almost astoundingly successful in that many writers have incorporated its philosophy and practice into their work, even though some have failed to acknowledge doing so. Some writers—including L. S. Barksdale (1972), Wayne Dyer (1977), Haim Ginott (1965), William Glasser (1965), Ken Keyes (1979), and Manuel Smith (1977)—have used RET's approaches in their own immensely successful and influential books.

Finally, several studies appearing in the professional literature have shown the enormous influence of Ellis and RET on today's psychotherapists and counselors. Thus, D. Smith (1982) found that Ellis was second to Carl Rogers and ahead of Sigmund Freud when 800 clinical and counseling psychologists ranked the psychotherapists whom they considered to be most influential in current practice. Smith also noted that "cognitive behavioral and/or rational therapy was the predominant representation among the ten most influential therapists. These findings suggest quite clearly that cognitive behavior therapy is one of the major trends in counseling and psychotherapy" (D. Smith, 1982, p. 807). Heesacker, Heppner, and Rogers (1982) did a frequency analysis of approximately 14,000 references cited in three major counseling psychology journals for the years 1979 and 1981 and found Ellis to be the most frequently cited author of works published after 1957, across three major counseling psychology journals.

Sprenkle, Keeney, and Sutton (1982) questioned 310 members of the American Association of Marital and Family Therapy as to whom they considered the 10 most influential theorists in the field of marriage and family therapy. The top four, in rank order, were Virginia Satir, Sigmund Freud, Carl Rogers, and Albert Ellis.

In view of the profound effect that RET has had on the mental health profession and the public during the last two decades, it seems reasonable to say that it has been, and still is, one of the most influential systems of psychotherapy (and of marriage and family therapy) of the twentieth century.

VALUES AND GOALS OF RET

RET does not pretend to be entirely objective and value free. Quite the contrary, it is a system of psychotherapy designed to help people live longer, minimize their emotional disturbances and self-defeating behaviors, and actualize themselves so that they live a more fulfilling, happier existence. Once these goals are chosen—and RET sees them as matters of choice rather than as absolute givens—then subgoals of the "best" ways for people to think, feel, and behave seem to follow from these main purposes. Whether or not the subgoals really work and actually result in longer and happier lives for most of the people most of the time can be scientifically (that is, logically and empirically) determined. Also, RET holds that the scientific (logical–empirical) method so far appears to be the best, most efficient way of discovering what techniques of psychotherapy are most workable for which people under what conditions, in order for their main goals and subgoals to be achieved (Ellis, 1962, 1971a, 1973, 1984a; Ellis & Grieger, 1977; Ellis & Whiteley, 1979).

The main subgoals of RET consist of helping people to think more rationally (scientifically, clearly, flexibly); to feel more appropriately; and to act more functionally (efficiently, undefeatingly), in order to achieve their goals of living longer and more happily. Consequently, RET defines rationality, appropriate feeling, and functional behavior in terms of these basic goals, and it tries to be as precise as it can be about these definitions.

Rational thoughts (or rational ideas or beliefs) are defined in RET as those thoughts that help people live longer and happier, particularly by (1) setting up or choosing for themselves certain (presumably) happiness-producing values, purposes, goals, or ideals; and (2) using efficient, flexible, scientific, logico-empirical ways of (presumably) achieving these values and goals and of avoiding contradictory or self-defeating results. It is assumed that for most of the people most of the time the employment of scientific thinking will help them choose and implement happiness-producing purposes; but it is also assumed that this is an hypothesis, not a proven fact, and that it may not hold true for some of the people some of the time.

APPROPRIATE NEG.
EMOTIONS:
SORROW/REGRET /
ANNOYANCE /
FRUSTRATION /
DISPLEASURE

Appropriate feelings are defined in RET as those emotions that tend to occur when human desires and preferences are blocked and frustrated and that help people minimize or eliminate such blocks and frustrations. Appropriate negative emotions include sorrow, regret, annoyance, frustration, and displeasure.

APPROPRIATE
POS. EMO
EMOTIONS:
LOVE/
HAPPINESS/
PLEASURE/
CURIOSITY

Appropriate positive emotions include love, happiness, pleasure, and curiosity, which largely tend to increase human longevity and satisfaction. Inappropriate feelings are defined in RET as those emotions—such as feelings of depression, anxiety, despair, inadequacy, and worthlessness—that tend to make obnoxious conditions and frustrations worse, rather than to help overcome them. Positive

DISAPPROPRIATE
NEG. EMOS →
DISAPPROPRIATE
POS. EMOS .

inappropriate feelings—such as grandiosity, hostility, and paranoia—are seen as those that temporarily tend to make people feel good (and often superior to others) but that sooner or later lead to unfortunate results and greater frustrations (such as fights, homicides, wars, and incarceration). One of the main assumptions of RET is that virtually all human preferences, desires, wishes, and longings are appropriate, even when they are not easily fulfillable; but that practically all absolutistic commands, demands, insistences, and musts, as well as the impositions on oneself and others that usually accompany them, are inappropriate and potentially self-sabotaging.

DISAPPROPRIATE
ACTIONS →
ARE SELF —
DEPENDANCY

RET defines inappropriate or self-defeating acts and behaviors as those human actions that seriously and needlessly interfere with life and with happiness. Thus, acts that are rigidly compulsive, addictive, and stereotyped tend to be against the

APPROPRIATE
ACTIONS →
ENHANCE
LIFE

interests of most people and the social groups in which they reside; and acts that are severely withdrawing, phobic, and procrastinating also tend to be self-defeating and socially damaging. Appropriate behaviors, on the other hand, tend to enhance survival and happiness.

RET sees irrational beliefs, inappropriate feelings, and self-defeating behaviors as interactional and transactional. For example, a woman may tell herself, "I must under all conditions do my job well! It's awful if I don't—and that makes me a bad person!" This almost always will lead to her feeling anxious, depressed, and inadequate, and she will most probably act poorly and inefficiently on job interviews and in employment situations. What is more, her inappropriate feelings of, say, depression, will then help her to think more irrationally and behave worse (e.g., not be able to function on a job at all). Her self-defeating behaviors, especially her behaving inefficiently on jobs, will tend to lead her on to more irrational beliefs (e.g., "I'll never be able to function at all on any kind of job!") and will enhance her feelings of anxiety and depression. RET does not see human thoughts, feelings, and behaviors as "pure" or monolithic, but almost always as inextricably merged with each other; and this may be particularly true of disturbed thinking, emoting, and behaving.

RET hypothesizes that if people's main goals are their staying alive, avoiding needless pain, and actualizing themselves, they had usually better strive for several important subgoals that help them in these respects:

Self-interest. Sensible and emotionally healthy people tend to be interested first or primarily in themselves and to put their own interests at least a little above the interests of others. They sacrifice themselves to *some* degree for those for whom they care, but not overweeningly or completely.

Social Interest. Social interest is usually rational and self-helping because most people choose to live and enjoy themselves in a social group or community. If they do not act morally, protect the rights of others, and abet social survival, it is unlikely that they will create the kind of world in which they themselves can live comfortably and happily.

Self-direction. Healthy people tend to assume primary responsibility for their own lives while simultaneously preferring to cooperate with others. They do not *need* or *demand* considerable support or succoring from others.

Tolerance. Rational individuals give both themselves and others the right to be wrong. Even when they intensely dislike their own and others' behavior, they refrain from damning themselves or others, as persons, for that obnoxious behavior.

Flexibility. Healthy and mature individuals tend to be flexible in their thinking, open to change, and unbigoted and pluralistic in their view of other people. They don't make rigid, invariant rules for themselves and others.

Acceptance of Uncertainty. Healthy men and women tend to acknowledge and accept the idea that we seem to live in a world of probability and chance, where absolute certainties do not exist and probably never will. They realize that it is often fascinating and exciting—and definitely not horrible—to live in this kind of probabilistic and uncertain world. They enjoy a good degree of order but don't whiningly demand it.

Commitment. Most people, especially bright and educated ones, tend to be healthier and happier when they are vitally absorbed in something outside themselves and preferably have at least one powerful creative interest, as well as some major human involvement, that they consider so important that they structure a good part of their daily existence around it.

Scientific Thinking. Nondisturbed individuals tend to be more objective, rational, and scientific than more disturbed ones. They are able to feel deeply and act concertedly, but they tend to regulate their emotions and actions by reflecting on them and their consequences and by applying the rules of logic and the scientific method to evaluating these consequences.

Self-acceptance. Healthy people are usually glad to be alive, accept themselves just because they are alive, and have some capacity to enjoy themselves. They refuse to measure their intrinsic worth by their extrinsic achievements or by what others think of them. They frankly *choose* to accept themselves unconditionally, and they try to avoid rating themselves—who or how they are. They attempt to enjoy rather than to prove themselves.

Risk Taking. Emotionally healthy people tend to take a fair amount of risk and to try to do what they want to do, even when there is a good chance that they may fail. They tend to be adventurous but not foolhardy.

Long-range Hedonism. People who are not emotionally disturbed tend to seek both the pleasures of the moment *and* those of the future, and they do not often court future pain for present gain. They are hedonistic—that is, happiness-seeking and pain-avoiding—but they assume that they will probably live for quite a few years and that they had therefore better think of both today and tomorrow, and not be obsessed with immediate gratification.

Non-utopianism. Healthy people accept the fact that utopias are probably unachievable and that they are not likely to get everything they want and to avoid all pain. They refuse to strive unrealistically for total joy or happiness or for total lack of anxiety, depression, self-downing, and hostility.

High Frustration Tolerance. People with minimal emotional disturbance tend to go along with St. Francis and Reinhold Niebuhr by changing obnoxious conditions that they can change, accepting those they cannot, and discerning the difference between the two.

Self-responsibility for Disturbance. Healthy individuals tend to accept a great deal of responsibility for their own upsets, rather than defensively blaming others or social conditions for their thoughts, feelings, and behaviors.

If, as RET hypothesizes (and as several other schools of therapy would also tend to agree) people had better strive for the basic goals of survival, for lack of emotional disturbance and the needless pain that accompanies it, and for maximum self-actualization and happiness, then therapists had better try to devise theories and practices that best serve their clients in achieving the subgoals just listed. RET has formulated several basic theories in this regard, which we shall now discuss.

THE EXPANDED ABC THEORY OF IRRATIONAL THINKING AND DISTURBANCE

RET is best known for its famous ABC theory of irrational thinking and emotional disturbance, which we shall now outline in its most recent expanded form (Ellis, 1984a). This theory of personality and of personality change accepts the importance of emotions and behaviors but particularly emphasizes the role of cognitions in human problems. It has a long philosophic history, as it was partially stressed by some of the ancient Asian thinkers, such as Confucius and Gautama Buddha; and it was especially noted, in startlingly clear form, by the ancient Stoic philosophers such as Zeno of Citium, Chrysippus, Panaetius of Rhodes, Cicero, Seneca, Epictetus, and Marcus Aurelius (Epictetus, 1899; Hadas, 1962; Marcus Aurelius, 1900). The ABC theory's most famous dictum was stated by Epictetus: "People are disturbed not by things, but by the views which they take of them." This was later beautifully paraphrased by Shakespeare, in *Hamlet:* "There's nothing either good or bad but thinking makes it so."

In the RET version of the ABC's of emotional disturbance, A stands for activating events that serve as a prelude to C, the cognitive, emotional and behavioral consequences of A (often known as neurotic symptoms). According to RET, people begin by trying to fulfill their goals (G's) in some kind of environment, and they encounter a set of activating events (A's) that tend to help them achieve or block these goals. The A's they encounter are usually current events or their own thoughts, feelings, or behaviors relating to these events; but A's also may consist of conscious or unconscious memories or thoughts about past experiences. When disturbed, people are prone to seeking out and responding ineffectually to these A's. They thus block the fulfillment of their goals because of (1) their biological or genetic predispositions, (2) their constitutional history, (3) their prior interpersonal and social learning, and (4) their innately predisposed and acquired habit patterns (Ellis, 1976a, 1979d).

Activating events virtually never exist in a pure or monolithic form but almost always interact with and partly include beliefs (B's) and consequences (C's). *People bring themselves* (their goals, thoughts, desires, and physiological propensities) *to bear on activating events*. To some degree, therefore, they *are* these activating events and their A's (their environments) are part of themselves. They only appear to think, emote, and behave in a material milieu; as Heidigger (1962) notes, they only have their being in the world. They also almost always exist in and relate to a *social* context—they live with and relate to other humans. They never, therefore, seem to be pure individuals but are *world-centered* and *social* creatures.

According to RET theory, people have almost innumerable beliefs (B's)—or cognitions, thoughts, or ideas—about their activating events (A's); and these B's tend to exert important, direct and strong influences on their cognitive, emotional, and behavioral consequences (C's) and on what we often call their "emotion-al" disturbances. Although activating events (A's) often *seem* directly to "cause" or contribute to C's, this is rarely true, because B's normally serve as important mediators between A's and C's and therefore more directly "cause" or "create" C's. This RET theory of human action and of disturbance is firmly held by RET followers (Bard, 1980; Bernard & Joyce, 1983; Ellis, 1957b, 1958, 1962, 1977c; Grieger & Boyd, 1980; Grieger & Grieger, 1982; Lembo, 1974, 1976, 1977; Walen, DiGiuseppe, & Wessler, 1980; Wessler & Wessler, 1980). It also is just as strongly held by virtually all the other main theorists and practitioners of cognitive behavioral therapy (CBT) (Beck, 1976; Goldfried & Davison, 1976; Guidano & Liotti, 1983; Mahoney, 1977; Meichenbaum, 1977; Raimy, 1975). RET holds that people largely *bring* their beliefs to A, so that they view or experience A's in the light of these biased beliefs (expectations, evaluations) and also in the light of their emotional consequences (C's) (desires, preferences, wishes, motivations, tastes, disturbances). Therefore, humans virtually never experience A's without B's and C's; but they also rarely experience B's and C's without A's.

People's B's take many different forms because they have many kinds of cognitions. In RET, however, we are mainly interested in their rational Beliefs (rB's), which we hypothesize lead to their self-helping behaviors, and in their irrational beliefs (iB's), which we theorize lead to their self-defeating (and society-defeating) behaviors. Some of the main kinds of B's are as follows:

1. Nonevaluative observations, descriptions, and perceptions (cold cogni-tions). Example: "I notice that people are laughing."

2. Positive preferential evaluations, inferences, and attributions (warm cogni-tions). Examples: "Because I prefer people to like me and they are laughing, (a) I see they are laughing with me, (b) I see they think I am funny, (c) I see that they like me, (d) I like their laughing with me, or (e) Their liking me has real advantages, which I love.

3. Negative preferential evaluations, inferences, and attributions (warm cognitions). Examples: "Because I prefer people to like me and not dislike me and they are laughing, (a) I see they are laughing at me, (b) I see they think I am stupid, (c) I see they don't like me, (d) I dislike their laughing at me, or (e) Their disliking me has real disadvantages, which I abhor.

4. Positive absolutistic evaluations, inferences, and attributions (hot cogni-tions; irrational beliefs). Examples: "Because people are laughing with me and presumably like me and I must act competently and must win their approval, (a) I am a great, noble person! *(overgeneralization),* (b) My life will be completely wonderful! *(overgeneralization),* (c) The world is a totally marvellous place! *(overgeneralization),* (d) I am certain that they will always laugh with me and that I will therefore always be a great person! *(certainty),* (e) I deserve to have only fine and wonderful things happen to me! *(deservingness and deification),* or

(f) I deserve to go to heaven and be beatified forever! *(deservingness and extreme deification).*

5. Negative absolutistic evaluations, inferences, and attributions (hot cognitions; irrational beliefs). Examples: "Because people are laughing at me and presumably dislike me and because I must act competently and must win their approval, (a) I am an incompetent, rotten person *(overgeneralization),* (b) My life will be completely miserable! *(overgeneralization),* (c) The world is a totally crummy place! *(overgeneralization),* (d) I am certain that they will always laugh at me and that I will therefore always be a rotten person! *(certainty),* (e) I deserve to have only bad and grim things happen to me! *(deservingness and damnation),* and (f) I deserve to roast in hell for eternity! *(deservingness and extreme damnation).*

6. Common derivatives of negative absolutistic evaluations (additional hot cognitions and irrational beliefs). Examples of disturbed ideas: "Because I must act competently and must win people's approval and because their laughing at me shows that I have acted incompetently and/or have lost their approval, (a) This is awful, horrible, and terrible! *(awfulizing, catastrophizing);* (b) I can't bear it, can't stand it! *(I-can't-stand-it-itis, discomfort anxiety, low frustration tolerance);* (c) I am a thoroughly incompetent, inferior, and worthless person *(self-downing, feelings of inadequacy);* (d) I can't change and become competent and lovable! *(hopelessness);* or (e) I deserve misery and punishment and will continue to bring it on myself *(deservingness and damnation).*

7. Other common cognitive derivatives of negative absolutistic evaluations (additional irrational beliefs). Examples of logical errors and unrealistic inferences: "Because I must act competently and must win people's approval and because their laughing at me shows that I have acted incompetently and/or have lost their approval, (a) I will always act incompetently and have significant people disapprove of me! *(overgeneralization);* (b) I'm a total failure and completely unlovable *(overgeneralization, all-or-none thinking);* (c) They know that I am no good and will always be incompetent, *(nonsequitur, jumping to conclusions, mind reading);* (d) They will keep laughing at me and will always despise me *(nonsequitur, jumping to conclusions, fortune telling);* (e) They only despise me and see nothing good in me *(focusing on the negative, overgeneralization);* (f) When they laugh with me and see me favorably that is because they are in a good mood and do not see that I am fooling them *(disqualifying the positive, nonsequitur);* (g) Their laughing at me and disliking me will make me lose my job and lose all my friends *(catastrophizing, magnification);* (h) When I act well and get them to laugh with me that only shows that I can occasionally do well, but that is unimportant compared to my great faults and stupidities *(minimization, focusing on the negative);* (i) I strongly feel that I am despicable and unlovable, and, because my feeling is so strong and consistent, this proves that I really am despicable and unlovable! *(emotional reasoning, circular reasoning, nonsequitur);* (j) I am a loser and a failure! *(labeling,*

overgeneralization); (k) They could only be laughing because of some foolish thing I have done and could not possibly be laughing for any other reason *(personalizing, nonsequitur, overgeneralization);* or (l) When I somehow get them to stop laughing at me or get them to laugh with me and like me, I am really a phony who is acting better than I am consistently able to do and will soon fall on my face and show them what a despicable phony I am! *(phonyism, all-or-nothing thinking, overgeneralization).*

People sometimes learn absolutistic evaluations, inferences, and conclusions (hot cognitions and irrational beliefs) from their parents, teachers, and others; for example, "I must have good luck, but now that I have broken this mirror fate will bring me bad luck and that will be terrible!" People tend to learn these irrational beliefs (iB's) easily and to retain them rigidly because they are probably born with a strong tendency to think irrationally. Actually, people often learn rational and practical *standards* (for example, "It is *preferable* to treat others considerately") and then overgeneralize, exaggerate, and turn these into dogmatic, irrational beliefs (iB's) (for example, "Because it is *preferable* for me to treat others considerately, I *have to* do so at all times, or else I am a *totally unlovable, worthless person!*"). Even if all humans were reared quite rationally, RET hypothesizes that they would often take their learned standards and irrationally escalate them into absolutistic demands on themselves, on others, and on the universe in which they reside (Ellis, 1958, 1962, 1971a, 1973, 1976a, 1977c, 1984a; Ellis & Grieger, 1977; Ellis & Whiteley, 1979).

Cognitive, affective, and behavioral consequences (C's) follow from the interaction of A's and B's. We may say, mathematically, that $A \times B = C$, but this formula is probably too simple and we may require a more complex one to express this relationship adequately. C is almost always significantly affected or influenced but not exactly caused by A, because humans naturally to some degree react to stimuli in their environments. Moreover, the more powerful A is (for example, a set of starvation conditions or an earthquake), the more profoundly it tends to affect C.

RET hypothesizes that when C consists of emotional disturbance (for example, severe feelings of anxiety, depression, hostility, self-deprecation, or self-pity), B usually mainly or more directly creates or causes A. Emotional disturbances, however, may at times stem from powerful A's, for example, from environmental disasters such as floods or wars. They also may follow from factors in the organism (such as hormonal or disease factors) that are somewhat independent of or may actually cause beliefs (B's). When strong or unusual A's significantly contribute to or "cause" C's and when physiological factors "create" C's, they are normally accompanied by contributory B's, too. Thus, if people are caught in an earthquake or if they experience powerful hormonal changes and they subsequently become depressed, their A's and their physiological processes probably strongly influence them to create irrational beliefs (iB's), such as: "This

[handwritten margin note: When emotional disturbance occurs — B usually contributes to cause]

earthquake *shouldn't* have occurred! Isn't it *awful!* I *can't stand* it!" These iB's, in turn, add to or help create their feelings of depression at C.

When C's (thoughts, feelings, and behavioral consequences) follow from A's and B's, they are virtually never pure or monolithic but partially include and inevitably interact with A and B. Thus, if A is an obnoxious event (e.g., a job refusal) and B is, first, a rational belief (for example, "I hope I don't get rejected for this job, as it would be unfortunate if I did") as well as, second, an irrational belief (for example, "I must have this job! I'm no good if I don't get it!"), C tends to be, first, a healthy feeling of frustration and disappointment and, along with the second irrational belief, unhealthy feelings of anxiety, inadequacy, and depression. So, A × B = C, but people also bring feelings (as well as hopes, goals, and purposes) to A. They would rarely apply for a job unless they desired or favorably evaluated it. Their A therefore partially includes their C. The two, from the beginning, are related rather than completely disparate.

At the same time, people's beliefs (B's) also partly or intrinsically relate to and include their A's and C's. Thus, when they tell themselves, at B, "I want to get a good job," they partly create the activating event (going for a job interview) and they partly create their emotional and behavioral consequence (feeling disappointed or depressed when they encounter a job rejection). Without their evaluating a job as good they would not try for it nor have any particular feeling about being rejected for it.

A, B, and C, then, are all closely related, and each almost always exists with the other two. Another way of stating this is to say that environments only exist for humans (and are quite different for other animals), and humans only exist in certain kinds of environments (where temperatures are not too hot or too cold) and are part of these environments. Similarly, individuals usually exist in a society (rarely as hermits) and societies are only composed of humans (and are quite different when composed, say, of ants or birds). As the proponents of systems theory point out, individual family members exist in a family system and change as this system changes, but RET also holds that the family system is composed of individuals and may considerably change as one or more of the individual family members change. In all these instances *interaction* is a key concept, probably essential to understanding how best to help people to change.

As with cognition, emotion, and behavior, thinking, as pointed out by Ellis in 1956 (Ellis, 1958, 1962), includes feeling and behaving. We largely think because we desire (a feeling) to survive (a behavior) and to be happy (a feeling). Emoting significantly includes thinking and behaving. We desire because we evaluate something as "good" or "beneficial" and, as we desire it, we move toward rather than away from it (act on it). Behaving to some degree involves thinking and emoting. We perform an act because we think it advisable to do so and because we concomitantly feel like doing it. Occasionally, as certain mystical people claim, we may have 100% *pure* thoughts, emotions, or behaviors that have no admixture of the other two processes. These seem to be exceptionally rare, and even when they occasionally appear to occur, as when a person is tapped below the knee and gives a knee-jerk response without any apparent concomitant thought or feeling, the original response (the knee jerk) seems to be immediately followed by a thought ("Look at that! My knee jerked!") and by a feeling ("Isn't that nice that my nerves function well?"). So, pure cognitions, emotions, and behaviors may exist, but rarely during normal waking (or conscious) states; and even when they do they are quickly followed by related cognitive-affective states (Schwartz, 1982).

Human thinking is unique, and their cognitions often instigate, change, and combine with their emotive and behavioral reactions. When they feel and behave, they almost always have some thoughts about their feelings and actions, and these thoughts lead them to have other feelings and behaviors. Thus, when they feel sad about, say, the loss of a loved one, they usually see or observe that they are sad, evaluate this feeling in some way (e.g., "Isn't it good that I am sad—this proves how much I really loved this person!" or "Isn't it bad that I am sad—this shows that I am letting myself be too deeply affected").

When people feel emotionally disturbed at C—that is, seriously anxious, depressed, self-downing, or hostile—they quite frequently view their symptoms absolutistically and awfulizingly and then irrationally conclude, "I should not, must not, be depressed! It's awful for me to be this way! I can't stand it! What a fool I am for giving in to this feeling!" They thereby develop a secondary symptom—depression about their depression or anxiety about their anxiety—that may be more severe and more incapacitating than their primary symptom and that may actually prevent them from understanding and working against this primary disturbance (Ellis, 1979a, 1980a).

RET assumes that people often use their cognitive processes in this self-defeating manner because this is the way they naturally, easily tend to think. RET therefore routinely looks for secondary symptoms and treats them prior to or along with dealing with clients' primary symptoms. The clinical observation that people tend to spy on themselves and condemn themselves when they have primary symptoms, and that they thereby frequently develop crippling secondary symptoms, tends to support the RET hypothesis that cognition is enormously important in the development of neurotic feelings and behaviors and that efficient psychotherapy had better include considerable rational–emotive methodology.

When people develop secondary symptoms—for example, feel very anxious about their anxiety, as agoraphobics tend to do—their secondary feelings strongly influence their cognitions and their behaviors. Thus, they feel so badly that they tend to conclude, "It really *is* awful that I am panicked about open spaces!" and they tend to behave more self-defeatingly than ever (e.g., they withdraw even more from open spaces). This again tends to demonstrate that A's (activating events), B's (beliefs), and C's (cognitive, emotive, and behavioral consequences) are interactive, that thoughts significantly affect feelings and behaviors, that emotions significantly affect thoughts and feelings, and that behaviors significantly affect thoughts and feelings (Ellis, 1962, 1984b).

In RET, we are concerned mainly with people's "emotional" disturbances, but the ABC theory also is a personality theory that shows how people largely create their own "normal" or healthy (positive and negative) feelings and how they can change them if they wish to work at doing so.

DISPUTING IRRATIONAL BELIEFS

A fundamental theory of RET is that when people seriously disturb themselves they almost always implicitly or explicitly accept or invent strong, absolutistic, *mus*turbatory irrational beliefs (iB's); and that one of the very best methods of helping them diminish or remove their emotional disturbances is to show them how to *dispute* (D) these iB's actively and to encourage them to do so, during therapeutic sessions and on their own, until they arrive at E—a new, effective philosophy that enables them to think and behave more rationally and self-helpingly. As Phadke (1982) has shown, D can be divided into three important sub-D's: (1) *detecting* irrational beliefs and clearly seeing that they are illogical and unrealistic, (2) *debating* these iB's and showing oneself exactly how and why they do not hold water, and (3) *discriminating* irrational beliefs (iB's) from rational beliefs (rB's) and showing oneself how the former lead to poor and the latter to much healthier results.

Disputing of irrational beliefs also may be effected in a number of other ways. Cognitively, they can be replaced by rational beliefs or sensible coping statements; they can be undermined by practicing some of the teachings of general semantics (Korzybski, 1933); they can be contradicted by being replaced by positive imagery (Maultsby, 1975; Maultsby & Ellis, 1974); they can be combatted by focusing on the distinct disadvantages they create and the advantages of giving them up; they can be supplanted by alternative problem-solving methods; and they can be put out of mind by cognitive distraction and by thought stopping. They may be alleviated by the use of many other kinds of thinking methods (Ellis, 1984b; Ellis & Abrahms, 1978).

RET theory and practice also hold that the best ways of disputing people's irrational beliefs and of helping them to change their feelings and behaviors in directions they consider more desirable are frequently emotive and behavioral techniques. In the emotive area it employs a number of selected experiential methods, including rational–emotive imagery (Maultsby, 1975; Maultsby & Ellis, 1974), shame-attacking exercises (Ellis, 1969, 1971b), role playing, unconditional acceptance by the therapist of her or his clients, the use of forceful self-statements and self-dialogues (Ellis, 1979c), and other evocative-dramatic techniques (Ellis, 1984b; Ellis & Abrahms, 1978). It also uses a variety of selected behavioral methods, including reinforcement, penalizing, activity homework assignments, implosive assignments, and skills training (Bernard & Joyce, 1983; Ellis, 1962, 1977e, 1984b; Ellis & Abrahms, 1978; Ellis & Becker, 1982; Ellis & Bernard, 1983).

Figure 1–1 demonstrates a typical method in which RET helps clients actively to dispute (D) their irrational beliefs and arrive at a new effective philosophy (E). It consists of a filled-out version of the recently revised Rational Self-Help Report Form, devised by Sichel and Ellis (1983) and commonly distributed to the regular individual and group therapy clients seen at the Institute for Rational–Emotive Therapy in New York City. We have filled in this form using some of the material mentioned previously in this chapter in connection with the irrational beliefs (iB's) an individual might well have if (let us say) he observed at point A (activating events) that people were laughing and if he felt anxious and depressed about this observation. Guided by an RET practitioner and some of the RET pamphlets and books—especially *A New Guide to Rational Living* (Ellis & Harper, 1975), *A Guide to Personal Happiness* (Ellis & Becker, 1982), and *Overcoming Procrastination* (Ellis & Knaus, 1977)—this person might well fill out the Rational Self-Help Report Form as it is filled out in Figure 1–1.

Unlike most other systems of cognitive behavioral therapy, RET emphasizes the use of active disputing (D) as the most elegant, though hardly the only, way of helping people to surrender their irrational beliefs (iB's). Rational–emotive therapists show clients (1) how to look for and detect their irrational beliefs, particularly their absolutistic shoulds and musts, their awfulizing, their I-can't-stand-it-itis, their can'ts, and their self-downing; (2) how logically and empirically to question and challenge their iB's and vigorously to argue themselves out of believing them; (3) how to replace iB's with alternate, rational beliefs (rB's) and coping statements; (4) how to think about these rational beliefs and show themselves why they are rational and in what ways they are different from irrational beliefs; and (5) how to internalize the scientific method, and steadily, for the rest of their lives, see that their irrational beliefs are hypotheses, not facts, and strongly challenge and question these hypotheses until they give them up. As noted earlier, RET uses many other cognitive, emotive, and behavioral methods for helping people to combat and to surrender their irrational beliefs, but it stresses the use of active and directive disputing.

UNIQUE FEATURES OF RET AND HOW IT IS DIFFERENT FROM OTHER COGNITIVE BEHAVIORAL THERAPIES

As already noted, RET has a number of unique features that make it differ significantly from most of the other popular forms of cognitive behavioral therapy (CBT). To conclude this introductory chapter, let us briefly note (and in some cases repeat) some of RET's main uniquenesses.

Figure 1–1 Completed RET Self-Help Form

RET SELF-HELP FORM

Institute for Rational-Emotive Therapy
45 East 65th Street, New York, N.Y. 10021
(212) 535-0822

(A) ACTIVATING EVENTS, thoughts, or feelings that happened just before I felt emotionally disturbed or acted self-defeatingly: _____
I noticed that people were laughing

(C) CONSEQUENCE or CONDITION—disturbed feeling or self-defeating behavior—that I produced and would like to change: _____
I felt anxious and depressed. I started to stay away from people.

(B) BELIEFS—Irrational BELIEFS (IBs) leading to my CONSEQUENCE (emotional disturbance or self-defeating behavior). Circle all that apply to these ACTIVATING EVENTS (A).	**(D) DISPUTES** for each circled IRRATIONAL BELIEF. Examples: *"Why* MUST *I do very well?"* *"Where is it written* that I am a BAD PERSON?" *"Where is the evidence* that I MUST be approved or accepted?"	**(E) EFFECTIVE RATIONAL BELIEFS (RBs)** to replace my IRRATIONAL BELIEFS (IBs). Examples: *"I'd* PREFER *to do very well but I don't* HAVE TO." *"I am a* PERSON WHO *acted badly, not a BAD PERSON."* *"There is no evidence that I* HAVE TO *be approved, though I would* LIKE *to be."*
1. I MUST do well or very well!		
2. I am a BAD OR WORTHLESS PERSON when I act weakly or stupidly.	How does it make me a bad person if people dislike me?	It doesn't! It only makes me a person who is less liked than I wish to be.
3. I MUST be approved or accepted by people I find important!	Why must I?	I don't have to be, though that would be desirable.
4. I am a BAD, UNLOVABLE PERSON if I get rejected.	In what way am I a bad person?	I am not! I am just a person who got rejected.
5. People MUST treat me fairly and give me what I NEED!		
6. People who act immorally are undeserving, ROTTEN PEOPLE!		
7. People MUST live up to my expectations or it is TERRIBLE!		
8. My life MUST have few major hassles or troubles.	Where is this law written?	Only in my head! Life will have major hassles. Tough!
9. I CAN'T STAND really bad things or very difficult people!		

(OVER)

Figure 1–1 *(cont.)*

10. It's AWFUL or HORRIBLE when major things don't go my way!		
11. I CAN'T STAND IT when life is really unfair!		
12. I NEED to be loved by someone who matters to me a lot!		
13. I NEED a good deal of immediate gratification and HAVE TO feel miserable when I don't get it!		
Additional Irrational Beliefs:		
14. These people must be laughing at me. If so, that makes me a fool!	Where is the evidence that they are laughing at me? If they are, how does that make me a fool?	There is none. They may be laughing for many other reasons! Even if I am acting foolishly, that doesn't make me a fool.
15. If they are laughing at me it's awful!	Why would it be awful if they were?	It wouldn't be. It would only be inconvenient!
16. They only despise me and see I am an undeserving person	Is this likely to be true?	No. A few of them may despise me but even if they do I can still accept myself.
17. They will talk badly about me and make me lose all my friends.	How do I know that this will happen?	I don't. They may not talk badly about me; and if they do I'll hardly lose all my friends.
18. Even if they are not laughing at me now, they will find me out and see how ridiculous I am later.	Where is the evidence that this will happen?	Nowhere! If they do later find me ridiculous, I can still see myself as a person with some foolish behavior but not a bad person.

(F) FEELINGS and BEHAVIORS I experienced after arriving at my EFFECTIVE RATIONAL BELIEFS: _Disappointment at people's laughing. Happy about overcoming my anxiety and depressions._

I WILL WORK HARD TO REPEAT MY EFFECTIVE RATIONAL BELIEFS FORCEFULLY TO MYSELF ON MANY OCCASIONS SO THAT I CAN MAKE MYSELF LESS DISTURBED NOW AND ACT LESS SELF-DEFEATINGLY IN THE FUTURE.

Joyce Sichel, Ph.D. and Albert Ellis, Ph.D.

Innate Predispositions to Disturbance. Although RET uses social learning theory and holds that external events and environmental influences significantly affect humans and contribute to their emotional disturbances, it stresses biological tendencies and innate predispositions to disturbance more than do most other forms of psychotherapy, including the cognitive therapies. Because it holds that people naturally and easily, as well as through cultural teaching, absorb and create irrational beliefs, RET stresses the importance of the therapist's vigorously and forcefully disputing these iB's and encouraging clients themselves to do so steadily and powerfully (Ellis, 1976a, 1979c, 1983a,b).

Secondary Disturbances. RET especially emphasizes the human disposition first to disturb oneself over some failure or frustration and secondarily to disturb oneself over one's disturbances. It assumes that secondary disturbances often exist, particularly with individuals who have had strong primary disturbances for a period of time; it looks for these secondary symptoms; and it usually deals with them first, before it then goes on to deal with the primary disturbances (Ellis, 1962, 1979a, 1980a, 1984b).

Assessment Procedures. RET at times employs all the assessment procedures of cognitive behavioral therapy, but it also favors rational–emotive therapy itself as an important means of assessment. It holds that in many cases the therapist can quickly zero in on some of the client's irrational beliefs (iB's) and make this therapeutic procedure highly diagnostic, that is, see how and under what conditions the client is likely to react to therapy (Ellis, 1984b).

Appropriate and Inappropriate Feelings. As indicated already, RET clearly defines inappropriate feelings, separates them from appropriate ones, and focuses (especially with new clients) on discovering what people's inappropriate feelings are, how they can learn to discriminate them from appropriate ones, and how they can work on changing them (Ellis, 1971a, 1973).

Absolutistic and Antiempirical Irrational Beliefs. RET holds that, although many kinds of human irrationalities and illogicalities exist and produce poor results, what we call "emotional disturbance" is most importantly a concomitant of absolutistic and unconditional shoulds, oughts, musts, demands, commands, and expectations. It hypothesizes that awfulizing, I-can't-stand-it-itis, damning, personalizing, all-or-nothing thinking, overgeneralizing, and other kinds of crooked thinking that disturbed individuals do and that lead to their emotional problems largely stem from explicit or implicit dogmatizing and absolutism. Therefore, if we merely dispute clients' derivative inferences and illogicalities alone, clients will not tend to make as profound and healthy a philosophic change as when we show them their intolerant demands and commands and induce them to surrender these, too. Preferential RET usually deals with absolutistic *and* unrealistic beliefs, and not merely with one or the other (Ellis, 1980b, 1984b).

Evaluative and Nonevaluative Dogmas. Although RET discloses and argues against all kinds of dogmas and unscientific postulates, it particularly looks for and opposes people's absolutistic evaluative judgments about themselves, others, and the world, as it holds that these are closely related to cognitive, emotive, and behavioral dysfunctioning that accompanies disturbed symptoms (Ellis, 1984a).

Relationship Processes. RET favors the building of a good rapport with clients, uses empathic listening and reflection of feeling, and emphasizes unconditional acceptance by the therapist of the client as well as strong encouragement by the therapist for clients to look at themselves and to change. It also takes a cautious attitude toward both therapists' and clients' dire need for each other's approval and continually explores the irrational beliefs (iB's) that they may have regarding needing this approval. Such approval needs interfere (1) with the clients' really working to change themselves and (2) with therapists' being firm enough with clients to help them change. RET also notably tries to induce clients to refuse to rate themselves poorly, whether or not they do well in therapy and win their therapist's approval; and it shows therapists how to accept themselves unconditionally, whether or not they are successful with various clients. While RET tries to show clients that they are equal and active collaborators with the therapist in changing themselves, it also encourages the therapist to be a highly active-directive teacher who had often better take the lead in explaining, interpreting, and disputing clients' iB's and to come up with better solutions to their problems (Ellis, 1983a).

Multimodal and Comprehensive Use of Techniques. RET has a distinct theory of human disturbance and of how it may be ameliorated most efficiently. This theory is interactive and multimodal and sees emotions, thoughts, and behaviors as transacting with each other and including one another. Hence it has always used many cognitive, emotive, and behavioral methods. Because it emphasizes the biological as well as social sources of disturbance, it frequently favors the use of medication and of physical techniques, including diet, exercise, and relaxation. At the same time, RET is selective in its methods and rarely uses one (such as positive thinking or religious conversion) just because it works. Instead, RET looks at the long-range as well as the short-range effects of various techniques, considers many methods (such as cognitive distraction) as more palliative than curative, and tries to emphasize those that tend to produce a profound philosophical change that helps clients not merely *feel* but *get* better (Ellis, 1972a, 1974, 1977c, 1983b). As noted previously, RET is famous for its cognitive and philosophical approaches to psychotherapy, but it also heavily emphasizes the use of a good many selective emotive and behavioral methods.

The Use of Force and Vividness. The theory of RET holds that emotionally disturbed people tend forcefully, vividly, vigorously, and with profound conviction to hold onto their main irrational beliefs (iB's); moreover, even when they have "insight" into these beliefs, they may still strongly believe them and refuse to give them up. Therefore, RET not only often emphasizes quite active-directive disputing of irrationalities but also stresses those emotive techniques (such as its shame-attacking exercises and rational–emotive imagery) and behavioral techniques (such as implosive *in vivo* desensitization) that powerfully contradict and work against people's disturbed thoughts, feelings, and behaviors (Dryden, 1983; Ellis, 1979c).

Ego Anxiety and Discomfort Anxiety. RET holds that people have two basic kinds of "emotional" disturbance that often significantly overlap and reinforce each other. The first is ego anxiety (or ego depression) arising from people's absolutistic and perfectionistic demands that they personally perform well and be approved by others, which lead to feelings of severe inadequacy when they perform poorly and are disapproved by significant others. The second is discomfort anxiety (or discomfort depression) arising from their absolutistic and perfectionistic demands that others do their bidding and that conditions be arranged so that they easily and quickly get what they demand. RET almost invariably looks for *both* these kinds of disturbance, reveals them to clients, and shows people various methods for effectively overcoming them (Ellis, 1979a, 1980a).

Humanistic Aspects. RET does not pretend to be "purely" objective, scientific, or technique centered but (unlike some of the other cognitive behavioral therapies) takes a definite humanistic–existential approach to human problems and their basic solutions. It primarily deals with disturbed *human* evaluations, emotions, and behaviors. It is highly rational and scientific but uses rationality and science in the service of humans, in an attempt to enable them to live and be happy. It is hedonistic but espouses long-range instead of short-range hedonism, so people may achieve the pleasure of the moment *and* the future, may arrive at maximum freedom *and* discipline. It hypothesizes that nothing superhuman exists and that devout belief in superhuman agencies tends to foster dependency and increase emotional disturbance. It assumes that no humans, whatever their antisocial or obnoxious behavior, are damnable nor subhuman. It particularly emphasizes the importance of will and choice in human affairs, even though it accepts the likelihood that some human behavior is partially determined by biological, social, and other forces (Bandura, 1980; Ellis, 1973, 1983b).

MOVES FROM SELF-ESTEEM TO
SELF-ACCEPTANCE

Views of Self-esteem and Self-acceptance. Where most other psychotherapies attempt to help people achieve self-esteem, RET is skeptical of this concept and tries, instead, to help them achieve what it calls self-acceptance. This means refusing to rate their oneself or one's being or essences at all, but rather to rate only their acts, deeds, and performances (Ellis, 1972b, 1973, 1976b, 1977c). RET shows people that, no matter what criteria they rate themselves upon, whether it be external (success, approval), internal (character or emotional stability), or supernatural (acceptance by Jesus or by God), they really *choose* these criteria. Therefore, they can more elegantly accept themselves, without any intervening variables, merely because they *choose* to do so.

Views of Efficient and Elegant Psychotherapy. RET especially strives for efficient and elegant forms of psychotherapy. It aims not merely for symptom removal but also for a profound change in people's basic philosophy. It tries to alleviate or remove most symptoms of disturbance permanently, not transiently, though it acknowledges that people have a strong tendency to retrogress and reinstitute their symptoms, even after they have once overcome them. It tries to develop methods of elegant therapy that require relatively little therapeutic time and that produce maximum results quickly and efficiently (Ellis, 1980b). It specializes in psychoeducational methods (such as bibliotherapy, audiotherapy, videotherapy, workshops, and other media presentations), in the course of which some of the main RET teachings can be effectively used with large groups of individuals for self-help purposes (Ellis, 1978a; Ellis & Abrahms, 1978).

Views on Behavioral Methods. RET favors *in vivo* rather than purely imaginative modes of systematic desensitization, and it often encourages implosive instead of gradual activity homework assignments. It uses reinforcement procedures but takes a somewhat different attitude toward them than do other cognitive behavioral schools. First, it is wary of using love or approval as a reinforcer, because that may help make people more suggestible and less autonomous and self-thinking. Second, it strives, in the last analysis, to help people choose their own goals and think for themselves, and hence become less suggestible and less reinforceable by external influences. It encourages some clients who are not easily reinforceable to use stiff penalties when they resist changing their dysfunctional behaviors, but it tries to make very clear that penalties are not to be used as punishments and must not include any ideas of undeservingness or damnation (Ellis, 1983b).

Insight and Behavioral Change. RET particularly stresses cognitive or intellectual insight, but it also shows the difference between intellectual and emotional insight and indicates how clients can achieve the latter and can effect behavioral change through achieving it (Ellis, 1962, 1963). Thus it shows clients that (1) when they have intellectual insight they usually believe something lightly

and occasionally and (2) when they have emotional insight they usually believe
this thing strongly and persistently and therefore, because of their powerful
belief, feel a need to act on it.

RET holds that before people can change their inappropriate feelings and
behaviors they normally require three main kinds of insight. The first kind
involves the acknowledgment that disturbances mainly or largely stem not from
past events but from the irrational beliefs (iB's) that people bring to such events.
In RET terms, activating events (A's) may contribute significantly to disturbed
consequences (C's), but their more important and relevant contribution of
"cause" comes from irrational beliefs (iB's) about what happens at A. The
second kind of insight is the realization that, no matter how we originally become
(or make ourselves) disturbed, we feel upset today because we are *still*
reindoctrinating ourselves with the same kinds of irrational beliefs that we
originated (or took over from others) in the past. The third kind of insight is the
full acceptance of the idea that, even if we achieve the first two insights by
realizing that we have created and keep carrying on our own disturbed feelings
and behaviors, these insights will not automatically make us change ourselves.
Only if we constantly *work on and practice,* in the present and future, thinking,
feeling, and acting *against* our irrational beliefs are we likely to surrender them
and make and keep ourselves less disturbed (Ellis, 1977c; Ellis & Knaus, 1977).

Use of Humor. RET hypothesizes that people had better give significant
meaning to their lives, as Frankl (1959) has ably shown, but that emotional
disturbance easily arises when they give exaggerated or overly serious significance to some of their thoughts, feelings, and actions (Ellis, 1962, 1971b, 1973).
RET therefore specializes in ripping up people's irrational beliefs (iB's)—and
not, of course, the people themselves—in many humorous ways (Ellis, 1977a,
1977b). For example, Ellis has composed a number of humorous songs that he
often employs with his clients and at his RET talks and workshops. Many other
RET (and non–RET) therapists and leaders also have adopted his song techniques (Ellis, 1981). Here are three examples:

Whine, Whine, Whine!

*(To the tune of the "Yale Whiffenpoof Song," originally
composed by Guy Scull—a Harvard graduate!)*
I cannot have all of my wishes filled—
Whine, whine, whine!
I cannot have every frustration stilled—
Whine, whine, whine!
Life really owes me the things that I miss,
Fate has to grant me eternal bliss!
And since I must settle for less than this—
Whine, whine, whine!
(Lyrics by Albert Ellis. © 1977 by Institute
for Rational–Emotive Therapy.)

Maybe I'll Move My Ass
(To the tune of "After the Ball," composed by Charles K. Harris)
After you make things easy and you provide the gas;
After you squeeze and please me, maybe I'll move my ass!
Make my life soft and easy, fill it with sassafras!
And possibly, if things are easy, I'll move my ass!
(Lyrics by Albert Ellis, © 1977 by Institute
for Rational–Emotive Therapy.)

I Wish I Were Not Crazy
(To the tune of "Dixie," composed by Dan Emmett)
Oh, I wish I were really put together—
Smooth and fine as patent leather!
Oh, how great to be rated innately sedate!
But I'm afraid that I was fated
To be rather aberrated—
Oh, how sad to be made as my Mom and my Dad!

Oh, I wish I were not crazy! Hooray, hooray!
I wish my mind were less inclined
To be the kind that's hazy!
I could agree to try to be less crazy,
But I, alas, am just too goddamned lazy!
(Lyrics by Albert Ellis, © 1977 by
Institute for Rational–Emotive Therapy.)

SUMMARY AND CONCLUSION

RET was originally developed as a pioneering form of cognitive behavioral therapy (CBT) to help clients overcome their "emotional" disturbances, including their primary and secondary problems. It also has developed into a personality theory that shows people how they largely create their own positive and negative feelings and how they can change them if they wish to work at doing so (Ellis, 1978b). It is psychoeducational as well as therapeutic and is now being applied, as the various chapters of this book show, to a large number of fields of human endeavor. It is based on the assumption that survival and happiness are of great value to most people and that these values can be achieved and enhanced appreciably by the use of flexible, undogmatic, rigorous, scientific thinking. It has already made significant contributions to psychotherapy and to self-actualization and, as it changes and develops (as scientifically based theories and practices almost invariably tend to do), it is hoped that it will have important and useful applications to still more fields of human striving.

REFERENCES

Adler, A. *Understanding human nature.* New York: Greenberg, 1927.

Adler, A. *The science of living.* New York: Greenberg, 1929.

Bandura, A. *Principles of behavior modification.* New York: Holt, Rinehart and Winston, 1969.

Bandura, A. The self system in reciprocal determinism. *American Psychologist,* 1978, *33,* 344–358.

Bard, J. A. *Rational–emotive therapy in practice.* Champaign, Ill.: Research Press, 1980.

Barksdale, L. S. *Building self-esteem.* Los Angeles: Barksdale Foundation, 1972.

Beck, A. T. *Depression.* New York: Hoeber-Harper, 1967.

Beck, A. T. *Cognitive therapy and the emotional disorders.* New York: International Universities Press, 1976.

Bedford, S. *Stress and tiger juice.* Chico, Calif.: Scott Publications, 1980.

Bernard, M. E., & Joyce, M. R. *Rational–emotive therapy with children and adolescents.* New York: John Wiley, 1983.

Blazier, D. *Poor me, poor marriage.* New York: Vantage, 1975.

Burns, D. *Feeling good.* New York: Morrow, 1980.

Butler, P. E. *Talking to yourself.* New York: Stein and Day, 1981.

Church, V. A. *Behavior, law and remedies.* Dubuque, Ia.: Kendall/Hunt, 1975.

Coué, E. *My method.* New York: Doubleday, 1923.

Diekstra, R., & Dassen, W. F. *Rationele therapie.* Amsterdam: Swets and Zeitlinger, 1976.

Dryden, W. *Rational–emotive therapy: Fundamentals and innovations.* London: Coors, 1983.

Dubois, P. *The psychic treatment of nervous disorders.* New York: Funk and Wagnalls, 1907.

Dyer, W. *Your erroneous zones.* New York: Funk and Wagnalls, 1977.

Ellis, A. Re-analysis of an alleged telepathic dream. *Psychiatric Quarterly,* 1949, *23,* 116–126. (a)

Ellis, A. Towards the improvement of psychoanalytic research. *Psychoanalytic Review,* 1949, *36,* 123–143. (b)

Ellis, A. *An introduction to the principles of scientific psychoanalysis.* Genetic Psychology Monographs. Provincetown, Mass.: Journal Press, 1950.

Ellis, A. The effectiveness of psychotherapy with individuals who have severe homosexual problems. *Journal of Consulting Psychology,* 1956, *20,* 191–195. (a)

Ellis, A. An operational reformulation of some of the basic principles of psychoanalysis. In H. Feigl & M. Scriven (Eds.), *Minnesota studies in the philosophy of science. Vol. I.: The foundations of science and concepts of psychology and psychoanalysis.* Minneapolis: University of Minnesota Press, 1956. (b)

Ellis, A. Outcome of employing three techniques of psychotherapy. *Journal of Clinical Psychology,* 1957, *13,* 344–350. (a)

Ellis, A. Rational psychotherapy and Individual Psychology. *Journal of Individual Psychology,* 1957, *13,* 38–44. (b)

Ellis, A. Rational psychotherapy. *Journal of General Psychology,* 1958, *59,* 35–49.

Ellis, A. *Reason and emotion in psychotherapy.* Secaucus, N.J.: Lyle Stuart and Citadel Books, 1962.

Ellis, A. Toward a more precise definition of "emotional" and "intellectual" insight. *Psychological Reports,* 1963, *13,* 125–126.

Ellis, A. *The art and science of love* (Rev. ed.). Secaucus, N.J.: Lyle Stuart; New York: Bantam, 1965. (a) Originally published, 1960.

Ellis, A. *Sex without guilt.* (Rev. ed.). Secaucus, N.J.: Lyle Stuart; North Hollywood: Wilshire Books, 1965. (b) Originally published, 1958.

Ellis, A. A weekend of rational encounter. In A. Burton (Ed.), *Encounter.* San Francisco: Jossey-Bass, 1969.

Ellis, A. *Growth through reason.* North Hollywood, Calif.: Wilshire Books, 1971. (a)

Ellis, A. *How to stubbornly refuse to be ashamed of anything.* Cassette recording. New York: Institute for Rational–Emotive Therapy, 1971. (b)

Ellis, A. Helping people get better rather than merely feel better. *Rational Living,* 1972, *7*(2), 2–9. (a)

Ellis, A. Psychotherapy and the value of a human being. In J. W. Davis (Ed.), *Value and valuation*. Knoxville: University of Tennessee Press, 1972. Reprinted, New York: Institute for Rational–Emotive Therapy, 1972. (b)

Ellis, A. Psychotherapy without tears. In A. Burton (Ed.), *Twelve therapists*. San Francisco: Jossey-Bass, 1972. (c)

Ellis, A. *Humanistic psychotherapy: The rational–emotive approach*. New York: Crown and McGraw-Hill, 1973.

Ellis, A. Cognitive aspects of abreactive therapy. *Voices*, 1974, *10*(1), 48–56.

Ellis, A. *How to live with a "neurotic"* (Rev. ed.). New York: Crown: North Hollywood: Wilshire Books, 1975. (a) Originally published, New York: Crown, 1957.

Ellis, A. The biological basis of human irrationality. *Journal of Individual Psychology*, 1976, *32*, 145–168. (a)

Ellis, A. RET abolishes most of the human ego. *Psychotherapy*, 1976, *13*, 343–348. Reprinted, New York: Institute for Rational–Emotive Therapy, 1976. (b)

Ellis, A. *Sex and the liberated man*. Secaucus, N.J.: Lyle Stuart, 1976. (c)

Ellis, A. Fun as psychotherapy. *Rational Living*, 1977, *12*(1), 2–6. (a)

Ellis, A. *A garland of rational songs*. Cassette recording and songbook. New York: Institute for Rational–Emotive Therapy, 1977. (b)

Ellis, A. *How to live with—and without—anger*. New York: Reader's Digest Press, 1977. (c)

Ellis, A. Skill training in counseling and psychotherapy. *Canadian Counselor*, 1977, *12*(1), 30–35. (e)

Ellis, A. Rational–emotive therapy and self-help therapy. *Rational Living*, 1978, *13*(1), 2–9. (a)

Ellis, A. Toward a theory of personality. In R. J. Corsini (Ed.), *Readings in current personalities theories*. Itasca, Ill.: Peacock, 1978. (b)

Ellis, A. Discomfort anxiety: A new cognitive-behavioral construct. Part 1. *Rational Living*, 1979, *14*(2), 3–8. (a)

Ellis, A. *The intelligent woman's guide to dating and mating*. Secaucus, N.J.: Lyle Stuart, 1979. (b)

Ellis, A. The issue of force and energy in behavioral change. *Journal of Contemporary Psychotherapy*, 1979, *10*, 83–97. (c)

Ellis, A. The theory of rational–emotive therapy. In A. Ellis & J. M. Whiteley (Eds.), *Theoretical and empirical foundations of rational–emotive therapy*. Monterey, Calif.: Brooks/Cole, 1979. (d)

Ellis, A. Discomfort anxiety: A new cognitive-behavioral construct. Part 2. *Rational Living*, 1980, *15*(1), 25–30. (a)

Ellis, A. Rational–emotive therapy and cognitive behavior therapy: Similarities and differences. *Cognitive Therapy and Research*, 1980, *4*, 325–340. (b)

Ellis, A. The use of rational humorous songs in psychotherapy. *Voices*, 1981, *16*(4), 29–36.

Ellis, A. Introduction to Windy Dryden's *Rational–emotive therapy: Fundamentals and innovations*. London: Coors, 1983. (a)

Ellis, A. The philosophic implications and dangers of some popular behavior therapy techniques. In M. Rosenbaum, C. M. Franks, & Y. Jaffe (Eds.), *Perspectives on behavior therapy in the eighties*. New York: Springer, 1983. (b)

Ellis, A. Expanding the ABCs of RET. In A. Freeman & M. Mahoney (Eds.), *Cognition and psychotherapy*. New York: Plenum, 1984. (a)

Ellis, A. Rational–emotive therapy and cognitive–behavior therapy. New York: Springer, 1984. (b)

Ellis, A., & Abrahms, E. *Brief psychotherapy in medical and health practice*. New York: Springer, 1978.

Ellis, A., & Becker, I. *A guide to personal happiness*. North Hollywood: Wilshire Books, 1982.

Ellis, A., & Bernard, M. (Eds.). *Rational–emotive approaches to the problems of childhood*. New York: Plenum, 1983.

Ellis, A., & Grieger, R. (Eds). *Handbook of rational–emotive therapy*. New York: Springer, 1977.

Ellis, A., & Harper, R. A. *A guide to rational living*. Englewood Cliffs, N.J.: Prentice-Hall, 1961. (a)

Ellis, A., & Harper, R. A. *A guide to successful marriage*. North Hollywood, Calif.: Wilshire Books, 1961. (b)

Ellis, A., & Harper, R. A. *A new guide to rational living*. North Hollywood, Calif.: Wilshire Books, 1975.

Ellis, A., & Knaus, W. *Overcoming procrastination*. New York: New American Library, 1977.
Ellis, A., & Whiteley, J. M. (Eds.). *Theoretical and empirical foundations of rational–emotive therapy*. Monterey, Calif.: Brooks/Cole, 1979.
Emery, G. *Own your own life*. New York: New American Library, 1982.
Emery, S. *Actualizations*. New York: Doubleday, 1978.
Epictetus. *The works of Epictetus*. Boston: Little, Brown, 1899.
Erhard, W. *What is the purpose of the EST training?* San Francisco: Erhard Seminars Training, 1976.
Eysenck, H. J. (Ed.). *Experiments in behavior therapy*. New York: Macmillan, 1964.
Frankl, V. *Man's search for meaning*. New York: Pocket Books, 1959.
Garcia, E., & Blythe, B. T. *Developing emotional muscle*. Atlanta: Georgia Center for Continuing Education, 1977.
Ginott, H. *Between parent and child*. New York: Macmillan, 1965.
Glasser, W. *Reality therapy*. New York: Harper & Row, 1965.
Goldfried, M. R., & Davison, G. *Clinical behavior therapy*. New York: Holt, Rinehart and Winston, 1976.
Goodman, D., & Maultsby, M. C., Jr. *Emotional well being through rational behavior training*. Springfield, Ill.: Charles C. Thomas, 1974.
Goulding, M. M., & Goulding, R. L. *Changing lives through redecision therapy*. New York: Brunner/Mazel, 1979.
Greenwald, H. *Decision therapy*. New York: Wyden, 1973.
Grieger, R., & Boyd, J. *Rational emotive therapy: A skills based approach*. New York: Van Nostrand Reinhold, 1980.
Grieger, R., & Grieger, I. *Cognition and emotional disturbance*. New York: Human Sciences Press, 1982.
Grossack, M. *You are not alone*. Boston: Marlborough, 1974.
Grossack, M. *Love and reason*. New York: New American Library, 1976.
Guidano, V. F., & Liotti, G. *Cognitive processes and emotional disorders*. New York: Guilford Press, 1983.
Hadas, M. *Essential works of stoicism*. New York: Bantam, 1962.
Heesacker, M., Heppner, P. P., & Rogers, M. E. Classics and emerging classics in counseling psychology. *Journal of Counseling Psychology*, 1982, *29*, 400–405.
Hauck, P. A. *Reason in pastoral counseling*. Philadelphia: Westminster, 1972.
Hauck, P. A. *Overcoming depression*. Philadelphia: Westminster, 1973.
Hauck, P. A. *Overcoming frustration and anger*. Philadelphia: Westminster, 1974.
Hauck, P. A. *Overcoming worry and fear*. Philadelphia: Westminster, 1975.
Hauck, P. A. *How to do what you want to do*. Philadelphia: Westminster, 1976.
Hauck, P. A. *How to stand up for yourself*. Philadelphia: Westminster, 1979.
Hauck, P. A. *Brief counseling with RET*. Philadelphia: Westminster, 1980.
Hauck, P. A. *Overcoming jealousy and possessiveness*. Philadelphia: Westminster, 1981.
Hauck, P. A. *Your inner therapist*. Philadelphia: Westminster, 1983.
Heidigger, M. *Being and time*. New York: Harper & Row, 1962.
Herzberg, A. *Active psychotherapy*. New York: Grune and Stratton, 1945.
Horney, K. *The neurotic personality of our time*. New York: Norton, 1939.
Jakubowski, P., & Lange, A. *The assertive option*. Champaign, Ill: Research Press, 1978.
Johnson, S. M. *First person singular*. New York: Signet, 1977.
Johnson, W. *People in quandaries*. New York: Harper, 1946.
Kelly, G. *The psychology of personal constructs*. New York: W. W. Norton, 1955.
Keyes, K. *Handbook to higher consciousness*. St. Mary, Ky.: Cornucopia Institute, 1979.
Knaus, W. J. *How to get out of a rut*. Englewood Cliffs, N.J.: Prentice-Hall, 1982.
Korzybski, A. *Science and sanity*. Lancaster, Pa.: Lancaster Press, 1933.
Lacey, L. A. *Effective communication with difficult people*. San Diego: Common Visions, 1982.
Lange, A., & Jakubowski, A. *Responsible assertive training*. Champaign, Ill.: Research Press, 1976.
Lazarus, A. A. *Behavior therapy and beyond*. New York: McGraw-Hill, 1971.
Lazarus, A. A. *The practice of multimodal therapy*. New York: McGraw-Hill, 1981.
Lazarus, A. A., & Fay, A. *I can if I want to*. New York: Morrow, 1975.

Lazarus, R. S. *Psychological stress and the coping process.* New York: McGraw-Hill, 1966.

Lembo, J. *Help yourself.* Niles, Ill.: Argus, 1974.

Lembo, J. *The counseling process.* New York: Libra, 1976.

Lembo, J. *How to cope with your fears and frustrations.* New York: Libra, 1977.

Little, B. L. *This will drive you sane.* Minneapolis, Minn.: Comp Care, 1977.

Losoncy, L. E. *You can do it.* Englewood Cliffs, N.J.: Prentice-Hall, 1980.

Low, A. *Mental health through will training.* Boston: Christopher, 1952.

Mahoney, M. Personal science: A cognitive learning therapy. In A. Ellis and R. Grieger (Eds.), *Handbook of rational–emotive therapy.* New York: Springer, 1977.

Maleske, H. *Natural therapy.* Reseda, Calif.: Mojave Books, 1976.

Marcus Aurelius. *The thoughts of the Emperor Marcus Aurelius.* Boston: Little, Brown, 1900.

Maultsby, M. C., Jr. *Help yourself to happiness.* New York: Institute for Rational–Emotive Therapy, 1975.

Maultsby, M. C., Jr. *A million dollars for your hangover.* Lexington, Ky.: Rational Self-Help Books, 1978.

Maultsby, M. C., Jr. *Rational behavior therapy.* New York: John Wiley, 1983.

Maultsby, M. C., Jr., & Ellis, A. *Technique of using rational–emotive imagery.* New York: Institute for Rational–Emotive Therapy, 1974.

Maultsby, M. C., Jr., & Hendricks, A. *Cartoon booklets illustrating basic rational behavior therapy concepts.* Lexington, Ky.: Rational Behavior Training Unit, 1974.

McMullen, R. E., & Casey, B. *Talk sense to yourself.* Champaign, Ill.: Research Press, 1975.

Meichenbaum, D. *Cognitive-behavior modification.* New York: Plenum, 1977.

Miller, J. *Headaches: The answer book.* Old Tappan, N.J.: Revell, 1983.

Morris, K. T., & Kanitz, J. M. *Rational–emotive therapy.* Boston: Houghton-Mifflin, 1975.

Nash, J. D. *Taking charge of your smoking.* Palo Alto, Calif.: Bull, 1981.

Perls, F. S. *Gestalt therapy verbatim.* Lafayette, Calif.: Real People Press, 1969.

Phadke, K. M. Some innovations in RET theory and practice. *Rational Living,* 1982, *17*(2), 25–30.

Powell, J. *Fully human, fully alive.* Niles, Ill.: Argus, 1976.

Raimy, V. *Misconceptions of the self.* San Francisco: Jossey-Bass, 1975.

Rotter, J. B. *Social learning and clinical psychology.* Englewood Cliffs, N.J.: Prentice-Hall, 1954.

Schutz, W. *Joy.* New York: Grove, 1967.

Schwartz, D. *RE-Therapie: So wird man sein eigener Psychologe.* Landsberg am Lech, Germany: Wolfgang Dummer, 1981.

Schwartz, R. M. Cognitive-behavior modification: A conceptual review. *Clinical Psychology Review,* 1982, *2,* 267–293.

Sichel, J., & Ellis, A. *RET self-help form.* New York: Institute for Rational–Emotive Therapy, 1983.

Silverstein, L. *Consider the alternative.* Minneapolis, Minn.: Comp Care, 1977.

Smith, D. Trends in counseling and psychotherapy. *American Psychologist,* 1982, *37,* 802–809.

Smith, M. *Why do I feel guilty when I say no?* New York: Dell, 1977.

Sprenkle, D. H., Keeney, B. P., & Sutton, P. M. Theorists who influence clinical members of AAMFT: A research note. *Journal of Marital and Family Therapy,* 1982, *8,* 367–369.

Thoresen, E. H. *Learning to think: A rational approach.* Clearwater, Fla.: Institute for Rational Living, 1975.

Tosi, D. J. *Youth: Toward personal growth.* Columbus, Ohio: Merrill, 1974.

Walen, S., DiGiuseppe, R., & Wessler, R. *A practitioner's guide to rational–emotive therapy.* New York: Oxford, 1980.

Wessler, R. A., & Wessler, R. L. *The principles and practice of rational–emotive therapy.* San Francisco: Jossey-Bass, 1980.

Wolfe, J. L., & Brand, E. (Eds.). *Twenty years of rational therapy.* New York: Institute for Rational–Emotive Therapy, 1977.

Young, H. *Rational counseling primer.* New York: Institute for Rational–Emotive Therapy, 1974.

2

Rational–Emotive Therapy and Cognitive Behavior Therapy: Similarities and Differences*

Albert Ellis

Rational–emotive therapy (RET) and cognitive behavior therapy (CBT) are both similar and different; and to dispel some of the existing confusion in this regard (Lazarus, 1979; Mahoney, 1979; Meichenbaum, 1979), I shall try to present in this article something of a systematic outline of their main similarities and differences. Let me first say what I have tried to make clear before (Ellis & Whiteley, 1979): that what I call general or unpreferential RET is synonymous with CBT, while what I have called elegant RET, but what may be more objectively called preferential RET, differs significantly from CBT in several important respects.

Preferential RET I shall define as that kind of rational–emotive therapy that RET practitioners usually prefer to use, particularly with relatively bright, neurotic, and reasonably well-motivated clients, because, they hypothesize, it is more efficient, thoroughgoing, self-maintaining, and productive of "deep" or "pervasive" personality change than is general RET. It is their therapy *of choice,* and it is a kind of RET that they will often choose *not* to use when restricted conditions of therapy and/or the limited resources of clients make it unfeasible or impractical. Preferential RET is always a form of general RET or CBT, but the latter may, and often does, include few aspects of the former. When, in this paper, I refer to RET without any modifier, I only mean *preferential* RET; when

*This chapter originally appeared in *Cognitive Therapy and Research*, 1980, *4*, 325–340.

I refer to CBT and *general* RET (which, again, I view as synonymous), I mean them as more generic terms that potentially but not necessarily include preferential RET. Let me now outline some significant differences between CBT and (preferential) RET under three major headings: cognitive, emotive, and behavioral differences.

COGNITIVE DIFFERENCES BETWEEN RET AND CBT

Some of the main cognitive differences between RET and CBT include the following.

Philosophical Emphasis

CBT of course emphasizes cognitive processes, but it does not have a specific philosophical emphasis, as RET does. Meichenbaum (1977), one of the leading proponents of CBT, covers many techniques, but he significantly omits any stress on a distinctly philosophical outlook. RET, on the other hand, emphasizes that humans are born (as well as reared) as philosophers (Ellis, 1962, 1973b) and that they are natural scientists (Kelly, 1955), creators of meaning (Frankl, 1966), and users of rational means to predict the future (Friedman, 1975). One of its main goals, therefore, is to help clients make a *profound philosophical change* that will affect their future as well as their present emotions and behaviors.

To this end, RET tries to help people comprehend and accept several ideas that are still revolutionary in our culture: (1) they largely (thought not exclusively) *create* their own emotional disturbances by strongly believing in absolutistic, irrational beliefs; (2) having a distinct measure of self-determination or "free will," they can actively *choose* to disturb or undisturb themselves; (3) to change, they had better actively *work* at modifying their thoughts, feelings, and behaviors; (4) if they decide to profoundly change one major philosophy, they may help modify many of their own emotional and behavioral reactions; (5) they will usually find a philosophy of long-range hedonism more healthful and productive of happiness than one of short-range hedonism; and (6) a scientific rather than an unscientific, devoutly religious, or mystical outlook is likely to bring them greater emotional health and satisfaction.

As I have shown (Ellis, 1962, 1971a, 1971b, 1973a, 1973c, 1974) and as Raimy (1975) has emphasized, all therapy techniques, when they are effective, probably work because clients, wittingly or unwittingly, change their underlying cognitions, ideas, assumptions, or philosophies. RET tries to help them specifically to see what their self-defeating views are, to question and challenge these, and to surrender them for more self-helping or happiness-producing outlooks. CBT may also include this RET philosophical approach, but it may not. In RET, it is central rather than optional or peripheral to personality change.

Humanistic Outlook

Not only is RET philosophical, but it includes the specific existential–humanistic outlook of some other therapeutic schools (Ellis, 1962, 1973b). To some degree, it incorporates the views of Alfred Adler, Kurt Goldstein, Karen Horney, Viktor Frankl, Carl Rogers, and other humanistic theorists. This view sees people as holistic, goal-directed individuals who have importance in the world just because they are human and alive; it unconditionally accepts them with their limitations; and it particularly focuses upon their experiences and values, including their self-actualizing potentialities. At the same time, RET favors ethical humanism, the philosophy of the American Humanist Association, which encourages people to live by rules emphasizing human interests over the interests of inanimate nature, of lower animals, or of any assumed natural order or deity. This outlook acknowledges people only as human, and in no way as superhuman or subhuman. It hypothesizes that devout faith in suprahuman entities and powers almost always leads to poor emotional health and to decreased long-range happiness. Although CBT (like behavior therapy or BT) is usually humanistically oriented, it does not have to be, while a humanistic outlook is intrinsic to RET.

Goals and Purposes

While RET, like CBT, is often interested in, or at least will settle for, symptom removal, it primarily strives for deep-seated emotional and behavioral change. It works for—but, of course, does not always achieve—a remarkably new psychological *set* on the part of its clients that will enable them not only to feel better and be relieved of their presenting symptoms but also to bring a radically revised outlook to all *new,* present and future, situations that will semiautomatically help them to stop disturbing themselves, in the first place, or to quickly undisturb themselves, in the second place.

This new outlook or *set* for which RET strives includes clients' acquiring philosophies of self-interest, self-direction, tolerance of self and others, acceptance of uncertainty, flexibility, scientific thinking, risk-taking, and commitment to vital interests (Ellis, 1973b, 1979a). RET hypothesizes that if clients achieve this kind of a changed perspective, they will minimally create present and future "emotional" problems.

Lack of Self-rating or of Ego

RET differs significantly from behavior therapy, from cognitive behavior modification, and from almost all other humanistic–existential therapies in that it does *not* espouse positive self-rating, or clients acquiring what is often called "self-confidence" or "self-esteem." Like these other therapies, it emphasizes the harm of self-downing or self-disesteem, but it takes the somewhat special position that all ratings or evaluations of the self tend to be mistaken and illegitimate. It holds, instead, that although people biologically and socially strongly tend to rate themselves as well as their acts and performances, they can learn to omit the first and to stick only with the second rating. That is, they can set up goals and values and then only rate what they do in terms of whether it helps them to achieve these goals, without giving any global rating to their "selves" for the achievement or nonachievement of such goals (Ellis, 1976a; Ellis & Abrahms, 1978; Ellis & Grieger, 1977; Ellis & Harper, 1975).

Various kinds of CBT—including the techniques of Goldfried and Davison (1976), Maultsby (1975), Meichenbaum (1977), and Rimm and Masters (1979)—teach rational coping statements, such as, "I am good because I exist" or "Even though I fail, I am still a good person." But the philosophical rationale for holding the belief "I am neither good nor bad, nor can I legitimately rate myself as a total person at all, even though some of my traits are good (efficient) or bad (inefficient) for some of my main purposes" can probably not be shown to clients without a fairly sophisticated analysis and socratic-type dialogue that is indigenous to RET.

Use of Humor

CBT, as well as certain other forms of therapy—such as Farrelly and Brandsma's (1974) provocative therapy—may include humor, or reducing irrational ideas to absurdity, as a therapeutic method. In principle, however, RET hypothesizes that almost all neurotic disturbance stems from taking things too seriously—from demanding, commanding, or *must*urbating about one's goals—and states that one of the main antidotes to this kind of irrational thinking is the strong therapeutic use of a sense of humor. Consequently, RET stresses (thought it does not mandate) the use of humor, including paradoxical intention, evocative language, irony, wit, cartoons, and rational humorous songs (Ellis, 1977a, 1977b).

Anti*must*urbatory Techniques

CBT practitioners—e.g., Beck (1976), Maultsby (1975), and Goldfried and Davison (1976)—often employ empirical arguments to show clients how to surrender their misperceptions of reality, and even Wolpe (1982) advocates helping clients to change their unrealistic, antiempirical perceptions. Going beyond this, however, RET hypothesizes that most antiempirical statements by which people disturb themselves stem from overt or implicit *musts,* from absolutistic premises that humans *bring to* many situations and that then almost compel them to misperceive these events.

Thus, if you begin with the irrational premise "I *must* not die dramatically in

an airplane accident," you will easily tend to make several antiempirical conclusions, such as: (1) "There is a *good chance* that the plane I fly in will get into
an accident," (2) "If I do get in an air crash, it will be awful (that is, more than
100% inconvenient)!" (3) "I *can't stand* even the thought of flying!" and (4)
"Everything connected with airplanes—even a photo of a plane—is exceptionally dangerous and horrible!" If, on the contrary, you start with the rational
premise "I definitely don't want to die in an airplane crash, but if I do, I do!" you
will most probably not make such antiempirical conclusions and will easily see
that there is little chance of your getting killed in a commercial flight (Ellis &
Harper, 1975; Ellis & Whiteley, 1979).

Because it hypothesizes the existence of underlying *musts* and of what Horney
(1965) called "the tyranny of the shoulds," RET not only tries to rip up clients'
antiempirical, unrealistic statements but also reveals and disputes the underlying
*must*urbatory premises out of which these statements usually arise. In this
respect, RET may be said to be "deeper" or more "radical" than related CBT
procedures.

Disputing Techniques

RET, like CBT, employs many cognitive methods, including the teaching of
rational or coping self-statements, cognitive distraction, thought stopping, bibliotherapy, semantic analysis, modeling, imagery, and problem solving (Ellis,
1969, 1976, 1978; Ellis & Abrahms, 1978; Ellis & Grieger, 1977; Ellis &
Knaus, 1977). Considerably more than CBT, however, it specializes in two
active forms of disputing: (1) the therapist's vigorously disputing or debating
clients' irrational thinking and (2) the therapist's teaching clients how to do their
own self-disputing and self-debating, so that they internalize the questioning,
challenging, skeptical method of science and use it to surrender their present and
future absolutistic cognitions (Phadke, 1976).

This is not to say that RET primarily or exclusively consists of arguing with
clients and showing them how to argue rationally with themselves, which has
been wrongly implied by critics such as Lazarus (1979), Mahoney (1974, 1979),
and Meichenbaum (1977, 1979). Often, RET practitioners hardly use disputation—as when they see young children, mentally retarded individuals, or
severely psychotic individuals who are hardly amenable to Socratic-type dialogues and who can be more efficiently reached by teaching them rational
coping statements. Whenever feasible, however, RET favors active disputation
for several reasons: (1) this is a highly democratic procedure that avoids in-
doctrinating clients with the therapist's "rational" beliefs; (2) it helps clients
make their own generalizations, which may lead to many and more profound
emotional and behavioral changes; (3) it appears to help clients not only achieve
but also sustain their improvement (though this hypothesis is yet to be clearly

tested); and (4) it shows clients how to dispute the irrationalities of their relatives, friends, and associates, and frequently to help these people and the clients' relationships with them (Ellis 1973b, 1975).

Recognition of Cognitive Palliative Methods

Like CBT, RET employs many cognitive distraction methods, such as teaching clients to use Jacobsen's (1958) progressive muscle relaxation technique or Benson's (1975) relaxation response. All these methods work at times, help clients to stop worrying temporarily, and thereby facilitate behavioral change. RET, because it focuses on the philosophies that often underlie cognitive behavioral methods, recognizes however that cognitive distraction methods are almost always palliative, for they sidetrack people momentarily from their self-defeating views instead of helping them truly to surrender these views. Moreover, there is the danger that, in feeling "good" or "relaxed" as a result of employing cognitive distraction, many clients may stop working at their underlying irrational beliefs and may therefore prevent themselves from making the thoroughgoing changes of which they are capable. RET practitioners, therefore, use distraction methods with caution, sometimes deliberately omit them, and encourage clients to employ them *in addition to* more penetrating and profound methods of cognitive behavioral therapy.

Problem-solving Methods

CBT stresses the use of problem-solving methods of treatment (D'Zurilla & Goldfried, 1971; Haley, 1977; Spivack, Platt, & Shure, 1976), while RET discourages such problem-solving at what it calls A (activating experiences in clients' lives) until *after* or at least *along with* clients' work to undermine and change B (their irrational beliefs about what is happening at A). Thus, if at point A (activating experience) your partner is giving you a hard time, and you are indecisive at point C (emotional and behavioral consequence) about whether or not to leave him or her, a typical CBT solution to this problem will be to have the therapist figure out with you how you can change your partner, reorganize the conditions under which you work with him or her, form a new partnership with someone else, and so forth. Instead, RET will first explore what you are telling yourself—at B, your belief system—to make yourself indecisive, and will turn up such irrational beliefs as "I *must* make a perfect decision, else I am contemptible!" "I can't stand making a disadvantageous decision!" and "It's *awful* if I lose my partner completely!"

   Once it helps you to see clearly and then to dispute and surrender these basic irrationalities, RET then will try to help you work out a better solution to the difficulties with your partner that exist at point A. For disturbed people almost always have, first, practical problems (e.g., "How can I get along better with my partner?") and emotional problems, or problems *about* problems (e.g., "How can I refuse to depress seriously or anger myself, even if the problem with my partner never goes away?"). Where CBT frequently concentrates on practical problem solving, RET much more frequently focuses on solving the emotional problem about the practical problem, and then (if required) helps the client with the original difficulty.

The Concept of Discomfort Anxiety

Most psychotherapies, including CBT and RET, deal largely with clients' ego anxiety: their downing themselves as total humans when they act incompetently and/or are disapproved of by significant others. RET, in addition, makes a special effort to work with clients' discomfort anxiety or low frustration tolerance. Discomfort anxiety is emotional hypertension that arises when people feel (1) that their life or comfort is threatened, (2) that they *must not* feel uncomfortable and *have to* feel at ease, and (3) that it is awful or catastrophic (rather than merely inconvenient or disadvantageous) when they don't get what they supposedly must (Ellis, 1978).

While dealing actively and directively with ego anxiety, RET deliberately looks for manifestations of discomfort anxiety and reveals and disputes the irrationalities that lie behind it. Because of its basic philosophy of long-range rather than short-range hedonism, it tends to be a more specific and stronger foe of low frustration tolerance than are more general forms of CBT.

Secondary Symptoms of Disturbance (ɪ.ᴇ, ᴀɴxɪᴇᴛʏ ᴏᴠᴇʀ ᴀɴxɪᴇᴛʏ)

The theory of RET says that not only do people tell themselves basic irrational beliefs (B) about the activating experiences (A) in their lives and thereby bring on disturbed emotional and behavioral consequences (C), but, because humans have a pronounced biosocial tendency to observe and evaluate virtually everything in their lives, including their emotional reactions, they also see, think about, and appraise their disturbed feelings and behaviors. In the process of *mustur*bating about their primary symptoms, they often create secondary symptoms, or disturbance about disturbance! Thus, by telling yourself, "I *must* succeed at this task!" you can make yourself anxious, and by convincing yourself, "I *should* not make myself anxious," you can produce the secondary symptom of anxiety about anxiety. You may also, at times, proceed to a third level: make yourself anxious about being anxious about being anxious!

RET, more than CBT, specifically looks for secondary and tertiary symptoms of disturbance, shows clients how they create these symptoms, and indicates what they can do to eliminate primary, secondary, and tertiary symptoms. Especially in the case of serious phobias, such as agoraphobia, RET works with original fear and, especially, the fear of fear: the horror *about* the original fear (Ellis, 1979a).

Selectivity of Techniques

[handwritten annotation: USES MOST EFFICIENT, AND LONGEST LASTING TECHNIQUES — IN VIVO/FLOODING]

Like CBT, RET is exceptionally electic in its methods of treatment and, although it favors cognition, also tries to encourage personality change through emotive and behavioral methods, recognizing that, if people force themselves to act and/or feel differently, they frequently will bring about cognitive modification (Ellis, 1968, 1970, 1979b; Wolfe & Fodor, 1977). RET, however, hypothesizes that *efficiency* is an important aspect of therapy and that, to achieve maximum efficacy and minimum harm with their clients, therapists had better be highly selective rather than indiscriminately eclectic in their use of various methodologies.

[handwritten annotation: RET FAVORS IN VIVO SENSITIZATION FLOODING HOMEWORK] Following its philosophy of therapeutic efficiency, RET favors *in vivo* desensitization and flooding homework assignments, and hypothesizes that they will usually result in more profound and lasting philosophical changes than will, say, imaginal and/or gradual desensitization. It also minimizes the use of catharsis and abreaction of anger, because it assumes that these techniques help people immediately feel better but ultimately get worse by encouraging them to reaffirm cognitively a philosophy of outrage while they are "releasing" their anger.

RET also avoids the use of transpersonal, mystical, and religious techniques because, again, these methods may sometimes help some clients to live "better" with their disturbed thinking but at the same time interfere with the full development of flexible, open, and scientific attitudes, which, according to RET, are core characteristics of optimum and sustained mental health (Ellis, 1970, 1972). RET, then, because of its basic assumptions about what really constitutes emotional health and disturbance, is more selective in choosing therapeutic methods than is general CBT. [Let me note, in passing, that one of the main differences between RET and Lazarus's (1976) multimodal therapy is that the latter somewhat compulsively uses all the main techniques in the BASIC ID model with virtually all clients all of the time, while RET more selectively uses some of these CBT techniques with some of the clients some of the time.]

EMOTIVE DIFFERENCES BETWEEN RET AND CBT

In principle, RET almost invariably employs emotive and behavioral methods of psychotherapy and has always done so. Because it is unusual in its emphasis of cognitive–rational methods, and is somewhat different in this respect from most other forms of therapy, I originally called it RT or rational therapy (Ellis, 1957, 1958, 1975), but I soon changed this to RET or rational–*emotive* therapy when I realized that the original name was leading critics to see it only (rather than in great measure) in rational terms (Ellis & Harper, 1961).

As noted already, RET is not merely a pragmatic approach to therapy that employs any and all techniques that "work" or that give good, tested results; it is also a philosophical system or theory of human nature and of personality change. As long as this theory seems valid, RET practitioners largely (though I hope not rigidly) follow it in their work with clients. Some of the main tenets of this theory follow. (1) Humans disturb themselves for biological as well as social or environmental reasons, because they are naturally and easily predisposed to think crookedly, emote inappropriately, and behave dysfunctionally in regard to their own goals and values. (2) Once they acquire or invent irrational thinking, they strongly and forcefully hold onto it and have great difficulty in giving it up. (3) Because their cognitions, affects, and actions significantly interact and transact with each other, only a multifaceted cognitive–emotive–behavioral approach to therapy is likely to help them overcome their neurotic symptoms, to maintain emotional health, and to be significant in preventing them from disturbing themselves again in the future. (4) Emotional maturity and behavioral efficacy largely consist of wishing, wanting, and preferring self-chosen, individualistic goals rather than absolutistically needing, necessitating, or *must*urbating about those goals. (5) Efficient—meaning quicker, simpler, longer-lasting, and more thoroughgoing—methods of personality change are usually preferable to less efficient means. Because of its being based on such theories as these—most or all of which, of course, may subsequently be revised or abandoned—RET favors certain emotive techniques and disfavors other emotive methods of therapy, while CBT is less selective in this respect. Some examples follow.

Discriminating Appropriate from Inappropriate Emotions

RET especially discriminates between negative emotions like sorrow, regret, frustration, and annoyance, which follow from people's not getting what they *desire* and which motivate them to try to change for the better an undesired or obnoxious situation, and negative emotions like depression, panic, rage, and feelings of inadequacy, which (it hypothesizes) follow from people's not getting what they irrationally think they *need* or *must have* and which interfere with their constructive motivation and action and usually sabotage their desires. Unlike many CBT and experiential practitioners, rational–emotive therapists do not accept an emotion as "good" merely because it exists, is genuine, and has a certain degree of intensity. Instead, RET specifically defines "healthy" emotions in terms of clients' goals and values, and not abstractly in their own right. Thus many followers of CBT—for example, Beck (1976)—think of depression as extreme sadness, and view both intense sadness and depression as harmful symptoms. But RET sees depressed people as commanding that their extreme sadness (which may be based on a real loss, and therefore quite legitimate) *must*

REMEMBER APPROXIMATELY SAD /
BUT →
SURRENDER not exist and as thereby illegitimately making themselves depressed. It con-
IN APPROPRE-sequently tries to help such individuals remain appropriately sad but surrender
ATE SAD —
NESS : their inappropriate, self-defeating feelings of depression.

Directly Working with and on Emotions

Like CBT, RET uses many evocative–emotive exercises that give clients an
opportunity to acknowledge, get in touch with, work on, and change their
feelings from inappropriate to appropriate ones. It particularly employs my
version of Maultsby's rational–emotive imagery (Maultsby, 1971, 1975; Maultsby & Ellis, 1974), where clients are asked to imagine intensely one of the worst
possible things that could happen, to let themselves feel strongly anxious,
depressed, or angry, and to work directly on changing these feelings to those of
sorrow, disappointment, or annoyance. It also, much more than does CBT,
creates and uses some encounter and marathon techniques (Ellis, 1977c, d; Ellis
& Whiteley, 1979; Wolfe & Fodor, 1977).

At the same time, RET avoids many emotive procedures, such as Reichian,
gestalt, bioenergetic, and primal technique, that some CBT practitioners (e.g.,
Palmer, 1973) use, because these procedures often help exacerbate rather than
ameliorate feelings that RET views as inapproprate, such as anger and "self-
esteem."

Relationship Procedures

USES EXTREME CAUTION ON GIVING LOVE, EMPATHY; SYMPATHY,
WARMTH → AS THESE FOSTER CONDITIONAL AND NOT
UNCONDITIONAL ACCEPTANCE

RET, CBT, and almost all other forms of psychotherapy involve some kind of
relationship between the therapist and clients, but RET tends to be more selective
than CBT in this respect and emphasizes the therapist's *accepting* rather than
giving warmth or approval to clients and stresses teaching them the philosophy
of self-acceptance. Although RET practitioners can, if they wish, give their
clients empathy, sympathy, warmth, and even love, they tend to do so with
extreme caution, recognizing that the therapist's expression of these feelings can
easily backfire and help clients think that they are "good people" *because* the
therapist approves of or loves them. Clients thereby tend to acquire conditional
rather than *un*conditional self-acceptance, and it is the latter that RET favors.

Forceful Emotive Interventions

Because it theorizes that humans are for the most part biologically predisposed to
disturb themselves and to perpetuate their own dysfunctional thinking, emoting,
and behaving, and that they have enormous difficulty in changing and keeping
changed their self-defeating emotional reactions, RET holds that it is often
important for therapists to use a great deal of force or vigor in interrupting their
clients' philosophies and behaviors (Ellis, 1979b). Consequently, RET employs

unusually strong rational coping statements that have a powerful emotive quality, and it uses dramatic exercises, such as its famous shame-attacking exercises, to induce many clients to flood themselves with positive or negative feelings that may be therapeutically useful (Ellis, 1974; Ellis & Abrahms, 1978). CBT may, of course, employ the same kind of forceful emotive procedures used in RET, but it tends to do so less often and to do so on pragmatic rather than theoretical grounds.

BEHAVIORAL DIFFERENCES BETWEEN RET AND CBT

Both CBT and RET include a wide range of behavioral procedures; in fact, they use almost all the common methods that are used in general behavior therapy (BT). Because, however, of the same kind of theoretical and philosophical assumptions mentioned earlier, RET is once again more selective than CBT in this connection. Thus it emphasizes relatively few behavioral methods while ignoring or deemphasizing some of the others.

Reservations about Operant Conditioning

Although RET often utilizes operant conditioning (Ellis, 1969, 1973a; Ellis & Abrahms, 1978), it takes a somewhat skeptical view of the effectiveness of social reinforcement, especially of kind and encouraging words from the therapist when clients do the "right" thing. For if I, as your therapist, keep telling you, "That's great!" or "I like that!" when you carry out your RET homework assignments, you may start to do them mainly for me and the praise I give you rather than for their intrinsic rewards. Moreover, you may falsely conclude, "Because I am doing so well at this therapy and because Dr. Ellis likes me for carrying it out satisfactorily, I am a good person!" You may thereby give yourself conditional rather than unconditional positive regard or acceptance and feel better but remain basically as disturbed as ever.

According to RET theory, most people—and especially most seriously disturbed people—are already, because of their biological nature and their social (reinforcement) upbringing, *too* reinforceable, *too* conditionable, and *too* suggestible. They much too easily do the "right" things for the wrong reasons. RET, therefore, is one of the few behavior therapies that consciously try to help clients acquire a basic philosophical outlook that makes them maximally nondependent, individualistic, and nonconformist. Although it often (for practical purposes) adopts Skinnerian methods, it also retains a fundamental individualistic–humanistic outlook that encourages clients to be less conditionable by outside (social) influences and more self-conditionable and self-controlling. In this respect, it is again more selective in its use of techniques than some of the other modes of CBT tend to be.

Use of Penalization

Although considerable research tends to show that reinforcing people for their "good" behavior works better than penalizing them for their "poor" behavior (Skinner, 1971), I have not found this to be consistently true in clinical practice, especially with adult D.C.'s (difficult customers!) whose degree of emotional disturbance, and especially their abysmally low frustration tolerance, almost forces them to go for immediate pleasures rather than long-term gains. RET practice has discovered that these individuals often do not alter their dysfunctional behavior unless they give themselves an immediate and somewhat drastic penalty immediately after repeating this behavior. Thus inveterate smokers frequently won't stop smoking if, say, they reinforce themselves with delicious food every time they desist from smoking; rather, they find, for physical and psychological reasons, that cigarettes are so "rewarding" that the food doesn't prove that reinforceable. But if they severely penalize themselves every single time they smoke, say, by burning a $100 bill (and lighting up the cigarette with it!), they usually stop smoking quite quickly!

On the basis of these and many similar observations concerning people's low frustration tolerance, RET theory states that humans frequently vigorously hold to and give in to irrational ideas, such as the idea that they can harmlessly get away with smoking, so that highly forceful emotive-behavioral intervention, such as their giving themselves stiff immediate penalties whenever they indulge in dysfunctional activities, is often required to help depropagandize them regarding these irrationalities. Whereas CBT and BT therefore tend to emphasize behavioral reinforcement methods, RET more often utilizes self-penalization.

In Vivo Desensitization

BT and CBT today often use *in vivo* desensitization rather than Wolpe's systematic desensitization, which is largely done imaginatively (Emmelkamp, Kuipers, & Eggeraat, 1978; Wolpe, 1958, 1982). RET, however, has always favored *in vivo* desensitizing homework assignments and does so more than general CBT (Ellis, 1962, 1979b). The two main homework assignments utilized in RET follow. (1) People who needlessly fear to do certain things, such as ride in elevators or encounter members of the other sex, are urged to do so many times, and preferably in a short period of time. (2) Clients who have low frustration tolerance and who cop out of difficult situations in order to feel better (e.g., quit unpleasant jobs or refuse to visit difficult relatives) are encouraged to stay in these situations until they overcome much of their low frustration tolerance or discomfort anxiety. Then perhaps they may be encouraged to leave these situations.

Flooding or Implosive Therapy

Because of its assumption that dramatic interruption of clients' irrational beliefs is often more effective than gradual and less dramatic interruption of these beliefs, RET tends much more than CBT to favor flooding or implosive therapy. It encourages disturbed individuals to engage—suddenly, implosively, and re-petitively—in "dangerous" or "phobic" behavior, not merely to desensitize themselves to the "pain" of undergoing this kind of action but also to impinge on their irrational ideas that they *can't* perform this behavior, that it will *destroy them* if they do, that it is *too* painful to bear, and so forth.

Skills Training Procedures → MUST FIRST SURRENDER iBs, THEN UNLEARN SKILLS

Both RET and CBT employ a good many skills training procedures, such as the teaching assertiveness, personal relating, and sexual proficiency, but RET also emphasizes the limitations of skills training when it is used mainly in its own right and does not include a basic change in clients' irrational beliefs (Ellis, 1977d). RET practitioners, when using skills training, strongly emphasize peo-ple's first surrendering their basic irrationalities, especially horror of failure and dire need for others' approval that blocks their acquiring assertiveness, sexual proficiency, and other skills. They then learn the skills themselves (Lange & Jakubowski, 1976; Wolfe & Fodor, 1975, 1977). The RET approach in this respect has a different emphasis from that used by most other CBT practitioners (Liberman, King, DeRisi, & McCann, 1977; Masters & Johnson, 1970).

CONCLUSION

I have tried to outline in this article some of the major differences between cognitive behavior therapy (CBT) or general RET, which I see as synonymous, and specialized or preferential RET, and to outline the somewhat distinct theory and practice of the latter form of psychotherapy. I have by no means covered all the possible differences between these two overlapping methods of therapy but have concentrated on the important ones that currently come to my mind. One of my main hypotheses is that the systematic use of CBT or general RET will be more effective for more clients more of the time than any form of treatment that exclusively stresses cognitive, emotive, or behavioral methods. But I also hypothesize that RET, when defined as it is in this chapter and when used in its preferential form, will also prove more effective than CBT (or than general RET) for more clients more of the time. Virtually no studies have yet been done to test this hypothesis, and it will be interesting to see what the outcome of such studies will be.

REFERENCES

Beck, A. T. _Cognitive therapy and the emotional disorders._ New York: International Universities Press, 1976.

Benson, H. _The relaxation response._ New York: Morrow, 1975.

D'Zurilla, T., & Goldfried, M. Problem solving and behavior modification. _Journal of Abnormal Psychology,_ 1971, _78,_ 109–126.

Ellis, A. Outcome of employing three techniques of psychotherapy. _Journal of Clinical Psychology,_ 1957, _13,_ 334–350.

Ellis, A. Rational psychotherapy, _Journal of General Psychology,_ 1958, _59,_ 35–49.

Ellis, A. Reason and emotion in psychotherapy. New York: Lyle Stuart; Citadel Press, 1962.

Ellis, A. What really causes therapeutic change? _Voices,_ 1968, _4_(2), 90–97.

Ellis, A. A cognitive approach to behavior therapy. _International Journal of Psychiatry,_ 1969, _8,_ 896–900.

Ellis, A. The cognitive element in experiential and relationship psychotherapy. _Existential Psychiatry,_ 1970, _28,_ 35–52.

Ellis, A. What does transpersonal psychology have to offer to the art and science of psychotherapy? _Voices,_ 1972, _8_(3), 10–20. (Revised version: _Rational Living,_ 1973, _8_(1), 20–28.)

Ellis, A. Are cognitive behavior therapy and rational therapy synonymous? _Rational Living,_ 1973, _8_(2), 8–11. (a)

Ellis, A. _Humanistic psychotherapy: The rational–emotive approach._ New York: Crown: McGraw-Hill Paperbacks, 1973. (b)

Ellis, A. _How to stubbornly refuse to be ashamed of anything._ Cassette recording. New York: Institute for Rational Living, 1974.

Ellis, A. How to live with a "neurotic" (Rev. ed.). New York: Crown, 1975. (Originally published, 1957.)

Ellis, A. _RET abolishes most of the human ego._ New York: Institute for Rational Living, 1976.

Ellis, A. _Discomfort anxiety: A new cognitive–behavioral construct._ Cassette recording. New York: BMA audiotapes, 1978.

Ellis, A. A note on the treatment of agoraphobics with cognitive modification versus prolonged exposure _in vivo. Behaviour Research and Therapy,_ 1979, _17,_ 162–164. (a)

Ellis, A. The use of force in psychotherapy. _Journal of Contemporary Psychotherapy,_ 1979, _10,_ 83–97. (b)

Ellis, A., & Abrahms, E. _Brief psychotherapy in medical and health practice._ New York: Springer, 1978.

Ellis, A., & Grieger, R. _Handbook of rational–emotive therapy._ New York: Springer, 1977.

Ellis, A., & Harper, R. A. _A guide to rational living._ Englewood Cliffs, N.J.: Prentice-Hall, 1961.

Ellis, A., & Harper, R. A. _A new guide to rational living._ Englewood Cliffs, N.J.: Prentice-Hall; Hollywood: Wilshire Brooks/Cole, 1975.

Ellis, A., & Knaus, W. _Overcoming procrastination._ New York: Institute for Rational Living, 1977.

Ellis, A., & Whiteley, J. M. (Eds.). _Theoretical and empirical foundations of rational emotive therapy._ Monterey, Calif.: Brooks/Cole, 1979.

Emmelkamp, P. M. G., Kuipers, A. C. M., & Eggeraat, J. B. Cognitive modification versus prolonged exposure _in vivo:_ A comparison with agoraphobics as subjects. _Behaviour Research and Therapy,_ 1978, _16,_ 33–41.

Farrelly, F., & Brandsma, J. _Provocative therapy._ Millbrae, Calif.: Celestial Arts, 1974.

Frankl, V. E. _Man's search for meaning._ New York: Washington Square Press, 1966.

Friedman, M. _Rational behavior._ Columbia, S.C.: University of South Carolina Press, 1975.

Goldfried, M. R., & Davison, G. S. _Clinical behavior therapy._ New York: Holt, Rinehart & Winston, 1976.

Haley, J. _Problem-solving therapy._ San Francisco: Jossey-Bass, 1977.

Horney, K. _Collected writings._ New York: Norton, 1965.

Jacobsen, E. _You must relax._ New York: Pocket Books, 1958.

Kelly, G. _The psychology of personal constructs._ New York: Norton, 1955.

Lange, A., & Jakubowski, P. _Responsible assertive behavior._ Champaign, Ill.: Research Press, 1976.

Lazarus, A. A. *Multimodal therapy.* New York: Springer, 1976.

Lazarus, A. A. A critique of rational–emotive therapy. In A. Ellis & J. M. Whiteley (Eds.), *Theoretical and empirical foundations of rational–emotive therapy.* Monterey, Calif.: Brooks/Cole, 1979.

Liberman, R. P., King, L. W., DeRisi, W. J., & McCann, M. *Personal effectiveness.* Champaign, Ill.: Research Press, 1977.

Mahoney, M. *Cognition and behavior modification.* Cambridge, Mass.: Ballinger, 1974.

Mahoney, M. A critical analysis of rational–emotive theory and practice. In A. Ellis & J. M. Whiteley (Eds.), *Theoretical and empirical foundations of rational–emotive therapy.* Monterey, Calif.: Brooks/Cole, 1979.

Masters, W. H., & Johnson, V. E. *Human sexual inadequacy.* Boston: Little, Brown, 1970.

Maultsby, M. C., Jr. Rational emotive imagery. *Rational Living,* 1971, *6*(1), 24–27.

Maultsby, M. C., Jr. *Help yourself to happiness.* New York: Institute for Rational Living, 1975.

Maultsby, M. C., Jr., & Ellis, A. *Technique for using rational emotive imagery.* New York: Institute for Rational Living, 1974.

Meichenbaum, D. *Cognitive behavior modification.* New York: Plenum, 1977.

Meichenbaum, D. Dr. Ellis, please stand up. In A. Ellis & J. M. Whiteley (Eds.), *Theoretical and empirical foundations of rational–emotive therapy.* Monterey, Calif.: Brooks/Cole, 1979.

Palmer, R. D. Desensitization of the fear of expressing one's own inhibited aggression: Bioenergetic assertive techniques for behavior therapists. *Advances in Behavior Therapy,* 1973, *4,* 241–253.

Phadke, K. M. *Bull fighting: A royal road to mental health and happiness.* Unpublished manuscript, Bombay, India, 1976.

Raimy, V. *Misunderstandings of the self.* San Francisco: Jossey-Boss, 1975.

Rimm, D. C., & Masters, J. C. *Behavior therapy* (Rev. ed.). New York: Academic Press, 1979. (Originally published, 1974.)

Skinner, B. F. *Beyond freedom and dignity.* New York: Knopf, 1971.

Spivack, G., Platt, J., & Shure, M. *The problem solving approach to adjustment.* San Francisco: Jossey-Bass, 1976.

Wolfe, J., & Fodor, I. G. A cognitive/behavior approach to modifying assertive behavior in women. *Counseling Psychologist,* 1975, *5,* 45–52.

Wolfe, J. L., & Fodor, I. G. Modifying assertive behavior in women. A comparison of three approaches. *Behavior Therapy,* 1977, *8,* 567–574.

Wolpe, J. Psychotherapy by *reciprocal inhibition.* Stanford, Calif.: Stanford University Press, 1958.

Wolpe, J. *The practice of behavior therapy* (3rd ed.). New York: Pergamon, 1982.

3

Varieties of Cognitions in the Cognitively Oriented Psychotherapies*

Richard L. Wessler

The cognitively oriented approaches to psychological therapy are based on the central assumption that "learned misconceptions (or faulty beliefs, or mistaken ideas) are the crucial variables that must be modified or eliminated before psychotherapy can be successful" (Raimy, 1975, p. 186). I have chosen the term *cognitively oriented psychotherapies* as a label for the various psychological approaches to explanation and treatment that share these theoretical assumptions. Among the approaches under this label are those of Ellis, Beck, Mahoney, Maultsby, Raimy, Kelly, and Bandura. I exclude those approaches that employ cognitions to control behavior without assigning importance to cognitions in the creation of emotions and behaviors.

The purpose of this chapter is to show the role of different types of cognitions in the understanding of emotions and behaviors, and to delineate what types of cognitions are important in producing therapeutic change.

The main figures in the cognitively oriented psychotherapies have used the term *cognition* to refer to several different mental activities. Cognitions include conceptions and ideas (Raimy, 1975), meanings (Beck, 1976), images (Lazarus, 1978), and beliefs (Ellis, 1962). Each leader has ascribed greater importance to one type of cognition without necessarily excluding the others. Some differences, then, exist in the theory of disturbance each has proposed and in the identification of the crucial cognitions that are the targets of intervention. There

*This chapter first appeared in *Rational Living*, 1982, *17*, 3–10.

are also differences in therapeutic procedures, but these, in my opinion, do not come from theories of disturbance but from convictions about the best ways to change the maladaptive cognitions.

A simple taxonomy of cognitions can clarify some of the main differences in emphasis among the cognitively oriented psychotherapies. The taxonomy I propose consists of five dimensions: evaluative–nonevaluative; general–specific; conscious–nonconscious; accurate–inaccurate; and decisions.

EVALUATIVE–NONEVALUATIVE

Any classification of cognitions should recognize a fundamental distinction used in attitude research, between knowing and appraising. Strictly speaking, the term *cognition* refers to the mental activity of knowing. For example, the statement "Portugal is a sovereign nation" is a cognition, a statement of knowledge. But "knowledge" can also be incorrect; for example, "Portugal is part of the continent of Asia."

The mental act of appraising adds evaluative information to what one assumes to be true. The statement "Portugal is beautiful" is not a statement of fact; it is an appraisal. The statement really means "I like the scenery of Portugal," since people often express appraisals in statements that attribute beauty or goodness to a thing or event, rather than using personal pronouns, as in "*I* judge this thing to be beautiful" or "This scene fits *my* idea of beautiful." Further confusion arises when a speaker combines knowledge and appraisal into one statement: "Portugal is a beautiful country."

Some 20 years ago, Abelson (1958) used the terms *hot* and *cold* cognitions to speak of the distinction between appraisals (hot) and knowledge (cold) of presumed facts. Zajonc (1980) revived these terms in an article that created some adverse reactions because he used the term *affect* to refer to appraisal, a common practice in social psychology. Zajonc's article, which offers strong indirect support for the cognitively oriented therapies, asserts that affect (appraisal) is possible without cognition (knowledge); one can appraise a thing or event without knowing what it is, for partial or even incorrect knowledge is sufficient to initiate a process of appraisal.

Strongly evaluative thinking is the chief contributor to emotions, according to Ellis (1962). Emotions, then, can be understood by discovering the hot cognitions associated with them. Unfortunately, many hot cognitions are not stated explicitly but are contained within what appears to be a cold cognition, for example, "I think I will fail if I attempt a new task." In this example, the speaker might (or might not) appraise failing as negative, or if negative to what extent (mild, moderate, strong), or mixed (some negative *and* some positive appraisals of failing at a certain task). If one attends only to the accuracy of the cold cognition, one misses the component of the statement that makes it active in an emotional process.

It seems likely that one does not appraise a cold cognition one believes to be untrue. While humans can imagine all sorts of things, only those that seem possible—however slight the possibility—stir emotions. Even the most remote possibility may stir emotion if the hot cognitions about it are strong enough. For example, the slight possibility that an airplane might crash is enough to produce an emotional response, provided the outcome is appraised as extremely negative. This may be one reason why merely convincing someone of the low probability of such an event's occurring is insufficient to reduce fear about the event; phobias do not result from cold cognitions alone. Hot cognitions are emphasized in Ellis's approach to psychotherapy, but receive less attention in other cognitively oriented psychotherapies.

There are a number of cold cognitions that are discussed in the cognitively oriented psychotherapies. Among these are anticipation of events (Kelly, 1955), expectancies (Rotter, 1954), anticipated outcomes (Bandura, 1969), and forecasts: "A unique characteristic of human beings is that their mental representations of the future powerfully affect their state of well-being in the present" (Frank, 1978, p. 1). In this view, behavior is not controlled by actual reinforcing consequences so much as by what one forecasts will happen and—implicitly or explicitly—whether the consequences are appraised as favorable or unfavorable.

Other cold cognitions include attributions or hypotheses people create to explain their own and others' behavior (Försterling, 1980), and conclusions based on logical operations (Beck, 1976). Beck has shown that failure to process information logically may lead a person to far different conclusions than the correct processing of the same basic information. Faulty generalizations and other misuse of evidence result in negatively experienced emotions, provided, if Ellis is correct, they are negatively appraised. Faulty conclusions (cold cognition) do not automatically result in emotional responses unless appraised (hot cognition).

GENERAL–SPECIFIC

Hot and cold cognitions can range from broad and pervasive to situation specific. Relatively enduring and generalized cognitions may be called *underlying beliefs* (Hafner, 1981) or *cognitive structures* (Meichenbaum, 1977), but, whatever they are labeled, they are abstractions about events and behavioral data. Specific thoughts about particular situations are derived from assumptions about self, people in general, the world, and similar abstract concepts.

General cold cognitions are presumed facts, for example, "People are inherently good" or "People cannot be trusted." Popularly held cultural maxims purport to speak truth about human behavior, such as "The world is fair, and people get rewarded and punished according to some divine or natural plan of justice." Such generalizations explain failures to aid persons in distress, because victims presumably deserve their fate. Such clichés can also be a source of comfort, as when one explains misfortune by saying that it is God's will.

General cold cognitions include correct information—for example, "Most people are right-handed"—as well as incorrect information—"*All* people are righthanded"—and other statements that cannot be empirically proven, such as "I am a worthless individual." The statement need not be correct for it to have impact on the person; rather, the person must *believe* that it is correct. As the sociologist W. I. Thomas said, if people define things as real, they *are* real in their consequences.

Several general cold cognitions may be combined, as, for instance, "Hard work brings desirable results, but I am not capable of hard work, therefore any good results I get are due to luck or other people's (rare) generosity." A person who holds this set of ideas will most likely conclude, when faced with a certain task, "I can't work hard enough to perform this task, so I'll put it off or not try it at all."

Generalized hot cognitions are simply values. They are acquired by learning and become personal guides for conduct and for making specific evaluations of things and events. I call them "personal rules of living" to emphasize their regulatory function in each person's life. Relatively enduring hot cognitions may also be called *evaluative premises,* and the specific appraisals derived from them are *evaluative conclusions* (Wessler & Wessler, 1980). Lists of irrational beliefs (Ellis & Harper, 1975) are generalized statements of evaluations and therefore evaluative premises.

The distinction between general and specific cognitions has implications for psychotherapy. Ellis distinguishes between elegant and inelegant solutions to emotional problems. Elegant solutions involve pervasive philosophical change, that is, change in one's general evaluative thinking or values. Inelegant solutions involve either a change in a situation-specific evaluation or in a cold cognition, but not *pervasive* philosophical change.

Taken together, general hot and cold cognitions constitute one's *world view* (Watzlawick, 1978). They form schemata for perceiving and acting, for attending and understanding. They may be inferred from specific statements about particular situations, as well as from behavior that, because of its regularity, seems to be following certain assumptions and rules.

CONSCIOUS–NONCONSCIOUS

It is a contradiction in terms to speak of unconscious cognitions. Cognition, by definition, refers to what is known, and unconscious thoughts are, also by definition, unknown, not in one's awareness. (By now it may also be apparent that evaluative cognition is also something of a contradiction, since cognition refers to what is known about something, not its evaluation or appraisal. It is probably better to use the term *thought* rather than cognition, but cognition is a byword in the cognitively oriented psychotherapies.) The writings of Ellis and Beck at least recognize that nonconscious thoughts that influence emotions and behaviors lie outside one's awareness and realization. Ellis (1962) describes these as unconscious or preconscious, and Beck (1976) calls them automatic thoughts. Neither imply a Freudian-structured unconscious with its emphasis on hidden motives and ego-protecting mechanisms.

The general hot and cold cognitions are probably not conscious much of the time. Indeed, when clients recognize one of their personal rules of living, it is often with the relief of recognition, an "ah-ha" of insight. Watzlawick (1978) states that perhaps the most salient portions of the person's world view lie outside his or her immediate awareness. Mahoney (1980) has forecast an important role for a network of unconscious thoughts in the future direction of the cognitively oriented psychotherapies: "The existence of such a network is not only possible but very probable, and . . . the practical implications are both challenging and inescapable" (p. 160).

Cognitions may be nonconscious because they are linked with other cognitions and only the first one or two thoughts are apparent. Moore (1980) hypothesizes that inferences very often appear linked, one to another, in roughly causal sequence. The terminal link in the inference chain contains the most definitive statement of the person's definition of the situation, and the definition of the situation may range from highly probable to highly improbable. The evaluation of the terminal link in the chain triggers the emotional response. There are emotional chains also (Wessler & Wessler, 1980): One may suffer from interpersonal anxiety, feel anger toward other people for "making" one feel anxious, unassertively not try to influence other people to act differently, feel helpless and depressed, and feel guilty for having angry thoughts and feelings. In this chain, one emotion is linked to another by the cognitions one has about each emotional state.

Recent evidence supports the notion that appraisals can be made without the fully conscious processing of stimuli (Zajonc, 1980). Evaluations, as noted earlier, may be imbedded in cold cognitions, without the person's awareness that he or she has made an evaluation. Thus, specific as well as general cognitions may fall outside immediate awareness. One implication of this assumption is that self-help approaches to psychotherapy are limited to those cognitions the individual is aware of and that one task of the therapist is to aid client discovery of unspoken and unthought-of assumptions and rules of living.

I do not mean to endorse a Freudian model of the mind which pictures the conscious and unconscious as two rooms, one above the other, connected by a trap door that must remain shut to prevent unacceptable thoughts from intruding. It seems far better to me to revive the pre–Freudian notion of parallel states of consciousness and to think of thoughts as molecules of water that move from stream to stream. Nor do I endorse dreams and free associations as the best ways to gain access to nonconscious thoughts; instead, they can be inferred from verbal and molar behavior in an *as-if* manner—people's behavior can be described as-if it follows certain rules.

ACCURATE–INACCURATE

The correction of misconceptions, to use Raimy's (1975) phrase, is the task of the cognitively oriented psychotherapies. This view of psychotherapy implies some standards by which accuracy of cognitions can be judged. Such a standard will differ depending on the type of cognition under scrutiny. Perhaps the easiest to judge are statements that describe a concrete situation or event. It is sometimes possible to verify independently a person's report of what occurred.

Even when this is not possible, it is relatively easy to identify statements that go beyond reporting into the realm of editorializing. Statements that attribute motives to people, forecast the future, add information to observed facts, and appraise the persons, situations, activities, and outcomes are clearly inaccurate as descriptions.

They might be accurate interpretations or inferences, but this cannot be known for certain without additional evidence. Statements of other people's intentions may indeed be correct, as can forecasts, generalizations, and other inferences from observations, but they usually require more data than are immediately at hand. Overgeneralizations are almost always inaccurate, for they are logical errors of inclusion. Accurate cognitions depend on reliable evidence and logical operations on one's observations. Statements of fact can be verified, including one's past observations and inferences, provided they are empirically testable, as sound hypotheses are supposed to be.

Hot or evaluative cognitions are not subject to verification. A personal value cannot be inaccurate, although it can be idiosyncratic and scorned by other people. Evaluations are personal statements of preferences, of likes and dislikes, and of notions of good and bad. They can be misstated, for example, by attributing goodness to a thing or event rather than taking personal responsibility for one's evaluative statement.

Evaluations can also be overgeneralized. For example, a complex situation can be oversimplified by labeling it *good* or *bad*. One also can think erroneously that absolute standards of good and bad exist, and even that they are universally agreed upon. Evaluations add appraisals to one's data about events and are not inherent in the events themselves.

This last idea, of course, is what Ellis has been saying for years and is, in my opinion, his greatest contribution to the cognitively oriented therapies. When he asks the question "Where is the evidence that you *must* . . .?" he knows that there can be no answer because values cannot be absolute or universal except by definition. A person can define himself as worthless but cannot prove it, or can label an event as awful but cannot verify the label. Evaluations have their own internal logic like mathematics, but are not empirical like science. Appraisals can be inconsistent with more general personal values, but cannot be inaccurate according to some external criterion.

DECISIONS

The final category of cognitions is labeled *decisions* (without an antonym, for I could think of none). The full title of the category is *decisions about behavior,* and implies thinking about one's actions, selecting courses of action to take, and instructing oneself to do this rather than that. Without this type of cognition, behavior might seem to result automatically from other cognitive activities. This somewhat existential dimension is, in fact, what makes therapeutic change possible, as one makes decisions to behave differently despite the anxiety generated by long-standing interpretations and evaluations, and to act against one's feelings rather than to go with them (and maintain a self-defeating pattern of anxiety reduction).

The adoption of this category of cognitions makes it possible to eliminate a seeming paradox that arises when cognitively analyzing therapeutic change. The cognitively oriented psychotherapies agree that cognitions must change in order for enduring behavioral change to occur. However, Bandura (1969), among others, has declared personal experiences such as the performing of new behaviors to be one of the most, if not the most, effective means of changing cognitions. Behaviors must change in order for cognitions to change, but cognitions must change in order for behaviors to change, and so on. The circle is broken by revising the statement to read that cognitive decisions to behave differently result in the performing of new behaviors that result in changes in one's hot and cold cognitions that in turn result in sustained behavioral change, and so on.

Among the cognitively oriented psychotherapists, Greenwald (1973) has had the most to say about decisions. Meichenbaum (1977) has shown that self-instructional statements can make the difference between behaviorally coping with otherwise disruptive emotions and allowing emotional arousal to result in better feelings but less productive actions.

INTEGRATION

Any statement about one's cognitions—and we work with statements about cognitions and not the cognitions themselves—can be classified according to the taxonomy just presented. Any statement can be categorized according to whether it is evaluative or nonevaluative, general or specific, conscious or nonconscious, accurate or inaccurate, and a decision to act. (These categories can be used as continua as well as dichotomies.)

These categories, especially the first and the last, can be used to show what is distinctive among the cognitively oriented psychotherapies, for there are differences and we might as well be aware of them. For instance, I have reviewed the work of therapists who claim they are practicing Ellis's approach but who are not doing so, even though they have done a fine job of correcting misconceptions, teaching problem-solving skills, and generally promoting clear thinking. To give further clarity to these differences, I will present a model of the cognitive–emotive–behavioral (CEB) episode (Wessler & Wessler, 1980), and then an example of clinical strategies using the model. This model recognizes that any arbitrary division of human processes is artificial: thoughts, emotions, and actions may occur simultaneously. They exist interdependently. There is mutual influence rather than a one-way action of thoughts causing emotional feelings.

THE MODEL

Step 1: Stimulus. The episode starts with a stimulus or stimulus complex that may come from either the external environment or the internal environment. An overt stimulus (from the external environment) might be other people's actions, a "phobic" object, or the loss of something tangible. Covert stimuli (from the internal environment) might be bodily sensations, that is, nausea or emotional arousal; or any of the remaining steps of this model, such as memories or anticipations. There are many potential stimuli in one's environment at any given time.

Step 2: Input and Selection. Individuals selectively attend to stimuli to focus on, ignoring many of the potential stimuli present in the environment. (It is here that perceptual defense occurs, the defensive maneuver so important in the theories of Rogers, Sullivan, and Perls, although failure to attend to a stimulus may simply be due to lack of conceptual categories for picking up the information [Neisser, 1976].)

Step 3: Perception and Symbolic Representation of Stimulus. This step is cognitive in character and can be divided into definition (the perception) and description (symbolic representation of perceptions). Descriptions are most accurate when they include the perceiver–describer in the account, as well as specification of time, place, and circumstances. Perception is temporally contiguous with stimuli, but descriptions need not be; they can come well after the fact or be about *images* that have no overt stimulus associated with them. This step is the earliest cognitive or symbolic representation in the CEB episode and is, in other words, the individual's phenomenological awareness of a stimulus.

Step 4: Nonevaluative Interpretation of Symbolic Representations of Stimuli. Interpretations, as defined here, are inferences about unobserved aspects of the perceived stimulus or about one's images. Inferences go beyond immediately observable facts and include such cognitive activities as logical operations, forecasts and expectations, attributions, and other examples of cold cognitions. They are conclusions drawn by the person. For example, "My friend did not speak to me" could carry the interpretation "He is not really my friend or he does not like me" (but he might not have seen me).

Step 5: Evaluative Interpretations of Processed Stimuli. This step consists of hot cognitions and is the process emphasized by Ellis in his view of emotions. If the appraisal is neutral, ambiguous, or indecisive, no affective response follows. The appraisal may be implicit rather than explicit, for example, when one reads a negative meaning into the interpretation "My friend did not speak to me."

Step 6: Emotional Response to Processed Stimuli. The arousal of the autonomic nervous system is hypothesized to follow nonneutral appraisal of stimuli (or images). (In a more complicated version of this model, arousal becomes a stimulus at step 1 and initiates a second emotional episode in which labeling of arousal occurs at step 4 and gets appraised at step 5.)

Step 7: Behavioral Response to Processed Stimuli. There is a tendency for action to accompany arousal based on appraisals at step 5. The tendency is to approach that which we evaluate positively and to eliminate that which we evaluate negatively, either by avoidance, escape, or modifying the stimulus. This, of course, is the "flight or fight" response. People tend to seek conditions that they believe will bring them *relative* comfort or discomfort, particularly immediate relief, although it may be only slightly more pleasant than its alternatives.

But such responses are only tendencies. Behavior is here conceived of as controlled by *decisions and self-directions,* based on anticipated outcomes. Behavior is usually consistent with emotional states, but not always. If humans always acted in accord with their emotional states there could be no therapeutic progress. Humans can choose to refuse the immediate relief of anxiety in order to receive later benefits of personal experiences.

Step 8: Functional Feedback or Reinforcing Consequences of Behavior. This step is not so much part of the CEB episode as a result of it. Reactions from the physical and social environment affect subsequent emotional experiences and behaviors. Defensive behaviors result in the reduction of anxiety and are therefore likely to be repeated due to their reinforcing value (or secondary gains). Experiences of mastery and personal efficacy occur when positive results are obtained through new behaviors.

AN EXAMPLE

Here is a specific example of a CEB episode. Let us say that a person suffers from test anxiety. The crucial variables are not the test (step 1) or his/her knowledge that it will occur at a scheduled time (steps 2 and 3). The person probably predicts poor performance (step 4) and evaluates this anticipated outcome as highly negative (step 5). The result is anxiety (step 6), which he/she may reduce by choosing to procrastinate (step 7), a behavior that brings immediate anxiety reduction (step 8) but is a neurotic choice if he/she has the goal of passing the test.

There are other ways to reduce the anxiety. One is to ignore the stimulus (step 1) by getting absorbed in some other activity. Another is to reconstrue failure by blaming the test or the test giver (step 4). One can change the appraisal (step 5): "It is not good to fail, but neither is it extremely bad." One can reduce the arousal at step 6 by taking drugs; or overprepare and reduce the chances of failing (altering the probability at step 4).

Among the cognitively oriented psychotherapies, Ellis's RET focuses largely on step 5, appraisals, both the specific appraisal and the underlying (general and possibly nonconscious) personal philosophical principles. Step 4 interventions are typical of the work of Beck, Maultsby, and others who emphasize the adopting of new attributions, new anticipated outcomes, new expectations, and more careful logical operations, such as avoiding overgeneralizations, dichotomous thinking, and the like.

Step 6 includes direct modifications of emotional responses through biofeedback, relaxation, and medication. Step 7 includes making decisions to endure discomfort, as well as increasing skills through training and modifying one's behavior by self-instructional messages. Step 8 includes any alteration of environmental contingencies. All can be used with step 5 interventions.

The complete therapist has skills to intervene at any point in the CEB episode and to offer help with many practical aspects of a client's problems as well as with psychological aspects. Lazarus's Multimodal Therapy is perhaps the most obvious example, but multiple interventions may be found in other approaches, too. What is distinctive among the cognitively oriented psychotherapies is the *relative* emphasis each places on one or more of the steps in the CEB episode.

What is distinctive about RET, the approach with which I am most familiar, is its explicit discrimination of nonevaluative and evaluative cognitions and its methods for promoting change. The distinctions are twofold.

First, there is an emphasis on changing extreme negative appraisals and the values on which they are based. RET does not seek to impose values on clients. Instead, RET seeks to help clients by showing them the advantages of changing the *form* of their values. "Irrational" evaluative thoughts are good ideas made bad by exaggeration. For example, a person may hold the cultural value that success at a certain task is better than failure, and know that success cannot always be obtained or that it often involves personal sacrifices. The person can also exaggerate the importance of success and "irrationally" demand success, perhaps as proof of his/her worth, and view failure as catastrophic. A major goal in RET is to reduce dysfunctional behaviors and emotions by substituting realistic versions of personal values for exaggerated ones. The RET therapist may also help clients examine some thoughts at steps 3 and 4, by presenting evidence, for example, that the anticipated failure is unlikely to occur or that they could cope if it did. However, when I say that someone is not practicing RET, I mean that the therapist devotes *no* part of the session to exploration and interventions directed to step 5 of the episode.

Second, what is distinctive about RET is Albert Ellis's philosophy of human nature at its best—tolerance, acceptance, and anti-absolutism that precludes exaggerated forms of personal values. The philosophy itself is not unique in psychotherapy; descriptions of Maslow's self-actualized person and Rogers's fully functioning individual show great similarities. How such ideas are conveyed is distinctive and is done by the application of a wide variety of cognitive and behavioral interventions. "As long as a basic RET framework is used, almost any kind of effective therapeutic technique may be used within this framework; and, in this respect, RET is perhaps the most eclectic of any system of therapy" (Wessler & Ellis, 1980, p. 185).

INSIGHT AND ACTION

Goldfried (1980) urges psychotherapies to look for commonalities among their clinical strategies and identifies two: direct feedback from the therapist, and corrective experiences. What is clear from the CEB episode is that there are four types of thought about which one can have corrective experiences; and eight aspects of a client's CEB episode about which to give feedback.

Corrective experiences require the attempting of new behaviors, but these are frequently inhibited by a fear of novelty and the possible discomfort or strong emotions that might accompany new activities. Inducing oneself to try new behaviors so that one may have corrective experiences is often more difficult than either gaining insights or intellectually questioning one's thoughts. Clients, before they act differently, choose to do so, and this involves a new set of thoughts.

This is the reason decisions and self-instructions to carry out new behaviors are included at step 7. Ellis's notion of hedonic calculus is basically a broad guideline for making decisions, as people try to strike a balance between long-range and short-range reinforcements. Maultsby's (1975) criteria for rational behavior are decision-making rules that help persons act in their own best interests. The three basic questions are: Will my action help me (1) remain alive, (2) reach my goal(s), and (3) avoid unwanted internal conflicts? While the answers are frequently difficult, in some cases they are obvious. It is in the best interests of persons who wish to overcome a phobia to experience fear in the presence of certain stimuli in order to free themselves from a pattern of avoidance behavior. It is better for a procrastinating person who wishes to accomplish certain tasks to do them rather than experience the comfort of putting them off.

If Goldfried and Bandura are correct in emphasizing corrective experiences and learning from one's efficacious performances, therapists can help clients develop decisions that promote their values and are consistent with therapeutic goals. Cognitive interventions such as teaching and verbal persuasion are not the only ways to change faulty thinking, nor the best. Experience may well prove to be the best teacher, decisions the most important cognitions in psychotherapy, and encouragement to make decisions and act on them the most challenging and significant task of psychotherapists.

REFERENCES

Abelson, R. P., & Rosenberg, M. J. Symbolic psychologic: A model of attitudinal cognition. *Behavioral Science*, 1958, *3*, 1–13.

Bandura, A. *Principles of behavior modification*. New York: Holt, 1969.

Beck, A. T. *Cognitive therapy and the emotional disorders*. New York: International Universities Press, 1976.

Ellis, A. *Reason and emotion in psychotherapy*. New York: Lyle Stuart, 1962.

Ellis, A., & Harper, R. A. *A new guide to rational living*. Englewood Cliffs, N.J.: Prentice-Hall, 1975.

Försterling, F. Attributional aspects of cognitive behavior modification: A theoretical approach and suggestions for modification. *Cognitive Therapy and Research*, 1980, *4*, 27–37.

Frank, J. D. Expectation and therapeutic outcome. In J. D. Frank, R. Hoehn-Saric, S. D. Imber, B. Lieberman, A. R. Stone (Eds.), *Effective ingredients of successful psychotherapy*. New York: Brunner/Mazel, 1978.

Goldfried, M. R. Toward the delineation of therapeutic change principles. *American Psychologist*, 1980, *35*, 991–999.

Greenwald, H. *Direct decision therapy*. San Diego: Edits, 1973.

Hafner, A. J. A problem-solving extension of the A-B-C format. *Rational Living*, 1981, *16*(2), 29–33.

Kelly, G. A. *The psychology of personal constructs*. New York: Norton, 1955.

Lazarus, A. A. *In the mind's eye*. New York: Rawson, 1978.

Mahoney, M. J. Psychotherapy and the structure of personal revolutions. In M. J. Mahoney (Ed.), *Psychotherapy process*. New York: Plenum, 1980.

Maultsby, M. C., Jr. *Help yourself to happiness*. New York: Institute for Rational Living, 1975.

Meichenbaum, D. H. *Cognitive behavior modification*. New York: Plenum, 1977.

Moore, R. H. Inference chaining. In M. S. Morain (Ed.), *Classroom exercises in general semantics*. San Francisco: International Society for General Semantics, 1980.

Neisser, U. *Cognition and reality*. San Francisco: W. H. Freeman, 1976.

Raimy, V. *Misunderstandings of the self: Cognitive psychotherapy and the misconception hypothesis*. San Francisco: Jossey-Bass, 1975.

Rotter, J. B. *Social learning and clinical psychology*. Englewood Cliffs, N.J.: Prentice-Hall, 1954.

Watzlawick, P. *The language of change*. New York: Basic Books, 1978.

Wessler, R. L., & Ellis, A. Supervision in rational–emotive therapy. In A. K. Hess (Ed.), *Psychotherapy supervision*. New York: John Wiley, 1980.

Wessler, R. A., & Wessler, R. L. *The principles and practice of rational–emotive therapy*. San Francisco: Jossey-Bass, 1980.

Zajonc, R. B. Feeling and thinking: Preferences need no inferences. *American Psychologist*, 1980, *35*, 151–175.

4

From a Linear to a Contextual Model of the ABC's of RET*

Russell M. Grieger†

When he first conceived of rational–emotive therapy (RET) in 1955, Albert Ellis formulated the ABC paradigm to explain human emotional disturbance and to direct psychotherapeutic efforts at change (Ellis, 1958, 1962). Simply and brilliantly, the ABC paradigm articulates the basic tenet that cognitions mediate and are central to the causation and amelioration of emotional, behavioral, and interpersonal disturbance. In this paradigm, A (an activating event in the world) does not directly produce or cause C (the cognitive, emotional, and/or behavioral consequences); rather, it is the B's (mediating thoughts, attitudes, or beliefs about A) that cause C.

Over the last three decades, the influence of Dr. Ellis's work on both the theory and practice of psychotherapy has become increasingly profound and pervasive. The premises posited by Ellis have spawned an enormous body of research and theoretical literature and have contributed immeasurably to the development of cognitive behavioral psychotherapy and to its emergence as a dominant force in psychology. A recent survey (Smith, 1982) concluded that the "cognitive-behavioral system represents one of the strongest, if not *the* strongest, theoretical emphasis today." Furthermore, the survey indicated that of the 10 individuals reported to have most powerfully influenced today's clinical trends,

*This chapter was first published in the *Journal of Rational Emotive Therapy,* 1985, *3*(2), 79–99.
†I want to express my deep appreciation to Ingrid Grieger for the many helpful suggestions she made on this chapter and for the many hours she spent in editorial work.

Albert Ellis ranked second, and five were either strongly or moderately identified with cognitive behavioral therapy (Ellis, Wolpe, A. Lazarus, Beck, and Meichenbaum).

As the amount of research on and conceptualization of the role of cognition on human psychology and psychopathology has grown, however, a parallel recognition has emerged regarding the need for greater understanding and more precise delineations of what constitutes the B's in the ABC paradigm (Bernard, 1980; Eschenroeder, 1982; Huber, 1985). Ellis himself has stated that the ABC's "are oversimplified and omit salient information about human disturbance and its treatment" (1984).

Partially in response to this recognition, a number of rational–emotive therapists have expanded the ABC model in attempts to describe more completely what takes place within humans that causes them to respond as they do (Diekstra & Dassen, 1979; Maultsby, 1975). A particularly impressive effort has been made by Wessler and Wessler (1980), who outline an eight-step model of an emotional episode: (1) a stimulus, which begins the episode; (2) selection of some aspects of the stimulus based on neural and physiological processes; (3) perception and symbolic representation of the stimulus; (4) cognitive interpretation of nonobservable aspects of the perceived stimulus; (5) cognitive appraisal or evaluation; (6 & 7) affective arousal and an action tendency caused by the appraisal; and (8) functional feedback (e.g., positive reinforcement) that affects future action. Among the attractive features of the Wessler and Wessler model is that it includes the focus of most all cognitive behavioral therapies and provides the therapist with the opportunity to assess and intervene cognitively at any or all of the eight steps.

In Ellis's (1984) expanded ABC model, he distinguishes between such various B's as nonevaluative observations and perceptions (cold cognitions), positive and negative preferential evaluations (warm cognitions), and positive and negative absolutistic evaluations and demands (hot cognitions). Most innovative, however, are his observations about how people's A's, B's, and C's reciprocally influence and "cause" each other. For example, he states that people are "prone to seek out and respond to their A's," that they "largely bring their beliefs to A, and they prejudicedly view or experience A's in light of these biased beliefs," and they "partly create the activating event at A."

As a practitioner and teacher of RET, I commend these rational–emotive therapists for their efforts in expanding the ABC model. At the very least, their efforts recognize the complexity of human thinking, provide the therapist with a framework from which to decide which cognitive behavioral strategies to employ and in what order, and offer a basis for the integration of the various cognitive behavioral therapies into an eclectic whole.

It is with this indebtedness that I offer my thinking on what I call the contextual ABC model of RET. Piggybacking on those who have already expanded the ABC's, I too wish to acknowledge the mutual influence among A, the B's, and C, to underscore the individual's ability to choose consciously, to act creatively, to take responsibility, and to emphasize the distinction between thinking that is specific to a particular situation and beliefs, philosophies, or life principles that are central to a person's way of functioning in the world across situations.

Despite the greater refinement and descriptiveness of the expanded ABC models just discussed, they remain essentially linear and therefore relatively static in nature. What appears to be missing from the RET and, indeed, from the cognitive behavioral literature is a more complete, graphic, dynamic, and three-dimensional model that more accurately captures the intricacies of the ABC process. This is the gap that the contextual ABC model attempts to fill. Specifically, in moving from a linear to a contextual model, it becomes increasingly possible to visualize and conceptualize the complexities of B, the reciprocity among the components of human functioning, and the power of the individual to create C's, B's and even A's independent of any environmental event.

What follows, then, is the contextual ABC model. First will be presented a section on the nature of activating events (A's), followed by a discussion of the nature of human cognition. After this I will describe how human cognitions variously influence and create action, feelings, thinkings, and even activating events. Finally, the chapter concludes with some implications for the practice of RET.

THE NATURE OF ACTIVATING EVENTS: "THE" REALITY VERSUS "OUR" REALITY

The contextual ABC model begins with the proposition that there exists a real world of objects and events; whether or not a person is physically present or mentally alert to experience what is there is irrelevant. In reality, literally, there is both a solid mass of, and a continual series of, available "things out there" that a person can select, perceive, symbolically represent, interpret, and evaluate.

A central distinction is made in RET between the circumstances *in* one's life (the A's) and the experiences one has *about* those circumstances (the C's). I argue that it is also crucial in RET to draw the distinction between the circumstances *in* one's life and the experience one has *of* the circumstances. While there is indeed a real world of circumstances (matter and events) that does exist "out there" (*the* reality), this real world differs from the one to which we relate and respond. What we as humans deal with are the circumstances as interpreted by us (*our* reality). In other words, as Mahoney (1980) has indicated, it is our representation of environments to which we respond, not the environments themselves.

As with the experiences people have *about* activating events, the experiences people have *of* activating events (their reality) is also mediated by the person's

B's. Coexistent with the fact that it is virtually impossible for people to not think, people are "thrown" to operate automatically, actively, and immediately on the real events they encounter, that is, to attend selectively, to perceive, to represent symbolically, and to infer about the events. In doing this, people "create" a reality of activating events for themselves that may be, but probably is not, identical to the real reality. In actuality, nothing exists *for us* without this selection/filtering/interpretation process; the rub is that people are usually unaware of that process and assume that what they "see" accurately represents what exists "in the world."

This re-creation of reality is represented in Figure 4–1, where A represents the actual events in the real world; B_1 represents the cognitive operations, including interpretations, that "create" the reality as experienced by the person; and A' represents the experienced or perceived events, as "created" by the person. I hypothesize that a very interesting, reciprocal process occurs at this point, in that the cognitive activity at B_1 and the experience of the event at A' mutually reinforce and ingrain each other. That is, after several such "creations" of the experienced event (A') by the cognitive activity at B_1, the two become yoked such that the presence of one confirms to the person the validity of the other. The perceived reality confirms and reinforces the validity of the cognitive process that generated the event, and the interpretation, in turn, confirms and reinforces the reality of the event. Then, finally, picking up the sequence in typical RET fashion, the person again operates on the new, perceived reality (the A') with evaluative thinking (B_2) to "create" the emotional and behavioral consequences or reactions at C.

Thus, people not only create their C's, but they create their A's as well. In the contextual ABC model, it is logical to help people understand and change the ways at B_1 that they create their reality of events, as well as to help them change the ways at B_2 that they create their feelings and behaviors at C.

THE NATURE OF HUMAN COGNITION

Among the objects in the universe are, of course, people, one such person represented in Figure 4–2 by a circle. Like all people, this person possesses a multitude of traits and attributes, including, among others, physical, interpersonal, intellectual, sexual, and cognitive ones. Imagine the person, the circle, filled with thousands of dots, each representing a separate attribute of the person. Among the various attributes people possess, the ones most uniquely significant for human functioning are those that are cognitive.

Central to the contextual ABC model is the premise that human cognition may be delineated by a number of categories that can be arranged, at least for the sake of discussion, from the most general and philosophical to the more specific. From this statement, three things are assumed: (1) the more general and philo-

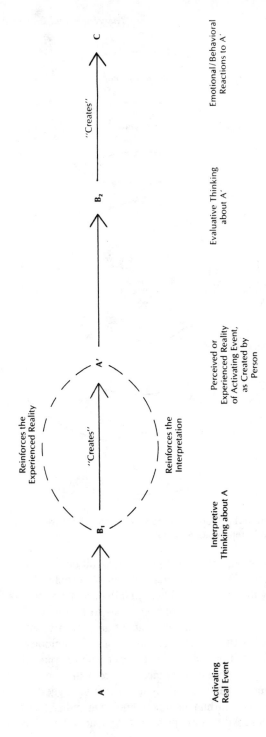

Figure 4-1 The Creation of Reality

| Activating Real Event | Interpretive Thinking about A | Perceived or Experienced Reality of Activating Event, as Created by Person | Evaluative Thinking about A' | Emotional/Behavioral Reactions to A' |

Reinforces the Experienced Reality

Reinforces the Interpretation

"Creates"

"Creates"

A   B₁   A'   B₂   C

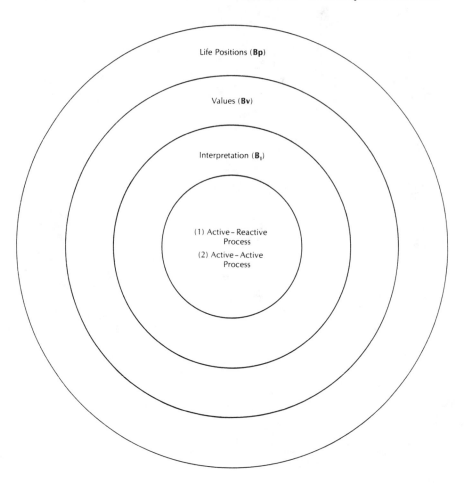

Figure 4–2 Person in the World (The page represents the world filled with objects *and* events and the circle represents a person.)

sophical the cognition, the more likely the cognition is to be unarticulated or beyond awareness; (2) the more general and philosophical the cognition, the more pervasively the cognition is likely to influence the person's life; and (3) the interplay of these various types of cognitions to a large extent directs what a person does in any given situation or about any given event.

In the contextual ABC model, three categories of cognition are delineated (see Figure 4–2): Life Positions (Bp), Values (Bv), and Interpretational Habits (B_I). Each will be briefly presented, proceeding from the most general and philosophical to the more specific. This is not meant to suggest a rigid progression from one to the other in human functioning, but rather that the more general cognitions form a backdrop or context that influences the less general ones, and, conversely, that the less general cognitions are influenced contextually by the more general ones.

Life Positions (Bp)

Most basic to all human beings is the existence of fundamental life positions. These positions, probably adopted when we are young, determine the scope and boundaries of both how we experience the world and how we act in it. These positions are not what we think, do, or feel on a moment-by-moment basis; rather, they are generalizations or abstractions, often unrecognized and unarticulated, that guide and set the boundaries of our thinking, doing, and feeling. They are the most basic assumptions, the context that most fundamentally guides our lives (Earle & Regin, 1980). I will delineate four life positions that have both the scope and the power to color virtually all of a person's life. Each of the four can be stated as a dichotomy between two poles, with no middle ground; the person at any moment stands either at one pole or the other, but rarely if ever with a foot in both.

Demandingness versus Affirmation. The first of the four dichotomous life positions comes primarily from RET and Albert Ellis (1962, 1971, 1974b, 1977, 1979) and can be termed *demandingness versus affirmation.* I direct the reader to almost any of Ellis's writings for an exposition of demandingness. Suffice it to say that, at the pole of demandingness, the person takes the childish, egocentric stance that the world automatically *must* be the way one wants and *must not* include what one does not want. It is, at one and the same time, an insistence for certain things to be ("I demand," "It must," "You should," "I have to") and a resistance to and a protestation against other things being as they are ("No! It mustn't be that way."). As the crux of most emotional disturbances, demandingness embodies the insistence that life be the way we want it, rather than the insistence that it be exactly the way it is.

At the polar opposite to demandingness is what I call affirmation. It is a rather complicated position that includes two subparts. Affirmation, first, includes being displeased in an anti-awfulizing way when something is not the way one wants it to be, preferring or desiring in a nondemanding way for something to be different than it is, and being willing in a nonself-pitying way to act to get what one wants regardless. So, affirmation is not a mere passive acceptance of what is, but an active position of power and potential action to get what one wants in the future. Second, affirmation includes, at any given moment in time, regardless of what that moment holds for a person, saying "Yes" or "I insist" to what, indeed, is there. Beyond acceptance, it is "choosing" what is there and what is not there. It is taking what one gets when one gets it, and not taking what one does not get when one does not get it (Rhinehart, 1976). This was stated well by a man serving a rather long prison term (Bry, 1976, p. 120):

Some days, my mind just can't stop wishing I were out. So then I say, "Why wish to be out there when I can't. No amount of resistance will change that. Now you have a choice. You can keep resisting and bitch about it, or you can choose it." I go through that maybe ten times a day and pull myself out of it. But it works. I tell myself, "This is all there is right now so just relax and quit fighting because you can't do anything but worry yourself to death trying to make it something it isn't."

Self as Object versus Self as Context. Rational–emotive therapy shares with all of psychology, and indeed with Western civilization, a view called *"self as object."* In this view, "the self is an abstraction that an individual develops about the attributes, capacities, objects, and activities which he possesses and pursues" (Coopersmith, 1967, p. 20). Different from the object of observations—the person—the self is a conceptualization *about* the object. Self as object is represented graphically in Figure 4–3, in which the large circle represents the person, the small circles represent the various roles the person plays in life (e.g., wife, mother, friend), and the dots represent the various attributes and performances of the person. Self, then, or self-concept, is the sum of the dots known to the person.

With a self-as-object model, it is easy for a person to identify his or her self as a role (e.g., psychologist), as an attribute (e.g., selfish), or as a particular behavior (e.g., an angry outburst). Thus, people identify themselves as such things as their jobs, their matehood or parenthood, their money, their education, their physical appearance, their good or bad deeds, and so on. From this process of identification, a person is likely to go the next step and evaluate or rate one's self as being either bad or good.

RET has made an enormous contribution in helping clients to stop this self-defeating process by making the important distinction between self-esteem and self-acceptance (Boyd & Grieger, 1982; Ellis, 1972, 1974a, 1974b; Ellis & Harper, 1975; Grieger, 1975). Self-esteem refers to the individual's evaluation or rating of self as being either good or bad, based on the presence or absence of certain traits, behaviors, or attributes (dots). RET advocates self-acceptance rather than self-esteem, based on the proposition that human beings are simply too complex to be accurately rated. It is recommended that people rate their individual performances but that they entirely dispense with rating their selves. What is suggested, instead, is that people decide to accept themselves, *a priori*, as fallible human beings who, like all human beings, do some things particularly well, some things poorly, and many things adequately.

Despite the obvious advantages in RET of advocating self-acceptance over self-esteem, the self-as-object model is still retained. I contend that there are problems inherent in the self-as-object viewpoint that can be avoided with an alternative framework. First of all, with this model, it is an easy progression from self-identification to self-esteeming or self-rating, a stance highly associ-

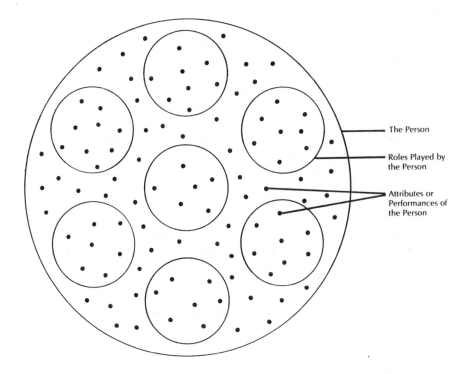

Figure 4-3 Self as Object

ated with a wide array of emotional and behavioral disturbances (Ellis, 1972). Second, in holding oneself to be what one does or what one has (one's dots), it becomes very difficult to avoid taking a variety of seemingly self-protective but actually self-defeating stances, such as justifying oneself as being right and thereby invalidating others, dominating and avoiding domination, and creating the extremes of euphoria and depression. Third, and perhaps most important, there is limited power to the person locked into the self-as-object viewpoint, for, in holding oneself as an object (a mass comprised of perceived attributes and performances), one easily sees oneself as what one already is. That is, one easily sees oneself as static, formed, inert, immovable, and unchangeable, and such a perception certainly creates barriers to therapeutic growth and change. In essence, then, with a self-as-object concept, one becomes a victim of one's own self-concept, which greatly diminishes the likelihood of acting creatively, courageously, and newly.

An alternative view of self, here called *self as context* or *self as potential,* is, I believe, a much more useful one, and one that contributes significantly to the contextual ABC model to follow. This view starts from the perspective that the self is *not* what one has or does; that is, it is not one's behavior; it is not one's traits; it is not one's intelligence; it is not one's body, hair, or other physical attributes; nor is it the roles one plays. A person certainly has and does all these things, but the person is *not* these things.

What, then, does the construct *self as context* mean? Very simply stated, self in this view is not a thing or an object; it has no substance, nor is it measurable. Rather, it is metaphysical. It, the self, is held as the background, the context or backdrop, out of which what the person has or does emerges. Referring again to Figure 4–3, self in this view is all of the empty space inside the person (the space between the dots), which always has the potential to be filled and that spawns the person's attributes and performances (the dots themselves). Rather than being an identity, self is the source of identities; rather than being the sum of one's attributes, self is the space in which attributes show up and develop; rather than being one's behavior, self is the clearing from which behavior comes; rather than being one's philosophies, values, and commitments, self is the place from which these emerge, flourish, and decline. Self as context, in sum, is "the context in which content is crystallized and process occurs, and it is not any individual content or process" (Bartley, 1978).

The importance of such a conceptualization will be seen further as the contextual ABC model is developed. For now, suffice it to say that the self-as-context viewpoint has several important benefits to it. First of all, it preserves and even enhances the self-acceptance position. Since one simply is not what one does or has, self-rating becomes blatantly nonsensical. Second, this model of self obviates the concept of self-identity, or the "Who am I?" issue. "Who a person is" is defined as potential—a clearing, an opportunity, a context—so that what one *does* and what one *wants to do* emerge as the central issues. Third, since self is seen as potential, the door is opened to creation, to taking the stance that "I can create my own beliefs, feelings, and behaviors out of an act of will (just because I want to), because there is the room and potential to do so." Fourth, self as potential conveys the position that change, psychotherapeutic or otherwise, is always possible and hence provides hope and motivation to the individual.

Living Psychologically versus Living Philosophically. The third of the four dichotomous life positions contrasts *living psychologically* with *living philosophically* (Siegel, 1984). At the pole of living psychologically, people identify themselves as exclusively psychological beings; they see themselves *as* their psychological attributes, as being their feelings, attitudes, wants, and goals, rather than seeing themselves as merely *containing* or *having* these *attributes*. The upshot of this position is that people become trapped by their psychological make up. Since they hold that their psychology is who they are, they assume that they have no choice but to respond according to how they feel and think. Thus, for example, a person living psychologically might have the intention of working on a project in the evening, then become anxious about something during the day, and conclude that it is not possible to work because of this anxiety.

The position of living philosophically does not deny the existence of psychological events, nor does it deny the coerciveness of these events. Living philosophically, however, is a position that has the effect of undeifying one's psychology; that is, it notes one's psychological state but puts it aside. Living philosophically means that one holds one's word, or one's promises and commitments, as being of paramount importance, regardless of how one feels at a given moment in time. In this rather unique philosophical position, one has declared that the stand one takes or the promises one gives are eminently more important than how one feels or even what one desires. Thus, when one makes a promise ("I will meet you for lunch at 12:00 P.M. on Tuesday"), one follows through despite how one feels ("I'm depressed, *and* I'll keep my word"), or what one wants ("I'd rather go jogging, *and* I'll keep my promise"), or what is convenient ("I'll get up an hour earlier to get paperwork done in order to keep my commitment to have lunch with her"). In genuinely taking this life position, a person can overcome procrastination, irresponsibility, and a whole hoard of passive, helpless stances in life.

Being at Effect versus Being at Cause. The fourth and final of the dichotomous life positions has been termed *being at effect versus being at cause* (Rhinehart, 1976). Being at effect is a position in which one believes that the circumstances in one's life control one's destiny and well-being. If articulated, this position would sound something like, "My well-being, my happiness, my goals getting met, are dependent on circumstances, by chance, working out." With such a philosophy, it is easy to imagine a person feeling like a leaf ready to be blown about at random, a hapless victim who is likely to respond with helplessness and depression, anger, and bitterness, when circumstances happen to be adverse.

The contrasting position, being at cause, starts from a position of personal responsibility for one's own well-being, for how one responds to events, and for the choices one makes in life, regardless of the circumstances. Responsibility, in this view, does not include credit or blame, right or wrong, good or bad; it is the "point of view" in which one "chooses" not to see oneself as a victim, but as being bigger than the circumstances. If articulated, being at cause would sound like this: "No one or no thing is put on this earth to make my life work; I am totally responsible for my own well-being, and I take that responsibility. Even though I may not know what to do to overcome this adverse circumstance, I am committed to doing whatever is necessary to make life work. I may now have this bad thing in my life, and I may not be able to change the circumstances, but I will go about living positively and hopefully anyway." To continue the analogy of the leaf, in this position the person holds oneself as the wind, or "cause in the matter," not as some helpless object buffeted by uncontrollable forces. In taking this position, a person is less likely to whine or to experience depression, rage, extreme frustration, low frustration tolerance, or other symptoms of emotional disturbance when circumstances are adverse.

It is my observation that most people, particularly those who have an emotional disturbance, take the first pole of each of the four dichotomies just discussed. They tend to endorse demandingness, self as object (accompanied by self-esteeming or self-rating), living psychologically, and being at effect. Until they become aware of the positions they hold and of their impact on their functioning, and until they take responsibility for them, they are likely to operate as victims who believe that they cannot bring about significant change in their lives.

Values (Bv)

I share with Ellis (1974b, 1984) the view that human beings are naturally motivated and goal oriented, but, in contrast with Freudians and others who hold that human motivation is largely biological, instinctual, and unconscious, I believe that motives can be understood best in terms of values (Peterson, 1968). That is, people come to value certain outcomes and so they are motivated to act by the values they hold. For example, if I value basketball and not opera, I will be spurred to attend basketball games rather than operas; if I value a single, intimate relationship over several more casual ones, I will act to get and maintain a committed relationship; if I value doing psychotherapy over psychological research, I will spend a great deal of time doing therapy and little or no time in conducting research.

According to Ellis (1984), human beings almost always hold the basic values of (1) remaining alive and (2) being happy while alive. Under the rubric of being happy, it seems that human values can be grouped in terms of (a) friendship, affection, and love, in both intimate relationships and more casual associations, (b) success in work and similar pursuits, (c) fun or pleasure in recreational activities and hobbies, and (d) comfort or ease in the general flow of life.

In the contextual ABC model, exactly how values influence actions depends on their interaction with the life positions a person holds, particularly vis-à-vis the demandingness–affirmation dichotomy (see previous section). When a person endorses the affirmation life position, values tend to be experienced and expressed in such terms as desires, wishes, wants, and preferences, such as "I want (or prefer) you to like me." With values held in this way, one is motivated to seek what is valued and, depending on whether or not the valued outcome is attained, is either pleased/happy or displeased/sorrowed. In endorsing the demandingness life position, values are held and expressed in terms of shoulds, oughts, musts, have to's, and needs, as in the statement "I need you to like me" or "You must like me." Values held this way are characterized by absoluteness, necessity, all-or-noneness, and either/or-ness, and they have been shown to be associated with desperation for what is valued; depression, guilt, and anger over being thwarted in attaining what is valued; and anxiety over getting and keeping what is valued.

Interpretational Habits (B_I)

The third and last of the categories of cognitions delineated in the contextual ABC model are interpretatonal habits (B_I). Contained contextually within peoples' life positions (Bp) and values (Bv), these have to do with the inferences and conclusions people make about the unobserved aspects of encountered objects and situations.

It is an assumption of the contextual ABC model that people naturally and regularly make situational interpretations. What is important here, however, are the *habitual, recurring* interpretations people have learned and make across situations, which color or create their "view of life." Furthermore, *interpretation* here refers both to a person's habitual style of processing data (e.g., general versus specific, logical versus nonsequitorial, realistic versus minimizing or magnifying) as well as to the content of the conclusions a person habitually draws. Examples of the latter include (1) internal versus external locus of control (Rotter, 1966), in which people either assume that a thing that happens to them is directly due to their actions (internal locus) or to luck, chance, or fate (external locus); (2) self-efficacy expectations (Bandura, 1977), the "conviction that one can successfully execute the behavior required to produce the outcomes" (p. 194); (3) outcome expectancy (Bandura, 1977), or a person's estimate that a given behavior will lead to certain outcomes; (4) a view of the world as friendly, supportive, and good versus overwhelming and making exorbitant demands (Beck, 1967); and (5) a view of the future as hopeful and positive versus bleak and difficult (Beck, 1967).

COGNITIVE CREATION OF CONSEQUENCES

Thus far in the contextual ABC model, two major elements have been delineated: (1) a real world that contains an unlimited number of potential activating events and that provides a "playground" for people to attempt to fulfill their goals or values; and (2) a person who, through the course of living, has acquired and retained a relatively stable variety of cognitive attributes that remain fairly constant across situations, the most important ones in determining one's experience in life here distinguished as life positions, values, and interpretational

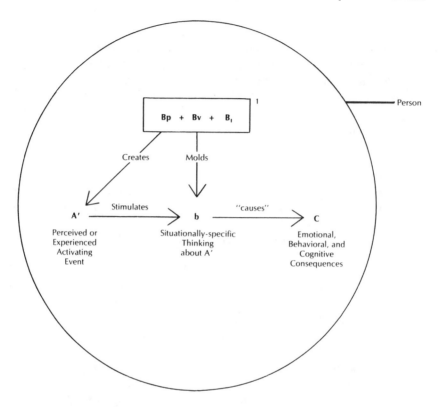

Figure 4–4 The Active–Reactive Process. (Bp = life positions; Bv = values; B_1 = interpretational habits.)

habits. I will now discuss the interaction of the two in the production of human actions and reactions, abstracted either as an *active-reactive* process or an *active-active* process. These processes are shown in the center of the person in Figure 4–2, are elaborated in Figures 4–4 and 4–5, and will be discussed in turn.

The Active–Reactive Process

After Ellis (1976, 1979, 1984), the contextual ABC model asserts that people can be understood best as trying to fulfill what they value in environments that contain numerous potential activating events. People do not merely react passively to the events they encounter, however; as discussed earlier, they actively operate to create their environments and then actively operate on their created environments in a way that "causes" their reactions.

This process can be seen in Figure 4–4, which is a blow-up of the center part of the person depicted in Figure 4–2. First, in part as a result of trying to satisfy their values (Bv), people seek out environments or parts of environments (A's) they think will fulfill their values. For example, people go to parties, bars, and

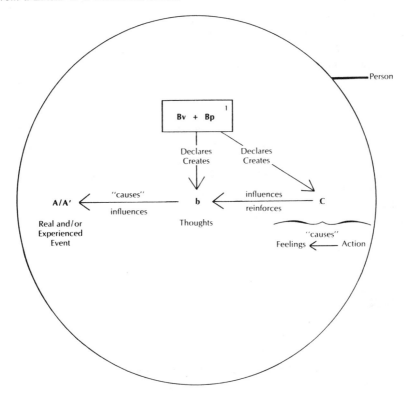

Figure 4–5 The Active–Active Process. (Here, Bv + Bp = life position of living philosophically.)

other social places because they value fun, attention, or stimulation. Then, in bringing their values (Bv), their life positions (Bp), and their interpretational habits (B_I) to these environments, they also selectively attend to and prejudicially perceive and interpret what they encounter. So, to begin with, people really create the activating events (referred to as the perceived or experienced activating event and designated as A') that they eventually operate on in causing their emotional and behavioral reactions.

As a next step in the process, people think about the experienced activating event (A'). Yet, while people can have any number of thoughts about their experienced activating event (A'), these thoughts are rarely random or accidental. To the contrary, the thinking that people do about A', designated in Figure 4–4 as b, is strongly molded by their higher-order cognitions, most prominently by their life positions (Bp), values (Bv), and interpretational habits (B_I). Most notable at b, then, are either preferential or demanding thinking (reflecting the life position of either demandingness or affirmation), either evaluative or nonevaluative thinking about oneself or other selves (self as object versus self as context), and either thinking that reflects a belief in one's being powerful and in control (the life positions of being at cause and living philosophically) or a belief that one is relatively powerless and helpless (being at effect and living psychologically). Thus, the thinking that goes on about any particular experience or event (A') may be unique and random but more probably is molded or formed by more basic, enduring cognitions carried with the person across situations.

Finally, following RET, the interaction of A' and b strongly influences the emotional, behavioral, and cognitive consequences or reactions. In other words, the thinking (b) that people do mediates between A' and C and therefore can be said to "cause" or "create" C. When thinking at b is done demandingly (as in "musts") and/or self-ratingly, C usually consists of emotional disturbance (e.g., severe feelings of anger, depression, guilt and self-denigration, and anxiety; and self-defeating or self-limiting behaviors like procrastination, phobias, compulsions, possessiveness, self-destruction, and aggression).

The Active–Active Process

The active–active process (see Figure 4–5) is, as far as I know, a new concept in the RET literature. It follows from the construct of self as context or potential and, most importantly, from the position of living philosophically. As will be recalled, a person who is living philosophically takes the stance that one's psychological response patterns are not as important as the commitments, promises, or declared stands taken. In living philosophically, one *believes* and *declares* that the promises one makes (to oneself or others) and the actions necessary to fulfill one's promises are more important than how one feels, and one listens to one's self-talk regarding these declarations.

In the active–active process, then, the concept of a *declaration* is crucial. In the spirit of the contextual ABC model, a declaration is an act of creation that has nothing to do with truth or empirical validity; by declaration something becomes so simply because a person says so, or declares it. Examples of declarations include the following: a judge declares a defendant guilty; a baseball umpire calls a strike; a parent names a child "Todd"; a priest pronounces someone married; a person forgives himself for a wrongdoing; a person says, "I love you," to someone else. All of these outcomes happen or become real simply because someone with authority says so.

The importance of the declaration process is that people, by endorsing the position of living philosophically, have the power to create out of their own self-initiated declarations how they will act, feel, and think without any immediate or prior stimulating event or condition. It may very well be that, once one declares that one will act a certain way and follows through on the declaration, a process of feeling and thinking consistent with the action occurs; that is, the self-initiated act will "cause" feelings and thoughts congruent with the action (see Figure 4–5). Furthermore, it also may very well be that events in the environment, formerly thought of as activating events, begin to respond in a way that is consistent with this process. The person, in the long run, has actually influenced the occurrence of events in the environment. Thus, these events become the consequences of the individual intervening directly at point C so that it is possible for the process to occur from C to B to A, rather than the usual A–B–C one.

Take, for example, a husband who is in a marriage that is conflictual and in crisis; he is often angry with his wife, he frequently acts ungraciously and hostilely toward her, and he regularly participates with her in bickering. Amidst this situation he may take the stance that she is at fault in the conflict and, furthermore, that she causes him to feel and act as he does (he believes that A causes C). Or, he may even go so far as to take responsibility for his actions and feelings (holding that his B's cause C), but he nonetheless believes that he has no choice but to act and feel as he does until he changes either her actions, his own thinking, or both (living psychologically). Either way, he will continue his marriage-defeating behavior.

Now, imagine a whole new scenario in which this same man lives philosophically: He believes that his commitments are more important than how he feels, and furthermore he believes that he can choose to act in certain ways simply because he declares he will. So, wanting to try to make his marriage once again viable, he *declares* that he will act in considerate, respectful, and even kind ways to his wife, even though his feelings or attitudes toward her are not consistent with this; in effect, he creates these behaviors at C from nothing except his value for the marriage and his self-generated declaration (see Figure 4–5). Imagine, further, that this husband also *declares* that he will mostly think about his wife's good attributes, that he will frequently remember the good times they had together, and that he will regularly imagine having fun with her in the future. Now he has created thoughts at b, with no activating event present or necessary to stimulate them. Before long, he will "cause" himself to feel in ways consistent with his actions, and he will influence and reinforce, by his positive actions and feelings, the positive thoughts, memories, and fantasies he has about his wife at b. What is likely to happen, as is often observed in marriage counseling, is that when one spouse (here, the husband) sustains positive behavior toward the other spouse, the spouse (here, the wife) tends to come around and act in ways consistent with the positive behavior she gets. In RET terms, this husband created the A. So, by creating C, he influences b, and both C and b "caused" A.

SOME IMPLICATIONS FOR PSYCHOTHERAPY AND WELLNESS

The contextual ABC model is *not* a new model of psychotherapy; rather, it is the ABC's of RET expanded in a way that represents the complexities of human cognitions; the diverse and fluid interrelationships among the A's, the B's, and the C's; and the power that people have to influence and even to create their beliefs, actions, and feelings, regardless of the external reality. This model is intensely cognitive and philosophical at its core and, as such, completely endorses and seeks to further the fundamental premises and techniques of rational–emotive therapy. Consistent with the goals and aims of RET, then, some of the contextual ABC model's implications for psychotherapy are as follows:

Forwarding Elegant Change

A feature that distinguishes RET from other cognitive behavioral therapies is its preferred goal of elegant change (Ellis, 1971, 1974b, 1977, 1979; Grieger & Boyd, 1980). *Elegant change* means first to lessen or reduce client endorsement of disturbance-producing cognitions, rather than mere symptom removal or environmental problem solving; moreover, elegant change means to lessen or reduce dysfunctional evaluative attitudes or beliefs (e.g., "I *must* be liked") rather than inaccurate, nonevaluative interpretations (e.g., "No one likes me"), although the latter are still deemed appropriate grist for the therapeutic mill.

The contextual ABC model goes beyond the exploration and amelioration of situational-specific b's to the uncovering and modification of the most profoundly held and enduring B's (life positions, values, and interpretational habits). By inviting clients to discover their (often unconscious) B's and by teaching them the enormous impact of those B's on how they perceive and respond to the events in their lives, and thus how they color the very quality of their lives, the "need" for elegant change of the most profound order is made absolutely clear and palpable.

Forwarding Philosophical Change

Closely related to and even concurrent with the endorsement and furthering of elegant change is the forwarding of philosophical change. Ellis (1962, 1971) has long contended that RET is much more a philosophical than a psychological endeavor, in that emotional and behavioral problems are essentially the result of holding dysfunctional or self-defeating beliefs or philosophies. Successful therapy therefore involves giving up these philosophies and replacing them with more workable ones. Indeed, most skilled RET practitioners spend a high percentage of time with their clients in philosophical exchanges.

The contextual ABC model is deeply wedded to this perspective. A rereading of the section in this chapter on life positions will show that each of the four dichotomies described are philosophical stances that can be said to guide and set the boundaries of our thinking, doing, and feeling. These form the backdrop or context out of which everything else comes. In the contextual ABC model, then, it would behoove the therapist to focus on the most elegant and far-reaching outcomes, that is, to make the correction of life positions (Bp) the first order of business, with interpretation (B$_I$) and thinking (b) change following.

Furthering Self-acceptance

A particularly powerful and unique aspect of RET is its endorsement of self-acceptance (*a priori,* nonevaluative acceptance of self) over self-esteeming (a criterion-based, conditional process of valuing the self). People are encouraged to rate their performances honestly but not to extend this to rating themselves (Ellis, 1971, 1972, 1974a, 1974b, 1977).

In articulating the concept of the self as context (or as potential), rather than as an object, the contextual ABC model provides an even clearer opportunity for clients to liberate themselves from self-assessment. For, when self is conceived as the potential *out of which* what one does and has emerges, but is not what one does or has, the absurdity of self-rating leaps out and we are left with the only viable alternative, a self-acceptance model.

Allowing Emotional Disturbance to Be Irrelevent

A phenomenon noted by many RET therapists is what has been called a "second-level problem" (Ellis, 1971, 1974a, 1977, 1979; Ellis & Harper, 1975; Grieger & Boyd, 1980). What this means is that, once people develop an emotional problem, a social phobia for instance, they often develop another emotional problem *about* the original problem, like depression or anger about being phobic. In RET we often find it necessary to help clients get rid of the second problem before tackling the original one.

The contextual ABC model takes this practice one step farther by advocating that people adopt and practice the life positions of living philosophically and being at cause. In deciding that they are ultimately responsible for what happens to them in life, despite barriers and adverse circumstances, and by determining that they will uphold their commitments regardless of how they feel at a particular moment in time, clients have the power to make their emotional problems irrelevant. These emotional problems then simply become barriers, circumstances, or psychological states, like many others, that can be overcome or even disregarded as clients continue to work toward creating satisfaction and happiness in their lives.

To illustrate this concept briefly, take the case of a 50-year-old woman who became rather depressed about several severe compulsions she developed following the untimely death of her 20-year-old daughter. While working on the irrational belief underlying her compulsions, I taught her the two life positions of living philosophically and being at cause. She, with encouragement, used them in her life successfully. To use her words, she convinced herself to take the following attitude: "These compulsions are stupid and are an annoyance in life, but they only occupy a part of my time. I'm determined to enjoy myself at times when I don't act this way, and I will actively find ways to do so despite them. My life is bigger than these compulsions." In no time her depression lifted and she and I are now concluding the therapy on her compulsions. The important point,

however, is that, even if she is unable to rid herself completely of her compulsions, she can still have a happy life, so long as she keeps this attitude. In
effect, then, she has made her compulsions irrelevant to her enjoyment of life.

Moving toward a Wellness Model

While we all would probably agree that there is a lot more to mental health than
the absence of symptoms (Ardell, 1979; Ellis, 1980a, 1980b; Phares, 1979;
Rogers, 1961), most of the field of psychotherapy is locked into a disease model
that emphasizes the remediation of emotional, behavioral, and/or social symp-
tomology. Although RET is certainly noteworthy for its didactic methods, its
appeal to the masses through self-help literature, and its willingness to use
radical vehicles to reach large groups of people (e.g., Ellis' famous Friday Night
Workshops), it by and large fits into the remediation framework. An alternative
approach is embodied in the wellness or holistic health movement, in which
therapy is defined as "any attempt to help the patient achieve a high level of
wellness" (Kaplan, Saltzman, & Ecker, 1979). Treatment then focuses on health
care instead of, or in addition to, disease care.

It seems to me that the contextual ABC model lends itself to the conditions of
the wellness model quite nicely. In addition to doing psychotherapy with "sick"
people, the model suggests ways to help people achieve high levels of wellness,
including teaching them healthy life positions (e.g., affirmation instead of
demanding; being at cause rather than being at effect), specific healthy attitudes
(e.g., "I do not need to always succeed"), and various helpful life skills (e.g.,
communication skills, skills in self-analysis), as well as self-acceptance and
anti-awfulizing stances.

Enhancing Personal Power

Most people who try to define a mentally healthy or "fully functioning" person
include terms that convey a person's ability to act independently, freely, self-
directedly, and powerfully. Examples include Rogers' (1961) concept of inner
directedness, Wessler & Wessler's (1980) focus on a person's ability to make
choices freely, and Ellis' (1980a) criteria of self-interest, self-direction, commitment, and risk taking.

If these features indeed characterize healthy people, then the contextual ABC
model provides a unique framework from which to help people attain these
attributes. For, in addition to helping people to rid themselves of irrational
demands and self-ratings, the therapist can help clients and others to adopt the
living philosophically and being at cause life positions, thereby teaching people
how to live creatively and declaratively, regardless of the inner or outer circumstances of their lives. By adopting these positions, people act because they

determine that they do so, not because it does or does not feel good or because others will or will not approve; that is, they come from positions of personal power, freedom, and complete autonomy.

CONCLUSION

The contextual ABC model represents a departure from the traditional ABC paradigm of RET. While in no way denouncing the theory or practice of RET, its intent is to capture in a three-dimensional and dynamic way the intricacies of human feeling, thinking, and acting and the complexities of human cognitions. Distinctions are made between situation-specific thoughts, ideas, and beliefs (small b's) and relatively enduring and constant philosophies and styles (large B's). The latter include life positions (expressed via the dichotomies of demandingness versus affirmation, self as object versus self as context, living psychologically versus living philosophically, and being at effect versus being at cause). The other B's are values and interpretational habits. Also delineated are the active–reactive and the active–active processes. The former relates to the power of B's to mold and create both the events in the world as perceived by the person and the situational-specific thinking a person does about these perceived events. The latter relates to the power a person has to create actions, feelings, and thoughts independently of a stimulating event.

It is hoped that the concepts and constructs presented in the contextual ABC model will further the basic goals of rational–emotive therapy, which are the promotion of elegant and philosophical change, the elimination of second-level problems or emotional problems about emotional problems, and the enhancement of personal wellness and power. Reactions and comments to this chapter are welcome, in the spirit of the continuing development of RET.

REFERENCES

Ardell, D. B. (1979). *High Level Wellness*. Emmaus, Pa.: Rodale Press.
Bandura, A. (1977). Self-efficacy: Toward a unifying theory of behavioral change. *Psychological Review, 84*, 191–215.
Bartley, W. W. (1978). *Werner Erhard: The transformation of a man; the founding of EST*. New York: Carkson N. Potter.
Beck, A. T. (1967). *Depression: Clinical, experimental, and theoretical aspects*. New York: Hoeber.
Bernard, M. E. (1980). Private thoughts in rational–emotive psychotherapy. *Rational Living, 15*, 3–8.
Boyd, J., & Grieger, R. (1982). Self-acceptance problems. In R. Grieger & I. Z. Grieger (Eds.), *Cognition and emotional disturbance*. New York: Human Sciences Press.
Bry, A. (1976). *EST*. New York: Avon Books.
Coopersmith, S. (1967). *The antecedents of self-esteem*. San Francisco: W. H. Freeman.
Dickstra, R., & Dassen, W. F. (1979). *Rationale therapie*. Amsterdam: Swets and Zeitlinger.
Earle, M., & Regin, N. (1980). *A world that works for everyone*. San Francisco: The EST Enterprise.

Ellis, A. (1958). Rational psychotherapy. *Journal of General Psychology, 59,* 35–49.

Ellis, A. (1962). *Reason and emotion in psychotherapy.* Secaucus, N.J.: Lyle Stuart; Citadel Press.

Ellis, A. (1971). *Growth through reason.* North Hollywood, Calif.: Wilshire Book Company.

Ellis, A. (1972). Psychotherapy and the value of a human being. In W. Davis (Ed.), *Value and valuation: Aetiological studies in honor of Robert A. Hartman.* Knoxville, Tenn.: University of Tennessee Press.

Ellis, A.(1974a). *How to stubbornly refuse to be ashamed of anything.* Cassette recording. New York: Institute for Rational Living.

Ellis, A.(1974b). *Humanistic psychotherapy: The rational–emotive approach.* New York: McGraw-Hill.

Ellis, A. (1976). RET abolishes most of the human ego. *Psychotherapy: Theory, research and practice, 13,* 343–348.

Ellis, A. (1977). The basic clinical theory of rational–emotive therapy. In A. Ellis & R. Grieger (Eds.), *Handbook for rational–emotive therapy.* New York: Springer.

Ellis, A. (1979). The theory of rational–emotive therapy. In A. Ellis & J. Whiteley (Eds.), *Theoretical and empirical foundation of rational–emotive therapy.* Monterey, Calif.: Brooks/Cole.

Ellis, A. (1980a). An overview of the clinical theory of rational–emotive therapy. In R. Grieger & J. Boyd, *Rational–emotive therapy: A skills-based approach.* New York: Van Nostrand Reinhold.

Ellis, A. (1980b). Rational–emotive therapy and cognitive behavior therapy: Similarities and differences. *Cognitive Therapy and Research, 4,* 325–340.

Ellis, A. (1984). Expanding the ABCs of RET. In A. Freeman & A. Mahoney (Eds.), *Cognition and psychotherapy,* New York: Plenum.

Ellis, A., & Harper, R. A. (1979). *A new guide to rational living.* Englewood Cliffs, N.J.: Prentice-Hall.

Eschenroeder, C. (1982). How rational is rational–emotive therapy? A critical appraisal of its theoretical foundation and therapeutic methods. *Cognitive Therapy and Research, 6,* 381–392.

Grieger, R. (1975). Self-concept, self-esteem, and rational–emotive theory. *Rational Living, 10,* 12–17.

Grieger, R., & Boyd, J. (1980). *Rational–emotive therapy: A skills-based approach.* New York: Van Nostrand Reinhold.

Huber, C. H. (1985). Pure versus pragmatic RET. *Journal of Counseling and Development, 63,* 321–322.

Kaplan, R., Saltzman, B., & Ecker, L. (1979). *Wholly alive.* Millbrae, Calif.: Celestial Arts.

Mahoney, M. J. (1980). Psychotherapy and the structure of personal revolutions. In M. J. Mahoney (Ed.), *Psychotherapy process.* New York: Plenum.

Maultsby, M. C. (1975). *Help yourself to happiness.* New York: Institute for Rational Living.

Peterson, D. R. (1968). *The clinical study of social behavior.* New York: Appleton-Century-Crofts.

Phares, E. (1979). *Clinical psychology: Concepts, methods and profession.* Homewood, Ill.: Dorsey Press.

Rhinehart, L. (1976). *The book of EST.* New York: Holt, Rinehart and Winston.

Rogers, C. (1961). *On becoming a person.* New York: Houghton-Mifflin.

Rotter, J. B. (1966). Generalized expectancies for internal versus external control of reinforcement. *Psychological Monographs, 80* (1, Whole No. 609).

Siegel, A. (1984). *Ideas.* Paper presented at The Forum Conference, San Francisco, Calif., July 2–6.

Smith, D. (1982). Trends in counseling and psychotherapy. *American Psychologist, 37,* 802–809.

Wessler R., & Wessler, R. L. (1980). *The principles and practice of rational–emotive therapy.* San Francisco, Calif.: Jossey-Bass.

5

A Review of Outcome Studies of Rational– Emotive Therapy from 1977 to 1982*

Terrance E. McGovern and Manuel Silverman

Rational–emotive psychotherapy, a major clinical model that has been adopted by many clinicians, social workers, and other mental health professionals, has generated considerable research (Corey, 1977; Ellis, 1977; Shertzer & Stone, 1980). In the most recent review of the literature assessing RET's effectiveness, DiGiuseppe and Miller (1977) divided 22 studies into noncomparative outcome studies, which did not compare RET with any other type of therapy, and comparative outcome studies, which did. This chapter will review the literature from 1977 through mid-1982 and will follow the organizational format used by DiGiuseppe and Miller (1977).

NONCOMPARATIVE STUDIES

The noncomparative studies discussed here are presented in Table 5–1.

Anxiety

Hymen and Warren (1978), focusing on test anxiety, used a subject base of 11 undergraduate students and divided them into two test groups: one group received RET plus imagery, and the other RET without imagery. Each group

*This chapter was originally published in the *Journal of Rational Emotive Therapy*, 1984, *2*, 1.

Table 5-1 Noncomparative Studies: 1977 through Mid-1982

Name/Year	Comparisons	Problem	Subjects	Outcome
Hymen & Warren (1978)	RET + imagery vs. RET – imagery	Test anxiety	11 undergrad.	No significant difference
Barabasz (1979)	Psychophysiological arousal: RET vs. placebo vs. no treatment	Test anxiety	148 students	RET significantly better than placebo & no treatment
D'Angelo (1978)	RET vs. control	Fear of neg. eval.	78 indiv.	RET significantly better
Katz (1978)	RET vs. placebo vs. no treatment	Test anxiety	30 students	RET significantly better
Rosenheim & Dunn (1977)	RBT alone	Multisymptomatic	5 M & 7 F in military health setting	Improvement but not significant
Roberts (1977)	RET vs. control	Multisymptomatic	48 students	RET significantly better
Krenitsky (1978)	REE vs. placebo vs. control	Relation of age/IQ to efficacy of REE	59 older (60–79) adults	Age IQ not a factor. REE significant in rational thinking and emotional adjustment; not significant on neuroticism scale
Ritchie (1978)	REE vs. control	Irrational beliefs; assertiveness; locus of control	200 5th-grade students	REE significant in irrational beliefs; improved in assertiveness/locus of control
Patton (1978)	RBT vs. control	Emotional disturbance	34 emotionally disturbed adolescents	RBT significant for RBT Concept Test/Common Perception Inventory/Internal-External scale/Time-Competence Scale of POI; improved but not significant for Inner-Directed Support Scale and all subscales of Observational Emotional Inventory

Study	Treatment	Target	Sample	Results
Savitz (1979)	RET vs. control	Emotional disturbance	35 outpatients	No dependent measures but improvement noted for all by referring physician
Bigney (1979)	RET vs. control	Personality/temperament changes	12 couples in marriage counseling	Improved but not significant
Rainwater (1979)	RET case study	Obsessive	Male obsessive	Significant improvement
Stevens (1981)	RBT alone	Stress	Individuals in USAF Security Service	Significant improvement
Cox (1979)	RBT alone	Alcohol abuse	15 criminal offenders	Improved—only 2 of 15 had parole revoked after treatment
Plachetta (1979)	RBT vs. control	Dating skills	17 volunteers	RBT significant on Dating Fear Scale & Social Avoidance & Distress Scale; improved on Fear of Negative Evaluation Scale
Zelie, Stone, & Lehr (1980)	RBT vs. control	School discipline	60 students	RBT significant for 2 behavior ratings and recidivism
Block (1980)	RET vs. placebo vs. control	Weight loss	40 overweight adults	Improved but not significant
Dye (1981)	REE vs. attention vs. no treatment	Self-concept	24 maternally deprived adolescents	Improved but not significant
Lee (1982)	RET group vs. control	Assertiveness	80 nurses	RET significantly better

received instruction over a three-week period, consisting of six one-hour sessions. Pre- and posttesting, with the anxiety scale of the Achievement Anxiety Test, showed no significant difference between the two groups, although anxiety was lowered for both. The researchers discussed the fact that the results were possibly due to the similarity in the treatment methods, plus the short treatment time. The small size of the subject population and the lack of a control group may be considered further weaknesses of this study.

Barabasz (1979), also using test-anxious students, measured psychophysiological arousal, dividing 148 subjects into a treatment, an attention-placebo, or a no-treatment group. The treatment group listened to four audiotaped RET counseling sessions over a two-week period. The dependent measures were skin conductance and pulse rate. Pre- to posttest measures found that RET was significantly better than both the placebo and no treatment. This study is interesting in that no direct instruction in RET was given, and yet even the short treatment time produced significant results. There was no follow-up study.

D'Angelo (1978) examined the effects of RET in reducing fear of negative evaluation. Seventy-eight subjects were divided into a treatment and a control group, with the treatment group receiving three one-hour presentations of RET on consecutive nights. Watson and Friend's Fear of Negative Evaluation Scale was used as a dependent measure. There was a significant reduction in fear of negative evaluation for the RET group, which was maintained at a one-month follow-up.

Katz (1978) studied RET with 30 test-anxious students, comparing a relaxation-placebo and a no-treatment control group. A multivariate analysis showed no differences among the groups at pretreatment, but the RET group showed significant gains at posttreatment. No follow-up was reported.

Multisymptomatic

There were a number of studies in which there were a variety of presenting complaints, with the subjects having been identified through psychological testing as being in need of help.

Rosenheim and Dunn (1977) examined the effectiveness of rational behavior therapy (RBT) in a military health setting. (RBT is a variation of RET that emphasizes greater examination of the accuracy of the perceptions and descriptions of activating events.) The subjects (18 to 36 years of age) consisted of five males and seven females who had requested treatment. Treatment involved both individual and group therapy for all subjects. Dependent measures were the Minnesota Multiphasic Personality Inventory (MMPI) and Rotter Incomplete Sentence Blank. Analyses of pre- and posttesting revealed no major personality changes but implied that RBT was successful in reducing excessive anxiety and defensive denial.

Roberts (1977) studied the effectiveness of RET with students who were identified via the Deichmann-Roberts Attitude Inventory (D-RAI) and the California Psychological Inventory (CPI) as being in need of help. Forty-eight students were assigned to a two-week experimental condition, while 27 other students served as a control group. A comparison of pre- with posttesting showed significant improvement for the experimental group on both the D-RAI and CPI.

Krenitsky (1978), in a somewhat different type of study, examined the relationship of age and verbal intelligence to the efficacy of rational–emotive education (REE, a method of preventive RET) with older adults. Fifty-nine older adults were assigned to one of three treatment conditions: an experimental, an attention-placebo, or a no-contact control. Within all the groups, distinctions were made with regard to levels of age (60 to 69 versus 70 to 79) and two levels of intelligence. Dependent measures were the Idea Inventory, the Adult Irrational Idea Inventory, the neuroticism scale of the Eysenck Personality Inventory, and the State–Trait Anxiety Inventory. There was a significant increase for the REE group in rational thinking and emotional adjustment when compared with the control group, but there was no significant difference on the neuroticism scale. Further, neither age nor intelligence were significant factors.

Ritchie (1978) researched the effect of rational–emotive education on irrational beliefs, assertiveness, and locus of control of 200 fifth-grade students. Subjects were assigned to an experimental or a control group, and three dependent measures were used in pre- and posttesting: the Children's Survey of Rational Concepts, Form C; the Revised Rathmus Assertiveness Schedule; and the Intellectual Achievement Questionnaire. The findings showed a significant difference in rational ideas between the experimental and control groups, and the experimental group proved better, though not significantly, in assertiveness and locus of control.

Patton (1978) examined the effects of rational behavior training (RBT) upon emotionally disturbed adolescents. The sample consisted of 34 adolescents in a special-education program who were diagnosed as "emotionally disturbed." The subjects were divided into an experimental or a control group. The experimental group received 40 minutes of RBT training for three days per week for 10 weeks. Five dependent measures were utilized: the RBT Concepts Test, the Common Perception Inventory, Rotter's Internal/External Locus of Control Scale, the Personal Orientation Inventory, and the Observational Emotional Inventory. Significant improvements for the experimental group were found on the RBT Concepts Test, the Common Perception Inventory, the Internal–External Scale, and the Time-Competence Scale of the Personal Orientation Inventory. Improvements, though not significant, were noted on the Inner-Directed Support Scale of the Personal Orientation Inventory, and all the subscales of the Observational Emotional Inventory.

Savitz (1979) studied the effects of RET on emotional disturbances. The subjects were 35 outpatient clients divided into a treatment and a control group. Treatment group subjects were given 50 minutes of RET group therapy each week for four weeks. This is a weak study, since no dependent measures were utilized; however, the referring physician did note improvement for treatment-group clients.

Other

Bigney (1979) tested the RET position in a marriage counseling situation. The subjects were 12 couples assigned randomly to either an experimental or a control group. Intrapsychic and interpersonal personality and temperament changes were measured after a 12-hour, six-week instruction in RET. Dependent measures included the California Psychological Inventory and the Taylor-Johnson Temperament Analysis. Results favored the experimental group, though none of the findings proved significant.

Rainwater (1979) conducted a case study utilizing RET to treat an obsessive individual. Measures used included self-reporting, self-monitoring, and peer reporting. Findings showed a significant improvement on all measures. The case study method, though valuable for in-depth study, possesses little value as an outcome study; it is included because it was the only study found that dealt specifically with the topic of obsessions.

Stevens (1981) studied stress with individuals in the Security Service of the U.S. Air Force. Each subject self-rated five stressful situations prior to treatment, and the ratings were evaluated using rational self-analysis for promoting rational cognitions. Treatment consisted of a six-hour workshop, with each subject additionally scheduled for three follow-up sessions. All subjects improved in their self-rating of satisfaction with 10 stressful situations in a test held two weeks after the workshop. Pre- to posttesting of the self-satisfaction scores revealed a significant improvement. Particular design weaknesses include the absence of a control group, in addition to the lack of a more objective measure.

Cox (1979) studied the effectiveness of rational behavior therapy on 15 criminal offenders with alcohol abuse problems. The site of the study was the Alcohol Rehabilitation Unit at the Federal Correction Unit in Lexington, Kentucky. Subjects, ranging in age from 21 to 62, with a mean age of 39, participated in RBT training prior to being paroled. A follow-up study showed that only two of the 15 individuals relapsed to the point where their parole was revoked. Again, the lack of a control group is a weakness of this study.

Plachetta (1979) examined the effectiveness of rational behavior therapy in improving the dating skills of 17 volunteers who were divided into an experimental and a control group. The RET group rated significantly better than the control on the Dating Fear Scale and the Social Avoidance and Distress Scale. It was also better, but not significantly, on the Fear of Negative Evaluation Scale.

Zelie, Stone, and Lehr (1980) studied the effectiveness of rational behavior therapy in problems of school discipline. Sixty students were divided into an experimental and a control group. Dependent measures were Teacher Behavior

Assessments and the recidivism rate. The experimental group was rated significantly better by teachers in regard to the initial problem behavior, class work, and homework. Also, the recidivism rate for the control group was three times that of the experimental group.

Block (1980) studied the effectiveness of RET with 40 overweight adults. Subjects were assigned to an experimental, an attention-place, or a no-treatment control group. The dependent measure was weight loss. Results indicated that RET subjects lost more weight, but these results were not significant.

Dye (1981) investigated the influence of rational–emotive education on the self-concept of maternally deprived adolescents living in a residential group home. Twenty-four subjects were divided into one of three groups: a treatment group, which received REE; a control group, which received nondirectional attention; and a no-treatment control group. Dependent measurement was made utilizing the Tennessee Self-Concept Scale. Though the results failed to demonstrate any significant findings, the treatment group did show greater gain scores.

Lee (1982) studied problems of assertiveness with a population of nurses. Eighty nurses were divided into an RET group or a control. Dependent measures used were the Assertion Inventory, the Rational Behavior Inventory, the Internal/External Locus of Control Scale, the State–Trait Anxiety Inventory, and the Wohler Physical Symptom Inventory. Pre- to posttesting showed that the RET group was significantly better on all measures.

In summary, the noncomparative studies generally support the efficacy of the RET position. Further, the studies go beyond those in the DiGiuseppe and Miller (1977) review in that there are more problem areas being researched and the subject pools are far more diverse.

COMPARATIVE STUDIES

The comparative studies are divided into two parts: those studies comparing RET with a single other therapy and those studies comparing RET with more than one other therapy. They are all presented in Table 5–2.

Part I: Single-therapy Comparisons

Behavior Assertion Training. Eades (1981) compared RET with behavioral assertion training in dealing with problems of assertion and irrational beliefs. The subjects in this study were 30 undergraduate students who were divided into one of three groups: an RET group, a behavioral assertion training group, or a control group. Dependent measures were the Assertion Inventory and the Irrational Beliefs Test, which were used for both pre- and posttesting. The results showed that both RET and behavioral assertion training were significant from pre- to posttesting on the Assertion Inventory. However, only the RET group demon-

Table 5-2 Comparative Studies: 1977 through Mid-1982

Name/Year	Comparisons	Problem	Subjects	Outcome
Eades (1981)	RET vs. behavioral assertion training	Assertion and irrational beliefs	30 undergraduates	Both RET and BAT significantly better pre to post; only RET significantly better compared with control
Cohen (1977)	RET vs. cognitive modification	Test anxiety	16 female undergraduates	RET better but not significant
Foley (1977)	RET vs. institutional program	Alcoholism	52 males	Both treatment groups improved but not significant
Block (1978)	RET vs. in-house school treatment program	School failure & misconduct	40 11th- & 12th-grade minority students	RET better but not significant
Kujoth & Topetzes (1977a, 1977b)	RET vs. psychodynamic insight therapy vs. eclectic therapy	Irrational ideas & negative emotions	115 community college students	RET significantly better wrt.* irrational ideas, anxiety, & depression
Warren (1979)	RET vs. RET + imagery vs. relationships-oriented counseling	Interpersonal anxiety	60 junior high school students	Both RET groups significantly better from pre to post & also wrt. control
Smith (1980)	RET vs. relationships-oriented counseling (ROC)	Test anxiety	60 junior high school students	No significant difference wrt. ROC; but, RET significantly better from pre to post, wrt. to self-report, & significantly better compared with control on sociometric measures
Baither Godsey (1979)	RET vs. relaxation training	Test anxiety	150 underachieving students	RET better, but not significant

Lipsky, Kassinove, & Miller (1980)	RET vs. relaxation training	Emotional adjustment	50 adults (20–60 yrs), actual patient population	RET significantly better
Jackson (1980)	RET vs. self-instructional (SI) coping therapy	Assertiveness	43 females	Both RET & SI significantly better from pre to post; RET better but not significant wrt. to SI
Jenni & Wollersheim (1979)	RET vs. stress management training (SMT)	Type A behavior	42 individuals	Both significantly better wrt. control; RET significantly better for high degree of Type A characteristics wrt. SMT.
Beck (1980)	RET vs. systematic desensitization (SD)	Speech anxiety	24 individuals	Both RET & SD better but not significant
Shackett (1980)	RET vs. systematic desensitization	Anxiety	60 individuals	RET & SD both significantly better wrt. control but not wrt. each other
Meyer (1982)	RET vs. recreational–educational programming group vs. control	Anxiety and self-esteem	100 children	RET significantly better for anxiety; no difference for self-esteem
Uzoka (1977)	RET vs. behavioral rehearsal vs. systematic desensitization	Test anxiety	69 male undergraduates	For defensive locus of control all treatment groups significantly better wrt. to control; for passive locus of control RET & behavioral rehearsal better but not significant
Carmody (1978)	RET vs. self-instructional coping therapy vs. behavior assertion training	Assertion	63 adults	All treatment better; only RET significant

Table 5-2 Continued

Name/Year	Comparisons	Problem	Subjects	Outcome
Manchester (1978)	RET vs. behavior modification vs. Gestalt vs. nutritive education	Obesity/nutrition	71 minority elementary school children	All improved, none significant wrt. each other
Rush, Beck, Kovacs, & Hollan (1977)	Cognitive therapy vs. pharmacotherapy	Depression	44 individuals	Cognitive therapy significantly better than pharmacotherapy
Lake (1978)	RET & digit temperature biofeedback vs. digit temperature biofeedback alone vs. EMG biofeedback vs. relaxation training	Migraine headache	24 individuals	All improved but none significant
N. J. Miller (1978)	REE vs. REE & behavioral rehearsal vs. REE & behavioral rehearsal & written homework	Content acquisition, neuroticism, anxiety	96 children	All treatment groups significantly better wrt. control but not wrt. each other
Saltzberg (1981)	RET vs. RET & bibliotherapy alone	Self-concept	30 students	Differences not significant
Taylor (1981)	RET & systematic desensitization & relaxation training	Test anxiety	143 high school students	Treatment group significantly better wrt. placebo & control

Study	Comparison	Focus	Sample	Results
Kassinove, Miller, & Kalin (1980)	Rational-emotive bibliotherapy vs. rational-emotive audiotherapy	Pre-treatment	34 adults	For neuroticism & anxiety bibliotherapy significant; for irrational ideas both significant
Zane (1979)	RET & behavioral rehearsal vs. behavioral rehearsal & RET	Assertion	12 M, 12 F	Both significantly better pre to post
Costello & Dougherty (1977)	RBT vs. control	RBT in classroom	63 individuals	RBT significant
Miller & Kassinove (1978)	REE vs. REE & behavioral rehearsal vs. REE & behavioral rehearsal & ABC homework vs. control	Emotional factors	96 4th graders of low/hi IQ	Improved, but not significantly; IQ not factor
T. W. Miller (1977)	RET self-acceptance group vs. self-esteem vs. control	Social anxiety	60 undergraduates	RET significantly better on Fear of Negative Evaluation Scale; RET better but not significant on Social Avoidance & Distress Scale
Hultgren (1977)	Rational child management vs. control	Parent education	16 mothers	Only partial significance

*wrt. means "with respect to."

strated gains that were significantly different from the control. Regarding the Irrational Beliefs Test, the findings showed that the RET group had significant gains from pre- to posttesting, compared with the behavioral assertion training and control groups. Follow-up studies were not indicated.

Cognitive Modification. Cohen (1977) compared RET to cognitive modification with test-anxious students, who were further identified as being open- or closed-minded. The subjects were 16 undergraduate females. Eight subjects were used as control group, while the remaining eight were divided into one of four treatment groups (of two persons per group): RET with open-minded subjects, cognitive modification with open-minded subjects, RET with closed-minded subjects, and cognitive modification with closed-minded subjects. Dependent measures were the Test Anxiety Scale and the Generalized Anxiety Scale. The findings, though lacking significance, demonstrated that RET open-minded subjects showed greater improvement on posttesting than either the cognitive modification or control groups.

Institutional Programs. Institutional programs employ elements of various therapeutic paradigms developed by the house staff of the particular institution. Two studies fall into this category.

Foley (1977) studied the self-concept of 52 male alcoholics. The subjects were divided into two treatment conditions: an institutional alcoholic treatment program, or this same program plus RET. The latter group received six hours of RET over a two-week period. The dependent measure was the Tennessee Self-Concept Scale. Though both groups improved from pre- to posttesting, the findings revealed no significant difference between the two groups on posttest scores. There were numerous design weaknesses in this study, including the absence of a control group, as well as the relatively short time of RET instruction.

Block (1978) studied the effectiveness of RET when compared with a school disciplinary/counseling program. The subjects were 40 eleventh- and twelfth-grade black and Hispanic students, identified by school personnel as high risk and failure and misconduct prone. Students were divided into one of three groups: a RET group, the school discipline/counseling program, and a control group. The RET group was given five weekly sessions spread throughout the entire semester. Dependent measures were grade-point average, incidents of disruptive behavior, and class cuts. The results indicated that the RET group demonstrated the greatest improvement on all variables over an extended period of time. Though this study supports the RET position, it is possible that a confounding variable may have been the RET group's identification as "special."

Psychodynamic Insight Therapy. Kujoth and Topetzes (1977a, 1977b) completed two studies comparing RET with psychodynamic insight therapy. In the first of these studies, 115 community college students were divided into two groups: an RET group and an insight therapy group. Two dependent measures were utilized: the Multiple Adjective Checklist and the Your Irrational Personality Trait Inventory Score. Pre- and posttesting demonstrated that the insight group showed no significant change, while the RET group was found significantly less irrational after treatment, with a decrease in undesirable emotionality also evidenced.

The second study was a partial replication of the first. In addition to the RET and insight groups, an eclectic therapy group was added. The findings revealed that, once again, only the RET group improved in variables related to mental health; moreover, this group was significantly less irrational after treatment and exhibited significantly less anxiety and depression. The absence of a control group in both studies is to be considered a weakness, though both studies appear to have been rigorous in other features of design.

Relationships-oriented Counseling. Warren (1979) compared RET, RET plus rational–emotive imagery, and relationships-oriented counseling in the treatment of interpersonal anxiety. The subjects were 60 junior high school students who were divided into one of four groups: one of the three treatment groups or a waiting-list control. All treatment groups met for seven 50-minute sessions over a period of three weeks. Self-report and sociometric measures were used for evaluation. Findings indicated that both RET groups showed significant improvement from pre- to posttesting, and also did better on the sociometric measures compared with the waiting-list control. Self-report measures showed no significant results.

Smith (1980) compared RET with relationships-oriented counseling in the treatment of test anxiety. In this study, 60 junior high school students were assigned to one of the treatment groups or a waiting-list control. Treatment consisted of seven 50-minute sessions over a three-week period. Sociometric and self-report measures were used for evaluation. Results showed that on self-report measures the RET group was significant in pre- to posttesting measures. On the sociometric measures the RET group proved significantly better than the control.

Relaxation Training. Baither and Godsey (1979) researched the relative effectiveness of RET compared with relaxation training in the treatment of test anxiety. Underachieving students (N=150) were assigned to one of the two treatment groups or a control group. The dependent measure utilized was the Alexander-Husak Anxiety Differential. Pre- and post measurements were taken, and the results were not significant.

Lipsky, Kassinove, and Miller (1980), in a pioneer study, researched the effectiveness of RET compared with relaxation training, using an actual patient population. The emotional adjustment of community mental-health-center patients of higher and lower intellectual ability was examined. In addition, the effects of rational role reversal and rational–emotive imagery were also studied. The subjects were 50 adults of both sexes ranging in age from 20 to 60. The subjects were first divided into lower and higher IQ groups, and then divided into one of five treatment groups: an RET group, an RET plus rational-role-reversal group, an RET plus rational–emotive imagery group, a relaxation training group, and a no-contact control. Four dependent measures were utilized: the Idea Inventory, the Multiple Adjective Checklist, the State–Trait Anxiety Inventory, and the Eysenck Personality Inventory. All RET groups proved significantly better than either the relaxation training or control groups on content acquisition. The RET-only group was significantly better than both the relaxation training and the control on measures of depression and neuroticism, and significantly better than either the relaxation training or the control on all dependent measures except the hostility scale, where both RET groups were significantly better than the control. RET plus rational role reversal was significantly better than RET alone on the depression, anxiety, and neuroticism measures, and RET plus rational–emotive imagery was significantly better than RET alone on the anxiety measures. In all cases, intelligence was not found to be a factor.

Self-instructional Coping Therapy. Jackson (1980) examined the effectiveness of RET compared with self-instructional coping therapy in problems of assertiveness and anxiety. The subjects were 43 adult women who responded to an assertion-training advertisement and were divided into one of three groups: an RET group, a self-instructional coping therapy group, and a waiting-list control. Results were to be determined by a behavioral-role-play test, a follow-up *in vivo* telephone call (to assess treatment generalizability), and self-report measures. In the role-play measure each subject was required to role play in 15 situations, 11 of which were so unreasonable that refusal behavior was anticipated. The follow-up *in vivo* telephone call, to assess refusal behavior, occurred approximately three weeks after treatment and consisted of requesting each subject to submit to a 45-minute on-the-spot interview. Both the RET and the self-instruction groups were significantly better than the control in the 11 refusal situations. No significant differences were found in the follow-up.

Stress Management Training. Jenni and Wollersheim (1979) compared cognitive therapy, based on RET, with stress management training in the treatment of Type A behavior patterns. There were 42 Type A subjects (determined by a structured interview) who were assigned to one of the two treatment groups or a waiting-list control. Dependent measures were self-report, the State–Trait Anxiety Inventory, and physiological arousal measures. Both treatment groups showed improvement on self-report measures and were significantly better than the control. For those subjects who initially had the highest degree of Type A characteristics, cognitive therapy was significantly more effective than the stress management and control groups. No treatment reduced the subjects' cholesterol level or blood pressure.

Systematic Desensitization. Beck (1980) compared RET with systematic desensitization in the treatment of speech-anxious repressors and sensitizers. Twenty-four subjects were assigned to one of the two treatment groups. No control was used. Two dependent measures were used: the Behavior Checklist and speaking time. Pre- to posttest measures showed improvement for both treatment groups, but these results were not significant.

Shackett (1980) compared RET with systematic desensitization in the treatment of anxiety. Thirty subjects were assigned to one of two treatment groups; a matched control group was also constructed. Both treatment groups received one hour of therapy for four weeks. The dependent measure was the IPAT Anxiety Scale. The results showed that both the RET and systematic desensitization groups were significantly better than the control, but there were no significant differences between the treatment groups.

Recreational–Educational Programming. Meyer (1982) studied the effects of rational–emotive group therapy upon the anxiety and self-esteem levels of learning-disabled children. The subjects were 100 children between the ages of 8 and 13 who were divided into one of three groups: an RET group, a recreational–educational programming group, and a no-contact control. All groups were further broken down into subgroups of from seven to nine subjects, based on age. Pre- to posttesting showed that the RET group proved significantly better on measures of anxiety; however, there were no differences found on measures of self-esteem.

Part II: Multiple Therapy Comparisons

RET, behavioral rehearsal, and systematic desensitization were compared by Uzoka (1977) in the treatment of test anxiety. Differences were also to be noted between defensive and passive locus of control. The subjects were 69 volunteer male undergraduates who were assigned to one of the three experimental conditions or a control. Dependent measures were the Alpert and Haber Achievement Anxiety Scale, the Spielberger State–Trait Anxiety Inventory, and a self-report inventory. The findings revealed that for defensive locus-of-control subjects there was significant improvement for all treatment groups when compared with the control; however, for passive subjects only the behavioral rehearsal and RET groups showed improvement, though this was not significant.

Carmody (1978) compared RET with self-instructional coping therapy and behavior assertion training in the treatment of assertion problems. The subjects were 63 subassertive adult outpatients, who were divided into one of the three experimental conditions or a control group. All treatment conditions received four 90-minute sessions. Results were evaluated by behavioral and self-report measures. All treatment groups showed improvement in short-term treatment; only the RET group proved significantly better on the self-report measure of unproductive cognitions; only the RET group demonstrated significant generalization of treatment gains in an *in vivo* test of transfer during a posttest follow-up; and treatment gains for all groups were maintained at a three-month follow-up.

Manchester (1978) compared RET with behavior modification, Gestalt awareness, and nutritive education in the treatment of obesity and nutrition problems among minority children. The subjects were 71 black, urban, elementary-school children ranging in age from 5 to 13. They were assigned to one of the four treatment groups, but a control group was, unfortunately, not employed. Dependent measures included measurement of weight, skinfold, self-esteem, and food consumption. Though all treatment groups were found to improve from pre- to posttest, there were no significant findings.

In these comparative studies, as with those in the prior section dealing with noncomparative studies, support for the RET position is given strength. A wide range of comparisons with regard to different therapies allows for greater generalizability of RET.

Other Outcome Studies of RET

This section includes those RET outcome studies that do not strictly fall into the headings of the prior two sections. These studies largely consist of RET combined with other therapies, measurements of specific elements of RET, or therapies that are very similar to or comprise a generic form of RET.

Rush, Beck, Kovacs, and Hollan (1977) performed one of the major studies of an RET-like therapy. The researchers examined and compared cognitive therapy and pharmacotherapy in the treatment of depressed outpatients. The subjects were 44 severely depressed individuals who were referred to the Mood Clinic of the University of Pennsylvania Medical Center. After initial matching and testing, 19 of the subjects were assigned to individual cognitive therapy; the remaining 25 received drug therapy. Both groups were treated for 12 weeks. Pre- and posttesting were measured via a battery of extensive psychological tests as well as by self-report, with different doctors performing the testing and treatment. Further testing at irregular monthly intervals up to one year after the completion of treatment was also performed. Seventy-five percent of the subjects were suicidal at the time of referral, with an average subject being depressed for a minimum of eight years. The findings significantly favored the cognitive therapy group at the end of treatment. Further, at a one-year follow-up, the results remained significant, with the cognitive therapy group showing less than half the relapse rate of the drug-therapy group. Up to the time of this study, no form of therapy was shown to be even *as effective* as drug therapy with this patient population.

Lake (1978) combined RET plus digit temperature biofeedback and compared it with digit temperature biofeedback alone, frontalis EMG biofeedback, and assisted relaxation training in the treatment of migraine headaches. The subjects were 24 classical migraine headache sufferers and were assigned to one of the four treatment groups or a control group. All treatment groups received four weeks of instruction. The dependent measure was a daily record of headache activity. Findings showed that, though all treatment groups improved, there were no significant differences among the groups or in comparison with the control.

N. J. Miller (1978) compared rational–emotive education with REE plus behavioral rehearsal, and REE plus behavioral rehearsal *and* written homework assignments, among 96 children of high and low intellectual levels. The subjects were divided into one of the three experimental conditions, or a control group. The dependent measures were two measures of content acquisition, one measure of neuroticism, and one measure of trait anxiety. Findings revealed that all three experimental groups were significantly better than the control on all measures. Further, intelligence was not found to be a factor in any of the findings.

Saltzberg (1981) compared RET to RET plus bibliotherapy to bibliotherapy alone in the treatment of self-concept problems among 30 students. The subjects were divided into three treatment groups, but no control group was used. Dependent measures were made utilizing Rotter's Locus of Control Scale, the Rational Behavior Inventory, the Tennessee Self-Concept Scale, the Self-Evaluation Scale, and the Ego Strength Scale of the MMPI. There were no significant differences among the groups. One shortcoming of this study was the absence of a control; further, pretesting was omitted.

Taylor (1981) combined RET with systematic desensitization and relaxation training in the treatment of test-anxious high school students. The combined therapeutic interventions form what Taylor calls the Lecture Verbal Interaction Method (LVIM). There were 143 subjects divided into three groups: treatment, placebo, and control. Pre- and posttesting were conducted using the Stimulus-Response Inventory, the State–Trait Anxiety Inventory, and algebra tests. The findings showed that the treatment group was significantly better on all measures.

Kassinove, Miller, and Kalin (1980) examined the efficiency of rational–emotive bibliotherapy for prospective psychotherapy clients. There were 34 subjects, ranging in age from 21 to 56, who were assigned to either the bibliotherapy, audiotherapy, or a no-contact control group. On neuroticism and trait anxiety, the bibliotherapy group showed significant results; on the acceptance of irrational ideas, both groups showed significant improvement.

Zane (1979) combined RET with behavioral rehearsal in the treatment of nonassertive behaviors. The subjects were 12 males and 16 females. Two groups were utilized: one was instructed first with RET and afterward with behavioral rehearsal; in the other group, the opposite regimen was used. There was no control group. Dependent measures were the Conflict Resolution Inventory and the Behavioral Role Playing Assertiveness Test, as well as telephone and self-report follow-up questionnaires. The results indicated both experimental groups showed significant improvement in pre- to posttest measurements, with the RET/behavioral rehearsal sequence being most effective.

Costello and Dougherty (1977) examined rational behavioral training in the classroom. There were three groups of 21 subjects each: group R, undergraduates enrolled in a 15-week course in rational behavior training; group A, adults enrolled in a six-week adult education course in rational behavior training; and group C, undergraduate students in a theology course, as a control. Pre- and postdependent measurement was accomplished utilizing the Personal Orientation Inventory. Findings on the inner-directedness scale showed significant results for both rational behavior training groups; but on the time-competency scale only group R changed significantly. This latter result, in addition to reflecting treatment time, also may suggest that greater emphasis is placed on inner-directedness than time competency in rational behavior training.

Miller and Kassinove (1978) studied the relative effectiveness of rational–emotive education among high- and low-IQ fourth graders. The subjects were 96 students divided into four groups: one group received only rational–emotive education lectures; a second group received both lectures and behavioral rehearsal; a third group received lectures, behavioral rehearsal, and ABC homework sheets; a fourth group served as a control. Pre- to posttest measurements showed no significant changes, although all rational–emotive education groups, particularly those that added behavioral components, showed improvement. Further, IQ proved not to be a factor.

T. W. Miller (1977) examined two different approaches to the problem of self-evaluation in the treatment of social-evaluation anxiety. Sixty undergraduates were divided into three groups: a self-acceptance group, a self-esteem group, and a waiting-list control. Being tested was the RET principle that self-acceptance, with its stated goal of nonrating, would produce better results than the self-esteem model. Treatment groups received 10 weeks of instruction. Dependent measures were the Fear of Negative Evaluation Scale and the Social Avoidance and Distress Scale. The findings revealed that the self-acceptance group was significantly more improved when compared with the self-esteem or control on pre- to postassessment for the Fear of Negative Evaluation Scale. On the Social Avoidance and Distress Scale, the self-acceptance group was also significantly better than the control, but not better than the self-esteem group.

Hultgren (1977) studied the effectiveness of RET in parent education. Sixteen mothers responded to an advertisement for a 10-week course and were divided into a rational child management group or a control. Posttesting showed that the rational child management group was more effective in changing the mothers' child-rearing attitudes, and knowledge of the causes of emotional responses, but was not effective in changing knowledge of child-management principles, childrearing practices, rationality of beliefs, or children's behavior.

These studies cover a varied range of problem situations and subject populations. Like the prior two sections, the efficiency of RET is maintained, with no significant results against the RET position.

DISCUSSION

DiGiuseppe and Miller (1977) assert that their review of research does support the efficiency of RET; and, specifically, they make the following points: (1) RET is more effective than client-centered therapy with introverted persons; (2) RET is more effective than systematic desensitization in the reduction of general or pervasive anxiety; (3) a combination of cognitive therapy and behavior therapy appears to be the most efficacious treatment for depression; (4) the relative effectiveness of RET versus assertiveness training is inconclusive, due to limited and confounded research.

This review agrees with their general findings supporting the efficacy of RET. Of the 47 studies reviewed, there were 31 with significant findings favoring the RET position. In the remaining studies, the RET treatment groups all showed improvement, and in no study was another treatment method significantly better than RET. Regarding DiGiuseppe and Miller's (1977) specific conclusions just stated: (1) There were no studies found comparing RET to client-centered therapy, thus, no conclusions may be drawn; (2) of the studies comparing RET to systematic desensitization, there were no significant findings supporting the conclusion that RET is more effective than systematic desensitization; (3) only one study was found that specifically dealt with the problem of depression (Rush, Beck, Kovacs, & Hollan, 1977), and the findings of that study do support the conclusion drawn by DiGiuseppe and Miller; (4) two studies compared RET to assertiveness training (Eades, 1981; Carmody, 1978). In the Eades (1981) study both RET and assertiveness training were significant in pre- to posttesting, but only RET was significant with respect to the control. In the Carmody (1978) study, RET was significant for some of the dependent measures. Thus, although RET is favored over assertiveness training, no definite conclusions seem warranted.

DiGiuseppe and Miller (1977) reported methodological shortcomings for many of the studies they reviewed. Specifically, they noted inadequate control groups and failures to make comparisons with other forms of therapy. Such shortcomings also existed, although to a lesser degree, in the studies currently reviewed. In addition to inadequate or missing control groups, some studies also only conducted posttesting.

Another point discussed by DiGiuseppe and Miller (1977) was the use of nonrepresentative subject pools, specifically college and high school students.

Although many of the studies in this review also utilized these school populations, many others broadened their population base, thus providing a wider
test of the RET position. The more diverse populations included clinical outpatients, elementary-school children, adults solicited through advertisements,
mothers, military personnel, older adults, emotionally disturbed adolescents,
minority students, high- and low-IQ populations, school underachievers, couples
in marriage counseling, criminal offenders, and overweight adults and children.
These additions represent an improvement over the studies reviewed by Di-
Giuseppe and Miller.

DiGiuseppe and Miller (1977) also noted the absence of studies in their review
that dealt with client variables such as socioeconomic status and IQ. Again, an
improvement may be noted in the studies currently reviewed. Miller and Kassinove (1978) and Krenitsky (1978) both performed studies isolating the variables
of IQ, demonstrating that it was not a factor in outcome. Block (1978) and Zelie,
Stone, and Lehr (1980) both addressed minority populations of low socioeconomic status, though no comparison was drawn to higher socioeconomic groups.
Nonetheless, no research has arisen that would dictate that RET is superior with
one socioeconomic group over another. But there does remain an absence of
studies examining racial/cultural factors.

Another area of concern discussed by DiGiuseppe and Miller (1977) is the lack
of adequate dependent variables and the weaknesses of existing psychometric
scales. This, indeed, remains a problem. In addition to self-report measures,
which are inherently weak dependent variables, the sheer number of different
scales renders objective comparisons virtually impossible; 61 different scales
were used in the 47 studies reviewed. DiGiuseppe and Miller suggest a greater
use of behavioral measures, which some of the studies in this review did use.
Block (1980), for example, in dealing with obesity, used "pounds lost" as a
dependent measure, and Barabasz (1979) used psychophysiological changes to
measure anxiety. Adequate follow-up remains a problem, however; only a small
number of the current studies reported a follow-up.

Two other limitations noted by DiGiuseppe and Miller (1977) concern the
short duration of therapy and the level of training of the therapist. The first of
these remains a problem, with some studies using only a single session. The level
of training of the therapist also remains a concern. In addition to the DiGiuseppe
and Miller argument that researchers publish therapist manuals describing the
techniques used in research, it would also be advantageous to have audiotaped
sessions reviewed by recognized practitioners of RET.

REFERENCES

Baither, R. C., & Godsey, R. (1979). Rational–emotive education and relaxation training in large
    group treatment of test anxiety. *Psychological Reports, 45,* 326.
Barabasz, M. (1979). Effects of rational–emotive psychotherapy on psychophysiological arousal
    measures of test anxiety. *Dissertation Abstracts International, 40*(3-B), 1348–1349.

Beck, K. E. (1980). Differential response of speech-anxious repressors and sensitizers to systematic desensitization and rational–emotive therapy. *Dissertation Abstracts International, 40*(12-B), 5800.

Bigney, R. E. (1979). Intrapsychic and interpersonal personality and temperament changes in marital dyads resulting from a marriage enrichment program based on rational–emotive therapy. *Dissertation Abstracts International, 39*(8-A), 4723–4724.

Block, J. (1978). Effects of a rational–emotive mental health program on poorly achieving, disruptive high school students. *Journal of Counseling Psychology, 25*, 61–65.

Block, J. (1980). Effects of rational–emotive therapy on overweight adults. *Psychotherapy: Therapy, Research and Practice, 17*, 277–280.

Carmody, T. P. (1978). Rational–emotive, self-instructional, and behavioral assertion training: Facilitating maintenance. *Cognitive Therapy and Research, 2*, 241–253.

Cohen, J. A. (1977). Effects of the client characteristics of open- and closed-mindedness in relation to rational–emotive therapy and cognitive-modification treatment of test-anxious subjects. *Dissertation Abstracts International, 37*(12-B), 6318.

Corey, G. (1977). *Theory and practice of counseling and psychotherapy.* Monterey, Calif.: Brooks/Cole.

Costello, R. T., & Dougherty, D. (1977). Rational behavior training in the classroom. *Rational Living, 12*, 13–15.

Cox, S. G. (1979). Rational behavior training as a rehabilitative program for alcoholic offenders. *Offender Rehabilitation, 3*, 245–256.

D'Angelo, D. C. (1978). The effects of locus of control and a program of rational–emotive therapy on fear of negative evaluation. *Dissertation Abstracts International, 38*(8-A), 4579.

DiGiuseppe, R. A., & Miller, N. J. (1977). A review of outcome studies on rational–emotive therapy. In A. Ellis & R. Grieger (Eds.), *Handbook of rational–emotive therapy.* New York: Springer.

Dye, S. O. (1981). The influence of rational–emotive education on the self-concept of adolescents living in a residential group home. *Dissertation Abstracts International, 41*(9-A), 3881.

Eades, J. M. (1981). The effects of the cognitive components of rational–emotive therapy and behavioral assertion training on assertiveness and irrational beliefs. *Dissertation Abstracts International, 41*(80A), 3422.

Ellis, A. (1977). Research data supporting the clinical and personality hypotheses of RET and other cognitive-behavior therapies. In A. Ellis & R. Grieger (Eds.), *Handbook of rational–emotive therapy.* New York: Springer.

Foley, J. D. (1977). Rational–emotive therapy compared with a representative institutional treatment program on the self-concept of male alcoholics. *Dissertation Abstracts International, 37*(9-A), 5607.

Hultgren, A. S. (1977). A rational child management approach to parent education. *Dissertation Abstracts International, 37*(9-A), 5607.

Hymen, S. P., & Warren, R. (1978). An evaluation of rational–emotive imagery as a component of rational–emotive therapy in the treatment of test anxiety. *Perceptual and Motor Skills, 46*, 847–853.

Jackson, J. S. (1980). Assertion training: Rational–emotive therapy vs. self-instructional coping therapy in the facilitation of refusal behavior among women. *Dissertation Abstracts International, 41*(6-A), 2517.

Jenni, M. A., & Wollersheim, J. P. (1979). Cognitive therapy, stress management training and the Type A behavior pattern. *Cognitive Therapy and Research, 3*, 61–73.

Kassinove, H., Miller, N. J., & Kalin, M. (1980). Effects of pretreatment with rational–emotive bibliotherapy and rational–emotive audiotherapy on clients waiting at community mental health center. *Psychological Reports, 46*, 851–857.

Katz, B. (1978). Treatment of test-anxious students by rational–emotive therapy, relaxation-placebo and no-treatment. *Dissertation Abstracts International, 38*(7-A), 4048–4049.

Krenitsky, D. L. (1978). The relationship of age and verbal intelligence to the efficacy of rational–emotive education with older adults, *Dissertation Abstracts International, 39*(5-B), 2506–2507.

Kujoth, R. K., & Topetzes, N. J. (1977a). A rational–emotive approach to mental health for college students: Study I. *College Student Journal, 11*, 1–6. (a)

Kujoth, R. K., & Topetzes, N. J. (1977b). A rational–emotive approach to mental health for college students: Study II. *College Student Journal, 11*, 7–11. (b)

Lake, A. E. (1978) Biofeedback and rational–emotive therapy in the management of migraine headache. *Dissertation Abstracts International, 39*(6-B), 2991–2992.

Lee, C. A. (1982). Cognitive behavioral group approach to assertiveness training for nurses. *Dissertation Abstracts International, 42*(10-B), 4197.

Lipsky, M. J., Kassinove, H., & Miller, N. J. (1980). Effects of rational–emotive therapy, rational role reversal, and rational–emotive imagery on the emotional adjustment of community mental health center patients, *Journal of Consulting and Clinical Psychology, 48,* 366–374.

Manchester, C. F. (1978). A study of the effects of three weight counseling techniques and one nutrition education technique on the weight, skinfold measures, and self-concepts of black, urban, obese elementary school children. *Dissertation Abstracts International, 38*(11-A), 6539–6540.

Meyer, D. (1982). Effects of rational–emotive group therapy upon anxiety and self-esteem of learning-disabled children. *Dissertation Abstracts International,* (10-B), 4201.

Miller, N. J., & Kassinove, H. (1978). Effects of lecture, rehearsal, written homework, and IQ on the efficacy of a rational–emotive school mental health program. *Journal of Community Psychology, 6,* 366–373.

Miller, T. W. (1977). An exploratory investigation comparing self-esteem with self-acceptance in reducing social-evaluative anxiety. *Dissertation Abstracts International, 37*(11-B) 5838.

Patton, P. L. (1978). The effects of rational behavior training on emotionally disturbed adolescents in an alternative school setting. *Dissertation Abstracts International, 38*(12-A), 7166.

Plachetta, L. J. (1979). The effects of rational-behavior training on dating skill level development with minimal daters. *Dissertation Abstracts International, 39,*(12-A), 7166.

Rainwater, G. D. (1979). A self-administered treatment for obsessing. *Dissertation Abstracts International, 39*(10-B), 5082.

Ritchie, B. C. (1978). The effect of rational–emotive education on irrational beliefs, assertiveness, and/or locus of control in fifth grade students. *Dissertation Abstracts International, 39*(4-A), 2069–2070.

Roberts, T. J. (1977). A rational–emotive approach to assessing and treating students enrolled in an undergraduate social work program. *Dissertation Abstracts International, 38*(2-A), 639–640.

Rosenheim, H. D., & Dunn, R. W. (1977). The effectiveness of rational behavior therapy in a military population. *Military Medicine, 142,* 550–552.

Rush, A. J., Beck, A. T., Kovacs, M., & Hollan, S. (1977). Comparative efficacy of cognitive therapy and pharmacotherapy in the treatment of depressed outpatients. *Cognitive Therapy and Research, 1,* 17–38.

Saltzberg, L. H. (1981). A comparison of RET group therapy, RET group therapy with bibliotherapy, and bibliotherapy-only treatments. *Dissertation Abstracts International, 41*(7-A), 3018.

Savitz, J. C. (1979). Diagnosis and treatment of emotionally disturbed clients using rational behavior therapy. *Dissertation Abstracts International, 39*(12-A), 7251.

Shackett, R. W. (1980). The relative effectiveness of rational–emotive therapy and systematic desensitization in the treatment of anxiety. *Dissertation Abstracts International, 40*(9-B), 4508–4509.

Shertzer, E., & Stone, S. C. (1980). *Fundamentals of counseling.* Boston: Houghton Mifflin.

Smith, G. W. (1980). A rational–emotive counseling approach to assist junior high school students with interpersonal anxiety. *Dissertation Abstracts International, 40*(12-A), 6157.

Stevens, R. J. (1981). The effects of RET/RBT principles as an instrument for stress management at a USAF Security Service base. *Dissertation Abstracts International, 41*(9-A), 3892.

Taylor, T. D. (1981). A multicomponent treatment model for reducing the test anxiety of high school mathematics students. *Dissertation Abstracts International, 41*(9-A), 3563.

Uzoka, A. F. (1977). Treatment of test anxiety in subjects with defensive and passive external locus of control orientation. *Dissertation Abstracts International, 38*(1-B), 384.

Warren, L. R. (1979). An evaluation of rational–emotive imagery as a component of rational–emotive therapy in the treatment of interpersonal anxiety in junior high school students. *Dissertation Abstracts International, 39*(12-B), 6103–6104.

Zane, P. K. (1979). The role of rational–emotive therapy and behavioral rehearsal in the treatment of nonassertiveness. *Dissertation Abstracts International, 39*(8-B), 4063.

Zelie, K., Stone, C. I., & Lehr, E. (1980). Cognitive-behavioral intervention in school discipline: A preliminary study. *Personnel and Guidance Journal, 59,* 80–83.

Part Two

The Dynamics of Emotional Disturbance

6

Discomfort Anxiety: A New Cognitive Behavioral Construct*

Albert Ellis

DISCOMFORT ANXIETY VERSUS EGO ANXIETY

For the past several years, largely on the basis of clinical evidence derived from my practice of rational–emotive therapy (RET), I have been distinguishing between two major forms of anxiety: discomfort anxiety (DA) and ego anxiety (EA). *Discomfort anxiety* I define as emotional tension that results when people feel (1) that their comfort (or life) is threatened, (2) that they *should* or *must* get what they want (and *should not* or *must not* get what they don't want), and (3) that it is *awful* or *catastrophic* (rather than merely inconvenient or disadvantageous) when they don't get what they supposedly *must*. *Ego anxiety* I define as emotional tension that results when people feel (1) that their self or personal worth is threatened, (2) that they *should* or *must* perform well and/or be approved by others, and (3) that it is *awful* or *catastrophic* when they don't perform well and/or are not approved by others as they supposedly *should* or *must* be.

Ego anxiety is a dramatic, powerful feeling that usually seems overwhelming; is often accompanied by feelings of severe depression, shame, guilt, and in-

---

*This chapter amalgamates two papers first published in *Rational Living:* Discomfort anxiety: A new cognitive-behavioral construct (Parts I and II), *14* (1979) and *15* (1980) respectively.

adequacy; and frequently drives people to therapy (or to suicide!). Discomfort anxiety is often less dramatic but perhaps more common. It tends to be specific to certain "uncomfortable" or "dangerous" situations, and consequently shows up in such phobias as fear of heights, open spaces, elevators, and trains. But it can also easily generalize to uncomfortable *feelings* themselves, such as feelings of anxiety, depression, and shame. Thus, DA may be a primary symptom (e.g., anxiety about elevators) or a secondary symptom (e.g., anxiety about feeling anxious about elevators).

As a secondary symptom, DA may generalize to almost *any* kind of anxiety. Thus, people may first feel anxious about feeling anxious about elevators; but they may later worry about whether they are *also* going to feel anxious about trains or escalators; and they may therefore actually make themselves exceptionally uncomfortable (anxious) about *many* forms of anxiety (discomfort) and may thereby become pandemically anxious. Or, they may at first feel anxious about a specific event (e.g., about entering an elevator) and later, realizing that they may well become anxious about that event, they may also make themselves anxious about any symbol of that event (e.g., a picture of an elevator) or about any thought of that event (e.g., the thought "Suppose I have to take an elevator when I visit my friend. Wouldn't that possibility be awful?").

Because it is often less dramatic than ego anxiety (or self-downing), and because it may be a secondary rather than a primary symptom, discomfort anxiety may easliy be unrecognized and may be somewhat wrongly labeled as general or free-floating anxiety. Thus, if people are anxious about going in elevators, they may clearly recognize their anxiety or phobia and label it "elevator phobia." But if they are anxious about being anxious (that is, fearful of the uncomfortable sensations they will probably feel if they enter an elevator or if they even think about entering an elevator), they may feel very anxious but may not see clearly *what* they are anxious about. Nor may their therapists!

The construct of discomfort anxiety helps to explain several phenomena relating to emotional disturbance in clearer and more therapeutic ways. Thus, if clients tell me they are so terrified of snakes that they feel extremely upset whenever they see even a picture of a snake, I can pretty well guess that they hardly think the *picture* will bite them. I can quickly surmise that they are not only afraid of snakes but also of their anxiety itself—of the uncomfortable *feelings* they will predictably have when they think about (or view a picture of) a snake.

My problem with these clients, therefore, is to get them first to stop awfulizing about their feelings of anxiety; to help them accept their discomfort (or potential discomfort) as a damned bother (and not as a holy horror!). Then, when they truly see that it's not awful to *feel* anxious, they can stop obsessing about this feeling and work on anti-awfulizing about the original feared object, the snakes. Their discomfort anxiety about their feelings helps keep them from confronting these feelings and working through them.

A research study that possibly shows the explanatory and therapeutic value of the construct of discomfort anxiety is that of Sutton-Simon (1979), who found some seemingly contradictory results that may be explained by the use of this construct. She noted that, in a study of subjects with fears of heights, subjects with social anxiety, and subjects with fears of heights plus social anxieties, those with fears of heights did not display significant irrationality on the Jones (1968) Irrational Beliefs Test (IBT), while those with social anxiety did show significant irrationality on the IBT.

This would be expected, according to the construct posited in this chapter, since fear of heights would presumably largely involve discomfort anxiety, while social anxiety would largely involve ego anxiety. Sutton-Simon (1979) observes that ego anxiety may be cross-situational, while discomfort anxiety may be specific to situations, although one person may experience discomfort anxiety in many situations. DA may be "hooked up" to the particular cues of the situation, while EA may be more of a quality of a person.

Although the construct of discomfort anxiety presented here seems to have some new and useful elements, it overlaps with several previous hypotheses about emotional disturbance and its treatment. Thus, Low (1952) pointed out that disturbed individuals often get upset about their symptoms of anxiety and panic, and that they may be helped by defining these symptoms as uncomfortable but not dangerous. Ellis (1962, 1979a,b) emphasized secondary symptoms of disturbance, such as anxiety about anxiety, and stressed the role of low frustration tolerance and short-range hedonism in disturbed behavior and in clients' resistance to changing this behavior. Weekes (1969, 1972, 1977) highlighted the importance of anxiety about anxiety, especially in agoraphobia. Rehm (1977) offered a self-control model of depression that stresses hedonic as well as ego factors in this disturbance. The present formulations go somewhat beyond these other theories in developing a construct of discomfort anxiety and in distinguishing it more clearly from ego anxiety.

DISCOMFORT ANXIETY AND DEPRESSION

The concept of discomfort anxiety also tends to give a better explanation of the origins and treatment of depression than many of the other explanations. Abramson and Sackheim (1977) point out a seeming paradox in depression. On the one hand, depressed individuals—as Beck (1976) emphasizes—blame themselves and look upon themselves as unable to help themselves; they are distinct self-downers. But on the other hand, they insist, in a somewhat grandiose manner, that they must have certainty and must control the outcome of the events in their lives; and they depress themselves when they don't actually have that kind of full control. They are therefore both self-denigrating and self-deifying, which seems to be something of a paradox.

In RET terms, and in terms of ego anxiety and discomfort anxiety, this paradox seems quite resolvable. In RET, it is hypothesized that the individual tends to have three basic irrational beliefs (iB's) about himself or herself and the universe: (1) "I *must* succeed at the important things that I do in life and win the approval of significant people in my life, and it is *awful* when I don't. I am therefore not as good as I *should* be, and I am therefore worthless." (2) "You *must* treat me kindly, fairly, and considerately, and it is *horrible* when you don't. You are therefore a crumb or a louse." (3) "The conditions under which I live *must* be easy, or at least not too difficult, and *must* give me all the things I really want quickly and without too much of a hassle; and it is *terrible* when they aren't that way. The world is a really rotten place in which to live and *should* not be the way it indubitably is."

Very often, depressed people have two of these basic ideas—the first and the third—and sometimes they have the second as well. There is no reason, of course, why they should not have two or three; and I also do not see why the first and the third, when they are strongly held, necessarily conflict with each other. The first one, "I *must* succeed at the important things that I do in life and win the approval of significant people in my life; and it is *awful* when I don't!" seems to be essentially self-downing. But its perfectionism is essentially grandiose, since the implication is that "I *must* be outstanding, perfect, and godlike; and if I am not what I must be in these respects, *then* it is *awful* and I am a worthless or rotten person." This same kind of grandiosity is also implied in the third irrationality; namely, "Because I am (or *should* be) a great person for whom everything goes easily and well in life, *therefore* the conditions under which I live must not be too difficult, and therefore it is *terrible* and the world is a horrible place if they are that difficult."

Implicit grandiosity, therefore, underlies virtually all emotional disturbance; namely, the unspoken (or spoken!) demand and command that "*I* must succeed and be universally approved; *you* must treat me kindly and fairly; and the *world conditions* must be easy and immediately gratifying for me. When these demands and commands are not met—as, of course, in reality, they usually are not—then I "logically" make myself anxious, despairing, depressed, or angry. Without these omnipotent insistences, I would only tend to make myself sorry, regretful, annoyed, and irritated.

Discomfort anxiety is particularly important in anxiety and depression, as I think will be shown in the following case illustration. Several years ago I saw a man of 28, who was severely anxious or panicked, as well as angry and depressed, virtually every day of the year, and had been so for 10 years prior to that time. He had been in intensive psychotherapy since the age of 15; and had improved moderately during this time, so that he at least had been able to go through college and work steadily as a bookkeeper. But he had been institutionalized twice, for a period of a year at a time; had not been able to achieve any intimate relations with women; and led a very restricted and highly routinized existence. He frequently became so depressed that he seriously considered suicide.

On the surface, this man's problem was ego anxiety, since he insisted that he had to do things well and win others' approval, and he put himself down severely whenever he failed to do so. He said that he hated himself, had no self-confidence, and had an enormous fear of failure; and he was afraid to make any major decisions, for fear that he might make a mistake and would then have to castigate himself for this mistake.

Actually, however, this client had benefited somewhat from previous therapy, particularly from reading Ellis and Harper's (1975) book, *A New Guide to Rational Living,* which he used virtually as his bible. In many respects, he felt relatively little shame or guilt as, for example, when he dressed sloppily and was criticized for not socializing, and when he acted quite selfishly, even with friends and relatives whom he most loved and respected. So I began to suspect that his main problem was discomfort anxiety, rather than ego anxiety, although he also had aspects of the latter (as perhaps almost every human does). In a typical fit of anxiety, depression, and anger, he would think and act in the following ways:

1. He would become exceptionally "anxious" or "panicked" when he had to wait in line at a store or wait to be served at a bar. Here, he seemed to be demanding that conditions be easier and that he be served immediately; he had fairly clear-cut low frustration tolerance or discomfort anxiety.

2. Once he became "panicked," he would tell himself, "I *must* not overreact in this manner; what a worm I am!" and would experience ego anxiety. But, often much more strongly, he would insist to himself, "I *must* not be panicked and feel such horrible discomfort at being panicked!" and would experience secondary symptoms of discomfort anxiety.

3. He would then notice that he was continually panicked over hassles and difficulties; and when he saw that this was so (largely as a result of the RET he was undergoing), he would then insist that life was *too* hard and that it *was* awful that he kept being set upon in these horrible ways. He would naively ask me, "Don't *you* feel terrible when people force you to do what you really don't want to do, such as wait on line for a long time at a store?" When I answered that I certainly did not like that kind of thing but that I accepted it and thereby was able to edit out almost entirely some of the inconvenience I was caused, he simply could not understand how I could accept it. He considered it intrinsically horrible to be balked in any desire, even relatively little ones like wanting to be waited on quickly at a store, and thought that everyone in the universe thought it equally horrible.

4. As he kept upsetting himself in these ways, he realized that he was, at least in the degree of his upsetness, different from other people. So he again put himself down for that and went back, once more, to ego anxiety. Then he also felt horrified about the uncomfortableness of continually feeling panicked and

reverted, once more, to discomfort anxiety about this continual discomfort; that is, he would not accept it and viewed it as being a virtually unlivable state. Again, he felt suicidal (though not actively so) because of these continued feelings; and again he wondered about his suicidalness, and whether he was a rotten person, much different from and worse than others, for having such feelings. At times, however, he merely accepted such feelings and thought that he was quite justified in thinking about killing himself because of the "horrible" discomforts of living.

5. Because this client defined almost all of his strong wants or desires as absolute needs—which is the philosophical essence of discomfort anxiety—he reemphasized his irrational belief, "I *must* do well!" For he devoutly believed that only by doing well would he get more of the things that he absolutely "needed." When he did not perform beautifully, therefore, he not only downed himself for his inadequacy but also felt that his performance was below his "need" level, and he thereby experienced discomfort anxiety as well as ego anxiety.

All in all, this client's DA continually intermingled with and helped reinforce his EA; and vice versa. Like many severely disturbed people, he probably would have functioned poorly with only EA, for he often seriously downed himself for his errors and for experiencing others' disapproval. But it is unlikely that he would have been as critically disturbed as he was without his suffering from both ego anxiety and discomfort anxiety. From observing him and many other clients like him, I hypothesize that some individuals suffer emotionally because of their ego anxiety and some because of their discomfort anxiety, and that those who have a combination of severe EA and DA are even more disturbed than those who have one or the other and are also less likely to change themselves or to benefit from any form of psychotherapy.

Another often-noted phenomenon that can be explained nicely by the hypothesis of discomfort anxiety is the observation that people who suffer severe depression frequently have lost their parents or other significant persons early in their lives; that this kind of depression is also related to job loss, to serious economic reversal, or to retirement from a satisfactory position; and that, as Levitt and Lubin (1975) show, depression proneness is not related to such traditional demographic variables as age, sex, and race, but instead increases as educational background, annual income, and ability to improve one's financial situation decrease. If these observations are true, we can easily conclude that people who are deprived of parental or economic satisfactions early or later in their lives suffer loss of status and consequent ego anxiety, and that they therefore are more prone to having severe feelings of depression. But we can perhaps more logically conclude that people who are deprived in these affectional and economic ways often (though not, of course, always) have low frustration tolerance or discomfort anxiety, and that a combination of actual frustration plus their discomfort anxiety *about* this frustration often drives them over the brink into the arms of severe depressive reactions. Frustration, Dollard, Doob, Miller, Mowrer, and Sears (1939) once wrongly claimed, leads to aggression. In itself, it doesn't. Nor does it lead to depression. But frustration *of people with abysmal discomfort anxiety* (for which there may exist a biological proneness or vulnerability, as well as a reinforcement or escalation resulting from unusually frustrating events) may lead to almost any kind of disturbed reaction, including aggression and depression.

As Beck (1967, 1976) and Ellis (1962) point out, depression is usually linked with ego anxiety, with people deprecating themselves for their poor performances and believing that, therefore, because *they* are worthless or hopelessly incompetent, they cannot handle life situations and particularly difficult situations that are occurring or may occur. But even in this ego anxiety aspect of depression, discomfort anxiety is probably also a factor, for depressed individuals are not merely telling themselves that they are so incompetent that they cannot master normal life situations and prove how "worthwhile" or "great" they are. They are also probably telling themselves that they are so hopelessly inept that they cannot ward off present and future *inconveniences* and *discomforts,* and that therefore their lives are, and will continue to be, terrible and horrible.

Depression also involves another and perhaps more common element of discomfort anxiety. For depressed people frequently have such abysmally low frustration tolerance that they refuse to accept ordinary or mild hassles, let alone unusual ones, and they can easily whine and wail when they don't have *good enough* events in their lives, or when they once had it easy and comfortable, but now that they have lost their jobs or lost money they don't any longer have it *that* good.

Years ago, before I realized how important a factor discomfort anxiety usually is in the case of severe feelings of depression, I mainly showed my depressed clients that they did *not* have to rate themselves for doing poorly in life (or for doing less well than others were doing) and that they could accept themselves unconditionally, *whether or not* they performed well and *whether or not* significant others approved of them. This helped them immensely in many instances, but in others I found that it was hardly sufficient.

I now *also* look for their discomfort anxiety, and I practically always seem to find it. If I am able to help them, as I often am, to give up their demanding and commanding that conditions be easier and more immediately gratifying, and their insisting that they get what they want quickly and effortlessly, I find not only that they get over their profound depressions, sometimes in fairly short order, but that they also have much less of a tendency to return to a depressed state when something unfortunate occurs in their lives at a later date.

TREATING DISCOMFORT ANXIETY

I do not find it easy to help people raise their level of frustration tolerance and thereby reduce or eliminate their discomfort anxiety. I am fairly convinced that virtually all human beings have a strong biological tendency to defeat themselves by being short-range hedonists and going for immediate rather than long-range gain (Ellis, 1976). That is why so many of them refuse to give up addictions such as smoking, overeating, alcohol abuse, and procrastination, which they "know" are harmful and which they keep resolving to overcome. But when they are induced by various kinds of therapy, including RET, to stay with discomfort, to see that it is *only* inconvenient and *not* unbearable, they often increase their frustration tolerance, overcome their discomfort anxiety, and make significant changes in their dysfunctional feelings and behaviors.

One reason for this lack of change in clients who have significant elements of both ego anxiety and discomfort anxiety is that they often bring up these two elements as if they were *one* problem. Consequently, their therapists mistakenly shuttle back and forth trying to help them with this supposedly *single* problem and end up trying, in a sense, to solve a quadratic equation with two unknowns— which is impossible to do! Thus, in the case of the client mentioned earlier, he could be said to have had two somewhat distinct problems, both of which started from the same premise. The premise would be, "I must get a good result at the things I do, especially a good result at producing my own feelings." This premise would lead to two rather different conclusions: (1) "When I do the wrong things and produce the wrong kind of feelings, I can't stand the *discomfort* I create. Under these conditions, the world is too hard for me to live in happily and I might just as well be dead!" (2) "When I do the wrong things and produce the wrong kind of feelings, I can't stand *myself* for acting so foolishly. Under these conditions, I am hopelessly inept, will always fail to get what I want, and hardly deserve to go on living!"

If clients with discomfort anxiety present material that shows these two irrational ideas, the therapist may get "hooked" into their system by trying to show them how to accept gracefully the discomfort that the world brings them and that they themselves produce. If the therapist fails to zero in on the client's problems *one at a time,* then the two will get confused with each other and the disputing of the client's irrational ideas will be so confounded that a satisfactory solution is unlikely.

It is important, therefore, for the therapist to recognize these two *different* (though perhaps overlapping) points clearly, and to deal first with one and then with the other, so that clients finally see that they have two disparate irrational ideas and that both of them produce dysfunctional emotional and behavioral results. Thus, if the therapist initially focuses on clients' discomfort anxiety, the clients may give up the idea that they *must* not experience "wrong" feelings because the discomfort of experiencing them is *too* difficult and *should not* be that difficult. After doing this, the therapist then probably has a better chance of zeroing in on clients' ego anxiety and helping them give up the idea that they *must not* experience "wrong" feelings because they are *lousy people* for acting ineptly. Either one of the irrational beliefs may be clearly seen and uprooted if the therapist considers them *independently*. But if they are tackled together, or if the therapist and client keep shuttling back and forth from one to the other, then there is a good chance that neither will be seen clearly nor given up.

If I am correct about the existence of discomfort anxiety (DA) and ego anxiety (EA) and their tendency to reinforce each other when they coexist in an individual, then these concepts serve to explain some other aspects of human disturbance and psychotherapy that have long been noted in the literature. For one thing, many indulgent forms of psychotherapy have often produced good, albeit temporary, results. Thus, large numbers of malfunctioning individuals have felt better for awhile and achieved transient symptom removal as a result of hypnosis, suggestion, reassurance, approval, and catharsis. I believe that most of these clients actually start to *feel* better rather than to *get* better in any permanent sense, but they definitely often do improve (Ellis, 1968, 1970, 1974). I would speculate that they do so largely because these indulgent techniques of therapy temporarily allay their discomfort anxiety. Even though it returns fairly soon— because their basic notion that they *must not* suffer frustration and deprivation has not been surrendered and may even be augmented—they at least feel significantly better and relatively symptom-free for a short period of time.

Another interesting phenomenon that can be partially explained by the concept of discomfort anxiety is the case of individuals who are converted to some highly implausible and probably irrational idea, such as the idea that God or Jesus has a personal interest in them and will save them from harm. Such people consequently achieve a distinct personality change, such as becoming recovered alcoholics. I hypothesize that these people, through their devout belief in some kind of magical cure, become highly motivated to work at their discomfort anxiety and to go through present pain to reap the rewards of future gain. Perhaps, for reasons that might be called wrong, they do the right thing: discipline themselves to give up alcohol, drugs, overeating, smoking, or gambling. They then see that they *can* control their own destiny, whereas previously they incorrectly thought that they could not. They may even acquire some sensible ideas along with the irrational ones that initially led them to discipline themselves and ameliorate their low frustration tolerance.

Still another aspect of therapy that can be explained by the concept of discomfort anxiety is the phenomenon of therapists leading many clients to believe in false or scientifically groundless ideas and thereby inadvertently helping these clients to become less disturbed. Thus, orthodox Freudians show people that their parents treated them cruelly when they were children and that this past cruelty makes them neurotic today (Freud, 1965); primal therapists go even further than this and teach their clients that they all suffered from intense primal pain as a result of their parents' iniquity and that if they now scream, yell, and release this pain, they will significantly improve their ability to function (Janov, 1970). Both these concepts are probably false, for they are largely stimulus–response rather than stimulus–organism–response theories, and they posit early childhood stimuli that were most likely nonexistent.

Interestingly enough, however, when a Freudian analyst or a primal therapist induces clients to mull over their past histories and experience feelings of intense distress in connection with these feelings, they are probably dealing with individuals who, because of their extreme discomfort anxiety, frequently refuse to face their anxious, angry feelings and instead suppress or repress them. Consequently, they do not give themselves a chance to deal with or change these feelings. In forcing such clients to get in touch with and face the discomfort of these feelings—albeit for the wrong reasons and often in a highly exaggerated way—Freudian and primal therapists may unwittingly help them see that feelings of anxiety and anger are *not* unbearable and horrible and may thereby help them to overcome some of their discomfort anxiety.

Several behavioral techniques, especially *in vivo* desensitization and implosion therapy, also seem explicable in terms of the concept of discomfort anxiety. Thus, I have found (Ellis, 1962), as have Marks, Viswanathan, Lipsedge, & Gardner (1972), that flooding or *in vivo* desensitization works much better with severely disturbed phobic or obsessive–compulsive individuals than more gradual or imaginal methods of therapy. I think this is because these individuals avoid discomfort at all cost and consequently will not confront their phobias or compulsions in order to overcome them. If they can be forced to do this, they eventually discover that doing what they intensely fear, or not doing what they absolutely think they *must* do, helps them to surrender some of their discomfort anxiety, enables them to start working on eliminating their dysfunctional behavior, and eventually helps them not only to *feel* better but actually to *get* better.

One of the persistent puzzles about neurotic individuals is that they can easily upset themselves by not only encountering a "fearful" situation but by imagining it, hearing about it, or seeing it (as in a radio broadcast or television show). Wolpe (1978) cites this as an indication that cognitive therapy often does not work because (1) "most neurotic patients are afraid of situations that they clearly know are not objectively dangerous"; (2) "the stimulus to a neurotic anxiety response may be such that it is inconceivable that it could be regarded as a threat—for example, anxiety at the sight of a test tube full of blood"; and (3) "a patient who is continually anxious may be found to have a specific persistent fear (e.g., fear of going insane); strong reassurance may convince him or her to the contrary, yet the anxiety may not materially diminish."

Wolpe (1978) may well be wrong here, because he uses the word "know" loosely, as if irrationality is totally "known." Thus, a neurotic individual may partly "know" that a situation is not objectively dangerous but also "know" that it is. She or he may be "convinced" that a fear of going insane is false but also be "convinced" that it is true. Rarely, in fact, do we "know" anything with 100% absoluteness; instead, we simultaneously partly believe it and partly do not.

More to the point, all of Wolpe's (1978) examples can be explained by the concept of discomfort anxiety. Thus, neurotic individuals may "know" that riding the rollercoaster at an amusement park is not threatening or dangerous; but they also may know that they are likely to experience anxiety if they ride it and therefore be afraid of their anxiety (and its consequent discomfort) rather than of the cars themselves. They may "know" that the sight of a test tube full of blood will not threaten them with pain of bloodletting, but they also may know that it reminds them of their anxiety about bloodletting and be threatened by this anxiety (discomfort) rather than by bloodletting. They may "know" that they have little chance of going insane, but they may still have both discomfort anxiety ("Wouldn't it be horribly uncomfortable if I *did* go crazy?") and ego anxiety ("I would be a weak, rotten person if I *did* go crazy!"). As noted already, when people have discomfort anxiety they tend to be afraid of any reminder of a "feared object," not because the representation of the object is seen as "frightening" but because their anxious, uncomfortable reaction to the object is viewed as "horrible" or "unbearable."

Mineka & Kihlstrom (1978) have reviewed the literature on experimental neurosis, including the experiments of Gantt (1944), Liddell (1944), Masserman (1943), Pavlov (1927), and Wolpe (1958), and have developed the hypothesis that the common thread running through the entire literature in this area is that in each case important life events become unpredictable, uncontrollable, or both. They also point out that there are striking parallels between experimental neurosis and learned helplessness following exposure to uncontrollable shock, which in turn has been linked to depression (Seligman, 1975). If there is some validity to the hypothesis of Mineka and Kihlstrom (1978) about experimental neurosis and to those of Seligman (1975) about learned helplessness, as I think there probably is, their theories can easily be related to my hypothesis of discomfort anxiety. I would guess that when humans (and several species of other animals) are faced with life events that they consider important to control and to succeed at, and when these events turn out to be consistently unpredictable, uncontrollable, or both, they not only tend to feel uncomfortable but they also conclude that these situations are *too* uncomfortable and there is no *use* trying to make them more comfortable. Therefore they give up completely or develop what G. V. Hamilton (1925) called a persistent nonadjustive reaction and become "depressed" or otherwise "neurotic."

I am hypothesizing that what I call discomfort anxiety (DA) is a biological tendency of humans and of certain other animals (e.g., rats or guinea pigs); that organisms of this sort innately strive to predict what is going on around them, to control their environments so that they get more of what they want and less of what they don't want, and thereby to survive satisfactorily or "happily." When they perceive that there is a high degree of probability that they will be able to do this, they persist in their adjustive reactions and therefore are "healthy" or "non-neurotic." When they perceive (rightly or wrongly) that they probably cannot control their life situations and get what they want, they either gracefully live with their continued frustrations (developing a philosophy of accepting the inevitable) or they refuse to accept this grim reality (whimpering and whining and developing a philosophy of desperate nonacceptance, a neurotic or nonadjustive outlook that frequently results in depression and withdrawal).

I am also hypothesizing that human phobias are particularly related to discomfort anxiety. When people have, for example, a phobia of airplanes, they usually have some element of ego anxiety; that is, they devoutly believe that *they*, now that they are alive, should live practically forever and *must* not die before their time; and they also frequently believe that it is shameful for them to display their fear of airplanes in front of others (e.g., flight personnel and plane passengers) and consequently they have to stay out of planes to avoid this "shameful" activity.

More important, however, they seem to have enormous discomfort anxiety about the supposed unpredictability of the plane's falling ("Yes, I know there is little chance of it's falling; but suppose it does!"), and they also have discomfort anxiety about their own initial anxiety reactions (which are often exceptionally uncomfortable). They therefore avoid plane flights, often to their own disadvantage.

In desensitizing these individuals to the thing they fear (e.g., plane flights), therapists have their choice of many methods, including systematic desensitization (Wolpe, 1958), imaginative implosion (Stampfl & Levis, 1967) and *in vivo* desensitization in the course of rational–emotive therapy (Ellis, 1962, 1971, 1973, 1979a; Ellis & Grieger, 1977). These seem to be radically different methods of desensitization, but as Teasdale (1977) points out, they have one thing in common: repeated presentation of a fear stimulus with no apparent disastrous consequence.

It seems that people with airplane (or other) phobias keep telling themselves, for one reason or another, "Going in a plane is too frightening, too painful; I can't stand it; I would practically fall apart at the seams if I had to experience this terrible event!" and they keep reindoctrinating themselves with this "fear" and reinforcing their belief in it by *not* going up in a plane. Every time they refuse to do so, they keep telling themselves (overtly or tacitly), "If I did fly, it *would* be horribly uncomfortable and now that I am avoiding flying, I can see how relatively comfortable I feel!" Moreover, by fearfully refusing to confront their phobia and *do* something to overcome it, it becomes almost impossible to get rid of it.

In virtually all kinds of desensitizing procedures, as Teasdale (1977) notes, they *do* something about their phobia: They actively confront it, either imaginatively or *in vivo,* and they *discover* that (1) the unpredictable event has more predictability than they originally thought it did; (2) nothing disastrous happens to them and they are *only* uncomfortable, and not, as they imagined, utterly *destroyed* by the confrontation; (3) they learn a technique such as SD, implosion therapy, or RET that gives them some possibility of *coping* with their anxiety in the future; (4) they learn that although they cannot control the feared event (the possibility of the plane's falling) they can definitely control some of their own *reactions* to it and therefore face a much "safer" kind of situation should they actually confront the feared object.

Let us make one other observation about the concept of discomfort anxiety (DA) in explaining and dealing with phobias. Emmelkamp, Kuipers, and Egger-aat (1978), in a study showing that *in vivo* desensitization works better with agoraphobics than do three different kinds of cognitive restructuring without *in vivo* retraining, point out that clinical agoraphobics probably differ from subjects in analog studies in that they have a higher degree of physiological arousal in anxiety-engendering situations (Lader, 1967) than do the former subjects. They note that "it is quite possible that cognitive restructuring constitutes an effective form of treatment for low physiological reactors (such as the subjects of analog studies), while such treatment will be effective for high physiological reactors (such as agoraphobics) only after the autonomic component has been reduced."

In a comment on the Emmelkamp et al. (1978) paper, I quite agree with their observation (Ellis, 1979b). For if it is true that agoraphobics (and many other serious phobics) are high physiological reactors—and my own clinical findings for many years lead me to strongly support this hypothesis—then I would assume that they tend to feel more discomfort, and presumably more discomfort anxiety, than certain other disturbed individuals. Consequently, it seems likely they would tend to develop more phobias and hold on to them more strongly than would "lighter" or less physiologically involved phobics. The discomfort anxiety theory helps explain why agoraphobics are somewhat different from other phobics and why they are so difficult to treat.

In many important respects, then, the concept of discomfort anxiety seems to shed light on human disturbance and on psychotherapeutic processes. It especially leads the way toward creating and utilizing more effective, more elegant, and more long-lasting forms of psychological treatment. I suggest, for example, that many or most of the therapeutic methods used today are in themselves forms of indulgence, and that in the long run they reinforce people's discomfort anxiety and possibly do more harm than good. Take, for instance, muscular relaxation methods, which are so popular among behavior therapists. While there is no question that such techniques frequently work and result in considerable symptom removal, like all methods of therapy, they also have ideological implications, some of which seem to be iatrogenic:

1. Usually, as in Wolpe's (1958, 1973) systematic desensitization, relaxation is used in a gradual way to interrupt clients' feelings of anxiety. The very

gradualness of this procedure, I suggest, may easily reaffirm these clients' beliefs that they *must* slowly, easily, and by comfortable degrees, tackle their anxieties, and that as soon as they experience any intense feelings of fear they *have* to relax their muscles and thereby distract themselves from these feelings. Such beliefs, of course, may well serve to increase, rather than to decrease, their discomfort anxiety.

2. Relaxation methods essentially consist of cognitive distraction rather than cognitive restructuring. If, for example, clients are afraid of elevators and they imagine themselves getting closer and closer to elevators and then, as they feel anxious about this imagined closeness, they focus on relaxing their muscles, they automatically distract themselves from the idea, "I *must not* enter elevators; it would be *awful* if something happened to me when I rode in them!" They may well decrease their anxiety by this distraction procedure, but they usually have not *worked at* really *giving up* their irrational beliefs about riding in elevators. Relaxation and other forms of cognitive distraction are almost always much easier than actively combating and rethinking one's basic irrationalities. They consequently reinforce people's notions of the horror of work, for instance, and thus may increase their discomfort anxiety.

3. Cognitive distraction, though a viable method of psychotherapy, probably is not as effective in most instances as *in vivo* desensitization. By employing it with clients, the therapist avoids getting them to face the actual elevators or other irrationally feared objects, and thereby gives them an inelegant method of solving their problems. Again, it tends to sustain or augment their discomfort anxiety.

It is tempting for me to overemphasize the significance of discomfort anxiety and to relate all forms of emotional disturbance to this concept. Thus, humans tend to believe that they *must* perform well and have approval, that others *must* treat them properly, and that the conditions under which they live *must* be easy and enjoyable. When these three *must*urbatory views are not affirmed by reality—which is often the case in this frustrating world—they usually conclude that they *can't stand* their own, others', or the world's imperfections and that it is *awful and terrible* that such unpleasantness is allowed to occur. In some respects, they seem to have low frustration tolerance (LFT) or discomfort anxiety as an aspect of virtually all their emotional disturbances—their self-downing, their hostility, and their self-pity. In a sense, then, we could say that virtually all "emotional" disturbances arise from LFT.

My clinical perception and judgment, however, tells me that this formulation omits some essential data about people and their disturbances. Although ego anxiety and discomfort anxiety are found in almost all individuals, and, as noted already, significantly interrelate and reinforce each other, I think it is best to view them as separate but interlocking behaviors. In that way, they have maximum explanatory and therapeutic usefulness.

REFERENCES

Abramson, L. Y., & Sackheim, H. A. A paradox in depression: Uncontrollability and self-blame. *Psychological Bulletin*, 1977, *84*, 838–851.

Beck, A. T. *Depression*. New York: Hoeber-Harper, 1967.

Beck, A. T. *Cognitive therapy and the emotional disorders*. New York: International Universities Press, 1976.

Dollard, J., Doob, L., Miller, N. E., Mowrer, O. H., & Sears, R. R. *Frustration and aggression*. New Haven: Yale University Press, 1939.

Ellis, A. *Reason and emotion in psychotherapy*. New York: Lyle Stuart, 1962. Paperback ed.: New York: Citadel Press, 1977.

Ellis, A. What really causes therapeutic change? *Voices*, 1968, *4*(2), 90–97.

Ellis, A. The cognitive element in experiential and relationship psychotherapy. *Existential Psychiatry*, 1970, *28*, 35–42.

Ellis, A. *Growth through reason*. Palo Alto, Calif. Science and Behavior Books and Hollywood: Wilshire Books, 1971.

Ellis, A. *Humanistic psychotherapy: The rational–emotive approach*. New York: Julian Press and McGraw-Hill Paperbacks, 1973.

Ellis, A. Cognitive aspects of abreactive therapy. *Voices*, 1974, *10*(1), 48–56.

Ellis, A. The biological basis of human irrationality. *Journal of Individual Psychology*, 1976, *32*, 145–168.

Ellis, A. *New developments in rational–emotive therapy*, Monterey, Calif.: Brooks/Cole, 1979. (a)

Ellis, A. A note on the treatment of agoraphobics with cognitive modification versus prolonged exposure *in vivo*. *Behavior Research and Therapy*. 1979, *17*(2), 162–163. (b)

Ellis, A., & Grieger, R. *Handbook of rational–emotive therapy*. New York: Springer, 1977.

Ellis, A., & Harper, R. A. *A new guide to rational living*. Englewood Cliffs, N.J.: Prentice-Hall, and Hollywood: Wilshire Books, 1975.

Emmelkamp, P. M. G., Kuipers, A. C., & Eggeraat, J. B. Cognitive modification versus prolonged exposure *in vivo:* A comparison with agoraphobics as subjects. *Behavior Therapy and Research*, 1978, *16*, 33–41.

Freud, S. *Standard edition of the complete psychological works of Sigmund Freud*. London: Hogarth, 1965.

Gantt, W. H. Experimental basis for neurotic behavior. *Psychosomatic Medicine Monographs*, 1944, Nos. 3 & 4.

Hamilton, G. V. *An introduction to objective psychopathology*. St. Louis: C. V. Mosby, 1925.

Janov, A. *The primal scream*. New York: Delta, 1970.

Jones, R. G. *A factored measure of Ellis' irrational belief system, with personality and maladjustment correlates*. Unpublished Ph.D. thesis, Texas Technological University, 1968.

Lader, M. H. Palmer skin conductance measures in anxiety and phobic states. *Journal of Psychosomatic Research*, 1967, *11*, 271–281.

Levitt, E. E., & Lubin, B. *Depression*. New York: Springer, 1975.

Lidell, H. S. Conditioned reflex method and experimental neurosis. In J. McV. Hunt (Ed.), *Personality and the behavior disorders*. New York: Ronald, 1944.

Low, A. A. *Mental health through will training*. Boston: Christopher, 1952.

Marks, I. M., Viswanathan, R., Lipsedge, M. S., & Gardner, R. Enhanced relief by flooding during waning diazepam effect. *British Journal of Psychiatry*, 1972, *121*, 493–505.

Masserman, J. H. *Behavior and neurosis*. Chicago: University of Chicago Press, 1943.

Mineka, S., & Kihlstrom, J. F. Unpredictable and uncontrollable events: A new perspective on experimental neurosis. *Journal of Abnormal Psychology*, 1978, *87*, 256–271.

Pavlov, I. P. *Conditioned reflexes*. London: Oxford University Press, 1927.

Rehm, L. P. A self-control model of depression. *Behavior Therapy*, 1977, *8*, 787–804.

Seligman, M. E. P. *Helplessness*. San Francisco: W. H. Freeman, 1975.

Stampfl, T. G., & Levis, D. J. Essentials of implosive therapy. *Journal of Abnormal Psychology*, 1967, *72*, 496–503.

Sutton-Simon, K. A study of irrational ideas of individuals with fears of heights, with social anxiety, and with fear of heights plus social anxieties. *Cognitive Therapy and Research*, 1979, *3*(2), 193–204.

Teasdale, J. D. Psychological treatment of phobias. In N. S. Sutherland (Ed.), *Tutorial essays in psychology* (Vol. 1). Hillsdale, N.J.: Erlbaum, 1977.

Weekes, C. *Hope and help for your nerves*. New York: Hawthorn, 1969.

Weekes, C. *Peace from nervous suffering*. New York: Hawthorne, 1972.

Weekes, C. *Simple, effective treatment of agoraphobia*. New York: Hawthorne, 1977.

Wolpe, J. *Psychotherapy by reciprocal inhibition*. Stanford: Stanford University Press, 1958.

Wolpe, J. *The practice of behavior therapy*. New York: Pergamon, 1973.

Wolpe, J. Cognition and causation in human behavior and its therapy. *American Psychologist, 1978, 33,* 437–446.

7

Anger Problems*

Russell M. Grieger

Aggression and violence have drawn more attention from the behavioral science and philosophical communities than perhaps any other human phenomena. Experimental studies on the psychology of aggression are legion, as attested by recent texts by Bandura (1973), Ellis (1977b), Geen and O'Neal (1976), Johnson (1972), and Novaco (1975). From a social perspective, aggression has been discussed in relation to such variables as criminal justice (Chappell & Monahan, 1975), social alienation (Daniels, Gilula, & Ochberg, 1970), and violence on television (Feshback & Singer, 1971). Indeed, the March 19, 1979 issue of *Look* magazine displayed a dramatic pictorial series showing English, German, Sicilian, Lebanese, and Irish children modeling the violence they directly and vicariously observed in their own countries. These pictures showed the children entertaining themselves with such games as "firing squad," "guillotine," and "soldier," among others.

Contrasted with aggression, anger is a rarely studied human reaction, except as it serves to instigate aggression or to reduce aggression through catharsis (Berkowitz, 1970; Feshback, 1961; Kahn, 1966). Novaco (1975) explains this by the fact that the dimensions of aggression can be easily observed and studied, whereas anger elements are more phenomenological in character. Regardless of the reason, anger problems populate clinical calendars, yet they are probably the least studied of human emotions (Novaco, 1975).

Three perspectives on anger, and indeed all emotions, have been articulated (Lazarus, Averill, & Opton, 1970). The biological perspective assigns emotion to the more phylogenetically old portions of the brain: the reticular formation

*This chapter originally appeared in R. Grieger and I. Grieger (Eds.), *Cognition and Emotional Disturbance* (New York: Human Sciences Press, 1982).

(Lindsley, 1950), the hypothalamus (Bard, 1950), and the limbic system (Mac-Lean, 1960). Ignoring the fact that these structures play as vital a role in cognitive functioning as in emotion (Douglas, 1967; Pribram, 1967), this perspective views emotion as basically instinctual and related to earlier steps on the phylogenetic ladder. Accordingly, anger control depends on the development of both intellectual and social forces for containing the beast in humans.

The cultural perspective suggests that emotions are shaped by various societies in order to provide for the affective needs of their citizens (Hebb & Thompson, 1954), and in turn to maintain their own existence. They do so in many ways, depending on economic, political, geographic, and historical factors, including influencing how people perceive or appraise emotional stimuli (Tursky & Sternbach, 1967) and how people can express emotions (LaBarre, 1947).

Following Magda Arnold (1960), Richard Lazarus (1966, 1968), and especially Albert Ellis (1962, 1971, 1973b, 1977a), the cognitive perspective is based on the conviction that cognitive theorizing, appraising, and evaluating are primary human functions and that emotional reactions are directly determined by such cognitive activity. Furthermore, the cognitive determinants of emotion can be either dispositional (reflecting the basic values, attitudes, or philosophies of an individual) or situational (an individual's interpretation and evaluation of specific situational cues) in nature. Thus, in understanding a particular emotional reaction, anger in this case, an understanding of the nature of the underlying cognitions is essential.

This chapter largely follows the cognitive model of emotional arousal in general and the RET model of emotional disturbance in particular. After first outlining this model, it will discuss in more detail the cognitive mediators of anger and suggest a distinction between anger that is healthy and that is not.

COGNITIVE MEDIATION OF ANGER

As an affective phenomenon, anger can be seen as both an autonomic (Ax, 1953; Funkenstein, King, & Drolette, 1954, 1957; Schacter, 1957) and a central (Moyer, 1971, 1973) nervous system reaction to some real or imagined event, plus a cognitive labeling of that arousal as anger based on both physiological and behavioral cues (Konocni, 1975a, 1975b; Lazarus, 1967; Schachter & Singer, 1962). Thus, on a descriptive level, anger is a combination of physiological arousal and cognitive labeling.

Etiologically speaking, cognitive theorists generally follow the maxim of the Stoic philosopher, Epictetus, who stated: "Men are disturbed not by things, but by the view they take of them." Accordingly, they define anger (and all other emotional reactions as well) not so much by physiological or affective arousal as by the cognitions or appraisals that prompt the arousal. To determine if a person is angry, the cognitive theorist looks to the person's thoughts or ideas, not to his or her feelings.

The cognitive model presented here is an extension of the now famous ABC theory of RET (Ellis, 1962, 1971, 1973, 1975, 1977a, 1977b). Echoing Epictetus, RET states that perceived, imagined, remembered, or anticipated events (at point A) do not directly provoke anger (at point C). They only serve to prompt cognitive activity which in turn determines the anger. Each anger reaction is mediated by some cognitive event that logically leads to that reaction.

As previously stated, cognitions are significant to emotional arousal in at least two ways (see Figure 7-1). First, cognitions act as dispositional traits or strongly learned, enduring, personal values or life philosophies that people carry with them across situations (B_1). As such, they variously influence emotional arousal (1) by providing a prejudicial set that leads people to search out and selectively attend to situational stimuli of a certain type; (2) by flavoring the evaluations or appraisals people make of particular experiences; (3) by directly keeping emotionally loaded past events "alive" and anticipated future happenings vivid; and (4) by indirectly creating events in the environment that prompt behavior from others consistent with the emotional reaction. In turn, consciously or unconsciously exercising the philosophy, and thus experiencing both the selectively perceived event and the emotional arousal, serves to further engrain it and make its activation more likely in the future.

Cognition plays a second significant role in emotional arousal by mediating aversive events (B_2). These situational attributions are the appraisals people make of the experienced event itself and of the likely outcome of various reactions to that event. They are in part determined by the characteristics of the event itself, but are also influenced by the person's life philosophies and past experiences in similar circumstances. The consequent emotional arousal and behavior reciprocally relate to these cognitive mediators by providing validating feedback to the appraisal and hence increasing its likelihood in the future. The situational mediators also serve to validate and reinforce the associated life philosophies.

Both varieties of cognition can lead to emotional arousal singularly, but it is more likely that they will act in concert with each other. In turn, emotional arousal and expressive behavior mutually influence each other. For example, anger arousal tends to prompt aggressive behavior (Rule & Nesdale, 1976). On the other hand, responding aggressively to negative events leads one to define one's emotional arousal as anger, which in turn increases anger (Konocni, 1975a, 1975b).

Having briefly outlined the model, I will now turn to a more detailed discussion of the cognitive mediators of anger. I will first discuss the irrational philosophies and situational attributions in anger and then present processes whereby people get angry about being angry.

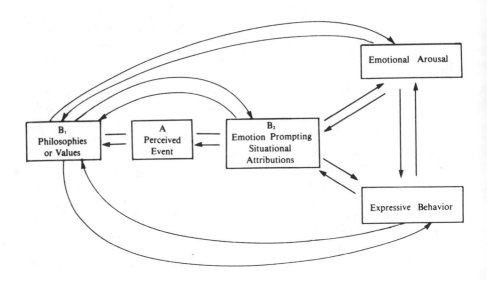

Figure 7–1. Cognitive Mediations of Anger

Irrational Philosophies in Anger

Consistent with rational–emotive theory (Ellis, 1962, 1971, 1975, 1976b, 1977b), anger, like all other emotional reactions, in large measure results from (and is maintained by) a person holding ideas or philosophies that logically lead to anger. Accordingly, people who ardently endorse angry (or anger instigating) ideas are prone to anger and to acting aggressively. Carrying these philosophies with them, they will tend to be oversensitive to elements of injustice or signs of hassle in situations; attribute hostile motivations to the actions of others; habitually evaluate situations in light of their angry philosophies; re-anger themselves by remembering (even obsessing about) past slights; and overreact to minor frustrations. In a very real sense, they are "programmed" time bombs ready to explode.

Albert Ellis (1973a, 1975) has proposed two separate yet conceptually similar forms of anger. In *autistic anger,* the individual childishly endorses the idea that because she or he does not personally like something or does not want something to happen, or because she or he finds someone's behavior undesirable or even obnoxious, it *should not* happen or that person *must not* behave that way. Then, when the event or act occurs, the person concludes that it is an *awful* thing that is too *unendurable* to bear. Finally, the person *condemns* either the world for allowing such a thing to happen or the offensive person for doing such a thing. The focus for these ideas is the "I": "Because *I* say so, it should not be."

In *impersonal anger,* the person invokes the magic of consensual validation. In this he or she concludes that, because everyone would agree that some event or action is bad, it *should not* have happened. Under this group umbrella, the person then goes on to conclude that it is *too awful to tolerate* and that he or she, like everyone, can legitimately rate the person as so thoroughly *rotten* as to deserve severe punishment. In this form of anger, then, the person is offended because of an allegiance to an implicit or explicit code of rules that pertain to some community, and he or she then acts as an avenging representative of that collective mass.

Both forms of anger have at least three common philosophical elements that directly lead to anger. The first is an assumption that an action or event that is deemed wrong *should not, must not* occur. In holding this view, the person acts as an arrogant, righteous rulemaker imposing laws over others and the universe that are absolute and incontrovertable. Ellis (1977a, pp. 12–13) states these as follows:

1. Others *must* behave the way I think best, in ways that I deem fair, moral, appropriate, ethical, considerate, or else . . .
2. The world, and particularly the conditions under which I live, *must* be arranged the way I think best, in ways that are just, compassionate, and hassle free, or else . . .

A second philosophical element common to both forms of anger is the person perceiving the action or event as negative (e.g., unfortunate, disadvantageous, inconvenient, deplorable) and then concluding that it is so *awful* to be virtually *unbearable.* When, for instance, a person is treated rudely at the theater and only concludes that it is a pain in the neck or an inconvenience to be subjected to such treatment, she or he will at worst be only irritated or annoyed. But, when she or he concludes that it is such a terrible thing that the offender had no right to do it, she or he will almost certainly become outraged and probably act in some revengeful way.

The third common philosophical element in both types of anger proposed by Ellis focuses on the person who performs the outlawed act itself. It consists of concluding that the offending person's acts are not only bad or rotten, but that the offending person is *rotten* and should therefore be severely punished for *being* that way. This attitude is expressed in statements such as, "Because you have done this terrible thing you should not have done, you are a *total shit* and I can justifiably condemn you to a lifetime of misery"; or, "Because we all agree that you should not have done such a horrid thing, we can condemn you and we can conclude that severe retribution must take place."

The assumption throughout all this is that people prone to anger take the philosophical position that they can Jehovistically impose absolute demands on others for certain behaviors and that it is legitimate for them to condemn the other if she or he violates the standards. Yet, while this is true for most if not all angry people, two other themes, already discovered to be central to a number of other emotional disturbances, underlie most all angry reactions (Grieger, 1977; Grieger & Boyd, 1979). These stimulate the irrational ideas proposed by Ellis and fuel the anger. One theme has to do with self-worth and the other with frustration tolerance.

Self-worth Anger

Often lurking behind anger is a perceived threat to one's sense of being worthwhile. Indeed, while not directly related to anger, experimental evidence suggests that subjects who report themselves high in self-esteem respond with less aggression to provocations than subjects who report the opposite (Green & Murray, 1973; Rosenbaum & de Charms, 1960; Rosenbaum & Stanners, 1961; Veldman & Worchel, 1961; Worchel, 1960). Toch (1969), for instance, suggested that low self-esteem was a significant determinant of both anger arousal and aggressive behavior in the interactions between the police and criminals he studied.

In cognitive therapy terms, people prone to self-worth anger believe that their self-worth depends on what others think of them and on how well they do in gaining the acknowledgment, acceptance, and love of others. In addition to autistic and/or impersonal anger themes, they ardently adhere to the idea that "I *must do well* and *win approval,* particularly from those I deem significant, *or else I rate as a rotten person.*" Individuals who hold this idea quite often interpret the negative actions of others as discounting them, as somehow threatening or taking away their self-worth. With the precious commodity of self-worth at stake, this person sees an unjust or insulting act as a horrible affront that absolutely *should not* happen and sees the perpetrator as a terrible person for doing that. Thus, when confronted with the slings and arrows of fortune, the person reflexively concludes, "His actions communicate that he finds me insignificant. If that is true, it does make me insignificant. He shouldn't do that to me, the SOB!"

A double-level problem thus operates in self-worth anger. On the more conscious, accessible level the typical should-ing and condemning takes place. At a less conscious, less accessible level looms the individual's predisposed tendency to generalize from the negative actions of others to his or her self-worth. Instead of simply accepting the validity of the insult and turning inward to condemn the self, this person turns on and condemns the other person in the picture. The important point is that the turning on the other person or event is a self-protective action designed to prevent the person from facing his or her fears of worthlessness. An analogy that I think captures the concept of self-worth anger has to do with two waitresses who serve a rude, critical customer. The waitress experiencing autistic or impersonal anger only carries food on the tray and strongly objects to the customer subjecting her to such behavior. The waitress experiencing self-worth anger carries her self-worth, as well as the customer's food, on the tray, and she strongly objects to the customer taking away her self-respect. She is personally hurt.

Let me illustrate what I am talking about through two clinical examples. In each instance, a significant feature of the client's anger was a perceived threat to self-worth.

Case 1. Carol was a member of a RET group, and she wanted to overcome her anger problems. Not a wilting lily, she quickly took advantage of the group situation. She readily acknowledged the fact that she should-ed other people and condemned them as rotten for behaving in the particular ways they did that she did not like. She also acknowledged the irrationality of these stances and, with our help, correctly thought them through. But, she did not improve.

Then in one group session Carol discussed how angry she had become at a woman who rented a room at her house. It seemed that this woman used Carol's iron and left her kitchen untidy, despite the fact that Carol repeatedly told her not to do either. After she and the group again went over the same ground as before, the following interchange took place between Carol and me.

THERAPIST: We don't seem to be getting anywhere here. Let me ask you a question, Carol. Do you find this woman's behavior positive, negative, or neutral?

CAROL: Well, negative of course.

THERAPIST: Then, finish this sentence for me. "I don't like her using my iron, particularly since I've told her not to, because . . ."

CAROL: (pause) Because it discounts me.

THERAPIST: What do you mean when you say it discounts you?

CAROL: She invalidates me.

THERAPIST: That sounds a little mystical to me. Do you mean that she somehow devalues your worth by ignoring your wishes?

CAROL: Yes. That's exactly right.

THERAPIST: Well, aren't you confusing her negative value of you, assuming that that is true, with your own value of yourself as a person? Aren't you putting your self-worth on the line depending on whether she obeys you or not?

CAROL: In a way, I guess I am.

THERAPIST: With that being at stake, I can see why you are so angry at her and why you would demand that she toe the line. It's a logical reaction from an illogical premise. But, isn't the real problem the fact that you don't really accept yourself?

CAROL: Yes. I guess that is the problem.

Case 2. Bill was a relatively new teacher on the faculty of a private school for emotionally disturbed and learning disabled youngsters to which I acted as a consultant. Following an in-service workshop on anger, Bill approached me to talk about his intense anger at the students. He expressed a concern that he might soon lose control and physically lash out. The following interchange took place.

> BILL: I've certainly lost my ideals around here. When I started work, I would ride home each night wondering how I could be more effective the next day. Now I fantasize getting even with them.
>
> CONSULTANT: Well, what exactly do they do that you find so irritating?
>
> BILL: Everything from the typical things like talking in class and fighting to not remembering my name. I've really worried about some of them and put extra effort into working with them, but they don't listen. They just don't appreciate me!
>
> CONSULTANT: Bill, it sounds like you might have an anger problem pretty much like we were talking about just a little while ago—a self-worth anger problem.
>
> BILL: How so?
>
> CONSULTANT: Well, you just said they don't appreciate you. Go with that for a minute. What if they don't? What if they don't? What does that mean to you?
>
> BILL: Look, I've put my life into this. If they don't appreciate what I'm doing, what's the use? My life is purposeless.
>
> CONSULTANT: Wow! That's quite a conclusion to draw—that your life's purposeless if some 12 year olds don't appreciate you. Doesn't that tell you what's at stake for you in their behavior?
>
> BILL: OK, you're right. I'm thinking that they take away my meaning by their acts. They steal away my insides, my worth. Just like what we talked about earlier.
>
> CONSULTANT: Right! That's what you think. And, what do you then do with that, in your head, when you think about those kids?
>
> BILL: It's: "Goddamn them! They're not going to get away with putting me down like that, the little bastards." And then I feel like lashing out.

Thus, a self-worth issue very often lies at the bottom of many anger problems. As with Carol and Bill, self-worth anger results, first, from a person believing that the negative treatment of others or the adverse conditions of the world threaten her or his self-worth or value, and, second, from vehemently *demanding* that different treatment result in order to recoup this loss of self. Given this, an interesting question is why a person who believes that she or he must have approval and acknowledgment to be worthwhile reacts with anger instead of anxiety and depression. In my clinical experience, people with self-worth anger are also prone to anxiety and depression as well, so that their negative emotional states are often more frequent and more complex. Beyond this, I frequently find that people with self-worth anger have what Cohen (1966) calls "defensive high self-esteem." That is, they have often been successful in getting people to approve of them so that they frequently feel good about themselves. They are, thus, often able to focus on the offensive agent and the insult in a blaming way, but their sense of well-being is fragile. It is so dependent on the continued good grace of others that prolonged or frequent assaults can easily shatter their façade. The result then is either an entrenchment of the anger and/or depression coupled with lowered self-esteem.

Low-Frustration-Tolerance Anger

Besides perceived threats to self-worth, a low tolerance for frustration or hassle also can prompt the should-ing, awfulizing, and other person rating that Ellis (1973a, 1975) has shown to fuel anger reactions. He (Ellis, 1976b) contends that low frustration tolerance (LFT), or overreacting to frustration, is a predictable consequence of a person holding one or more of the following ideas in the face of difficult, hassling, or frustrating circumstances: (1) the world *has* to be arranged so that I get pretty much what I want, when I want it, without too much hassle; (2) it is *awful, horrible,* and *terrible* when I am thwarted or presented with such difficult circumstances; and (3) I *can't stand it* when things go wrong. By holding these ideas, the person creates an unrealistic exaggeration of the badness of aversive events and connotes a gross underestimation of his or her ability to tolerate or deal with the event, thus making an emotional and/or behavioral overreaction likely.

To test these contentions, Nolan, Boyd, and Grieger (1979) had subjects who scored in the upper and lower quartiles on the frustration-reactive subscale of Jones's (1968) Irrational Beliefs Test try to solve three problems that, unbeknownst to them, were insolvable. Following this task, subjects who scored in the upper quartile reported significantly higher negative affect, as measured by the Multiple Affect Adjective Checklist (Zuckerman & Lubin, 1965), than did subjects who scored in the lower quartile. The results of this investigation lend strong support to the contention that the mediating cognitive appraisals of frustrating situations have a profoundly instrumental effect upon people's emotional reactions to those frustrating circumstances.

For the purpose of this discussion, it is important to note that the subjects in this study who highly endorsed the beliefs in the frustration-reactive subscale reported significantly more anger ($p < .025$) than did subjects who only minimally endorsed this belief. To understand this, it is helpful, as with self-worth anger, to think of frustration-related anger as a double-level problem. On the first or more surface level, the LFT-angry person engages in the should-ing toward, awfulizing about, and condemning of the frustrating person or set of circumstances. On the second, perhaps less conscious level, the person strongly *demands* that things be easy, smooth, and hassle free, and then evaluates the frustration as awful, saying, for example, "This hassle is *too much to bear;* it is such a hassle that it *shouldn't* exist, particularly for me; and you (or the world) are *rotten* for subjecting me to such a thing." All in all, low-frustration-tolerance anger is a scream of outrage against any interruption of the smooth flow of events.

Again let me illustrate LFT anger with a clinical example. Michael was a client I previously showed to have a profound case of self-worth anger (Grieger, 1977). What precipitated his decision to seek psychological help was his increasing anger that resulted in his physically abusing his 12-year-old son. After confronting and making significant inroads into his self-worth issues, he then turned to the element of low frustration tolerance, or, to say it another way, to his belief that he should not have to contend with the hassles that his children, his wife, his house, and his job inevitably presented. Note the following interchange.

MICHAEL: This damn thing just keeps coming at me. If I'm not angry at one thing its another.

THERAPIST: What happened this week, Michael?

MICHAEL: Nothing in particular. I just seem to get madder as the day wears on. It starts sometime in the afternoon and really gets to me at night.

THERAPIST: What's going on at work in the afternoon?

MICHAEL: Nothing, really. Students just keep coming by my office and wanting to talk to me. And I have this stupid report to write for the Dean, and . . .

THERAPIST: So, you keep getting interrupted from doing what is important for you to do at work, and you also seem to see the report as an inane, bureaucratic thing. And, what goes through your head at these times?

MICHAEL: (pauses) That I have to do this and it's a pain in the ass.

THERAPIST: Is that all?

MICHAEL: No. I also think that I shouldn't be bothered by all this nonsense. The Dean's report is basically just busywork, and the student interruptions are pointless.

THERAPIST: And they *shouldn't* hassle me like this.

MICHAEL: Right! They shouldn't! It's all a bunch of shit.

THERAPIST: And what about home?

MICHAEL: That just continues it. It's one thing after another. The gutters need painting, the lawn needs mowing, and . . .

THERAPIST: And what? "I . . ."

MICHAEL: . . . shouldn't have to put up with it either! It's such a pain in the ass.

THERAPIST: Those things are indeed a pain in the ass. But, Michael, I hear you really holding two philosophies, one that feeds into or actually mirrors the other. The one is that I shouldn't have to deal with these hassles. Right?

MICHAEL: Right.

THERAPIST: But I also hear you holding another idea, which I suspect includes the first. It is that life should always be easy and simple for you. It simply should not be difficult! How does that sound to you?

MICHAEL: Pretty accurate.

SITUATIONAL ATTRIBUTIONS IN ANGER

What has been discussed so far are the enduring irrational philosophies people endorse and carry with them accross situations, which prompt them to become angry. Individuals who hold these philosophies may be seen as angry people because they have adopted ideas that (1) are scientifically invalid and (2) logically and predictably lead to frequent anger reactions.

In addition to irrational philosophies, another set of cognitive variables also play an important role in mediating anger. These are situationally based and reflect current appraisals of a situation. Appraisal here refers to the cognitive interpretations and evaluations of situations that may not be but probably are influenced by one's more enduring philosophies. These include attributions about an aggressor's intent, the perceived arbitrariness of another's actions, one's own perceived power and control in the situation, expectation of outcome, and the badness of one's anger.

Aggressor's Intent

One of the more consistent findings in the literature has been that the magnitude of anger arousal and aggression relates to the perceived intent of an attacker (Epstein & Taylor, 1967; Greenwell & Dengerink, 1973; Taylor, 1967). That is, if a person determines that another intended to be aggressive or frustrating, then he or she is very likely to respond with anger and aggression. On the other hand, if the person decides that the aggressor's behavior was accidental, then the probability of anger and counterattack is significantly lessened.

This proposition has been ingeniously explored by Nickel (1974). He first had confederates give subjects high-intensity shocks for incorrectly guessing a color. Just prior to changing places with the confederate, the experimenter explained to half the subjects that the buttons had accidentally been reversed so that while the subjects had received high-intensity shocks the confederate had intended to give low-level shocks. Those subjects who were led to believe that the confederate's intent was opposite to what they had received gave significantly lower shocks to the confederate than those not given this information. Thus, subjects responded more to their perception of the opponent's intent than to the intensity of shock or the received aggression. It therefore appears that the attribution of hostile intent is a major mediator of anger and aggression: You will be much less likely to respond with anger and aggression if you perceive the obnoxious behavior of another as being accidental than if you see it as preplanned.

Perceived Arbitrariness versus Mitigating Circumstances

Several investigators have found that attributing arbitrary, nonjustifiable, or selfish motivations to an aggressor will more likely lead to anger and counteraggression than when the aggressor's behavior is seen otherwise. Mallick and McCandless (1966), for instance, had a confederate child interfere with the performance of half of their subjects on a task for which they could earn money. All subjects were then given the opportunity to play, to chat with the experimenters about irrelevant topics, or to be given a reasonable explanation for the confederate's frustrating behavior. Consistent with predictions, the experimenters found that, when the subjects were given an opportunity to retaliate, those frustrated were more likely to interfere in kind than those who were not frustrated, unless they had been given a reasonable explanation for the confederate's behavior. It therefore seems that when a frustrator's behavior is labeled as inappropriate and arbitrary, children are more likely to behave aggressively.

It also appears that the specific motivations attributed to an aggressor are important in anger arousal. Using paper-and-pencil measures of anger and hostility, Frodi (1976) assessed the effects of different types of attributed mitigating circumstances on the anger of junior-high students. After being highly criticized by an experimenter, students were told that he was either sick (sympathy condition), a high-achieving expert (achiever condition), or habitually obnoxious (habit condition). The sympathy and habit conditions produced the least anger, while the achiever condition produced the greatest anger. In order to obtain a measure of perceived intentionality, a second group of students was given a typed description of the experiment and asked to judge whether, given the mitigating circumstances, the experimenter acted intentionally or not. The sympathy condition was seen as least intentional, and the achievement condition most intentional. The results confirmed an earlier study by Frodi (1973) that found high school students were relatively less hostile when the investigator's behavior was attributed as being beyond his control.

To determine whether perceived mitigating circumstances result in response inhibition to already aroused anger or an actual failure to arouse anger, Zillman and Cantor (1976) measured the effects of mitigating circumstances on levels of physiological arousal and retaliatory behavior. The mitigating circumstance (E worrying about an exam) was told to subjects either prior to an aggressive act, following it, or not at all. On the physiological measures (heart rate), prior knowledge resulted in little change in arousal level in response to aggression, and knowledge following aggression resulted in a significant drop in arousal, which had risen to high levels in response to aggression. In the no-knowledge condition, arousal levels remained high following aggression. On the retaliatory measure (an evaluation of the aggressor that would purportedly influence his job), subjects with prior knowledge showed comparatively little retaliatory behavior, while subjects with postaggression mitigating knowledge and subjects with no knowledge showed significant levels of retaliation. With regard to retaliation by subjects who had mitigating knowledge after the aggressive act, the authors suggest that intensely aroused anger may produce a disposition to retaliate that lasts beyond the physical excitatory residues. Once this commitment is made, the mitigating information is ignored on a conscious level.

Perception of Personal Power and Control

It seems that a person's perception that she or he can control or cope with a situation containing provocation serves to diminish the negative response to that situation. Davison (1967) made the observation that relaxation procedures not only teach a person to identify and undo anxiety but also teach the person the comforting idea that she or he can control and regulate the anxiety. In a broader context, Lefcourt (1973), after reviewing the literature, concluded that the perception of control ameliorates negative situational reactions across species. He stated, "Pain-producing stimuli prove less painful and disruptive to individuals who can predict and control these stimuli, and these findings are obtained with different types of data" (p. 420).

With regard to anger arousal, Rimm, DeGroot, Bourd, Reiman, and Dillow (1971) taught subjects how to reduce their anger effectively through muscle relaxation. Novaco (1975), following Meichenbaum and Cameron (1973), successfully taught subjects to dissect angry provocations into stages and to use self-instructional techniques to regulate the anger. More important to this discussion, Novaco (1975) asserts that learning nonangry and nonantagonistic responses to provocations reduces the probability of future anger in provocative circumstances. He reasons that "as one learns to handle provocations with nonantagonistic behavior, he develops a new sense of competence and discovers that he can take charge without being angry" (p. 10).

An interesting variation on this theme is offered by Brehm (1966). He suggested that anger and hostility can be reduced by convincing a person that he or she has the option or freedom to aggress. His reasoning is based on the assumption that, whenever a person has a freedom (e.g., to become angry) and that freedom is denied, he or she is motivated to restore it. In testing this out, Nezlek and Brehm (1975) found that leading a victim to perceive that he or she had the opportunity to counteraggress against an instigator resulted in a significant decrease in counterhostility, in comparison to those who did not have this perception. Thus, a perception of personal power or choice in a situation mediated angry and hostile responses.

Expectation of Outcome

The term *expectation* refers to the prediction a person makes about current or future events, based on appraisals of past situations. According to Rotter (1954, 1972), the potential for a behavior in a particular situation is a function of the person's expectations for reward or punishment in that situation and the value of those consequences for that person. Accordingly, action is likely when there is a high expectation for reward plus a high value for that reward. Contrarily, a low expectation for reward, a low value for the rewards that seem available, or a high expectation for punishment would make an action highly improbable.

Expectation of outcome or consequence can be predicted to influence anger in at least three ways. First, high expectations for rewarding or desirable consequences that do not occur can make an outcome aversive, resulting in anger and even in aggression (Novaco, 1978). What happens in this case is that the person takes the positive outcome for granted and hence overreacts to the frustration.

Second, a perception or belief that anger and aggression will be rewarded, or alternatively that failing to respond with anger or aggression will be punished, will raise the probability of an angry and/or aggressive response. The now famous study by Stanley Milgram (1963), in which a subject "mercilessly" shocked confederates in response to pressure from the experimenter, dramatically demonstrates this.

Third, high expectations that anger or aggressive behavior will result in negative consequences of some kind will predictably reduce the probability of anger and aggression. Burnstein and Worchel (1962) and Mosher (1965), for instance, show that expectations for social disapproval, particularly among those with high approval needs, will inhibit anger and aggression in the presence of environmental cues indicating the existence of such negative consequences. Mosher (1965) has further suggested that an extremely powerful inhibitor of anger and aggression is the expectation of personally suffering guilt as a result of experiencing anger or acting aggressively. Studies by Buss (1966a, 1966b), Baron (1971), James and Mosher (1967), and Knott, Lasater, and Shuman (1974) seem to bear this out. Finally, experimental evidence has shown that expectation of physical retaliation (but only if it is powerful or massive) will result in an inhibition of anger and aggression (Shortell, Epstein, & Taylor, 1970; Dengerink & Levendusky, 1972).

Self-evaluation of Anger

A final situational-specific cognitive mediator of anger and aggression to be mentioned is the person's negative evaluation of her or his own anger arousal. Thus, when a person becomes aware of being angry and sees it as bad (i.e., unwarranted by the circumstances), the likelihood that she or he will nullify the anger and antagonism is increased. Indeed, Borden (1975) showed this to be true, as did Berkowitz, Lepinski, and Angulo (1969). By manipulating awareness of anger level, Berkowitz et al. found that subjects very aware of their high level of anger had a significantly lowered incidence of aggression to a confederate instigator. They speculated that awareness of extreme anger causes people to conclude that their reactions are not justified.

COGNITIVE ELEMENTS IN ANGER ABOUT ANGER

It is an axiom of RET that people rarely display only primary symptoms of emotional disturbance; they also typically present secondary symptoms about their primary symptoms (Ellis, 1962, 1978, 1979a, 1979b; Ellis & Abrahms, 1978; Ellis & Grieger, 1977; Ellis & Harper, 1975; Grieger & Boyd, 1979). That is, they first make themselves emotionally upset or disturbed and then they frequently make themselves emotionally upset about being emotionally upset.

Secondary symptoms usually exacerbate primary problems and serve to interfere with solving the original problem.

The ABC theory of RET provides a nice framework with which to conceptualize this. Following the theory, people first experience some aversive event at point A and they then disturb themselves at point C by thinking (and believing) some irrational, disturbance-producing idea at point B. Not content to stop there, they then observe their own disturbed reaction at C, in effect making it a new A (or A_2); and they then create a new disturbance (a C_2) by again thinking (and believing) irrational, disturbance-producing ideas (at B_2) about their disturbed state. In effect, they create a double-level problem, or an emotional problem about an emotional problem (Grieger & Boyd, 1979).

Ellis has shown this to be a particularly powerful phenomenon in anxiety problems. In addition, human beings, after becoming angry, are very likely to observe their anger and to disturb themselves further about it. Some note their anger and make themselves anxious by holding what Ellis has labeled ego anxiety thoughts ("Isn't it terrible to be so angry? I shouldn't be feeling this way!"). Others create guilt for themselves by putting themselves down ("Its an awful thing to feel this way. I'm a real heel.")

Those who make themselves angry about being angry are likely to hold ideas or philosophies that characterize low frustration tolerance (Ellis, 1976b; Nolan et al., 1979). Thus, one first makes oneself angry via some situational attribution or some irrational philosophy that logically leads to the anger. Then, noting and experiencing the anger as displeasurable or aversive, one evaluates the emotional upset as *too much* of a hassle, which one *shouldn't have to* bear. One consequently experiences anger about having to bear the burden of experiencing the anger itself.

HEALTHY AND UNHEALTHY ANGER[1]

What has so far been presented is a cognitive mediation model of anger arousal and maintenance. An implication of all this is that it is very easy for human beings to become angry, and, given the myriad frustrations that everyday life indubitably presents, it is very likely that every person will periodically experience anger. Ignoring the issue of whether or not people must as a consequence of their existence feel angry, a question remains as how to differentiate between healthy and unhealthy, or rational and irrational, anger. How do we conceptualize those anger reactions that are appropriate and those that are not?

To answer this, it is helpful first to consider the basic values that humans hold. Most people seem to hold a fairly limited number of basic values, including (1) staying alive, (2) living happily or with an acceptable amount of pleasure and a

[1]This section is modeled after a paper by Albert Ellis titled "Healthy and Unhealthy Aggression," presented at the 1973 Annual Meeting of the American Psychological Association.

minimum of pain, (3) living comfortably in a social group or community in which one is basically accepted, and (4) relating intimately and lovingly with one person or a selected few individuals (Ellis, 1973a). People do indeed adopt many subvalues or subgoals, such as listening to music, playing golf, and the like, but these can be easily catalogued under one or more of the basic four just listed.

Assuming that humans do generally adopt these basic values and that it is legitimate for them to do so, it follows that "any thoughts, emotions, or actions [that] aid or promote these goals are rational, sensible, or healthy; while, by the same token, any behavior [that] blocks or sabotages these goals are irrational, insane, or unhealthy" (Ellis, 1973a, p. 2). Therefore, healthy anger can be seen as anger that aids and abets the human values (or goals) of remaining alive, being happy, successfully relating to a small social group, and relating intimately and pleasurably to one person or a few select individuals. Unhealthy anger, then, is anger that thwarts, blocks, or undermines these basic goals. Neither the definition of healthy or unhealthy anger is offered in an absolute form, but rather in terms of probabilities.

Going beyond this, a cognitive therapist further defines healthy and unhealthy anger by the thoughts or ideas that lie behind and prompt the anger, rather than by the quality of the affective experience itself or by some behavioral correlate like aggression. Healthy anger (or, better, irritation or annoyance) is defined as a person holding thoughts that predictably (although not inevitably) lead to the realization of one's basic goals, with the opposite being true for unhealthy anger. So, using the ABC's of rational–emotive therapy, if I am insulted by you at point A, and feel angry at point C, I may be thinking both rational and irrational thoughts at point B: (1) "I don't like the rotten thing you did, and I wish you would refrain from doing it in the future; (2) You *shouldn't* have done that *terrible* thing to me, and you're a *rotten person* for doing it!"

The first of these thoughts is healthy or rational because it logically derives from my basic values. Being insulted, I can still survive, but to some degree it has interfered with my happiness and may possibly have interfered with my successfully relating with others. I can therefore legitimately conclude that I don't like to be insulted, that it was a bad thing to do, and that it was obnoxious. And I will probably behave in some self-assured, determined, and assertive ways that will least likely do me in, to get my message across.

My second thought is unhealthy or irrational because it does not derive from my basic human values, it has no empirical or objective basis, and it probably will lead me to behaviors that further undermine my goals (Ellis, 1973a; Ellis & Abrahms, 1978; Goodman & Maultsby, 1974). There is absolutely no evidence that you shouldn't behave badly, that behaving badly is more than bad or inconvenient, or that you are totally rotten for behaving badly (Ellis, 1977a). Holding these beliefs, however, I will probably become oppositional, combative, insulting, argumentative, and perhaps even violent. In the process, I will further undercut my happiness and interfere with my interpersonal relationships.

The implications for treatment of differentiating healthy anger (or irritation) from unhealthy anger in this way are obvious. Common sense argues against a squelching or denying of anger, for this makes people ignore the irrational ideas behind the anger. It also argues against a program designed to teach people to express their anger "creatively," for this teaches people that anger is both unavoidable and acceptable. Finally, it argues against the free expression of anger, for evidence shows that such expression, by providing the person with an opportunity to rehearse the anger-producing philosophies, tends to further ingrain the philosophies and abet the anger (Bandura & Walters, 1963; Feshback, 1971).

Rather, such a differentiation suggests treatment strategies that help unhealthy angry people radically change their irrational philosophies (Ellis, 1973a). It argues for therapies, like RET and other cognitive behavioral treatment programs, that first help people acknowledge their unhealthy anger and then encourage them to (1) assume full responsibility for their anger; (2) look for and find their anger-instigating philosophies; (3) dispute these philosophies via cognitive, emotive, and behavioral means; and (4) act on and practice ideas that are contrary to the unhealthy ones (Ellis, 1976b).

SUMMARY

I have outlined in this chapter an RET-based, cognitive mediation model of how anger is developed and maintained. Within this model, anger is seen as being aroused when an individual holds irrational ideas or philosophies and/or when a person makes situationally specific assumptions that logically lead to anger. By the same token, a person can be said to have an anger problem when she or he strongly endorses these irrational philosophies or habitually and frequently makes these assumptions across situations. The irrational ideas articulated by Ellis (1977b) to be behind anger are buttressed either by self-worth and/or low-frustration-tolerance issues, and situational assumptions include attributions regarding the intent of an aggressor, the perceived arbitrariness of another's actions, the sense of personal power one has in a situation, outcome expectations for getting angry, and the perceived badness of being angry. Finally, following Ellis (1973a), healthy anger (i.e., irritation, annoyance) is differentiated from unhealthy anger by the different cognitions that lie behind the two, one set being rational and goal facilitating and the other being irrational and goal blocking.

REFERENCES

Arnold, M. B. *Emotion and personality*. New York: Columbia University Press, 1960.

Bandura, A. *Aggression: A social learning analysis*. New York: Prentice-Hall, 1973.

Bandura, A., & Walters, R. H. *Social learning and personality development*. New York: Holt, Rinehart & Winston, 1963.

Bard, P. Central nervous mechanisms for the expression of anger in animals. In M. L. Reymert (Ed.), *Feelings and emotions: The Mooseheart symposium*. New York: McGraw-Hill, 1950.

Baron, R. A. Magnitude of victim's pain and level of prior anger arousal as determinants of adult aggressive behavior. *Journal of Personality and Social Psychology*, 1971, *17*, 236–243.

Berkowitz, L. Experimental investigations of hostility catharsis. *Journal of Consulting and Clinical Psychology*, 1970, *35*, 1–7.

Berkowitz, L., Lepinski, J., & Angulo, E. Awareness of our anger level and subsequent aggression. *Journal of Personality and Social Psychology*, 1969, *11*, 293–300.

Borden, R. J. Witnessed aggression: Influence of and observer's sex and values on aggressive responding. *Journal of Personality and Social Psychology*, 1975, *31*, 567–573.

Brehm, T. *A theory of psychological acceptance*. New York: Academic Press, 1966.

Burnstein, E., & Worchel, P. Arbitrariness of frustration and its consequence for aggression in a social situation. *Journal of Personality*, 1962, *30*, 528–541.

Buss, A. H. The effect of harm on subsequent aggression. *Journal of Experimental Research in Personality*, 1966, *1*, 249–255. (a)

Buss, A. H. Instrumentality of aggression, feedback and frustration as determinants of physical aggression. *Journal of Personality and Social Psychology*, 1966, *3*, 153–162. (b)

Chappell, D., & Monahan, J. Violence and criminal justice. Lexington, Mass.: D. C. Heath, Lexington Books, 1975.

Cohen, A. R. Some implications of self-esteem for social influence. In I. L. Janis & C. I. Houland (Eds.), *Personality and persuasibility*. New Haven, Conn.: Yale University Press, 1966.

Daniels, D. N., Gilula, M. F., & Ochberg, F. M. *Violence and the struggle for existence*. Boston: Little, Brown, 1970.

Davison, G. C. Anxiety under total curarization: Implications for the role of muscular relaxation in the desensitization of neurotic fears. *Journal of Mental and Nervous Diseases*, 1967, *143*, 443–448.

Dengerink, H. A., & Levendusky, P. G. Effects of massive retaliation and balance of power on aggression. *Journal of Experimental Research in Personality*, 1972, *6*, 230–236.

Douglas, R. J. The hippocampus and behavior. *Psychological Bulletin*, 1967, *67*, 416–442.

Ellis, A. *Reason and emotion in psychotherapy*. New York: Lyle Stuart, 1962.

Ellis, A. *Growth through reason*. Palo Alto, Calif.: Science and Behavior Books, 1971; Hollywood, Calif.: Wilshire Books, 1974.

Ellis, A. *Healthy and unhealthy aggression*. Paper presented at the First Annual Convention of the American Psychological Association, Montreal, Canada, August, 1973. (a)

Ellis, A. *Humanistic psychology: The rational–emotive approach*. New York: Julian Press, 1973. (b)

Ellis, A. *How to live with a neurotic*. New York: Crown, 1975.

Ellis, A. The biological basis of human irrationality. *Journal of Individual Psychology*, 1976, *32*, 145–168. (a)

Ellis, A. Techniques of handling anger in marriage. *Journal of Marriage and Family Counseling*, 1976, *2*, 305–315. (b)

Ellis, A. The basic clinical theory of rational–emotive therapy. In A. Ellis & R. Grieger (Eds.), *Handbook of rational–emotive therapy*. New York: Springer, 1977. (a)

Ellis, A. *How to live with and without anger*. New York: Reader's Digest Press, 1977. (b)

Ellis, A. *Discomfort anxiety: A new cognitive-behavioral construct*. Invited address to the Association for Advancement of Beharior Therapy Annual Meeting, November 17, 1978. New York: BMA Audio Cassettes, 1978.

Ellis, A. A note on the treatment of agoraphobics with cognitive modification versus prolonged exposure *in vivo*. *Behavior Research and Therapy*, 1979, *17*(2), 162–163. (a)

Ellis, A. *A theoretical and empirical foundation of rational–emotive therapy*. Monterey, Calif.: Brooks/Cole, 1979. (b)

Ellis, A., & Abrahms, E. *Brief psychotherapy in medical and health practice*. New York: Springer, 1978.

Ellis, A., & Grieger, R. *Handbook of theory and practice*. New York: Springer, 1977.

Ellis, A., & Harper, R. A. *A new guide to rational living*. Englewood Cliffs, N.J.: Prentice-Hall, 1975.

Epstein, S., & Taylor, S. P. Instigation to aggression as a function of degree of defeat and perceived aggression intent of the opponent. *Journal of Personality*, 1967, *35*, 265–289.

Feshback, S. The stimulating vs. cathartic effects of a vicarious aggressive activity. *Journal of abnormal and social psychology,* 1961, *63,* 381–385.

Feshback, S. Dynamics and morality of violence and aggression. *American Psychologist,* 1971, *26,* 281–292.

Feshback, S., & Singer, R. D. *Television and aggression.* New York: Jossey-Bass, 1971.

Frodi, A. Alternatives to aggressive behavior for the reduction of hostility. *Guteborg Psychological Reports,* 1973, *3,* 11.

Frodi, A. Effects of varying explanations given for provocation on subsequent hostility. *Psychological Reports,* 1976, *38,* 659–669.

Geen, R. G., & O'Neal, E. C. *Perspectives on aggression.* New York: Academic Press, 1976.

Goodman, D., & Maultsby, M. C. *Emotional well-being through rational behavior training.* Springfield, Ill.: Thomas Press, 1974.

Green, R., & Murray, E. Instigation to aggression as a function of self-disclosure and threat to self-esteem. *Journal of Consulting and Clinical Psychology,* 1973, *40,* 440–443.

Greenwell, I., & Dengerink, H. The role of perceived vs. actual attack in human physical aggression. *Journal of Personality and Social Psychology,* 1973, *26,* 66–71.

Grieger, R. M. An existential component of anger. *Rational Living,* 1977, *12,* 3–8.

Grieger, R., & Boyd, J. *Rational–emotive therapy: A skills-based approach.* New York: Van Nostrand Reinhold, 1979.

Hebb, D. O., & Thompson, W. R. The social significance of animal studies. In G. Lindzey (Ed.), *Handbook of social psychology. Vol. 1; Theory and method.* Cambridge, Mass.: Addison-Wesley, 1954.

James, P., & Mosher, D. Thematic aggression, hostility-guilt, and aggressive behavior. *Journal of Projective Techniques,* 1967, *3,* 61–67.

Johnson, R. *Aggression in man and animals.* Philadelphia: W. B. Saunders, 1972.

Jones, R. G. *A factored measure of Ellis's irrational belief system, with personality and maladjustment correlates.* Unpublished doctoral dissertation, Texas Technological College, Lubbock, Texas, 1968.

Kahn, M. The physiology of catharsis. *Journal of personality and social psychology,* 1966, *3,* 278–286.

Knott, P. D., Lasater, L., & Shuman, R. Aggression-guilt and conditionability for aggressiveness. *Journal of Personality,* 1974, *3,* 332–344.

Konocni, V. T. Annoyance, type, and duration of post-annoyance activity, and aggression: "The cathartic effect." *Journal of Experimental Psychology,* 1975, *104,* 76–102. (a)

Konocni, V. T. The mediation of aggressive behavior: Arousal level vs. anger and cognitive labeling. *Journal of Personality and Social Psychology,* 1975, *32,* 706–712. (b)

LaBarre, W. The cultural basis of emotions and gestures. *Journal of Personality,* 1947, *16,* 49–68.

Lazarus, R. S. *Psychological stress and the coping process.* New York: McGraw-Hill, 1966.

Lazarus, R. S. Emotions and adaptation: Conceptual and empirical relations. In W. J. Arnold (Ed.), *Nebraska symposium on motivation.* Lincoln, Neb.: University of Nebraska Press, 1968.

Lazarus, R. S., Averill, J. R., & Opton, E. M. Towards a cognitive theory of emotion. In M. Arnold (Ed.), *Feelings and emotions.* New York: Academic Press, 1970.

Lefcourt, H. The functions and illusions of control and freedom. *American Psychologist,* 1973, *28,* 417–425.

Lindsley, D. B. Emotions and the electroencephalogram. In M. R. Raymert (Ed.), *Feelings and emotions: The Mooseheart symposium.* New York: McGraw-Hill, 1950.

Look, March 19, 1979, pp. 18–24.

MacLean, P. D. Psychosomatics. In H. W. Magoun (Ed.), *Handbook of physiology. Action 1: Neurophysiology* (Vol. 3.). Washington, D.C.: American Physiological Society, 1960.

Mallick, S. K., & McCandless, B. R. A study of catharsis of aggression. *Journal of Personality and Social Psychology,* 1966, *4,* 591–596.

Meichenbaum, D., & Cameron, R. *Stress inoculation: A skills-training approach to anxiety management.* Unpublished manuscript, University of Waterloo, Ontario, Canada, 1973.

Milgram, S. Behavioral study of obedience. *Journal of Abnormal and Social Psychology,* 1963, *67,* 371–378.

Mosher, D. K. Interaction of fear and guilt in inhibiting unacceptable behavior. *Journal of Consulting Psychology.* 1965, *29,* 161–167.

Nezlek, T., & Brehm, W. Hostility as a function of the opportunity to counteraggress. *Journal of Personality*, 1975, *43*, 421–433.

Nickel, T. W. The attribution of intention as a critical factor in the relation between frustration and aggression. *Journal of Personality*, 1974, *42*, 482–492.

Nolan, E. J., Boyd, J. D., & Grieger, R. M. *Influences of irrational beliefs and expectancy of success on frustration tolerance.* Unpublished manuscript, 1979.

Novaco, R. W. *Anger control: The development and evaluation of an experimental treatment.* Lexington, Mass.: D.C. Heath, Lexington Books, 1975.

Novaco, R. W. Anger and coping with stress. In J. P. Foreyt & D. P. Rathjew (Eds.), *Cognitive behavior therapy.* New York: Plenum Press, 1978.

Rimm, D. C., DeGroot, J. C., Bourd, P., Reiman, J., & Dillow, P. V. Systematic desensitization of an anger response. *Behavior Research and Therapy*, 1971, *9*, 273–280.

Rosenbaum, M. E., & de Charms, R. Direct and vicarious reduction of hostility. *Journal of Abnormal and Social Psychology*, 1960, *60*, 105–111.

Rosenbaum, M. E., & Stanners, R. F. Self-esteem, manifest hostility, and expression of hostility. *Journal of Abnormal and Social Psychology*, 1961, *63*, 646–649.

Rotter, J. B. *Social learning and clinical psychology.* Englewood Cliffs, N.J.: Prentice-Hall, 1954.

Rotter, J. B. An introduction to social learning theory. In J. Rotter, J. E. Chance, & E. J. Phares (Eds.), *Applications of a social learning theory of personality.* New York: Holt, Rhinehart and Winston, 1972.

Rule, B., & Nesdale, A. Emotional arousal and aggressive behavior. *Psychological Bulletin*, 1976, *83*, 851–863.

Shortell, J. R., Epstein, S., & Taylor, S. P. Instigation to aggression as a function of degree of defeat and the capacity for massive retaliation. *Journal of Personality*, 1970, *38*, 313–328.

Taylor, S. P. Aggressive behavior and physiological arousal as a function of provocation and the tendency to inhibit aggression. *Journal of Personality*, 1967, *35*, 297–310.

Toch, H. *Violent Men.* Chicago: Adline, 1969.

Turksy, B., & Sternbach, R. S. Further physiological correlates of ethnic differences in response to shock. *Psychophysiology*, 1967, *4*, 67–74.

Veldman, D., & Worchel, P. Defensiveness and self-acceptance in the management of hostility. *Journal of Abnormal and Social Psychology*, 1961, *63*, 319–325.

Worchel, P. Status restoration and the reduction of hostility. *Journal of Abnormal and Social Psychology*, 1960, *63*, 443–445.

Zillman, D., & Cantor, J. R. Effects of timing of information about mitigating circumstances on emotional responses to provocation and retaliatory behavior. *Journal of Experimental Social Psychology*, 1976, *12*, 38–55.

Zuckerman, M. & Lubin, B. *Manual for the Multiple Affect Adjective Check List.* San Diego: Educational and Industrial Testing Service, 1965.

8

An Addendum to the Understanding and Treatment of Individuals with Motivational Deficits*

Barry A. Bass

Patients typically arrive at a psychotherapist's office wanting to change either themselves or their circumstances. When self-change is the stated goal, they frequently either want to stop an undesirable behavior (e.g., smoking, drinking) or start a desirable one (e.g., exercise). The only thing preventing them from doing what it is they want, they often tell us, is a lack of willpower. That is, they—along with most therapists—believe that one needs to be motivated in the here and now in order to change.

Quite often these individuals will tell us that, although they really "want" to change, they are simply "stuck" and need a "push." In this regard it's not unusual for clients to request that they be hypnotized so that they can receive that extra boost of motivation necessary to allow them to carry out their desires. Our more sophisticated clients might describe the dilemma as one in which short-term payoffs interfere with long-term motivation. Thus lack of motivation almost never means a lack of desire but rather an inability to convert long-term motivation or desire into the short-term effort required to realize a goal.

This point of view is certainly endorsed in the cognitive behavioral literature as well. The cognitive sequence that both clients and therapists seem to agree is necessary for behavior change to occur can be diagramed as follows:

*This chapter is reprinted from the *Journal of Rational Emotive Therapy,* 1984, 2.

Long-term motivation	→	short-term motivation,	→	behavior
precedes		which precedes		change.
(value, goal)		(want, desire, willpower)		(action)

In this vein, May and Yalom (1984), two prominent existential therapists, have written that "decision is the bridge between wishing and action" (p. 375). Ellis, founder of rational–emotive therapy (RET) and an existential therapist in his own right, asserts that most unmotivated clients are simply individuals with low frustration tolerance (LFT). Frequently these individuals suffer from what Ellis (1982) has labeled "discomfort anxiety" and believe that they cannot and should not have to tolerate pain, discomfort, or adversity. Essentially LFT is characterized by a lack of motivation. RET addresses this problem by encouraging clients to surrender their LFT philosophies of life and by insisting that clients can stand what they don't necessarily like. The authors of a highly respected RET text (Walen, DiGiuseppe, & Wessler, 1980) have written that "LFT is perhaps the main reason that clients do not improve after they have gained an understanding of their disturbance and how they create it" (p. 12).

Thus the assumption of both the traditional existential therapist as well as the RET existentialist is that once our clients stop expecting or demanding that life be easy or painless, they will go about doing what they had been avoiding. My experience as a rational–emotive therapist, however, has not always borne this out. In more than one instance patients have discarded their LFT philosophy and have learned to accept the fact that life need not be easy, pain-free, and nonfrustrating. However, they often have not changed their behavior. In one case a client said, "Yes things in life are often difficult and painful. And to the best of my ability I'll try not to whine and complain about the pain and difficulties I encounter. However, I still refuse to accept the pain of changing and so I am still stuck."

This apparent attitude shift, accompanied by the failure to change a behavioral pattern, is far from an uncommon occurrence in therapy. That is, although "humans tend to perceive, think, emote, and behave simultaneously" (Ellis, 1984), it is also clear that a change in cognition is often not sufficient to produce a change in behavior.

My assertion is that short-term motivation is not required in order to bring about a change in behavior. All that is required is the goal (long-term motivation) to change, a commitment to it, and possession of the skills necessary to produce the desired result. In this regard it is asserted that an irrational belief frequently held by both clients and their therapists is that one must "want" to do something *now* in order to produce that behavior now or in the immediate future. That is, we often believe that only by being motivated in the present can we produce the action in the near future that we had desired in the past.

It is here asserted that "wanting" and "doing" are concepts located in separate domains and are related causally only for those individuals who mistakenly believe that wants must precede actions. Everyday experience tells us that we often engage in behavior that has no immediate short-term payoff. For example, we may decide the night before to arise at 6:00 AM and then do so even though in the morning we may have no real desire to get out of bed. In other words, we do not need to feel motivated (in the short-term sense being used here) to change any behavior we had previously decided upon.

Thus it is asserted that the individuals who have the most difficulty keeping commitments to themselves are not only those with low tolerance for frustration but also those who believe that wanting must immediately precede acting. The following exchange between myself and a patient complaining of lack of sexual motivation can serve to illustrate this point.

Bob and Doris had been married for six years and had not yet consummated their marriage. Bob stated that it was his long-term goal to have an ongoing sexual relationship with his wife. However, he found it impossible to do any sexual homework assignments because he reported no attraction (or short-term motivation) at all to his wife.

THERAPIST: It's now been five weeks in a row in which you promised to take a shower with Doris and yet have not kept your word. We seem to be at an impasse.

BOB: Each week that I make the promise I have really good intentions. But then I get home and the reality of who Doris is hits me, and I realize once again that I'm not attracted to her—not even in the slightest. I'm just not motivated.

THERAPIST: So you believe you must be motivated or *want* to take a shower with Doris in order for you to get into the shower with Doris?

BOB: Yes. Once I get home I realize that I really don't *want* to take a shower with Doris—at least not now.

THERAPIST: So let's see if I have this right. As a long-term goal you would like to want to take a shower with Doris, but you don't *want to now*.

BOB: Yes, As a long-term goal I do want to take a shower with her. But not this week.

THERAPIST: Well, Bob, in light of what you are saying I think I have a strategy that you could use to get yourself to take a shower with Doris this week. Don't want to take a shower with Doris . . . and take a shower with Doris.

BOB: But I don't want to.

THERAPIST: That's fine. Just continue to not want to, but do it anyway.

BOB: But I can't.

THERAPIST: That's not quite correct. It's true you have not yet gotten into the shower with Doris, but that might have been because you thought that you needed to be motivated, or thought you needed to want to get into the shower with Doris, in order for you to get into the shower with her. But you know you can decide today to do something tomorrow, and even though you may change your mind and even if you no longer want to do it tomorrow you *can* do it just because you said you would.

BOB: But I wouldn't enjoy doing something I didn't want to do.

THERAPIST: You may be right about that. But we'll never find out for sure unless you do the experiment. This week, continue to not want to take a shower with Doris *and* take a shower with her anyway.

That conversation was a breakthrough for this patient. He did in fact take the shower with his wife and, subsequently, used similar reasoning to help himself overcome obstacles to other sexual goals. A similar approach has been helpful in breaking the destructive pattern of drug abuse in an individual who believed that as long as he wanted (in the short-term) to use drugs he could not keep his long-term commitment to staying drug-free. Likewise, other clients have learned to ignore short-term desires temporarily in order to accomplish previously unattainable goals.

Based upon my experiences with these and other "unmotivated" and easily frustrated clients, I have developed the following three-phase therapeutic regimen for helping individuals to attain their goals. It should be emphasized that this approach is meant to be used in conjunction with and not instead of those cognitive behavioral techniques already shown to be of benefit to individuals with willpower deficits.

1. *Problem Identification.* This phase consists of a cognitive behavioral analysis of the presenting problem areas. Since one of the things that clients with avoidance problems do is avoid looking carefully at problems, it is not uncommon for these individuals to arrive in treatment long after others might already have sought and received help. As a result, problems are so thoroughly entrenched that even taking a thorough case history can elicit both avoidance and anxiety from most clients. It is particularly important that we do not allow these individuals to avoid examining all relevant issues, including their LFT personality characteristics. It is equally important to target motivational deficit problems at this time.

2. *Pedagogic.* This phase includes the disputation of irrational beliefs. For LFT clients these beliefs often focus on their demanding that things be the way they wish, catastrophizing about difficult circumstances, and avoiding the experience of discomfort that is often necessary for change. In addition this phase includes drawing the distinction for our clients between the domains of want, desire, or willpower and of action. In drawing this distinction it is often helpful to define lack of motivation as the unfortunate result of believing that the two domains must be connected. In this regard we might point out that, although we might not want something, we can still act on getting it anyway, as per the earlier example of Bob. Similarly, we may have something we do not want, like tiredness or depression, but we can still act to acquire goals anyway, such as getting up to go to work when we are tired.

3. *Homework.* Homework assignments, pursued outside of the therapy office, allow patients to demonstrate to themselves the validity and utility of their newly acquired philosophy. In addition to accomplishing a skill-practicing function, homework is always presented as an experiment or opportunity to discover the limits to which a cognitive and philosophical belief system can be stretched. For this reason the emphasis is less on obtaining certain results than on taking risks, collecting data, and, perhaps most important of all, keeping commitments.

CONCLUSION

In brief I have attempted in this paper to present a philosophical addendum to the traditional cognitive behavioral treatment of individuals with motivational deficits. I have drawn the distinction between long-term goals and short-term willpower. It has been asserted that willpower deficit is typically self-defined by individuals who report they do not wish to and therefore believe they are unable to act upon a previous commitment or goal. In addition to utilizing the already established strategies for treating these individuals, it is suggested that drawing the distinction between motivation and action can often serve to move unmotivated clients.

REFERENCES

Ellis, A. (1982). Psychoneurosis and anxiety problems. In R. Grieger & I. Z. Grieger (Eds.), *Cognition and emotional disturbance*. New York: Human Sciences Press.

Ellis, A. (1984). Rational–emotive therapy. In R. J. Corsini (Ed.), *Current psychotherapies* (3rd ed.). Peacock.

May, R., & Yalom, I. Existential psychotherapy. In R. J. Corsini (Ed.), *Current psychotherapies* (3rd ed.) (pp. 354–391). Itasca, Ill.: Peacock.

Walen, S. R., DiGiuseppe, R., & Wessler, R. L. (1980). *A practitioner's guide to rational–emotive therapy*. New York: Oxford University Press.

9

Self-acceptance Problems*

John Boyd and Russell M. Grieger

Self-esteem is a concept that mental health professionals endorse as central to understanding personality and psychopathology. It is among those rare concepts that almost all therapeutic approaches seem intent on enhancing or improving (Adler, 1974; Berne, 1964; Branden, 1971, Freud, 1963; Jung, 1954; Perls, 1969; Rogers, 1961).

Cognitive systems in general, and RET in particular, take a rather radical position with regard to self-esteem. Simply stated, a major premise of RET is that pursuing or promoting self-esteem is an indubitably destructive endeavor and that therapeutic efforts had best be made to get people to give up their self-esteem (Ellis, 1973, 1974, 1975, 1976). We support this position and will endeavor to define what self-esteem is and why it is destructive. We will then describe an alternative concept, self-acceptance, and show why being self-accepting, rather than self-esteeming, is more theoretically valid and pragmatically tenable. Following this, we will discuss emotional disturbances in which self-esteem issues are both central and secondary.

SELF-ESTEEM

The first personality theorist to focus on self-esteem as a central theoretical concept was Alfred Adler (1927). He posited that humans have an innate inferiority resulting from their infantile experience of complete helplessness, and that the remainder of their lives are motivated to a great extent by strivings to overcome their basic sense of inadequacy. From this point of view, much human behavior is motivated by a drive to compensate for low self-esteem.

*This chapter was originally published in 1982 in R. Grieger and I. Grieger (Eds.), *Cognition and Emotional Disturbance*, published by Human Sciences Press (New York, 1982).

Other early theorists attending to self-esteem, such as James (1890), Mead (1934), Horney (1950), and Fromm (1947), did not give the concept as primary a position as did Adler, and usually self-esteem was treated as one of several divisions of the total self, or the product of other fundamental personality processes. These theorists also tended to view self-esteem as a function of one's *learned attribution of worth.* One of the strongest contemporary explanations for the acquired nature of self-esteem comes from Rogers (1951, 1961). He has stressed that during the formative years children internalize the attitudes that they perceive significant others to have toward them. From these perceptions and internalizations they form self-attitudes that are carried for the remainder of their lives. "Self-regard" was Rogers's term for the personal worth that individuals create from their perceptions of others' reactions toward them.

This brief review is by no means exhaustive. There are numerous personality theories that include self-esteem as a major construct, and each one has a somewhat different explanation for the antecedents of one's self-attribution of worth. Yet there are similarities and common dimensions among these theories, and Coopersmith's (1967) analysis of them has yielded four interrelated and overlapping factors that contribute to the development of self-esteem: (1) treatment from significant others, (2) history of successes, (3) values and aspirations, and (4) style of defending self-esteem.

The first antecedent factor has already been mentioned in regard to the position of Rogers and other phenomenologists. Rogers stresses that the facilitative relationship conditions of empathy, unconditional acceptance, and honesty, expressed through the behavior of significant others, encourage recipients to value themselves. Our self-esteem is built upon the attitude that others value us, and this attitude is most likely to arise when we receive facilitative relationship conditions.

History of success is the second antecedent of self-esteem. This refers to the extent to which we have accomplished what we set out to do and have received social recognition for these accomplishments. By achieving valued goals we develop an "I can do it" belief or a sense of power and competence, and respectful treatment from other people is usually a byproduct as well. But underlying success experiences are values and aspirations, the criteria by which we determine if a success has been achieved. One person's attainment of a sought-after goal may be viewed as a success by that individual but be meaningless to someone else who does not aspire to or value the goal. Consequently, the development and constellation of one's values and aspirations is a prime determinant in self-esteem.

The fourth antecedent factor is one's manner of responding to negative personal events, such as failing at an important task, receiving negative appraisals from significant others, and having personal limitations. Sullivan (1953) has set forth the widely accepted notion that people continually guard against a loss of self-esteem, and they experience anxiety when they anticipate devaluation or are demeaned by others or themselves. Individuals differ in their ability to deal successfully with threatening circumstances and in their styles of responding. Many resort to distortions of reality as a defensive measure and thereby relinquish a degree of sanity. They lack the crucial mental health skill of "[defining] an event filled with negative implications and consequences in such a way that it does not detract from [one's] sense of worthiness, ability, or power" (Coopersmith, 1967, p. 37).

These four antecedents of self-esteem offer an eclectic foothold on the question of from where self-esteem comes. But in RET these antecedents are viewed as experiences that give rise to several *faulty* and *self-defeating* propositions, including the following major three (Ellis, 1974, 1976).

First is the notion that people are equal to their traits, particularly their character traits. Thus, if they have significantly bad traits, then they rate as bad people and justifiably have low self-esteem; if they have good traits, however, they rate as good people and can rightfully claim positive self-esteem.

This proposition represents faulty reasoning because it is predominantly an overgeneralization, suggesting that any individual trait or cluster of traits can legitimately generalize to the whole person. But, how can one or several aspects of a person equal all of him or her? It is like saying that a whole basket of fruit is rotten because one apple is spoiled. Do not people have almost unlimited traits that change from day to day? How can any person know all his or her traits in order to make a judgment? Where is the table of weights by which to value certain traits over others? By what formula do we do the weighing—addition, geometry, multiplication? The questions such a proposition raises are many, and the answers suggest that the proposition itself is senseless.

The second faulty proposition is that people must succeed in life, must win the love of those whom they find significant, and must survive comfortably and happily. To do so gives them personal worth or high self-esteem; to fail to do so makes them unworthy or of low esteem.

This proposition is blatantly false for a number of reasons. For one, it sets up absolute standards for self-worth, all of which are magical and tautological (Ellis, 1974, 1976). There are simply no universal, scientific standards for success. Furthermore, if people have low self-worth because of failures in their various enterprises, love affairs, and efforts for contentment, then by definition we must define all people as worthless, for all have surely failed in one or more of these at some point in their lives. No one is so totally outstanding or infallible as to succeed all the time. Finally, there are numerous practical disadvantages of holding such a view, not the least of which are anxiety over failure and loss of creativity and spontaneity.

Third, people must have self-worth, or prove to themselves that they have self-worth, in order to accept and respect themselves. Furthermore, they must be convinced that they are worthwhile in order to be happy and enjoy their lives.

In addition to all the fallacies of the first two propositions, this one is blatantly tautological, for it argues that self-worth is a criterion for happiness where no evidence exists that this is the case. In fact, as we shall soon discuss, those who are most happy, fulfilled, and free from psychological symptoms are those who basically stop worrying about whether or not they are worthwhile.

These, then, are the faulty propositions upon which self-esteeming is based, but what about the consequence of the esteeming process? What happens when an individual rates himself or herself as unworthy and ends up with low self-esteem (LSE)?

A review of the self-esteem literature, a monumental task because of the plethora of articles and books on the subject, will produce many personality and psychopathological characteristics that have been clinically and/or empirically associated with LSE. For example, research has shown that individuals with high self-esteem (HSE) versus those with LSE exhibit a greater degree of interpersonal influence, are less likely to identify with their negative attributes, are less easily persuaded by threatening communications, and improve more after a success (Schneider & Turkat, 1975).

Coopersmith's (1967) overview of his and others' self-esteem studies extends the foregoing profile even further. Evidence suggests that, when compared with LSE people, those with HSE tend to:

1. Have lower anxiety and less psychosomatic symptoms, and in general are better at dealing with threatening situations;
2. Be more emotionally active and responsive, and are more likely to have deep interpersonal relationships;
3. Be more competent and effective and have more positive expectations for success and less anticipation of failure and helplessness;
4. Set higher goals for themselves and be prone to reach them;
5. Be more independent and creative;
6. Be more likely to be socially accepted and have poise and social skills.

In view of the characteristics described, it is clear that LSE is a psychological liability. It should be stressed, however, that LSE certainly does not guarantee an inadequate personality, for there are those who struggle with a feeling of low worth yet maintain stable and productive lives. There are probably many LSE-ers who have only a few of the problematic characteristics that have been described. Furthermore, LSE seems to exist in degree (Coopersmith, 1967), and a moderate level of LSE may not be as destructive to one's functioning as a chronic level. But substantive empirical and clinical evidence does indicate that LSE is a dimension within psychopathology that is widespread, deleterious to psychological health, and worthy of therapeutic treatment.

Holding ourselves in high self-esteem is the other side of the coin. Is not this, however, unquestionably a desirable goal, one to strive for? The answer is no! When people hold themselves in high esteem, they are engaging in the same irrational process of evaluating their total worth based on some personal characteristic or on the affection offered by another. Thus, to maintain HSE, people *must* continue to display their characteristic of worth and to maintain affection from others—a highly anxious state of affairs. If they fail in this task, they lose their tenuous hold on self-esteem.

Those people who are blessed with many of the characteristics we associate with personal worth sometimes create a particularly troublesome problem for themselves. They become egotistical and narcissistic. Genuinely though neurotically believing they have more value than others, they act upon this belief in selfish and self-centered ways. When their criteria for aggrandizement slip away, as is eventually the case, their grandeur vanishes and they fall quickly to the depths of LSE. Suicides consequent to commercial failings are everpresent in contemporary society.

SELF-ACCEPTANCE

The concept of self-acceptance is central to the theory of RET and a primary goal of a good many RET endeavors. Contrasted with self-esteem, self-acceptance starts from the premise that human beings are too multifaceted to be rated or evaluated as a total entity. With such human complexity, and with no means or tools to do such a rating anyway, self-acceptance means giving up the philosophical set of person rating and simply attending to one's traits, skills, or performances, either individually or in small clusters.

Given that self-acceptance is more philosophically sound and psychologically helpful than self-esteem, there are several basic propositions that follow (Ellis, 1976). These are objective and valid statements about human nature which replace self-rating and a sense of self based on evaluative thinking.

1. Despite the almost infinite individual manifestations, people generally have two major goals or purposes in life: (a) to remain alive and (b) to live with a maximum degree of happiness and a minimum degree of pain.
2. People have an ongoing aliveness that continues for a certain period of time and then comes to an end.
3. People have a multitude of traits that make them separate and different from others, giving them uniqueness. Although some of these traits change, a good many have consistency over time, giving people an "identity" or "self" all their own.
4. People have awareness of their ongoingness and their traits. They can, therefore, within limits, plan for their future, change some of their traits, discover what they enjoy, and work to realize their enjoyment.
5. People have awareness of themselves. They can choose to value themselves based on how well they do in meeting their goals; they can choose to

value themselves on the grounds that it simply feels better and makes more practical sense to do so; or they can choose to accept themselves unconditionally, simply because they are alive and because they realize that *self*-rating is both impossible and pernicious.

To summarize these propositions, RET strongly advises people to stop their self-rating process, never jumping from self-acceptance and trait-rating to self-esteeming and self-rating. Why? Because self-acceptance follows the rules of scientific evidence; because a self-acceptance stance does not hinder people from attaining their basic goals and, in fact, serves to facilitate them; and because self-acceptance certainly does not lead to the emotional problems that self-esteeming sooner or later does.

In the final analysis, RET proposes two alternatives to self-rating (Ellis, 1976; Ellis & Harper, 1975). The less elegant alternative is for people to define themselves arbitrarily as good or esteemable simply because they exist, thus making themselves feel worthwhile. The more elegant alternative is for people to recognize their extreme complexity, to acknowledge that any attempt at rating is scientifically doomed, and to recognize that they have no intrinsic worth, but rather aliveness. People can and certainly "should" rate their traits, for this will facilitate their meeting their goals; but in addition they can fully accept themselves no matter what helpful or harmful traits they discover.

SELF-RATING AND EMOTIONAL DISTURBANCE

RET places a central focus on LSE and considers it to be a primary etiological factor in many forms of psychopathology. In the words of Ellis (1965), "Perhaps the most common self-defeating belief of a highly disturbed patient is his conviction that he is a worthless, inadequate individual who essentially is undeserving of self-respect and happiness" (p. 1).

We endorse Ellis's statement and suggest that most clients who seek mental health treatment have self-esteem problems that are either primary or concomitant to other concerns. An explanation of how LSE fits into various emotional–behavioral problems is given later in this chapter, but first it is appropriate to describe self-rating more extensively.

As mentioned earlier, the ideational process by which individuals create LSE and accompanying emotional disturbance is termed "self-rating"—the tendency to rate one's acts, behaviors, and performances as good or bad and to generalize this evaluation to one's entire worth. It is a habitual tendency that may occur without the individual's awareness and can exist in episodic bursts or as a chronic and continuous stream of meaning that may monopolize the mind.

Ellis (1977b) contends that all human beings are predisposed to self-rating, and there is a significant amount of support for his claim. The clinician need not ask *if* the client self-rates, but rather *how much* and *in what manner*. Poorly adjusted individuals chronically engage in self-rating and make it a way of life, and even the most stable people self-rate now and then. For example, we therapists might only rarely put ourselves down for making an everyday goof, but if someone else criticizes our therapy they'd better look out! We tie our self-worth to our therapeutic expertise, and we angrily defend our perceived competence and/or criticize ourselves for not reaching high standards of success.

Self-rating varies not only in degree but also in form. While each person probably has her or his own way of self-rating, and it is imperative that the empathic therapist decipher these unique pathologies, it is also possible to identify common forms of self-rating. One fairly standard form for adolescents is a preoccupation with physical appearance. A male college student in therapy with one of the authors is an illustrative case. He walks across campus with his eyes darting from one male to the next, continuously comparing his appearance to theirs. He gives particular attention to couples, asking himself the question, "Would that girl choose me over the guy she's with?" This form of self-rating is not unusual, and for most adolescents it passes as they learn to accept their physical appearance.

Another common form of self-rating was demonstrated by a female client who drove herself toward an ideal self-image. When her performances and character- istics were not close approximations of the ideal person she *demanded* she be, she would experience acute depression. At other times, when fearing that she would not measure up to her ideal image, she would have anxiety attacks. The seriousness of her striving was directly expressed one day when the therapist asked, "How would you feel if I told you there was a ceiling on your develop- ment and you would never reach your ideal self, and that you must live the rest of your life just the way you are?" The client thought for a moment and then said in a very convincing and determined tone, "I wouldn't want to live any longer."

This case is a classic example of what Horney (1950) has termed the "ideal self" in neurotic adjustment. Some people have such a deficit in self-esteem that they create a perfect self to strive toward, a self that is undeniably of high worth. It represents an overcompensation for their perceived low worth and serves as the criterion for self-rating.

A third form of self-rating, which usually leads to LSE, guilt, and depression, is comparing oneself to inflexible and unrealistic moral and religious standards and then condemning oneself for not being perfectly moral and saintly. The pathology in this form of self-rating does not lie in morality or religion but in the idea that one is first and foremost worthless and that the only redemption and route to self-worth is attainment of perfect morality and sainthood.

Recently a client sought help for just such a problem. He was a bright and overly conscientious graduate student who was being strongly influenced by a fundamentalist religious sect. He was laden with guilt and anxiety, and had periodic flights of panic. Every day offered him more evidence that he was a "lost soul": he had not *totally* given his life to the church; he suspected that some of his behavior was motivated by unconscious, immoral motives; and he couldn't read God's "signs" as well as his religious friends. Seeking therapy for his emotional problems was also a sinful act, because he had been told that true Christians "put their lives in the hands of the Lord."

Within the forms and styles of self-rating there are some similar cognitive characteristics. Excessive personalization and introspection are usually present, as an overabundance of stimuli are examined for their relationship to one's self and value. Also, Beck (1976) and Berger (1974) advise clinicians to look for thinking disorders such as overgeneralization, dichotomous reasoning, polarized thinking, and adherence to absolutistic rules. These mechanisms create distortions of reality, and compounding this genesis are existing irrational beliefs noted earlier.

To summarize, RET theory says that self-rating is a uniquely human trait that causes defensiveness and LSE and precipitates a host of other emotional–behavioral disturbances. Self-rating is an irrational cognitive process based on unprovable self-esteem questions, illogical reasoning, and bonafide thinking disorders.

Approval and Performance Anxiety

Two criteria that people frequently use as indicators of self-worth are approval from others and successful performances. The irrational inferences are "I'm of value if others value me" and "I'm worthwhile because I am good at this performance and because others tell me I'm good when I perform well."

People who use others' approval and excellent performances as self-rating criteria are putting their self-worth on the line at all times. They are constantly under threat, and therefore experience an abundance of anxiety. Unfortunately this anxiety tends to fulfill their worst expectations because it causes them to be socially inept and clumsy and overly subservient and to behave in other unattractive ways. As for performances, anxiety can ruin proficiency, and even if individuals can somehow produce a high-level performance their anxiety is hardly worth the price. In RET the stream of meaning behind approval and performance anxiety is brought to awareness, challenged, and worked through. Although each person has unique properties in her or his mediational flow, the four themes of irrationality are usually prominent, as expressed in the following statements:

1. "I must have their approval; it would be *terrible* to have them dislike me. I *couldn't stand* that; if they don't like me it must mean there's something wrong with me—that I'm *not worthy* of their approval."
2. "Since this performance is terribly important to me, I've just *got to* do well; I *can't* be satisfied with a mediocre showing; if I don't do well it will prove how ordinary I am, that I'm not really good at anything, just an *incompetent*."

Approval and performance anxiety are LSE symptoms brought on by self-rating. They sometimes indicate a primary self-esteem problem, and frequently they reveal LSE as a concomitant to other first-order problems.

Self-downing Depression

Most clinicians are trained to treat depression solely as an affective disturbance with secondary symptoms. In contrast to this view, the work of Beck (1972, 1976), Ellis (1962), and Seligman (1975) posits that the distorted views of depressed persons are central to the development and maintenance of their disturbance.

Self-rating is one of the major cognitive dimensions associated with depression. While anticipation of being shown to be worthless leads to anxiety, actually putting yourself down or rating yourself as bad for an act or any other reason will produce guilt and depression. In fact, the anxiety–depression sequence is a typical pattern for people with long-standing emotional problems, for they get anxious before a performance because they may find themselves worthless, and they make themselves depressed afterward by concluding they are worthless.

Clinicians make a critical mistake when they fail to see self-downing in depression. It is easier to see the client's demandingness and awfulizing, such as in the following monologue: "Life is just overwhelming; I lost my job, my wife left me, what's the use in going on. . . . There's nothing to live for." In this brief expression the depressed person exhibits the attitude that life should be easier, a catastrophic fate has been unfairly dumped on him, and the future will be just as bad. Also hidden among these depressive ideas is self-downing:

- Life is just overwhelming, *and I'm too weak to handle it.*
- I lost my job, *because I'm so incompetent.*
- My wife left me, *showing that I'm unlovable; she discovered what a louse I am.*
- There's nothing to live for, *I'm so worthless my life doesn't have a value to anyone else, not even to me.*

Sometimes depressed individuals are also guilty, and they do more than advocate their own lack of value; in fact, they promote their badness. By "self-blaming" they entertain the nonsequitur of "I am despicable, totally and forever, because I did a bad act." This attitude leads to acute guilt and depression, and the clinician should watch for suicidal thoughts and plans.

Secondary Gain and Self-rating

Genuine self-rating and blaming leads to serious levels of anxiety, guilt, and depression—a level of distress that is debilitating. The people doing this self-rating are often not aware of their cognitive habit, and they ignorantly express a true belief in their unworthiness without realizing what they are saying. Their irrational beliefs and self-rating are hidden between the lines and symbolically expressed, and only on occasion do they slip out.

Another type of self-rating has different signs. The level of emotional distress is problematic but not chronic, and the self-raters openly discuss their LSE. These are often signs of self-rating that have become a neurotic way of life, a mode of behavior that is rewarded by secondary gains such as sympathy and attention from others, relief from responsibilities, and an avoidance of other impending problems such as marital difficulties, decisions, or career failures. Masochistic self-blamers have a particularly interesting secondary gain. They admonish themselves but then follow up this condemnation with the hidden idea that "I'm good for recognizing how bad I am and punishing myself."

Secondary gains are not the only reason for clients to dwell on their LSE during therapy. Their self-flagellating tactic may actually be camouflaging more threatening issues, and the therapist must cut through this defensive maneuver.

In a recent supervision session one of the authors listened to an audiotape of a female client who initiated and engaged the therapist in a discussion of her LSE. The supervisor's sense of "something amiss" grew; after finally learning that the LSE discussion had extended over two sessions, the pieces fell together. By reevaluating the case a new diagnosis was reached; the client had been *demanding* rather than self-rating. Shoulds, oughts, and musts were responsible for more distress than self-rating, and when the therapist followed this diagnostic path the case quickly improved. Though the client offered some resistance at first, she quickly gained insight into her demandingness, and emotional and behavioral changes followed as the therapist and client entered the "working-through stage" of RET.

Self-rating and Anger Problems

Another set of problems that often involves self-rating has to do with anger. Grieger (1977) has described an anger reaction that has LSE and self-rating at its core (see Chapter 7). The syndrome begins with one's self-esteem being tied to external criteria (approval, performance, etc.) and the anxiety one feels when these criteria are threatened. Instead of focusing on one's self-worth and feeling anxious or depressed, however, the angry individual takes the protective course of condemning the threatening agent. With defensively aggressive behavior the individual attacks to protect his or her self-esteem.

This kind of defensive anger is difficult to diagnose, because the irrational themes of demandingness, awfulizing, and condemnation of others are all involved. But the reason for these themes—the reason most hidden from the angry person—is a threat to self-esteem. For example, in response to disrespectful treatment the person with ego or self-worth anger concludes, "Their actions show disrespect, like I'm not significant and therefore I must not be significant. Those bums shouldn't do such an awful thing to me; I'll show them!"

Self-worth anger illustrates how self-rating interacts with other irrational themes to create a formidable emotional–behavioral problem. It also shows how self-rating and LSE can be hidden at the deepest levels of a neurotic difficulty that seems to belie insecurity. When dealing with anger and aggression clinicians may want to heed Ellis's (1977a) advice: "The first, and perhaps the most important of the emotive methods of overcoming anger, consists of unconditional self-acceptance or self-acknowledgment" (p. 8).

Procrastination and Self-esteem

Procrastination is one of those "little problems" that can mirror larger psychological difficulties. That is, clients at mental health centers and other psychiatric facilities frequently present themselves as "basket cases," completely debilitated by anxiety, depression, or whatever. As they describe their symptoms and complaints, they say in passing, "I can't get anything done; I'm always late; I've put off this appointment for months; somehow I just can't get myself to do the things I want to do," and so forth. Therapists don't give procrastination as the diagnosis in such cases, but procrastination may well be a microcosm of the client's overall difficulties.

At counseling centers and guidance clinics procrastination is more often the sole presenting concern; sometimes it is so commonplace that counselors take it for granted. In academic settings where deadlines abound for tests and term papers, procrastination is indigenous to student life.

There are many ideational antecedents for procrastination, and Ellis and Knaus (1977) have devoted an entire book to the subject. A lack of self-discipline and low frustration tolerance are the most well-known causes of procrastination, but self-rating and LSE also give rise to procrastination, and in a two-step manner. First, individuals are afraid to do a certain act because they unknowingly fear failure or rejection and sense a threat to their self-esteem. So they put off the threatening act, even though its completion would have desirable consequences for them, for fear of proving their worthlessness. Second, they observe the delay they have chosen, find it disgusting, and condemn themselves for it, further fostering LSE.

Miscellaneous Emotional Disturbances and Self-rating

As mentioned earlier, there is a host of emotional disturbances and symptoms that can be precipitated, primarily or in part, by self-rating. In some of these disturbances self-rating is so obvious that laypeople can spot it, but in others the client's symptoms may seem too bizarre or serious to be linked with LSE. The following case examples will be offered to show how self-rating can be unobtrusively present in psychopathology.

Frank was a young man in his early twenties whose complement of problems justified the label "obsessive–compulsive neurosis." Of keenest concern to Frank were sensory obsessions that interfered with and sometimes prohibited his work and social life. These obsessions consisted of counting eyeblinks, swallows, breaths, and having obsessive bladder sensations that prompted dry-run bathroom trips. Frank was also susceptible to worrying in general, and an irrational fear about being accosted by homosexuals caused paranoialike suspicions.

There were a few situational/learning circumstances in Frank's background that could explain some of the origins for his symptoms. The onset of bladder sensations was traced back to an academic examination that was critical to his professional career; he sat through four hours of testing while fighting off bladder pains, the urge to urinate, and a fear of impairing his performance if he took time to go to the bathroom. Another historical origin was a childhood experience involving an apparent pedophiliac, and a joking comment years later from an adolescent friend who commented that Frank had the physical appearance of a "fag." Frank put these two experiences together and created the fear that he somehow attracted homosexuals and that he might have latent homosexual strivings.

The mediational core of Frank's obsessional symptoms was twofold. A symptom would always begin with "awfulizing" thoughts about something that he feared might happen, such as flunking a test, being socially criticized, or becoming a homosexual. As he then became anxious he would begin to fear that this anxiety would bring on an obsession and, true to his prophesy, it would. The scenario ended as Frank obsessed for hours.

Relaxation training, desensitization, and RET were successful in helping Frank to reduce his awfulizing and his approval and performance anxieties. He learned to dispute many of his irrational ideas; through homework assignments he confronted and worked through obsessional tendencies, and after 10 sessions his symptoms were minimal. Even when anxiety and obsessions did crop up he could effectively send them away with concentrated rational thinking. Both Frank and the therapist were pleased with the success of their efforts: Presenting problems were overcome. There had been a costly omission in therapy, however. They did not work long enough or hard enough on Frank's LSE and self-rating. Though this aspect of Frank's problems was touched, most of their time in therapy was taken up with other forms of distortion.

Two years later Frank returned to therapy with what seemed like a new set of obsessional tendencies. He was being influenced by a fundamentalist religious sect, experienced excessive-guilt and anxiety, and found himself going to extreme lengths to prove his honesty and morality to others. To make a long story short, this time the therapist directly challenged Frank's self-rating practices, and together a successful assault was made on his low opinion of himself. This strategy should have been vigorously employed in Frank's first therapy stint, for self-rating had always been behind his sensory obsessions. It was the irrational foundation that fostered the approval and performance anxiety that eventually escalated into obsessions.

Another set of emotional disturbances that can obfuscate self-rating is relationship and sexual difficulties. Symptoms such as volatile emotions, poor communication, and psychosomatic ailments tend to mask the fact that the self-esteem of both partners is critical to their relationship. When one or both partners have LSE and use the other's behavior for self-rating purposes, a weak and dependent relationship will develop. This point has been beautifully expressed in Gibran's (1976, p. 16) *The Prophet:*

> Give your hearts, but not into each other's keeping.
> For only the hand of life can contain your hearts.
> And stand together yet not too near together:
> For the pillars of the temple stand apart,
> And the oak tree and the cypress grow not in each others shadow.

Hank and Millie's is a tragic story of a couple in which both parties had LSE. They had been married for 18 years, were in their middle forties, and throughout their marriage had maintained an ongoing series of hostile battles. Each partner felt insecure and demanded a constant flow of affection from the other. They expected each other to be completely devoted and to meet their every whim. When their partner failed to meet these demands and expectations, they felt hurt (a loss of esteem), condemned the partner, and retaliated by withholding affection (including sex) and making cruel, derogatory remarks.

Marital therapy for Hank and Millie was unsuccessful because in each other's presence they refused to do anything but battle. Individual therapy for each one has been of limited success, but only when the therapist exerts full intervention to self-esteem. Relative calm arrives in their marriage only on rare occasions, when each has had a profitable therapy session and has temporarily stopped self-rating and rating the other party.

RET FOR SELF-ESTEEM PROBLEMS

The bulk of this chapter has explained self-esteem from an RET perspective, and the outline of a diagnostic structure has been sketched. Left untouched, however, has been therapeutic treatment. How can self-esteem problems be effectively resolved through psychotherapy? Grieger and Boyd (1979) have answered this "how" question at length; to conclude this chapter an overview of RET for self-esteem problems will be offered. As has been presented, the demon that generates LSE is the human predisposition to self-rate, and the ideal solution to the self-rating is a cessation of self-rating and the introduction of self-acceptance. To bring about this, or an approximation thereof, RET progresses through four stages that influence the client to make constructive changes in the cognitive, emotive, and behavioral realms.

The first stage of RET, *psychodiagnosis,* is aimed at helping clients describe their emotional disturbances while the therapist simultaneously is soliciting diagnostically relevant information. A diagnosis is reached when the therapist understands the overall disturbance via the A-B-C paradigm. Diagnosis can be made quickly by experienced RET therapists when client problems are typical, though the therapist remains open and may alter a diagnosis later in therapy. A longer diagnostic stage may be required for unfamiliar or complex disturbances. Regarding self-esteem problems, the diagnostic tasks are to categorize self-rating as a primary or secondary cognitive process, to ferret out the client's idiosyncratic content in self-rating, and to determine if and how other irrational beliefs are contributing to the disturbance.

Following diagnosis is the *insight* stage of RET. Here the objective is to promote clients' understanding of their irrational beliefs and the way they use them to create emotional disturbance. Insights pertaining to LSE revolve around self-rating; clients learn that they do self-rate, how they self-rate, and the emotional and behavioral consequences of self-rating. Attention is given to the antecedents of LSE only if there is an unusual clinical reason to do so. Awareness of past history does not lift present-day disturbances or the self-rating habit, but sometimes a client gains motivation to overcome self-rating if she or he can see that it was encouraged and practiced by significant others.

The *working-through* stage of RET overlaps with the insight stage. Working through consists of persistently exerting efforts that are therapeutically designed to rehabilitate the cognitive, emotional, and behavioral aspects of a psychological problem. RET is directed at the tripartite constitution of self-esteem problems: irrational beliefs and cognitive distortions, emotional and imaginal operations, and overt behavior. There is a host of techniques for each modality, such as cognitively disputing irrational beliefs and replacing them with rational attitudes, practicing emotive-imagery exercises, and behavioral homework assignments that force one to confront and give up self-defeating actions. To illustrate, clients having LSE are usually asked within the RET session to challenge and logically argue against their self-rating ideas, or perhaps to switch roles with the therapist and solve a mock LSE problem that parallels their own. Shame-attacking assignments, an emotive method, encourage LSE clients deliberately to do something they neurotically consider shameful and to thus confront, experience, and defuse a self-rating criterion. A procrastinating self-rater might use the behavioral technique of self-managed reward and penalty in order to get things done.

As the working-through stage progresses there are therapeutic changes in the ideas, emotions, and behavior of LSE clients. A most important change is to slow down the self-rating process and to wage a battle against it. Clients learn to notice when they are self-rating and to dispute these cognitions actively *in vivo.*

Behavior begins to shift toward the confident–assertive realm, through effort rather than magic. New actions may feel foreign and take clients into threatening experiences, such as assertively returning a malfunctioning apparatus to a sharp-tongued store clerk, or entering a competition where your error-laden performance will be seen by a crowd of spectators. From such experiences comes the psychological freedom to be oneself.

As cognition and behavior are changing, so also is emotion. Anxiety, guilt, depression, and anger lift in proportion to the decrease in self-rating and the increase in self-acceptance. The tripartite resolution to LSE problems can snowball upward, cognitively, emotively, and behaviorally, just as the self-rating process takes one downward.

The last RET stage, *re-education,* is entered and becomes conjoint with working through, when clients' therapeutic changes have begun. The purpose of re-education is to strengthen and ingrain rational ways of thinking and behaving, to help clients acquire additional skills (e.g., assertion, decision making) that will assist them in overcoming their disturbances, and to help them synthesize their therapeutic learnings and generalize these to their lives and future.

Elegant RET solutions are developed in the re-education stage, as clients make changes in their life philosophies. The obsessive–compulsive client cited twice in this chapter has made significant shifts in his career aspirations and religious beliefs. He has taken much of the irrationality out of both. No longer a work-aholic, he does not feel compelled to be corporate president and has chosen a life based on personal rather than commercial values. Spiritually, his RET assault on self-condemnation has opened up an inner world of self-acceptance that he now supports through his religion.

EPILOGUE

Self-esteem problems are one of our oldest and deadliest enemies—the price we pay for being the only animal species with self-consciousness. For over 2,000 years we have known the enemy is within us, that certain interpretations of events lead to emotional disturbance; yet we have done so little about this phenomenon. It seems fitting and certainly overdue that the same cognitive capacity by which we have berated ourselves for so long is turned toward logic and reason for the attainment of self-acceptance, happiness, and contentment. This is an ideal worth our best efforts, and our emotional health is riding on the outcome.

REFERENCES

Adler, A. *The practice and theory of individual psychology.* New York: Harcourt, 1927.
Adler, A. *Understanding human nature.* New York: Fawcett World, 1974.
Beck, A. T. *Depression: Causes and treatment.* Philadelphia: University of Pennsylvania Press, 1972.

Beck, A. T. *Cognitive therapy and the emotional disorders.* New York: International Universities Press, 1976.

Berger, E. Irrational self-censure: The problem and its correction. *Personnel and Guidance Journal,* 1974, *53*(3), 193–198.

Berne, E. *Games people play.* New York: Grove Press, 1964.

Branden, N. *Psychology of self-esteem.* New York: Bantam, 1971.

Coopersmith, S. *The antecedents of self-esteem.* San Francisco: W. H. Freeman, 1967.

Ellis, A. *Reason and emotion in psychotherapy.* New York: Lyle Stuart, 1962.

Ellis, A. *Sex without guilt.* New York: Lyle Stuart, 1965.

Ellis, A. *Growth through reason.* Hollywood, Calif.: Wilshire Books, 1973.

Ellis, A. *Humanistic psychotherapy: The rational–emotive approach.* New York: McGraw-Hill, 1974.

Ellis, A. *How to live with a "neurotic."* New York: Crown, 1975.

Ellis, A. RET abolishes most of the human ego. *Psychotherapy: Theory, Research and Practice,* 1976, *13*(4), 343–348.

Ellis, A. *How to live with and without anger.* New York: Thomas Y. Crowell, 1977. (a)

Ellis, A. Rational–emotive therapy: Research data that supports the clinical and personality hypotheses of RET and other modes of cognitive-behavior therapy. *The Counseling Psychologist,* 1977, *7,* (1), 2–42. (b)

Ellis, A., & Harper, R. A. *A new guide to rational living.* Hollywood, Calif.: Wilshire Books, 1975.

Ellis, A., & Knaus, W. *Overcoming procrastination.* New York: Institute for Rational Living, 1977.

Freud, S. *Collected papers.* New York: Collier, 1963.

Fromm, E. *Man for himself.* New York: Rinehart, 1947.

Gibran, Kahlil. *The prophet.* New York: Knopf, 1976.

Grieger, R. M. An existential component of anger. *Rational Living,* 1977, *12*(2), 3–8.

Grieger, R. M., & Boyd, J. *Rational–emotive therapy: A skills-based approach.* New York: Van Nostrand Reinhold, 1979.

Horney, K. *Neurosis and human growth.* New York: W. W. Norton, 1950.

James, W. *Principles of psychology.* New York: Holt, 1890.

Jung, C. *The practice of psychotherapy.* New York: Pantheon Press, 1954.

Mead, G. H. *Mind, self and society.* Chicago: University of Chicago Press, 1934.

Perls, F. *Gestalt therapy verbatim.* Lafayette, Calif.: Real People Press, 1969.

Rogers, C. R. *Client-centered psychotherapy.* Boston: Houghton Mifflin, 1951.

Rogers, C. R. *On becoming a person.* Boston: Houghton Mifflin, 1961.

Schneider, D. J., & Turkat, D. Self-presentation following success or failure: Defensive self-esteem. *Journal of Personality,* 1975, *43,* 127–135.

Seligman, M. *Helplessness: On depression, development and death.* San Francisco: W. H. Freeman, 1975.

Sullivan, H. S. *The interpersonal theory of psychiatry.* New York: W. W. Norton, 1953.

10

Application of Rational– Emotive Therapy to Love Problems*

Albert Ellis

Rational–emotive therapy (RET) is largely a theory and practice of interpersonal relationships and most probably would never have been created and developed had I not been absorbed, from childhood onward, with my own love and relating problems (Ellis, 1965a, 1972b, 1983). Because of my personal interest in love, I was motivated to do a considerable amount of pioneering research on the emotion of love (Ellis, 1949a, 1949b, 1949c, 1950, 1951, 1954, 1961). I also began in 1955 to focus RET clinical work on helping people with their love, marital, and sex problems (Ellis, 1957, 1958, 1960, 1962, 1963a, 1963b, 1963c, 1965b, 1965c, 1972, 1973c, 1975b; Ellis & Harper, 1961a, 1961b). Some of the early RET clinicians also devoted themselves to problems of love and interpersonal relations and made significant contributions to these areas (Ard, 1967; Ard & Ard, 1969; Blazier, 1975; Demorest, 1971; Grossack, 1976; Harper, 1960, 1963; Harper & Stokes, 1971; Hauck, 1972, 1975, 1977, 1981; Hibbard, 1975, 1977; Maultsby, 1975; McClellan & Stieper, 1973; and Shibles, 1978).

As a result of this emphasis, RET has always been especially concerned with the diagnosis and treatment of love problems, and I shall present in this chapter relevant theories and practices.

---

*This chapter was originally published in Albert Ellis & Michael Bernard (Eds.), *Clinical Applications of Rational Emotive Therapy* (New York: Plenum, 1985).

SUPER-ROMANTIC LOVE

Romantic, passionate love, or intense in-lovedness has existed from time immemorial but received an enormous boost in the Middle Ages and has become a near-requisite of mating or marriage in the twentieth century (Burgess & Locke, 1953; de Rougemont, 1956; Ellis, 1954, 1961; Ellis & Harper, 1961a; Finck, 1887; Folsom, 1935; Hunt, 1959; Lucka, 1915; Murstein, 1974). It has enormous advantages, in that romantic lovers often experience extremely pleasurable feelings and are motivated to great efforts and outstanding performances.

Romantic love generally is acknowledged to include several strong factors, especially idealization of the beloved; a high degree of exclusivity; intense feelings of attachment, usually with a strong sexual component; the powerful conviction that the love will last forever; obsession with thoughts of the beloved; a strong desire to mate with the beloved; an urge to do and to sacrifice almost anything to win the beloved; the conviction that romantic love is the most important thing in the world; and the belief that one can practically merge with one's beloved and become one with him or her (Christie, 1969; Ellis, 1949a, 1949b, 1949c, 1950, 1951, 1954, 1961; Hunt, 1959; Katz, 1976; Kremen & Kremen, 1971; Stendhal, 1947; Tennov, 1979).

Devotees of romance tend to create and maintain a number of irrational beliefs (iB's) or myths that interfere with their intimate relationships and with their happiness. Here, for example, are some of the common romantic myths of our culture:

1. You can passionately love one, and only one, person at a time (Ellis, 1954).
2. True romantic love lasts forever.
3. Deep feelings of romantic love insure a stable and compatible marriage.
4. Sex without romantic love is unethical and unsatisfying. Sex and love always go together (Bach & Wyden, 1969; Ellis, 1954, 1961).
5. Romantic love can easily be made to develop and grow in marital relationships.
6. Romantic love is far superior to conjugal love, friendship love, nonsexual love, and other kinds of love, and you hardly exist if you do not experience it intensely.
7. If you lose the person you love romantically you must feel deeply grieved or depressed for a long period of time and cannot legitimately fall in love again until this long mourning period is over.
8. It is necessary to perceive love all the time to know someone loves you (Katz, 1976).

When people devoutly hold these kinds of myths they tend to put them into personal rules of behavior and to imbed them into absolutistic *shoulds* and *musts*.

Thus they tell themselves (or implicitly believe), "I must only romantically love one person at a time and am a phony if I love other persons simultaneously." "I have to marry only a person I romantically love and will be desolate if he or she does not mate with me." "My romantic feelings must last forever, and there is something very wrong with me if they fade after a relatively short time. That proves I did not *really* love." "If I do not experience enduring, intense romantic love, I cannot be satisfied with other kinds of love feelings and will have, at most, only a mildly happy existence." "My partner must love me completely and passionately at all times or else he or she doesn't really love me."

RET, when faced with highly unrealistic romantics who make themselves anxious, depressed, hostile, or self-pitying because of their holding myths and irrational beliefs like those just listed, uses two main modes of disputing:

1. It shows people how their beliefs are anti-empirical and gives them evidence of their invalidity. Thus, it presents data that one can positively love two or more people simultaneously (Murstein, 1974); that romantic love usually fades, especially when the lovers live together (Finck, 1887); that deep feelings of love not only do not insure a stable and compatible marriage but often interfere with it (de Rougemont, 1956); and that romantic love is by no means always superior to and more happiness producing than other kinds of love (Lederer & Jackson, 1968).

2. As it does with people's irrational beliefs about other aspects of their lives, RET particularly reveals and disputes their absolutistic *shoulds* and *musts* about romantic love. It shows them that, no matter how much they legitimately *prefer* passionate involvements, they do not *have to* achieve or maintain them; and that when they lose out in the early or later stages of romance, that is highly inconvenient and very sad and deplorable but is not *awful* and *terrible* (Ellis, 1957, 1962, 1975b, 1984; Ellis & Becker, 1983; Ellis & Grieger, 1977; Ellis & Harper, 1975).

In addition to these cognitive techniques for helping people surrender their self-defeating myths and musts about romantic love, RET uses a number of other emotive and behavioral methods. Thus, it may show clients that their relationship with their therapist is nonromantic but still satisfying and helpful; it demonstrates that the therapist can respect and accept them *whether or not* they are romantically successful; it gives them *in vivo* homework assignments, such as allowing themselves to become romantically involved with some "wrong" partners and to see that they do not have to live with or marry these partners; and it may provide them with skill training to help them encounter, communicate with, and win the love of romantic partners (Ellis, 1962, 1973b, 1976, 1979b, 1984). It specifically deals with obsessive–compulsive love, as shown in the next section of this chapter.

OBSESSIVE–COMPULSIVE LOVE, OR "LIMERENCE"

Extreme obsessive–compulsive love, or what Tennov (1979) has called "limerence," is usually but not necessarily romantic. Thus, a mother can obsessively love her son or daughter, an entrepreneur may compulsively love his work, and an adolescent may obsessively and compulsively worship his or her same-sex friend without wanting to have sex with or to marry this friend. For the most part, however, "limerence" is an extreme form of romantic love that frequently includes:

1. Disturbed behaviors such as obsessive and intensive thinking about the beloved;
2. The dire need for reciprocation;
3. Mood swings dependent on the lover's interpretation of the beloved's reciprocation;
4. Severe feelings of anxiety and depression when the beloved doesn't seem to requite one's love;
5. Idealization of the beloved and refusal to see or abide by some of his or her deficiencies;
6. Eagerness to do foolhardy things to win or keep the beloved's favor (Tennov, 1979).

According to RET, obsessive–compulsive love or limerence normally includes lovers' devoutly and absolutistically holding one or more of these irrational beliefs (iB's):

1. "I *must* have my beloved's reciprocation, or else I am an undeserving, inadequate person!"
2. "It is *horrible* to lose my beloved. I *can't stand* it!"
3. "If my beloved does not care for me, or if he or she dies, life has no value and I might as well be dead!"
4. "My beloved is the *only* one in the world for me, and his or her love *alone* can make me and my life worthwhile!"
5. "Because I *must* win my beloved's favor and *have to be* miserable without it, it is worth doing *anything,* including seriously risking my life, to win him or her!"

These iB's have been presented throughout the RET literature (Ellis, 1962, 1973b, 1973c, 1979b, 1984; Ellis & Grieger, 1977; Ellis & Whiteley, 1979).

RET employs a number of cognitive methods in helping people overcome their obsessive–compulsive disturbances about love, including these:

1. It shows them how actively and persistently to dispute their irrational beliefs (iB's) and to exchange them for relative preferences (Ellis, 1957, 1962, 1973a, 1973b, 1975b, 1984).

2. RET shows them how to use rational beliefs (rB's) or coping statements and how to think them through and keep repeating them until they truly feel them. Typical rational self-statements are: "I would like to have my beloved's reciprocation but I don't *need* it to live and be happy!" "It would be *unfortunate* if I lost my beloved, but it wouldn't be *horrible* and I *could* stand it!" "My beloved is not the *only* one I could care for, and I could have a worthwhile existence even if she or he did *not* love me!"

3. RET shows people how to use cognitive distraction techniques—such as Jacobsen's (1942) progressive relaxation method, Yoga, or meditation—to divert them from intrusive thoughts about their beloved.

4. RET shows obsessive–compulsive lovers how they can *also* focus on caring for other people besides their one "true" beloved and can thereby be less obsessive.

5. RET helps people to make out a list and steadily review several disadvantages of their overattachment to their beloved and several advantages of caring for some other people, interests, and involvements, helping them to become less obsessed with one special beloved.

6. RET particularly shows obsessive–compulsive lovers (or "limerents") how to work on their secondary symptoms of disturbance. On the primary level, they make themselves obsessed and compulsive; and then, secondarily, they note this and tell themselves irrational beliefs (iB's) such as, "I *must* not be obsessed! It's stupid of me to be irrationally in love, and I am therefore a *stupid, worthless person!*" RET shows them how to dispute these self-downing iB's by asking themselves "Why *must* I not be obsessed?" and "Where is the evidence that I am a *stupid, worthless person* for being compulsively in love?" By thereby helping them to accept themselves in spite of their foolish behavior, RET alleviates their secondary disturbances and gives them leeway to return to working against and surrendering their primary obsessive–compulsive attachments (Ellis, 1962, 1979a, 1980; Ellis & Harper, 1975).

RET also employs a number of emotive and behavioral methods with obsessive–compulsive lovers. To begin with, the RET practitioner is expected to accept such lovers unconditionally, in spite of their crazy addiction to love. Then, through role-playing methods, RET shows them how to resist the unreasonable demands of their partners; it gives them the homework assignments of resisting these demands and shows them how to reinforce themselves for resisting; and it shows them how to penalize themselves (e.g., by burning money) when they indulge too much in thinking about their beloved or in phoning him or her too frequently (Ellis & Abrahms, 1978).

JEALOUSY AND POSSESSIVENESS

We may distinguish between two forms of jealousy: rational and irrational. We are rationally jealous when we desire a continuing, and sometimes a monogamous, relationship with our beloved and when we are concerned about its being disrupted by his or her loving (or paying too much attention to) someone else, thereby depriving us of the lover's presence and probably threatening us with complete loss. When we are rationally jealous, we feel frustrated and disappointed when our beloved pays "too much" attention to others, but we are not severely disturbed.

We are irrationally (or insensately) jealous when we absolutistically demand or command that our beloved almost exclusively care for and pay attention to us and when we are horrified at the thought of his or her being emotionally intimate with and perhaps leaving us for another person. When irrationally jealous, we tend to feel seriously anxious, hostile, and/or depressed; to ruminate obsessively about the grave danger of losing our beloved; to be very suspicious of her or his actions; to keep demanding tokens and words of affection from him or her; and to try to be with him or her practically all the time (Clanton & Smith, 1977; O'Neill & O'Neill, 1972).

RET hypothesizes that insensately jealous and possessive people tend to have several dogmatically held irrational Beliefs (iB's) that create their jealousy, such as:

1. "I must have a guarantee that you strongly love only me and will continue to do so indefinitely!"
2. "If you do not love me as I love you, there must be something radically wrong with me, and I hardly deserve your affection."
3. "Because I love you intensely and keep being devoted to you, you have to return my love always, you will cause me great suffering if you don't, and you then will be a rotten, damnable person."
4. "Unless I have the absolute certainty that you adore me and always will, my life is too disorganized and unpleasant and it hardly seems worthwhile going on with it" (Ellis, 1972a; Harper, 1963; Hauck, 1981).

When people are irrationally jealous, RET particularly tries to help them recognize their irrational beliefs (iB's) and change them for rational beliefs (rB's). Thus, it shows them how to dispute their irrationalities and to wind up with these more realistic and undogmatic philosophies of love and life:

1. "I would very much like you to care for me as I care for you, but there is no reason you *have to* do so. I can still be happy, though not as happy, if you don't."
2. "You may well be the best love partner I am likely to find during my lifetime and I therefore highly value your love and companionship. But if I

somehow lose you, I can almost certainly love others and achieve a satisfying, loving relationship with one of them."

3. "Although I love you dearly and am quite willing to devote myself to you, my love does not oblige you to love me in return or to restrict yourself for me. You have a perfect right to your own feelings and behaviors regarding me, and, since I cannot make you change them, I will try to accept them as best I can and still keep loving you."

4. "If you lie to me or otherwise contradict the feelings of love you say you have for me and betray our relationship, I shall consider your behavior unloving and untrustworthy, but I shall not damn you as a person for acting in this undesirable manner" (Ellis, 1972a; Harper, 1963; Hauck, 1981).

RET uses several other cognitive methods in helping people combat their self-defeating feelings of jealousy:

1. It encourages them to make a comprehensive list of the disadvantages of jealousy, possessiveness, and hatred and a list of the advantages of rational jealousy and feelings of concern and frustration. It also encourages them to make a list of the advantages of agreed-upon open relationships that allow both partners to engage in nonmonogamous relationships and to review these advantages carefully when one of the partners feels jealous. Some of the advantages of open relationships are (a) they lead to a greater variety of sex and love experiences and to the alleviation of boredom and monotony, (b) they provide maximum freedom and minimum restriction on both partners, (c) they provide satisfactions when the two mates are apart for days or weeks, (d) they sometimes help the mates appreciate each other more and become more intimate and trusting, (e) they may provide sexual love and experiences and learning that may significantly help both partners grow and mature and relate better to each other, (f) they may satisfy the curiosity of partners who previously have had restricted sexual love and experiences, (g) they may compensate for the sexual and/or love deprivation of one of the mates who may have higher libidinous drives than the other mate, and (h) they may help build the feelings of self-efficacy or achievement confidence of relatively inexperienced partners.

2. RET shows jealous lovers how to set a specific time of day and/or time-limit during which to allow themselves to indulge in jealous thoughts each day. For example, they can permit themselves to indulge in jealous (and homicidal!) ruminations from 8:00 to 8:15 PM each day and can force themselves to think of other things at other times.

3. RET encourages reading assignments that show jealous people that it is possible for people to live intensely and not feel irrationally jealous. Thus, it recommends books like *Sex without Guilt* (Ellis, 1958), *The Civilized Couple's Guide to Extramarital Adventure* (Ellis, 1972a), *Infidelity* (Boylan, 1971),

Jealousy (Clanton & Smith, 1977), *Overcoming Jealousy and Possessiveness* (Hauck, 1981), and *Open Marriage* (O'Neill & O'Neill, 1972).

Emotively, RET uses several methods of helping people to give up their feelings of insensate jealousy, one of which is to employ rational–emotive imagery (Maultsby, 1975; Maultsby & Ellis, 1974). With one of my recent male clients I used it as follows:

THERAPIST: Close your eyes. Now imagine, as intensely as you can, that your wife is actually, as you sometimes now think she is, having an affair with one of your best friends and that she cares for him a great deal but keeps denying that she has any interest in him. But you find love letters from her to him, proving she is in love with him and having steady sex with him. Can you vividly imagine this happening.

CLIENT: Easily! I often imagine something like this.

THERAPIST: Good! How do you honestly feel as you vividly imagine this?

CLIENT: Very incensed. Practically homicidal!

THERAPIST: Good! Now keep imagining this happening and, as you do so, make yourself feel *only* disappointed, *only* sorry—but *not* angry and homicidal.

CLIENT: I'm having difficulty changing my feelings.

THERAPIST: I know. It's hard. But you can do it. I know you can do it. Now change your feeling *only* to disappointment and sorrow.

CLIENT
(AFTER A FEW
MINUTES): All right.

THERAPIST: You're now *only* feeling disappointed and sorry and not incensed? Is that right?

CLIENT: Yes.

THERAPIST: Very good! Open your eyes. Now how did you do that? What did you do to change your feeling?

CLIENT: I . . . think I saw them making love . . . and in our own bed, where my wife and I sleep. And I got very angry! Then I relaxed. Then I got unangry.

THERAPIST: That will work. Relaxing will take away your anger. But it won't make you feel disappointed. What did you do to make yourself feel disappointed?

CLIENT: Oh, yes. That's right. After relaxing I said to myself, "That's really very bad. I can't trust her. But she has a right to love anyone she wants, even him. I hate her making love to him. But it's only sad, it isn't the end of the world. And if she keeps that up, I'll just get another woman who really loves me."

THERAPIST: That was very good! Now what I want is for you to continue to do just what you just did, rational–emotive imagery, at least once a day for the next 30 days. First imagine the worst and let yourself feel very jealous, very angry. Then change your feeling to one of disappointment and sorrow, the same way you just did and other ways that will occur to you. There are many things you can tell yourself to create feelings of disappointment. Yours was a good one, but you can find others, too.

CLIENT: I can?

THERAPIST: Yes, you can. Now will you do this rational–emotive imagery at least once a day for the next 30 days until you become automatically practiced in making yourself feel appropriately disappointed instead of inappropriately homicidal when you imagine your wife being unfaithful?

CLIENT: Yes, I will. But suppose I start feeling anxious and insecure instead of angry?

THERAPIST: Oh, fine. Those feelings usually go with jealousy, too. So if you feel them, do the same things. Let yourself feel very anxious and insecure. Implode those feelings. Then change them to feelings of real concern about your possibly losing your wife—but not of anxiety or overconcern. Make yourself feel very regretful about her possible loss—but not self-downing. Understand?

CLIENT: Yes, I think so.

THERAPIST: Fine. Now go practice rational–emotive imagery at least once a day for the next 30 days.

Emotively, as well, RET uses role playing to help jealous clients confront and work through jealousy-provoking situations. It shows them how to tell themselves, very forcefully, such coping statements as "I *want* my mate to love me and only me, but I can still be happy if he (or she) doesn't!" It gives them unconditional acceptance, even when they are very foolishly jealous, and it shows them how to accept themselves fully when they are at their worst in this respect.

Behaviorally, RET gives clients homework assignments that help contradict their jealous thoughts and feelings. Thus, it encourages them to date partners who are also involved emotionally with other partners. At times, it encourages them to arrange an open relationship with a mate, in the course of which they can actively work through some of their jealous feelings. RET would tend to endorse the behavioral rules of Taylor (1982), who advises jealous lovers: (1) Don't spy or pry. (2) Don't confront or entrap. (3) When you think your partner is having an affair, stay out of it. Or, as we would add in RET, if you are determined to confront or get into a partner's affair, first get rid of your hostility and whining self-pity, and then, and then only, do your confronting.

Using, then, several cognitive, emotive, and behavioral methods, RET helps people retain rational or appropriate feelings of jealousy but to minimize insensate, irrational jealousy and possessiveness.

ENCOUNTERING SUITABLE PARTNERS

Because satisfactory love relationships are often difficult to find, because most people are much more selective about love than they are about companionship and sex, and because long-term high-level love partnerships are hard to maintain, literally millions of would-be lovers rarely or never enjoy enduring intimacy. Social shyness, unassertiveness, and fear of rejection are important blocks to encountering suitable love partners, and RET has always specialized in helping people overcome their blocks.

People who block themselves from meeting a good many potential partners and from eventually narrowing down their intimacies to one or a few almost always profoundly hold the same kind of iB's as other self-defeating individuals hold, especially these three: (1) "I must win the approval of all the highly desirable lovers I encounter, and I am pretty worthless if I don't!" (2) "The partners I select must be considerate and loving to me, and they are rotten people if they aren't!" (3) "Conditions must be arranged so that I fairly easily meet potential lovers; and it is *awful* and I *can't stand* it when these conditions are quite difficult and when they put real blocks in my way!" RET shows shy and procrastinating would-be lovers that they explicitly or implicitly hold these iB's and it teaches them active methods of disputing and overcoming them (Ellis, 1957, 1962, 1971, 1973b, 1973c, 1975b, 1984).

The following is an example of a cognitive dialogue that an RET practitioner would be likely to have with a female client who wants to meet men she might relate to emotionally but who rarely does very much to initiate or facilitate encounters.

THERAPIST: When you see what you consider to be an attractive and personable man at a dance, a party, or other social situation, and you want to talk to him but run away from doing so, what do you tell yourself to make yourself retreat?

CLIENT: I tell myself that he's not for me, that he already has a woman, or something like that.

THERAPIST: Well, that's a rationalization. You're giving yourself an excuse, which seems to be plausible (but really isn't), so that you don't have to talk to him. But what's your *reason* behind your rationalization? What are you really telling yourself that makes you afraid to talk to him?

CLIENT: I don't know.

THERAPIST: Yes, you do! "If I go over and talk to him . . .?" What?

CLIENT: "He may not like me. He may reject me."

THERAPIST: Right! That's what you're saying to yourself. "And if he doesn't like me, if he rejects me . . .?" What?

CLIENT: "I'll never get anyone I want. No good man will want me."

THERAPIST: Yes, that's what you're saying to yourself. But that's an anti-empirical or unrealistic statement that follows from some absolutistic philosophy, from some should or must. What do you think that absolutistic philosophy is?

CLIENT: "I *must* not ever get rejected by a man I really want. I *should* win them all. Otherwise, I'm unlovable and will never get one."

THERAPIST: Right. Now let's go over that set of irrational beliefs. At A, the activating event, you encounter a man you really would like to talk to, probably date, and maybe eventually mate with. At B, your irrational set of beliefs, you tell yourself that you *must* not get rejected by him or any other decent man; that you *should* win every man who is good for you. Then, at C, emotional and behavioral consequence, you feel anxious and you withdraw and refuse to talk to this man.

CLIENT: Yes, that's the way it always seems to go.

THERAPIST: That's the way you *make* it go. But let's get you to make it go otherwise; let's help you to approach many or most men you find desirable.

CLIENT: How?

THERAPIST: First, by going on to D—disputing. Let's you and I now do some active disputing. First of all, why *must* you get all the desirable males you meet? Where is it written that you *should* not get rejected by them?

CLIENT: Uh . . . because it's so uncomfortable not to get what I want.

THERAPIST: So it's uncomfortable! Why *must* you be comfortable?

CLIENT: Because I *want* to be.

THERAPIST: Why *must* you get what you want?

CLIENT: Uh . . . I guess I don't have to.

THERAPIST: "But I really *should!*"

CLIENT (LAUGHS): Yes. I guess I feel I really should.

THERAPIST: And where will that *should* and *must* get you?

CLIENT: Anxious—and withdrawing.

THERAPIST: Exactly! But you'd better go over that, better show yourself, very carefully and in detail, that, as long as you insist that you *must* do well and get what you want, you'll almost inevitably be anxious and withdrawing.

CLIENT: Mmm.

THERAPIST: Yes—Mmm! Suppose you don't get this attractive man—you really try and you still don't get him? How would you feel about that?

CLIENT: Awful!

THERAPIST: Why would it be *awful* to get rejected?

CLIENT: Because I wouldn't like it.

THERAPIST: That's why it would be *bad*. Uncomfortable. A pain in the ass. But why would that badness be *awful?*

CLIENT: Well, I guess it really wouldn't be.

THERAPIST: Why *wouldn't* it be?

CLIENT: Well . . . uh . . . because it would only really be inconvenient. And there are other men available.

THERAPIST: Right. And if it were *awful,* it would be *totally* bad or inconvenient—or 101% bad. And it hardly is that! No matter how inconvenient it is, you can probably always live and be happy, and then look for something *less* inconvenient.

CLIENT: Yes, I suppose so.

THERAPIST: You'd better say that more enthusiastically!

CLIENT: Yes, I guess I could be happy without this one man. But suppose I *never* got a good lover or husband? Could I *then* be happy?

THERAPIST: Why not? You wouldn't be *as* happy as if you did get one. But you could certainly be happy in *some* way, couldn't you?

CLIENT: Oh, yes. I see what you mean. Even if I never succeeded in love I could still be happy in other ways, with other things.

THERAPIST: Damned right!

In this manner, cognitively and philosophically, the therapist keeps showing the client that she *can* risk rejection, and that if she doesn't she's likely to be much *less* happy than if she does. The RET practitioner takes her absolutistic views and her unrealistic derivatives of them, rips them up, and shows her how to dispute them herself and to use the scientific method to keep proving to herself that: (1) She doesn't *have to* find love; (2) it's hardly *horrible* if she doesn't; (3) she *can* stand males rejecting her; (4) her worth as a human doesn't decrease when she gets rejected; (5) men who treat her badly when she encounters them are inconsiderate but are not total bastards; and (6) it would be nice if conditions made it easy and enjoyable for her to meet a good many men until she finally found a suitable love partner, but the world is hardly a terrible place if things are difficult and if she has to keep trying in order to get what she wants.

With clients like this one, RET uses some of its other common cognitive techniques. The client can be shown how to make a list of all the advantages of taking risks and probably getting many rejections while doing so, and all the disadvantages of "comfortably" refusing to take such risks and waiting like a sitting duck for personable men to come to her. She can be given information on some of the best places to go to meet men and what methods of approach she can use to encounter them. She can be taught to use techniques of cognitive distraction—such as Jacobsen's (1942) relaxation techniques—when she makes herself quite anxious in an encountering situation. She can be shown how to imagine herself encountering men and talking to them in a sustained manner. Finally, she can be given bibliotherapy materials to read on RET and encountering, such as *The Intelligent Woman's Guide to Dating and Mating* (Ellis, 1979) and *First Person Singular* (Johnson, 1977).

With clients who are having trouble encountering others and finding love partners, RET uses its common emotive techniques. These include

1. *Forceful self-statements:* Clients are taught to say to themselves, very forcefully, statements such as, "It's hard to encounter new potential partners, but it's much harder if I don't!" "If I fail in my encountering methods, too damned bad! It's better to have tried and lost than never to have encountered at all!"
2. *Rational–emotive imagery.* Clients are shown how to imagine themselves failing miserably at encountering others and *only* feeling sorry, regretful, frustrated, and annoyed, *not* depressed or self-downing.
3. *Role playing.* Clients are given practice, through role playing, in meeting partners they consider suitable and showing them how they make themselves anxious, and need not do so, when they do encountering.

4. *Shame-attacking exercises.* Clients are deliberately induced to do something they consider foolish or shameful in their encountering procedures, such as wearing outlandish clothing or deliberately saying the wrong thing. They are shown how to feel unashamed and self-accepting when they do so.

RET uses a number of behavioral methods in helping clients overcome their fear of encountering possible love partners:

1. *In vivo desensitization.* They do homework assignments involving actually encountering potential partners at least several times a week, until they become desensitized to rejection.
2. *Implosive assignments.* Clients are induced to encounter potential partners many times in a row—say, 20 times a day—until they soon see that there is no real "danger" in doing so.
3. *Reinforcement.* Clients are shown how to reinforce themselves every time they carry out one of their encountering homework assignments.
4. *Penalization.* Clients are shown how to penalize themselves every time they refuse to carry out an encountering homework assignment.
5. *Skills training.* Clients are given skills training (or sent to someone who gives it) that will help them encounter others. This includes assertiveness training, communication training, and sex training.

LOSS OF LOVE

One of the main love problems is that of losing the love of a chosen partner, either at the beginning, when one first loves and is rejected by the beloved, or later, after one has experienced reciprocation for awhile but then loses it because one's partner rejects one's love or dies. In any of these instances, the loss of love may lead to anxiety, depression, self-pity, self-downing, rage, or even (in not a few cases) suicide or homicide. RET theory postulates that, in most of the cases where people suffer greatly from loss of love and are not merely extremely sorrowful or mournful but also self-hating and self-pitying, they tend to create and strongly maintain several iB's, such as:

1. "I must not be rejected by you, for if you reject me there is something radically wrong with me, and if that is so I am a quite inadequate person, most probably not worthy of winning any good person's love in the present or future."
2. "I would, if I were truly attractive and competent, be able to win the love of practically any person whom I really wanted; and since I have never gained or have lost the love of my beloved, I am gruesomely unattractive and incompetent!"

3. "I really am an excellent person, and you do not appreciate me and favor me as you should! You're mean and nasty for rejecting me, and I will have to get even with you if it's the last thing I do!"

4. "Conditions should be arranged so that I am always able to win the love of a person I really desire and so that I do not have to go to too much trouble to win it. When conditions are against me, life is perfectly awful, I can't stand it, and I can be nothing but perfectly miserable!"

5. "When someone whom I love and who loves me dies or is otherwise taken away from me it is totally unfair, and I can't bear a world that is that unfair and cruel! There is no one else in the world who can have with me the kind of relationship I had with this person. I cannot be happy at all, and I might as well kill myself!"

When people possess these iB's and rigidly cling to them, they will tend to feel exceptionally upset emotionally; they will do little to continue to win the love of a chosen partner; they will, when this partner is unavailable, sit on their rumps and refuse to look for other love partners; and they will frequently make themselves so upset as to interfere with their work, school, and social lives, often to the point of incompetence. They sometimes will be obsessed with the lost partner for many years; they will compulsively (and often foolishly) keep doing everything to try to get this partner back; and they will practically insure that they do not have any kind of a future intimate relationship with anyone else.

As usual, RET employs its most popular and effective cognitive methods with people who are not merely bereaved but are exceptionally anxious and depressed about the loss of love:

1. It shows them their major iB's and actively disputes these beliefs; teaching them how to do this kind of scientific disputing on their own.

2. It gives them coping or rational beliefs (rB's) that they can tell themselves and think about, over and over, such as, "My beloved was a fine partner, but there are always other partners with whom I can have a good relationship." "The person whose love I lost has her or his own reasons (or prejudices) for rejecting me, and these reasons may have little to do with me or the ways in which I act."

3. RET shows clients many techniques of cognitive distraction they may use when they have lost a beloved, such as meditation, sports, creative activity, seeking a new partner, and absorption in work.

4. RET may give clients considerable information about love and its myths (as noted earlier) and may help them with practical problem-solving techniques to use in obtaining new partners to replace lost ones.

5. RET helps clients do "referenting," that is, to focus on the disadvantages of the person whose love they have lost and the advantages of other possible partners.

6. It shows people how to reframe rejection and loss, seeing it as a challenge instead of a horror and seeing its benefits rather than only its disadvantages.

7. RET uses bibliotherapy to help clients overcome their dire need for another person. For example, it recommends books like *How to Break Your Addiction to a Person* (Halpern, 1982), *Letting Go* (Wanderer & Cabot, 1978), and *How to Survive the Loss of a Love* (Colgrove, Bloomfield & McWilliams, 1981). It offers tape recordings like *Conquering the Dire Need for Love* (Ellis, 1974), *Conquering Low Frustration Tolerance* (Ellis, 1975a), and *Twenty-two Ways to Brighten Your Love Life* (Ellis, 1983).

8. RET particularly shows clients how to accept themselves *with* their anxiety and horror over their loss of love, how to rid themselves of their depression over their depression, and how to deal with their guilt about their anger at their lost beloved (Ellis, 1979a, 1980; Ellis & Whiteley, 1979).

RET uses the same kind of emotive techniques for overcoming depression over loss of love as it uses with other love problems; these include rational–emotive imagery (Maultsby, 1975; Maultsby & Ellis, 1974), rational role playing (Ellis & Abrahms, 1978), shame-attacking exercises (Ellis, 1969, 1971), forceful self-statements (Ellis, 1979), and devotion to other pleasurable pursuits (Ellis & Becker, 1982). Behaviorally, it uses the kinds of favored RET methods listed previously in this chapter, such as *in vivo* desensitization (Ellis, 1962; Ellis & Abrahms, 1978), reinforcement and penalization (Ellis, 1969, 1973a), skills training (Ellis, 1956, 1962, 1977d), and self-control methods (Ellis, 1982).

KEEPING LOVE ALIVE

Lest it be thought that RET deals only with love problems and pathologies, I shall conclude this chapter with some of its applications to the "normal" human desire to keep love alive. RET is dedicated to helping humans to survive and to survive happily, thus it focuses on alleviation of emotional misery in order to abet happiness and self-fulfillment (Ellis, 1984; Ellis & Whiteley, 1979). As part of its double-barreled emphasis, first on abetting self-actualization and growth and second on therefore minimizing disturbance, it gives serious thought to devising methods of creating and enhancing feelings of love and of keeping these feelings alive once they have developed. Because space limitations preclude my discussing all the salient things that RET has to contribute in these applications of positive love making, I shall conclude with some of its contributions to keeping love alive.

Several writers have recently written optimistic views of how people can infinitely perpetuate and deepen romantic love in marriage or in living-together arrangements, but they tend to define romance in fairly unrealistic ways (Branden, 1982). RET therapists, educators, and writers tend to take a quite realistic and nonutopian view, leaving aside the dubious issue of indefinitely prolonging romantic attachments. RET makes the following recommendations to those who would enhance and perpetuate their intense love feelings:

1. Let your expectations be optimistic, but don't let them run riot. Assume that you can *steadily* and *continuingly* but not *always* and *ecstatically* love.

2. Although you may spontaneously love or fall tumultuously in love, realize that the continuation of your passions frequently requires unspontaneous *work*. Plot and scheme; yes, give some real thinking, emoting, and believing *effort* to maintaining your love feelings and sometimes to enhancing them.

3. Ask yourself, "What do I and can I find lovable about my partner? What are this partner's good traits that I can focus upon? What are the things I can enjoy with him or her? What loving thoughts can I have, and what caring things can I do for my beloved?"

4. Practice loving feelings. Remember and imagine situations that make you feel affectionate, caring, tender, ardent, and desirous. Spend time, perhaps some amount each day, thinking about these situations and working up your amative feelings about them.

5. Deliberately act in loving ways toward your beloved. Send flowers, buy gifts, write poems, say loving words, tell others how much you care. No matter how difficult you find saying "I love you," say it, again and again (Ellis & Harper, 1961b; Hauck, 1977).

6. Plan and carry out mutually enjoyable pursuits with your beloved, such as reading aloud together, engaging in sports, attending movies and plays, visiting friends, having sex, and camping out (Buscaglia, 1982).

7. Observe your feelings of anger, irritation, resentment, boredom, and frustration with your beloved. See when they spring from desires or preferences ("I wish my partner would be more attentive to me") or from absolutistic demands and commands ("My partner at all times *must* pay more attention to me").

8. If you mainly desire your beloved to think, act, or feel differently, try to express your desire as a preference, warmly and without hostility, encouraging your partner to fulfill it. If you cannot arrange this kind of fulfillment, work at accepting your frustration and refrain from making too much of it (Ellis, 1979b; Garrity, 1977).

9. If you feel resentful about your beloved's frustrating you, look for your authoritarian commandingness, your insistence that she or he absolutely *must* give you what you demand, and use RET disputing techniques to surrender your demands. Virogously tell yourself, "I would *prefer* very much to have my partner fulfill my desire, but she (or he) never *has* to" (Blazier, 1975; Ellis, 1977c; Hauck, 1974, 1977).

10. If you have low frustration tolerance about the conditions blocking you from fully enjoying yourself with your beloved, look for your *musts* and *shoulds*

about these conditions and actively use RET to dispute them. Strongly tell yourself, "It would be nice if economic, social, and other conditions helped me to enjoy myself more with my beloved, but if they are frustrating and sabotaging, tough! I can stand it!"

11. Being considerate is not the same as loving, but it certainly helps. If you go out of your way to discover what your beloved likes and to abet those preferences, and if you especially go out of your way to discover what your beloved dislikes or hates and to avoid doing those things, you will go a long way toward keeping his or her love for you alive (Taylor, 1982).

12. Don't be compulsively honest about everything! Silence is often golden, especially when your partner keeps doing irritating things that you can well put up with. Don't think you *have to* speak up, express yourself, or be perfectly honest. But if she or he does something that is against your basic goals and values and that can be changed, *then* speak up.

13. Keep a good sense of humor! Reduce your own overly serious ideas about your beloved's "obnoxious" behavior to absurdity. Learn some RET rational humorous songs about love and disturbance and lustily sing them to yourself on appropriate occasions (Ellis, 1977a, 1977b). Try, for example, these songs:

Love Me, Love Me, Only Me!

(To the tune of "Yankee Doodle")
Love me, love me, only me, or I'll die without you!
Make your love a guarantee, so I can never doubt you!
Love me, love me totally; really, really try, dear;
But if you must rely on me, I'll hate you till I die, dear!

Love me, love me all the time, thoroughly and wholly;
Life turns into slushy slime 'less you love me solely!
Love me with great tenderness, with no ifs or buts, dear;
For if you love me somewhat less I'll hate your goddamned guts, dear!
(Lyrics by Albert Ellis. © 1977 by Institute for Rational–Emotive Therapy.)

I Love You Unduly

(To the tune of "I Love You Truly" by Carrie Jacobs Bond)
I love you unduly, unduly, dear!
Just like a coolie I persevere!
When you are lazy and act like a bore,
I am so crazy, I love you more!
I love you truly, truly, dear!
Very unduly and with no cheer!
Though you're unruly and rip up my gut,
I love you truly—for I'm a nut!
(Lyrics by Albert Ellis. © 1977 by Institute for Rational–Emotive Therapy.)

I Am Just a Love Slob
(To the tune of "Annie Laurie" by Lady Scott)
Oh, I am just a love slob,
Who needs to have you say
That you'll be truly for me
Forever and a day!
If you won't guarantee
Forever mine to be,
I shall whine and scream and make life stormy,
And then la–ay me doon and dee!
(Lyrics by Albert Ellis. © 1977 by Institute for Rational–Emotive Therapy.)

14. Frankly acknowledge your own and your partner's sexual desires and proclivities. Recognize that sex does *not* equal intercourse but includes many noncoital enjoyments, and in collaboration with your mate arrange for your *both* achieving regular sexual satisfaction (Ellis, 1960, 1965c, 1976, 1979b).

15. Be with and share with your partner to a considerable degree, but try to arrange that you both *also* maintain appreciable individuality and personal identity.

16. Make consistent efforts to communicate well with your beloved, especially by using the RET method of facilitating communication developed by Ted Crawford (1982). This includes actively listening to your partner, using a revolving discussion sequence (where you make sure you understand each other's views before you agree or disagree with them), and eliminating the shoulds and musts that block real communication (Brainer, 1976; Ellis, 1983b).

17. Love requires some sacrifices, particularly of time and effort. You may legitimately love—be quite devoted to—your work (as Edison was) or to a cause (as Lenin was). But if you want primarily to love and be loved by another person, you had better be devoted, first, to accepting (and I could say loving) yourself and to caring for that person. Let yourself be devoted to work and to a cause— yes, somewhat, but not too much. Work hard to find a compromise and strike some balance in this respect (Blazier, 1975; Ellis, 1979b; Ellis & Harper, 1961b; Fromme, 1965; Kelley, 1979; Murstein, 1974)?

SUMMARY AND CONCLUSION

RET has its own theories about love, including how it is blocked and how it is fulfilled. It particularly has applications for individuals having serious love problems, such as people possessed by super-romantic love, "limerents" who are mired in obsessive–compulsive feelings, insensately jealous and possessive lovers, people who needlessly interfere with or prevent themselves from encountering suitable partners, and those who suffer anguish and depression when they lose love. On the more positive side, RET has important things to teach about "normal" human desires to enhance love and keep it alive. Naturally, RET doesn't have all the answers to love or to anything else, but it is making significant contributions to this fascinating field of human endeavor and endearment.

REFERENCES

Ard, B. N., Jr. The A-B-C of marriage counseling. *Rational Living*, 1967, *2*(2), 10–12.
Ard, B. N., Jr. & Ard, C. C. (Eds.). *Handbook of marriage counseling.* (2nd ed.). Palo Alto, Calif.: Science and Behavior Books, 1976.
Bach, G. R., & Wyden, P. *The intimate enemy.* New York: Morrow, 1969.
Blazier, D. C. *Poor me, poor marriage.* New York: Vantage, 1975.
Boylan, B. R. *Infidelity.* Englewood Cliffs, N.J.: Prentice-Hall, 1971.
Brainerd, G. *Basic marriage communication training.* Pasadena, Calif.: Basic Communication Marriage Training, 1976.
Branden, N. *The psychology of romantic love.* New York: Bantam, 1971.
Burgess, E. W., & Locke, H. T. *The family.* New York: American Book Company, 1953.
Buscaglia, L. *Living, loving and learning.* New York: Ballantine, 1982.
Clanton, G., & Smith, L. (Eds.). *Jealousy.* New York: Holt, Rinehart and Winston, 1977.
Colgrove, M., Bloomfield, H. H., & McWilliams, P. *How to survive the loss of love.* New York: Bantam, 1981.
Crawford, T. *Communication and revolving discussion sequence.* Rosemead, Calif.: Unpublished manuscript, 1982.
De Rougemont, D. *Love in the western world.* Greenwich, Conn.: Fawcett, 1956.
Demorest, A. F. Love, romance and neurosis. *ART in Daily Living*, 1971, *1*(3), 6–7.
Ellis, A. Some significant correlates of love and family behavior. *Journal of Social Psychology*, 1949, *30*, 3–16. (a)
Ellis, A. A study of human love relationships. *Journal of Genetic Psychology*, 1949, *75*, 61–76. (b)
Ellis, A. A study of the love emotions of American college girls. *International Journal of Sexology*, 1949, *3*, 15–21. (c)
Ellis, A. Love and family relationships of American college girls. *American Journal of Sociology*, 1950, *55*, 550–556.
Ellis, A. *The folklore of sex.* New York: Boni, 1951.
Ellis, A. *The American sexual tragedy.* New York: Twayne, 1954.
Ellis, A. *How to live with a neurotic.* New York: Crown, 1957.
Ellis, A. *Sex without guilt.* New York: Lyle Stuart, 1958.
Ellis, A. *The art and science of love.* Secaucus, N.J.: Lyle Stuart, 1960.
Ellis, A. *The American sexual tragedy* (2nd ed.). New York: Lyle Stuart and Grove Press, 1961.
Ellis, A. *Reason and emotion in psychotherapy.* Secaucus, N.J.: Lyle Stuart and Citadel Press, 1962.
Ellis, A. *The intelligent woman's guide to mate-hunting.* New York: Lyle Stuart and Dell Books, 1963. (a)
Ellis, A. *Sex and the single man.* New York: Lyle Stuart and Dell Books, 1963. (b)
Ellis, A. Sick and healthy love (part 1). *Independent*, *132*, April 1963, pp. 1, 8–9. (c)
Ellis, A. Sick and healthy love (part 2). *Independent*, *132*, May 1963, pp. 4–6. (d)
Ellis, A. *Suppressed: Seven key essays publishers dared not print.* Chicago: New Classics House, 1965. (a)
Ellis, A. *Sex without guilt* (2nd ed.). Seacaucus, N.J.: Lyle Stuart, 1965. (b)
Ellis, A. *The art and science of love* (2nd ed). New York: Bantam, 1965. (c)
Ellis, A. A weekend of rational encounter. In A. Burton (Ed.), *Encounter.* San Francisco: Jossey-Bass, 1969.
Ellis, A. *Growth through reason.* North Hollywood: Wilshire Books, 1971. (a)
Ellis, A. *How to stubbornly refuse to be ashamed of anything.* Cassette recording. New York: Institute for Rational–Emotive Therapy, 1971. (b)

Ellis, A. *The civilized couple's guide to extramarital adventure.* New York: Wyden, 1972. (a)

Ellis, A. Psychotherapy without tears. In A. Burton (Ed.), *Twelve therapists.* San Francisco: Jossey-Bass, 1972. (b)

Ellis, A. Are cognitive behavior therapy and rational therapy synonymous? *Rational Living,* 1973, *8*(2), 8–11. (a)

Ellis, A. *Humanistic psychotherapy: The rational–emotive approach.* New York: Crown and McGraw-Hill, 1973. (b)

Ellis, A. Unhealthy love: Its causes and treatment. In M. E. Curtin (Ed.), *Symposium on love.* New York: Behavioral Publications, 1973. (c)

Ellis, A. *Conquering the dire need to be loved.* Cassette recording. New York: Institute for Rational–Emotive Therapy, 1974.

Ellis, A. *Conquering low frustration tolerance.* Cassette recording. New York: Institute for Rational–Emotive Therapy, 1975. (a)

Ellis, A. How to live with a neurotic (2nd ed.). North Hollywood: Wilshire Books, 1975. (b)

Ellis, A. *Sex and the liberated man.* Secaucus, N.J.: Lyle Stuart, 1976.

Ellis, A. Fun as psychotherapy. *Rational Living,* 1977, *12*(1), 2–6. (a)

Ellis, A. *A garland of rational humorous songs.* Songbook and cassette recording. New York: Institute for Rational–Emotive Therapy, 1977. (b)

Ellis, A. *How to live with—and without—anger.* New York: Reader's Digest Press, 1977. (c)

Ellis, A. Skill training in counseling and psychotherapy. *Canadian Counselor,* 1977, *12*(1), 30–35. (d)

Ellis, A. Discomfort anxiety: A new cognitive behavioral construct. Part 1. *Rational Living,* 1979, *14*(2), 3–8. (a)

Ellis, A. *The intelligent woman's guide to dating and mating.* Secaucus, N.J.: Lyle Stuart, 1979. (b)

Ellis, A. Discomfort anxiety: A new cognitive behavioral construct. Part 2. *Rational Living,* 1980, *15*(1), 25–30.

Ellis, A. Self-direction in sport and life. *Rational Living,* 1982, *17*(1), 27–34.

Ellis, A. My philosophy of work and love. *Psychotherapy in Private Practice,* 1983, *1*(1), 43–49. (a)

Ellis, A. *Twenty-two ways to brighten your love life.* Cassette recording. New York: Institute for Rational–Emotive Therapy, 1983. (b)

Ellis, A. *Rational–emotive therapy and cognitive-behavior therapy.* New York: Springer, 1984.

Ellis, A., & Abrahms, E. *Brief psychotherapy in medical and health practice.* New York: Springer, 1978.

Ellis, A., & Becker, I. *A guide to personal happiness.* North Hollywood: Wilshire Books, 1983.

Ellis, A., & Grieger, R. (Eds.). *Handbook of rational–emotive therapy.* New York: Springer, 1977.

Ellis, A., & Harper, R. A. *A guide to rational living.* Englewood Cliffs, N.J.: Prentice-Hall, 1961. (a)

Ellis, A. & Harper, R. A. *A guide to successful marriage.* North Hollywood: Wilshire Books, 1961. (b)

Ellis, A., & Harper, R. A. *A new guide to rational living.* North Hollywood: Wilshire Books, 1975.

Ellis, A., & Whiteley, J. M. *Theoretical and empirical foundations of rational–emotive therapy.* Monterey, Calif.: Brooks/Cole, 1979.

Finck, H. T. *Romantic love and personal beauty.* New York: Macmillan, 1877.

Fromme, A. *The ability to love.* New York: Pocket Books, 1966.

Grossack, M. *Love and reason.* New York: New American Library, 1976.

Halpern, H. M. *How to break your addiction to a person.* New York: McGraw-Hill, 1982.

Harper, R. A. Marriage counseling as rational process-oriented psychotherapy. *Journal of Individual Psychology,* 1960, *16,* 197–207.

Harper, R. A. Jealousy—Its prevention and cure. *Sexology,* 1963, *29,* 516–518.

Harper, R. A., & Stokes, W. R. *Forty-five levels to sexual understanding and enjoyment.* Englewood Cliffs, N.J.: Prentice-Hall, 1971.

Hauck, P. A. *Overcoming depression.* Philadelphia: Westminster, 1973.

Hauck, P. A. *Overcoming frustration and anger.* Philadelphia: Westminster, 1974.

Hauck, P. A. *Marriage is a serious business.* Philadelphia: Westminster, 1977.

Hauck, P. A. *Overcoming jealousy and possessiveness.* Philadelphia: Westminster, 1981.

Hibbard, R. W. A rational approach to treating jealousy. *Rational Living,* 1975, *10*(2), 25–27.

Hunt, M. M. *The natural history of love.* New York: Grove, 1959.

Jacobsen, E. *You must relax*. New York: McGraw-Hill, 1942.

Johnson, S. M. *First person singular*. New York: New American Library, 1977.

Katz, J. M. How do you love me? Let me count the ways. *Sociological Inquiry*, 1976, *46*, 17–22.

Kelley, H. H. *Personal relationships: Their structures and processes*. Hillsdale, N.J.: Erlbaum, 1979.

Kremen, H., & Kremen B. Romantic love and idealization. *American Journal of Psychoanalysis*, 1971, *31*, 134–143.

Lederer, W. J., & Jackson, D. D. *The mirages of marriage*. New York: W. W. Norton, 1968.

Lucka, E. *Eros*. New York: Putnam, 1915.

Maultsby, M. C., Jr. *Help yourself to happiness*. New York: Institute for Rational–Emotive Therapy, 1975.

Maultsby, M. C., Jr., & Ellis, A. *Technique for using rational–emotive imagery*. New York: Institute for Rational–Emotive Therapy, 1974.

McClellan, T. A., & Stieper, D. R. A structured approach to group marriage counseling. *Rational Living*, 1973, *8*(2), 12–18.

McDonald, P., & McDonald, D. *Loving free*. New York: Ballantine, 1973.

Murstein, B. I. *Love, sex and marriage through the ages*. New York: Springer, 1974.

O'Neill, N., & O'Neill, G. *Open marriage*. New York: Evans, 1972.

Shibles, W. *Rational love*. Whitewater, Wis.: Language Press, 1978.

Stendhal (M. H. Beyle). *On love*. New York: Liveright, 1947.

Taylor, R. *Having love affairs*. Buffalo, N.Y.: Prometheus, 1982.

Tennov, D. *Love and limerence*. New York: Stein and Day, 1979.

Wanderer, Z., & Cabot, T. *Letting go*. New York: Putnam, 1978.

11

Cognitive Factors in Sexual Behavior*

Janet Wolfe and Susan Walen

It has been said that while sex is perfectly natural it is rarely naturally perfect. This statement implies that a great deal of our sexual behavior entails utilizing new learning. Learning can be broadly conceptualized into two major forms: that in which stimuli acquire new meaning for the individual (classical conditioning) and that in which new responses are added to the individual's repertoire (operant conditioning). It is likely that many of the changes we observe in our overt sexual behaviors are mediated by the principles of operant conditioning (reinforcement and punishment). Overt sexual behavior, however, is usually elicited by external events (e.g., a sexual approach by a partner) or by internal events (e.g., sexual thoughts or feelings of arousal). These eliciting stimuli for sexual behavior probably acquire their erotic meaning for the individual through the principles of classical conditioning. Thus, it seems that people learn not only (a) "how to do sex," but also (b) to give certain external stimuli sexual meaning, and (c) to identify and label certain internal stimuli (physiological arousal) as erotic.

It is common knowledge by now that our greatest sex organ is not located below the belt, but between our ears. The cognitive activity of our brain can either augment or inhibit the sexual response cycle. The two major forms of cognitive behavior that we will examine in this chapter are perception and evaluation.

---

*This chapter was first printed in R. Grieger & I. Grieger (Eds.), *Cognition and Emotional Disturbance* (New York: Human Sciences Press, 1982).

PERCEPTION

Perception entails three processes: detection, labeling, and attribution. Let us briefly review each in turn. *Detection* simply refers to the individual's ability to note the presence of a stimulus or to discriminate it from other stimuli. For example, an individual may note a change in heart rate. Obviously, unless this step is accomplished the stimulus is functionally "not there" for the individual. *Labeling* refers to the descriptors that the individual uses to categorize the stimulus event; it is a classifying operation. The person who notes the sensations in heart activity may label it, "my heart just skipped a beat." The third step is *attribution,* finding an explanation for the perception. The attribution selected by the individual may depend most heavily on contextual cues (Schachter & Singer, 1962). Using the preceding example, the skipped heart beat may be attributed to "true love" or fear, depending, at least in part, on the situational cues of the moment.

Perception, therefore, is a process of gathering data correctly and drawing accurate conclusions from the data. In a sense, the perceiver is functioning as a data collector and had better scientifically check out the accuracy of her or his reality testing. Inability to detect sexual stimuli, incorrect labeling, or misattribution of them may significantly impede sexual performance.

Aaron Beck (1976, 1978) has done a great deal of work on cognitive errors of perception in problems of depression. Let us now take Beck's work out of the mood clinic and usefully apply it in the sex clinic. The major cognitive errors described by Beck are the following:

Selective abstraction: focusing only on certain details from a complex situation and using the detail to describe the entire experience.
Arbitrary inference: drawing a conclusion without evidence or in the face of evidence to the contrary.
Overgeneralization: drawing a conclusion on the basis of a single incident.
Personalization: relating events to oneself without clear evidence.
Dichotomous thinking: classifying events into either/or or all/none categories instead of as existing on a continuum.

We will return to these cognitive errors later and illustrate their role in perception as part of the sexual response cycle.

EVALUATION

The second major cognitive behavior that can affect sexual functioning is evaluation, which in essence entails rating events on a continuum from good to bad. The cognitive theory of RET, as evolved by Albert Ellis (Ellis & Harper, 1975), has focused primarily on evaluative beliefs.

Obviously, when an individual evaluates a sexual stimulus as good or positive, sexual functioning will be enhanced. Equally obvious, when a stimulus is evaluated negatively, sexuality will be diminished. Still more destructive are exaggerated negative evaluations, which Ellis refers to as "awfulizing" or "catastrophizing." If a man fails to get an erection during sex play, he can rationally evaluate this event as bad. Such an evaluation would be sensible if he had held expectations of intercourse in the sexual encounter, but may not inhibit other sexual behaviors that do not require an erection. Irrationally, however, he may go on to evaluate his flaccid state as "terrible, awful, and horrible." Such an overly negative evaluation will typically set up an intense cycle of anxiety or guilt, which in turn will probably block further attempts at sexual arousal of the individual or his partner.

A NEW CONCEPTION OF THE SEXUAL AROUSAL CYCLE

While arousal need not preceed the initiation of overt sexual behaviors, it certainly will affect the individual's enjoyment of a sexual encounter and thus will affect how she or he behaves. Arousal, we suggest, is a product of both *perception* and *evaluation* of events and in turn leads to further cognitive appraisal. Thus, we propose the arousal cycle (see Figure 11–1). Note that this system suggests a feedback model, in which each of the eight links in the chain functions as both a cue for the next link and a reinforcer for the preceding event. Let us take each succeeding link and discuss its contribution to a positive sexual experience.

Link 1: Perception of a Sexual Stimulus

The perception or identification of a stimulus as erotic in large part is learned, a conclusion that seems clear from an examination of cross-cultural studies of sexual behavior. Ford and Beach (1951), for example, state:

> Human sexuality is affected by experience in two ways: First, the kinds of stimulation and the types of situations that become capable of evoking sexual excitement are determined in large measure by learning; second, the overt behavior through which this excitement is expressed depends largely upon the individual's previous experience (p. 263).

How does this happen? How do we learn to identify certain people or body parts or inanimate objects as erotic? A number of processes may come into play, one of which involves modeling and social reinforcement. The culture in which we live sets the stage for detection and labeling of a stimulus as erotic. For example, Americans for many years have focused much erotic energy on women's breasts, much to the amazement of many Europeans and certainly to

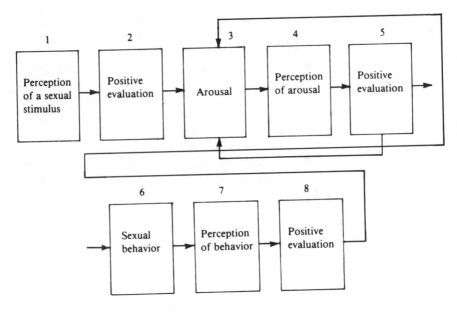

Figure 11–1. Proposed feedback loop of a positive sexual experience

many African tribes in which breasts are usually bared, and despite the fact that for a large percentage of women the breasts are not erotically sensitive.

Not only cultural expectations, but the existence of an adequate vocabulary are important to the perception process. For instance, the dearth of words (synonyms or descriptors) in our language for the female sex organ, the clitoris, may contribute in large part to the relatively high percentage of women who are sexually dysfunctional in our society.

Finally, through a process of stimulus pairing, an event that has been repeatedly experienced with arousal or orgasm will acquire erotic potential. The study by Rachman and Hodgson (1968) provided a laboratory model that suggests how this process may work. An analogue of a fetish was created through classical conditioning by repeatedly pairing slides of high black boots with slides of attractive naked women. Using normal male subjects and measuring changes in penile volume, conditioning, stimulus generalization, extinction, and spontaneous recovery were all demonstrated.

Link 2: Evaluation of the Sexual Stimulus

Once the stimulus is identified as erotic, it will be evaluated by the individual. If the evaluation is positive, arousal will proceed. If, however, the individual evaluates the stimulus negatively, arousal may be blocked. Thus, an individual who evaluates a sexual picture or sexual approach as "disgusting," "not nice," or "unseemly" will probably fail to be aroused by it. When the range of sexual stimuli that are considered acceptable to the individual is very restricted, the probability of arousal will be low and the sexual repertoire will be perforce limited.

Link 3: Arousal

Physiological arousal is a generalized phenomenon, and much the same kind of responses will be noted after a variety of human experiences, both negative and positive. The early stages of sexual arousal (e.g., increased heart rate, blood pressure, muscle tension) show the same responses as do those that occur under a number of conditions ranging from simple physical exertion to painful stimulation to anxiety-arousing events.

According to Schachter's (1964) model of emotion, two elements are required for the experience of emotion: (a) a physiological state of arousal and (b) situational cues that enable the individual to label the arousal as a specific emotion. In the classic study of this model by Schachter and Singer (1962), physiological arousal was induced in subjects by injections of epinephrine. Subjects were then exposed to highly emotional displays of behavior (euphoria or anger) by a confederate of the experimenters. Those subjects who were correctly informed of the expected phenomenologic effects of the drug were less affected by the confederate's behavior than were subjects who were misinformed or uninformed. The latter subjects displayed more emotional responses, modeling those of the confederate, presumably because the context allowed them to provide an emotional label for their aroused state.

By derivation, we presume that appropriate environmental cues can help an individual to label physiological arousal as the sensations of love or sexual excitation. Because the arousal is nonspecific, however, inaccurate labeling may easily result. For example, a young woman may be dating a man whose approach behaviors are extremely unpredictable. He might court her avidly for a few days and then not phone again for weeks, following which the cycle is repeated. The young woman's hopes and expectations would be very confused, and her partner's inconsistent and inconsiderate behavior might result in a strong state of arousal. If she labels her arousal as feelings of intense love rather than those of anxiety or anger, she may remain in what may be an unfulfilling relationship. The accurate perception of arousal, therefore, will be an extremely important aspect of good erotic functioning. Once correctly perceived, arousal may lead to further focusing on erotic sensations and to increased sexual behavior, which will further increase arousal.

Link 4: Perception of Arousal

Research by Julia Heiman (1977) has indicated a significant sex difference in the ability to detect and report erotic arousal. Male and female college students were presented with erotic and nonerotic auditory stimuli. Their reactions were measured by objective recordings of genital vasocongestion and by subjective reports of arousal. A significant discrepancy between these two measures was found for the female subjects, indicating either that they are less able to discriminate their own arousal and/or are less likely to report it. What factors could be responsible for this difference between the sexes?

Cultural taboos and rigid sexual norms for females may certainly play a role. Women are known to engage less frequently in masturbation; in fact, commonly a first step in the treatment of sexually dysfunctional women is permission giving and instruction in masturbation, thus providing a training ground for recognizing and labeling genital sensations.

Young women frequently do not attend to their own arousal, concentrating instead on making sure that their partner doesn't "go too far." While she is busy policing his behavior, she is distracted from monitoring her own sensations. When women are fully sexually active, they may still be inattentive to their arousal because they may be more attuned to pleasing their partners, thus following the cultural model of women as passive caretakers of others.

Also, quite simply, a woman's vasocongestive arousal is often not as obvious as is a man's. One can hardly miss detecting an erection, but many of a woman's early arousal signals are internal, subtle, and ambiguous. A slight dampening of the vulva, if detected, could be interpreted as perspiration or urine, and nipples certainly erect to the cold. Many women, in fact, are not even certain if they have had an orgasm. Since women tend to do less verbal or physical sharing of early masturbatory experiences or other sexual behaviors than do men, their ability to detect and correctly label their arousal may be hindered.

Another important aspect of the identification of arousal in both men and women relates to the criteria used in the inspection process. The earliest physiological changes in sexual arousal consist of increases in heart rate, muscular tension, skin temperature, and respiration. All of these, however, are fairly nonspecific, and research indicates that we are not particularly adept at discriminating them (Heiman, 1977). With the addition of more intense and localized vasocongestive changes (copious lubrication or erection) the signals become clearer.

Trouble can still arise, however, if the individual sets the criteria for signs of physiological arousal too stringently. How full must an erection be before the male identifies it as a "sure" sign of arousal? How much lubrication must be noticed in the woman? What, in fact, happens if he or she *only* uses the magnitude of erection or lubrication as the signal? One possibility is that the individual may engage in further sexual behavior before arousal is maximal, thus often leading to nonattainment of orgasm or a relatively anhedonic orgasm. Or, if the specific signal is delayed or doesn't match rigid criteria, the individual may conclude that he or she is not aroused at all and may abandon further attempts at the sexual pursuit.

Attending to multiple cues and not setting rigid criteria for these cues would seem to be the most helpful. If the individual is focusing on only one cue, particularly a genital cue, she or he may not augment the arousal cycle by self-reinforcing and arousal-facilitating cognitions, but instead may further reduce arousal with inhibitory cognitions.

The attribution for a perceived state of arousal will also be important, since arousal is so nonspecific. Two studies of misattribution cited by Rook and Hammen (1977) are relevant to this point. Cantor, Zillman, and Bryant (1975) found that male subjects' subjective reports of sexual arousal and liking of an erotic film were enhanced by residual physiological arousal produced by physical exercise. Dutton and Aron (1974) arranged to have male subjects approached by an attractive female experimenter while on a fear-arousing suspension bridge. These men gave more sexual responses to Thematic Apperception Test (TAT) cards and made more attempts to contact the experimenter after the study than did male subjects tested on a less threatening bridge or those approached by a male experimenter.

It may be suggested, therefore, that situational cues are an important determinant in the interpretation or attribution that an individual makes to a perception of arousal. Possibly such a phenomenon is involved in the establishment of problematic or unusual sexual behaviors. Misattribution of an arousal sequence as sexual may come to elicit sexual arousal or ultimately restrict the individual to the unusual eliciting stimuli.

Link 5: Evaluation of Arousal

If an individual has learned to label arousal as bad, the negative emotional consequences to this evaluation may block the sexual arousal cycle. Thus, the woman who thinks of her vulva as dirty or smelly and evaluates her own lubrication as merely "sticky" or, worse, as "disgusting" may end up feeling embarrassed by her arousal, an emotion hardly compatible with a positive sexual experience. Similarly, the man who decides that he "shouldn't" have erections in certain situations may find himself consumed with guilt rather than further arousal. It is for these reasons that much of the work of the sex counselor consists of instilling a new set of sex-positive attitudes vis-à-vis arousal.

Link 6: Overt Sexual Behavior

If arousal is present and is accurately labeled and evaluated, typically the individual moves on to initiate or to further engage in sexual behavior and thereby augments arousal. Here again, however, differences between the sexes may emerge. Many women inhibit themselves at this stage, blocking their pursuit of sexual arousal with cognitions such as "I can't take over the control." "I couldn't do that (or ask for that)." "He won't like it if I do that." "As long as he's happy, I'm happy." "It's not nice (or ladylike) to do that." "What will he think of me if I do?" Thus, while the man is liable to time his behaviors and movements to his state of arousal, the woman may not. She may even be repeatedly engaging in sexual behavior when she is at a low or even zero level of arousal. If so, it is easy to imagine how this pairing could result in further sexual difficulties.

Link 7: Perception of Sexual Behavior

Individuals react to their own spontaneous expressions as indicators of their arousal. They may monitor cries, laughter, tears, or movements. If accurately perceived and labeled, and if evaluated positively, they may further augment the perception of arousal. In addition, since movement and other expressive behaviors may increase cardiac output, they may directly contribute to the general arousal level.

At this link, however, an important distinction needs to be made between *observation* of sexual or expressive behaviors and *spectatoring* them. The latter implies not merely detection and labeling, but a *self-rating* process that has a goal-oriented focus. When the individual is spectatoring his or her performance, the here-and-now experience of pleasure is lost and sex becomes work rather than play. When the self-rating of the individual is critical, the results can certainly be a troublesome distraction from the arousal cycle.

Link 8: Evaluation of Sexual Behavior

Evaluation of one's sexual behavior is the core problem in the majority of the common sexual dysfunctions brought to the sex counselor. In fact, rational–emotive therapists make a distinction between sexual *dysfunction* and sexual *disturbance*. The individual may have a dysfunction (e.g., erectile difficulty) and yet choose to be relatively undisturbed about it emotionally. If disturbed, of course, the emotional turmoil will further inhibit good sexual functioning. The disturbance, according to RET, stems from the individual's *evaluation* of the sexual difficulty.

The erectile failure will be problematic to the man and his partner only if they evaluate it as "awful." If they go on to attribute the failure to some enduring characteristic of themselves and evaluate this characteristic as horrid, they will not only impede their performance at the moment but will be making dire and probably self-fulfilling prophesies of the future. On the other hand, if they are able to conclude that the erectile failure is not catastrophic, that they can still function as good sex partners using other techniques, that their "self" is still intact even if the erection is not, the erection may very well be recovered, or at least the couple may go on to their next sexual encounter unencumbered by fear, anxiety, or self-downing.

SYNTHESIS

Positive sexual experiences are a smooth amalgam of stimuli and responses, the flow between them guided by correct perceptions and positive evaluations. When this process occurs, the emotional climate of the individual will be untroubled, and sex play will be pleasant or even joyful.

Negative sexual experiences occur when the linkages between stimuli and responses are blocked by incorrect or negative cognitions. The following are some examples of these kinds of cognitive errors:

Perceptual Errors

1. Selective abstraction: "I don't see a sex flush on my chest . . . I guess I'm not aroused."
2. Arbitrary inference: "I haven't come yet . . . I'm probably not going to."
3. Overgeneralization: "My erection is smaller . . . I knew I was becoming impotent."
4. Personalization: "I've taken off my clothes and he doesn't have an erection. He doesn't find me attractive any more."
5. Dichotomous thinking: "I'm not orgasmic." "I'm not a real man."

Evaluative Errors

None of the preceding five statements need to impede the process of the arousal cycle, unless the individual ascribes an exaggerated negative evaluation to the cognition. For instance, in the first example, the woman could conclude that she is not aroused and evaluate this finding nonhurtfully: e.g., "Well, so I'm not aroused. There's always next time. I'll just make this a super loving session for my partner." On the other hand, consider what would occur if perceptions such as the preceding were followed by an evaluation such as "How awful!" "It shouldn't be this way!" "I can't stand it!" "I've got to do better!" "What a sad sack I am!" "It's all my (or his or her) fault!" The flooding of anxiety, misery, guilt, or anger will certainly get in the way of happy, playful sex.

With regard to sexual dysfunctions, it is interesting to note that sex therapists have developed various classificatory systems for the common sexual dysfunctions, typically delimiting premature ejaculation, retarded ejaculation, and impotency among men and preorgasmia, dyspareunia, and vaginismus among women. These categories are often broken down still further into primary dysfunctions (occurring under all conditions) and situational dysfunctions (occurring only under specific conditions).

Closer examination of these categories, however, suggests that the same dysfunctional processes are operative in virtually all cases. For example, most premature ejaculators *assume* that they orgasm rapidly because they are too highly aroused, and the typically ineffective self-help procedures they evolve consist of distracting themselves from the sexual encounter (e.g., by reciting multiplication tables) or minimizing stimulation (e.g., not allowing their partner to touch their genitals). Counselors who have worked with premature ejaculators find, however, that rather than being overaroused, they are usually underaroused. In fact, when such clients acquire the ability to exert some control over the reflex, they typically report that the orgasm, when it occurs, is significantly more pleasurable.

It appears, then, that the core ingredients in all of the diagnostic categories are a high level of emotional distress induced by *cognitive errors of evaluation*, often coupled with *cognitive errors of perception*. The end product is an individual who approaches the job of sex (rather than the joy of sex) as a way to prove him- or herself (rather than to enjoy him- or herself)—certainly a very unsexy attitude.

SEX THERAPY

For roughly the first half of the twentieth century the treatment of sexual disorders consisted largely of psychoanalytically or psychodynamically oriented therapy. Treatment was posited on the notion that healthy sexual functioning could be achieved by gaining insight into early psychosexual problems and resolving the oedipal conflicts and the penis envy or castration anxiety resulting from them, which normally would require years of individual probing. While essentially cognitive in nature, psychoanalytically oriented therapies rarely focus directly (or even indirectly) on inaccurate perceptions and dysfunctional evaluations of sexual stimuli, arousal, or behavior. To the extent that any of these links are discussed, they are typically not followed by instruction for remediation. For example, if an oedipal conflict is identified as a "reason" for premature ejaculation, the patient is rarely instructed in techniques that could effectively influence the perception and evaluation of the stages of arousal leading to ejaculation, or reduce the emotional distress following a rapid ejaculation. To date there has been little evidence of the success of this type of treatment in significantly altering dysfunctional sexual behavior, and in innumerable instances, especially in cases of women in classical psychoanalysis, there may actually be a further increase in sexual disturbance during and following treatment.

More practical forms of sex therapy also have existed since at least the early part of the twentieth century, largely practiced by nonanalytic physicians and often described in detail in manuals for the general public. Sexologists, including August Forel (1922), Havelock Ellis (1935), Magnus Hirschfeld (1935), William J. Robinson (1929), W. F. Robie (1925), Theodore Van de Velde (1926), G. Lombard Kelly (1948), and Hannah and Abraham Stone (1935), contributed works read by millions who wanted to learn what to do to feel more sexually adequate. Although their approaches were largely ignored by psychoanalytic practitioners, there is some evidence that their writings dealt more directly with the various links in our model and had positive effects in terms of attitudinal and behavioral changes.

Still more recently, the focus in sex research and sex therapy has followed a more-or-less explicit behavioral model. One of the first modern psychologists to break completely from the Freudian model and emphasize an active cognitive and behavioral approach to sex therapy was Albert Ellis (1953, 1960). Subsequently, the experimental and clinical work of Masters and Johnson (1970) established the efficacy of directed behavioral change and *in vivo* practice as important ingredients in improved sexual functioning. The carefully documented procedures and effectiveness of the work of Masters and Johnson received wide publicity and significantly influenced even the work of psychoanalytically oriented practitioners such as Kaplan (1974). From the work of Masters and Johnson, Ellis, and other pioneers, behavior therapy procedures began to be applied systematically to problems of sexual inadequacy and disturbance (Annon, 1974; Barbach, 1975; Feldman & MacCulloch, 1971; Hartman & Fithian, 1972; Heiman, LoPiccolo, & LoPiccolo, 1976; Lazarus, 1971; Semans, 1956; Wolpe & Lazarus, 1966).

In addition to the often highly creative behavioral methods used in contemporary sex therapy, a significant component of behavior change used by most of these theorists and practitioners is a focus on altering cognitions. Directly or indirectly, cognitions about sexual stimulation and sexual behavior are addressed. Clients' attitudes based on myth and misinformation about themselves, their bodies, and their sexual functioning are replaced with more accurate beliefs about sex and sexuality. Ellis (1960, 1976, 1979), in particular, has elaborated cognitive restructuring techniques that focus on changing attitudes toward sexual performance in general and toward oneself when a sexual dysfunction is present. The goal of such procedures is to reduce anxiety and self-downing, thus providing a better psychological set for approaching the more technical behavioral aspects of a sex therapy program.

Let us now examine some of the current and most widely practiced sex therapy approaches in terms of our eight-stage model, focusing on two of the more common sexual disorders.

Female Orgasmic Dysfunction

The main treatment modality for both primary and secondary orgasmic dysfunction is a series of graduated masturbation homework assignments (Barbach, 1975; Heiman, LoPiccolo, & LoPiccolo, 1976; Kaplan, 1974). Adjunctive techniques for secondary orgasmic dysfunction may include sensate focus (Masters & Johnson, 1970), systematic desensitization (Wolpe, 1969), and assertiveness training (Wolfe, 1976).

In a variety of ways, treatment focuses on getting the woman to develop an expanded set of situations and stimuli capable of evoking sexual excitement (Link 1). This is done in a number of ways. Through giving corrective information about the female pelvic anatomy and physiology, women are urged to think of their clitoris, and not the vaginal walls, as being the site of erotic stimulation most likely to lead to orgasm. The use of fantasy (and not just romantic thoughts of one's husband of 30 years) is encouraged. Fantasies, often previously used with anxiety (or perhaps not used at all) are relabeled by the therapist as good, fun, healthy sexual stimuli. And fingers, vibrators, pillows, and other physical stimuli are given "status" as valid sexual stimuli. While expanding their set of stimuli that can potentiate sexual arousal and enjoyment, clients also are learning a new vocabulary with which to describe these stimuli, both to themselves and to their partners. Through repeated pairing of the new sexual stimuli with higher arousal, the new erotic potential of these stimuli gets better established. In addition, clients are helped to identify those stimuli that "turn them off" rather than turn them on (e.g., body odor, unresolved hurts and anger) and to bring about changes in these stimuli and/or in their evaluation of them, in order to reduce or eliminate their turning-off potential.

Corrective information is also given regarding Link 4, perception of arousal, by information giving coupled with masturbatory practice. Thus the client may be looking for exploding skyrockets, copious lubrication, or shockwaves through her body as signals of arousal. Failing to experience these, by selective abstraction she may fail to label and acknowledge her body's far more subtle indications of arousal (e.g., a tickling or tingling sensation in her vulva, tensing of her thigh muscles, contractions of her abdominal and perineal muscles, or increased breath rate). By providing the client with a variety of indicators of arousal, with accompanying labels for them, and by encouraging her to look for her own changes in sensation during her masturbatory practice sessions, she becomes trained to perceive more accurately a wide variety of sexual sensations.

At Link 5, positive evaluation of arousal is facilitated through various kinds of verbal coaching aimed at re-educating and reassuring the client about her sexual arousal and the things that aid or interfere with it. In addition, the client is helped to identify and label those physical and mental signals that distract her from tuning in to her arousal (e.g., discomfort from too-hard clitoral stimulation, anxiety about rejection, overfocus on pleasing her partner, or more general mind-wandering), and is provided with ways of reducing her interfering thoughts and feelings.

Kaplan (1974), Barbach (1975), and Heiman, LoPiccolo, and LoPiccolo (1976) aid this process of positive evaluation of arousal by telling the client that it's all right to take as long as she needs, by showing her that her feelings and fears are normal and that she's not such a bad person, since lots of other women have this problem. However, perhaps no therapy as effectively and directly attacks the negative evaluation and attendant anxiety, guilt, or depression that block arousal and interfere with orgasm as well as Ellis' (1960, 1975, 1979) RET, in which the client is taught vigorously and actively to debate her ideas that "It's awful not to feel excited"; "I should be coming more quickly"; or "What a hopeless sexual failure I am."

One of the staples in the armamentarium of the sex therapist, especially useful in the treatment of secondary anorgasmia, is sensate focus. This procedure consists of a two-phased sequence of mutual partner stimulation exercises designed to take the focus off intercourse and to redirect it to sensual pleasure from many parts of the body. It also provides a means for the sexual partners to communicate their likes and dislikes and feelings to each other. In the first phase, first one partner, then the other, caresses the partner's body from head to toes, experimenting with different touches and receiving feedback on what feels good and what produces discomfort. Breasts and genitals are excluded. In the second part, breasts and genitals are added, with additional instruction to experiment not with producing orgasm but with finding ways of touching that produce higher states of arousal. Again, both participants learn to reduce their rigid fixation on the usual erogenous zones and to extend their sources of erotic stimulation and arousal to a variety of areas often not previously perceived as stimulating. They learn to talk about these places in a new way, to touch them in new way, and to evaluate the arousal and sexual behavior positively (e.g., sensations in the scalp, feet, ears, etc.). The overall cognitive/emotive effect is generally a reduction in tension in sexual interactions, a freeing of the pressure to have an orgasm (or an erection) or intercourse. Because it becomes almost impossible to fail when the sexual goals of orgasm, erection, and intercourse are eliminated, all the kinds of stimulation and arousal that occur tend to become more positively evaluated, with a concomitant reduction of interfering negative thoughts and feelings.

If the woman is to transmit to her partner some of the new information about what sexual behaviors feel arousing to her so that they may be incorporated into their sexual encounters, she may profit from assertiveness training, to help her become more skilled and comfortable in communicating sexual preferences and feelings. Assertiveness training consists of helping the individual—via the techniques of behavior rehearsal, modeling, and coaching—to communicate feelings and preferences in a direct, clear fashion (for example, that she would like her partner to perform oral–genital contact, or that she'd like to rub her clitoris during intercourse to facilitate orgasm). A usual part of this process involves the uncovering of feelings that block communication (e.g., anxiety about sounding foolish or about being rejected) and helping the client to develop a new set of beliefs that support assertive expression ("I have a right to express my preferences"; "I have a right to sexual satisfaction"; "If the other person feels put upon by my request, it's disappointing and frustrating, but not awful"). The process of expanding the repertoire of stimuli, arousal cues, and overt sexual behaviors and of evaluating them positively is thus extended to the woman's partner.

Experimentation in a wide variety of sexual behaviors (Link 6) is encouraged between the partners, with the therapist giving permission to talk about what's liked and what's uncomfortable as a further means of helping the clients to develop more comfortable and positive feelings and evaluations of their newly extended set of sexual behaviors. The woman also may be encouraged to practice new behavioral expression on her own (e.g., stimulating herself to a noisy orgasm, or role-playing orgasm), to help her strengthen both the behavior and the positive experience of it.

Premature Ejaculation

Let us now apply our model to a common male problem, that of premature ejaculation. A core condition in cases of premature ejaculation is an inability to recognize (and consequently control) the sensations premonitory to ejaculation (Link 4). An important step in treatment may involve *in vivo* training, in which the client learns to "get in touch" with his preorgasmic sensations, with the goal of increasing his threshold of excitability. As Walen, Hauserman, and Lavin (1977, p. 301) state, "It appears that the active ingredient of the successful therapy methods consists of overcoming the immediate obstacle to ejaculatory continence by inducing the man to experience the previously avoided perception of high levels of erotic arousal while he is with his sexual partner." The therapist also helps the client to focus on the thoughts and feelings e.g., fear of failure, anger, or insensitivity toward his partner) that interfere with this sensual focus, and replace them with more positive evaluations. The client is also helped to identify and positively evaluate other stimuli and behaviors (e.g., fantasies, ways of stimulating himself) that will aid him in becoming aroused and better controlling the pacing of the arousal (Links 1 and 6).

When, as is frequently the case, there is an additional problem of negative evaluation of the problem behavior (Link 8), the client may be greatly helped by the addition of an RET approach (Ellis, 1976) in which he is counseled to challenge his anxiety-creating thoughts ("It's awful if I come too fast") or self-attacking thoughts ("What an inadequate sexual partner I am for coming so fast"). This work on countering possible negative evaluations of sexual behavior is also done by most of the leading sex therapists, by reassuring the client that it is not necessary for him to be able to have prolonged intercourse or an erect penis in order to be able to enjoy sex or to satisfy his partner.

A CASE EXAMPLE

What is evident from the preceding examples is that the links in the proposed feedback-loop model do not necessarily follow each other in a step-by-step, sequenced fashion, but rather reverberate to each other in different ways. What we hope the model can facilitate is the identification of which links may be especially problematic in an individual case, so that therapeutic strategies may thereby be more clearly selected.

The following case illustrates a session in which various links in the model are dealt with, within a rational therapy framework, as the therapist helps the client to clarify her misperceptions and exaggeratedly negative evaluations and to dispute these irrationalities to produce cognitive, emotive, and behavioral changes. The client is a 32-year-old woman with secondary orgasmic dysfunction. The woman has been divorced for four years, during which she has had several sexual partners but has become increasingly "turned off" by sex. In the session, she is discussing a man she has dated three times with whom she enjoys talking and going out, but at whom she is beginning to feel angry as he has orgasms easily and she does not. Though a major goal is helping her to identify the kinds of stimulation she likes and to become more assertive in going after her preferences, the larger goal is to help the client to develop a belief system that supports her right to have pleasure and helps her anti-awfulize about the possibility of being rejected (the underlying issue that is probably the root of a large percentage of sexual disturbances).

C: I don't know what's wrong with me. I really liked Bob—but after we had sex the other night, I just felt angry and crummy and couldn't wait for him to get out the door. Maybe I'm just too fussy or messed up and won't ever find anyone I can relate to.

T: You seemed to feel so positively about him. What happened, do you think, that led up to your feeling angry?

C: Hmmmm. I think it was when we had sex. We did a lot of necking. . . . I really like that a lot and was getting very turned on. Then we started having intercourse. He came in about 3 minutes, then we sort of lay in bed and talked for awhile and I just wished he'd disappear. I think that's the thing that really made me mad.

T: *It* made you mad? Remember. . . . How is it that we cause our feelings in reaction to certain things, according to RET?

C: Oh, yeah . . . by my thoughts about what happened. . . . Let me see. I guess I told myself he should have been more interested in my pleasure. And that he was a pretty selfish person . . . he doesn't really give a damn about me at all.

T: Gee, that doesn't sound like the way you were describing him a couple of weeks ago. Let's assume he may be acting selfishly or insensitively with you sexually; that is, not taking the time to check with you and see if you are satisfied. Can you see how this selfish behavior doesn't mean he's a totally selfish person?

C: I guess he's not really a selfish person. He's actually been very nice and generous to me, and from what I've seen, to his family and friends. But he *shouldn't* just have his orgasm and roll over, should he? I mean, I don't like that!

T: And where is it written that he *must* behave the way you'd like him to?

C: I guess he doesn't *have* to . . ., but I want him to.

T: Great! Now, I'd like to check things out and see if you have some handle on how to dispute your "should," your demands that he must give you an orgasm. Because if you want at least to explore the possibility of a relationship with him, and improve your sexual enjoyment, I think it's important that you really learn how to stop this kind of "should-ing," else you probably are going to get so angry you're just going to want to run, a pattern you've said you'd like to break.

C: I guess I can tell myself, I don't like his neglecting my orgasm, but I can stand it. I already have—three times! (Laughs) And I can try to remember he's not a rotten selfish person . . . just somewhat fallible.

T: Good. Now, let's see if we can brainstorm some ways of going about trying to see if you can wind up with more orgasms. Any thoughts in this? What are some of the things that turn you on, some of the ways you think you're most likely to orgasm?

C: Uh . . . (awkwardly) uh . . . well, I can just about always have an orgasm with my vibrator. And almost always . . . uh . . . if a guy does oral sex on me. And I love when he touches my body, rubs my back.

T: Good, so you've got some pretty good ideas to give him.

C: Yeah . . . but I could *never* ask him to do . . . like, go down on me. He'd probably think I was a weirdo, to need these kinds of things, and to just come out and ask for them. Just the thought makes me really anxious.

T: Let's assume that he might, though lots and lots of men I've talked to have said just the opposite, that they'd welcome some feedback from their partners, 'cause half the time they don't know if she's really turned on, or if she's come. And they say that if she'd open her mouth, he wouldn't have to go through so much mind-reading or spend half an hour screwing her when she'd really like her back massaged and her nipples licked! But anyway . . . Let's assume Bob does think you're a weirdo. What do you suppose you're telling yourself about this to create anxiety?

C: That's easy: that it would be awful if he thought that, and that he'd never want to see me again.

T: And if he didn't want to see you again?

C: I guess, when I think about it, it wouldn't be so awful. Pretty disappointing, 'cause I guess I do think he's one of the nicest guys I've met in a long time, but I guess if I've survived without him all this time, I could still get by if he split.

T: Good. Now if you can keep those rational thoughts firmly planted in your mind—and especially at the times you're anxious about letting him know where you're at sexually—you'll be in a better place to take the risk of speaking up.

Because of the client's religious background and awkwardness in discussing her sexual preferences, behavior rehearsal was done to help reduce her anxiety and increase her facility in expressing herself. At the next session, she reported great success: Bob had expressed surprise at learning that she hadn't been satisfied, since her noises had led him to assume she had come, and he was eager to do the things she indicated she liked.

CONCLUSION

Positive sexual experiences are a result of more than good sexual technique. They result from accurate and realistic perceptions and positive evaluations. Without these mediating links, no amount of "sexpertise" can overcome inhibitions, guilt, anxiety, depression, and anger. Sexual dysfunctions of the male or the female client can therefore be regarded as stemming from blockages in these final common pathways.

It will seem obvious that good diagnosis will maximize the selection of an appropriate treatment procedure, which in turn may enhance the probability of successful treatment. It is suggested that a diagnosis based on the proposed feedback-loop model of a positive sexual experience may enable the therapist to (1) select the most relevant cognitive behavioral procedures for the client, and (2) emphasize the most relevant aspects of these procedures for an individual case.

REFERENCES

Annon, J. S. *The behavioral treatment of sexual problems. Vol. 1. Brief therapy.* Honolulu: Enabling Systems, 1974.

Barbach, L. G. *For yourself: The fulfillment of female sexuality.* New York: Doubleday, 1975.

Beck, A. T. *Cognitive therapy and the emotional disorders.* New York: International Universities Press, 1976.

Beck, A. T., Rush, A. J., Emery, G. & Shaw, B. F., *Cognitive therapy of depression.* New York: Guilford Press, 1979.

Cantor, J., Zillman, D., & Bryant, J. Enhancement of experienced sexual arousal in response to erotic stimuli through misattribution of unrelated residual excitation. *Journal of Personality and Social Psychology,* 1975, *32,* 69–75.

Dutton, D., & Aron, A. Some evidence for heightened sexual attraction under conditions of high anxiety. *Journal of Personality and Social Psychology,* 1974, *30,* 510–517.

Ellis, A. Is the vaginal orgasm a myth? In A. P. Pillay & A. Ellis (Eds.), *Sex, society and the individual.* Bombay: International Journal of Sexology Press, 1953.

Ellis, A. *The art and science of love.* New York: Lyle Stuart, 1960.

Ellis, A. *Sex and the liberated man.* New York: Lyle Stuart, 1976.

Ellis, A. *Intelligent woman's guide to dating and mating.* Secaucus, N.J.: Lyle Stuart, 1979.

Ellis, A., & Harper, R. A. *A new guide to rational living.* Hollywood, Calif.: Wilshire Books, 1975.

Ellis, H. *Studies in the psychology of sex.* New York: Random House, 1936.

Feldman, M. P., & MacCulloch, M. J. *Homosexual behavior: Therapy and assessment.* New York: Pergamon, 1971.

Ford, C., & Beach, F. *Patterns of sexual behavior.* New York: Paul Hoeber, 1951.

Forel, A. *The sexual question.* New York: Physician's and Surgeon's Book Co., 1922.

Hartman, W., & Fithian, M. *The treatment of the sexual dysfunctions.* Long Beach, Calif: Center for Marital and Sexual Studies. 1972.

Heiman, J. R. A psychophysiological exploration of sexual arousal patterns in males and females. *Psychophysiology,* 1977, *14,* 266–274.

Heiman, J. R., LoPiccolo, L., & LoPiccolo, J. *Becoming orgasmic: A sexual growth program for women.* Englewood Cliffs, N.J.: Prentice-Hall, 1976.

Hirschfeld, M. *Sex in human relationships.* London: Lane, 1935.

Kaplan, H. S. *The new sex therapy: Active treatment of sexual dysfunctions.* New York: Brunner/Mazel, 1974.

Kelly, G. L. *Sexual manual for those married or about to be.* Augusta, Ga.: S. Medical Supply Co., 1948.

Lazarus, A. *Behavior therapy and beyond.* New York: McGraw-Hill, 1971.

Masters, W. H., & Johnson, V. E. *Human sexual inadequacy.* Boston: Little, Brown, 1970.

Rachman, S., & Hodgson, R. J. Experimentally-induced "sexual fetishism": Replication and development. *Psychological Record,* 1968, *18,* 25–27.

Robie, W. F. *The art of love.* Ithaca, N.Y.: Rational Life Press, 1925.

Robinson, W. *Woman: Her sex and love life.* New York: Eugenics Publishing Co., 1929.

Rook, K. S., & Hammen, C. L. A cognitive perspective on the experience of sexual arousal. *Journal of Social Issues*, 1977, *33*, 7–29.

Schachter, S. The interaction of cognitive and physiological determinants of emotional state. In L. Berkowitz (Ed.), *Advances in Experimental Social Psychology*. New York: Academic Press, 1964.

Schachter, S., & Singer, J. Cognitive, social, and physiological determinants of emotional state. *Psychological Review*. 1962, *69*, 379–399.

Semans, J. H. Premature ejaculation: A new approach. *Southern Medical Journal*, *49*, 353–357.

Stone, H., & Stone, A. *A marriage manual*. New York: Simon & Schuster, 1935.

Van de Velde, T. H. *Ideal marriage*. New York: Covici-Friede, 1926.

Walen, S. R., Hauserman, N., & Lavin, P. *A clinical guide to behavior therapy*. New York: Oxford University Press, 1977.

Wolfe, J. *How to be sexually assertive*. New York: Institute for Rational Living, 1976.

Wolpe, J. *The practice of behavior therapy*. New York: Pergamon Press, 1969.

Wolpe, J., & Lazarus, A. *Behavior therapy techniques*. New York: Pergamon Press, 1966.

Part Three
Primary Techniques and Basic Processes

12

The Process of Rational–
Emotive Therapy*

Russell M. Grieger

Rational–emotive therapy has become one of the major approaches to psychotherapy during the last 20 years and is a foremost contributor to the emergence of
what Mahoney (1977) has called the cognitive behavioral model of intervention.
The accord given to RET in its early phase of development was largely due to the
clinical efforts and writings of its founder, Albert Ellis, and to his psychotherapeutic success as well as that of other RET practitioners. This face
validity has now been supported by an impressive body of empirical evidence
(Ellis, 1977; DiGiuseppe, Miller, & Trexler, 1977; McGovern & Silverman,
1984), so that the scientific community has joined practicing therapists in
acknowledging RET as an innovative and viable approach to cognitive behavioral intervention.

As RET has gained recognition, the theory and methods have been adopted
and applied, in part or large measure, by thousands of mental health professionals. Parallel to this growing practice has been an increasing clamor for a
description of what RET is all about, from start to finish, and also for an
explanation of its many techniques.

In part as a response to this clamor, I and a colleague of mine, John Boyd,
published a text that both outlined the steps or stages in RET and, for each step,
described its goals and techniques (Grieger & Boyd, 1980). In this text, we

*This chapter is a highly condensed and somewhat revised version of a text written by Russell M.
Grieger and John Boyd, *Rational–emotive therapy: A skills-based approach* (New York: Van
Nostrand Reinhold, 1980). The reader is encouraged to refer to that text for an expanded discussion
of what is in this chapter, as well as for a description of many of the major techniques used by RET
practitioners. In its present form, this chapter appeared in the *Journal of Rational–Emotive Therapy*,
1986, *4*(1), 138–148.

delineated a four-step, skills-based model that is based on the proposition that psychotherapy is a "craft" consisting of highly developed and refined skills that are employed strategically to influence the psychological state and behavior of clients constructively. In our skills-based model, which we believe is reflective of RET practice now being performed, we outlined the stages of rational–emotive psychodiagnosis, insight, working through, and re-education, which is now called working through II. Under ideal circumstances the techniques employed in these four skill groups sequentially lead the client through the RET process.

Now, some five years later, as many new RET techniques are being published and as cognitive behavioral therapy in general continues to expand in scope and complexity, I thought it timely to restate what takes place in RET. This chapter, then, while not technique oriented, serves again to describe the process of RET, and, coincidentally, to orient the reader of this text to the chapters to follow in this part. Thus, it outlines RET as a four-step process, although the steps have been somewhat revised since 1980.

RATIONAL–EMOTIVE PSYCHODIAGNOSIS

All psychotherapies begin with an attempt to understand the nature and dynamics of the client's problems. So too with RET. In almost complete contrast to most other types of psychotherapy, however, RET's primary diagnostic focus is on uncovering the client's disturbance-producing beliefs or philosophies, understanding how these uniquely contribute to the client's emotional problems, and setting realistic goals to which both the therapist and client can agree. The tools the therapist uses to accomplish these tasks are fourfold: (1) a thorough knowledge and appreciation of the crucial role that cognitions play in impacting behavior and affect, (2) an understanding of and sensitivity to the basic irrational ideas that create the various emotional disturbances, (3) confidence in the validity of the RET premises and a commitment to understanding clients from this perspective, and (4) general interview skills that are part of all clinicians' repertoires.

Rational–emotive psychodiagnosis encompasses four separate yet overlapping chores, which I will now briefly discuss in turn.

Categorizing Problems

Determining what does and does not constitute psychopathology and therefore what would be best dealt with through psychotherapy is a debatable point, but it is one that is essential in deciding how best to help people. Some problems clearly call for psychotherapy, while others could be handled better with guidance, advice, case management, or some form of environmental manipulation.

In making this determination, we find it useful to distinguish external from internal problems. External problems include such things as career concerns (e.g., do I or do I not change my job?), problems in living (e.g., financial difficulties), and relationship difficulties (e.g., an "obnoxious" spouse). In RET these are often termed *activating events,* or A's, in the ABC formula. While these are often weighty concerns that certainly deserve attention, they hardly constitute psychopathology and, unless accompanied by emotional problems, certainly are not the province of psychotherapy. By contrast, internal problems include the emotional disturbances (depression, anger, guilt, and anxiety) and the dysfunctional behaviors (addiction, procrastination, and the like) to which psychotherapy generally attends and which are the distinct province of RET. Internal problems are often problems about external problems, and in RET these are termed the *consequences* and noted with the letter C in the ABC formula.

A typical categorizing situation frequently encountered is the client who presents multiple problems, both external and internal. If this client presents internal or emotional problems about external problems, then the RET therapist ferrets out the emotional–behavioral aspects and earmarks these as first or primary targets for change. The reasons for this are several: (1) to relieve clients of external, practical problems before resolving the emotional problems about the practical problems often robs them of the motivation to work on the emotional problems; (2) people generally can solve or better cope with environmental problems on their own after they resolve their emotional problems; and (3) emotional problems are simply the realm of psychotherapy, not career choice and so on.

Thus, first in psychodiagnosis, the therapist determines whether or not the client has an internal, emotional problem about some external problem. If not, then the request for psychotherapy is denied and an appropriate, alternative referral is made. But, if an emotional problem is uncovered, or if an emotional problem is found to be superimposed on an external problem, then attention is first given to this, and the next step is to detect what irrational beliefs the client holds that causes him or her to be disturbed.

Detecting Irrational Beliefs

An RET therapist assumes on theoretical and empirical grounds that emotional disturbance stems from the irrational beliefs (iB's) a person holds, most particularly the four themes of demandingness, awfulizing, I-can't-stand-it-itis, and self-rating. From the moment the client begins talking, then, the RET therapist will listen for hints of these themes and will begin to determine which ones go with and cause which presented emotional problems.

The detection of iB's is probably the most crucial of the diagnostic steps in the diagnostic process, for what is detected here will be the center of the RET change efforts to come later. Before therapists can hear or inquire about the iB's, then, they must truly understand the dynamics of psychopathology, be familiar with how people express the ideas behind their pathology, and have the skills for eliciting these ideas. The purpose of this chapter is not to present the RET literature of psychopathology; however, almost all of Ellis' writings are directed toward this and should be read. In addition the reader may want to review Grieger and Grieger (1982) and Grieger and Boyd (1980) for in-depth discussions of these matters.

Detecting Problems about Problems

It is the rare client who presents only a single emotional problem. Rather, people usually develop secondary symptoms that overlie their primary symptoms. To say it differently, they usually develop emotional problems about their emotional problems. When people feel and behave in a disturbed manner at C (for example, they experience depression), this C itself becomes another event in their lives (they notice their depression), and then they most often create a secondary disturbance (shame and depression about being depressed) about the original problem.

Secondary symptoms of emotional disturbance usually exacerbate primary symptoms; they also largely interfere with people clearly perceiving how they create their primary symptoms and what they can do to eliminate them. In RET we are careful to look for evidence of both primary and secondary problems. If we find both, which is usually the case, we are able to organize more accurately the client's disturbance and to be more effective at helping her or him surrender them.

Goal Setting

The end product of the processes delineated here is the development of a conceptual schema that categorizes the client's problems in terms of their composite ABC's. This psychodiagnosis conceptualizes the events (A's), the irrational beliefs (iB's), and the emotional and behavioral consequences (C's) that comprise the symptomatic picture. Immediately after formulating the diagnosis proper, the therapist tells the client what options are available and which one(s) are recommended. The options available to RET clients, in order of preference, are: (1) to work on emotional–behavioral problems about other emotional–behavioral problems, if present; (2) to work on emotional–behavioral concerns and, when resolved, turn therapy toward any environmental and career problems remaining; (3) to work on environmental concerns before working on emotional–behavioral problems, an option usually not recommended for the reasons already given. Goal setting in RET directs the client to option one or two, or both one and two, the latter most often being the choice.

RATIONAL–EMOTIVE INSIGHT

Facilitating client insight is a second major chore in RET. It would be a mistake, however, to conclude that insight necessarily follows diagnosis. It sometimes does, but often it overlaps the diagnostic process; that is, the therapist helps the client gain insights concurrently with psychodiagnosis. Regardless, for the sake of discussion, it is helpful to think of rational–emotive insight facilitation as an independent and separate activity, for several reasons: It clarifies issues for the client, it helps the client make sense of what follows in the therapy, and it teaches the client what to do to make positive therapeutic changes.

In RET there are five insights that clients had better acquire in order to get the most out of their therapy. Some people require education in all of them, while other, more sophisticated people need to learn only selected ones. Nevertheless, it is important to check each client on all five to make sure each insight is in place:

1. Peoples' current ideas and beliefs play an extremely important role in causing their emotional and behavioral problems. This, of course, represents the basic premise underlying RET and is conceptualized in terms of the ABC theory. This insight, then, explains the "real" cause of emotional problems and helps people take responsibility for them. Coincidentally, it also helps clarify both the purpose and focus of RET.

2. Again, people are encouraged to take responsibility for their emotional problems by understanding that, regardless of the historical events surrounding the original acquisition of the iB's, people feel upset and are disturbed today because they continue to indoctrinate themselves with the same iB's they learned in the past. Through this insight, they learn that their ongoing self-conditioning is more important than their early experiences.

3. Clients "need" to have an awareness, acknowledgment, and appreciation of what particular irrational ideas or beliefs cause their emotional problems. All three parts of this insight are important because an awareness without an acknowledgment and appreciation is unmotivating; indeed, some people can readily find their irrational beliefs, but they put little or no stock in the relevance of their irrational beliefs and hence the awareness is unimpactful. This insight then, not only shows what one specifically has to change in order to get over the problems, but it also promotes hope and power in the client. Since clients cause their problems by endorsing the iB's, they are not dependent on the good will of external forces to get better.

4. Clients can accept themselves even though they have created and maintained their emotional problems all by themselves. Many novice therapists have had clients with whom they failed to discuss this and who later ended up guilt ridden and depressed by blaming themselves once they realized their role in causing their own problems. So, I recommend taking time to discuss this.

5. By the time most people enter therapy they have so propagandized themselves to their own beliefs that they blindly accept them as truth and rarely question their validity. Unfortunately an energetic and sustained assault on them is necessary if they are to give them up. This insight, then, says that the first four insights are not sufficient; rather, people must work long and hard to give up their irrational beliefs, if they are to get over their emotional problems. Furthermore, they had better plan to keep working at giving them up indefinitely, if they are to maintain their gains.

These five insights are necessary but insufficient ingredients for constructive change. They orient clients to rational–emotive theory, teach them the bases of their problems, and facilitate motivation for the hard work required to give up emotional problems. Next comes the change stages, or working through, parts 1 and 2.

RATIONAL–EMOTIVE WORKING THROUGH, PART 1: TEACHING A RATIONAL KNOWLEDGE BASE

Rational–emotive working through constitutes the heart of RET. Helping clients work through their emotional–behavioral problems means helping them systematically to give up their irrational ideas and adopt rational, self-enhancing ones. This is where most of the therapist's energy and time are directed and where long-lasting change takes place. Successful working through leads to significant change, whereas unsuccessful working through leads to no gain or superficial gain at best.

Helping people to give up their irrational ideas is often a very difficult and arduous undertaking. This is so for at least three reasons. First, because people have typically believed these ideas for years and have thought about and dealt with scores of situations consistent with them, they often vigorously cling to their irrational ideas. In effect, they have deeply endorsed and practiced believing their irrational ideas until these ideas have become "second nature." Changing anything so well learned, therefore, requires repeated, energetic efforts, even for those who are willing and committed to change.

The fact that sometimes people do not want to change provides a second reason why working through can be difficult. For some, the prospect of relinquishing the existing, albeit self-defeating ways of thinking, feeling, and acting elicits fears and resistances that in and of themselves represent significant cognitive distortions and require therapeutic attention. Some of these unrealistic and/or irrational fears include fear of losing one's identity or becoming a phony by adopting new ideas, fear of becoming emotionally dulled or machinelike by thinking rationally, fear of becoming mediocre and losing one's specialness by giving up perfectionistic ideas, and fear of losing sources of gratification or secondary gain by relinquishing the pathological ways of thinking and acting.

Successful working through can be blocked and even defeated if the therapist does not respond to these issues in an adequate manner.

And, third, the working through process often proves to be very difficult because people generally are not very adept at critical thinking. This is often because of resistance, a lack of skills in critical thinking, or simple ignorance about different ways to think than the ways they already do. Very often, however, it is because people are, as Ellis (1967) has said, "allergic to thinking." That is, people tend to be lazy and intolerant of frustration and pain and therefore want a magical, facile solution to their problems that requires little effort. Thus, left to their own devices, they drift, goof, and act on their acknowledged irrational, self-defeating beliefs, even though they know better.

So, in rational–emotive working through, part 1, we recognize that clients have the worst of two worlds: they tend to cling to their irrational thinking while at the same time they tend to be poor at doing what is important in order to change. The goals at this stage are: (1) to help clients clearly comprehend what is illogical and false about the ideas or philosophies that underpin their disturbances; (2) to show clients the foolhardiness or self-defeating consequences of their irrational ideas; (3) to teach clients new, alternative ideas that are contrary to their irrational ideas; and (4) to convince them of both the logic behind and the benefits of these new ideas, in order to motivate them to commit themselves to and take responsibility for adopting these new ideas. Through these efforts, we try (1) to get clients to acquire a rational knowledge base that can be learned, endorsed, and adopted in the future, thereby effecting a significant therapeutic change; and (2) to further their motivation to work at actualizing these changes.

The Institute for Rational–Emotive Therapy in New York City has an extensive professional tape library that contains many tapes of Albert Ellis and other RET practitioners doing this part of RET. Listening to these tapes will show that, to help clients gain a rational knowledge base, the rational–emotive therapist acts as a nonsense-annihilating teacher who persuades, cajoles, encourages, and teaches the client to suspend judgment, to consider each currently held idea as a proposition or hypothesis to be tested, to consider new ideas (and which ones) that are accurate and beneficial, and to work hard to give up the old and take on the new ideas. In sum, at this stage the therapist is highly didactic, using teaching, reasoning, persuasion, and Socratic dialogues to accomplish therapeutic results.

RATIONAL–EMOTIVE WORKING THROUGH, PART 2: FACILITATING A NEW PHILOSOPHY

It would be a mistake to think of the two parts of rational–emotive working through as distinct and separate processes; rather, they both constitute the heart of change and in practice overlap and compliment each other. For the sake of understanding and clarity, however, it is best to discuss working through, part 2, as an entity in and of itself.

Having set the stage with the three preceding processes, rational–emotive psychodiagnosis, insight, and working through 1, then, the therapist puts her or his energies into helping the client get rid of the old, irrational philosophies and replace them with new, rational ones. The end product is almost always for the person to believe new rational ideas or philosophies and to act on them automatically.

Rational–emotive working through, part 2, can be subdivided into the following two components: disputation and habit strengthening.

Disputation

The disputation process employs the logico-empirical method of repeated and persistent scientific experimentation and questioning. Through a whole host of cognitive, behavioral, and emotive strategies, the therapist helps clients do three things, all of which are designed to assist them in determining whether their ideas are valid or invalid (Ellis & Grieger, 1977). First, the therapist raises rhetorical questions (e.g., Where is the evidence to support this?), devises behavioral and emotive experience, and teaches clients to do likewise. In this way, clients are assisted in debating their irrational ideas. To say it another way, clients are encouraged to play devil's advocate with themselves, vigorously engaging in an internal debate about the tenableness of the idea in question. The therapist also helps clients discriminate, or make distinctions, between the rational and irrational parts of their ideas—between their wants or desires and their "musts"; between undesirable and "awful" consequences; between doing bad deeds and "being" a bad person; between logical conclusions and nonsequiturs; and the like. By this process, people learn to siphon off the parts of their thinking that make no sense and lead to their own harm. And, third, the therapist helps clients to clearly and precisely define terms. They are helped to make finer and finer definitions of terms until logical fallacies and illogical conclusions are seen as absurd.

This disputation process is critical in RET. Not only is it the cornerstone of change, but it also is fraught with a variety of hazards for both the client and therapist. For that reason it is well for the therapist to be versed in a wide variety of techniques by which to accomplish the goals of this stage. Many such techniques have been developed, though space does not allow for their presentation. Some worth mentioning now, though, are the logical analysis and evaluation of irrational ideas through Socratic questioning, empirical analysis and evaluation through data collection, functional analysis (or an analysis of the positive and negative consequences of holding the belief), the use of humor, the use of paradox and of the taking an idea to a ludicrous extreme, rational–emotive imagery, behavioral experimentation, risk-taking exercises, shame-attacking exercises, and bibliotherapy.

2) Habit Strengthening

Working through, part 2, also serves to ingrain or habituate in people their new, rational ideas. Clients are therefore shown ways (and indeed encouraged to find ways on their own) to convince themselves, over and over again, of both the validity and pragmatic value of what they have learned. Thus, RET therapists teach them a habituating type of rational–emotive imagery (Maultsby, 1975), encourage them to preach rational thinking to others, suggest that they reward themselves for rational thinking and punish themselves for irrational thinking, suggest that they read rational bibliotherapeutic material, and, of course, strongly urge them to continue to do their disputation, both in mental and written form, for the rest of their lives. Perhaps most important, RET therapists do anything they can to get their clients to act in ways consistent in their daily lives with their new rational philosophy; in other words, they are encouraged to have as many direct experiences in life that express the rational, self-enhancing ideas or philosophies learned through the course of their rational–emotive therapy. This is probably when and where lasting change occurs.

SUMMARY AND CONCLUSION

This is the process of RET. Rather than telling exactly what the rational–emotive therapist does in RET, however, the aim of this chapter has been to orient the reader to the process of RET, to its stages and the goals or purposes of each stage. In this chapter, four stages are distinguished: rational–emotive psychodiagnosis, rational–emotive insight, and rational–emotive working through, parts 1 and 2.

Practitioners interested in doing RET will find this chapter a very nice overview; however, to do RET well, it is, of course, advised that readers familiarize themselves with the multitude of techniques and skills in the RET arsenal, in addition to studying with and being supervised by a qualified RET practitioner. Readers are advised to read the remaining chapters in this unit and to turn to several of the prominent RET books already published, which tell in great detail what RETers do, including Bard (1980), Ellis (1962, 1971, 1973), Ellis and Grieger (1977), Grieger and Boyd (1980), Walen, DiGuiseppe, and Wessler (1980), and Wessler and Wessler (1980).

REFERENCES

Bard, J. A. (1980). *Rational–emotive therapy in practice*. Champaign, Ill.: Research Press.
DiGiuseppe, R., Miller, N., & Trexler, L. (1977). A review of rational–emotive outcome studies. *The Counseling Psychologist, 7,* 64–72.
Ellis, A. (1962). *Reason and emotion in psychotherapy*. New York: Stuart.
Ellis, A. (1967). Goals of psychotherapy. In A. R. Maurer (Ed.), *The goals of psychotherapy*. New York: Appleton-Century Crofts.

Ellis, A. (1971). *Growth through reason*. Palo Alto, Calif.: Science and Behavior Books.

Ellis, A. (1973). *Humanistic psychotherapy: The rational–emotive approach*. New York: McGraw-Hill.

Ellis, A. (1977). Rational–emotive therapy: Research data that supports the clinical and personality hypotheses of RET and other modes of cognitive behavior therapy. *The Counseling Psychologist, 7*, 2–42.

Ellis, A., & Grieger, R. (1977). *Handbook of rational–emotive therapy: Volume I*. New York: Springer.

Grieger, R., & Boyd, J. (1980). *Rational–emotive therapy: A skills-based approach*. New York: Van Nostrand Reinhold.

Grieger, R., & Grieger, I. Z. (1982). *Cognition and emotional disturbance*. New York: Human Sciences Press.

McGovern, T. E., & Silverman, M. A. (1984). A review of outcome studies of rational–emotive therapy from 1977 to 1982. *Journal of Rational–Emotive Therapy, 2*, 7–18.

Walen, A. R., DiGuiseppe, R., & Wessler, R. L. (1980). *A practitioner's guide to rational–emotive therapy*. New York: Oxford University Press.

Wessler, R. A., & Wessler, R. L. (1980). *The principles and practices of rational–emotive therapy*. San Francisco: Jossey-Bass.

13

Didactic Persuasion Techniques in Cognitive Restructuring*

Thomas H. Harrell, Irving Beiman, and
Karen LaPointe

Therapeutic procedures that emphasize the role of cognitive variables have been increasingly employed in recent years. Unfortunately, the proliferation of cognitive treatment techniques has not, in general, been accompanied by systematic empirical evaluation of their effectiveness (Mahoney, 1974). This deficiency of controlled research may be explained, at least in part, by the relatively few attempts to specify the procedures found in the diversity of techniques and approaches encompassed by the label "cognitive therapy."

Attempts at specification have been notably limited and have not addressed all relevant aspects of cognitive treatment. Mahoney (1974) suggests at least the following components operative in Ellis's rational–emotive therapy (RET) approach: (1) didactic persuasion toward a belief system that recognizes the role of irrational thoughts in subjective distress and deficient performance, (2) training in the observation and discrimination of self-statements, (3) training in the logical and empirical evaluation of self-statements, (4) graduated performance assignments, (5) immediate social feedback, (6) instructions and selective reinforcement for alteration of self-statements, and (7) therapist modeling and role-playing of recommended cognitive mediation styles. Similar components have been delineated by authors attempting to integrate RET into a behavior therapy framework (Beck, 1970; Goldfried & Davison, 1976; Goldfried, Decenteceo, & Weinberg, 1974; Meichenbaum, 1972; Rimm & Masters, 1974). These latter proposals have resulted in specification of those techniques, such as

*This chapter is reprinted from *Rational Living*, 1980, *15*(1), 3–8.

graduated performance assignments and therapist modeling, that are most amenable to behavioral assessment.

Mahoney's (1974) recognition of didactic persuasion as one of the active components of RET is an important step, since many practitioners of RET, including Ellis himself, rely heavily on methods of verbal persuasion to help clients recognize the role of irrational thoughts in subjective distress and to facilitate the development of a more "rational" belief system. Although the area has been recognized, the specific techniques involved in didactic persuasion have not been explicated in any systematic fashion. Consequently, didactic methods are noted as haphazard procedures (Goldfried, et al., 1974), unsupported by empirical data substantiating their effectiveness. We believe the haphazard and empirically unverified state of verbal persuasion methods is a consequence of the failure to operationalize these procedures. Since many of the cognitive techniques previously mentioned occur within or along with various verbal persuasion methods, clear specification of the latter is essential if adequate teaching and implementation of cognitive therapy, and research in cognitive therapy, are to occur.

Explication of procedural components is an initial and essential step toward methodologically sound outcome research (Fiske et al., 1970; Paul, 1967). Without operationalized treatment procedures, the reliability and validity of therapist implementation of the procedures cannot be empirically verified. In turn, without evidence that those procedures were consistently and correctly employed, they cannot be specified as the treatment variables responsible for the observed effects. Additionally, without clear specification of cognitive therapy procedures, the communicability of these strategies among therapists is reduced. This limits teachability, as well as the certainty of reliable implementation, of cognitive treatments.

The purpose of the present chapter is to specify verbal persuasion methods that may be utilized in cognitive therapy. Although verbal persuasion techniques may be found in such diverse areas as attitude change and persuasion, and argumentation and debate, as well as cognitive restructuring and self-control, only those procedures considered applicable within the context of a therapeutic relationship will be presented here. This explication of didactic persuasion techniques is intended to facilitate clinical application of cognitive therapy procedures, as well as future research efforts investigating their individual or collective effectiveness.

DIDACTIC PERSUASION TECHNIQUES

Explanation of Therapeutic Rationale

The basic assumptions, relevant theoretical considerations, and empirical support for the treatment procedure are explained to the client in clear, nontechnical terms. The persuasive value of this explanation lies in diminishing the client's unfamiliarity with the treatment methods and explicating his role in the therapy process. The rationale also prepares the client for acceptance of the appropriateness of the chosen treatment method(s) and avoids the "contrarient idea" (resistive ideas elicited by presentation of conclusions without prior discussion or explanation) (McBurney & Mills, 1964).

Therapeutically, a number of elements are active in the presentation of the rationale. Cognitions are placed in a formal symbol system that enables the client to represent his cognitions tangibly and directs him to focus attention on both their content and consequences as critical elements in the therapeutic procedure (Mahoney, 1974). The formal paradigm and rationale allow a "shared conceptual system" between therapist and client (Frank, 1961). By accepting the paradigm, the client essentially agrees to the overall therapeutic plan, increasing the probability of more extensive cognitive change.

The rationale stresses the client's personal responsibility for his thoughts and feelings, thus encouraging the client's perception that he, in fact, is responsible for and exerts control over his maladaptive cognitions. This element is essential to insuring the active participation of the client in the therapeutic plan, and to placing treatment within a self-control model (Kanfer & Karoly, 1972; Mahoney and Thoresen, 1974). An excellent example of a therapeutic rationale is presented by Bernstein and Borkovec (1973), although the procedure described is progressive relaxation training.

Logical Analysis and Evaluation

The principles of logic are applied by the therapist to the alteration of client maladaptive cognitions (Beck, 1976; Ellis, 1962, 1971, 1973). Logical discussion or formal argument can be directed toward two issues: (1) the logical validity of the client's premise (i.e., maladaptive belief or assumption); and (2) the incongruity, with his behavior, of the client's premise.

Ellis (1962) lists multiple reasons for the logical invalidity of common irrational premises. These reasons are used in logical argument to challenge the client's irrational premises.

When dealing with incongruity of belief and behavior, two forms of reasoning are applicable. In applying a generalization to a specific instance, deductive reasoning is used to show how the behavior does not follow from the basic premise. For example, "Last week we discussed how it was not possible for anyone to live up to all the expectations others have for us. Yet today you seem to be degrading yourself as a mother because you weren't able to give your daughter all the attention she wanted while you were fixing dinner. It appears to be particularly hard for you realistically to accept your limitations in the relationship with your daughter. Is it possible for you to meet all of your daughter's demands on a daily basis?"

There are occasions when a client engages in adaptive behavior that is inconsistent with a maladaptive belief. In this case inductive reasoning, drawing a generalization from specific instances, is used to show how the belief does not follow from the behavior. For example, "It sounds like you were able to handle that situation very well. You went into a crowded room and said to yourself, 'I'm new here, and I feel a little nervous, but most people are somewhat apprehensive in a new situation, so my feelings are natural and to be expected.' It seems to me that you're handling new social situations in a much more realistic manner."

Reduction to Absurdity

The therapist appears to assume, for the moment, that the irrational premise of the client is accurate. Then, by carrying the faulty premise to its logical extreme, its absurdity is illuminated (Ellis, 1962, 1971, 1973). For example, "You're telling me that you feel you really need to have other people's approval and can't stand it if you feel you've offended anyone. Let's assume that you actually can live your life without offending anyone and can gain everyone's approval. What would that take? Well, you'd have to dress in a way that everyone approved of, wear your hair in a way everyone approved of, eat what other people approved of, drink what other people approved of, say things that other people approved of, and always act in a way other people found acceptable. Of course, in order to know that you wouldn't offend anyone, you'd have to know all about what each person you were with liked. So you couldn't be with anyone until you knew them well enough never to offend them. And then you could never be with people who approved of different things because in order to be what one person approved of, you might offend another."

Empirical Analysis and Evaluation

The cognition is compared with real-life observations and/or empirical evidence related to the content of the cognition. The comparison allows an evaluation of the degree to which the cognition is a realistic expression of the known facts of a situation (Beck, 1970, 1976; Ellis, 1962, 1971, 1973). For example, "You seem to be saying that you have failed at everything you've ever tried in your life. It occurs to me that one way to determine if this is actually the case would be to look back over your life and see if you can't identify some accomplishments, as well as some failures. Let's try to be very objective as we do this and see if this examination really bears out your belief."

This technique would seem to be particularly effective when supplemented by homework assignments arranged in such a manner that the client makes observations and collects information that indicate the degree to which the cognition realistically reflects everyday life experiences (Ellis, 1962).

Contradiction with Cherished Value

The therapist introduces a dissonant situation for the client by demonstrating that a particular cognition contradicts or is incongruent with a valued belief or quality (Crabb, 1971). For example, "You're far too intelligent to believe that any one person could meet all your needs 100% of the time." Acknowledging the incompatibility of the two cognitions can lead the client to reduce the resulting dissonance by modifying the maladaptive one. Unless the dissonance is resolved, a cognition that is inconsistent with a personally valued quality or belief will be maintained.

Incredulous Therapist Response

The therapist attempts to induce dissonance by simply expressing, in an incredulous manner, his disbelief that the client could actually maintain such a maladaptive or irrational cognition (Ellis, 1962, 1971, 1973). For example, "You don't *really* expect her to respond to your every whim, do you?" Therapeutic utilization of this technique requires that the therapist direct incredulity toward the client's *attitude* and not toward the client; otherwise, the client is likely to respond with defensiveness and resistance.

Appeal to Negative Consequences

The client's maladaptive behaviors and the negative consequences of those behaviors are portrayed as resulting from maladaptive cognitions (Ellis, 1962, 1971, 1973). The technique involves specifying the negative consequences of the maladaptive cognition and encouraging the client to avoid or escape from the unpleasant consequences by modifying the problematic cognition. Affective consequences, such as depression and anxiety, as well as behavioral outcomes, such as poor performance on an exam or the continued avoidance of potentially pleasurable activities, are frequently specified. For example, a client's unfounded belief that he is much less competent in heterosexual relationships than his peers might be responded to in this manner: "I know you really wanted to enjoy yourself when you went out on a date last weekend, but can you see how your constant self-evaluation of your performance prevented you from being relaxed and spontaneous? When you're constantly convincing yourself that you are incompetent and unable to do the right thing, you are making yourself so nervous that you're certain to look unsure of yourself and make mistakes."

Negative Analogies

The therapist verbalizes an analogy that pairs the client's maladaptive cognition with a negative stimulus; i.e., an unpleasant imaginal scene aroused by the analogy (Crabb, 1971). The analogy is designed to elicit negative feelings with respect to the cognition. For example, the client's belief that he needs his mother for security, which results in his lack of independent behavior when away at college, might be responded to in the following manner: "Your behavior reminds me of a two-year-old kid walking down the street looking over his shoulder to see if Mom is still watching from the door. If she is, you'll go on, knowing that faithful Mom will pick you up if you fall. If she isn't, you'll run home and not attempt any independent activity."

The analogy should be developed so that the client's negative feelings are associated with the maladaptive cognition and not directed toward himself as a person. Otherwise, the analogy is likely to increase defensiveness or elicit hostility.

Appeal to Positive Consequences of Change

The positive consequences of alternative, adaptive cognitions are developed by therapist and client (Brehm & Cohen, 1962). The therapist may specify the adaptive affective and behavioral consequences of cognitive change, focusing initially on the most apparent and immediate consequences and gradually developing those of a long-term nature. For example, "Let's look at how things would be if you assumed that you were capable of being confident and relaxed in more varied social situations. For one thing, you could attend parties and meet new people; you could also start dating instead of staying home all weekend. As you gained greater confidence in your abilities, you could begin to take more initiative in determining your own social life by actively arranging those situations you enjoy most."

The intent of the procedure is to induce the client to evaluate the positive consequences of more adaptive cognitions across a variety of situations. Successful application, however, is dependent upon insuring that the client perceives the relationship between cognitive change and the anticipated positive consequences. Graduated performance assignments in which the client experiences positive consequences contingent upon adaptive cognitive modifications should serve to exemplify the validity of this relationship and facilitate more permanent change. This method also should be more effective if used in conjunction with the techniques that stress negative aspects of maintaining maladaptive cognitions.

CONCLUSION

Despite the current proliferation of cognitive treatment techniques, those falling within the category of verbal persuasion procedures have generally remained unspecified. This lack of specification has led didactic persuasion techniques to be labeled haphazard and unverified (Goldfried, et al., 1974). In order to increase communicability among therapists and facilitate research, various didactic persuasion techniques have been operationalized in this chapter. To facilitate clarity in the presentation, these techniques have been delineated without reference to additional therapeutic procedures. However, with respect to clinical application, these didactic procedures should be conceptualized as one of several components within a comprehensive cognitive behavioral treatment strategy (e.g., Beck, 1976; Goldfried & Davison, 1976; Mahoney, 1974).

A final point addresses the issue of how cognitive persuasion strategies can be most effectively implemented. A client–therapist relationship that embodies the qualities of respect, trust, empathy, and congruence is frequently noted as a prerequisite for successful implementation of therapeutic procedures (Frank, 1961; Goldstein, 1975). Although the importance of the client–therapist relationship is emphasized in almost every approach to psychotherapy, persuasive and logical evaluation techniques require particularly careful attention to the therapist's interpersonal style and ability to develop a therapeutic relationship. Specific pitfalls for inexperienced therapists include engaging in nonproductive argument, communicating disrespect for the client, and failing to maintain the distinction between the client as a person and the client's cognitions. Difficulties of this nature may be avoided most effectively by striving for a therapeutic relationship in which the client and therapist are working together to establish a more effective style of living for the client.

REFERENCES

Beck, A. T. Cognitive therapy: Nature and relation to behavior therapy. *Behavior Therapy*. 1970, *1*, 184–200.

Beck, A. T. *Cognitive therapy and the emotional disorders*. New York: International Universities Press, 1976.

Bernstein, D., & Borkovec, T. *Progressive relaxation training: A manual for the helping professions*. Champaign, Ill.: Research Press, 1973.

Brehm, J. W., & Cohen, A. R. *Explorations in cognitive dissonance*. New York: Wiley, 1962.

Crabb, L. J. Sensible psychotherapy. Unpublished manuscript, University of Illinois at Champaign-Urbana, 1971.

Ellis, A. *Reason and emotion in psychotherapy*. New York: Lyle Stuart, 1962.

Ellis, A. *Growth through reason*. Palo Alto, Calif.: Science and Behavior Books, 1971.

Ellis, A. *Humanistic psychotherapy: The rational–emotive approach*. New York: Julian Press, 1973.

Fiske, D. W., Hunt, H. F., Luborsky, L., Orne, M. T., Parloff, M. B., Reiser, M. F., & Tuma, A. H. Planning for research on effectiveness of psychotherapy. *American Psychologist*, 1970, *25*, 727–737.

Frank, J. D. *Persuasion and healing*. Baltimore: Johns Hopkins University Press, 1961.

Goldfried, M. R., & Davison, G. C. *Clinical behavior therapy*. New York: Holt, Rinehart & Winston, 1976.

Goldfried, M. R., Decenteceo, E. T., & Weinberg, L. Systematic rational structuring as a self-control technique. *Behavior Therapy*, 1974, *5*, 247–254.

Goldstein, A. P. Relationship-enhancement methods. In F. H. Kanfer & A. P. Goldstein (Eds.), *Helping people change*. New York: Pergamon Press, 1975.

Hanson, R. W., & Adesso, V. J. A multiple behavioral approach to male homosexual behaviors: A case study. *Journal of Behavior Therapy and Experimental Psychiatry*, 1972, *3*, 323–325.

Heintz, A. C. *Persuasion* (Rev. ed.). Chicago: Loyola University Press, 1974.

Humphreys, L., & Beiman, I. The application of multiple behavioral techniques to multiple problems of a complex case. *Journal of Behavior Therapy and Experimental Psychiatry*, 1975, *6*, 311–315.

Kanfer, F. H., & Karoly, P. Self-control: A behavioristic exploration into the lion's den. *Behavior Therapy*, 1972, *3*, 398–416.

Kanfer, F. H., & Phillips, J. S. *Learning foundations of behavior therapy*. New York: Wiley, 1970.

Karlins, M., & Abelson, H. I. *Persuasion* (2nd. ed.). New York: Springer, 1970.

Karoly, P. Multicomponent behavioral treatment of fear of flying: A case report. *Behavior Therapy*, 174, *5*, 265–270.

Mahoney, M. J. *Cognition and behavior modification*. Cambridge, Mass.: Ballinger, 1974.

Mahoney, M. J., & Thoresen, C. E. *Self-control: Power to the person*. Monterey, Calif: Brooks Cole, 1974.

McBurney, J. H., & Mills, G. E. *Argumentation and debate* (2nd ed.). New York: Macmillan, 1964.

Meichenbaum, D. Ways of modifying what clients say to themselves: A marriage of behavior therapies and rational–emotive therapy. *Rational Living*, 1972, *7*, 23–27.

Meichenbaum, D. *Cognitive behavior modification*. Morristown, N.J.: General Learning Press, 1974.

Paul, G. L. The strategy of outcome research in psychotherapy. *Journal of Consulting Psychology*, 1967, *31*, 109–118.

Rehm, L. P., & Rozensky, R. H. Multiple behavior therapy techniques with a homosexual client. *Journal of Behavior Therapy and Experimental Psychiatry*, 1974, *5*, 53–57.

Rimm, D. C., & Masters, J. C. *Behavior therapy*. New York: Academic Press, 1974.

14

Vivid Methods in Rational–Emotive Therapy*

Windy Dryden

The fundamental goal of rational–emotive therapy is to enable clients to live effective lives by helping them change their faulty inferences and irrational evaluations about themselves, other people, and the world. While there are many ways of achieving this goal, the purpose of this chapter is to highlight ways in which rational–emotive therapists can make the therapeutic process a more vivid experience for their clients so that they may be stimulated to identify and change their faulty inferences and irrational evaluations more effectively. A number of rational–emotive and cognitive therapists have already written on the use of vivid methods in therapy (Arnkoff, 1981; Ellis, 1979; Freeman, 1981; Knaus & Wessler, 1976; Walen, DiGiuseppe, & Wessler, 1980; and Wessler & Wessler, 1980). However, a comprehensive account of the uses, advantages, and limitations of such methods has yet to appear in the literature on rational–emotive therapy. In this chapter, attention will be given to the use of vivid methods in *problem assessment,* vivid *disputing* methods, and vivid ways in which clients may *work through* their emotional and behavioral problems.

RATIONALE FOR VIVID METHODS IN RET

Rational–emotive therapists aim to help clients achieve their goals through the systematic application of cognitive, emotive, and behavioral methods. However, therapist and client rely heavily on verbal dialogue in their in-session encounters.

*This chapter combines three articles by Dr. Dryden: (1) "Vivid RET: Problem assessment," *Rational Living,* 1983, *18,* 7–12; (2) "Vivid RET: Disputing methods," *Journal of Rational–Emotive Therapy,* 1983, *1,* 9–14, and (3) "Vivid RET: The working through process," *Journal of Rational–Emotive Therapy,* 1984, *1,* 27–31. Reproduced by permission of *Rational Living* and the *Journal of Rational-Emotive Therapy.*

The tone of such dialogue in rational–emotive therapy sessions can be rich, stimulating, and arousing, but it is far too often dry and mundane (as supervisors of novice rational–emotive therapists will testify). While the role of emotional arousal in the facilitation of attitude change is complex (Hoehn-Saric, 1978), it is my contention that the majority of clients can be helped best to reexamine faulty inferences and irrational beliefs if we as therapists gain their full attention and make therapy a memorable experience for them. While there are no studies that are addressed to this point in the rational–emotive therapy literature, there is some suggestion from process-and-outcome studies carried out on client-centered therapy that vivid therapist interventions are associated with successful client outcome and with certain client in-therapy behaviors that have in turn been linked to positive outcome (Rice, 1965; Rice, 1973; Rice & Gaylin, 1973; Rice & Wagstaff, 1967; Wexler, 1975; Wexler & Butler, 1976). At present we do not know whether any client in-therapy behaviors are associated with successful outcome in RET. Yet, it is possible to hypothesize that such client in-session behaviors as attending to and being fully involved in the therapeutic process and making links between in-session dialogue and out-of-session activities will be associated with therapeutic gain in RET. If this proves correct, then it is my further contention that vivid methods in RET may more effectively bring about such client behavior.

Given the dearth of much-needed studies on these points, anecdotal evidence will have to suffice. This involves feedback from my clients, who frequently related incidents of (1) how my own vivid therapeutic interventions helped them to reexamine a variety of their dysfunctional cognitions and (2) how they, with my encouragement, improved by making the working-through process a more stimulating experience for themselves.

It should be stressed at the outset that, while there is a place for vivid methods in RET, these are best introduced into therapy at appropriate times and within the context of a good therapeutic alliance between therapist and client.

PROBLEM ASSESSMENT

Effective rational–emotive therapy depends initially on the therapist gaining a clear understanding of (1) the client's problems in cognitive, emotional, and behavioral terms and (2) the contexts in which the client's problems occur. To a great extent, the therapist is dependent on the client's verbal reports in gaining such an understanding. It is in this area that many obstacles to progress may appear. Some clients have great difficulty identifying and/or accurately labeling their emotional experiences. Other clients are in touch with and able to report their emotions but find it hard to relate these to activating events (either external or internal). Yet a further group of clients is easily able to report problematic activating events and emotional experiences but has difficulty seeing how these may relate to mediating cognitions. Vivid methods can be used in a variety of ways to overcome such obstacles to a valid and reliable assessment of client problems.

Vividness in Portraying Activating Events

With some clients, traditional assessment procedures through verbal dialogue do not always yield the desired information. When this occurs, rational–emotive therapists often use imagery methods. They ask clients to conjure up evocative images of activating events. Such evocative imagery often stimulates the client's memory concerning her or his emotional reactions or indeed in some instances leads to the reexperiencing of these reactions in the session. While focusing on such images, the client also can begin to gain access to cognitive processes below the level of awareness that cannot be easily reached through verbal dialogue.

One particularly effective use of imagery in the assessment of client problems is that of bringing future events into the present. This is illustrated by the following exchange between myself and a client who was terrified that her mother might die, which led her to be extremely unassertive with the mother.

THERAPIST: So you feel you just can't speak up to her. Because if you did, what might happen?

CLIENT: Well, she might have a fit.

THERAPIST: And what might happen if she did?

CLIENT: She might have a heart attack and die.

THERAPIST: Well, we know that she is a fit woman, but let's go along with your fear for the moment. Okay?

CLIENT: Okay.

THERAPIST: What if she did die?

CLIENT: I just can't think . . . I . . . I'm sorry.

THERAPIST: That's okay. I know this is difficult, but I really think it would be helpful if we could get to the bottom of things. Okay? (Client nods.) Look, Marjorie, I want you to imagine that your mother has just died this morning. Can you imagine that? (Client nods and begins to shake.) What are you experiencing?

CLIENT: When you said my mother was dead I began to feel all alone . . . like there was no one to care for me . . . no one I could turn to.

THERAPIST: And if there is no one who cares for you, no one you can turn to . . .?

CLIENT: Oh, God! I know I couldn't cope on my own.

Instructing clients to imagine vividly something that has been warded off often leads to anxiety itself. It is important to process this anxiety, as it is sometimes related to the client's central problem. Issues like fear of loss of control, phrenophobia, and extreme discomfort anxiety are often revealed when this anxiety is fully assessed. However, some clients do find it difficult to imagine events spontaneously and require therapist assistance.

While imagery methods are now routinely used in cognitive behavior therapy (e.g., Lazarus, 1978), there has been little written on how therapists can stimulate clients' imagery processes. I have used a number of the following vivid methods to try and help clients utilize their potential for imagining events.

Vivid, Connotative Therapist Language. One effective way of helping clients to use their imagery potential is for the therapist to use rich, colorful, and evocative language while aiding clients to set the scene. Unless the therapist has gained prior diagnostic information, he or she is sometimes uncertain about which stimuli in the activating event are particularly related to the client's problem. Thus, it is best to give clients many alternatives. For example, with a socially anxious client I proceeded thus, after attempting without success to get him to use his own potential for imagery.

THERAPIST: So at the moment we are unclear about what you are anxious about. What I'd like to suggest is that we use your imagination to help us. I will help you set the scene based on what we have already discussed. However, since we have yet to discover detailed factors, some of the things I say might not be relevant. Will you bear with me and let me know when what I say touches a nerve in you?

CLIENT: Okay.

THERAPIST: Fine. Just close your eyes and imagine you are about to walk into the dance. You walk in and some of the guys there glance at you. You can see the *smirks* on their *mocking* faces and one of them *blows* you a kiss. (Here I am testing out a hypothesis based on previously gained information.) You start to *seethe* inside and . . .

CLIENT: Okay, when you said I was starting to seethe, that struck a chord. I thought I can't let them get away with that but if I let go I'll just go berserk. I started feeling anxious.

THERAPIST: And if you went berserk?

CLIENT: I couldn't show my face in there again.

THERAPIST: What would happen then?

CLIENT: I don't know. I . . . It's funny—the way I see it, I would never go out again.

Here I was using words like "smirks," "mocking," "blows," and "seethe" deliberately in my attempt to stimulate the client's imagination. It is also important for the therapist to vary his or her tone so that this matches the language employed.

Photographs. I have at times asked clients to bring to interviews photographs of significant others or significant places. These are kept on hand to be used at relevant moments in the assessment process. I have found the use of photographs particularly helpful when the client is discussing an event in the past that is still bothering her or him. Thus, for example, one client who spoke without feeling about being rejected by his father who died seven years earlier, broke down in tears when I asked him to look at a picture of him and his father standing apart from one another. Feelings of hurt and anger (with their associated cognitions) were expressed, which enabled us to move to the disputing stage.

Other Mementoes. In a similar vein, I have sometimes asked clients to bring in mementoes. These may include pictures they have drawn, paintings that have meaning for them, and poems either written by themselves or other people. The important point is that these mementoes are to be related to issues that the client is working on in therapy. A roadblock to assessment was successfully overcome with one client when I asked her to bring in a memento that reminded her of her mother. She brought in a bottle of perfume that her mother was accustomed to wearing. When I asked her to smell the perfume at a point in therapy when the assessment process through verbal dialogue was again breaking down, the client was helped to identify feelings of jealousy toward her mother, which she experienced whenever her mother left her to go out socializing. Moreover, my client was ashamed of such feelings. This issue was centrally related to her presenting problem of depression.

Another of my clients was depressed about losing her boyfriend. I had great difficulty helping her to identify any related mediating cognitions through traditional assessment procedures. Several tentative guesses on my part also failed to pinpoint relevant cognitive processes. I then asked her to bring to our next session anything that reminded her of her ex-boyfriend. She brought in a record of a popular song that had become known to them as "our song." When I played the song at an appropriate point in the interview, my client began to sob and expressed feelings of abandonment, hurt, and fear for the future. Again a vivid method had unearthed important assessment material where traditional methods had failed.

It should be noted from these examples that quite often such dramatic methods lead to the expression of strong affective reactions in the session. This is often an important part of the process, because such affective reactions are gateways to the identification of maladaptive cognitive processes that are difficult to identify through more traditional methods of assessment.

The "Interpersonal Nightmare" Technique. Rational–emotive and cognitive therapists sometimes employ methods originally derived from gestalt therapy and psychodrama to assist them in the assessment phase of therapy. These have been adequately described (Arnkoff, 1981; Nardi, 1979) and will not be discussed here. I would like to describe a related technique I have developed (Dryden, 1980), which I call the "interpersonal nightmare" technique. This technique may be best used with clients who are able to specify only sketchily an anticipated "dreaded" event involving other people but are neither able to specify in any detail the nature of the event nor how they would react if the event were to occur. First the client is given a homework assignment to imagine the "dreaded" event. He or she is told to write a brief segment of a play about it, specifying the exact words that the protagonists would use. The client is encouraged to give full rein to imagination while focusing on what he or she fears might happen. An example will suffice. The following scenario was developed by a 55-year-old woman with alcohol problems who was terrified of making errors at the office where she worked as a typist.

SCENE:	Boss's office where he sits behind a very large desk. He has found out that one of the typists has inadvertently filed a letter wrongly and sends for her. She comes in and is made to stand in front of the boss.
BOSS:	Have you anything to say in this matter?
TYPIST (ME):	Only that I apologize and will be more careful in the future.
BOSS:	What do you mean by saying you will be more careful in the future—what makes you think you have a future? (At this point he starts banging on the desk.) I have never yet met anyone less competent or less suited to the job than you are. You mark my words, I will make life so uncomfortable for you that you will leave. When I took over this job I intended to have the people I wanted working for me, and you are not on that list. I have already gotten rid of two typists, and I shall see that you are the third. Now get out of my office you stupid, blundering fool, and remember I shall always be watching you and you will never know when I shall be behind you.

I then read over the scene with the client, making inquiries about the tone in which she thought her boss would make these statements and asking her to identify which words the boss would emphasize. I then arranged for a local actor who was the same age as the boss to enact the scene realistically on cassette. In the next session I instructed my client to visualize the room in which the encounter might take place. She briefly described the room, paying particular attention to where her boss would be sitting and where she would be standing. I then played her the cassette, which evoked strong feelings of fear of being physically harmed and humiliated. Again, important data had been collected that traditional assessment procedures had failed to uncover.

These examples have shown how rational–emotive methods can employ various visual, olfactory, language, and auditory methods to help clients vividly imagine appropriate activating events. This in turn helps them more easily identify maladaptive emotional experiences and related cognitive processes that are not readily identified through the verbal interchange of the psychotherapeutic interview. It is important to note that the use of such methods is not being advocated for its own sake. They are employed with specific purposes in mind.

Rational–Emotive Problem Solving

Knaus and Wessler (1976) have described a method that they call rational–emotive problem solving (REPS). This method involves the therapist creating conditions in the therapy session that approximate those the client encounters in her or his everyday life and which give rise to emotional problems. Knaus and Wessler contend that this method may be used either in a planned or impromptu fashion and is particularly valuable when clients experience difficulty in identifying emotional experiences and related cognitive processes through verbal dialogue with their therapists. I employed this method with a male client who reported difficulty in acting assertively in his life and claimed not to be able to identify the emotions and thoughts that inhibited the expression of assertive responses. During our discussion I began to search around for my pouch of pipe tobacco. Finding it empty, I interrupted my client and asked him if he would drive to town, purchase my favorite tobacco, adding that if he hurried he could return for the last five minutes of our interview. He immediately got up, took my money and walked out of my office toward his car. I rushed after him, brought him back into my office and together we processed his reactions to this simulated experience.

It is clear that this technique must be used with therapeutic judgment and that its use may threaten or even destroy the therapeutic alliance between client and therapist. However, since rational–emotive therapists value risk taking, they are often prepared to use such techniques when more traditional and less risky methods have failed to bring about therapeutic improvement. It is further important, as Beck et al. (1979) have stressed, for the therapist to ask the client for the latter's honest reactions to this procedure, to ascertain whether it may have future therapeutic value for the client. When a client indicates that she or he has found the rational–emotive problem-solving method unhelpful, the therapist had better then explain the rationale for attempting such a procedure and disclose that he or she intended no harm but was attempting to be helpful. Normally clients respect such disclosures, and in fact the therapist in doing so provides a useful model for the client, namely, that it is possible to nondefensively acknowledge errors without damning oneself. However, with this method, it is apparent that therapists cannot realistically disclose their rationale in advance of initiating the method, since this would detract from its potential therapeutic value.

Dreams

Although Albert Ellis has recently written a regular column for *Penthouse* magazine providing rational–emotive interpretations of readers' dreams, rational–emotive therapists are not generally noted for using dream material. However, there is no good reason why dream material cannot be used in RET as long as (1) it does not predominate in the therapeutic process and (2) the therapist has a definite purpose in mind in using it.

Freeman (1981, pp. 228–229) has outlined a number of further guidelines for the use of dreams for assessment purposes:

1. The dream needs to be understood in thematic rather than symbolic terms.
2. The thematic content of the dream is idiosyncratic to the dreamer and must be viewed within the context of the dreamer's life.
3. The specific language and imagery are important to the meaning.
4. The affective responses to the dreams can be seen as similar to the dreamer's affective responses in waking situations.
5. The particular length of the dream is of lesser import than the content.
6. The dream is a product of and the responsibility of the dreamer.
7. Dreams can be used when the patient appears stuck in therapy.

I inadvertently stumbled on the usefulness of dream material for assessment purposes when working with a 28-year-old depressed student who would frequently reiterate, "I'm depressed and I don't know why." I had virtually exhausted all the assessment methods I knew (including those described in this chapter) to help her identify depressogenic thoughts in situations when she experienced depression, but without success. In a desperate last attempt, I asked her if she could remember any of her dreams, not expecting in the least that this line of inquiry would prove fruitful. To my surprise she said yes, she did have a recurring dream. In this dream she saw herself walking alone along a river bank, and when she peered into the river, she saw a reflection of herself as a very old woman. This image filled her with extreme sadness and depression. On further discussion she said that she believed that this dream meant that she had no prospect of finding any happiness in her life, either in love relationships or in her career and that she was doomed to spend her years alone, ending up as a sad, pathetic, old woman. This account of the dream and subsequent discussion of its meaning enabled me to help her identify a number of inferential distortions and irrational beliefs, which provided the focus for subsequent cognitive restructuring.

Daydreams may also provide important material for assessment purposes. For some people, particular daydreams occur in response to and as compensation for a negative activating event. Thus, one client reported having the daydream of establishing a multinational corporation after failing to sell insurance to prospective customers. The use of such daydreams by clients may not necessarily be dysfunctional but may impede them (as in the preceding example) from getting to the core of their problems. Often daydreams are an expression of our hopes and aspirations, and I have found it valuable to ask clients not only about the content of such material but also what would stop them from actualizing their goals. Much important assessment material is gathered in this manner, in particular concerning ideas of low frustration tolerance.

In Vivo Therapy Sessions

Sacco (1981) has outlined the value of conducting therapy sessions in real-life settings in which clients experience emotional difficulties. I have found moving outside the interview room to such settings particularly useful in gaining assessment material when traditional methods have failed to provide such data. For example, I once saw a male student who complained of avoiding social situations. He did so in case others would see his hands tremble. Traditional assessment methods yielded no further data. To overcome this treatment impasse, I suggested to him that we needed to collect more data and we eventually conducted a therapy session in a coffee shop where I asked him to go and get us both a cup of coffee. He refused because he feared that his hands might tremble, but I firmly persisted with my request. He was able to identify a stream of negative cognitions on the way from our table to the service counter. He returned without our coffees but with valuable information, which we processed later in my office. It is important for therapists to explain their rationale for conducting *in-vivo* sessions in advance, in order to gain client cooperation. In addition, obtaining clients' reactions to these sessions is often helpful, particularly if *in-vivo* sessions are planned for use later in the therapeutic process.

DISPUTING

In this section, various vivid disputing methods will be outlined. The purpose of these methods is (1) to help clients see the untenable basis and dysfunctional nature of their irrational beliefs and to replace them with more rational ones and (2) to help them make more accurate inferences about reality. These methods often demonstrate the rational message powerfully but indirectly, and they do not necessarily call upon the client to answer such questions as "Where is the evidence . . .?"

It is important for the therapist to make certain preparations before initiating vivid disputing methods, since the success of such methods depends upon (1) the client clearly understanding the link between thoughts, feelings, and behaviors and (2) the therapist ascertaining particular biographical information about the client.

Preparing for Vivid Disputing

The Thought–Feeling–Behavior Link. After the therapist has undertaken a thorough assessment of the client's target problem, the next task is to help the client see the connections among thoughts, feelings, and behaviors. Here again vivid methods can be employed. Thus the therapist, while speaking with the client, might pick up a book, drop it to the floor, and continue talking to the client. After a while, if the client has made no comment, the therapist can ask for both affective and cognitive reactions to this incident. Thus, the client is given a vivid here-and-now example of the thought–feeling link.

Biographical Information. Before initiating the vivid disputing process, I often find it helpful to gather certain information about the client. I like to find out about my client's *interests, hobbies,* and *work situation.* I have found this information often helps me adapt my interventions, using phrases that will be meaningful to my client, given her or his idiosyncratic life situation. Thus, if my client is passionately interested in boxing, a message utilizing a boxing analogy may well have greater impact than a golfing analogy.

I also find it helpful to discover *who my client admires.* I do this because later I may wish to ask my client how he or she thinks these admired individuals might solve similar problems. This prompts the client to identify with a model to imitate. Lazarus (1978) has employed a similar method with children. For example, I asked a male client to imagine that his admired grandfather experienced public speaking anxiety, and I inquired how he would have overcome it. This helped him identify a coping strategy that he used to overcome his own public speaking anxiety problem. This approach is best used if the client also can acknowledge that the admired individual is fallible and thus prone to human irrationality. In addition, it is important that the client sees the feasibility of imitating the model.

I find it invaluable to ask my clients about their *previous experiences of attitude change.* I try and discern the salient features of such change for possible replication in my in-session disputing strategies. For example, one anxious female client told me she had changed her mind about foxhunting after reading a number of personal accounts offering arguments against foxhunting. As part of my disputing plan, I directed this client to autobiographies of people who had overcome anxiety. Another client claimed she had in the past received help from speaking to people who had experienced problems similar to her own. I arranged for this client to speak to some of my ex-clients who had experienced but overcome comparable problems.

I now propose to outline a number of ways in which rational–emotive therapists can vividly employ disputing techniques. The importance of tailoring interventions to meet the specific, idiosyncratic requirements of clients should be borne in mind throughout.

Vivid Disputing Methods

Disputing in the Presence of Vivid Stimuli. In a previous article (Dryden, 1983), I outlined a number of ways of vividly portraying activating events to help clients identify their emotional reactions and the cognitive determinants of these reactions. I outlined various visual, language, auditory, and olfactory methods. These same methods can be used as context material in the disputing process. For example, one client brought along a drawing of herself and her mother. She portrayed her mother as a very large, menacing figure and herself as a small figure crouching in fear in front of her mother. I asked the client to draw another picture where she and her mother were of the same height, standing face-to-face, looking each other in the eye. When she brought in this drawing, I inquired how her attitude toward her mother differed in the two pictures. This not only provided her with a demonstration that it was possible for her to evaluate her mother differently but also led to a fruitful discussion in which I disputed some of her irrational beliefs inherent in the first drawing while having her focus on the second.

A similar tactic was employed using the "interpersonal nightmare" technique with the 55-year-old woman mentioned earlier. After disputing some of the irrational beliefs uncovered when the technique was employed for assessment purposes, I repeatedly played the woman the tape while having her dispute some of the irrational beliefs it revealed. A similar method can be used when *in-vivo* sessions are conducted. In my 1983 article I reported the case of a student who was anxious about his hands shaking in public. Both assessment and later disputing of his irrational beliefs were carried out in a coffee bar. Indeed he practiced disputing his irrational beliefs while carrying two shaking cups of coffee back from the service counter to our table. Disputing in the presence of vivid stimuli enables the client to build bridges from in-session to out-of-session situations.

Imagery Methods. One very effective imagery method that can be used in the disputing of irrational beliefs is that of time projection (Lazarus, 1978). When a client makes grossly exaggerated negative evaluations of an event, he often stops thinking about it and therefore cannot see beyond its "dreaded" implications. The purpose of time projection is to enable clients to see vividly that time and the world continue after the "dreaded event" has occurred. Thus, for example, a Malaysian student whose tuition fees were paid for by his village concluded that it would be terrible if he failed his exams because he couldn't bear to face his fellow villagers. I helped him to imagine his return to his village while experiencing shame. I then gradually advanced time forward in imagery. He began to see that it was likely that his fellow villagers would eventually come to adopt a compassionate viewpoint toward him, and even if they did not, he could always live happily in another part of the country or in another part of the world.

Imagery methods that focus on helping clients think more carefully and critically about "dreaded" events are also extremely valuable. For example, another client who had a fear of other people seeing his hands shake was asked to imagine going into a bar, ordering a drink, and drinking while his hands shook. He said that he would be extremely anxious about this because other people in the bar would stare at him. He was asked to imagine how many people would stare at him. Would they stare in unison, or would they stare one at a time? He was asked to imagine how often they would stare at him, how long they would stare at him, and how often in the evening they would resume staring at him. He concluded that everybody would not stare at him and those who did stare would possibly only stare for about 30 seconds and he could stand that. This and other methods illustrate that it is possible to simultaneously help clients dispute both their faulty inferences and irrational evaluations. Another technique I employed with this same client was "imagery to exaggeration." He was asked to imagine his hands shaking while consuming drink and with everybody in the bar staring at him continually for three hours. At this point he burst out laughing and realized the exaggerated nature of his inference.

Rational–emotive imagery is a frequently employed technique and has been fully described by Maultsby and Ellis (1974) and Ellis (1979). It often has dramatic impact and thus qualifies as a vivid method. It is worthwhile noting at this point that some clients have difficulty conjuring up images and may have to be trained in a stepwise fashion to utilize this ability. Furthermore, while helpful, it is probably not necessary for clients to imagine with extreme clarity.

The Rational–Emotive Therapist as Raconteur. Wessler and Wessler (1980) have outlined the therapeutic value of relating various stories, parables, witty sayings, poems, aphorisms, and jokes to clients. The important factor here is that the therapist modifies the content of these to fit the client's idiosyncratic situation. Telling identical stories to two different clients may well have two different effects. One client may be deeply affected by the story, while for another the story may prove meaningless. It is important that rational–emotive therapists become acquainted with a wide variety of these stories and be prepared to modify them from client to client, without introducing unwarranted distortions.

Active Visual Methods. Active visual methods combine therapist or client activity with a vivid visual presentation. Young (1980) has outlined one such method, which he uses to help clients see the impossibility of assigning a global rating to themselves. He asks a client to describe some of his behaviors, attributes, talents, and interests. Every answer the client gives Young writes on a white sticky label and sticks the label on the client. This continues until the client is covered with white sticky labels and can begin to see the impossibility of assigning one global rating to such a complex being. Wessler and Wessler (1980) outline similar active visual methods to communicate a similar point. For example, they ask their clients to assign a comprehensive rating to a basket of fruit or a desk. Clients are encouraged to explore actively the components of the fruit basket or desk while attempting to assign a global rating to it.

Visual Models. I have previously described the use of visual models I have devised, each of which demonstrates a rational message (Dryden, 1980). For example, I employ a model called the "LFT Splash." In the model a young man is seated at the top of a roller coaster with a young woman standing at the bottom. I tell clients that the young man does not move because he is telling himself that he can't stand the splash. Clients are asked to think what the young man would have to tell himself in order to reach the woman. This model is particularly useful in introducing to clients the idea of tolerating acute time-limited discomfort which, if tolerated, would help them achieve their goals.

Flamboyant Therapist Actions. A common disputing strategy that rational–emotive therapists use in verbal dialogue when clients conclude they are stupid for acting stupidly is to ask some variant of the question "How are you a stupid person for acting stupidly?" Alternatively, instead of asking such questions, the therapist could suddenly leap to the floor and start barking like a dog for about 30 seconds, resume her or his seat, and then ask the client to evaluate this action. Clients usually say that the action is stupid. The therapist can then ask whether that stupid action makes him or her a stupid person. Such flamboyant actions often enable clients to discriminate more easily between global self-ratings and ratings of behaviors or attributes.

Rational Role Reversal. Rational role reversal has been described by Kassinove and DiGiuseppe (1975). In this technique, the therapist plays a naive client with an emotional problem that is usually similar to the client's. The client is encouraged to adopt the role of the rational–emotive therapist and help the "client" dispute his or her irrational belief. As Kassinove and DiGiuseppe point out, this technique is best used after the client has developed some skill at disputing some of his or her own irrational ideas. A related technique has been devised by Burns (1980), which he calls "externalization of voices." In this technique, which is again used after the client has displayed some skill at disputing irrational beliefs, the therapist adopts the irrational part of the client's personality and supplies the client with irrational messages. The client's task is to respond rationally to the irrational messages. When clients show a high level of skill at this, the therapist, in role, can try hard to overwhelm the client with a barrage of quick-fire irrational messages, thus helping the client to develop an automatic ability to respond to his or her own irrational messages. This method also can be used to help clients identify those negative thoughts to which they experience difficulty in responding.

Therapist Self-Disclosure. Some clients find therapist self-disclosure an extremely persuasive method, while for others it is contraindicated. One way of attempting to ascertain a client's possible reactions to therapist self-disclosure is to include an appropriate item in a pretherapy questionnaire. It may well be wise to avoid using therapist self-disclosure with clients who respond negatively to the item. In any case, the therapist had better ascertain the client's reaction to any self-disclosing statements she or he might make. The research literature on this topic indicates that therapists had better not disclose personal information about themselves too early in the therapeutic process (Dies, 1973). When therapists do disclose information about themselves it is my experience that the most effective forms of self-disclosure are those in which they portray themselves as coping rather than mastery models. Thus, for example, it is better for the therapist to say to the client, "I used to have a similar problem, but this is how I overcame it," rather than to say, "I have never had this problem, because I believe . . ."

Paradoxical Therapist Actions. This method is often best used when clients, through their actions, communicate messages about themselves to the therapist that are based on irrational beliefs. For example, I once saw a female client who experienced a lot of rheumatic pain but had an attitude of low frustration tolerance toward it. Her behavior toward me in sessions indicated the attitude, "I am a poor soul, feel sorry for me." This prompted me to adopt an overly sympathetic and diligent stance toward her. Thus at the beginning of every session I treated her as if she could hardly walk and escorted her by arm to her chair and made frequent inquiries about her comfort. This eventually prompted her to make statements like, "Don't treat me like a child," "I can cope," or "It's not as bad as all that." I then helped her to identify and dispute some of the original implicit irrational messages. Whenever she began to lapse back into her self-pitying attitude, I began to behave in an overly solicitous manner again, which provided a timely reminder for her to attend to the behavioral components of her philosophy of low frustration tolerance and then to the philosophy itself.

Paradoxical Therapist Communications. Ellis (1977) has written on the use of humor in RET, where the therapist humorously exaggerates clients' irrational beliefs. He points out the importance of using humor against the irrational belief, rather than as an *ad hominem* attack. Taking clients' beliefs and inferences to an absurd conclusion is another paradoxical technique that can be used. Thus, for example, with clients who are scared that other people may discover one of their "shameful" acts or traits, therapists can take this to its illogical conclusion by saying, "Well there is no doubt about it, they will find out, then they will tell their friends, some of whom will call up the local television station, and before you know it you will be on the six o'clock news." Again, it is important that clients perceive that such communications are being directed against their beliefs rather than against them. Thus, feedback from clients on this matter had better be sought.

Rational Songs. Ellis (1977) has written about the use of his now-famous rational songs in therapy. For example, the therapist can hand a client a song sheet and sing, preferably in an outrageous voice, a rational song that has been carefully selected to communicate the rational alternatives to the client's target irrational belief. Since Ellis tends to favor tunes that were written many years ago, it may be more productive for the therapist to rewrite the words to more up-to-date and popular songs, for clients not familiar with some of the "old favorites."

In-session Inference Tests. Clients are likely to make faulty inferences about their therapist similar to those they make about other people in their lives. For example, one of my clients saw me talking to a fellow therapist at the end of one of our sessions. At our next session she told me that she was anxious about this because she was convinced I had been talking about her and laughing about what she had told me in the session (she was not in fact paranoid). I proceeded to pull out two pieces of paper, kept one for myself and gave the other one to her. I told her that I wanted to find out whether she indeed had extraordinary mind-reading powers. I thus wrote down the word "chicken" on my piece of paper and asked her to concentrate very carefully for the next three minutes and to write down what she thought I was thinking about. I said that I would keep thinking about the word I had written down to make it a fair experiment. After the three minutes, she wrote down the word "baseball." This became known as the "baseball–chicken" interview, which she recalled frequently when she made arbitrary inferences concerning the meaning of other people's behavior.

Using the Therapist–Client Relationship. Wessler (1982) has written that it is important for the rational–emotive therapist to inquire about the nature of his client's reactions to him or her, that is, to examine some of the client's here-and-now attitudes. Little has been written about this approach in the rational–emotive literature, and thus relatively little is known about its potential as a framework for disputing inaccurate inferences and irrational beliefs. Wessler (1982) also advocates that therapists give clients frank feedback about this impact on them and explore whether clients have a similar impact on other people. Such generalizations must of course be made with caution, but such discussion is often a stimulus for clients to become more sensitive to their impact on other people and often leads them to ask other people about their interpersonal impact (Anchin & Kiesler, 1982).

The advantage of using the therapist–client relationship in this way is that it provides both parties with an opportunity to process the client's inferences and beliefs in an immediate and often vivid fashion. The outcome of such strategies is often more memorable for clients than the outcome of more traditional disputing methods, where client inferences and beliefs about recent past events are processed.

Therapist Paralinguistic and Nonverbal Behavior. When rational–emotive therapists want to emphasize a point, one important way of doing so is for them to vary their paralinguistic and nonverbal behavior. For example, Walen et al. (1980, p. 178) note that when Ellis in his public demonstrations talks about something being "awful" he drops his voice several notes, stretches out the word and increases his volume, producing a dreary and dramatic sound, for example, "and it's AWWWWWFULL that he doesn't like me." Later, when he changes the word "awful" to "unfortunate" or a "need" to a "want," Ellis again pronounces the words now reflecting rational concepts in a distinct way. He says the key word slowly, enunciates very clearly, and raises the pitch of his voice as well as the volume. In addition, the therapist might associate some dramatic nonverbal behavior with the paralinguistic clue. For example, when the word "awful" is pronounced, the therapist might sink to the floor, holding his neck as if strangling himself.

Therapeutic Markers. Another way of emphasizing a point is to draw the client's attention to the fact that an important point is about to be made. For example, I might say to a client when I want to emphasize a point, "Now I want you to listen extremely carefully to this point because if you miss it it would be awwwfull" (therapist sinks to the floor again). I call such interventions "therapeutic markers." Another way of emphasizing statements is to change one's body position. For example, by moving their torsos forward toward clients, therapists can indicate the importance of their following statements. Whenever I want clients to become aware of important statements they have made, particularly when they make more rational statements at the beginning of the disputing process, I may, for example, pause and say, "Excuse me, could you just repeat what you said—I really want to make a note of this." If I am recording a session, I might say, "Hold on a minute, I really want you to hear what you have just said, I can't believe it myself, I just want to check it out."

Pragmatic Disputes. One major way of encouraging clients to surrender their irrational beliefs in favor of more rational ones is to point out to them, and in this context in dramatic terms, the implications of continued adherence to their irrational beliefs. Ellis counsels that for particularly resistant and difficult clients this tactic is often the most effective (Ellis, 1982). Quite often I have heard Ellis tell clients something like, "If you continue to cling to that belief you'll suffer for the rest of your life." Here, as before, he changes his paralinguistic and nonverbal behavior when he states the conclusion, "You'll suffer for the rest of your life." In a similar vein, when clients state that they can't (or rather, won't) change their beliefs, he points out to them the logical implications of not doing so when he says forcefully: "So suffer!" In this regard it would be interesting to determine under what conditions pragmatic disputes are more effective than philosophical ones.

WORKING THROUGH

This final section focuses on how therapists can help clients to vividly work through some of their emotional problems. Ellis (1980) has criticized some popular behavioral techniques on the grounds that they do not necessarily encourage clients to make profound philosophical changes in their lives. In particular he criticizes those methods that encourage the client to confront a dreaded event very gradually. He posits that this gradualism may indeed reinforce some clients low-frustration-tolerance ideas. Whenever possible, then, rational–emotive therapists encourage their clients to act in dramatic and vivid ways because they believe significant attitude change is more likely to follow the successful completion of such tasks. I will outline the vivid methods that clients can put into practice behaviorally and cognitively in their everyday lives. First, however, rational–emotive therapists face a further problem, which has received insufficient attention in the RET literature: how to encourage clients to carry out their homework assignments.

Vivid Cues for Encouraging Clients to Do Their Homework

While some clients conscientiously do the homework assignments they and their therapists have negotiated, other clients do not. It is true that some clients do not follow through on these assignments because of low-frustration-tolerance ideas; still other clients do not follow through, particularly early on in the working-through process, because they require some vivid reminders to initiate this process. With such clients, I have found it particularly helpful to ask them what they generally find memorable in everyday life experiences. For example, some people find the printed word memorable, while others have visual images on which they cue. Yet others focus primarily on auditory stimuli. I find that it is profitable to capitalize on whatever channel the client finds memorable.

Vivid Visual Cues. There are a number of ways clients can remind themselves to initiate the disputing process. A number of rational–emotive therapists encourage clients to carry around small $3'' \times 5''$ cards with rational self-statements written on them, to which clients can refer at various times. Other therapists have encouraged clients to write reminders to themselves either to initiate a homework assignment or to refer to a rational message. These clients are encouraged to pin up such messages at various places around the home or in their work situation.

I find it helpful to encourage those clients who find visual images powerful to associate a particular dysfunctional feeling with a visual image that would enable them to initiate the disputing process. Thus one client found it helpful to conjure up a sign in her mind that said "Dispute" when she began to feel anxious. Another client, who was depressed, began to associate the onset of depression with a road sign on which was written "Act now."

Another strategy I have used is to ascertain from clients what, if any, in-session experiences they have found particularly memorable. I try to help them encapsulate some of these experiences as a cue either to initiate the disputing process or to remind themselves of the relevant rational principle to which this experience referred. One client who was prone to thinking himself an idiot for acting idiotically found it memorable when I made strange faces at him to help him get the point that concluding he was an idiot for acting idiotically was an overgeneralization. Whenever he began to make such an overgeneralization in everyday life, he would get the image of my making faces and quickly remember to what this referred. This helped him accept himself regardless of any idiotic act he actually made or thought he might make in the future.

Another client who did virtually no cognitive disputing or behavioral assignments outside the sessions was helped in the following manner. First, this issue was made the focus of therapy. Instead of asking her traditional disputing questions, I asked her to imagine what I would say to her were I to respond to her irrational beliefs. She in fact had understood rational principles because her answers were very good. Her problem was that she would not employ these principles. I then asked her if there was any way she could conjure up a picture of me giving her rational messages at various emotionally vulnerable times in her everyday life. She hit on the idea of imagining that I was perched on her shoulder whispering rational messages into her ear. Additionally she began to carry around a small card that said "Imagine that Dr. Dryden is on your shoulder." This proved a particularly effective technique where all else had failed.

Vivid Language. Wexler and Butler (1976) have argued in favor of therapists using expressive language in therapy. I have found that one of the major benefits of using vivid nonprofane language is that clients remember these vivid expressions or catch-phrases and use them as shorthand ways of disputing irrational beliefs in their everyday lives. For example, in the case where I helped a client dispute a particular distorted inference by having her attempt to read my mind (the "baseball–chicken" interview), whenever the client concluded that other people were making negative inferences about her without supporting data, she would remember the phrase "baseball and chicken." This served (1) as a timely reminder that she might be making incorrect conclusions from the data at hand, and (2) as a cue for her to start examining the evidence.

In a related technique, the therapist asks the client to give his or her own distinctive name to a faulty psychological process. Wessler and Wessler (1980) give such an example where a client came to refer to himself as "Robert the Rule Maker," to describe his tendency to make demands on himself and other people. A knowledge of clients' subcultural values is particularly helpful here. I work in a working-class area in Birmingham, England, and one word my clients frequently use, which was unfamiliar to me, was the word "mather."[1] I helped one client who was angry with her mother to see her mother as a fallible human being with a worrying problem, and that she could be accepted for this rather than be damned for it. My client suddenly laughed and said, "Yes! I guess my mother is a matherer." I encouraged her to remember this catchy phrase whenever she began to feel angry toward her mother.

Auditory Cues. Rational–emotive therapists often make tape recordings of their sessions for clients to replay several times between sessions. This often serves to remind clients of rational principles they have understood in the session but may have since forgotten. Using personal recording systems, clients also can be encouraged to develop auditory reminders to initiate either cognitive or behavioral homework assignments. In addition, they can be encouraged to put forceful and emphatic rational statements on cassettes and play these while undertaking behavioral assignments. For example, I once saw a client who was anxious about other people looking at her for fear they might think her strange. I suggested that she do something in her everyday life that would encourage people to look at her so she could dispute some of her underlying irrational beliefs. She decided to wear a personal stereo system in the street, which she thought would encourage people to look at her. I suggested that while walking she play a tape on which she had recorded the rational message "Just because I look strange doesn't mean that I am strange."

The use of rational songs in therapy has already been described. Several of my clients have found that singing a particular rational song at an emotionally vulnerable time has been helpful for them. It has reminded them of a rational message they might not ordinarily have been able to focus on while being emotionally distressed. Another client told me that her sessions with me reminded her of a particular song and whenever she hummed this song to herself it helped bring to mind the fact that she could accept herself even though she did not have a man in her life. The song, ironically, was "You're No One Till Somebody Loves You." In fact she rewrote some of the words and changed the title to "You're Someone Even Though Nobody Loves You."

Olfactory Cues. It is possible for clients to use various aromas as cues to remind themselves to do a homework assignment or to initiate the disputing process. One client said that she found my pipe tobacco particularly aromatic and distinctive. Since we were both seeking a memorable cue, I suggested an experiment whereby she purchased a packet of my favorite tobacco and carried this around with her to smell at various distressing times. This aroma was associated in her mind with a particular rational message. This proved helpful, and indeed my client claimed that by saying to herself the phrase "Pipe up" she

[1]This is pronounced "my-the" and means to be worried or bothered.

now no longer has to take the tobacco out of her handbag to smell. Just the phrase is enough to remind her of the rational message.

THE WORKING-THROUGH PROCESS

From its inception, RET has strongly recommended that clients undertake "some kind of activity which itself will act as a forceful counterpropagandist agency against the nonsense he believes" (Ellis, 1958). Ellis has consistently stressed that for clients who will agree to do them, dramatic, forceful, and implosive activities remain the best forms of working-through assignments. Such assignments emphasize either cognitively based or behavioral activities.

Cognitive Assignments

In cognitive assignments, clients are encouraged to find ways in which they can convince themselves (outside therapy sessions) that rational philosophies which they can acknowledge as correct in therapy sessions are indeed correct and functional for them. Ellis has always urged clients to dispute their ideas vigorously, using such aids as written homework forms (Ellis, 1979). Other vivid cognitive techniques that clients can use include the following.

Rational Proselytizing (Bard, 1973). Here clients are encouraged to teach RET to their friends. In teaching others, clients become more convinced themselves of rational philosophies. This technique, however, had better be used with caution, and clients should be warned against playing the role of unwanted therapist to friends and relatives.

Tape-recorded Disputing. In this technique, clients are encouraged to put a disputing sequence on tape. They are asked to play both the rational and irrational parts of themselves. Clients are further encouraged to try and make the rational part more persuasive and more forceful in responding to the irrational part.

Passionate Statements. For those clients who are intellectually unable to do cognitive disputing in its classical sense, *passionate rational self-statements* can be used. Here client and therapist work together to develop appropriate rational self-statements that the client can actually use in everyday life. Clients are encouraged to repeat these statements in a very forceful manner instead of in their normal voice tone. Another variation of this technique is to have clients say rational self-statements to their reflection in a mirror, using a passionate tone and dramatic gestures to again reinforce the message.

Behavioral Techniques

Behavioral techniques that rational–emotive therapists particularly favor have clients do cognitive disputing in actual settings that vividly evoke their fears. The purpose is to enable clients to have the success experience of doing cognitive disputing while exposing themselves to feared stimuli. In addition, dramatic behavioral assignments are recommended to help clients overcome their low-frustration-tolerance ideas. Here the focus is oriented toward clients changing their dysfunctional attitudes toward their internal experiences of anxiety or frustration. Behavioral assignments include the following.

Shame-Attacking Exercises. Here the client is encouraged to do some act that she or he has previously regarded as "shameful." The client is encouraged to act in a way that will encourage other people in the environment to pay attention to her or him without bringing harm to self or other people and without unduly alarming others. She or he is encouraged to engage simultaneously in vigorous disputing, such as, "I may look weird, but I'm not weird." In my opinion, one of the drawbacks of encouraging a client to do shame-attacking exercises in a group is that the group serves to reinforce the client positively for doing the exercise. Doing shame-attacking exercises together can become a game that is not taken seriously. However, shame-attacking exercises are extremely valuable in promoting change, and, while humor is an important component, my experience is that greater and longer-lasting change is effected when clients do shame-attacking exercises on their own as part of their individual therapy, without the social support of a group.

Risk-Taking Assignments. In risk-taking assignments clients are encouraged to do something they regard as being "risky." For example, a client may be encouraged to ask a waiter to replace a set of cutlery because it is too dirty. In preparing clients for risk-taking exercises, identification and disputing of faulty inferences and consequent irrational evaluations needs to be done. The problem, however, is to get the client to prompt the aversive responses from others that he or she predicts will occur. In order for evaluative change to take place the client had better be prepared to do such risk-taking experiences repeatedly over a long period of time so that he or she eventually encounters the "dire" response. This is because such aversive responses from others occur far less frequently than the client predicts. Again the client is encouraged to undertake cognitive disputing along with the behavioral act.

Step-out-of-Character Exercises. Wessler (1982) has modified this exercise from Kelly (1955). Clients are encouraged to identify desired behavioral goals that are not currently enacted with frequency. For example, one group member chose the goal of eating more slowly, which for him was a desirable, nonshameful, nonrisky exercise, but one that involved monitoring of eating habits and cognitive disputing of low-frustration-tolerance ideas.

In Vivo *Desensitization*. These methods require clients to confront their fears repeatedly in an implosive manner. For example, clients with elevator phobia are asked to ride in elevators 20 to 30 times a day at the start of treatment, instead of gradually working their way up to this situation either in imagery or in actuality. Again, simultaneous cognitive disputing is urged. Neuman (1982) has written on and presented tapes of short-term group-oriented treatment of phobias. In his groups clients are encouraged to rate their levels of anxiety. The most important goal is for clients to experience a "level 10," which is extreme panic. Neuman continually points out to people that it is important to experience "level 10" because only then can they learn that they can survive and live through such an experience. Similarly, if inroads to severe phobic conditions are to be made, it is important for rational–emotive therapists to work toward helping clients tolerate extreme forms of anxiety before helping clients to reduce this anxiety.

Stay-In-There Activities. Grieger and Boyd (1980) have described a similar technique, which they call "stay-in-there" activities, the purpose of which is to have clients vividly experience that they can tolerate and put up with uncomfortable experiences. One of my clients wanted to overcome her car-driving phobia. One of the things she feared was that her car would stall at a set of traffic lights and she would be exposed to the wrath of motorists who were stuck behind her. After eliciting and disputing her irrational ideas in traditional verbal dialogue, I encouraged her actually to turn off her engine at a set of lights and to stay there for about 20 minutes, thus creating the impression her car had broken down. Fortunately, the other car drivers did react in an angry fashion and she was able to practice disputing her dire needs for approval and comfort in a situation in which she remained for fully half an hour.

Some clients tend to do these dramatic exercises once or twice and then drop them from their repertoire. Therapists are often so glad and so surprised their clients will actually do these assignments that they do not consistently show them the importance of *continuing* to do them. One of the reasons for continued practice has already been mentioned, namely, that clients are more likely to make inferential changes than evaluative changes by doing these assignments infrequently. This is largely because the "dreaded" event has a far lower probability of occurring than clients think. However, sooner or later, if clients consistently and persistently put into practice these assignments, they may well encounter such events that will provide a context for disputing of irrational beliefs. Thus, if therapists really want to encourage clients to make changes at "B" as well as at "A," they had better be prepared to encourage clients consistently to do these dramatic assignments over a long period of time.

Operant Conditioning Methods

Ellis (1979) has consistently employed operant conditioning methods to encourage clients to take responsibility for being their own primary agent of change. Here clients are encouraged to identify and employ positive reinforcements for undertaking working-through assignments, and apply penalties when they do not do so. While not all clients require such encouragement, difficult and resistant clients, whose resistance is due to low-frustration-tolerance ideas, can be encouraged to take full responsibility for not putting into practice assignments that would stimulate change. Thus, dramatic experiences like burning a $10 bill, throwing away an eagerly awaited meal, and cleaning a dirty room at the end of a hard day's work are experiences that are designed to be so aversive that clients would choose to do the assignment previously avoided rather than undergo the penalty. Of course clients can, and often do, refuse to do the assignment and refuse to employ operant conditioning methods. However, many clients who have been resistant in the working-through process have, in my experience, begun to move when the therapist adopts this no-nonsense approach.

LIMITATIONS OF VIVID METHODS IN RET

While the basic thesis in this chapter has been to show the possible efficacy of vivid RET, there are, of course, limitations on such an approach.

First, it is important for therapists to determine the impact on clients of introducing vivid methods into the therapeutic process. Thus, using the guidelines of Beck, Rush, Shaw, and Emery (1979), it is perhaps wise for the therapist to ask the client at various points in the therapy to give frank feedback concerning the methods and activities used. While the therapist may not always agree not to use such techniques just because a client has a negative reaction to them, we had better obtain and understand our clients' negative reactions to our procedures.

Second, it is important in the use of vivid dramatic techniques not to overload the client. One vivid and dramatic method carefully introduced into a therapy session at an appropriate time is much more likely to be effective than several dramatic methods employed indiscriminately in a session.

Third, it is important that rational–emotive therapists be clear about the rationale for using vivid methods and not see the use of such methods as a goal in itself. The important thing to remember is that vivid methods are to be used as vehicles for promoting client attitude change and not to make the therapeutic process more stimulating for the therapist. It is also extremely important to ascertain what the client has learned from the vivid methods the therapist has employed. The client will not magically come to the conclusion the therapist wants. It is also important that therapists not promote "false" change in their clients. Change is "false" when the client feels better as a result of some of these vivid methods but does not get better. Ellis (1972) has written an important article on such a distinction. Thus therapists should invariably ask questions like, "What have you learned from doing this vivid method?" and "How can you strengthen this learning experience for yourself outside of therapy?"

Fourth, dramatic and vivid methods are not appropriate for all clients. They are particularly helpful for those clients who use intellectualization as a defense and/or who use verbal dialogue to tie rational–emotive therapists in knots. While there are no data at the moment to support the following hypothesis, I would speculate that dramatic and vivid methods had better not be used with clients who have overly dramatic and hysterical personalities. It is perhaps more appropriate to assist such clients to reflect in a calm and undramatic manner on their experiences than to overstimulate an already highly stimulated personality.

REFERENCES

Anchin, J. C., & Kiesler, D. J. (Eds.). *Handbook of interpersonal psychotherapy*. Oxford: Pergamon Press, 1982.

Arnkoff, D. B. Flexibility in practicing cognitive therapy. In G. Emery, S. D. Hollon, and R. C. Bedrosian (Eds.), *New directions in cognitive therapy*. New York: Guilford. 1981.

Bard, J. A. (1973). Rational proselytizing. *Rational Living*. 8(2), 24–26.

Beck, A. T., Rush, A. J., Shaw, B. F., & Emery, G. (1979). *Cognitive therapy of depression*. New York: Guilford.

Burns, D. D. *Feeling good: The new mood therapy*. New York: Morrow, 1980.

Dies, R. R. Group therapist self-disclosure: An evaluation by clients. *Journal of Counseling Psychology*, 1973, *20*, 344–348.

Dryden, W. Nightmares and fun. Paper presented at the Third National Conference on Rational–Emotive Therapy, New York, June 7, 1980.

Ellis, A. (1959). Rational psychotherapy. *Journal of General Psychology*, *59*, 35–49.

Ellis, A. (1972). Helping people get better, rather than merely feel better. *Rational Living*, 7(2), 2–9.

Ellis, A. (1977). Fun as psychotherapy. *Rational Living*, *12*(1), 2–6.

Ellis, A. (1979). The practice of rational–emotive therapy. In A. Ellis & J. M. Whiteley (Eds.), *Theoretical and empirical foundations of rational–emotive therapy*. Monterey, CA: Brooks/Cole.

Ellis, A. (1980, July 15). *The philosophic implications and dangers of some popular behavior therapy techniques*. Invited address to the World Congress on Behavior Therapy, Jerusalem.

Ellis, A. (1982). Personal communication.

Freeman, A. Dreams and imagery in cognitive therapy. In G. Emery, S. D. Hollon, and R. C. Bedrosian (Eds.), *New directions in cognitive therapy*. New York: Guilford, 1981.

Grieger, R. & Boyd, J. (1980). *Rational–emotive therapy: A skills-based approach*. New York: Van Nostrand Reinhold.

Hoehn-Saric, R. Emotional arousal, attitude change and psychotherapy. In J. D. Frank, R. Hoehn-Saric, S. D. Imber, B. L. Liberman, and A. R. Stone (Eds.), *Effective ingredients of successful psychotherapy*. New York: Brunner/Mazel, 1978.

Kassinove, H., & DiGiuseppe, R. Rational role reversal. *Rational Living*, 1975, *10*(1), 44–45.

Kelly, G. A. (1955). *The psychology of personal constructs*. New York: Norton.

Knaus, W., & Wessler, R. L. Rational–emotive problem simulation. *Rational Living*, 1976, *11*(2), 8–11.

Lazarus, A. A. *In the mind's eye*. New York: Rawson, 1978.

Maultsby, M. C., Jr., & Ellis, A. *Technique for using rational–emotive imagery*. New York: Institute for Rational Living, 1974.

Nardi, T. J. The use of psychodrama in RET. *Rational Living,* 1979, *14*(1), 35–38.

Neuman, F. (Leader). (1982). *An eight-week treatment group for phobics* (Series of eight cassette recordings). White Plains, NY: F. Neuman.

Rice, L. N. Therapist's style of participation and case outcome. *Journal of Consulting Psychology,* 1965, *29,* 155–160.

Rice, L. N. Client behavior as a function of therapist style and client resources. *Journal of Counseling Psychology,* 1973, *20,* 306–311.

Rice, L. N., & Gaylin, N. L. Personality processes reflected in client and vocal style and Rorschach processes. *Journal of Consulting and Clinical Psychology,* 1973, *40,* 133–138.

Rice, L. N., & Wagstaff, A. K. Client voice quality and expressive style as indexes of productive psychotherapy. *Journal of Consulting Psychology,* 1967, *31,* 557–563.

Sacco, W. P. Cognitive therapy in-vivo. In G. Emery, S. D. Hollon, & R. C. Bedrosian (Eds.), *New directions in cognitive therapy.* New York: Guilford, 1981.

Walen, S. R., DiGiuseppe, R., & Wessler, R. L. *A practitioner's guide to rational–emotive therapy.* New York: Oxford University Press, 1980.

Wessler, R. A. (1982, September 5). *Alternative conceptions of rational–emotive therapy: Toward a philosophically neutral psychotherapy.* Paper presented at the twelfth European Congress of Behavior Therapy, Rome.

Wessler, R. A., & Wessler, R. L. (1980). *The principles and practice of rational–emotive therapy.* San Francisco: Jossey-Bass.

Wexler, D. A. A scale for the measurement of client and therapist expressiveness. *Journal of Clinical Psychology,* 1975, *31,* 486–489.

Wexler, D. A., & Butler, J. M. (1976). Therapist modification of client expressiveness in client-centered therapy. *Journal of Consulting and Clinical Psychology, 44,* 261–265.

Young, H. S. *Teaching rational self-value concepts to tough customers.* Paper presented at the Third National Conference on Rational–Emotive Therapy, New York, June 8, 1980.

15

Rational–Emotive Therapy Approaches to Overcoming Resistance*

Albert Ellis

Resistance to psychotherapy, even by those who strongly aver that they want to help themselves change and who spend considerable time, money, and effort in pursuing therapy, has been observed for many years. Ancient philosophers—such as Confucious, Gautama Buddha, Epictetus, Seneca, and Marcus Aurelius—recognized that people voluntarily pursuing personality change often resist their own and their teachers' best efforts. When modern psychotherapy began to develop in the nineteenth century, some of its main practitioners—such as James Braid, Hippolyte Bernheim, Jean-Martin Charcot, Auguste Ambroise Liebault and Pierre Janet—made the theory of resistance and the practice of overcoming it key elements in their psychotherapies (Ellenberger, 1970).

Early in the twentieth century, psychotherapeutic resistance particularly came into its own with the elucidation of the Freudian concept of transference (Freud, 1912/1965) and with Freud expanding his earlier concept to include five main varieties of resistance: resistances of repression, of transference, and of secondary gain (all stemming from the ego), resistance of the repetition compulsion (arising from the id), and resistance of guilt and self-punishment (originating in the superego) (Freud, 1926/1965). Since this time, psychoanalysis (and many

*This chapter combines two previously published articles: (1) Ellis, A., Rational–emotive therapy (RET) approaches to overcoming resistance, part 1, *British Journal of Cognitive Psychotherapy*, 1983, *1*(1), 28–38, and (2) Ellis, A., Rational–emotive (RET) approaches to overcoming resistance, part 2, *British Journal of Cognitive Psychotherapy*, 1983, *1*(2), 1–16. Reprinted by permission of *British Journal of Cognitive Psychotherapy*.

related forms of therapy) have, we might say, almost been obsessed with problems of resistance.

As several recent writers have aptly noted (Wachtel, 1982), views on what resistance is and how it can best be resolved in therapy largely depend on one's definition of this fascinating phenomenon. Personally, I like Turkat and Meyer's (1982, p. 158) definition: "Resistance is client behavior that the therapist labels antitherapeutic," since it is both simple and comprehensive; and, as its authors suggest, it can also be operationalized to each client's individual experience and be seen as that specific form of behavior that is observed when this particular client acts nontherapeutically according to his or her therapist in these particular situations.

However accurate such a definition of resistance may be, it is too general to be of much clinical use, and it hardly explains the main "causes" of resistance, nor what can be done to overcome it. Rational–emotive therapy (RET), together with cognitive behavioral therapy (CBT), assumes that when clients self-defeatingly and irrationally resist following therapeutic procedures and homework assignments, they largely do so because of their explicit and implicit cognitions or beliefs. RET, which tends to be more philosophical and more persuasive than some other forms of CBT—such as those of Bandura (1977), Mahoney (1980) and Meichenbaum (1977)—assumes that resisting clients have an underlying set of powerful and persistent irrational Beliefs (iB's), as well as an innate biosocial tendency to create new irrationalities, that frequently block them from carrying out the therapeutic goals and contracts that they overtly agree to work at achieving. Although RET does not agree with psychoanalytic and psychodynamic theory, which holds that client resistance is based on deeply unconscious, repressed thoughts and feelings, it does hypothesize that many—perhaps most—of the iB's that underlie client resistance are (1) at least partially implicit, unconscious, or automatic; (2) tenaciously held; (3) held concomitantly with strong feelings and fixed habit patterns of behavior; (4) to some extent held by virtually all clients; (5) difficult to change; and (6) likely to recur once they have been temporarily surrendered (Bard, 1980; Ellis, 1962, 1971, 1973, 1976, 1979, 1983b, 1984; Ellis & Grieger, 1977; Ellis & Whitely, 1979; Walen, DiGiuseppe, & Wessler, 1980; Wessler & Wessler, 1980).

More specifically, RET assumes that clients who self-defeatingly resist therapy implicitly or explicitly tend to hold three main irrational Beliefs (iB's) or philosophies: (1) "I *must* do well at changing myself, and I'm an incompetent, hopeless client if I don't"; (2) "You (the therapist and others) *must* help me change, and you're rotten people if you don't"; and (3) "Changing myself *must* occur quickly and easily, and it's horrible if it doesn't!" Concomitantly with these irrational beliefs, resisters feel anxious, depressed, angry, and self-pitying about changing, and these disturbed feelings block their forcing themselves to change. Behaviorally, resisters withdraw, procrastinate, remain inert, and sabotage their self-promises to change. RET practitioners are largely concerned with helping resisters (and other clients) make a profound philosophic change so that they adopt a cooperative, confident, determined attitude toward self-change, rather than the self-blocking views that they hold. To effect this kind of cognitive restructuring, RET uses a wide variety of thinking, feeling, and activity methods.

Having said all of this, I shall spend the first part of this chapter trying to show, from an RET standpoint, what are the principal kinds of resistance, in what ways they usually arise, and what RET (and, hopefully, other) practitioners can do to understand and help themselves and their clients overcome therapy-sabotaging resistance. I shall first deal with common, "normal," or "usual" resistance; and in the later sections with unusual or highly stubborn resistances.

COMMON FORMS OF RESISTANCE

Some of the statistically common kinds of resistance that therapists encounter include the following:

"Healthy" Resistance

Clients sometimes resist change because therapists have their own fish to fry and mistakenly see these clients as having symptoms (e.g., hostility to their parents) or as having origins of their symptoms (e.g., oedipal feelings "causing" their sexual inadequacy) that the clients view as figments of the therapists' imagination. Rather than allow these therapeutic "authorities" to lead them up the garden path, such clients refuse to accept these interpretations and healthfully resist or flee from "treatment" (Basch, 1982; Ellis, 1962; Ellis & Harper, 1975; Lazarus & Fay, 1982).

From a rational–emotive view, clients who resist for healthy reasons are explicitly or implicitly telling themselves rational beliefs (rB's), such as, "My therapist is probably wrong about my having this symptom or about the origins of my having it. Too bad! I'd better ignore his or her interpretations and perhaps get another therapist!" In the ABC theory of RET, at A (activating event) the clients experience their therapist's interpretations and directives (e.g., "You think you love your mother very much but unconsciously you really appear to loathe her"). At B (belief system), the clients tell themselves the rational beliefs just noted, and at C (emotional and behavioral consequences) they feel appropriately sorry about their therapist's misperceptions about their disturbances and they actively resist these misperceptions. They are therefore acting rationally and sanely and, according to RET, their resistance is self-helping and healthy. The one who has the real problem in these cases—and is "resisting" doing effective treatment—is their therapist!

Resistance Motivated by Client–Therapist Mismatching

Clients sometimes are "naturally" mismatched with their therapists, that is, manage to pick or be assigned to a therapist whom they just do not like, for whatever reasons. Thus, they may have a therapist who, to their idiosyncratic tastes or preferences, is too young or too old, too liberal or too conservative, too male or too female, too active or too passive. Because of this mismatching, they don't have too much rapport with their therapist and therefore resist him or her more than they would resist a more preferable therapist. If this becomes obvious during the therapy (which it never may), the therapists may try to compensate for what these clients see as their "flaws," and may succeed in doing so by being extra nice to or hardworking with such clients. Or the clients may naturally overcome their antitherapist prejudices as the course of therapy intimately proceeds (just as husbands and wives may become more attached to their physically unattractive mates as time goes by and more emotional intimacy is achieved). Or the clients and/or their therapists may (often wisely) bring the relationship to a close.

Resistance Stemming from Clients' Transference Disturbances

Following Freud (1900/1965; 1912/1965), psychoanalytic therapists assume that clients will unconsciously reenact with or transfer to their therapists the same kind of highly prejudiced relationships that they experienced with their parents during their early childhood. Thus, if a young woman has a middle-aged male analyst, she will strongly tend to fall in love with him (as she presumably once loved her father); will be jealous of his wife; will hate him when he refuses to go to bed with her; will try to control him as she tried to control her father; and so forth.

In RET, we take the view that these disturbed transference relations *sometimes* but not *necessarily* occur and that, when they do, they are usually sparked by some irrational beliefs (iB's). Thus, if this young woman strongly transfers her relationship from her father to her analyst, she is probably telling herself (and strongly believing) iB's like these: "Because my analyst is helpful and fatherly to me in some ways, he *must* be a complete father to me, and he *must* love me dearly!" "Because being loved by my father is enjoyable, I absolutely *must* be loved by my own father and by all fatherly people, including my therapist!" "If my father and my therapist do not totally love me—as I utterly *need* them to do—I am a worthless person!"

If and when, then, disturbed transference relations occur in therapy, rational–

emotive practitioners look for the irrational beliefs (iB's) *behind* these disturbances, show clients how to see and change these ideas, and thereby teach them how to surmount these kinds of relationship resistances.

Resistances Caused by Therapists' Relationship Problems

Therapists, like clients, also sometimes have their relationship difficulties. These may be of three major kinds: (1) Therapists may naturally not like some of their clients, particularly those who are nasty, stupid, ugly, or otherwise unprepossessing. (2) Therapists may have what the psychoanalysts call severe countertransference difficulties and may therefore be bigoted against their clients. Thus, if a therapist hates her mother and one of her clients looks and acts like this mother, she may unconsciously want to harm rather than help this client. (3) Therapists may not have personal negative feelings toward their clients but may be insensitive to these clients' feelings and may not know how to maintain good therapeutic relations with them (Goldfried, 1982; Lazarus & Fay, 1982; Meichenbaum & Gilmore, 1982).

If the first or third of these therapist problems exists, it can be met by therapists' becoming aware of their own limitations and by compensating for them. Thus, therapists who personally do not like their clients can still focus on suitable helpful procedures and thereby surmount this handicap. I particularly notice that in using RET I can focus so well on my clients' problems, and especially on showing them how to correct their thinking errors, that it hardly matters that I personally do not like some of them and would never select them as my friends (Ellis, 1971, 1973).

RET therapists can also, especially with certain supersensitive clients, go out of their way to give these clients positive verbal reinforcement, to listen carefully and reflectively to their difficulties, to be open and honest with them, to give them active encouragement, to deliberately point out their good (as well as some of their self-defeating) characteristics, and otherwise to empathize with them in an almost Rogerian manner (Dryden, 1982; Ellis, 1977; Johnson, 1980; Walen, DiGiuseppe, & Wessler, 1980; Wessler & Wessler, 1980; Wessler, 1982). Although this kind of positive reinforcement has its distinct dangers (Ellis, 1983; Turkat & Meyers, 1982), it can also at times be constructively used to overcome resistance.

If therapists are victims of countertransference and are negative to clients because of their own problems and bigotries, these can be resolved by looking for and disputing the irrational beliefs (iB's) creating their prejudices. Therapists who, for example, hate their clients who resemble the therapists' obnoxious mothers, are irrationally telling themselves ideas like these: "Because my mother treated me badly, I can't stand *any* person who has some of her traits!" "This client *must not* behave the obnoxious way in which my mother acted! She's a horrible *person* for behaving in this crummy way!" Such irrational beliefs are fairly easily revealed if therapists use RET to probe their negative reactions to their clients. The kinds of overgeneralizations that lead to these beliefs are particularly uprooted through rational–emotive therapy (RET) and cognitive behavioral therapy (CBT) (Ellis, 1962; Beck, 1976).

Resistance Related to Moralistic Attitudes of Therapists

In addition to the therapist-related resistances just mentioned, a common trait that many therapists possess and that blocks them in helping clients is their moralism: the profound tendency to condemn themselves and others for evil or stupid acts. Even though they are in the helping profession, they frequently believe that their seriously disturbed clients *should* not, *must* not be the way they are, especially when these clients abuse their therapists, come late, refuse to pay their bills, and otherwise behave obnoxiously or antisocially. Many therapists therefore overtly or covertly damn their clients for their wrongdoings and consequently help these clients damn themselves and become more, instead of less, disturbed. Naturally many such clients often resist therapy.

RET practitioners particularly can combat this kind of resistance, since one of the key tenets of RET is that all humans, including all clients, merit what Rogers (1961) calls unconditional positive regard and what RET calls unconditional acceptance (Ellis, 1962, 1972, 1973, 1976, 1984). This means that rational–emotive therapists look at their own (and other's) moralism and the irrational beliefs (iB's) that underlie them, such as: "My client *should* work at therapy! She *must* not sabotage my efforts! How *awful* if she does! I *can't stand* it!" And RET practitioners work hard at extirpating these ideas and giving all their clients, no matter how difficult they are, unconditional self-acceptance. In this manner they help minimize therapist-encouraged resistance.

Resistance Linked to Clients' and Therapists' Other Love–Hate Problems

Although the Freudians assume that love–hate problems between clients and their therapists are invariably sparked by and intimately involved with transference difficulties—that is, stem from clients' and therapists' early family relationships—this is questionable. Client–therapist difficulties, and the resistance to which they sometimes lead, may be based on reality factors that have nothing to do with anyone's childhood experiences. Thus, a young female client may just happen to have an exceptionally bright, attractive, and kindly therapist who would be an ideal mate for her (or almost any other woman) if she met him socially; and she may quite realistically fall in love with him, even though he has virtually nothing in common with her father, her uncles, or her brothers. Similarly, her therapist may fall in love with her not because she resembles his mother but because, more than any other woman he has met and gotten close to in his entire life, she truly *is* charming, talented, and sexy to him.

When nontransference, reality-based feelings occur in therapy, and when they lead to intense warm or cold feelings on the part of the therapists and/or clients, they can easily foment resistance problems. Thus, a female client who intensely loves her therapist may resist improving in order to prolong the therapy; and a therapist who intensely loves his or her client may also (consciously or unconsciously) foment resistance to ensure that the therapy indefinitely continues.

These nontransference relationship feelings that encourage resistance are sometimes difficult to resolve, since they are reality based and therefore both therapists and clients may derive special gains (or pains) from them that may interfere with effective therapy. But they also may include iB's that can be disputed, such as: "Because I love my therapist and it would be great to mate with him, I *can't bear* giving up therapy. So I'll refuse to change!" Or: "Because I really care for my client and enormously enjoy the sessions with her, I *must* not help her improve and bring these sessions to an end!" These iB's can be sought out and disputed, until the client and/or therapist gives them up and thereby removes motivation for resistance.

Fear of Disclosure Resistance

One of the most common forms of resistance stems from clients' fear of disclosure. They find it uncomfortable to talk about themselves freely (e.g., engage in free association) or to confess thoughts, feelings, and actions that they view as "shameful" (e.g., lusting for their mothers or sisters). They therefore resist being open in therapy and getting at the source of some of the things they find most bothersome (Dewald, 1982; Freud, 1926/1965; Schlesinger, 1982).

Where psychoanalysis finds this kind of resistance exceptionally common and attributes it to deeply unconscious and often repressed feelings of guilt, RET holds that clients who resist therapy because they are afraid to reveal "shameful" thoughts about themselves usually do so because they are quite aware of these feelings or else have them just below their level of consciousness (in what Freud called their preconscious realm of experience). Thus, if a male client resists talking about sex because of his incestuous feelings for his mother or sister, he usually (though not always) is consciously aware of these feelings but deliberately suppresses rather than expresses them. He resists talking about such feelings in therapy because he is usually telling himself irrational beliefs such as "It's wrong to lust after my mother; and I *must* not behave that wrongly!" "If I told my therapist that I lust after my sister, he would think I was a sex fiend and wouldn't like me. I *have to* be liked by my therapist, and would be a shit if even he didn't like me!"

In RET, we help clients reveal these iB's and, more important, to dispute and surrender them. We help them to see that their "shameful" feelings may not even be wrong (for to lust after your mother is hardly to copulate with her!); and that even when they are self-defeating (as having continual obsessive thoughts about incest would be), human *behaviors* never make one a totally rotten *person*. By helping clients to give up just about *all* shame and self-downing, RET sees that they rid themselves of what Freud would call superego-instigated resistance and are considerably more open in therapy than they would otherwise be (Dryden, 1983; Ellis, 1957, 1962, 1971, 1973, 1984; Ellis & Grieger, 1977; Ellis & Whiteley, 1979).

Resistance Created by Fear of Discomfort

Probably the most common and strongest kind of resistance in therapy is that motivated by low frustration tolerance or what RET calls discomfort anxiety (Ellis, 1979, 1980). Even psychoanalysis, albeit reluctantly, recognizes this form of resistance. Blatt and Erlich (1982) acknowledge it as broad and basic, a fundamental resistance to change and growth. They call it an expression of the basic wish to maintain familiar and predictable modes of adaptation, even though these are uncomfortable and painful in the long run. Dewald (1982) talks about strategic resistance, that is, clients' efforts to seek fulfilment of childhood wishes and to demand unrealistic or impossible goals.

In RET this important form of resistance is attributed to short-range hedonism—clients' short-sighted demands that they achieve the pleasure of the moment even though this may well defeat them in the long run. The main irrational beliefs that lead to low frustration tolerance (LFT) or discomfort anxiety are "It's *too hard* to change, and it *shouldn't be* that hard! How *awful* that I have to go through pain to get therapeutic gain!" "I *can't tolerate* the discomfort of doing my homework, even though I have agreed with my therapist that it is desirable for me to do it." "The world is a *horrible place* when it forces me to work so hard to change myself! Life *should be* easier than it is!"

RET shows clients how to dispute these grandiose ideas and to accept the realistic notion that no matter how hard it is for them to change in therapy, it's harder if they don't. It teaches them that there is rarely any gain without pain and that the philosophy of long-range hedonism—the seeking of pleasure for today *and* for tomorrow—is likely to result in therapeutic change. It shows them how to use their natural hedonistic tendencies by reinforcing themselves for therapeutic progress (e.g., overcoming procrastination) and penalizing themselves when they refuse to work at therapy (e.g., when they procrastinate) (Ellis & Knaus, 1977; Knaus, 1982). RET also stresses problem-solving skills that help clients to achieve more successful solutions to their problems with an expenditure of minimum unnecessary effort (D'Zurilla & Goldfried, 1971; Ellis, 1962, 1977; Ellis & Harper, 1975; Ellis & Whiteley, 1979; Spivack & Shure, 1974).

Secondary Gain Resistance

Several nineteenth-century and early-twentieth-century therapists noted that many clients receive secondary gains or payoffs from their disturbances and that they therefore are very reluctant to give them up (Ellenberger, 1970). Thus, if a factory worker who hates his job develops hysterical paralysis of the hand, he may resist psychotherapy because if it succeeds he will have to return to the work he hates. Freud (1926/1965) and some of his followers (A. Freud, 1936; Fenichel, 1941; Berne, 1964) emphasized the unconscious aspects of this defensive process and insisted that if clients have direct gains to make by improving but have important unconscious secondary gains to maintain by refusing to improve, they will stubbornly resist treatment for deeply unconscious, and often repressed, reasons. Thus, a woman will refuse to lose weight or to have good sex with her husband because of her underlying hatred of her mother and the strong unconscious payoff she is receiving by spiting this mother (who wants her to be thin or to have a good marriage).

Although Freudians usually exaggerate the deeply unconscious (and very dramatic) element in secondary gains, it seems clear that many clients do resist change because the payoffs they are getting from their disturbances are (or at least *seem* to be) considerable. Goldfried (1982) puts this kind of resistance in behavioral terms by pointing out that when clients change for the "better" they sometimes discover hidden penalties. Women may overcome their unassertiveness, for example, only to find that assertiveness is often ill rewarded in our society. Hence, they may "logically" fall back again to being unassertively neurotic!

Using RET analysis, we often find that secondary gain resistance is spurred by several iB's, such as "Because my mother *must not* try to make me lose weight, and is a *rotten person* for criticizing me for being overweight, I'll fix her wagon by remaining a fat slob!" Or, "Because macho men will put me down if I am an assertive woman, and I *can't stand* their put-downs, I'll give up my desire for assertiveness and remain fairly submissive for the rest of my life." Using RET, we show clients how to dispute and surrender these iB's and thereby to be able to achieve the *greater* payoff of losing weight rather than the neurotic one of spiting their mother. And we may encourage women to achieve the *primary gain* of being assertive rather than the *secondary gain* of winning the approval of macho men.

Resistance Stemming from Feelings of Hopelessness

A sizeable number of clients seem to resist therapeutic change because they strongly feel that they are *unable* to modify their disturbed behavior, that they are *hopeless* and *can't* change (Ellis, 1957, 1962; Turkat & Meyer, 1982). Such clients sometimes at first make good progress; but as soon as they retrogress, even slightly, they irrationally tend to conclude, "My falling back like this proves that it's *hopeless* and that I'll *never* conquer my anxiety!" "Because I *must* not be as depressed and incompetent as I now am, and am therefore a *complete depressive,* what's the use of my trying any longer to conquer my depression? I might as well give in to it and perhaps kill myself!"

Thoughts and feelings about the hopelessness of one's disturbed state are part of what RET calls the *secondary symptoms of disturbance.* As I have noted elsewhere (Ellis, 1962, 1979, 1980, 1984) these secondary symptoms tend to validate the RET or cognitive behavior theory of neurosis. For on the level of primary disturbance, people desire to achieve their goals (such as success and approval), fail to do so, and instead of sanely concluding, "It would have been nice to achieve what I wanted but since I didn't, too bad! I'll try again next time," they irrationally conclude, "I *should* have achieved success and approval, and since I didn't do what I *must* do, it's *awful* and I'm no damned good as a *person!*" They then become, or, in RET terms, *make* themselves, disturbed. But once emotionally upset, they *see* their upsetness and cognize about it in this vein: "I *shouldn't* disturb myself as I am now doing! How *awful!* I am a *total fool* for acting this foolishly, and a fool like me *can't* change. It's hopeless!"

RET, because of its theory of secondary disturbance, particularly shows clients how they falsely *invent* their thoughts and feelings of hopelessness and how they can dispute and give them up. It uses (as will be indicated later in this series of articles) many cognitive, emotive, and behavioral methods of dispelling feelings of hopelessness that lead to resistance (Ellis, 1984; Ellis & Abrahms, 1978).

Resistance Motivated by Self-punishment

Freud (1926/1965) held that one of the main forms of resistance originates in the superego or in our guilt-creating tendencies. Thus, a female client who is jealous of her more accomplished sister and who may become more conscious of her hatred during therapy may strongly feel that she deserves to be punished for her meanness and may therefore resist giving up her self-defeating neurotic behavior (such as overeating or compulsive handwashing). During my 40 years of clinical practice I have rarely found this kind of self-punishing resistance among neurotics (though I have found it a little more often in psychotics and severely borderline clients).

Assuming this kind of resistance does exist, it would seem to stem from irrational beliefs along these lines: "Because I have done such evil acts, which I absolutely *should not* have done, I am a thoroughly *worthless individual* who *deserves* to suffer. Therefore, I deserve to be continually disturbed and will make no real effort to use therapy to help myself." If clients actively have these ideas, RET would be most appropriate to show them how to combat their iB's. Psychodynamic therapies, on the other hand, might well be contraindicated, because, although they might show clients how self-punishing they are, they might not teach them how to eradicate the irrational beliefs behind this kind of masochism.

Resistance Motivated by Fear of Change or Fear of Success

Psychodynamic therapists, from Freud onward, have often held that resistance sometimes stems from fear of change, from fear of the future, or fear of success (Blatt & Erlich, 1982). This is probably true, since many disturbed people have a pronounced need for safety and certainty and, even though their symptoms are uncomfortable, at least they know and are familiar with their negative limits and may be afraid that if they lose them they may experience even *greater* discomfort. So they prefer to stick with the tried and true discomfort.

More important, perhaps, many symptoms (such as shyness and fear of public speaking) protect clients against possible failure (such as failing in love or giving a laughable speech). To surrender these symptoms would therefore mean to risk subsequent failure and disapproval, and many clients would find this much more "catastrophic" or "awful" than they find retaining their symptoms.

What has been labeled "the fear of success" is almost never really that, but a fear of *subsequent* failure. Thus, if a withdrawn teenage boy stops withdrawing and begins to succeed at school, at sports, and at social affairs, he may (1) lose the comfort and indulgence of his overprotective parents, (2) gain the enmity of his siblings, (3) risk later failure at the activities in which he has now begun to succeed, and (4) be forced to take on much more responsibility and effort than he would like to assume. He may *view* his academic, athletic, and social "gains," therefore, as actual "dangers" or "failures," and may resist or retreat from them. Does he, then, really have a "fear of success"—or of failure?

When clients do resist psychotherapy, because of fear of change or fear of success, RET looks for their iB's, such as, "I *must* not give up my symptoms, since change would be *too* uncomfortable and I *can't stand* such change!" "I cannot change my neurotic behavior and do better in life because that would be too risky. I might encounter greater failure later, as I *must* not; for that would be *awful!*" These and similar iB's that underlie the fear of change or fear of success are revealed and eliminated during rational–emotive therapy, thus minimizing this kind of resistance to change.

Resistance Motivated by Reactance and Rebelliousness

A number of clinicians have observed that some clients react or rebel against therapy because they see it as an impingement on their freedom. Especially if it is active and directive, they perversely fight it, even when they have voluntarily asked for it (Brehm, 1976; Goldfried, 1982). Noting this form of resistance, several therapists have invented or adopted various kinds of paradoxical or provocative therapy to try to trick these perversely rebellious clients into giving up their resistance (Dunlap, 1928; Erikson & Rossi, 1979; Farrelly & Brandsma, 1976; Fay, 1978; Frankl, 1960; Haley, 1963; Watzlawick, Weakland, & Fisch, 1974).

When clients resist therapy because of reactance, RET looks for their irrational beliefs, such as "I *have to* control my entire destiny; and even though my therapist is on my side and is working hard to help me, I *must not* let him or her tell me what to do!" "How *awful* if I am directed by my therapist! I *can't bear* it! I should have perfect freedom to do what I like, even if my symptoms are killing me!" RET reveals and helps clients rip up their iB's, but it also selectively (and not cavalierly!) makes use of paradoxical intention. For example, it gives some clients the homework assignment of failing at a certain task, to show them that failure is not world shattering (Ellis & Abrahms, 1978; Ellis & Whiteley, 1979).

As can be seen by the foregoing survey of some of the common kinds of resistance, clients frequently come to therapy because they are plagued with symptoms of emotional disturbance and yet they stubbornly resist the best efforts of their therapists to relieve their suffering. In many instances their "resistance" is partly attributable to therapeutic fallibility—to the poor judgment, inept theories, and emotional rigidities of their therapists. But often (perhaps more often) they have their own reasons for resisting the therapist-directed procedures that they voluntarily seek. As noted, these reasons are varied and wide-ranging.

While some aspects of the rational–emotive approach to treating common resistances have already been briefly outlined, the next section will discuss RET's cognitive antiresistance techniques in considerably more detail.

DISPUTING CLIENTS' IRRATIONAL, RESISTANCE-CREATING BELIEFS

RET employs a number of cognitive methods to interrupt, challenge, dispute, and change the irrational beliefs (iB's) that are found to underlie clients self-sabotaging resistances. These include the following techniques:

Cognitions That Underlie Resistance

Virtually all RET clients are taught the ABC's of emotional disturbance and dysfunctional behavior. Thus, when clients have a neurotic symptom or self-defeating consequence (C), such as depression and self-hatred, following their experiencing an unfortunate activating event (A), such as rejection by a significant person, they are shown that while A (rejection) probably contributes to and influences C (depression), it does not directly (as they tend to falsely "see" or infer) *create* or *cause* C. Rather, the more direct (and usually more important) "cause" of C is B, their belief system, with which they mainly "create" or "cause" C. Although they mistakenly believe that their depression and self-hatred directly and inevitably follow from their being rejected (A), they actually have a *choice* of B's and C's, and they foolishly *choose* to make themselves inappropriately depressed and self-hating (neurotic) at C, when they theoretically could have *chosen* instead to make themselves feel only appropriately disappointed and frustrated (self-helping and unneurotic) (Ellis, 1957, 1962, 1973, 1984; Ellis & Harper, 1961, 1975).

According to the ABC theory of RET, when these clients want to be accepted and approved at A (activating event) and are unpleasantly, instead, rejected, they *can* choose to manufacture or resort to a set of sensible or rational beliefs (rB's) and *can* thereby conclude, "How unfortunate that so-and-so disapproved of some of my traits and therefore rejected my friendship or love. Too bad! But I can still find significant others to approve of and accept me. Now how do I go about finding them?" If they rigorously create and stay with these rB's, these clients would, as stated, feel appropriately disappointed and frustrated, but *not* depressed and self-hating.

Where, then, do their inappropriate and disturbed feelings of depression and self-hatred come from? RET shows clients that these neurotic consequences (C's) mainly or largely (though not exclusively) stem from their iB's. These iB's almost invariably consist of absolutistic, dogmatic, illogical, unrealistic beliefs. Instead of being expressions of flexible desire and preference (as rB's seem to be), they are inflexible, rigid commands and demands—absolutistic and unconditional shoulds, oughts, musts, and necessities. Thus, feelings of depression and self-hatred (at C) that follow disapproval and rejection (at A) are largely the result of iB's like (1) I *must* not be disapproved of and rejected by a person I deem significant"; (2) "If I am rejected, as I must not be, it's *awful* and *terrible*"; (3) "I *can't stand* being disapproved, as I *must* not be;" and (4) "If I am rejected by a significant other, as must *never,* under *any* conditions, occur, there has to be something horribly rotten about me, and that rottenness makes me a thoroughly *despicable, undeserving person!*"

RET, using its cognitively oriented ABC theory of human disturbance, first tends to show depressed and self-hating clients how they (and not their parents, teachers, society, or culture) unwittingly (and largely unconsciously) *choose* to *disturb themselves;* how they can therefore *decide* to change their iB's and thereby undisturb themselves; and how they can mainly (though not completely) acquire a realistic philosophy of *preference* rather than an absolutistic philosophy of *demandingness* and consequently rarely seriously disturb themselves in the future.

In combatting clients' self-defeating resistances, RET puts them into the ABC model and shows them that when they promise themselves and their therapists that they will work at therapy at point A (activating event) and when they act dysfunctionally at point C and achieve the self-defeating consequence of resistance, they have both rational beliefs and irrational beliefs at point C. Their rB's tend to be "I don't like working at therapy. It's hard to change myself! But it's hard*er* if I don't; so I'd damned well better push myself, and do this hard work right *now* to make my life easier and better later." If, says the theory of RET, they *only* believed and felt these rational beliefs at B, they would not be especially resistant at C.

No such luck! When clients seriously and self-injuriously resist, they usually *also* create and indulge in irrational beliefs such as these: (1) "It's not only hard for me to work at therapy and change myself, it's *too* hard! It *should not, must not* be that hard"; (2) "How *terrible* that I have to work so hard and persistently to change myself"; (3) "I *can't stand* working at therapy that is harder than it *should be*"; and (4) "What a *rotten therapist* I have, who makes me work harder than I *should!* And what *crummy methods* he or she inflicts on me! I'm sure there is some easier, more enjoyable method of changing, and until I find it I'll be damned if I'll make myself so uncomfortable with this one!"

These iB's of resistant clients, which mainly consist of a devout philosophy of low frustration tolerance (LFT) or discomfort anxiety (DA) (Ellis, 1979, 1980), can also be supplemented with a philosophy of self-downing or ego anxiety (EA). Resistant clients' iB's then tend to run along these lines: (1) "I absolutely *must* work hard and succeed at therapy"; (2) "If I don't change as much and as quickly as I *must*, it's *awful* and *terrible*"; (3) "When I don't make myself change as well as I *must*, I *can't* stand it and life is *intolerable*"; and (4) "Unless I do as well as I *must* in therapy, I am an inadequate, hopeless, worthless person!" One might think that these self-blaming iB's would help spur on clients to work at therapy and to overcome their resistance. Occasionally, this may be true, but usually these iB's sabotage clients, lead them to feel that they *can't* change, and result in still greater resistances.

RET's primary cognitive technique of combatting resistance, therefore, consists of showing clients that they do not "just" resist and that they do not *merely* resist *because* they find it difficult to change, but that they *choose* to subscribe to a philosophy of low frustration tolerance and/or of self-deprecation which, in turn, largely "causes" their resistance. The main cognitive message of RET, of course, is that they can instead choose to *dis*believe and to *surrender* their iB's and can exchange them for rB's that will help them work at rather than resist therapeutic change.

Disputing Irrational Beliefs

The basic disputing techniques of RET can be employed to show clients that the iB's behind their absolutistic *shoulds, oughts,* and *musts,* and behind the inferences, attributions, overgeneralizations, nonsequiturs, and other forms of crooked thinking that tend to stem from these *musts,* can be annihilated or ameliorated by vigorous scientific thinking (Ellis, 1958a, 1962, 1971, 1973,

1984; Ellis & Becker, 1982; Ellis & Grieger, 1977; Ellis & Harper, 1975; Ellis & Whiteley, 1979). Thus registers are challenged by the therapist and are induced to keep challenging themselves with scientific questions like, "Where is the evidence that I *must* succeed at changing myself?" "Why is it *awful* and *horrible* that it is difficult for me to change?" "Prove that I *can't stand* my having to work long and hard at therapy." "Where it is written that it's *too hard* to change and that it *should not* be that hard?" This kind of scientific disputing is persisted at, by both therapists and clients, until resisters start changing.

After A (activating event), B (rational and irrational beliefs), and C (emotional and behavioral consequences), RET goes directly (and often quickly) on to D: disputing. As just noted, D is the scientific method. Science accepts beliefs as hypotheses, constructs, or theories, not as facts. Furthermore, scientific theories are not dogmatic, inflexible, absolutistic or devout. Otherwise they are religious rather than scientific (Ellis, 1983a; Rorer & Widiger, 1983). RET not only tries to be scientific about its own theories and to set them up so that they are precise and falsifiable (Barley, 1962; Mahoney, 1977; Popper, 1962; Weimer, 1979), but it is one of the new forms of cognitive behavioral therapy that attempts to teach clients how to think scientifically about themselves, others, and the world in which they live. If, RET contends, people were consistently scientific and nonabsolutistic, they would rarely invent or subscribe to dogmatic *shoulds* and *musts*, would stay with their flexible wishes and preferences, and would thereby minimize or eliminate their emotional disturbances.

RET, therefore, encourages all clients, and particularly resistant ones, actively and persistently to dispute (at point D) their iB's and to arrive at point E, which is a new effect or effective philosophy. Where D consists of clients' disputing their iB's, E consists of the logical and empirical answers they then give to this disputing. Thus, to perform D and to arrive at E, a client's internal dialogue in regard to her or his resistance would go something like this:

IB: "I *must* succeed at changing myself during therapy!"

D: "Where is the evidence that I *have* to succeed?"

E: "There is no such evidence! Succeeding at changing myself would have several distinct advantages and I'd definitely like to get these advantages. But I never *have* to get what I desire, no matter how much I desire it."

IB: "If I don't succeed in overcoming my resistance and working at therapy, I am an incompetent, hopeless person who can never stop resisting!"

D: "Prove that I am an incompetent, hopeless person who can never stop resisting."

E: "I can't prove this. I can only prove that I am a person who has *so far* failed to stop resisting but not that I have, or always will have, *no* ability to do so in the future. Only my *belief* in my total incompetence to change myself will make me *more* incompetent than I otherwise would probably be!"

IB: "It is *awful* and *horrible* that I have to work at therapy and to change myself."

D: "In what way is it *awful* and *horrible* to work at therapy and to change myself?"

E: "In no way! It is distinctly difficult and inconvenient for me to work at therapy, and

I'd rather it be easy. But when I label this work *awful* or *horrible* I mean that (1) it *should not* be as inconvenient as it is, (2) it is *totally* or *100%* inconvenient, and (3) it is *more than* (101%) inconvenient. All these conclusions are wrong, since (1) it should be as inconvenient as it is because that's the way it is, (2) it virtually never can be 100% inconvenient because it invariably could be worse, and (3) it obviously cannot be 101% inconvenient because nothing can be *that* bad! Nothing in the universe is *awful* or *terrible* or *horrible,* since these are magical terms that go beyond reality and have no empirical referents. If I invent such antiempirical "descriptions" of my experience, I will thereby make my life *seem* and *feel* "awful" when it is only highly disadvantageous and inconvenient; and I will then make myself suffer *more* than I would otherwise suffer."

IB: "I *can't stand* my having to work long and hard at therapy."

D: "Why can't I stand having to work long and hard at therapy?"

E: "I definitely *can* stand it! I don't *like* working that long and hard and wish that I could change myself easily and magically. But I *can* stand what I don't like, as long as (1) I don't die of it and (2) I can still in some ways enjoy myself and be happy. Fairly obviously I won't die because I work at therapy (though I may kill myself if I don't!). And even though this kind of work is often unenjoyable, it leaves me time and energy for other pleasures. In fact, in the long run, it helps me to achieve *greater* life enjoyment. So I clearly *can* stand, *can* tolerate the therapeutic work that I don't like."

IB: "Because there is no easy way for me to work at therapy and I'd better uncomfortably persist at it until I collaborate with my therapist and change myself, the world is a *horrible* place and life is hardly worth living. Maybe I'd better kill myself."

D: "Where is it written that the world is a horrible place and that life is hardly worth living because there is no easy way for me to work at therapy?"

E: "It is only written in my self-defeating philosophy! It seems evident that, because of the way I am and because of the way the world is, I will often have trouble changing myself through therapy. Too bad! Really unfortunate! But if that's the way it is and that's the way I am, I'd better accept (though still dislike and often try to change) the world's limitations and my own fallibility, and I'd better attempt to live and to enjoy myself as much as I can with these undesirable realities. I can teach myself, as St. Francis recommended, to have the courage to change the unpleasant things that I can change, to have the serenity to accept those that I can't change, and to have the wisdom to know the difference between the two."

RET's most famous and most popular technique is the one just outlined: that of teaching resistant clients to find their main irrational beliefs that significantly contribute to or "cause" their resistances; to actively dispute these iB's by rigorously using the logico-empirical tools of the scientific method; and to persist at this disputing until they arrive at E, an effective philosophy that is self-helping rather than irrational and self-downing. As Kelly (1955) brilliantly noted, humans are natural predictors and scientists. RET, along with other cognitive behavioral therapies, tries to help them be better and more productive scientists in their personal affairs (Ellis, 1962, 1973, 1984; Ellis & Becker, 1982; Ellis &

Grieger, 1977; Ellis & Harper, 1975; Ellis & Whiteley, 1979; Friedman, 1975; Mahoney, 1974, 1977).

Rational and Coping Self-statements

RET, following the leads of Bernheim, (1886/1947) and Coue (1922), teaches resistant clients to say to themselves, repetitively, rational or coping statements and to keep actively autosuggesting these statements until they truly believe them and feel their effect. Thus, they can strongly say to themselves rB's such as "Therapy doesn't *have* to be easy. I can, in fact, *enjoy* its difficulty and its challenge." "Sure it's hard to work at changing myself; but it's much harder if I don't." "Too bad if I am imperfect at changing myself. That only proves that I am still, and will continue to be, a highly fallible person. And I *can* accept myself as fallible!" Unlike positive thinking, however, RET encourages resisters to think through, and not merely parrot rational and coping statements.

Referenting

RET uses the general semantics method of referenting (Danysh, 1974) and teaches resistant clients (1) to make a comprehensive list of the disadvantages of resisting and the advantages of working at therapy and (2) to keep regularly reviewing and thinking about this list (Ellis & Abrahms, 1978; Ellis & Becker, 1982; Ellis & Harper, 1975). Thus, under disadvantages of resisting, clients can list: "(1) It will take me longer to change. (2) I will keep suffering as long as I resist changing. (3) My refusing to change will antagonize some of the people I care for and will sabotage my relationships with them. (4) My therapy will become more boring and more expensive the longer I take to change myself. (5) Continuing to afflict myself with my symptoms will make me lose much time and money. (6) If I continue to resist, I may well antagonize my therapist and encourage him or her to put less effort into helping me. (7) My refusing to work hard at therapy and thereby continuing to remain irrationally fearful and anxious will force me to forego many potential pleasures and adventures and make my life much duller." Similarly, using this referenting technique, clients are shown how to list the advantages of working harder at therapy and thereby abetting their own personality change. By reviewing and examining these disadvantages of resistance and these benefits of nonresistance, they are helped to resist considerably less.

RET often forcefully brings to clients' attention not only present but probable later disadvantages of resisting therapy. Thus, the RET practitioner can reward the client: "Yes, you don't have to work right now at overcoming your low frustration tolerance, since your parents are still around to help support you economically. But how are you going to earn a decent living after they are gone unless you prepare yourself to do so now?" "Of course, you may be able to get away with your drinking and staying up late at night at present, but won't it eventually sabotage your health? And do you really want to keep making yourself fat, tired, and physically ill?"

Challenge of Self-change

RET tries to sell some resistant clients on the *adventure* and *challenge* of working at changing themselves. Thus, it gives clients the homework exercise of disputing irrational beliefs (DIBS) which helps them debate their iB's and to reframe some of the difficult things they do with therapy by asking themselves questions like, "What good things can I feel or make happen if I work hard at therapy and still don't succeed too well?" (Ellis, 1974; Ellis & Harper, 1975). Rational–emotive therapists also prod resistant clients with questions like, "Suppose you pick the wrong therapy technique and work hard at it with few good results. Why would that be great for you to do?" By these paradoxical questions they hope to help resisters see that (1) trying something and at first failing at it is usually better than not trying at all; (2) striving to change leads to important information about oneself that may result in later success and pleasure; (3) action can be pleasurable in its own right, even when it does not lead to fine results; (4) trying something and at first failing at it is usually better than not trying at all; (5) trying to change oneself and *accepting* delayed results increases one's frustration tolerance, and (6) the *challenge* of striving for therapeutic change (like the challenge of trying to climb Mount Everest) may be exciting and enjoyable in its own right.

Although ego-enhancing methods of therapy are seen by RET as having their distinct dangers (since if clients are led to think of themselves as good or worthy individuals when they succeed at therapy they will also harmfully view themselves as bad or worthless individuals when they fail), some elements of verbal reinforcement can be used to combat resistance. Thus, therapists can show clients that *it* is good and desirable (and not that *they* are good or worthy) if they use their energy and intelligence to work at therapy. This technique can be combined with the challenging method. For example, the therapist can say to the client, "Yes, many people are prone to sitting on their asses and to stupidly resisting changing themselves. But anyone who fortunately has *your* intelligence, talent, and ability *can* overcome this kind of resistance and show how competent he or she is at changing. Not that you *have to* use your innate ability to change. But wouldn't you get much better results if you did?"

Proselytizing Others

One of the regular RET cognitive techniques that can be especially helpful with resistant and difficult clients consists of inducing them to use RET methods with others (Bard, 1980; Ellis, 1957; Ellis & Abrahms, 1978; Ellis & Harper, 1975;

Ellis & Whiteley, 1979). If, using RET, you have clients who resist giving up anger, you can try to get them to talk others—relatives, friends, employees—out of *their* anger. If your clients refuse to do their RET homework, you can try to induce them to give homework assignments to others and to keep checking to see if these people actually do their homework.

Cognitive Distraction

Cognitive distraction frequently is used in RET to divert clients from anxiety and depression (Ellis, 1973, 1984; Ellis & Abrahms, 1978; Ellis & Whiteley, 1979). Thus, clients are shown how to relax, to meditate, to do yoga exercises, and to use other forms of distraction when they upset themselves. Distraction, however, is often not that useful with resistant clients, since it only temporarily diverts them from rebelliously and defensively persisting with their disturbed behavior and they therefore soon return to it. One form of distraction that works well if you can get these clients to use it is in the form of a vital, ongoing interest that really absorbs them. Thus, if you can help them get absorbed in writing a book, being an active member of a self-help group, or volunteering to help others, they can sometimes find such constructive enjoyment as to minimize their need for self-defeating behavior like alcoholism, drugs, or stealing.

Use of Humor

Many resistant clients have little sense of humor, and that is precisely why they find it so hard to see how they are defeating themselves and how absurd their thoughts and behaviors are. But some, in spite of their severe disturbance, do have a good sense of humor that can be used to interfere with their resistance. Thus, I kept showing one of my stubborn clients how ironic it was that she railed and ranted against cold weather and thereby made herself suffer *more* from the cold. I also frequently tell resistant clients, "If the Martians ever come to visit us and they're really sane, they'll die laughing at us. For they'll see bright people like you vainly insisting that they can do something they can't do—such as change your parents—while simultaneously saying they can't do something that they invariably can do, namely, change yourself. They won't be able to understand this and will probably fly back to Mars because we're so crazy!" RET frequently uses humor and rational humorous songs to combat therapeutic resistance (Ellis, 1977c, 1977d, 1981).

Paradoxical Intention

With highly resistant and negative clients, as Erikson (Erikson & Rossi, 1979), Frankl (1960), Haley (1963), and others have shown, paradoxical intention sometimes works and is therefore a cognitive method of RET (Ellis & Whiteley,

1979). Thus, you can tell depressed clients to loudly wail and moan about everything that occurs in their lives. Or you can have highly anxious people take the assignment of only allowing themselves to worry from 8:00 to 8:15 AM every day. Or you can insist that resistant clients refuse to do *anything* you tell them to do, such as refuse to come on time for their sessions and refuse to do any homework assignments. Perversely, resisters may then stop resisting. But don't count on this! Paradoxical intention is a shocking but limited method that tends to work only occasionally and under special conditions.

Suggestion and Hypnosis

You may deliberately use strong suggestion or hypnosis with some difficult clients, even though these are inelegant techniques that somewhat interfere with clients' independent thinking. Resistant clients who *think* hypnosis works may allow themselves to change with hypnotic methods when they would not allow this without hypnosis. RET has included hypnosis methods from its inception in 1955 (Ellis, 1958, 1962). Stanton (1971), Tosi (Tosi & Marsella, 1977; Tosi & Reardon, 1976), and other researchers and clinicians have shown how it can sometimes be used effectively with resistant clients.

Philosophy of Effort

The usual practice of RET is to explain to all clients, right at the beginning of therapy, that they have enormous self-actualization powers (as well as self-defeating tendencies) and that only with hard work and practice will they be able to fulfill these powers (Ellis, 1962; Grieger & Boyd, 1980; Grieger & Grieger, 1982; Walen, DiGiuseppe, & Wessler, 1980; Wessler & Wessler, 1980). Clients are also shown that they can easily fall back to old dysfunctional patterns of behavior and that they therefore had better persistently keep monitoring themselves and working to change. With resistant clients this realistic message is often repeated with the aim of both prophylaxis and cure. A favorite RET slogan is, "There's rarely any gain without pain!" This philosophy is steadily promulgated to combat the low frustration tolerance of resisters (Ellis, 1979, 1980, 1982).

Working with Clients' Expectations

As Meichenbaum and Gilmore (1980) have shown, clients bring cognitive expectations to therapy and may see what is helping in their sessions with the therapist as disconfirming these expectations. Consequently, they may resist changing themselves. If so, you can accurately and empathically perceive and share your clients' expectations, make sense out of their unproductive resistant behavior, and thereby help overcome resistance. Using RET, you might well go one step further and, as you help your clients explore and understand the reasons for their resistance (and the iB's that often underlie this resistance), you can actively push, encourage, and persuade them to surrender their resistant ideas and behaviors.

Irrational Beliefs Underlying Primary and Secondary Resistance

Clients frequently have both primary and secondary resistance. Primary resistance stems largely from their three main musts: (1) "I *must* change myself quickly and easily, and I'm an incompetent person if I don't"; (2) "You *must* not force me to change, and I'll fight you to death if you do;" and (3) "Conditions *must* make it easy for me to change, and I won't try to help myself if they don't!" Once humans resist changing themselves for any of these three (or a combination of these three) reasons, they *see* that they resist and have another set of irrational beliefs about this resistance, such as (1) "I *must* not incompetently resist change, and I'm a pretty worthless person if I do"; (2) "I *must* not resist change in a hostile or rebellious manner, and it's *awful* if I do"; and (3) I *must* not have low frustration tolerance that makes me resist change, and I can't stand it if I do!" Their secondary disturbance, that is, their guilt or shame *about* resisting, tends to tie up their time and energy and incite *increased* resistance. In RET, therefore, we look for and try to eliminate secondary as well as primary resistances; and we do so by showing clients their primary and secondary iB's and by disputing both these sets of iB's, just as we would dispute any other irrational beliefs. By helping them first to undo their disturbances *about* their resistance, we show them how to remove these secondary problems and then how to get back to changing the ideas and feelings that constitute the primary resistance.

Irrational Beliefs underlying Avoidance of Responsibility

Resistance may sometimes stem from clients' trying to avoid responsibility for change and from their deliberately (though perhaps unconsciously) fighting the therapist's efforts to help them change. This form of childish rebelliousness can arise from ego irrationalities ("I must thwart my therapist and 'win out' over him to show what a strong, independent person I am!") or from low frustration tolerance irrationalities ("I must not have to work too hard at therapy, because if I assume full responsibility for changing myself life becomes too rough and unsatisfying!"). When avoidance of responsibility and concomitant rebellion against the therapist or against working at therapy result in resistance, RET tries to show clients the irrational beliefs (iB's) behind this kind of avoidance and rebellion and teach them how to combat and surrender these iB's.

Use of Quick and Active Disputation

Although RET therapists may sometimes help create resistance by actively and quickly disputing their clients' irrational beliefs, they may also, by "poorly" employing this technique, promptly smoke out clients' resistances, see exactly what kind of D.C.'s (difficult customers) these clients are, and promote more efficient and effective therapy methods. Active disputing, though risky, may uncover resistances rapidly, save therapists and clients considerable time and effort, lead to vigorous countermeasures by the therapist, and sometimes lead to a suitable quick (and inexpensive!) end to therapy.

Some cognitive behavioral therapists (e.g., Meichenbaum & Gilmore, 1980) recommend that resistance be overcome by graduating the change process into manageable steps and by structuring therapeutic intervention so that the therapist maximizes the likelihood of success at each stage. This will sometimes work but also has its dangers with those who resist because of abysmal LFT. With these individuals gradualism may easily *feed* their LFT and help them believe that it is *too* hard for them to change and that they *must* do so in a slow, gradual manner (Ellis, 1983c).

Disputing Impossibility of Changing

When clients contend that they *can't* change, RET can show them that this is an unrealistic, antiempirical view not supported by any facts (which merely show that *it is difficult* for them to change). But RET therapists do not use only this realistic, scientific refutation but also employ the more elegant anti*mus*turbatory form of disputing. Clients usually tell themselves "I *can't change* because they start with the basic proposition, "I *must* have an ability to change quickly and easily, and I'm incompetent and pretty worthless if I don't do what I *must*." RET disputes this *mus*turbatory, absolutistic thinking by showing them that they *never* have to change (though that would be highly desirable) and that they are *people who act incompetently* rather than *incompetent people*. This disputing of the idea "I can't change" is therefore more profound and more elegant than the simple antiempirical disputing of Meichenbaum (1977), Beck (1976), Maultsby (1975), and other proponents of CBT.

Helping Clients Gain Emotional Insight

RET often shows resistant clients that they falsely believe they are working hard to improve and to overcome their own resistance, when they really aren't. Thus they frequently say, "I see that I am telling myself that therapy should be easy, and I see that that is wrong." They then mistakenly think that because they have *seen* how they are resisting and have *seen* the error of their ways, they have worked at changing this error and thereby *overcome* their resistance. But they have usually done nothing of the sort. Their "insight" has not been used to help them *fight* the idea that therapy should be easy. They can now be shown that they'd better see and fight this idea, that is, dispute it by asking themselves, "*Why* should therapy be easy?" and by vigorously answering, "There's no damned reason why it should be! It often is—and should be—*hard!*"

RET tries to distinguish clearly between so-called intellectual and emotional insight (Ellis, 1963). Resistant clients often say, "I have intellectual insight into my hating myself but this does me no good, since I still can't stop this self-hatred. What I need is emotional insight." What these clients mean is that they hate themselves and may even see the irrational self-statements they make to bring about this feeling (e.g., "I must always succeed at important tasks and I am worthless when I don't!"), but they do not know how to change their iB's or they know how to change them but refuse to do the persistent and strong disputing that is required to give them up.

In RET we try to show clients, particularly resistant ones, three main kinds of insight:

1. People mainly disturb themselves rather than get upset by external conditions and events.

2. No matter when they first started to destroy themselves (usually in childhood) and no matter what events contributed to their early *disturbance,* people *now,* in the present, continue to make themselves upset by *still* strongly subscribing to irrational beliefs similar to those they held previously. They now keep their old disturbances alive by continually reindoctrinating themselves with these iB's.

3. Since people are born with the tendency to accept iB's from others and to create many of their own; and since they consciously and unconsciously reinstill these iB's in themselves from early childhood onward; and since they easily, automatically, and habitually actualize these ideas in their feelings and actions and thereby powerfully reinforce them over long periods of time, there is usually no simple, fast, easy and complete way to change them. Only considerable work and practice to challenge and dispute these irrational beliefs, and only long, concerted *action* that contradicts the behavioral patterns that accompany them will be likely to minimize or extirpate them.

RET, then, teaches clients that insights #1 and #2 are important but not sufficient for profound philosophical and behavioral change; and that they had better be accompanied by the most important insight of all—#3.

More specifically, RET shows resistant clients who say that they have intellectual insight into their symptoms (such as self-hating) but can't give it up because they don't have emotional insight, that they usually only have insight

#1—and even that, often, partially. Thus, a young woman may say, "I see that I hate myself," but may not see what she is irrationally believing to create her self-hatred (e.g., "Because I am not as competent as I *must* be, I am a thoroughly *inadequate person*"). Even when she sees what she is believing to create her self-hatred she only has achieved #1; and she may falsely believe that she obtained her self-hating belief from her parents and *that* is why she now hates herself.

In RET, we would therefore help her achieve insight #2: "No matter how I got the irrational belief that I *should* be more competent and am an *inadequate person* if I'm not, *I* now continue to indoctrinate myself with it so that *I* am fully responsible for believing it today; and therefore *I* had better give it up."

RET doesn't stop there, since she still might be left with only mild or "intellectual" insight, but pushes her on to insight #3: "Since *I* keep actively believing that I *should* be more competent and am an *inadequate person* if I'm not, and since I tend to keep recreating and newly inventing similar irrational beliefs (because it is my basic nature to do so), I had better keep steadily and forcefully *working and practicing* until I no longer believe this. For only by *continually* disputing and challenging this belief and only by *forcing myself* to keep acting against it will I be able *finally* to give it up and replace it with rational beliefs and effective behaviors."

Insight #3, plus the determination to act on this level of understanding, is what RET calls "emotional" insight or "willpower." It is this kind of cognitive restructuring or profound philosophical change that RET particularly employs with resistant clients.

Bibliotherapy and Audiotherapy

RET employs bibliotherapy with resistant clients and encourages them to read RET-oriented pamphlets and books, such as *Reason and Emotion in Psychotherapy* (Ellis, 1962), *A New Guide- to Rational Living* (Ellis & Harper, 1975), *Humanistic Psychotherapy: The Rational–Emotive Approach* (Ellis, 1973), and *A Guide to Personal Happiness* (Ellis & Becker, 1982). RET practitioners also give a good many talks, courses, workshops, marathons, and intensives that help clients understand theory and use the techniques of rational–emotive therapy. I have especially found that some RET cassette recordings, films, and TV cassettes are useful with resistant clients, who are urged to listen to them many times until the presentations on these materials sink in. Notably useful in this respect are the cassette recordings, *Conquering the Dire Need for Love* (Ellis, 1977d), *Conquering Low Frustration Tolerance* (Ellis, 1977a), *Overcoming Procrastination* (Knaus, 1974), *I'd like to Stop, But . . .* (Ellis, 1974), *Self-Hypnosis: The Rational–Emotive Approach* (Golden, 1982), *Twenty-One Ways to Stop Worrying* (Ellis, 1972b), and *How to Stubbornly Refuse to be Ashamed of Anything* (Ellis, 1972a).

Imaging Methods

One of the main modes of human cognition is imagery, and RET frequently employs imaging methods. These are sometimes especially useful with resistant clients, since some of them resist because they see and feel things more incisively through pictorial than through verbal means (Coue, 1922; Lazarus, 1978, 1981). Consequently, when they block on or find difficulty with verbal self-statements and philosophical disputing of irrational beliefs, they can sometimes be reached more effectively by imagery methods. To this end, RET, following Coue (1922) and a host of his disciples, can teach resisters to use positive imagery to imagine themselves doing things that they negatively contend that they can't do (e.g., successfully giving a public talk), and it can help them imagine bearing up under frustrating conditions when they normally think that they absolutely can't bear such conditions. Also, RET frequently employs Maultsby's technique of rational–emotive imagery (Maultsby, 1975; Maultsby & Ellis, 1974), by which resistant (and other) clients are shown how to imagine one of the worst things that could happen to them, to implode their disturbed feelings about this happening, and then to work at changing these to more appropriate negative feelings.

Modeling Techniques

Bandura (1969, 1977) has pioneered in showing how modeling methods can be used to help disturbed individuals, and RET has always used such methods (Ellis, 1962, 1971, 1973, 1984; Ellis & Abrahms, 1978; Ellis & Whiteley, 1979). In the case of resistant and difficult clients, RET practitioners not only teach them how to accept themselves unconditionally and fully, no matter how badly or incompetently they behave, but they also model this kind of acceptance by displaying firm kindness to these clients and showing by their attitudes and demeanor (as well as their words) that they can fully accept such clients, even when they are nasty to the therapist, when they come late to sessions, when they fail to do their homework, and when they otherwise stubbornly resist the therapist's efforts (Ellis, 1962, 1973, 1984; Ellis & Whiteley, 1979). RET also sponsors public workshops, such as my famous Friday night workshops that are given regularly at the Institute for Rational–Emotive Therapy in New York, where live demonstrations of RET are given for large audiences, so that the members of the audience can see exactly how RET is done and can model their own self-help procedures after this model. Resistant clients who serve as volunteer demonstratees at these workshops are often particularly helped by the public session they have with me (or other RET therapists, when I am out of town) and by the feedback and the comments they receive from 15 or 20 members of the audience.

Recorded Playback of Therapy Sessions

Carl Rogers (1942) pioneered in using recordings of therapy sessions to help therapists understand exactly what they were doing and how to improve their techniques. RET, beginning in 1959, pioneered the use of audiotapes for two other purposes: (1) to show therapists throughout the world exactly how RET is done, so that they could model their own use of it after the practices of its originator and other RET practitioners (Ellis, 1959, 1966a, 1966b; Elkin, Ellis & Edelstein, 1971; Wessler & Ellis, 1979), and (2) to give clients recordings of their own sessions so that they could listen to them several times and thereby hear and internalize some of the therapeutic messages that they would otherwise miss or forget. This second use of recordings, which also can be done with video equipment if this is available, has been found very useful with resistant clients. If they are given homework assignments of listening to their own taped sessions (and sometimes the taped session of others), they often get across to themselves some of the elements of RET that they otherwise easily miss (Ellis, 1979, 1984; Ellis & Abrahms, 1978; Ellis & Whiteley, 1979). One of my borderline clients, for example, who argued vigorously against almost every point I made about his needlessly upsetting himself, accepted these same points almost all the time when he listened to a cassette recording of each session several times during the week following this session.

CONCLUSION

As can be seen from the material just presented, RET cognitive methods, when carefully selected and employed with resistant and difficult clients, can often be effective. Also, RET often employs a variety of emotive and behavioral techniques, in addition to many cognitive methods, with resistant clients. Rarely, if ever, would it compulsively stick to one favored method. In fact, the more resistant a client is, the more cognitive, emotive, and behavioral methods are usually employed. RET is designed to be not only effective but efficient and therefore to solve clients' problems as quickly as feasible, utilizing minimal therapist time and effort (Ellis, 1980). With average clients who are not resistant, it can therefore often employ a relatively small number of techniques and can help these clients to improve significantly in a fairly short period of time. It invariably uses some cognitive, emotive, and behavioral modalities but doesn't have to utilize many of them compulsively, as is sometimes done in multimodal therapy (Lazarus, 1981) or in holistic psychotherapy. With resistant clients, however, RET is often done more comprehensively and intensively because that is what such clients may require.

REFERENCES

Bandura, A. *Principles of behavior modification.* New York: Holt, Rinehart and Winston, 1969.

Bandura, A. *Social learning theory.* Englewood Cliffs, N.J.: Prentice-Hall, 1977.

Bard, J. *Rational–emotive therapy in practice.* Champaign, Ill.: Research Press, 1980.

Bartley, W. W. *The retreat to commitment.* New York: Knopf, 1962.

Basch, M. F. Dynamic psychotherapy and its frustrations. In P. L. Wachtel (Ed.), *Resistance.* New York: Plenum, 1982.

Beck, A. T. *Cognitive therapy and the emotional disorders.* New York: International Universities Press, 1976.

Berne, E. *Games people play.* New York: Grove, 1964.

Bernheim, H. *Suggestive therapeutics.* New York: London Book Company, 1947. Originally published, 1886.

Blatt, S. J., & Erlich, H. S. Levels of resistance in the psychotherapeutic process. In P. L. Wachtel (Ed.), *Resistance.* New York: Plenum, 1982.

Brehm, S. S. *The application of social psychology to clinical practice.* Washington, D.C.: Hemisphere, 1976.

Coue, E. *My method.* New York: Doubleday, Page, 1922.

Danysh, J. *Stop without quitting.* San Francisco: International Society for General Semantics, 1974.

Dewald, P. A. Psychoanalytic perspectives on resistance. In P. L. Wachtel (Ed.), *Resistance.* New York: Plenum, 1982.

Dryden, W. The therapeutic alliance: Conceptual issues and some research findings. *Midland Journal of Psychotherapy,* June, 1982, *1,* 14–19.

Dryden, W. Vivid RET II: Disputing methods. *Rational Living.* 1983, *1,* 9–14.

Dunlap, K. A revision of the fundamental law of habit formation. *Science, 1928, 67,* 360–362.

D'Zurilla, T. J., & Goldfried, M. R. Problem solving and behavior modification. *Journal of Abnormal Psychology,* 1971, *78,* 107–126.

Elkin, A., Ellis, A., & Edelstein, M. *Recorded sessions with RET clients (C2025).* New York: Institute for Rational–Emotive Therapy, 1971.

Ellenberger, H. F. *The discovery of the unconscious.* New York: Basic Books, 1970.

Ellis, A. Hypnotherapy with borderline psychotics. *Journal of General Psychology,* 1958, *59,* 245–253. (a)

Ellis, A. Rational psychotherapy. *Journal of General Psychology,* 1958, *59,* 35–49. (b)

Ellis, A. *Recorded sessions with adolescent and child RET clients (C2011).* New York: Institute for Rational–Emotive Therapy, 1959.

Ellis, A. *Reason and emotion in psychotherapy.* Secaucus, N.J.: Lyle Stuart and Citadel Books, 1962.

Ellis, A. Toward a more precise definition of "emotional" and "intellectual" insight. *Psychological Reports,* 1963, *13,* 125–126.

Ellis, A. *Recorded sessions with RET neurotic clients (C2004).* New York: Institute for Rational–Emotive Therapy, 1966. (a)

Ellis, A. *Recorded sessions with RET severely disturbed clients (C2004).* New York: Institute for Rational–Emotive Therapy, 1966. (b)

Ellis, A. *Growth through reason.* Palo Alto, Calif.: Science and Behavior Books; Hollywood: Wilshire, 1971. (a)

Ellis, A. *How to stubbornly refuse to be ashamed of anything.* Cassette recording. New York: Institute for Rational–Emotive Therapy, 1971. (b)

Ellis, A. *Psychotherapy and the value of a human being.* New York: Institute for Rational–Emotive Therapy, 1972. (a)

Ellis, A. *Twenty-one ways to stop worrying.* Cassette recording. New York: Institute for Rational–Emotive Therapy, 1972. (b)

Ellis, A. *Humanistic psychotherapy: The rational–emotive approach.* New York: Crown and McGraw-Hill Paperbacks, 1973.

Ellis, A. *Disputing irrational beliefs (DIBS).* New York: Institute for Rational–Emotive Therapy, 1974. (a)

Ellis, A. *I'd like to stop, but.* . . . Cassette recording. New York: Institute for Rational–Emotive Therapy, 1974. (b)

Ellis, A. *How to live with a "neurotic."* New York: Crown, 1957. Rev. ed., 1975.

Ellis, A. RET abolishes most of the human ego. *Psychotherapy,* 1976, *13,* 343–348.

Ellis, A. *Conquering low frustration tolerance.* Cassette recording. New York: Institute for Rational–Emotive Therapy, 1977. (a)

Ellis, A. *Conquering the dire need for love.* Cassette recording. New York: Institute for Rational–Emotive Therapy, 1977. (b)

Ellis, A. *Fun as psychotherapy.* Cassette recording. New York: Institute for Rational–Emotive Therapy, 1977. (c)

Ellis, A. *A garland of rational songs.* Songbook and cassette recording. New York: Institute for Rational–Emotive Therapy, 1977. (d)

Ellis, A. *How to live with—and without—anger.* New York: Reader's Digest Press, 1977. (e)

Ellis, A. Discomfort anxiety: A new cognitive behavioral construct. I. *Rational Living,* 1979, *14*(2), 3–8.

Ellis, A. Discomfort anxiety: A new cognitive behavioral construct. II. *Rational Living,* 1980, *15*(1), 25–30.

Ellis, A. The use of rational humorous songs in psychotherapy. *Voices,* 1981, *16*(4), 29–36.

Ellis, A. *The case against religiosity.* New York: Institute for Rational–Emotive Therapy, 1983. (a)

Ellis, A. Failure in rational–emotive therapy. In E. Foa & P. M. Emmelkamp (Eds.), *Failures in behavior therapy.* New York: Wiley, 1983. (b)

Ellis, A. The philosophic implications and dangers of some popular behavior therapy techniques. In M. Rosenbaum and C. M. Franks (Eds.), *Perspectives on behavior therapy in the eighties.* New York: Springer, 1983. (c)

Ellis, A. *Rational–emotive therapy and cognitive behavior therapy.* New York: Springer, 1984.

Ellis, A., & Abrahms, E. *Brief psychotherapy in medical and health practice.* New York: Springer, 1978.

Ellis, A., & Becker, I. *A guide to personal happiness.* North Hollywood: Wilshire Books, 1982.

Ellis, A., & Grieger, R. (Eds.). *Handbook of rational–emotive therapy.* New York: Springer, 1977.

Ellis, A., & Harper, R. A. *A new guide to rational living.* Hollywood: Wilshire; Englewood Cliffs, N.J.: Prentice-Hall, 1975.

Ellis, A., & Knaus, W. *Overcoming procrastination.* New York: Institute for Rational–Emotive Therapy; New York: New American Library, 1977.

Ellis, A., & Whiteley, J. M. (Eds.). *Theoretical and empirical foundations of rational–emotive therapy.* Monterey, Calif.: Brooks/Cole, 1977.

Erikson, M. H., & Rossi, E. L. *Hypnotherapy: An exploratory casebook.* New York: Irvington, 1979.

Farrelly, F., & Brandsma, J. M. *Provocative therapy.* Fort Collins, Colo.: Shields, 1974.

Fay, A. *Making things better by making them worse.* New York: Hawthorn, 1978.

Fenichel, O. *Psychoanalytic theory of neurosis.* New York: Norton, 1945.

Frankl, V. Paradoxical intention: A logotherapeutic technique. *American Journal of Psychotherapy.* 1960, *14,* 520–535.

Freud, A. *The ego and the mechanisms of defense.* New York: International Universities Press, 1936.

Freud, S. *The interpretation of dreams. Standard Edition.* New York: Basic Books, 1900/1965.

Freud, S. *The dynamics of transference. Standard Edition.* New York: Basic Books, 1912/1965.

Freud, S. *Inhibitions, symptoms and anxiety. Standard Edition.* New York: Basic Books, 1926/1965.

Friedman, M. *Rational behavior.* Columbia, S.C.: University of South Carolina Press, 1975.

Goldfried, M. R. Resistance and clinical behavior therapy. In P. L. Wachtel (Ed.), *Resistance.* New York: Plenum, 1982.

Grieger, R., & Boyd, J. *Rational–emotive therapy: A skills-based approach.* New York: Van Nostrand Reinhold, 1980.

Grieger, R., & Grieger, I. Z. (Eds.). *Cognition and emotional disturbance.* New York: Human Sciences, 1982.

Haley, J. *Strategies of psychotherapy.* New York: Grune and Stratton, 1963.

Johnson, N. Must the rational–emotive therapist be like Albert Ellis? *Personnel and Guidance Journal,* 1980, *59,* 49–51.

Kelly, G. *The psychology of personal constructs.* New York: Norton, 1955.

Knaus, W. *Rational–emotive education.* New York: Institute for Rational–Emotive Therapy, 1974.

Knaus, W. *How to get out of a rut.* Englewood Cliffs, N.J.: Prentice-Hall, 1982.

Lazarus, A. A. *In the mind's eye.* New York: Rawson, Wade, 1978.

Lazarus, A. A. *The practice of multimodal therapy.* New York: McGraw-Hill, 1981.

Lazarus, A. A., & Fay, A. Resistance or rationalization? In P. L. Wachtel (Ed.), *Resistance.* New York: Plenum, 1982.

Mahoney, M. J. *Cognition and behavior modification.* Cambridge, Mass.: Ballinger, 1974.

Mahoney, M. J. Personal science: A cognitive learning therapy. In A. Ellis & R. Grieger (Eds.), *Handbook of rational–emotive therapy.* New York: Springer, 1977.

Mahoney, M. J. Psychotherapy and the structure of personal revolution. In M. J. Mahoney (Ed.), *Psychotherapy process.* New York: Plenum, 1980.

Maultsby, M. C., Jr., & Ellis, A. *Technique for using rational–emotive imagery.* New York: Institute for Rational–Emotive Therapy, 1974.

Maultsby, M. C., Jr. *Help yourself to happiness.* New York: Institute for Rational–Emotive Therapy, 1975.

Meichenbaum, D. *Cognitive behavior modification.* New York: Plenum, 1977.

Meichenbaum, D., & Gilmore, J. B. Resistance from a cognitive-behavioral perspective. In P. L. Wachtel (Ed.), *Resistance.* New York: Plenum, 1982.

Popper, K. R. *Objective knowledge.* Oxford: Clarendon, 1972.

Rogers, C. R. *Counseling and psychotherapy.* Boston: Houghton Mifflin, 1942.

Rorer, L., & Widiger, L. Personality assessment. *Annual Review of Psychology,* 1983, *34,* 431–463.

Schlesinger, H. J. Resistance as process. In P. L. Wachtel (Ed.), *Resistance.* New York: Plenum, 1982.

Spivack, G., & Shure, M. *Social adjustment in young children.* San Francisco: Jossey-Bass, 1974.

Stanton, H. E. The utilisation of suggestions derived from rational emotive therapy. *Journal of Clinical and Experimental Hypnosis,* 1977, *25,* 18–26.

Tosi, D., & Marzella, J. N. Rational stage directed therapy. In J. L. Wolfe & E. Brand (Eds.,), *Twenty years of rational therapy.* New York: Institute for Rational–Emotive Therapy, 1977.

Tosi, D., & Reardon, J. P. The treatment of guilt through rational stage directed therapy. *Rational Living,* 1976, *2*(1), 8–11.

Turkat, I. D., & Meyer, V. The behavior-analytic approach. In P. L. Wachtel (Ed.), *Resistance.* New York: Plenum, 1982.

Walen, S., DiGiuseppe, R., & Wessler, R. L. *A practitioner's guide to rational–emotive therapy.* New York: Oxford, 1980.

Watzlawick, P., Weakland, J., & Fisch, R. *Change.* New York: Norton, 1974.

Wessler, R. A., & Wessler, R. L. *The principles and practice of rational–emotive therapy.* San Francisco: Jossey-Bass, 1980.

Wessler, R. L. *Alternative conceptions of rational–emotive therapy: Towards a philosophically neutral psychotherapy.* Paper presented at the Twelfth European Congress on Behaviour Therapy, Rome, September, 5, 1982.

Wessler, R. L., & Ellis, A. Supervision in rational–emotive therapy. In A. K. Hess (Ed.), *Psychotherapy supervision.* New York: Wiley, 1980.

16

The Use of Psychodrama in RET*

Thomas J. Nardi

The Socratic dialogue is a characteristic feature of rational–emotive therapy (RET) and is therefore often used in clinical demonstrations. Such demonstrations accurately capture the distinguishing aspects of RET and yet, ironically, produce a somewhat myopic view of it. Techniques that could add more vitality and variety to RET sessions are often purposely excluded because they fail to "fit" the presented model. The purpose of this chapter is to offer the use of psychodrama techniques to illustrate, teach, and advance RET concepts in both didactic presentations and clinical practice.

Psychodrama was developed by Jacob Moreno (1946) and represents a blending of group psychotherapy and traditional stage drama. The members of the therapy group stage and act out personal concerns and problems. Group members serve as actors and audience. The rationale of psychodrama is succinctly described by Harper (1959, p. 273): "Psychodramatists contend that irrational and compulsive patterns are more readily seen and treated in the situation which involves action rather than just conversation."

My own experience confirms that actions at times do indeed speak louder than words. I have found certain psychodrama techniques to be useful in reaching clients when direct verbal exchanges have proven ineffective. Psychodrama often serves to experientially illustrate an RET concept in a way that transcends direct dialogue.

*This chapter first appeared in *Rational Living,* 1979, *14*(1), 35–38.

Psychodrama also serves to promote and facilitate group interaction. This is particularly important in advanced or ongoing growth groups that have gone beyond solving the immediate problems that brought the clients to therapy. Psychodrama can serve to provide these clients with a variety of experiences in which to develop and apply RET concepts.

The closest many RET practitioners come to psychodrama is in the use of role playing, behavioral rehearsal, and assertiveness training. There are other psychodrama techniques that can be readily applied to RET groups. The remainder of this chapter will focus upon some of these techniques and their unique use in RET. A preliminary caveat, however, is in order: Do not confuse techniques with theory. The techniques are taken from psychodrama, but their method comes from RET theory.

DEMONSTRATION OF INSIGHT

Ellis (1973) has noted that there are three types of psychotherapeutic insight. The first insight is that our problems have certain antecedent causes in our near or distant past. In childhood we are first exposed to irrational beliefs by parents, teachers, and peers. The second insight is that our problems are maintained in the present because of our current thinking. We create our own emotional upset by continuing to keep our irrational beliefs. The third insight is that change will only come about if we assume the responsibility for change and then work at it.

These concepts can be very effectively illustrated for a therapy group or workshop audience. You need a cotherapist and a foam encounter bat. The scene is set with one therapist assuming the role of a child and the other the role of a parent. The parent loudly berates the child for not doing well enough in school. The parent's yelling includes a liberal sprinkling of irrational ideas, particularly those related to self-worth and perfectionism. The tirade against the child is punctuated with blows from the foam bat, until finally, in disgust, the parent throws the bat at (to) the child. The parent then storms away. The child now takes the bat and begins to echo the irrational beliefs. While striking himself with the bat he moans, "I've got to be perfect! I'm no good if I don't achieve perfection. I can never be good enough."

The group is then asked, "Who has done the damage to the child? Who continues to do the damage? Who can stop it? Are *you* carrying around an emotional club? What irrational beliefs are you using to beat yourself?" This demonstration is a powerful and effective way of making people aware of their self-talk, how they first got it, and, most important, how they continue to defeat themselves with it.

THE DOUBLE

The double is another technique that can be used to uncover irrational ideas and to make clients more aware of their self-talk. The double voices the irrational beliefs that lie behind a spoken statement. The therapist can be the double, or the members of a group can double for one member. They reflect what was said plus the unvoiced irrational ideas underlying the statements.

Typically, two group members sit facing each other in the center of the group and role-play a situation that is problematic for both of them. Group members try to tune in to what is being said and relate it to their own irrational beliefs. They may then stand behind either of the two and double for them.

> WIFE: I get really mad because I know you don't fully support my job change.
>
> DOUBLE: I demand that you support the change! That's why I am making myself angry.
>
> HUSBAND: I am trying to support your switch. I just want you to realize the possible disadvantages.
>
> WIFE: I know about the dangers. That's why I'm so apprehensive. It's really a big move. I'll be the first woman in that department.
>
> DOUBLE: I'm really scared. If I don't do well it will be terrible—I'll be terrible! What will people think of me?

The person involved in the role-playing has the responsibility of letting the double know if he is inaccurate. Usually it is reported that the double is surprisingly on target. The impact of the double's comments is even greater when they come from a group member rather than the therapist. The accuracy of the group member's doubling can even be seen as a measure of his grasp of RET.

EMPTY CHAIR TECHNIQUES

Harold Greenwald recently remarked that for clients who request psychoanalysis he has a couch; for those who want gestalt therapy, he has an empty chair. The empty chair is a well-known gestalt therapy technique, but few people realize that it was first used by Moreno and later adopted by Fritz Perls.

The empty chair technique can be used in various ways to dramatize RET concepts. For example, it is quite useful in dealing with indecision. Recently a young woman complained about her indecisiveness regarding returning to college. She had dropped out several years earlier and now felt fairly determined to return. There was, however, a sense of foreboding that she was unable to identify. Two chairs were placed before her. She was told that the chair on the right represented her rational side. When she sat in that chair she was to speak aloud her rational thoughts about returning to school. The chair on her left was to represent her irrational side. When sitting there she was to voice her irrational beliefs about returning. She was told to switch chairs as she debated the decision with herself.

RIGHT CHAIR: It will require work and effort, but it is what I want. I had problems in school before, but that's in the past. If I apply myself, I'll probably do well. There's no reason to be afraid to try.

LEFT CHAIR: That may be true, but I failed before so I'll probably fail again. I'd be a complete waste if I failed again. I'd be no damn good at all, and I'm afraid to risk having to face this.

RIGHT CHAIR: Even if I fail it doesn't mean that *I am* a failure. If school is important to me, I owe it to myself to try. If I make it—fine. If I don't—I'm still O.K.

Changing chairs as she voiced her beliefs was a powerful experience for her. It helped her to realize more clearly what her self-talk really was.

A variation on this can be done with two participants. I have found it particularly useful in couples groups. A couple sits in the center of the group. Each person has two chairs available—a "rational belief chair" and an "irrational belief chair." They begin by sitting in their rational chairs. They discuss their problems and switch to the irrational belief chairs as they become aware of their irrational self-talk. Members of the group have the option of moving either participant to the irrational chair when they detect the intrusion of irrational ideas. Once the participant adopts a more rational belief, he or she is allowed back into the original chair.

This has proved to be an effective and pleasant way of showing the couple how they drift easily into irrationally motivated interactions. It also helps them learn to stay on a more rational track in their interactions. The technique also helps the group members to sharpen their skills.

ROLE REVERSAL

Role reversal means assuming another person's position in order to gain a better perspective on the interaction. Husbands and wives, parents and children, employees and employers may act out troublesome situations and then actually change chairs. The shift in seating is accompanied by a shift in roles. The participants are asked to play the role associated with the new chair. After a few minutes they are asked to state the rational and irrational beliefs motivating the role they have assumed. For example, a mother and her teeanage daughter role-played a typical situation regarding dating. They then switched chairs and the mother played her daughter's part while the daughter took on the mother's role.

THERAPIST: O.K., stay where you are and answer as the role you're playing would. What is the self-talk you're aware of now?

DAUGHTER
(AS MOTHER): If my daughter doesn't listen to me, I'm a failure as a mother. If anything happens to her, I can never forgive myself.

THERAPIST: And how can you dispute that?

DAUGHTER
(AS MOTHER): I can't make her listen to me. If anything happens I *can* forgive myself. Even if I fail as a *mother,* I can't fail as a *person.*

THERAPIST: O.K. (To the actual mother) And how about you?

MOTHER (AS
DAUGHTER): I can't stand it when she tries to force her old-fashioned ideas on me. No one's going to tell me what to do. Since I don't like her rules, she should stop.

THERAPIST: And how can you challenge that?

MOTHER (AS
DAUGHTER): I *can* stand it. It would be nice if Mom were more with it, but she's not. Let me try to change her thinking without antagonizing her and making things worse.

Participants often have an easier time identifying the other person's irrationality. Discussion and awareness of how another person views the participant are then facilitated.

PARADOXICAL INTENTION

Paradoxical intention is a technique used in psychodrama as well as in other therapeutic approaches (Frankl, 1960; Haley, 1963; Lazarus, 1976). Basically, paradoxical intention involves prescribing the symptom. The client is told to practice repeatedly and indeed to exaggerate the very problem he faces. For example, the woman who worries about not achieving orgasm is directed to purposely try *not* to climax. This technique, plus the anticatastrophizing of RET, is often quite effective in treating a variety of clinical problems. It also can be seen in many of the shame-attacking exercises used in RET.

A variation of paradoxical intention can be used during role playing. The client is told to role-play a problem he faces but to exaggerate the influence of his irrational beliefs. This *reductio ad absurdum* dramatically (and often humorously) illustrates the catastrophizing behind the irrational belief. The exaggerated aspects of the irrational belief are often more accurate appraisals of what the client is actually anticipating. When the client is able to verbalize and laugh at his catastrophizing, he has indeed made progress.

FUTURE PROJECTION

In psychodrama, future projection is considered a "rehearsal for living" (Starr, 1977). It consists of acting out an upcoming situation in order to be better prepared for it. I have taken this concept a step further in "rational future projection," which I use with clients who have reached an impasse in therapy. Often the client will report a situation that he thinks will be too difficult for him to handle. The client often says, "I'm not ready to deal with this situation yet." This usually means that there is some irrational belief that he is not ready to give up. I have found it helpful to instruct the client to imagine himself in the future. He is told to imagine that two or three years have passed. During these years he has continued to progress in his understanding and disputation of his irrational beliefs. He has completely overcome the belief that had been problematic to him. Then I ask him to role-play the problem situation from the vantage point of the future, when he is no longer maintaining the irrational belief.

The client then can usually role-play and deal with his problem in a much more realistic and self-enhancing way. He is shown that he doesn't have to wait two or three years, since the new beliefs and behavior are already in his repertoire. Some clients then report being able to deal with difficult situations (e.g., job interviews) by "pretending" that they are indeed further advanced in control of their self-talk.

Future projection, like all of the other techniques described, obviously will not be effective with every client. Moreover, these techniques can lose their effectiveness if they are overused or used in a mechanical way. RET is a comprehensive and dynamic system of therapy. A willingness to explore new avenues of application of RET is, in my opinion, essential not only for one's personal and professional growth, but also for the advancement of RET.

REFERENCES

Ellis, A. *Humanistic psychotherapy*. New York: McGraw-Hill, 1973.
Frankl, V. E. Paradoxical intention. *American Journal of Psychotherapy*, 1960, *14*, 520.
Haley, J. *Strategies of psychotherapy*. New York: Grune and Stratton, 1963.
Harper, R. A. *Psychoanalysis and psychotherapy: 36 systems*. Englewood Cliffs, N.J.: Prentice-Hall, 1959.
Lazarus, A. *Multimodal behavior therapy*. New York: Springer, 1976.
Moreno, J. L. *Psychodrama*. New York: Beacon, 1946.
Starr, A. *Rehearsal for living: Psychodrama*. Chicago: Nelson Hall, 1977.

17

Rational–Emotive Hypnotherapy: Principles and Techniques*

William L. Golden

The basic premise of Rational–Emotive Therapy (RET), as well as many of the other cognitive behavioral therapy approaches, is that neurotic suffering is largely the result of misconceptions and misperceptions (Ellis, 1962). The various treatment techniques used in RET are based on the assumption that one can produce emotional and behavioral changes by directly modifying these misperceptions and maladaptive cognitions.

Rational–emotive hypnotherapy (REH) is based on the same premises as RET. Several writers (Araoz, 1981; Ellis, 1962) have pointed out that one's neurotic self-defeating thoughts can be viewed as a negative or irrational type of self-hypnosis. Emotions such as anxiety and depression result from self-indoctrination (i.e., what one repeatedly tells or suggests to oneself). Imagery has a similar effect. Beck (1976), another cognitive behavioral therapist, has studied the role of imagery in the development and maintenance of emotional disturbance.

Barber and his associates (Barber, 1979; Barber, Spanos, & Chaves, 1974) claim that all hypnotic phenomena are a result of cognitive processes (i.e., attitudes, expectations, thoughts, and imagery). In a number of investigations it was found that suggestions and task-motivated instructions alone were as effective as hypnotic induction procedures in producing phenomena such as age

*This chapter was originally published in the *British Journal of Cognitive Psychotherapy,* 1983, *1*(1). The author would like to thank Gerald Albert, Ph.D., Albert Ellis, Ph.D., and Fred Friedberg, Ph.D., for their reviews of the manuscript, and Carolyn McCarthy for her secretarial assistance.

regression, amnesia, hallucinations, catalepsy, arm levitation, and analgesia (see Barber, 1979; Barber et al.; 1974; Spanos & Barber, 1976 for reviews). These findings have been interpreted by Barber and his associates as meaning that hypnotic induction procedures and hypnotic trance are unnecessary in order to experience the phenomena usually attributed to a hypnotic state. They have proposed a cognitive behavioral model of hypnosis as an alternative to the traditional trance model.[1] According to Spanos and Barber (1976), "hypnotic" behavior is the result of four primary conditions that are also important in cognitive behavioral therapy techniques:

1. The motivation and cooperation of the individual receiving the treatment or the suggestions
2. The attitudes and expectations of the individual, toward the treatment
3. The wording of the instructions or suggestions
4. The individual's involvement or "absorption" in "suggestion-related" thoughts and imagery

Research has demonstrated that behavior therapy and hypnotic procedures are more effective when a client has positive attitudes toward treatment and expects it to be successful. Research also has shown that suggestions are more likely to be experienced when they provide a client with cognitive strategies such as instructions to engage in "suggestion-related" thoughts and imagery (i.e., thoughts and images that are consistent with the goals of a particular suggestion) (see Spanos & Barber, 1974, 1976, for reviews of the literature). For example, anesthesia of the hand is produced by imagining receiving novocaine and telling oneself that one's hand is becoming numb, while, at the same time, blocking out competing thoughts such as "this is ridiculous, it really isn't happening." Spanos (1971) and Spanos and Barber (1972) found that clients who did respond to suggestions after undergoing a trance induction procedure were those who, on their own, employed "suggestion-related" fantasies like the one just described. In several other investigations hypnotizability was enhanced by teaching clients to block out incompatible thoughts and to become "absorbed" in "suggestion-related" thinking and imagining (see Diamond, 1974, 1977). Katz (1979) found that training in the application of cognitive strategies, such as how to think and imagine, along with suggestions, was more effective than a traditional hypnotic induction procedure, in enhancing suggestibility.

These laboratory studies demonstrate that cognitive processes are involved in hypnosis and that cognitive behavioral methods are effective in enhancing suggestibility. However, so far, there have been no clinical studies comparing the effectiveness of cognitive behavioral and traditional approaches. Because

---

[1]Nevertheless, some REH therapists who follow Tosi's (1974) rational stage-directed therapy appear to subscribe to a traditional trance model. According to Boutin (1978), the rationale for using hypnosis is that it intensifies imagery and cognitive restructuring.

REH is only one of several possible cognitive behavioral approaches to hypnotherapy, research is also needed to determine which of the various techniques might enhance the efficacy of hypnotherapy. Rational–emotive procedures are the ones most often integrated with hypnotherapy; therefore, this chapter will focus on REH and the techniques that are more commonly used by REH therapists.

The basic approach in REH is to reverse the effects of negative and irrational self-suggestions through a combination of hypnotic, cognitive, and behavioral strategies. Ellis (1962) has proposed that hypnosis is therapeutic when it interferes with the irrational self-indoctrination process that is at the core of neurosis and neurotic behavior. According to Ellis, "All hypnotic suggestion that is therapeutically successful probably works through autosuggestion—since, unless the patient himself takes over the suggestions of the hypnotherapist, and consciously or unconsciously keeps thinking about them when the therapist is no longer present, only the most short-lived kind of results are likely to follow" (1962, p. 276). Barber (1978) and Ruch (1975) have also emphasized that hypnosis or suggestions are effective only to the degree that individuals accept them and incorporate them as their own self-suggestions.

REH procedures can be categorized as either (1) "uncovering" techniques that are used for increasing a client's awareness of self-defeating thoughts and their emotional and behavioral consequences, or as (2) cognitive restructuring techniques that help clients rationally reevaluate and modify misperceptions and misconceptions. Eventually clients are taught to engage in a rational self-hypnotic process. REH therapists teach their clients cognitive restructuring as well as self-hypnotic techniques. The survey of techniques that follows is representative of those that REH therapists use and is not intended to be an exhaustive list.

UNCOVERING TECHNIQUES

Hypnotic Induction and Relaxation

Sometimes clients are unable to pinpoint their maladaptive thoughts and emotions. However, once they close their eyes and relax, many of these same individuals appear to be more aware of their thoughts and feelings. This does not necessarily mean that hypnotic trance provides these individuals with powers that they do not usually possess. Other explanations that are more consistent with a cognitive behavioral viewpoint are possible.

According to Barber and his associates (1974), heightened recall as well as other "hypnotic" phenomena are not special abilities that are created from the hypnotic state or trance. They have concluded that the sensory, perceptual, and behavioral modifications that occur in hypnosis are "capabilities and potentials" that most normal individuals can experience and are the result of cognitive processes. Heightened recall is produced by vividly imagining past events. The ability to accomplish this feat is affected by the individual's expectations, motivation, and involvement in the task.

Another possible explanation for heightened recall in therapy situations is that most hypnotic induction procedures elicit the relaxation response (see Benson, Arns, & Hoffman, 1981) and are therefore effective in reducing anxiety, making it easier for the clients to think about and discuss material that they were previously too anxious or distracted to confront. After reviewing the research literature, Benson et al. (1981) concluded that hypnotic induction procedures produce a physiological state similar to relaxation procedures. Edmonston (1979, 1981), after his reviews of the literature, concluded that hypnosis and relaxation are the same.

Nevertheless, clinical experience suggests that hypnotic trance induction procedures are useful for those clients who believe in their efficacy. Lazarus (1973) found this expectancy effect in a clinical study on hypnosis and behavior therapy. Clients who requested hypnosis were assigned to a treatment that was defined as either relaxation therapy or hypnosis. Although the treatments were actually the same for both groups, the clients who received "hypnosis," as they requested, showed greater improvement than the group that received "relaxation." On the other hand, clients who did not state a preference for either type of therapy did equally well with the two differently labeled treatments. Barber (1978) has said that when hypnotic induction is helpful it is not because of the powers of a hypnotic state or trance but because of the individual's expectation or belief in the efficacy of the procedure.

Imagery Techniques

Imagery is routinely employed by cognitive behavioral therapists as an assessment device. Clients are instructed to close their eyes and imagine themselves in various problematic situations or, as they are called in RET, activating events. This tends to elicit the same disturbing thoughts, fantasies, and feelings that are experienced in the real situations. Once their awareness is increased, clients are able to report what they are thinking and feeling in each activating event.

Imagery assessment techniques can be applied with or without hypnotic induction procedures. However, as mentioned earlier, according to Barber et al. (1974), it is the imagery and the individual's expectations, motivation, and involvement in the task, rather than "trance," that are responsible for the heightened awareness that is observed in hypnosis and in cognitive behavioral therapy. Future research is needed to test the validity of this hypothesis.

There are other hypnotic techniques that can be understood from a cognitive behavioral viewpoint and can be used in REH to uncover maladaptive thoughts, fantasies, and feelings. In dream induction, suggestions are given that the client will have a dream, a daydream, or a fantasy that will relate to the client's problem. In traditional hypnotherapy the client is given suggestions under hypnosis that he or she will have the dream during trance or posthypnotically at night during natural sleep. However, trance induction is not necessary in order to induce dreams or to produce vivid imagery. As Barber (see Barber & Hahn, 1966; Barber et al., 1974) has pointed out, it is possible to influence the content of one's dreams through simple instructions and suggestions alone. Barber and his associates (Spanos, Ham, & Barber, 1973) also found that visual hallucinations can be produced by suggestions and task-motivated instructions, without a prior trance induction. Starker (1974) found that subjects given task-motivated instructions to imagine various scenes rated their imagery as being as vivid as hypnotized subjects who were given suggestions to imagine various scenes. Contrary to what is usually assumed about hypnosis, Ham and Spanos (1974) found in their study that nonhypnotized subjects, who were given task-motivated instructions to hallucinate, rated their auditory hallucinations as more believable than a group of hypnotized subjects.

Regression is a technique that many hypnotherapists use for providing clients with insight. Regression is viewed by traditional hypnotists as involving a special state that makes it possible for a subject to return to a past experience. On the other hand, from a cognitive behavioral viewpoint, regression can be considered to be simply another imagery technique for evoking memories, thoughts, and emotions. Barber and Calverly (1966) found that nonhypnotized subjects who were given suggestions to regress back to an earlier age were able to experience age regression equally as well as hypnotized subjects could.

In REH, although there is a preference for "here-and-now" imagery of recent activating events, sometimes regression imagery is used to explore the remote past with clients. Decisions about these choices can be made on the basis of the requests and expectations of a client. When clients want and expect hypnosis, dream induction, or regression to provide them with answers, it is often effective to "join" them and use their motivation to get them to cooperate. This "joining" approach can serve as a "foot in the door" for self-monitoring maladaptive thoughts and feelings. Although cognitive behavioral therapists often borrow techniques from different orientations, their viewpoint remains cognitive behavioral, and they employ these procedures for the purpose of either examining or modifying maladaptive cognitions, emotions, and behaviors.

Self-monitoring

RET therapists and other cognitive behavioral therapists typically have their clients monitor thoughts, fantasies, feelings, and behaviors in between therapy sessions. Clients are asked to record the frequency, intensity, duration, and pervasiveness of their symptoms. In addition they are trained to observe the thoughts that elicit these reactions. These therapeutic activities are also important in REH, where the client is taught that his or her symptoms are produced through negative and irrational self-suggestions, a process that often takes place without one's full awareness, and that it is possible to observe the process and modify it. In REH, as in RET and other cognitive behavioral approaches, clients are instructed to monitor and record these maladaptive self-suggestions (i.e., their self-statements).

COGNITIVE RESTRUCTURING

Cognitive restructuring techniques are usually employed without the aid of formal hypnotic induction procedures. Nevertheless, hypnotic interventions share elements in common with cognitive restructuring procedures, and there may be benefits that result from purposely integrating the two approaches. As an example, expectations have been found to be important in cognitive behavioral therapy as well as in hypnosis (see Spanos & Barber, 1976). One could predict from a cognitive behavioral viewpoint that, for individuals who believe in the "powers of hypnosis," employing a hypnotic induction procedure prior to utilizing cognitive restructuring techniques would add to the credibility, and hence the efficacy, of treatment. As another example, resistance to cognitive restructuring procedures might be reduced by incorporating some of Milton Erickson's ideas about the wording of suggestions and the impact of various communication devices on facilitating compliance to therapeutic suggestions (see Bandler & Grinder, 1975; Erickson & Rossi, 1979; Erickson, Rossi, & Rossi, 1976; Watzlawick, 1978). In addition, cognitive restructuring techniques have been found to enhance behavior therapy (see Meichenbaum, 1977) and may have a similar effect on hypnotherapy, as suggested by the laboratory studies cited earlier. These are areas for future research.

It is beyond the scope of the present article to describe all of the various cognitive restructuring techniques. The reader is advised to refer to Beck (1976), Ellis (1962), Ellis & Harper (1975), Goldfried & Davison (1976), Meichenbaum (1977), and Raimy (1975) for further information. The remainder of the chapter will concern itself with a description of the cognitive restructuring techniques that are most commonly employed by REH therapists.

Disputing Irrational Beliefs

Ellis' (1962) disputation of irrational beliefs is a technique for helping clients to rationally reevaluate and modify their misconceptions and maladaptive thoughts. When integrating this technique with hypnosis, one begins the disputation after first going through a hypnotic induction procedure. A didactic or Socratic approach can be used. The didactic approach involves direct teaching. The therapist corrects misconceptions (such as "I must be perfect at everything") and explains why the client's misperceptions and irrational thoughts are incorrect and self-defeating. The Socratic method entails self-discovery. The beliefs are challenged, with the intention of encouraging the client to reevaluate them. A therapist may combine or alternate between using these two styles of rational reevaluation. For example, the therapist may start out didactic, and, as a client learns the technique, become more Socratic. Or alternatively, whenever clients have difficulty responding to reflective questions or are unable, on their own, to rationally reevaluate particular beliefs or perceptions, the therapist can switch to a didactic approach. Eventually clients are taught to question and challenge misperceptions and misconceptions, on their own, as part of their practice in using self-hypnotic procedures.

Mood Induction

An effective method for getting clients to realize how they contribute to their disturbance is through mood induction. This technique is particularly useful with resistant clients or those who have difficulty understanding the connection between thoughts and emotions. Typically, although it is probably not necessary, a relaxation or hypnotic induction procedure is employed prior to any suggestions for mood induction. Then, the therapist suggests that the client purposely think the maladaptive thoughts that usually elicit the client's symptoms. Through these suggestions, the client's disturbing emotions are induced, providing the client with the opportunity to experience how certain thoughts produce symptoms. Finally, the client is encouraged to experiment with more rational points of view and to observe the effect of rational thinking in reducing emotional distress.

Rational–Emotive Imagery (REI)

Through REI, clients practice coping with activating events. There are different ways of doing REI (see Ellis & Harper, 1975; Maultsby, 1975). One style of REI is to imagine oneself in an activating event (e.g., taking an examination) and practice using rational self-statements (such as "I will probably do well on the test, as long as I study. But even if I did fail I would not be a worthless person") to modify maladaptive emotions (e.g., test anxiety). The individual can also imagine him- or herself coping with the situation and responding appropriately (e.g., calming down and doing well on the exam). A relaxation or hypnotic induction procedure can be used prior to the imagery. At first, the therapist guides the client through the imagery. Later, the client practices REI as a self-control or self-hypnotic technique.

Coping Desensitization

The coping skills approach to desensitization is similar to REI in several ways. Both procedures involve having clients practice coping techniques, such as self-suggestions and relaxation procedures, while imagining themselves confronting difficult situations. However, in desensitization a hierarchy (i.e., a list of situations, rank-ordered from least to most disturbing) is employed for the purpose of providing clients with graded exposures to the situations in which they experience distress. Although more time consuming, graduated exposures are particularly helpful with extremely anxious and phobic individuals who are resistant to more direct approaches. For more information on this technique, see Goldfried and Davison (1976) and Meichenbaum (1977).

Desensitization can be integrated with REH. In REH, a hypnotic induction procedure is used prior to having clients imagine items from their hierarchy. While imagining these scenes, clients are given rational suggestions that are intended to counteract the effect of their misperceptions and maladaptive cognitions. The clients are also encouraged to practice using rational suggestions and relaxation techniques as coping strategies during the procedure.

Flooding

In flooding, a client is confronted with an anxiety-provoking situation or image until the situation or imagery no longer elicits anxiety. Behavior therapists have explained flooding and desensitization in terms of counterconditioning, extinction, or habituation. Cognitive behavioral therapists view these procedures as methods that help clients to reevaluate their fears and provide them with opportunities to develop coping strategies. For example, after confronting a feared situation, an individual may have a "corrective experience" and realize that the situation is not really dangerous. Research has demonstrated that desensitization and flooding are, in fact, more effective when subjects are encouraged purposely to use coping and rational self-statements and relaxation techniques during their exposure to anxiety-provoking situations (see Golden, Geller, & Hendricks, 1981; Meichenbaum, 1977).

When flooding is used in hypnotherapy, a hypnotic induction procedure is used prior to the presentation of the anxiety-provoking stimulus. In REH, clients also may be encouraged to use rational suggestions and relaxation techniques to reduce their anxiety during the flooding.

Rational Self-Hypnosis

Training in self-hypnosis is very important in REH. Self-hypnosis can be used by clients as a way of rehearsing or preparing for difficult situations (i.e., activating events) or for *in vivo* coping. During self-hypnotic sessions, either with or without the benefit of relaxation or a hypnotic induction procedure, clients practice various imagery and cognitive restructuring techniques such as the ones described in this chapter. In addition, they concentrate on the new thoughts that they want to internalize. During this meditation clients mentally rehearse rational thoughts and practice giving themselves constructive suggestions that will help them to cope with activating events. During *in vivo* exposures they can apply what they practiced during their imagery exercises.

In Vivo Exposure

Usually, after having had some practice through imagery techniques, clients are instructed to apply their skills to real-life situations. While in the situation they use relaxation techniques and rational suggestions to reduce negative feelings, control habits and compulsions, or pursue their goals, despite feeling uncomfortable. Direct exposure (*in vivo* flooding) or graded exposure (*in vivo* desensitization) can be used, depending on the client and the situation.

DISCUSSION

Although the techniques described here are used by most REH therapists, the cognitive behavioral model of hypnotic phenomena that is described is not the paradigm that all REH therapists accept. This is true despite the fact that REH therapists generally subscribe to the rational-emotive theory of emotional disturbance and therapeutic change.

Recently, the "uniformity myth" that all cognitive behavioral therapies are alike or are equally effective has been questioned (see Meichenbaum, 1977). It is important to avoid a similar myth about cognitive behavioral hypnotherapy. REH is only one of several possible cognitive behavioral approaches to hypnotherapy. The REH that is presented here is an integration of RET, techniques from some of the other cognitive behavioral therapies, and techniques from various approaches to hypnotherapy. It is based on a nontrance model of hypnosis, whereas rational stage-directed hypnotherapists seem to accept a traditional trance model (Boutin, 1978).

In terms of consistency, RET and REH are more theoretically compatible with a nontrance model of hypnosis. REH and Barber's (1979) cognitive behavioral model of hypnosis emphasize self-control and how one's cognitions affect one's emotions, behaviors, and physiological responses. Research is needed not only to evaluate the effectiveness of the various REH techniques but also the validity of the different models.

REFERENCES

Arboz, D. L. Negative self-hypnosis. *Journal of Contemporary Psychotherapy*, 1981, *12*, 45–52.

Bandler, R., & Grinder, J. *Patterns of the hypnotic techniques of Milton H. Erickson, M.D.* Cupertino Calif.: Meta Publications, 1975.

Barber, T. X. Hypnosis, suggestions, and psychosomatic phenomena: A new look from the standpoint of recent experimental studies. *The American Journal of Clinical Hypnosis*, 1978, *21*, 13–27.

Barber, T. X. Suggested ("hypnotic") behavior: The trance paradigm versus an alternative paradigm. In E. Fromm & R. E. Shor (Eds.), *Hypnosis: Developments in research and new perspectives*. (2nd rev. ed.). New York: Aldine, 1979.

Barber, T. X., & Calverly, D. S. Effects on recall of hypnotic induction, motivational suggestions, and suggested regression: A methodological and experimental analysis. *Journal of Abnormal Psychology*, 1966, *71*, 169–180.

Barber, T. X., & Hahn, K. W., Jr. Suggested dreaming with and without hypnotic induction. Medfield Mass.: Medfield Foundation, 1966.

Barber, T. X., Spanos, N. P., & Chaves, J. F. *Hypnosis, imagination and human potentialities*. New York: Pergamon Press, 1974.

Beck, A. T. *Cognitive therapy and the emotional disorders*. New York: International Universities Press, 1976.

Benson, J., Arns, P. A., & Hoffman, J. W. The relaxation response and hypnosis. *The International Journal of Clinical and Experimental Hypnosis*, 1981, *29*, 259–270.

Boutin, G. E. Treatment of test anxiety by rational stage directed hypnotherapy: A case study. *American Journal of Clinical Hypnosis*, 1978, *21*, 52–57.

Diamond, M. J. Modification of hypnotizability: A review. *Psychological Bulletin*, 1974, *81*, 180–198.

Diamond, M. J. Hypnotizability is modifiable: An alternative approach. *International Journal of Clinical and Experimental Hypnosis*, 1977, *25*, 147–166.

Edmonston, W. E. The effects of neutral hypnosis on conditioned responses: Implications for hypnosis as relaxation. In E. Fromm & R. E. Shor (Eds.), *Hypnosis: Developments in research and new perspectives*. (2nd rev. ed.). New York: Aldine, 1979.

Edmonston, W. E. *Hypnosis and relaxation: Modern verification of an old equation*. New York: John Wiley, 1981.

Ellis, A. *Reason and emotion in psychotherapy*. New York: Lyle Stuart, 1962.

Ellis, A., & Harper, R. A. *A new guide to rational living*. Englewood Cliffs, N.J.: Prentice-Hall, 1975.

Erickson, M. H., & Rossi, E. L. *Hypnotherapy: An exploratory casebook*. New York: Irvington, 1979.

Erickson, M. H., Rossi, E. L., & Rossi, S. L. *Hypnotic realities*. New York: Irvington, 1976.

Golden, W. L., Geller, E., & Hendricks, C. A. A coping-skills approach to flooding therapy in the treatment of test anxiety. *Rational Living*, 1981, *16*, 17–20.

Goldfried, M. R., & Davison, G. C. *Clinical behavior therapy*. New York: Holt, Rinehart and Winston, 1976.

Ham, M. W., & Spanos, N. P. Suggested auditory and visual hallucinations in task-motivated and hypnotic subjects. *American Journal of Clinical Hypnosis*, 1974, *17*, 94–101.

Katz, N. W. Comparative efficacy of behavioral training, training plus relaxation, and sleep/trance hypnotic induction in increasing hypnotic susceptibility. *Journal of Consulting and Clinical Psychology*, 1979, *47*, 119–127.

Lazarus, A. A. "Hypnosis" as a facilitator in behavior therapy. *International Journal of Clinical and Experimental Hypnosis*, 1973, *21*, 25–31.

Maultsby, M. C., Jr. *Help yourself to happiness through rational self-counseling*. Boston: Marlborough House, 1975.

Meichenbaum, D. *Cognitive-behavioral modification: An integrative approach*. New York: Plenum Press, 1977.

Raimy, V. *Misunderstandings of the self: Cognitive psychotherapy and the misconception hypothesis*. San Francisco: Jossey Bass. 1975.

Ruch, J. C. Self-hypnosis: The result of heterohypnosis or vice versa? *International Journal of Clinical and Experimental Hypnosis*, 1975, *23*, 282–304.

Spanos, N. P. Goal-directed phantasy and the performance of hypnotic test suggestions. *Psychiatry*, 1971, *34*, 86–96.

Spanos, N. P., & Barber, T. X. Cognitive activity during "hypnotic" suggestibility: Goal-directed fantasy and the experience of non-volition. *Journal of Personality*, 1972, *40*, 510–524.

Spanos, N. P., & Barber, T. X. Toward a convergence in hypnosis research. *American Psychologist*, 1974, *29*, 500–511.

Spanos, N. P., & Barber, T. X. Behavior modification and hypnosis. In M. Hersen, R. M. Eisler, & P. M. Miller (Eds.), *Progress in behavior modification*. New York: Academic Press, 1976.

Spanos, N. P., Ham, M. W., & Barber, T. X. Suggested ("hypnotic") visual hallucinations: Experimental and phenomenological data. *Journal of Abnormal Psychology*, 1973, *81*, 96–106.

Starker, S. Effects of hypnotic induction upon visual imagery. *Journal of Nervous and Mental Disease*, 1974, *159*, 433–437.

Tosi, D. J. *Youth toward personal growth: A rational–emotive approach*. Columbus, Ohio: Charles Merril, 1974.

Watzlawick, P. *The language of change*. New York: Basic Books, 1978.

Part Four

Applications of Rational–Emotive Therapy

18

Rational–Emotive Therapy in Groups*

Richard L. Wessler

Rational–emotive therapy (RET) as group psychotherapy began almost as early as individual RET. In 1955, Albert Ellis, who had been trained as a psychoanalyst and who already was well known as a sex and marriage counselor, became dissatisfied with the results he obtained from employing psychoanalytic principles. Therefore, he took the bold step of directly confronting patients with their self-defeating philosophies, of actively arguing against their ideas, and of assigning behavioral and cognitive homework for their use in practicing their newly adopted ways of thinking and acting (Ellis, 1962).

The goals of RET, whether done in groups or individually, are to teach clients how to change their disordered emotionality and behavior and to cope with almost any unfortunate event that may arise in their lives. RET holds that humans can employ their conscious thought processes to their own benefit by solving their problems and rethinking the self-defeating assumptions about their own and other people's presumed perfectability.

The ideal outcome of RET would be for the individual to adopt an attitude of self-acceptance rather than of self-judgment; to accept life's realities, including grim realities, by acknowledging their existence and not attempting to avoid or prevent them with magical thinking and superstitious maneuvers. It would involve refraining from judging other people in a global manner and especially from damning them for their shortcomings and transgressions. It would mean

---

*Dr. Wessler originally published this chapter in Arthur Freedman (Ed.), *Cognitive therapy with couples and groups* (New York: Plenum Press, 1983).

independently thinking out for oneself an ethical philosophy rather than childishly depending upon other people or on religion for absolute rules about right and wrong; unashamedly pursuing pleasure in both long-term and short-term interests, rather than unpleasurably conforming to rigid rules, or shortsightedly indulging oneself with no heed for the future.

RET seeks to help people reduce or eliminate strong negative emotions (e.g., anxiety, depression, and hostility) so they can live more personally satisfying lives. To accomplish this goal, RET seeks to help people identify the beliefs that produce and sustain dysfunctional emotional experiences and maladaptive behaviors and to change them to beliefs that promote rather than thwart their personal objectives.

The goal of change, in other words, is an elegant philosophical restructuring that will enable the individual to pursue more efficiently the common human goals of survival and happiness.

BASIC CONCEPTS

The label *rational–emotive therapy* refers to two different activities of psychological therapists. First, the label stands for classical RET, characterized by the extensive writings of Albert Ellis. In this form of RET, neurotic disturbance is postulated to be caused by irrational thinking, which the client is taught to identify. The process is highly directive, confrontive, and educative. It has been illustrated amply by Ellis in transcripts of therapy sessions (Ellis, 1971) and in tape recordings issued by the Institute for Rational Living in New York City and in films and videotapes.

The second meaning of the label *RET* is coextensive with the cognitive learning approaches to therapy. It has been called comprehensive RET (Walen, DiGiuseppe, & Wessler, 1980) to distinguish it from classical RET. In this form of RET, neurotic disturbance is postulated to be caused by irrational thinking as well as by faulty perceptions, muddled inferences, arbitrary definitions, and illogical reasoning.

The classical version is highly philosophical in the sense that it focuses explicitly on human values, on issues of right and wrong (i.e., morality), and a philosophy of living that includes tolerance for one's imperfections, other people's transgressions, and the world's ample supply of frustration.

Like classical RET, comprehensive RET is highly directive, confrontive, and educative; but it is in addition persuasive and makes use of techniques and procedures developed by cognitive learning and other forms of treatment. It tends to be a good deal more eclectic, but without losing the philosophical core that distinguishes RET from its allied approaches. Unfortunately, there are fewer examples of comprehensive RET available for reading, listening, and viewing.

However, comprehensive RET is what most RET practitioners, including Albert Ellis, do, especially in group therapy.

THERAPY

Theory

The theory of RET as a treatment of disturbance is quite simple: If a person changes her or his irrational beliefs to rational beliefs, she or he will suffer less and enjoy life more. The evaluation of self, of other people, and of the world in general are the major targets of change.

RET treatment is based on an educational and persuasive model. Clients are taught to identify how they are disturbing themselves by uncovering their irrational beliefs, then they are informed about why their beliefs are irrational and how to change them. If they change their philosophical rules of living and then live according to those changes, they will lead more satisfying and enjoyable lives. There is no assumption that some deep or mysterious forces keep them from changing their philosophy of living. People are postulated to have innate tendencies to retain or readopt their irrational beliefs (Ellis, 1976), and because there is widespread social approval for some of them, to readily retain those.

Since people often resist change or fail to change when new information is presented to them, persuasive attempts other than information giving are typical of RET sessions (Wessler & Ellis, 1980). These persuasive attempts are better labeled *dissuasive methods* because their aim is to help people give up their dysfunctional ones (Wessler & Wessler, 1980).

Dissuasive methods are based on theories of attitude formation and change. The evaluative component of attitudes is the particular target of change because in RET the belief system consists of evaluations. Information giving is directed at the knowledge component of an attitude, but because many attitudes are not based upon knowledge, information giving has its limitations.

Attitudes often are represented as having three components (knowledge, evaluation, and action) in interdependent relationship. A change in one may result in a change in the other two. A major theory of attitude change, *cognitive dissonance* (Festinger, 1957), proposes that changes in evaluations will follow changes in knowledge or action or both. The RET theory of treatment makes use of this principle by offering arguments against rigidly held absolutistic beliefs and assigning homework between therapy sessions. Homework usually consists of the client's doing something that is inconsistent with his or her beliefs and thus inducing dissonance. As Festinger pointed out, it is difficult to deny that you did something against your evaluative beliefs, especially if there are witnesses. People tend to adjust their evaluative beliefs to fit what they have done, or to fit what they have learned, or both.

Many other dissuasive maneuvers will be presented later in this chapter. All can be understood as attempts to change attitudes. RET does not depend upon rational discussion alone to produce therapeutic change. In the broadest sense of RET, anything within the bounds of professional ethics that helps people change their minds in favor of a more personally satisfying philosophy of living is a legitimate part of RET. RET assumes that the individual changes his or her own mind and can choose to do so. It is not the therapist's responsibility to force change.

Therapy Process

In broad outline, RET proceeds as follows: The individual client identifies explicitly or implicitly that she or he wants certain changes or goals. The therapist shows the client that the goals of personal change can be attained by cognitive change. The therapist goes on to show what the client's maladaptive beliefs are and how they can be changed. The client then can choose to work to change her or his thinking.

This simply stated process can occur over one session or many. Some people never change much, despite genuine efforts. (Why their thinking is so difficult to change is not known, but Ellis suspects biological diathesis.)

There is no assumption that any special relationship must be established with the therapist before change can occur. The therapist exhibits nondamning acceptance of the client, though she or he may express judgments about some of the client's actions.

The therapist probably has to be seen in certain ways by the client in order to be effective. The literature on attitude change and persuasion (Karlins & Abelson, 1970; McGuire, 1969; Zimbardo & Ebbesen, 1969) suggests some perceptions of the therapist that promote effective RET. The therapist probably is more effective if seen as credible by the client. A perception of credibility can be promoted by showing expertise and trustworthiness. A confident manner and a belief in what he or she says tend to communicate such expertise (cf. Frank, 1978), as do educational degrees and professional reputation. Trustworthiness may occur when clients see therapists as genuinely interested in helping them and not working for the therapist's sole benefit. The beginning of trustworthiness is to have genuine concern for the client's improvement and welfare. The list of characteristics includes warmth and empathic ability.

The relationship with the client is important for another reason that is unrelated to any presumed curative aspects. Therapist characteristics that are irrelevant to the client's belief system probably influence acceptance of rational thinking. In other words, clients may change their minds for reasons unrelated to logic and evidence presented to them. Just as college students say they like a course or expect to do well because they like the professor, clients may believe a therapist because they like him or her or reject a therapeutic message because they do not.

In group therapy the same concerns are multiplied. If the individual does not like, respect, or believe the group members and the therapist, the chances of his or her being helped are reduced greatly.

An issue in any group is its dynamics. Since the individual is the focus of change in RET groups, dynamics are important insofar as they affect the individual's thinking, feelings, and behaving. The norms of the group and its communication patterns and emerging leadership roles can be used therapeutically or, if they encourage continued irrational thinking, can function iatrogenically. Thus, in an RET group, cohesiveness is allowed, promoted, or discouraged, depending on whether the therapeutic aims of the individuals in the group are helped or hindered by group cohesiveness.

Group therapy provides opportunities for observing a client's interactions and making comments about them. At times the teaching of interpersonal skills is the chief concern of an RET group. This, however, usually occurs in conjunction with or after attention has been given to the client's belief system. For example, the teaching of assertive communication skills may aid a person in his or her everyday life, but by itself it is a palliative. Assertive skills may help increase the chance for getting what one wants, but that does not reduce exaggerating the unfairness of not getting what one wants. Similarly, the improvement of communications skills between couples, so often cited by couples and counselors as a serious difficulty, is a secondary aim in RET. The primary aim is to reduce personal disturbance; then the couple can be shown how to improve communications.

Treatment Tactics

The initial considerations in the process of RET in groups are the same as with individuals. The individual is the focus of change and therefore an assessment of the individual's problems is necessary. Assessment here means understanding the cognitive dynamics—the person's main rational and irrational beliefs and their resulting emotional and behavioral consequences. Facts about the individual's social status, marital status, birth order, height, weight, and age are of little or no importance in RET. To an extent, even the practical problems in a person's life (the A's in the ABC model) are of little importance, at least initially. Later, after dealing with the belief system, the practical problems may be taken up.

The therapist who leads the group is in a better position than group members to make an assessment of problem diagnosis in terms of the ABC model. However, group members, as they learn the ABC model, often become adept at spotting each others' irrational beliefs and defenses. There is the risk that group members may tacitly agree not to confront each other or to offer only practical problem-solving suggestions, but an experienced leader–therapist will recognize such actions, comment on them, and try to prevent their recurrence.

In order to make an assessment or problem diagnosis, the therapist and group members actively ask questions, probe answers, offer comments, and test hypotheses inferred from a focal client's in-group behavior and self-reports of thoughts, feelings, and actions. The general strategy is to follow the ABC model. The focal client, in presenting a personal problem, usually starts with the A or activating experience. Then the C or emotional consequences are sought and clarified. Sometimes both A and C are revealed in the initial presentation of a specific problem, for example, "I got very angry at my boss when he asked me to work overtime last night!" In this illustration the individual identifies the A (the boss's asking the person to work overtime) and C (hostility). The group members, led by the therapist, then may ask questions about both A and C, for example, "What reasons did the boss give?" (an A probe); "Did you have something else to do?" (another A probe); "Has this happened very often?" (yet another A probe). And, "Did you let him know you were angry?" (C probe); "How did you know it was anger that you experienced?" (another C probe). These questions clarify and add richness to the report and are especially helpful if the client has difficulty recognizing and reporting emotional experiences, as is sometimes the case.

The therapist then leads the group in focusing on the belief system. Using the model of anger presented earlier in this chapter, the therapist asks questions about the demands the client placed upon the boss's behavior ("He must not ask me to work overtime"), blame ("He's a rotten bastard for making such a request"), intolerance ("He shouldn't have a responsible position if he's going to make such requests"), and grandiosity ("He has no right to ask me to work overtime"). One by one the client's evaluative thinking about the situation would be uncovered. He or she might be asked to challenge the truth of the self-statements, or the group members might offer reasons why the self-statements were untrue.

In addition to the approach of presenting personal problems, RET groups also may be experiential. Group exercises adopted from many sources may be used to "produce" emotional consequences. The following exercise might easily be used with a new group; its purpose is to "produce" emotional consequences (usually anxiety); to expose defenses; to introduce the notion that thinking, especially evaluative thinking, largely determines emotional experiences; and that a great deal of such thinking is automatically done without much awareness. The therapist addresses the group:

> I'm going to ask you to think of some secret, something about yourself that you normally would not tell anyone else. It might be something you have done in the past, something you're doing now in the present. Some secret habit or physical characteristic. *(Pause)* Are you thinking about it? *(Pause)* Good. Now I'm going to ask someone to tell the group what they have thought of, . . . to describe it in some detail. *(Short pause)* But since I know everyone would want to do this, and we

don't have enough time to get everyone in, I'll select someone. *(Pause, looking around the group)* Yes, I think I have someone in mind. *(Pause)* But, before I call on that person, let me ask you, what are you experiencing right now?

Answers such as "tense," "anxious," and "nervous" are commonly mentioned. Ideas such as "I hope you don't call on me!" are expressed. At this point the therapist shows the group that it is the *thought* of doing something, not the doing itself, that leads to their feelings. The therapist then asks questions about what kinds of thoughts led to these feelings. Typical responses are, "If they would find out something about me I wouldn't want them to know, that would be awful!" Once the discussion has begun, it often picks up momentum as people realize that their strongly evaluative thinking about what might happen led to their anxious reactions. As the discussion progresses, the therapist can show the group members that they may be demanding that they follow social norms implicit in the situation, for example, "I must do what the leader says." The anxiety-producing conclusions are obvious: "And if I don't do what she says, she and the others will think that I've copped out or can't take it or have some other weakness. That would be awful and prove what a worthless person I truly am!"

Further discussion may show people their defensiveness and self-protectiveness. For example, some people will admit that they would not have revealed anything too embarassing, just something that sounds risky but really is "safe." Others will admit that they thought of leaving the room. Such responses often are generalized to other situations as well and can be uncovered by asking, "Is your reaction typical of the way you usually act when put on the spot?"

An imaginative RET group leader can incorporate almost any exercise into the process. The "secret" is how the experience is processed, not how it is conducted. Any experience or exercise intended to generate "here-and-now" feelings can be processed using the ABC model. And, of course, awareness of one's belief system or insights into one's behavior are not the end of the processing of an experience. Dissuasion—helping the person change dysfunctional evaluative thinking—is the crucial activity.

Nardi (1979) has combined elements of psychodrama with RET. For example, a group member playing another member's parent shouts irrational beliefs and hits the focal person with a foam rubber bat; then the focal client takes the bat and hits him- or herself while shouting the same beliefs. Although this exercise overstates the importance of early socializing agents in acquiring of irrational beliefs, it is an effective demonstration of what the client does *today* to create his or her own misery. In another psychodrama-inspired exercise, group members acting as alter egos speak the irrational beliefs of the main characters in a psychodrama; this exercise gives members opportunities to clarify what irrational thinking is and how it affects behavior.

Didactic exercises can teach RET principles, such as the following demonstration that I created to teach the notion of human complexity and the illegitimacy of self-evaluation. It is most conveniently introduced after a client's saying some self-deprecating remark. The therapist says, "Before we respond to John's remark, I'd like to ask everybody to do something for me. Do you see this table? I'd like someone to measure it for me." If no one responds, he asks someone, especially John, to attempt the task. Ambitious group members will report the table's length, width, height, or weight. None of this is accepted by the therapist. It is not the length, width, height, or weight that is of interest, but the table itself. Of course, there is no way to measure the table itself; *partis por toto,* the part–whole error in self-evaluation can then be discussed. To measure one's whole worth on the basis of a few dimensions is illegitimate, a form of self-prejudice. Humans, of course, are considerably more complex than tables.

Cognitive and behavioral rehearsal, especially in the form of role playing, readily may be used in an RET group. The group often provides a "safe" environment in which to try out new behaviors acquired through skills training and to reinforce new rational ways of thinking. When a client's problems involve a good deal of interpersonal anxiety, the group provides a forum to try out interpersonal skills; more important, it provides a forum for attacking the shame that in RET theory is at the heart of interpersonal anxiety. Shame is hypothesized to occur as one fearfully anticipates or experiences real or attributed criticism by other people of one's weaknesses. In the group one can learn not to feel shame about any of his or her characteristics and can work at improving those characteristics that can be modified.

To summarize, the initial activity in the rational–emotive therapy process is assessment of the individual's problem. To do this, questions are framed in a way that yields information to support or refute the hypotheses about the individual's cognitive dynamics as formulated by the therapist and group members. The next step is to make the individual aware of how she or he is creating self-sabotaging emotional and behavioral consequences. The next step is dissuasion, any activity intended to help the individual change her or his maladaptive, unrealistic, irrational beliefs to ones that promote individual survival and happiness. The two most common approaches are (1) education and (2) direct and indirect methods of influence. The principal direct methods are Socratic dialogue and logical disputation. When direct methods do not seem to be effective, indirect methods may be used.

Homework has been a characteristic part of RET since its inception. Its use in groups differs little from its use with individuals. The client agrees to do some activity during the time between sessions. The activity might be reading RET literature (bibliotherapy), writing out challenges to his or her irrational thinking (written homework), or some shame-attacking or risk-taking experiential assignment.

To aid in getting rid of irrational ideas that lead to shame (interpersonal anxiety over real or fictitious inadequacy), the client is asked to do something foolish in public. The violation of social norms is an effective shame-attacking exercise. For example, most people seem unaware that they conform to custom when riding elevators and almost always face the front of the elevator, even though they are not sure whether it is illegal not to do so. A shame-attacking exercise, then, would consist of asking someone who says she or he would feel anxious riding in elevators while facing the back instead of the front, to do so. Anticipation can be probed; people may have images of the other passengers giving them strange looks or thinking that the deviant was crazy or stupid. The therapist can show that looks or thoughts cannot directly affect anyone, and even spoken words are ineffective unless taken seriously.

The RET practitioner urges shame-attacking experiences for yet another reason. Even if the client has correctly interpreted the meaning of people's glances or read their minds accurately, it is the B or belief system that leads most directly to the anxiety. Thus, one's evaluative philosophy about harmlessly breaking social rules and receiving criticism for so doing is the main concern of this exercise. RET teaches self-acceptance—the ability to follow one's own conscience despite others' disapproval. Thus, the shame-attacking exercise is aimed at increasing self-acceptance and mature responsibility, not simply at achieving comfort while doing a specific zany activity. Although these exercises often are humorous because they involve harmless social rule breaking, they have a serious purpose. Shame-attacking exercises can be done not only within the group but also as an assignment to all group members to perform outside the group and to report during the next group meeting.

The risk-taking exercise is any activity that the individual defines as "a risk." Since the risk referred to is psychological, what is risky is both idiosyncratic and objectively nondangerous. Thus, in the final analysis, it is not truly a risk, but the discovery of this fact is a main purpose of risk-taking exercises. A man who fears striking up conversations with women may be asked to do so. A person who "must" do everything perfectly is asked to make mistakes. Through their experience, if they carry out the activity, they learn that their dire prophecies do not come to pass, that the anticipation is worse than the doing, and that what they once have done they can do again, thus building confidence.

These activities are assigned with the person's consent. The group often can exert influence on the individual to do the assignment and can provide a forum for rehearsal and practice. It is important to note that the group may misunderstand the shame-attacking and risk-taking homework assignments. The point is not to do them well or to overcome uncomfortable situations by gaining mastery over them. The point is to gain mastery over oneself by actively confronting self-limiting philosophies of living. Thus the woman who refuses to initiate contacts with men because she would feel worthless if she were rejected is encouraged to approach men *not* because she can become better at it with time and thereby escape rejection, but to accept herself *even if* she receives rejections. In fact, were she to approach men and not receive rejections, an experienced RET therapist might comment, "That's too bad. Try again!" These exercises are deliberately counterphobic because they are some of the best ways to overcome irrational thinking about life's "horrors."

Consistent with the aim of risk taking, the RET group leader does not try to create a climate of support in which people are reinforced for their neurotic "need" for love and approval. Group members are encouraged to adopt and express nonjudgmental attitudes toward each other, to practice what Ellis calls nondamning acceptance. This is somewhat different from positive regard and is closer to affective neutrality. Given time and the freedom to communicate with each other, group members often develop warm feelings and cohesiveness, even though these sentiments have not been promoted by the leader. So, although some initial attempts to encourage people to reveal personal facts and to "trust" each other are desirable to get the group started, their continued use is seldom necessary.

The whole issue of *trust,* which some group members (and some therapists, too) overemphasize, requires reassessment. Trusting involves several things. First, it means trusting you with information about myself because I believe that you will not practically disadvantage me because of your privileged communication. This is essentially an ethical issue having to do with confidentiality. Second, most clients worry about the *psychological* harm they might suffer at the hands (or is it mouth?) of another person. Since psychological reactions are of our own making, however, and based upon our belief systems, there is in fact nothing to "trust" another person with. Trust also means that I can trust you to help me. But this issue, which is by far the more realistically important one, seldom is mentioned in therapy groups.

Discomfort with strangers is another way that group members justify remaining silent, when actively working on their problems would be better for their purposes. Some people have a life philosophy that says, "I must never feel uncomfortable," known in RET jargon as low frustration tolerance, or LFT. Both trust and discomfort are socially respectable ways of labeling shame. They are better dealt with as B's to be changed than as conditions the group has to fulfill. In other words, speaking up about oneself is both a shame-attacking and risk-taking experience. Clients are done a disservice when allowed to avoid anxiety-provoking situations either within or outside the group.

PRACTICE

Problems

Almost all neurotic problems can be treated in a RET group. Psychosis, whether of organic or of unknown origin, cannot be treated in an RET group, but its sufferers frequently can benefit from working on their neurotic problems or, more simply, on their problems of living.

It is better, then, to specify what cannot be treated in an RET group. Psychosis itself cannot be, but some of its symptoms—for example, egocentric thinking— can be by a vigorous leader and group members who feel free to point out the self-centeredness. Disorders in which the individual does not seek change are not appropriate for an RET group. Some involuntary referrals can be "hooked" into therapy by showing that RET can help them achieve some goals, but many cannot. Criminals are not necessarily imprisoned because of neurosis. Although they stupidly may think they can get away with crime in the long run, they hardly are driven to commit it by anxiety, depression, or hostility. The latter factors might be a reason in some cases, and the skillful therapist might show how the criminal's life would be better without enraged hostility; such persuasion would be a first step in eventually doing RET with the law breaker.

Other involuntary referrals can be treated similarly. It is necessary first to "motivate" the client by showing that she or he can benefit in some way from taking RET seriously. RET or any therapy is a means to an end; if the end can be seen as one that is important to the person, she or he will tend to see therapy as somewhat valuable. In involuntary referrals, the therapist might be seen as the agent of society, and in fact may so act to try to get the person to become the "standard" socially acceptable model of a human. In my opinion it is unethical to use therapy in this way. It is the client's goals that we can work on, not society's. In fact, RET often goes *against* societal norms and explicitly asks people to decide for themselves what is right and wrong rather than passively accepting "society's" (or someone's version of "society's") rules. Oversocialization creates neurosis. Undersocialization creates sociopathy, but that, strictly speaking, falls outside the scope of RET.

Assessment

Precise differential diagnosis usually is not done in RET. Rough categorization based on an initial individual interview is enough to screen out persons who are blatantly psychotic, overly egocentered, withdrawn to the point of perpetual silence, or talkative to the point of compulsiveness. A psychotic individual would not be excluded because of the psychosis but because he or she might be too withdrawn or otherwise unable to interact with other group members.

Evaluation of a different kind is done as the leader sorts through the client's reports and actual behavior, to discover the main irrational philosophies he or she lives by. This is more discriminating than simply asking a person about his or her troubles. If clients could report all of their beliefs when asked, there would be little for therapists to do. But a person with an anger problem over his or her boss's behavior may have several problems, for example, putting him- or herself down when the boss behaves unfairly, or taking the boss's unreasonable request as a lack of respect and then "awfulizing" about that. We often get angry at others because they say or do things that "cause" us to feel ashamed or anxious. Within a few sessions, the RET leader can give fairly complete accounts of each person's main life difficulties, belief system, main symptoms, and how hard he or she works to change.

This last point, how hard the client works at change, is particularly important. Most people can uncover or recognize their beliefs and can understand how those beliefs are leading to upset and goal-defeating behaviors. Some people, however, find it exceptionally difficult to overcome their irrational thinking or to do what would help them effect significant changes. It is one thing when an individual does not change thought habits of a lifetime; this takes time and practice. It is quite another when the person does not attempt to carry out behavior-experiential homework assignments. The reason may be LFT or discomfort anxiety.

When a person claims that something is too difficult or too inconvenient, she or he is expressing a philosophy of low frustration tolerance, that life should not be so hard. Most people want to change easily and comfortably. Others fear the discomfort they might experience in doing, say, a risk-taking assignment. They want to feel better *before* changing, instead of changing to feel better.

One of the important evaluation tasks of the therapist is to discover what the person fears and to help reduce the fear before they attempt to make significant behavioral changes. To accomplish this, imagery and time projection can be employed: imagery to discover exactly what the person fears and time projection to help him or her develop some confidence in coping.

In one example, a young woman who refused to dance in public despite the repeated requests from her husband to go to a disco reported that she imagined everyone would laugh at her. Rather than reassure her that this would not happen, the therapist asked her to imagine the details: How many people would be there? Would they all laugh? Would they laugh simultaneously or consecutively? How long would each laugh? The therapist then deliberately exaggerated the scene and asked her to imagine all 30 patrons consecutively laughing for 10 seconds. To illustrate the length of a 10-second laugh, the therapist laughed for 10 seconds and was joined by the client in laughter during the last 3 seconds. She was then asked if she could stand this "horrible torture" for 300 seconds and to imagine what it would be like. She decided that she could stand it for 5 minutes, even though she previously had been convinced that she could not stand it at all. Armed with this cognitive rehearsal she successfully carried out her homework assignment of dancing in public and later used the same approach to overcome other social phobias without the help of the therapist.

If it is apparent after a group has begun that one or more members do not participate and seem unlikely to, they may be excused from the group and referred for individual treatment. Each is there for help; if they are neither giving nor getting help they would best be excused from the group.

Treatment

The process and mechanisms of treatment have been described in the previous section. In this section the beginning of a group will be illustrated. Assume that the group members are unknown to each other but have had an initial screening interview with the therapist.

The initial task is to get the group members acquainted with each other. This can be accomplished by each person's simply saying his or her name and mentioning a little about him- or herself, or it can be the focus of an exercise in which pairs get acquainted with each other, then form larger groups.

An early issue is trust. It can be handled by the leader's discussion of the issue or by an experiential exercise such as the one of asking for secrets. The secrets exercise also can be used to introduce the ABC model.

Another introduction to the ABC model is one I developed and labeled the *emotional dictionary*. It is especially useful with groups that are not accustomed to talking about their emotional experiences. A chalkboard or other large writing surface is required. Group members are asked to name common English words that stand for emotions, which are listed on the board. If any controversies arise from the choice of a word, they are discussed to discover common meanings (one of the points of the exercise).

The group then is asked to vote on whether each word stands for a negative or positive emotional experience (not whether it can have positive or negative outcomes). In case of doubt, the leader can ask, "Would you look forward to experiencing (say) anxiety?" A plus or minus sign is placed next to each word.

Then the group is asked to indicate whether the word stands for an experience that is usually extreme and dysfunctional, or mild-to-moderate, or perhaps even motivating. Again a vote is taken and disagreements discussed. A 2 or a 1 is placed next to the plus or minus sign for each word. Then the leader tells the group that in RET we make the assumption that -2 emotions are due to *iB's,* and that -1 emotions are due to *rB's.* Although this is something of an oversimplification, it presents the idea of discriminating rational from irrational beliefs and discriminating negative emotions from goal-defeating ones.

The processing of additional exercises or personal problem solving using the ABC model can be done with greater awareness on the part of the group members. In all of RET there is an emphasis on the nonmysterious: Therapy and counseling are seen as educational and dissuasive processes without intentions or "insights" that must be concealed from the client or carefully timed. If an individual client or group member asks a question about theory, philosophy, or procedure, it is answered unless the question is an obvious attempt to sidetrack the discussion; even then, it might be answered and the discussion refocused on the topic.

Treatment may be either time limited or open ended. Ellis's therapy groups at the Institute for Rational–Emotive Therapy have been in existence for many years, with several complete turnovers of membership. New members are incorporated rather easily into the group, partly because the leader discourages a "we-are-special" attitude among group members and partly because established group members seem eager to work with new people.

Termination, as already mentioned, is a matter of individual decision, although both therapist and group members may comment on the decision and even try to dissuade the individual from her or his choice if further treatment seems warranted. Good questions for the therapist to ask are: What are you not doing that you would like to do? And what are you doing that you would like to stop? These concrete questions can assist an individual in reviewing her or his own desire for further treatment. Some clients remain in group long after they have ceased to create significant problems in their lives, usually because they enjoy the group experience and it helps them to keep their own thinking clear. When obvious dependence on the group is detected, the therapist will move to encourage greater independence, perhaps insisting that the person leave the group. Termination in time-limited groups is not an issue in RET.

Therapist's Tasks

The leader of an RET group is a therapist, not a facilitator. The term *facilitator* implies that the leader merely creates conditions for positive growth potentials to become fulfilled. Since no positive growth potentials thwarted by society or other people are assumed in RET theory, the notion of facilitator is inappropriate.

Nor is the leader first among equals. His or her job is to provide structure for group experience or problem-solving attempts. The clients, of course, furnish the specific content.

The communication pattern in problem solving within groups is one of therapist to focal client, with other group members either observing if the therapist is especially active or directing their messages to the therapist or to the focal client. There is little interaction among nonfocal clients in this situation.

Another communication pattern emerges when the therapist teaches inductively; then, most of the messages are exchanged between the therapist and the other group members. Again, little interaction among the group members occurs.

However, the therapist deliberately can withdraw from the discussion and assume the role of coach rather than teacher–therapist. The group members are left to process an exercise or attempt to apply the ABC model to a focal client's problem. As long as the group does well and remains on target, the therapist does not intervene. When the group wanders or proposes practical solutions without attempting to work with the individual's belief system, the therapist can redirect their efforts. Simple comments such as, "I wonder who can guess what John's beliefs are that lead to his anger" can redirect the discussion.

The therapist also is active in seeing that one or two people do not dominate the discussion or that no one becomes disruptive. Since there is no assumption in RET that anyone "has" to talk or has a "right" to be heard, the therapist can manage the group discussion diplomatically and head it into productive areas.

Group members may socialize with each other outside the therapy sessions (and frequently do), but the therapist does not. The therapist's relationship is professional, not social. The therapist may see individuals from the group for private sessions. Clients who require hospitalization for psychosis or suicide attempts are referred to a suitable facility, and their re-entry to the group is assessed upon their release. Occasionally, clients may be referred for medication, and this practice could be a condition for remaining in the group, depending on the attitude of the specific RET therapist.

APPLICATION

Group Selection and Composition

There are no special rules regarding group selection. Some practical guidelines are to exclude persons who are likely to be disruptive because of active psychosis or compulsive talking and to include members of both sexes, because many problems of interpersonal anxiety involve relations with the other sex. These guidelines might be disregarded if, for example, the person diagnosed psychotic were only occasionally disruptive or if therapy were combined with consciousness raising, as in a men's or women's sexuality group.

It is probably unwise to have all depressed persons in the same group, although a group having the same phobia (e.g., flying) might work well as a time-limited, topic-limited therapy group.

Group Setting

There are no special space requirements. A circular seating arrangement facilitates interactive communications. Sufficient space for role playing and psychodrama experiences also is desirable, and the space should be private enough to preserve confidentiality.

Group Size

No special rules apply. If there are fewer than 6 group members, discussions may lag. If there are more than about 12, it is difficult to include everyone.

For the teaching of RET principles and illustrating their application to selected problems, the group size could amount to several hundred. Ellis frequently demonstrates the use of rational principles in daily life to groups of 100 or more, although these demonstrations are not thought to be group therapy. Similarly, the public education workshops held at the Institutes for Rational Living in New York City and Los Angeles and elsewhere may be attended by scores of people. These workshops lie somewhere between therapy and education and focus on specific topics, for example, overcoming creative blocks and designing future life goals and plans.

Therapy Frequency, Length, and Duration

Most RET groups meet weekly. They may be open ended with changes in membership or they may be time limited. For time-limited workshops, about six to eight weeks seems typical. The length of session varies from an hour and a half to three hours. An exception is an RET group marathon, which might range from 10 to 14 hours or longer. There are no prescriptive guidelines for frequency, length, or duration.

Media Usage

There are no restrictions or requirements for media in RET groups. Videotape equipment might be used for giving feedback to participants about their mannerisms and style of presentation, but this probably is rarely done. Chalkboards and flip charts also could be used, but are not required. "Props," for example, foam bats, might be used. Ellis has conducted group therapy for years without any media aids, although he uses printed homework forms that clients may fill out. Some RET therapists (e.g., Maultsby, 1975) make more extensive use of written forms.

Leader Qualifications

A leader should be professionally qualified to practice counseling and/or psychotherapy in his or her state and be competent in conducting rational–emotive psychotherapy. Although many professionals may meet these requirements and competently perform RET, certain ones are recognized by the International Training Standards and Review Committee in RET as associate fellows and fellows. They have demonstrated their abilities and are recognized as qualified in the practice of rational–emotive methods.

Ethics

Practitioners of RET are bound by the ethical code of their respective professional groups. The majority of recognized rational–emotive therapists are psychologists bound by the ethical code of the American Psychological Association. Violations of ethical standards also may be referred to the International Training Standards and Review Committee for action if the professional is certified to practice rational–emotive methods.

RESEARCH

There have been many research studies published that deal with RET and other cognitive learning approaches to psychotherapy. These studies focus either on the cognitive hypothesis as a factor in psychological disturbance (Ellis, 1979), or on therapeutic outcome (DiGiuseppe, Miller, & Trexler, 1979). Very few studies have investigated group therapy *per se*.

In general, the studies cited in the following summaries lend support to the role of cognition in emotional–behavioral processes. The analog studies support RET treatment claims about the efficacy of its interventions. The problem revealed by these research summaries is that very few studies investigate pure or classical RET.

The studies that Ellis (1979) cites in support of his theoretical claims come from a wide variety of sources. Relatively few of them test hypotheses specifically derived from RET theory. It seems safe to conclude from the volume of studies cited by Ellis that cognitions play an important role in human behavior and experience; that neurotic behavior is correlated with unrealistic ideas and illogical thinking; and that mood is affected by cognitive processes. However, the fundamental hypothesis of RET—that irrational beliefs lead to self-defeating emotions and that rational beliefs do not—has not been adequately investigated.

The outcome studies of RET suffer from the same deficiency: Few of them have studied pure or classical RET as an independent variable. DiGiuseppe et al. (1979) review about 50 studies, noting their limitations. Some used no behavioral outcome measures, obtaining data only on changes in irrational beliefs as measured by a paper-and-pencil test, a practice Wessler (1976) warned against. Some study the outcome of educational efforts, not psychotherapy or counseling. Others report outcomes of cognitive approaches, not pure RET. Comprehensive RET is the kind actually practiced, and it overlaps significantly with the approaches of Meichenbaum (1974), Beck (1976), and others. Although some of the outcome research is impressive (especially Rush, Beck, Kovacs, & Hollon, 1977), the therapy is not exclusive RET in nature. The few RET studies support its effectiveness with such specific problems as public-speaking anxiety and test-taking anxiety.

One difficulty in conducting research on RET, whether group or individual, is that RET is not a single technique in the sense that, for example, desensitization is. RET is a theory of disturbance that emphasizes the roles of maladaptive perceptions, misconceptions, and evaluations. RET is a growing collection of tactics for helping people change their maladaptive cognitions; some tactics are very direct, some indirect. What makes research difficult is that a skilled RET therapist may use several cognitive, behavioral, and affective–expressive tactics within a few minutes while working with a client (Wessler & Ellis, 1980). If the direct disputing of irrational beliefs seems to get nowhere, the therapist quickly can switch to imagery or role reversal, or analogies, or even parables and poetry. It is very difficult to duplicate this therapeutic flexibility under controlled conditions.

If one accepts RET as an attitudinal theory of neurotic disturbance, then a different research question emerges, namely, can attitudes be influenced in dyads and larger groups? The answer is yes, and it is supported by several decades of research in attitude change and persuasion. RET employs these tactics to bring about evaluative and other cognitive changes (Wessler & Wessler, 1980).

STRENGTHS AND LIMITATIONS

RET is most easily used with clients who recognize their own responsibility in creating their difficulties or who really come to accept this fact. RET takes the individual and his or her problems as its focus. It can be used for specific problems, for example, a phobia, and thus functions very much like behavior therapy. Or it can take personality exploration and self-awareness as its goal, as do traditional psychotherapy, nondirective counseling, and other self-awareness approaches. As a system of therapy, RET easily incorporates specific techniques developed in other systems into its tactics of therapeutic dissuasion. Versatility and applicability to a wide range of neurotic problems of living are among RET's outstanding strengths.

RET makes no claim that the person was a victim of her or his parents, society, or past passive conditioning. Clients who wish to become undisturbed, rather than discovering on whom to place blame for disturbance, benefit most quickly.

RET works well with clients of at least average intelligence, but can be used with less intelligent people in a more or less rote fashion (which is probably how they learned their philosophy of living initially). Clients who are rigidly religious often resist the humanistic ethical message central to RET, but one need not give up all religion to do RET or to benefit from it. Almost all religions offer a rational version that deemphasizes or eliminates the absolutistic thinking found in its very conversative or orthodox counterparts.

RET is no cure-all. It does not cure psychosis or psychopathy. It will not stop crime, delinquency, or social problems. Since RET depends on the cooperation of the client, it will not help the uncooperative. Therapists may try to encourage cooperation by many means, including their personal charisma, but not everyone is willing to cooperate.

Group RET has additional limits. The very disturbed client many be better helped in individual sessions. A client whose activities require weekly or more frequent monitoring would benefit more from individual sessions than from group.

On the other hand, for certain clients, particularly shy ones, group treatment is better than individual treatment. For many clients, the advantages of group therapy far outweigh the disadvantages. Most clients' problems involve other people, and therefore the group is an ideal setting in which to work on their problems. True, there is the disadvantage that there will be less attention from the therapist, but the advantages of group therapy are many:

1. Groups are cost efficient; the therapist can see several clients at one time and teach rational principles to many people at one time.
2. Members of the group can learn that they are not unique in having a problem or in having specific kinds of problems.
3. The group can provide a forum for preventative psychotherapy, since members can hear others discussing problems that they may not have faced or may not be currently facing in their lives.
4. Group members can learn to help each other. It is a well-established educational principle that one of the best ways to learn a skill is to try to teach it to someone else. Clients learn rational thinking while trying to teach it to others in a group setting.
5. Some experiences, activities, and exercises can be done only in groups. The group also provides a forum for practicing shame-attacking or risk-taking exercises.
6. Some group exercises may be advantageous in bringing out specific emotions that then can be dealt with *in vivo* in the group setting.
7. Certain problems are dealt with more effectively in a group, for example, interpersonal or social-skills deficits. The client can practice new social behaviors and ways of relating to people.
8. A group setting allows clients to receive a great deal of feedback about their behavior, which may be more persuasive in motivating them to change than that of a single therapist in an individual situation.
9. When therapeutic efforts are focused on practical solutions to life problems, the presence of many heads in a room may result in more suggestions than an individual therapist could muster.
10. The group members can provide a source of peer pressure that may be more effective in promoting compliance with homework assignments than that of the individual therapist.

Finally, the group can provide a phasing out experience for clients who have been in individual therapy. Such clients may have discovered their irrational ideas and how to dispute them but require additional practice to complete the process.

REFERENCES

Beck, A. T. *Cognitive therapy and the emotional disorders*. New York: International Universities Press, 1976.

DiGiuseppe, R., Miller, N. J., & Trexler, L. D. A review of rational-emotive psychology outcome studies. In A. Ellis & J. M. Whiteley (Eds.), *Theoretical and empirical foundations of rational–emotive therapy*. Monterey, Calif.: Brooks/Cole, 1979.

Ellis, A. *Reason and emotion in psychotherapy*. New York: Lyle Stuart, 1962.

Ellis, A. *Growth through reason*. Palo Alto: Science and Behavior Books, 1971.

Ellis, A. The biological basis of irrational thinking. *Journal of Individual Psychology*, 1976, *32*, 145–168.

Ellis, A. The basic clinical theory of rational-emotive therapy. In A. Ellis & R. Grieger (Eds.), *Handbook of rational emotive therapy*. New York: Springer, 1977.

Ellis, A. Rational-emotive therapy: Research data that support the clinical and personality hypotheses of RET and other modes of cognitive-behavior therapy. In A. Ellis & J. M. Whiteley (Eds.), *Theoretical and empirical foundations of rational-emotive therapy*. Monterey, Calif.: Brooks/Cole, 1979.

Festinger, L. *A theory of cognitive dissonance*. Evanston, Ill.: Row, Peterson, 1957.

Frank, J. D. *Psychotherapy and the human predicament*. New York: Schocken, 1978.

Maultsby, M. C., Jr. *Help yourself to happiness*, New York: Institute for Rational Living, 1975.

McGuire, W. M. The nature of attitudes and attitude change. In G. L. Lindzey & E. Aronson (Eds.), *The handbook of social psychology* (Vol. 2). Reading, Mass.: Addison-Wesley, 1969.

Meichenbaum, D. H. *Cognitive-behavior modification*. Morristown: N.J.: General Learning Press, 1974.

Nardi, T. J. The use of psychodrama in RET. *Rational Living*, 1979, *14* (1), 35–38.

Rush, A., Beck, A. T., Kovacs, M., & Hollon, S. Comparative efficacy of cognitive therapy and pharmacotherapy in the treatment of depressed outpatients. *Cognitive Therapy and Research*, 1977, *1*, 1–8.

Walen, S., DiGiuseppe, R., & Wessler, R. L. *A practitioner's guide to rational-emotive therapy*. New York: Oxford University Press, 1980.

Wessler, R. L. On measuring rationality. *Rational Living*, 1976, *11*(1), 25.

Wessler, R. L., & Ellis, A. Supervision in rational-emotive therapy. In A. K. Hess (Ed.), *Psychotherapy supervision*. New York: Wiley-Interscience, 1980.

Wessler, R. A., & Wessler, R. L. *The principles and practice of rational-emotive therapy*. San Francisco: Jossey-Bass, 1980.

Zimbardo, P., & Ebbesen, E. G. *Influencing attitudes and changing behavior*. Reading, Mass.: Addison-Wesley, 1969.

ADDITIONAL READING

Arnold, M. B. *Emotion and personality: Psychological aspects*. New York: Columbia University Press, 1960.

Berkowitz, L. *Roots of aggression*. New York: Atherton, 1969.

Davison, G., & Neale, J. *Abnormal psychology: A cognitive experimental approach*. New York: Wiley, 1974.

Ellis, A. *Humanistic psychotherapy: The rational-emotive approach*. New York: Julian, 1973.

Ellis, A. The basic clinical theory of rational-emotive therapy. In A. Ellis & R. Grieger (Eds.), *Handbook of rational emotive therapy*. New York: Springer, 1977.

Ellis, A. Discomfort anxiety: A new cognitive behavioral construct. *Rational Living,* 1979, *14*(2), 1–7.

Ellis, A., & Greiger, R. *Handbook of rational-emotive therapy.* New York: Springer, 1977.

Ellis, A., & Harper, R. A. *A new guide to rational living.* Englewood Cliffs, N.J.: Prentice-Hall, 1975.

Hauck, P. A. *Overcoming depression.* Philadelphia: Westminster, 1973.

Hauck, P. A. *Overcoming frustration and anger.* Philadelphia: Westminster, 1974.

Hauck, P. A. *Overcoming worry and fear.* Philadelphia: Westminster, 1975.

Horney, K. *The neurotic personality for our time.* New York: Norton, 1939.

Izard, C. E. *Human emotions.* New York: Plenum, 1977.

Karlins, M., & Abelson, N. I. *Persuasion* (2nd ed.). New York: Springer, 1970.

Katz, D., & Kahn, R. L. *Social psychology of organizations* (2nd ed.). New York: Wiley, 1978.

Knaus, W. J. *Rational emotive education.* New York: Institute for Rational Living, 1974.

Knaus, W. J. *Do it now: How to stop procrastinating.* Englewood Cliffs, N.J.: Prentice-Hall, 1979.

Lazarus, A. *Multimodal behavior therapy.* New York: Springer, 1976.

Lazarus, A. *In the mind's eye.* New York: Rawson Associates, 1977.

Lazarus, R. S. *Psychological stress and the coping process.* New York: McGraw Hill, 1966.

Mahoney, M. J. Reflections on the cognitive-learning trend in psychotherapy. *American Psychologist,* January 1977, *32,* 5–13.

Mahoney, M. J. A critical analysis of rational-emotive therapy and therapy. In A. Ellis & J. M. Whiteley (Eds.), *Theoretical and empirical foundations of rational-emotive therapy.* Monterey, Calif.: Brooks/Cole, 1979.

Moore, R. The E-priming of Albert Ellis. In J. Wolfe & E. Brand (Eds.), *Twenty years of rational emotive-therapy.* New York: Institute for Rational Living, 1975.

Raimy, V. *Misunderstandings of the self.* San Francisco: Jossey-Bass, 1975.

Rimm, D. C., & Masters, J. C. *Behavior therapy: Techniques and empirical findings.* New York: Academic, 1974.

Schachter, S., & Singer, J. E. Cognitive, social and physiological determinants of emotional states. *Psychological Review,* 1962, *9,* 379–399.

Watzlawick, P. *The language of change: Elements of therapeutic communication.* New York: Basic, 1978.

19

A Rational–Emotive Approach to Family Therapy*

Albert Ellis

Family therapy began to make its mark a number of years ago based on a psychoanalytic or psychodynamic model (Ackerman, 1966), and for a while this model reigned supreme in the field. Sparked by Gregory Bateson, Don Jackson, Jay Haley, and other prominent theoreticians and therapists, however, family therapy began to take on a systems and a problem-solving approach. Today most practitioners emphasize this approach, which holds that family members become disturbed largely within the framework of the entire system in which they live and operate. An understanding of this system, gained primarily through a therapist's seeing all the family members simultaneously to see how they interact with each other, will lead to the therapist's being able to suggest important changes in the system. Once these changes are heeded by the members of a disturbed family unit and put into practice (this systems-oriented theory of family therapy states), not only do these members manage to get along much better with each other, but also any seriously disturbed individuals (such as "schizophrenics") in the family setup will have their functioning significantly improved (Guerin, 1976; Haley, 1977; Watzlawick, Beavin, & Jackson, 1967; Watzlawick, Weakland, & Fisch, 1974).

The psychoanalytic and the systems-oriented views of family therapy have been criticized by various family therapists, including Levant (1978), who points

*This chapter combines two articles that were published in *Rational Living, 13,* 15–20, and *14,* 23–28, respectively.

out that they both tend to neglect the individuals who reside in a family system, and they fail to acknowledge the important ways in which individuals react to other family members because of their own phenomenological views. Levant, citing the clinical experience and the theories of existentialist, humanistic, experiential, and client-centered therapists such as Raskin and van der Veen (1970), Rogers (1961), and Truax and Carkhuff (1967), points out that people bring *themselves* to any system, including the family, and that what seriously affects them is not what actually goes on within a family framework, but rather their *view* or *interpretation* of what goes on. Levant, therefore, calls for a "third" force in family therapy that would make up for the grave deficiencies of the psychoanalytic and systems approaches.

As might be expected, I tend to agree with many of Levant's points, although I do not endorse his specific Rogerian outlook. If I were to present the phenomenological and humanistic view of family therapy, which can be seen from both a rational–emotive and a client-centered framework, I would tend to make the following points, virtually all of which would probably be endorsed by Levant and his fellow Rogerians:

1. Disturbed marital and family relationships do not stem mainly from what happens among family members or the kind of family system that exists for these members, although these events and that system may *contribute* to such disturbances in important ways. Instead, they primarily, or more directly, stem from the perceptions that family members have and the views they take of the happenings within the family system. Note that, stated in this way, this proposition merely translates the ABC's of RET into family relationships and hypothesizes that an activating experience (A) occurring within a family setup does not directly or primarily cause the emotional consequence (C) that arises when this setup exists in a disturbed or disordered fashion. Rather, the belief system (B) of the individual family members about what happens at A largely and more directly tends to "cause" C.

2. Assuming that obnoxious or unpleasant events are transpiring (at point A) in a family and that, therefore, the family is beset with difficulties or problems, no matter what the family members (individually or collectively) do to bring about more favorable events and relationships within the family context, they are not likely to succeed too well at this task, nor are they likely to *maintain* a favorable family system in the future if any of the members perceive themselves and/or the other participants in a highly distorted, negative way. In other words, changing the family conditions (at point A) may temporarily help some or all of the family members to get along better with each other (at point C), but this kind of change will tend to be exceptionally palliative and short-lived unless some of the family members somehow radically change B, the belief systems about what often transpires within the marital and child-rearing setup.

3. Practically all people who live in family settings have innate tendencies to

think crookedly, thereby unduly upsetting themselves emotionally and consequently finding it difficult to get along consistently with other family members. But they also have strong innate self-correcting and self-actualizing tendencies; they can frequently see what is wrong with their own and their close relatives' behavior and can often voluntarily change this behavior so as to improve family functioning. Adult heads of families, in particular—no matter how distorted, self-defeating, and sabotaging their perceptions and (consequent) behaviors—are still usually remarkably able, by dint of their own resources or with the help of a therapist, to change some of their thoughts, feelings, and actions, and thereby to bring about more favorable events and relationships within the family system.

4. As Rogers (1961) and his followers have pointed out, and as Levant (1978) specifically shows, a therapist can be of considerable help to family members who see themselves as being in trouble by: (1) conveying to them his or her empathic understanding of their misperceptions of themselves and others; (2) fully accepting them, even though they still behave in foolish and destructive ways; (3) encouraging them to accept and forgive themselves unconditionally, even with their poor behavior; and (4) serving as a model of an open, genuine, congruent individual who accepts himself or herself in spite of personal deficiencies and in spite of the hassles and uncertainties that life presents to virtually all of us.

The phenomenologically oriented points that I have just listed are, as Levant points out, indigenous to client-centered family therapy, but they are rather neglected in most psychodynamic and systems-oriented therapies. Levant, however, like many Rogerians, tends to take a somewhat passive existential approach to therapy, and he therefore neglects to note that the phenomenological and humanistic methodology that he espouses is also part and parcel of several kinds of active–directive therapy. It is emphasized, for example, in Frankl's (1966) brand of existential therapy, in Perls' (1969) gestalt therapy, and of course in rational–emotive therapy (Ellis, 1962, 1971, 1973, 1977; Ellis & Grieger, 1977).

Not only does an active–directive mode of psychological treatment remain highly compatible with a phenomenological approach to family therapy, but, I would contend, it also includes just about all the advantages Levant claims for client-centered family therapy, and it is a decidedly more efficient form of treatment than the Rogerian and other passive–nondirective methods. Some of my reasons for believing this are

1. Virtually all humans seem to be born with strong tendencies toward misperception, overgeneralization, self-damning, deifying and damning others, omnipotence, magical thinking, low frustration tolerance, and other forms of irrationality (Ellis, 1962, 1976, 1977b, 1977c; Beck, 1976; Hoffer, 1951; Korzybski, 1933; Levi-Strauss, 1970). Passive or nondirective methods of family treatment, therefore, are too namby-pamby to help them face and overcome these

innate tendencies, which particularly seem to flower when family members continually live together under the same roof.

2. Once family members begin to think and act in self-defeating and family-defeating ways, they tend to become habituated to doing so and resist changing their ways, in spite of their desire to do so and in spite of therapeutic intervention. This is not, as the psychoanalytic school would hypothesize, because of their unconscious motivation or their secret wishes to "do in" other family members (or to sabotage the therapist) but rather because it is very hard for most humans to change their habitual dysfunctional thinking, feeling, and behaving (Ainslie, 1974; Ellis, 1962, 1977b, 1977c; Ellis & Grieger, 1977; Ellis & Harper, 1975; Ellis & Knaus, 1977; Mischel & Mischel, 1975). Consequently, passive or wishy-washy methods of therapy, especially during its initial stages, tend to be wasteful or useless (Mahoney, 1977).

3. The most serious kinds of family problems probably stem from people's misperception of reality and from their faulty personal constructs (Ellis, 1962, 1977b; Kelly, 1955; Raimy, 1975). But a good deal of sex, love, and marital difficulty also arises from misinformation and lack of training for marital and family living (Dreikurs, 1974; Ellis, 1971, 1973, 1976, 1977b; Ellis & Harper, 1961; Kaplan, 1974; Knox, 1975; Masters & Johnson, 1970). Marital and family therapy, therefore, had better include a good degree of directively presented information and skills training.

4. Especially when they are living within a troublesome family network, people with emotional problems almost always require concrete, monitored homework assignments to help them overcome their personal and family difficulties (Ellis, 1954, 1962, 1977b; Ellis & Harper, 1961, 1975; Herzberg, 1945; Masters & Johnson, 1970; Maultsby, 1975; Salter, 1949; Shelton & Ackerman, 1974; Wolpe, 1958, 1973). Therapists who take a nondirective or client-centered approach to family therapy cannot very well provide for their clients these kind of homework assignments.

5. A good many individuals and families who could use family therapy have special handicaps, such as a low educational and/or low socioeconomic status, and there is evidence that such handicapped people would seldom work at changing themselves or improving their family structures if they were treated only with passive, client-centered methods of counseling (Aponte, 1976; Minuchin & Montalvo, 1967). It seems likely that even if a phenomenological and nondirective form of family therapy can appreciably help some educated, middle-class clients, many or most other types of clients require a more active–directive approach.

The foregoing reasons why I favor an active–directive, RET-oriented procedure in family counseling are hardly exhaustive, but they will suffice. As for RET procedures in family therapy, these usually follow the integrated cognitive-emotive-behavioral forms of treatment.

COGNITIVE FAMILY THERAPY

The main cognitive approach used in RET family therapy follows the usual ABCDE's of rational–emotive methodology. If all the members of a given family are old enough and mature enough to take part in the therapy sessions (which is usually the case, though very young children may often be excluded), they are shown that it is not primarily their past history of activating events or activating experiences (A's) that has caused their emotional consequences (C's) or disturbances today. Moreover, RET does not encourage any of the family members to cop out by attributing their current emotional consequences (C's) to the activating experiences (A's) that they are presently undergoing with other members of the family.

The rational–emotive therapist tries instead to show these family members that in the course of both their past and present lives, they *make themselves* disturbed, at C, by telling themselves irrational beliefs (iB's) about what occurs at A. The therapist demonstrates that if they rationally dispute (at D) their own irrational beliefs (iB's), and if they determinedly act against them, they will end up with a new set of cognitive, emotive, and behavioral effects (E's) that will largely solve their emotional problems. Then, while they are helping themselves emotionally, they can also go back to A and do their best to instigate changes in these activating experiences (their own and those of other family members as well, especially those of young children who are not very likely to change under their own power).

Let me illustrate some of the cognitive aspects of rational–emotive family therapy by using material from the work I did with a husband, a wife, and their 13-year-old son, Johnny. I'll call them the Jones family. I saw this family because the husband and wife kept fighting with each other about Johnny's behavior. Mr. Jones was very angry at Johnny for playing hooky from school. Mrs. Jones was anxious and self-downing because she couldn't control Johnny and because she was worried that her husband might leave her if they kept fighting and if Johnny kept acting the way he did. Johnny was exceptionally rebellious and refused to stop playing hooky, no matter what penalties his parents or the school laid on him. He felt that he was being done in by the family's not supporting him in his need to stay away from schooling in which he had no interest and which he found very boring.

Mr. Jones, at the start of therapy, stoutly believed that Johnny was acting very obnoxiously, for no good reason whatever, and that Johnny's behavior was "making me very angry. He has no right to act that way and create so much trouble for all of us. If he continues to act this way, I hope he runs away from home and we never see him again. I'm afraid that he's going to turn out to be just like my youngest brother—a no-good bastard who has never done any good for anybody and who hardly deserves to live!"

I quickly tried to show Mr. Jones, during the very first session of therapy when he came with his wife and son, that Johnny was *not* making him angry. On the contrary, he was definitely—and foolishly—*angering himself*. And, if he could see exactly what he was doing to create this anger, he could give it up.

He was very skeptical and insisted that, no, Johnny really *was* making him angry, just as his no-good bastard of a brother had, years ago, made Mr. Jones, his parents, and his brother and sisters very angry by his uncalled-for behavior. I did not give ground but showed Mr. Jones that when he felt the emotional consequence (C) of anger, it did not stem from the activating event (A), Johnny's playing hooky and defying him and the school authorities.

While working with Mr. Jones on his anger, I also, during the first few sessions of family therapy, worked with Mrs. Jones on her anxiety. Her activating experience (A) was basically the same as her husband's, namely, Johnny's playing hooky from school. But instead of being angry about this, she was anxious, because she had a set of irrational beliefs (iB's) about Johnny: "I *must* get Johnny to stop playing hooky, because it would be *awful* if my husband continued to blame me for Johnny's delinquency and finally left me. Failing with both Johnny, whom I *should* have brought up better, and with my husband, whom I *should* have been able to pacify and keep, would make me a *rotten person!*"

I helped Mrs. Jones dispute (at D) this set of irrational beliefs by having her ask herself: "Why *must* I get Johnny to stop playing hooky, even though it would be highly desirable if he did?" "In what way would it prove utterly *awful* if this situation continued and my husband left me because of it?" "Where is the evidence that I *should* have brought up Johnny better and *should* have thereby pacified my husband?" "How do I become a thoroughly *rotten person*, even if it can be shown that I have acted poorly in these respects?"

When she disputed her own irrational beliefs in this manner, it didn't take long for Mrs. Jones to end up with a new effect (E) along these lines: "There's no reason why I *must* get Johnny to stop playing hooky, though that would be highly desirable. If this situation continues and my husband continues to blame me and finally leaves me, that would be most inconvenient, but hardly *awful* or *more than* inconvenient. And even failing with Johnny and my husband hardly makes me a *rotten person*, but, at worst, a person who is failing in these two important areas." As she began reaching this new cognitive effect, Mrs. Jones lost her anxiety and her depression. She still felt quite sorry about the existing state of affairs and was able to work more effectively at trying to change it.

Finally, as I was working in the family sessions with his mother and father, I also spoke to Johnny about his reasons for playing hooky from school, and I was soon able to help him see that, like his parents (whose irrational beliefs he clearly was able to perceive, as I pointed them out to them in his presence), he also had a set of basic ideas that kept driving him to self-defeating behavior: "I *have to* get the immediate gratification of playing hooky rather than the long-range gains of going to school and avoiding trouble. It's *terrible* to be bored in school! Life is utterly miserable when I can't get exactly what I want when I want it!"

Getting Johnny to see that he had these ideas was not very difficult, but inducing him to give them up was much harder! I have to admit that I only succeeded in this respect to a mild and highly intermittent degree. Only at times, and usually for a short period of time at that, would Johnny dispute his irrational beliefs and come up with a new basic philosophy or cognitive effect. When he did so, he then would tell himself something like, "I don't *need* immediate gratification, though I certainly prefer it. It's a pain in the ass to go to school and be bored, but it's probably a greater pain to play hooky and get into trouble. Life isn't great when I don't get exactly what I want, but at least I can make it somewhat passable and enjoyable." When he reached this kind of conclusion, Johnny acted less rebelliously at school and with his parents. But then he would slide back to his basic attitudes of low frustration tolerance and would begin to get into trouble again. Fortunately, however, since I was having an easier time with Mr. and Mrs. Jones than with Johnny in helping them effect attitudinal changes, they were usually able to take his retrogressions fairly well and not upset themselves too much about his backsliding.

In any event, I continued to show all three family members that they'd better place the responsibility for their disturbed feelings and actions squarely on themselves, and not on their early upbringing nor on the events that were presently occurring in their lives. I attempted to get all of them, including Johnny, to accept this responsibility and to change their disturbance-creating outlooks, so that no matter what happened to them in or outside of the family setup they would tend to avoid feeling inappropriately angry, self-damning, and undisciplined and would instead feel appropriately sorry, regretful, and irritated at each other's and their own troublesome behavior.

At the same time, I was employing various other cognitive techniques of RET to help the members of the Jones family—particularly information-giving and problem-solving methods. Both in Johnny's presence and on some occasions when he was not in the therapy sessions, I explained to Mr. and Mrs. Jones why he acted in some of the ways that he did and how they could stop condemning him and instead reinforce his desirable behavior and perhaps penalize his undesirable acts. I also discussed how they could help Johnny get vitally absorbed in some constructive pursuits such as carpentry, which would serve to make his life less boring and give him more of an incentive to attend school. We further discussed how Mr. and Mrs. Jones could arrange to spend more time together in recreational pursuits that they both enjoyed, so that their conversations would not have to be concerned almost exclusively with what to do about Johnny and the troubles he was causing.

While working with the Joneses in these problem-solving ways, I fully recognized (as RET practitioners normally do) that I was mainly helping them to change A, their activating experiences, rather than to change B, their irrational beliefs about these experiences. So from time to time I pointed this out to them and tried to get them to give up the illusion that if I provided them with better ways of "handling" Johnny, all their emotional difficulties would be solved.

I used with the Jones family one of the unique aspects of cognitive RET procedures that I emphasized in my first book on rational–emotive therapy, *How to Live with a "Neurotic,"* originally published in 1957 and thoroughly revised in 1975. Once RET family clients learn how to surrender their own *must*urbatory demands and commands on themselves and others, they are often taught how to use this same kind of anti-awfulizing and anti*must*urbatory thinking to do RET with other family members and thereby help these others become less disturbed.

Thus, I showed Mr. Jones not only how to help himself with his anger but how to help his wife with her anxiety and her self-downing. And I showed Mrs. Jones how to encourage her husband to be less angry at Johnny when Mr. Jones tended to blow up at him. When, for example, Mr. Jones began to rail at Johnny in an angry fashion, Mrs. Jones was shown that she could say to her husband, "Let us assume that you are right, dear, and that Johnny really is acting badly, against both of us and himself, when he plays hooky. That's certainly poor behavior on his part. But his behavior cannot by itself make you angry and upset. What irrational beliefs are you telling yourself to upset yourself *about* his behavior?"

When Mrs. Jones induced her husband to stop and think about creating his own anger at Johnny, and to see that he was instigating it by demanding that his son *must* not behave badly, she would then (I showed her) be able to act as a therapist to her husband and ask, "Why *must* he not? Where is the evidence that he *has* to act well?" She could thereby help her husband to stop and think—she could encourage him to use RET on himself when he neglected to do so.

I helped both these marriage partners to use RET on each other and, at times, with Johnny. They reported that not only did this method of doing therapy with other family members often help the others but, perhaps more important, it helped Mr. and Mrs. Jones get a full grasp of the RET principles and be able to use them more effectively for self-treatment.

EMOTIVE FAMILY THERAPY

RET family therapy tends to include a number of highly emotive techniques. In the case of the Jones family (Ellis, 1978), I used several emotive techniques, including (1) my fully accepting all the family members and refusing to condemn them, even when their behavior was obviously foolish or antisocial; (2) shame-attacking and risk-taking exercises; (3) rational–emotive imagery; (4) role-playing methods; (5) dramatic and evocative confrontation; (6) the use of force-ful language by me and of vigorous self-statements by the clients; and (7) a pronounced emphasis on humor.

As is also the case with individual RET, none of the affective methods used in family therapy are employed just because they work in their own right, and none are employed to help clients feel better rather than to get better. They are closely intertwined with the philosophical and phenomenological-humanistic aspects of RET. The main goal, as with virtually all rational–emotive treatment, is to try to help the family members, both as individuals and as part of a cohesive group, to make profound changes in themselves and in their own ways of viewing themselves and the family setup. The goal, once again, is not to help them only or mainly to change their family environment or to make a low-level adjustment to a fairly crummy family life.

Just about all of the emotive techniques just listed, moreover, are done actively rather than passively, and directively rather than nondirectively by RET practitioners. Even when I or other RET professionals give our clients full acceptance or unconditional positive regard, we try to not only give it and model it for them in an indirect way, but to directly and actively teach them how to give it to themselves.

BEHAVIORAL FAMILY THERAPY   *RET – Active & Directive*

Although Levant (1978) discusses three major types of family therapy (psychodynamic, systems-oriented, and client-centered), he says nothing about the use of behavioral methods, in which all three of these schools are notably deficient. RET, partly because it is active–directive, nearly always employs a good measure of behavior therapy with both individual and family clients. Some of the main behavioral methods of RET include the following:

1. Activity homework assignments, most of them to be done by clients *in vivo,* are continually given to members of a family group. Thus, in the case of Mr. and Mrs. Jones, Mr. Jones and I agreed that he would deliberately stay at home every time he felt very angry at Johnny and refrain from running out of the house to a chess club or a neighborhood bar, as he had regularly been doing before he came to family therapy. He was also given a batch of the Rational Self-Help Forms (Ellis, 1977d) and was given the assignment of filling out one of them as well as he could every time he felt himself getting angry at Johnny.

As for Johnny himself, he contracted with me and with his mother and father to go to school every day for a month, whether he felt like going or not; and to fill out a Rational Self-Help Form every time he did not go or every time he went and felt depressed or self-pitying about going. Mrs. Jones was given the assignment of confronting her husband with each of Johnny's serious misbehaviors, no matter how panicked she felt about getting criticized by him when she did so; and of disputing her irrational belief that she absolutely had to have his approval, so that she would be able to keep confronting him in this connection.

2. Operant conditioning or self-management principles are frequently employed in RET marriage and family therapy and are used to reinforce self-helping behaviors and to penalize self-defeating ones. Thus, Johnny's parents agreed with him and with me to reward him (with money or food he especially liked) every day that he attended school and did not play hooky. Mr. Jones accepted the penalty of burning a $20 bill every time he avoided facing his wife and Johnny. Mr. and Mrs. Jones agreed that if Mrs. Jones would tell her husband all the worst details about Johnny's behavior, holding nothing back from him in this regard, Mr. Jones would make a special effort to discuss these details with her in a noncondemning, problem-oriented manner.

3. Skills training is often employed in RET to help members of families overcome their irrational beliefs or change the unfortunate activating experiences that they have. Thus, I worked with Mrs. Jones on her problem of nonassertion with both her husband and her son. I helped her give up the irrational beliefs (iB's) that she *could not* handle difficult, painful situations with Mr. Jones and Johnny, and that it was shameful for her to run away from handling such situations. As she began to see that it was distinctly disadvantageous, but hardly *terrible,* when she avoided handling things with Johnny and her husband, I role-played with her the new behavior of speaking up more assertively to both of them when she wanted to raise some issues that she knew they would avoid or would condemn her for raising. As a result of her assertiveness training during therapy, she began to take less responsibility for disciplining Johnny, and persuaded her husband to take more responsibility.

4. RET often uses distraction or diversion techniques of therapy to help some clients cope with their anxieties and hostilities. I employed such methods on several occasions with members of the Jones family. Thus, I taught Mr. Jones to use Jacobsen's (1942) progressive relaxation technique when he felt very angry at his son or his wife; he found this method a useful one for interrupting his anger and giving himself a chance to deal with it, a little later, in a philosophically disputing way. I also encouraged Mrs. Jones to use yoga relaxing exercises when she felt too anxious about being criticized for Johnny's poor behavior. I explained to both these clients that distraction techniques like these are palliative, rather than curative, but that they are nonetheless useful at times, if not too much is expected of them.

Other deconditioning and reconditioning forms of behavior therapy are often used in RET, including Cautela's (1966, 1967) covert desensitization; Ramsey's (1974) emotional training; and Heiman, LoPiccolo, and LoPiccolo's (1976) resensitization methods. These methods, as Masters and Johnson (1970) and Annon (1974, 1975) especially note, may be particularly effective in helping couples with sexual problems. In the case of the Jones family, the one main sexual problem they had was that Mrs. Jones could come to orgasm in intercourse if her husband actively copulated with her for a minimum of five minutes, while he usually came to orgasm in less than two minutes and consid-ered himself to be suffering from premature ejaculation. I explained to them that he was merely a "fast" and not a "premature" ejaculator, and that nothing was *awful* or *horrible* (but only inconvenient) about that. I also got them to use the stop-start method of intercourse, until he trained himself to last five or more minutes almost all the time that they had sex (Ellis, 1975).

Let me note again, in this connection, that although I and other RET prac-titioners use several different kinds of behavioral procedures, we put them squarely within a phenomenological and humanistic framework. We prefer to teach *self*-control behavioral methods, rather than resort to direct conditioning or reconditioning by a therapist, as many classical behavior therapists do (Goldfried & Merbaum, 1973; Kanfer & Goldstein, 1975).

RET, moreover, also acknowledges the possible drawbacks and harmfulness of social reinforcement, which is not only used continually by scores of behavior therapists (Bandura, 1969) but has also been shown to be one of the main hidden factors in the results of therapy obtained by many client-centered therapists. Thus, it has been found that although Rogerian therapists attempt to help their clients to achieve unconditional positive regard, they frequently give quite conditional positive regard. They reinforce their clients with appropriate "uh-huhs" or nods of approval when they say the things that the client-centered therapists consider "right," and they thereby often encourage these clients to strive, perhaps more than they did before, for decidedly conditional positive regard. This helps them to remain hooked, perversely, on their dire love needs, which compel them to think that they must have others' approval.

RET, on the other hand, uses reinforcement procedures, including social reinforcement, in a realistic, hard-headed manner and with full realization of its limitations and drawbacks. Thus, I will often arrange for my family therapy clients to be reinforced for their healthy or improved behavior by me, by other family members, or by outside individuals, but I rarely use reinforcement by itself. For, although it is tempting to get the quick changes that may occur in clients as a result of their being reinforced for doing one behavior and/or penalized for performing another, they may often become more reinforceable and less self-directional in the course of this process. The goal of therapy, of course, is personality change on the part of the clients. But the goal of *elegant* therapy is self-change and self-direction more than change that is manipulated or practically forced from without. Moreover, there is some evidence to show that clients who lose their symptoms because of being conditioned to change their ways by a therapist or by external conditions often do very well for a while but then tend to slip back into their old habits of cognitive, emotive, and behavioral dysfunctioning, while clients who work at effecting a basic form of cognitive restructuring are more likely to maintain their therapeutic gains and even go beyond them when therapy is ended (Beck, 1976; Ellis, 1977a, 1977c; Lazarus, 1971, 1976; Meichenbaum, 1977).

With the use of RET, therefore, we try to teach family (as well as individual) clients to be less manipulatable by social conformity and hence to be somewhat less conditionable. We would like to see them strongly *desire,* but not absolutely or compulsively *need,* the approval of others, including members of their own family group. RET focuses—as few other major systems of family therapy do—on helping people relate to each other better on a preferential, rather than an obligatory or *mus*turbatory, basis. It analyzes and disputes their oversuggestibility and avoids fostering (as several other therapeutic systems do) the childish dependency of family members on the therapist and/or on each other. In these ways, RET goes out of its way to help people train themselves to be more responsible, self-sufficient, and self-accepting—yes, even when they are part of a family structure and would like to become more closely related to other family members.

SUMMARY

RET takes a "third force" position in family therapy, that is, a phenomenological-humanistic approach that is highly active–directive. This approach first attempts to help family members see and surrender their misperceptions of themselves and others and to make profound philosophical changes in their intrapersonal and interpersonal attitudes and behaviors. In welding a phenomenological-humanistic approach to an active–directive approach to family therapy, RET uses—as it does with individual clients—a combined cognitive, emotive, and behavioral methodology. RET family therapy shows clients how to acknowledge, understand, and minimize their own emotional problems while at the same time helping other family members become more rational, experience more enjoyable and appropriate emotional responses, and act in a less self-defeating and family-defeating way.

REFERENCES

Ackerman, N. *Treating the troubled family.* New York: Basic Books, 1966.
Ainslie, G. Specious reward: A behavioral theory of impulsiveness and impulse control. *Psychological Bulletin,* 1974, *82,* 463–496.
Annon, J. *The behavioral treatment of sexual problems* (Vol. 1 and Vol. 2). Honolulu: Enabling Systems, 1974 and 1975.
Aponte, H. J. Underorganization in the poor family. In P. J. Guerin, Jr. (Ed.). *Family therapy: Theory and practice.* New York: Gardner Press, 1976.
Bandura, A. *Principles of behavior modification.* New York: Holt, Rinehart and Winston, 1969.
Beck, A. *Cognitive therapy and the emotional disorders.* New York: International Universities Press, 1976.
Cautela, J. R. A behavior therapy approach to pervasive anxiety. *Behavior Research and Therapy,* 1966, *4,* 99–111.
Cautela, J. R. Covert sensitization. *Psychological Reports,* 1967, *20,* 459–468.

Dreikurs, R. *Psychodynamics, psychotherapy, and counseling* (Rev. ed.). Chicago: Alfred Adler Institute, 1974.

Ellis, A. *The American sexual tragedy.* New York: Twayne, 1954.

Ellis, A. *Reason and emotion in psychotherapy.* New York: Lyle Stuart, 1962.

Ellis, A. *Growth through reason.* Palo Alto: Science and Behavior Books; and Hollywood: Wilshire Books, 1971.

Ellis, A. *Humanistic psychotherapy: The rational–emotive approach.* New York: Julian Books and McGraw-Hill, 1973.

Ellis, A. The rational–emotive approach to sex therapy. *Counseling Psychologist,* 1975, *5*(1), 14–21.

Ellis, A. Techniques of handling anger in marriage. *Journal of Marriage and Family Counseling,* 1976, *2,* 305–316.

Ellis, A. *Fun as psychotherapy.* Cassette recording. New York: Institute for Rational Living, 1977. (a)

Ellis, A. *How to live with—and without—anger.* New York: Reader's Digest Press, 1977. (b)

Ellis, A. Rational–emotive therapy: Research data that supports the clinical and personality hypotheses of RET and other modes of cognitive-behavior therapy. *Counseling Psychologist,* 1977, *7*(1), 2–42. (c)

Ellis, A. *Rational self-help form.* New York: Institute for Rational Living, 1977. (d)

Ellis, A. A rational–emotive approach to family therapy. Part I: Cognitive therapy. *Rational Living,* 1978, *13*(2), 15–20.

Ellis, A., & Grieger, R. *Handbook of rational–emotive therapy.* New York: Springer, 1977.

Ellis, A., & Harper, R. A. *Creative marriage.* New York: Lyle Stuart, 1961. Paperback edition, retitled *A guide to successful marriage.* Hollywood: Wilshire Books, 1971.

Ellis, A., & Harper, R. A. *A new guide to rational living.* Englewood Cliffs, N.J.: Prentice-Hall; Hollywood: Wilshire Books, 1975.

Ellis, A., & Knaus, W. *Overcoming procrastination.* New York: Institute for Rational Living, 1977.

Frankl, V. *Man's search for meaning.* New York: Washington Square Press, 1966.

Goldfried, M., & Merbaum, M. (Eds). *Behavior change through self-control.* New York: Holt, Rinehart and Winton, 1973.

Guerin, P. J., Jr., (Ed.). *Family therapy: Theory and practice.* New York: Gardner, 1976.

Haley, J. *Problem solving therapy.* San Francisco: Jossey-Bass, 1977.

Heiman, J., LoPiccolo, L., & LoPiccolo, J. *Becoming orgasmic.* Englewood Cliffs, N.J.: Prentice-Hall, 1976.

Herzberg, A. *Active psychotherapy.* New York: Grune and Stratton, 1945.

Hoffer, E. *The true believer.* New York: Harper, 1951.

Jacobsen, E. *You must relax.* New York: McGraw-Hill, 1942.

Kanfer, F. H., & Goldstein, A. P. (Eds.). *Helping people change.* New York: Pergamon Press, 1975.

Kaplan, H. S. *The new sex therapy.* New York: Brunner/Mazel, 1974.

Kelly, G. *The psychology of personal constructs.* New York: Norton, 1955.

Knox, D. *Dr. Knox's marital exercise book.* New York: McKay, 1975.

Korzybski, A. *Science and sanity.* Lancaster, Pa.: Lancaster Press, 1933.

Lazarus, A. A. *Behavior therapy and beyond.* New York: McGraw-Hill, 1971.

Lazarus, A. A. *Multimodal behavior therapy.* New York: Springer, 1976.

Lembo, J. *The counseling process: A rational behavioral approach.* New York: Libra, 1976.

Levant, R. Family therapy: A client-centered perspective. *Journal of Marriage and Family Counseling,* 1978, *4,* 42–49.

Levi-Strauss, C. *Savage mind.* Chicago: University of Chicago Press, 1970.

Mahoney, M. Reflections on the cognitive learning trend in psychotherapy. *American Psychologist,* 1977, *32,* 5–114.

Masters, W. H., & Johnson, V. E. *Human sexual inadequacy.* Boston: Little, Brown, 1970.

Maultsby, M. C., Jr. *Help yourself to happiness.* New York: Institute for Rational Living, 1975.

Meichenbaum, D. *Cognitive behavior modification.* New York: Plenum, 1977.

Minuchin, S., & Montalvo, B. *Families of the slums: An exploration of their structure and treatment.* New York: Basic Books, 1967.

Mischel, W., & Mischel, H. A cognitive social learning approach to morality and self-regulation. In

T. Lickana (Ed.), *Morality: A handbook of moral behavior*. New York: Holt, Rinehart and Winston, 1975.

Perls, F. *Gestalt therapy verbatim*. Lafayette, Calif.: Real People Press, 1969.

Raimy, V. *Misunderstandings of the self*. San Francisco: Jossey-Bass, 1975.

Ramsey, R. W. Emotional training. *Behavioral Engineering*, 1974, *1*, 24–26.

Raskin, N. J., & Van der Veen, F. Client-centered family therapy: Some clinical and research perspectives. In J. T. Hart & T. M. Tomlinson (Eds.), *New directions in client-centered therapy*. Boston: Houghton-Mifflin, 1970.

Rogers, C. R. *On becoming a person*. Boston: Houghton-Mifflin, 1961.

Salter, A. *Conditioned reflex therapy*. New York: Creative Age, 1949.

Shelton, J. L., & Ackerman, J. M. *Homework in counseling and psychotherapy*. Springfield, Ill.: Charles C. Thomas, 1974.

Truax, C. B., & Carkhuff, R. R. *Toward effective counseling and psychotherapy: Training and practice*. Chicago: Aldine, 1967.

Watzlawick, P., Beavin, J. H., & Jackson, D. D. *Pragmatics of human communication*. New York: Norton, 1967.

Watzlawick, P., Weakland, J. H., & Fisch, R. *Change*. New York: Norton, 1974.

Wolpe, J. *Psychotherapy by reciprocal inhibition*. Stanford, Calif.: Stanford University Press, 1958.

Wolpe, J. *The practice of behavior therapy*. New York: Pergamon Press, 1973.

20

Involving the Family in the Treatment of the Child: A Model for Rational– Emotive Therapists*

Nina Woulff

The ideas in this chapter arise from a desire to develop a model of rational–emotive therapy for children that accounts for the family's contribution to the child's problem and suggests a rationale and techniques for incorporating the family into the treatment of the child. Working primarily in a child guidance setting, where the referred client is always a child, I noticed that changes in presenting problems were most efficiently accomplished when the child's family was involved in assessment and treatment. However, I found no rigorous model in either the rational–emotive therapy (RET) or the family therapy literature that demonstrated how the two therapy approaches may be successfully integrated. Having been trained in both RET and structural-strategic family therapy, and believing strongly in the efficacy of both, I felt challenged to see whether the two theories were capable of mating to produce effective and successful results.

Rational–emotive therapy primarily addresses the issue of changing the client's irrational beliefs. This therapy focuses on the internal events of the problem bearer and de-emphasizes the context of the problem or the client. This focus has been helpful in demonstrating the idiosyncratic manner in which clients contribute to, create, and maintain their misery. RET literature only rarely discusses the manner in which humans living in groups influence and affect one

*This chapter was first published in A. Ellis and M. E. Bernard (Eds.), *Rational–emotive approaches to the problems of childhood* (New York: Plenum Press, 1983).

another (Ellis, 1978, 1979, 1982; McClellan & Protinsky, 1977; Stieper, 1977; Young, 1979).

When the client is a child, it becomes crucial that the therapist acknowledge the effect of the child's human environment because children are extremely dependent upon adults for meeting needs and learning the ways and means of relating and functioning in this world. Structural-strategic therapy (Haley, 1976, 1980; Papp, 1977; Selvini, 1978; Andolfi, 1979; Madanes, 1981) demonstrates how this human environment—specifically, how the interaction between people in groups—is crucial to problem creation and maintenance.

The model of therapy proposed in this chapter is a hybrid of rational–emotive therapy and structural-strategic therapy and shall henceforth be described as rational–emotive family therapy, or REFT.

RATIONALE FOR REFT

There are several reasons that REFT is preferable to individual RET with referred children. When parents refer their child to a mental health clinic, it is not unusual that the parents are more distressed than the child. Thus, to work individually with the child in these situations is often not productive because the child is not particularly motivated to change. Even if the child is motivated to change, the therapist has relatively little influence compared with the influence of the parents. Parental reinforcement is extremely powerful, and it is highly unlikely that a child who has learned rational thinking with her or his individual therapist will continue to maintain this change when her or his parents and other family members still strongly reinforce the old irrational beliefs and consequent behavior. This problem is exemplified in the following case.

Several years ago, I worked with a 10-year-old boy who exhibited persistent behavior problems at school and home. His parents insisted that he needed individual therapy and that they could meet with me only sporadically because of their busy schedules. Being a relatively young and unassertive therapist at the time, I agreed to their conditions. The young boy happily came to his individual sessions, during which we engaged in games and discussion aimed at correcting many misperceptions he had about his "badness." The boy was the only adopted child in his family and also had diabetes, which was controlled by medication. He had interpreted these unique characteristics as meaning that he was completely unlovable and that nothing he could do would change how adults thought about him and acted toward him. The boy was quite bright, and within several sessions was able to develop a more rational outlook about himself and plan how to change his behavior in order to get into less trouble. However, when I periodically spoke with the child's teacher or parents I would hear that his behavior had remained virtually unchanged except for brief and fleeting "good spells." I was quite perplexed but continued working with the boy. Some time later, during a session with the parents, some interesting factors emerged. Although there had been little progress in the therapy, the mother insisted that the boy continue because she believed that he had a very pathological personality and was the cause of most of the other problems in the family. She said that the fact that this boy was the only family member going for therapy proved this point. The father disagreed with the mother's manner of disciplining the boy and would give him special attention whenever the mother attempted to be firm with him. The father's justification was "but he is such a pathetic little chap—he does not need to be disciplined on top of everything else he has to deal with in life—with problems like his he can't help himself." It thus became obvious to me that the parents were actively reinforcing the boy's irrational beliefs about his innate "badness" and his misbehavior. The parents were very committed to their attitudes; they became quite irritated when I attempted to challenge their beliefs, and they argued that I should limit my therapeutic efforts to changing their son. I saw the boy for several additional sessions and then told the parents that I would not continue unless the whole family would attend regularly. They refused and I closed the case.

I believe much time was wasted in working with this boy and that, in effect, my agreeing to work with him individually was interpreted by the parents as further evidence that he was really bad and helpless. The case demonstrates some of the hazards of not working with families when a child is referred. In addition, it suggests the need for several important skills when doing rational–emotive family therapy. Specifically, the therapist needs to have a conceptual model of the problems that includes the interaction among family members, do a thorough assessment, be able to overcome resistance to family treatment, and motivate family members to follow through on tasks.

CONCEPTUAL SCHEMATA FOR REFT

The REFT therapist conceptualizes well-functioning families as groups of people who are able to accomplish the task of aiding the personality and social development of their offspring. This difficult task is hampered when the system has unclear or inappropriate rules, boundaries, and/or hierarchy. In an effective family system, the parents comprise a cooperative working team that operates as the "executive" unit of the system, and the children are a subsystem of clearly secondary power and status. The tasks of the parental subsystem are to work cooperatively in socializing the children and to be able to modify rules and expectations as children grow older. The task of the sibling system is to offer its members the opportunity to learn how to negotiate, cooperate, share, compete, and make friends with peers.

In order for each subsystem to carry out its specific functions, the boundaries between subsystems must be clear. The term *boundaries* refers to the intensity of interaction between people and to how responsibilities are delegated. When boundaries are enmeshed between subsystems or individuals, family members experience little sense of separateness. This lack of separateness contributes to difficulties in the development of independent activities and thinking, and in problem solving. When boundaries are disengaged, there is little helpful communication between members, and this lack can hamper the development of the capacity for living interdependently with others.

When a family presents with a problem child, the REFT therapist investigates the possibility of hierarchical incongruities and inappropriate boundaries within a family. Examples of such problems are (1) a parent is relating to his child as a peer; (2) a child is closely enmeshed with one parent while the other parent is relatively distant; (3) an older child makes most of the decisions for a family; (4) or all members of a family relate to each other as equals in status.

The REFT therapist believes that these organizational and relationship problems are primarily created and maintained by individual family members' irrational assumptions about themselves and each other. Thus, although the REFT therapist may have structural reorganization as the objective goal for the family with a symptomatic child, the means by which this goal is achieved is the altering of irrational assumptions. To accomplish this task, the REFT therapist utilizes a wide repertoire of RET techniques, including direct cognitive disputation, imaginal and behavioral disputation, jokes and parables, paradoxical prescriptions, and problem transformation (Bergner, 1979).

STAGES OF REFT

It is suggested that the REFT therapist follow specific stages in working toward goals. The case of Michael P. will be used throughout this section to demonstrate the crucial stages in REFT therapy. Michael P., age 11, was brought to the clinic by his mother and father. There was one younger sister in the family, who was seemingly problem-free. Mr. and Mrs. P. were concerned about Michael because he was sleeping and eating poorly, was very antagonistic toward his father, stated that he was very miserable, and expressed intense disgust and anxiety about the idea of his parents' having sexual relations. Michael's father was concerned about his lack of friends, although Mrs. P. did not agree with this. His behavior and performance in school were not a problem. Michael had a history of problems similar to these. His parents had taken a course in parenting skills and had been in family therapy before. At the assessment session, they staunchly maintained that Michael should be seen in individual therapy because they feared that talking about their concerns in front of him would hurt him. They also said that they were dissatisfied with their previous therapy because the therapist focused almost exclusively on their marriage and the problems with the boy did not go away.

Assessing the Problem

At this point, the REFT therapist will want to obtain certain information that will reveal structural anomalies in this group of people and will help to identify the irrational beliefs that are maintaining the symptoms and the dysfunctional structure. In order to do this, the therapist should ask herself or himself the following questions:

- Are the parents united in the way in which they attempt to solve the problem?
- How may the attempted solutions be actually reinforcing the child's problem rather than solving it?
- Does the problem child have an inappropriate amount of power and influence in the family?
- Do the parents behave assertively with their child?
- Do the family members have any practical problems that could be contributing to the presenting problem (e.g., lack of child management or negotiation skills, financial problems, communication problems with the school, physical or neurological handicaps)?
- What irrational assumptions could be influencing the way in which each member of this family reacts to the problem and to the other members of the family?
- How do the family members irrationally blame themselves or others for the problem?
- How do the child's beliefs maintain his or her symptoms?

The REFT therapist elicits the answers to these questions by direct questioning, by observing the nonverbal behavior of individuals in the family and interactions between family members, and by assigning homework. Questions that the therapist can ask the family directly might include:

- Do you (the parents) discuss this problem? What happens when you discuss it?
- Specifically, what does each person in the family do when the problem occurs? What has been done in the past?
- What does each family member think is the cause of the problem?
- What does each family member think is needed in order to solve the problem?
- What do these problems mean about the child (e.g., is he sick, bad, stupid, evil)?
- What does each family member feel and think when the problem occurs?
- What is happening around you and what are you thinking about when you experience your problems? (Asked of the child.)
- What does each family member want from therapy?

In observing nonverbal behaviors during the session, the therapist listens for irrational emotions and for incongruities between what a person says and how he or she behaves. In addition, the therapist observes the interaction of the family members for clues about family structure and irrational beliefs. While observing, the therapist keeps the following questions in mind:

- Who answers questions first?
- Does one parent seem more involved with the symptomatic child?
- Do the parents seem intimidated by the child, or vice versa?
- Who talks to whom in the family?
- What tone of voice is used when the family members address each other?
- How are the family members seated, and how do they look at each other?

Finally, in giving homework assignments, the therapist is attempting to elicit cognitive and behavioral data that will further help in providing the information that is needed in order to make a hypothesis about what is creating and maintaining the problem. This information is not all gathered at once. The REFT therapist must be prepared to revise his or her understanding of the problem throughout the duration of therapy. As the therapist gives directives and as family members change, irrational beliefs are activated that the therapist must be prepared to reassess and to deal with.

This information-gathering scheme was used in the assessment of Michael P. and his family. Both parents were spending a great deal of time with their son when he experienced his problems. The mother spent hours talking to Michael about his various anxieties, and she reported that he was very dissatisfied with his father. The father would invite Michael to participate in activities with him, but Michael would refuse. At night, when Michael entered the parents' bedroom and accused them of having sexual relations, they would both reassure him that they were only sleeping and allow him to sleep in their room for the rest of the night. At mealtime, both the mother and the father would gently coax Michael to eat his food. Both parents expressed great concern that their child was emotionally disturbed and possibly suicidal. The mother thought that the cause of the problem was that he was fearful of his father and that he had a very "sensitive" personality like hers. The father thought that Michael was too close to his mother and stayed in the house too much. Both parents discussed their son's problems *ad nauseum,* but they could not decide on an effective solution. They seemed to be rather confused about practical child-management techniques.

When Michael was home, he was almost always in a bad mood, and there seemed to be no clearly identifiable precipitating factors. He said that when he walked home from school he began to feel depressed as he approached his home. He said that he was aware of thinking that his father was mean and unfair and that his mother was worried and upset. He said that he also thought it was terrible to have these problems and to be coming to a child guidance clinic. The mother said that she vacillated between feeling intensely worried about her son, annoyed at him for being such a problem, and then guilty and depressed. The father said that he often felt guilty, helpless, and occasionally angry at his son. The parents said that their son needed individual therapy, and Michael said that he didn't know what would help him. Both parents stated that their goal in coming to therapy was to free their son of his problems.

In observing the family's nonverbal behavior, I noticed several interesting patterns. The mother tended to answer questions before anyone else did, and her body was turned toward her son. Whenever she spoke to him, her voice sounded pleading and childlike. Although the boy stated that he was quite miserable, he sounded very assertive and would correct his parents when they were telling me about the problem. The parents did not get annoyed at the boy when he did this but would meekly defend themselves to him. The boy frequently rolled his eyes and sighed.

Formulating a Hypothesis about the Problem

With this information, I formulated a hypothesis about the problem. In terms of the structure of the family, it appeared that the boy had a great deal of power and influence over his parents. Thus, the hierarchy was reversed because the child seemed to influence his parents, rather than vice versa. He determined where he slept, what they did in their bedroom, and how they spent much of their time. In addition, the boundary between mother and son seemed enmeshed, in that they shared common problems and worries and did not solve problems on their own. The boundary between son and father seemed disengaged, because they had little interaction with each other. In their attempted solutions, the parents were inadvertently reinforcing the problem, because the boy was obtaining much special time and attention from his mother. He was treated as though he were king.

In understanding how this dysfunctional structure is maintained, the REFT therapist looks to the misconceptions of individuals within the family system. It seemed apparent that each member of the family had irrational beliefs that were creating distressing feelings and causing them to behave in ways that reinforced the symptom. The mother had irrational fears and expectations of herself and her son. At times, she believed, "I must worry about my son all the time and help him overcome his problems; when I don't, I am a complete failure," and "The poor boy—he cannot help his problems; I am terrible to be so annoyed at him." The husband believed, "I am a worthless father because my son has so many problems," "I must not do anything that would upset my son," and "My son shouldn't be so difficult to help." The son believed, "I cannot stand it if my father doesn't act exactly as I want him to act," "I can't help myself—I am hopeless," "It is terrible for my mother to be so upset," and "I am a bad, evil person because I have all these problems." In addition, the boy had a very low frustration tolerance and believed, "I cannot stand to be worried and anxious—

my mother must calm me immediately." In addition, all family members shared the irrational belief that the source of and the solution to their problems was in each other and that they each had little ability to control the unhappiness they were experiencing. Families who come to a mental health clinic frequently blame each other, teachers, principals, neighborhoods, early history, babysitters, and even the weather for their problems. Although these factors may, in fact, be influential in activating a difficulty, I have usually found that there are a good number of irrational beliefs operating in families with a problem child.

In analyzing the irrational beliefs of the individuals in the family, the reasons for the dysfunctional structure become apparent. When parents are depressing themselves by irrational self-downing they are unlikely to behave in ways syntonic with an effective parental subsystem. If their child has low frustration tolerance and is quite demanding and if the parents believe that their self-worth rests in producing a happy child, they will probably give in to many of the child's demands. In a sense, these parents live in fear of their own child as a result of the connotations they place on her or his behavior. Thus, the child becomes the "boss" and the parents become the "child."

In the family of Michael P., the symptoms were maintained by a cycle of interactions in which the more Michael complained of his difficulties, the more his parents got upset and doted on him; and the more this happened, the more the boy acted up. The parents kept themselves indecisive and overinvolved with him by being caught in their own cycles of internal thinking, in which they would depreciate themselves for getting annoyed and angry with their son. In analyzing a family's problem, it is helpful for the REFT therapist to look for repetitive cycles of thinking in the minds of individuals and repetitive cycles of behavior between individuals.

In addition, it is helpful for the REFT therapist to be cognizant of constellations of irrational beliefs that occur in families with certain structural dysfunctions. For example, in most families where boundaries are enmeshed, the therapist will find that at least two family members share several of the following irrational beliefs:

- "It is terrible to be different from other people in my family. I must not think, behave, or feel differently from the way they do."
- "It is awful to fight or to be annoyed or angry with someone in my family."
- "I must be able to change people in my family."
- "I can't stand it if someone in my family has a problem."
- "It would be horrible if a member of my family left. We all *need* each other."

Careful identification of irrational beliefs will assist the therapist in planning the focus of treatment.

Defining Goals

My goals for the family of Michael P. were that the parents become an effective and assertive team in dealing with their son and that Michael learn how to solve many of his emotional problems. In order to accomplish this, I had to help the family members identify, challenge, and replace the irrational beliefs that were creating their emotional problems and preventing them from solving the practical problems of effective child management. The goals sound fairly clear and straightforward; however, in order to reach these goals, the REFT therapist must be somewhat creative in introducing the family to the notion of therapy and change.

Motivating the Family for Treatment and Dealing with Resistance

Parents who bring their children for treatment often state, as in the example of Michael P., that they want their child changed. At the beginning of treatment, the parents are usually very reluctant to admit that they need treatment themselves and often become early treatment dropouts if the therapist prematurely attempts to demonstrate to the parents how they are irrationally upsetting themselves. Family therapy literature contains several rather exotic theories and methodologies for dealing with families' resistance to treatment (Hoffman, 1976; Papp, 1977; Selvini, 1978; Watzlawick, 1978). For example, Andolfi (1979, p. 123) wrote:

> The therapist is thereby drawn into a *game* in which every effort on his part to act as an agent of change is nullified by the family group. In systemic terms, these apparently contradictory attitudes derive from the dynamic equilibrium existing between opposite and interacting forces: the tendency toward change, which is implicit in the request for help, and the preponderant tendency toward homeostasis, which leads the family to repeat its habitual behavioral sequences.

Suggested techniques for dealing with this problem include using a team of therapists and prescribing paradoxes and counterparadoxes.

From an RET viewpoint, resistance can be understood as a cluster of irrational beliefs that are activated when family members perceive the therapist as suggesting that the entire family participate in the change process. Resistance can occur at the beginning of family therapy, when the therapist attempts to involve the parents, and throughout the therapy, whenever the therapist gives the family specific tasks. When parents resist becoming involved in therapy, there are several irrational beliefs that commonly occur. Sometimes these beliefs are easy to uncover, and the therapist can then challenge them directly. However, resistance, by its very nature, tends to be difficult to deal with directly, and the reasons for initial resistance often are not disclosed until later in therapy. The therapist must then infer the underlying irrational beliefs.

In the case of Michael P., both parents wanted only individual therapy for their son. When asked about this, the parents gave the following reason: "When Michael hears us discussing these problems, he becomes more upset, and we cannot bear it when he is upset." In addition, the mother indicated that the idea of coming to sessions made her feel depressed. When I asked her what she was telling herself about coming to therapy, she said, "I guess then I would think that the problems were all my fault and responsibility." Mrs. P.'s response leaves out the evaluative component of her self-statement, which later emerged as being "and that would prove I am a terrible mother." This irrational belief is not uncommon among parents of referred children. The irrational beliefs of parents that contribute to resistance to family treatment include:

"It is a sign of complete failure to have to come for help on family matters."
"The therapist might ask us to talk about other problems we have, and that would be disastrous."

Children in families also can be resistant to treatment, and some of their common irrational beliefs are:

"If anyone knew I was coming to this place, I would die."
"If my family comes here for therapy, then that is absolute proof that I am a bad person."
"I don't want anything to change, because things could get worse, and I couldn't stand that."

The therapist has at least two ways of dealing with this resistance to treatment. One way is to challenge the irrational inferences and evaluations directly. The therapist can also choose to "sidestep" the resistance. For example, the therapist can tell the parents that their involvement in the therapy is crucial because they are the most significant people in their child's life and because they, more than anyone else in the world, are best equipped to help their child. When parents hear this, they tend to think of coming to therapy as an honor rather than as a curse. In addition, I suggest that the therapist state that the goals of therapy are to help the child become free of his or her problems and that the therapist will assist the parents in helping their child. By stating the goals of treatment in this way, the therapist is likely to engage the cooperation of the parents in the therapy process. There will be many opportunities later in therapy to teach the family members how to identify and rigorously challenge their irrational evaluations.

Implementing the Treatment Plan

Once the family has agreed to treatment, the therapist is advised to follow these steps: (1) negotiate the treatment form and frequency; (2) transform the presenting problem when necessary; (3) give behavioral homework; (4) deal with resistance to homework; and (5) help the referred child to develop strategies for independent problem solving.

Negotiate Treatment Form and Frequency. It is not necessary, nor is it always advisable, to see all family members conjointly when doing REFT. In determining the form of treatment, the therapist should ask himself or herself the following questions:

- Through what means will the goals of therapy be most efficiently and effectively achieved?
- What form of treatment is the family likely to agree to?

With the family of Michael P., I decided on a "mixed" form of treatment. I gave the family a 90-minute appointment every two weeks. During the first half hour, I saw Michael individually, then met with the parents for the next 45 minutes, and saw all three for the remaining 15 minutes. This decision was based on my assumptions that (1) it would be easier to encourage Michael to develop independent thinking and problem solving if I saw him alone; (2) initially, the parents would be more likely to express their own feelings and thoughts if they were free from the influence of their powerful son; (3) the last 15 minutes would give the parents the opportunity to rehearse dealing effectively with their son; and (4) the parents would be likely to accept this format.

Transform the Presenting Problem. Bergner (1979) wisely pointed out that it is important for therapists to be aware that clients can have very destructive definitions of their problems, which lead to depression and ineffective solutions. In these cases, Bergner suggested that the therapist attempt to replace these destructive problem definitions with more constructive ones. This approach is similar to reframing (Watzlawick, 1974, 1978) and positive connotation (Selvini, 1978). In REFT, the therapist will want to transform a problem definition if she or he believes that the family members will be more likely to carry out new solutions to their problem if they think about it in a new way.

With the family of Michael P., I thought it important to change the parents' inference that their son was emotionally disturbed, suicidal, and overly sensitive, because this way of perceiving the problem resulted in the parents' overprotecting him. I told the parents that, based on the evidence, it seemed clear that their son was suffering from "separation anxiety which was precipitated by approaching adolescence" and that the only way he would overcome this problem was if his parents were "willing and able to wean him away from them." I assured the parents that this would not be an easy process. In transforming the problem this way, I created a new path for the family to follow, a path that I hoped would lead them away from the self-defeating cycle in which they were stuck.

Give Behavioral Homework. The overall goal of behavioral homework is to reverse incongruent hierarchies and to eliminate the reinforcers that are maintaining the symptom. The therapist should keep the homework tasks as simple, as clear, and as inexpensive as possible.

Deal with Resistance to Homework. Therapists should not become discouraged when parents resist or sabotage homework directives. In REFT, it is this very resistance that is the royal road to the irrational beliefs that are perpetuating the cycle of interactions around the symptom. Also, the REFT therapist should be prepared to help family members solve the emotional and practical problems that may surface when the presenting problem improves.

In the family of Michael P., I directed the parents to stop allowing their son to sleep in their bedroom; to cease sympathizang, cajoling, and encouraging him; and to apply positive consequences if he ate his meals. In addition, the father was instructed to discipline his son firmly when the boy was rude. These tasks were relatively simple and straightforward; however, it took more than a dozen sessions before the parents could comfortably and effectively carry out these new solutions. At the beginning of therapy, Mrs. P. resisted the directive that her husband take firm control of her son because she claimed it would result in a wider rift between father and son. It was necessary to identify and challenge her irrational belief: "It is terrible if a child does not love his father all the time." In addition, the father was rather fearful of disciplining his son, claiming that he thought he would lose control of himself and beat the boy. It was necessary to teach the father the difference between irrational anger and rational annoyance and to suggest some practical child-management techniques.

Although at first it seemed as though Mrs. P. was following the directive to become less involved with her son, it soon became clear that this was not the case. Mrs. P. was talking less to her son about eating, sleeping, and sexual problems. Michael, however, was a rather clever boy and developed new problems, such as fighting with his sister and his grandmother, and Mrs. P. would fall back into her old ways of dealing with him. It thus became clear that something was preventing Mrs. P. from generalizing effective solutions. It emerged that Mrs. P. harbored the beliefs that "If I don't attend to all my son's problems, I will be a bad mother and that is devastating," and "I must be the opposite of my own mother, who was neglectful and awful." In challenging these beliefs and arriving at more rational alternatives, Mrs. P. was able to be more appropriately involved with her son in a variety of situations.

In working with these parents, a curious phenomenon developed. As Michael's problems became less severe, his parents became mildly depressed and claimed that "the situation was just hopeless." Because the parents kept an objective record of Michael's behavior, I knew that their response was triggered by something else. In questioning the parents about their thoughts regarding their situation, it became evident that they were evaluating themselves as failures because their child was not 100% problem free! It emerged that the parents were both perfectionists and needed help in defining rational goals for themselves and their son.

In addition, Mrs. P. complained that her husband emphasized her difficulties in dealing with her son and never recognized her successes. In investigating this problem, I found that Mrs. P. had an irrational need for approval from her husband. However, in addition, Mr. P. was very frightened of his wife's anger and disapproval. Mr. P. was worried that as she became tougher with her son, she would also become tougher with him, not need him as much, and possibly leave him. It was necessary to help both parents challenge these beliefs before they could work cooperatively, supportively, and authoritatively in helping their son.

At the beginning of therapy with these parents, I was quite specific in my directives. During later sessions, however, I encouraged the parents to generate their own solutions to specific difficulties. As the parents became free of their incapacitating irrational beliefs, they began negotiating with each other in developing plans to deal with their son's behavior. For example, during one of the last sessions, the father and mother developed their own plan for dealing with the problem of the son's avoidance of peer contact.

Help the Referred Child to Develop Strategies for Independent Problem Solving. When working individually with the referred child in REFT, the therapist must help the child to identify her or his faulty emotional and practical problem-solving techniques and must be aware that the child may experience new difficulties when the transactions in the family change.

Returning to our example, in working with Michael P. I discovered that he was quite a "pro" at irrational thinking. Although his parents' reactions had certainly helped him maintain his irrational thinking and behavior, it seemed clear that Michael was very adept at helping himself remain miserable. My first job was to show Michael how to overcome downing himself for seeing a therapist. Michael believed that he had the devil inside him because he felt so angry at times. Slowly Michael learned that it was not the devil, but irrational thoughts over which he had control, that produced his anger. In addition, Michael also believed, as did his parents, that it was awful to not love his father. Paradoxically, as Michael learned to dispute this belief, he reported a greater number of positive interactions with his father. As his mother became more authoritative, Michael became angry and depressed. He learned how to challenge his demandingness and awfulizing related to this change in his relationship with his mother. He also came to realize that he could solve many of his problems without her help.

One of Michael's most persistent problems was his lack of friends. Although he seemed to want to spend more time playing with peers, he took little action to rectify the problem. After spending considerable time making direct suggestions and attempting to challenge his low frustration tolerance, I decided to transform the problem. I told him that it seemed to me that he had a much more serious problem than I had thought. Based on the evidence, it appeared that he had a deep-seated fear of fun. His reaction to this problem transformation was quite dramatic: He became very annoyed with me and at his next visit returned with several examples of enjoyable experiences with friends.

Terminating REFT

Termination of REFT occurs when the presenting problems have decreased and when the therapist is convinced that the family members have made significant changes in their thinking. I suggest that the REFT therapist delineate an end stage of therapy. This need not be more than two sessions, and the goals are to reinforce the changes that family members have made and to avoid future reactivation of symptoms. At this stage, it is very helpful for therapists to ask families the following questions:

- How do you explain the changes that have occurred?
- How could you slip back into your old patterns? Specifically, how would you each have to think and react to each other in order to get back into the old rut?

In responding to these questions, family members demonstrate their ability to understand how they have contributed to the problem and whether they have developed a more internal locus of control. If family members respond to the first question by saying that their child has changed because the weather is better or the teacher is nicer, then the therapist knows that her or his job is not over. At the end of REFT, parents sometimes request help with individual difficulties that are not directly related to the problem with their child. It is suggested that, if the therapist agrees to continue working with this parent, a new therapeutic contract be established.

CHARACTERISTICS OF REFT THERAPISTS

Training in RET theoretically equips therapists with many of the skills that are needed to conduct effective family therapy sessions. Family therapists need to be (1) directive and focused in leading sessions; (2) able to plan sessions; (3) willing to challenge realities that family members accept; (4) persistent in encouraging people to change; (5) able to focus on present-oriented methods of coping and problem solving and not be sidetracked by the intricacies of past history; (6) clearly goal oriented; (7) able to design creative homework assignments; and (8) willing to make a flexible use of themselves in order to engage and motivate the family members (Minuchin, 1974; Haley, 1976; Watzlawick, 1974; Minuchin & Fishman, 1981). These are all skills that are basic to the repertoire of the RET therapist (Ellis & Grieger, 1977; Grieger & Boyd, 1980; Walen, DiGiuseppe, & Wessler, 1980; Wessler & Wessler, 1980). A family therapist must be able not to get distracted by the morass of content that family members present during a session. Because RET therapists are trained to look for the B underlying the A, they are less likely to get absorbed by the details of a problem.

The importance of the therapist's taking a nonblaming stance is frequently emphasized in family therapy literature (Selvini, 1978; Andolfi, 1979; Minuchin & Fishman, 1981). Stanton (1981) wrote, "Blaming, criticizing and negative terms tend to mobilize resistance, as family members muster their energies to disown the pejorative label. Such negative or depressive maneuvers by the family can render the therapist impotent" (p. 376). RET therapists are unlikely to fall into the trap of perceiving some family members as "victims" and others as "bullies," because they understand all dysfunctional human behavior as stemming from irrational cognitions. Thus, the RET therapist would tend to perceive family members as all "victims" of their own individual irrational ideologies.

HAZARDS AND PITFALLS OF REFT

Despite the skills that an RET therapist brings to working with families, she or he still faces several potential hazards and pitfalls.

One of the most common problems is underdiagnosing the extent of irrational thinking in family members. This is a particular problem in families in which one family member—often the mother—flagrantly expresses irrational emotions and ideas while the other family members appear quite rational in comparison. I once worked with a family in which the mother was clearly self-downing and irrationally angry in relation to her difficult 4 year old. The father appeared to be quite rational and reasonable relative to the mother. I spent considerable time and energy in helping the mother become more self-accepting, less depressed and angry, and more effective in child management techniques. However, the management strategies never lasted very long, and the old dysfunctional patterns of coping would quickly reemerge. When I took a second look at the problem, I discovered that this seemingly reasonable husband was undermining the strategies because he had a good number of misconceptions about his child's vulnerability, as well as irrational expectations of his wife.

Another problem with which family therapists contend is the tendency to become "inducted" into the family if the therapist tends to agree with the family's perception and definition of its problem and to do the parents' job. In other words, the therapist becomes susceptible to the group pressure exerted by the family. For example, she or he may take over the role of leader of the family in establishing rules or may fall into the unfortunate trap of acting as judge for the family in deciding what is "fair" or who is "right" or "wrong." The RET therapist who remembers the basic values and goals of RET will be somewhat protected from this pitfall. RET therapists are trained to assume that clients' statements about their problems, themselves, and others are rarely purely descriptive; rather, they are colored by inferences and evaluations. The therapists are thus unlikely to accept these statements as "truth" and to agree with family's perception and definition of their problem. Also, because RET therapists believe that the goal of therapy is to teach clients to own the responsibility for emotions and behavior, they do not run in and try to "fix" clients' problems for them.

Another problem that occasionally occurs is that one parent denigrates the other for having irrational beliefs by inferring that to have these beliefs is "weak," "bad," or "crazy." The therapist must be able to identify and interrupt this interaction quickly, because it can lead to therapy failure or a worsening of the situation. The therapist can interrupt this interaction by de-awfulizing the concept of irrational thinking and by looking for the issues underlying this one-upmanship game. The therapist will often find that the "superior" mate secretly has a horde of irrational fears and expectations.

SUMMARY

Although it seems at times a complicated and arduous task to conduct REFT effectively, there are many benefits to working in this mode. In terms of dealing with child-related problems, the family therapy approach can be very time efficient. Many of the advantages of doing RET in groups apply to working with families: Several family members can learn RET at one time, family members can reinforce their own learning by challenging each other's beliefs, and family therapy sessions can function as a live laboratory in which family members experiment with new interactions. In addition, by having family members interact together, certain emotions can be activated during the session so that the therapist can deal with them directly.

By working with the whole family, family members develop a much stronger belief in their ability to function competently and to solve their own problems. It is arguable that a therapist who works solely with children inadvertently reinforces the parents' belief that the solution to their problems rests with an outside agent, the therapist, thereby discouraging the development of an internal locus of control.

This model offers a means by which the therapist can unravel the tangled web of irrational beliefs and interactions that surround symptoms, and it suggests a direction for therapy. It is recommended that the therapist be able to assess both the functional attributes of the family as a human system and the individual cognitive and emotional makeup of its members. By changing the irrational beliefs that sustain dysfunctional organizations and destructive cycles of interaction, the therapist will be able to help families efficiently and effectively over-come their presenting problems and develop the skills necessary to maintain such changes.

REFERENCES

Andolfi, M. *Family therapy: An interactional approach*. New York: Plenum Press, 1979.

Bergner, R. M. Transforming presenting problems. *Rational Living*, 1979, *14*(1), 13–16.

Ellis, A. A rational–emotive approach to family therapy: I. *Rational Living*, 1978, *13*(2), 15–19.

Ellis, A. A rational–emotive approach to family therapy: II. *Rational Living*, 1979, *14*(1), 23–27.

Ellis, A. Rational–emotive family therapy. In A. M. Horne & M. M. Ohlsen (Eds.), *Family counseling and therapy*. Itasca, Ill.: Peacock, 1982.

Grieger, R., & Boyd, J. *Rational–emotive therapy: A skills-based approach*. New York: Van Nostrand Reinhold, 1980.

Haley, J. *Problem-solving therapy*. San Francisco: Jossey-Bass, 1976.

Haley, J. *Leaving home*. New York: McGraw-Hill, 1980.

Hoffman, L. Breaking the homeostatic cycle. In P. J. Guerin (Ed.), *Family therapy: Theory and practice*. New York: Gardner Press, 1976.

McClellan, T. A., & Stieper, D. R. A structured approach to group marriage counselling. In A. Ellis & R. Grieger (Eds.), *Handbook of rational–emotive therapy*. New York: Springer, 1977.

Minuchin, S. *Families and family therapy*. Cambridge, Mass.: Harvard University Press, 1974.

Minuchin, S., & Fishman, H. C. *Family therapy techniques*. Cambridge, Mass.: Harvard University Press, 1981.

Papp, P. The family who had all the answers. In P. Papp (Ed.), *Family therapy: Full length case studies*. New York: Gardner Press, 1977.

Protinsky, H. Marriage and family therapy: Cognitive and behavioral approaches within a systems framework. *Family Therapy*, 1977, *4*(1), 85–91.

Selvini Palazzoli, M., Boscola, L., Cecchin, G., & Prata, G. *Paradox and counterparadox*. New York: Jason Aronson, 1978.

Stanton, M. D. Strategic approaches to family therapy. In A. S. Gurman & D. P. Kniskern (Eds.), *Handbook of family therapy*. New York: Brunner/Mazel, 1981.

Walen, S., DiGiuseppe, R., & Wessler, R. *A practitioner's guide to rational–emotive therapy*. New York: Oxford University Press, 1980.

Watzlawick, P. *Change*. New York: W. W. Norton, 1974.

Wessler, R., & Wessler, R. *The principles and practices of rational–emotive therapy*. San Francisco: Jossey-Bass, 1980.

Young, H. S. "Is it RET?" *Rational Living*, 1979, *14*(2), 9–17.

21

RET Intervention with Younger Populations: Systematic and Practical Guidelines*

Michael E. Bernard and Marie R. Joyce

It is quite interesting to note that up until this time there has been only one other book, *Rational–Emotive Approaches to the Problems of Childhood* (Ellis & Bernard, 1983) which demonstrates how RET and other allied cognitive behavioral approaches can be utilized to help resolve the emotional problems of children and adolescents. While there has been a fair amount of work that discusses and illustrates how cognitive approaches can be employed to modify childhood *behavioral problems* such as aggression and hyperactivity (e.g., Kendall & Hollon, 1979b), scant attention has been paid in the cognitive literature to *emotional problem solving*. As a rule, child-oriented cognitive behavioral theorists and therapists act as though emotions play little or no role in child behavior problems, and it is almost as if these scientists and practitioners have forgotten that emotions exist!

In this chapter we will describe the third and fourth stages of RET therapy: *skill acquisition* and *practice and application*. After relationship building and problem assessment have been undertaken, the practitioner begins to teach the basics of emotional and practical problem solving, which include helping the young client to become aware of self-talk, teaching the ABC's of RET, and illustrating the basic principles of cognitive change (skill acquisition). Once the

*This chapter was originally published in Michael Bernard and Marie Joyce, *Rational–emotive therapy with children and adolescents* (New York: John Wiley, 1984). Reprinted by permission of John Wiley & Sons, Inc.

basic skills of RET have been introduced, the practitioner shifts attention to helping the client practice and apply these skills in as wide a variety of situations as possible.

The decision as to which rational–emotive intervention procedure to employ depends upon a host of factors, including the extent of the emotional and practical problems uncovered during assessment, the "cognitive maturity" of the young client, the willingness of the client to change, whether parents and teachers are willing to (and capable of) participating in a change program, and time available for intervention. For example, Claudio, aged 10, was referred for being aggressive, hyperactive, and for a negative approach to his school. Claudio's father, an unemployed machinist, drank a great deal and spoke little English, while his mother, a part-time house cleaner, appeared extremely depressed as a consequence of the continued family arguments, her long working hours, and her family's poor economic circumstances. After several frustrated attempts at family intervention, it became clear that the father was not interested in changing so that his son might improve, and his mother appeared a "poor risk" for successful family counseling. Claudio was willing to see the practitioner and, with the help of his teachers, a cognitive behavioral program was implemented. His teachers set up a school-based response-cost token system where Claudio was rewarded and punished for appropriate/inappropriate academic/social behaviors (response-cost procedures appear more effective with children with impulse-control disorders). At the same time, a cognitive program was instituted with the goals of encouraging Claudio to (1) interpret specific situations at school more accurately through an empirical analysis of his conclusions and predictions; (2) acquire more rational language concepts for interpreting and describing experiences; (3) develop a more rational picture of his self-concept; and (4) through the use of verbal self-instructions to aid his approach to his school work. As this illustration demonstrates, there are no "cookbook" approaches to applying RET with school-age children. For RET practitioners to be successful, they had better be sensitive to the unique characteristics of each case and be prepared to vary their approach accordingly.

THE BASICS OF INTERVENTION

Goals

RET is largely geared to teaching an attitude of emotional responsibility, that is, each of us has the capacity to change how we feel. Through the teaching of skills of rational self-analysis and critical thinking, RET instructs people how to become better solvers of their own emotional problems. The main goal of emotional problem solving is to teach children and adolescents how to change inappropriate feelings to appropriate ones. As Waters (1982a) indicates,

> Appropriate feelings are generated by rational beliefs, are an appropriate response to the situation, facilitate goal achievement, and are usually moderate as opposed to extreme reactions; whereas inappropriate feelings are generated by irrational beliefs, are an inappropriate response to the situation, impede goal achievement, and are usually extreme reactions. [p. 72]

Examples of inappropriate and unhelpful emotions are when children feel very angry, enraged, hostile, depressed, and anxious, while more appropriate feelings would be irritation, annoyance, disappointment, sadness, apprehensiveness, and concern.

For younger children, the goals of RET can be expressed as follows (Waters, 1981, p. 1):

1. Correctly identify emotions.
2. Develop an emotional vocabulary.
3. Distinguish between helpful and hurtful feelings.
4. Differentiate between feelings and thoughts.
5. Tune into self-talk.
6. Make the connection between self-talk and feelings.
7. Learn rational coping statements.

For older children and adolescents, a more complex set of goals may be pursued in addition to the ones already listed (Young, 1983):

1. Teach the ABC's.
2. Dispute "awfulizing."
3. Dispute "shoulds, oughts, and musts" (personal imperatives).
4. Challenge "I-can't-stand-ititis" (low frustration tolerance).
5. Teach self-acceptance.
6. Correct misperceptions of reality.

We would again like to emphasize that RET does not lead to young clients becoming passive automatons who conform to the sometimes pernicious social influence of parents and teachers. One basic objective of RET is to teach young people to live as comfortably as possible in situations that cannot be significantly changed. We shall illustrate how a young client can be taught different ways to solve problems that, up until the present, he or she either has done nothing about or dealt with in a nonproductive way.

An Overview of Intervention Strategies

There are two aspects of cognitive activity that can lead to emotional and behavioral disturbance and are corrected through RET. *Distorted interpretations and perceptions of reality* are brought about by errors of logical inference and reasoning (arbitrary inference, selective abstraction, overgeneralization, magnification and minimization, personalization, and absolutistic/dichotomous reasoning), and can lead to moderately maladaptive levels of emotional arousal. Misinterpretations frequently can be retained by people as invalid assumptions about themselves and their world. A second and, from an RET point of view, major aspect of dysfunctional cognitive activity is the evaluations and appraisals the individuals make of their misinterpretations. These *evaluations of interpretations,* which can be rational or irrational, are seen to be the main source of emotional disturbance, since rational appraisals of a distorted perception of reality will generally not lead to extreme and unproductive levels of emotional arousal.

An example provided by DiGiuseppe and Bernard (1983) will illustrate the differences between faulty inferences that lead to misinterpretations and self-defeating appraisals of distortions of reality.

> George, a ten year old, moved to a new neighbourhood and has not met new friends. He is sitting quietly in the neighbourhood playground while the other children are running about. He feels frightened and his associated action potential (behavior) is withdrawal. He sits alone leaning up against a wall reading a book. As he sees the other children coming, George thinks, "They'll never like me, they'll think I'm not very good at their games and they won't play with me, no matter what I do." George has drawn these inferences about the other children's behavior. In fact they are predictions about what might happen, but which never actually have. Inferences alone are not sufficient to arouse fear. Some children, although not George, might be perfectly happy to sit by themselves and read books, but George appraises the situation quite negatively and catastrophizes "It's awful that I don't have anyone to play with, I must be a jerk if they won't play with me." [pp. 48–49]

RET practitioners decide on the basis of the age of and goals for a young client whether they wish to target the client's interpretation of reality ("They'll never like me") for change, which Ellis would consider a limited solution, or whether the evaluative assumptions and beliefs ("It's awful . . . I must be a jerk") are challenged. Once again, teaching clients to accept life as it comes without exaggerating its unpleasantness is a preferred goal of treatment.

There are a few basic strategies that RET practitioners typically employ to modify dysfunctional interpretations and appraisals and to teach rational thinking skills. *Empirical analysis* involves the practitioner and young client working collaboratively to design a simple experiment to test the client's interpretation of reality (Ellis, 1977; DiGiuseppe, 1981). In arriving at an *empirical solution,* the "truth" of the client's inference is tested by having the client collect data that the client and the practitioner agree would be sufficient to either confirm or reject the client's assumption. In George's case, George and the practitioner could define those reactions of other children that would indicate that George was liked and those that would suggest dislike. George could then test his prediction that

"No one will like me and play with me" by initiating a limited number of contacts with the children in the neighborhood he would like to know, to see if, in fact, there was any evidence to support his self-defeating interpretative conclusions that he would be rejected. If little or no evidence was collected that supported George's conclusion, then his anxiety would, hopefully, decrease to a point where he would feel free and more relaxed to pursue other contacts. The practitioner could point to the fact that George's thinking was untrue and could help him to restate his ideas more objectively.

A second basic cognitive approach for changing cognitions is what Ellis calls *philosophical disputation* and is the core and distinctive RET intervention. Disputation can occur at a number of levels of abstraction (DiGiuseppe & Bernard, 1983). The client can be taught to question the specific appraisals of particular interpretations by examining the irrational content (and concepts) contained in the appraisal. This limited form of disputation is appropriate for children who are not able to discuss irrational concepts and beliefs in the abstract. George might be able to rationally reevaluate his appraisal of social rejection by disputing concepts of "awful" and "jerk" in the context of the presenting problem, whereas discussion of concepts such as "exaggeration" and "self-acceptance" as they apply in the general case might be well beyond his grasp. If George was 12 or older, he might be a better candidate for a more general consideration and application of philosophical disputation to the irrational concepts and beliefs that underly his negative appraisals.

Both empirical analysis and philosophical disputation, at whatever level they are applied, constitute the basic components of *rational thinking* skills taught in RET. There are two other general approaches that RET practitioners frequently employ. *Rational self-statements* (De Voge, 1974; DiGiuseppe, 1975) are provided by the practitioner to the client for rehearsal and subsequent utilization in situations that tend to occasion in the client inappropriate levels of affectivity. The contents of the self-statement incorporate rational concepts and help the client overcome whatever emotions are interfering with behavior. George might be instructed through modeling to verbalize covert self-statements that would compete with his social anxiety: "Just relax, George, just go up and introduce yourself. Don't worry, you can cope with whatever happens; be brave."

Another cognitive procedure that is being increasingly employed by RET practitioners with younger clients is rational–emotive imagery (REI). This involves asking the young client to recreate as vividly as possible in his mind a mental picture of a situation in which he experiences an extreme emotional reaction. When the feeling is as strong as possible, the client is asked to try to change the feeling from being extreme (eight, nine, or ten on the feeling thermometer) to a more moderate level (four, five, or six). For example, the change could be from extreme anxiety to moderate worry and concern. When the client is able to do this, it is pointed out that the way the emotional change took place is through a change in thoughts. REI can be employed both during *skill building* and *practice and application* phases of RET.

In addition to these four cognitive approaches RET practitioners, in helping young clients to solve practical problems that are not emotional (not knowing what to do in a situation, being overly aggressive), teach *practical problem-solving skills*. Practical problem solving may vary from helping younger children to think about different alternatives (and their consequences) for handling a *specific* problem, to a broader set of cognitive strategies for thinking about and solving problems in general (Spivack & Shure, 1974). Because George is only 10, emphasis would be placed on encouraging, and, where necessary, teaching friendship-making skills that he could use to solve his problem.

SKILL ACQUISITION

We shall now describe in some detail the flow of rational–emotive intervention, commencing with the decision, made by the practitioner as a consequence of RET assessment, that the young client "has a problem." It is at this point that the different cognitions, emotions, and behaviors that are to be changed are listed and goals for initial, intermediate, and final sessions are tentatively formed. It is in fact the case that from this point onward assessment and intervention are interwoven. As the young client begins to internalize at whatever level of complexity the ABC's of RET and as the therapeutic relationship develops, the quality of introspective detail provided improves and the specific identity of automatic cognitions and irrational beliefs becomes clearer. Thus, the specific goals for a young client will necessarily alter in response to new information uncovered during intervention. As new problems arise the practitioner continues to assess, as a prelude to intervention, the relationships among cognitions, feelings, and behaviors.

In the discussion that follows we illustrate how the RET goals that we have just described for both children and adolescents are accomplished. The practitioner will be guided as to the level at which RET shall be introduced by the variety of mediating factors we have already enumerated.

Basic Insights for the Younger Client

Before the practitioner begins the teaching of emotional and problem-solving skills, it is most important to make young clients aware that not only are changes in their emotions and behaviors possible, but also that change is desirable (DiGiuseppe, 1981). Many children can only conceive of one way of dealing with and feeling in a situation, and some find it illuminating to learn both the possibility of alternative courses of action and emotional change.

Many children have few words for emotions, and a narrow vocabulary may limit their ability to conceptualize a situation. DiGiuseppe (1981) has recounted:

> Recently, while discussing a child's depressed reaction to the withdrawal of some of her privileges, I made the suggestion that she could have thought or felt differently about the situation than she did. The child responded, "What's the matter with you? Do you want me to be happy about it?" The child only conceptualized happy or sad as possible reactions. Frequently children's schema of emotional reactions are dichotomous and are limited to happy–sad or happy–mad constructs. It will be impossible to convince a child to change his or her automatic thoughts if the child believes the therapist wants him or her to be pleased with a situation that is obviously negative. [pp. 58–59]

We agree with DiGiuseppe that one of the first steps in cognitive therapy with children is to provide them with a schema that incorporates a continuum of responses and feelings and contains a vocabulary for these reactions.

In introducing the idea that one does not always have to feel the same way, and that feelings can vary in intensity from weak (a little) to strong (the most), we find it instructive to have younger children place their hands and arms close together to indicate feeling a little upset and to spread their arms as wide as possible to express extreme upset.

Discussing the negative consequences of present behavior in relation to the positive consequences (or less negative consequences) that may derive from different alternatives sometimes provides young clients with a "way out" of a chronic problem situation that they have been looking for desperately. Grieger and Boyd (1983) illustrate in Figure 21–1 how a diagram can be employed to emphasize the relationship between varying levels of upset and positive and negative consequences. In conjunction with such an activity, it is frequently helpful to explain to the client, as Virginia Waters suggests, that being very upset is like being in an "emotional fog" and that until one calms down, one will not be able to see how best to solve a given problem.

For example, Craig, a 13 year old, became very angry when he was told by the bus driver that he had to sit in his seat rather than on the arms of the seat.

THERAPIST: Well, how angry, from 1 to 10, did you feel on the bus yesterday when the driver turned around and told you to sit down?

CLIENT: Almost 10 (arms stretched out wide).

THERAPIST: And do you always feel that angry when he tells you to sit down?

CLIENT: Yes.

THERAPIST: And yesterday you got off the bus, cursed the driver, and took the train home?

CLIENT: Uh-huh.

THERAPIST: Do you ever feel anything differently when he picks on you?

CLIENT: No.

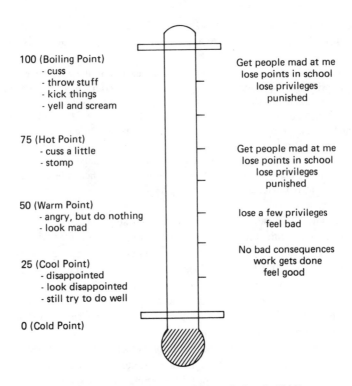

Figure 21–1. Jeff's mad thermometer (from Grieger & Boyd, 1983).

THERAPIST: What do you think will happen if you continue to get angry at the driver?
CLIENT: I won't be able to use the bus.
THERAPIST: Is that a good thing or a bad thing?
CLIENT: Bad.
THERAPIST: Well, I will show you how you can make yourself less angry—let's say from a 9 to a 6—and, hopefully, by feeling less angry, you'll be able to keep on riding the bus.

Teaching the ABC's of RET

After a young client is made aware of the possibility and desirability of change, the next step is frequently teaching the basic RET insights concerning thoughts, feelings, and behavior. Before the young client is actually instructed in the ABC's, however, it is most important that she possess some understanding of emotions. Children of all ages vary a great deal in their ability to understand and express emotions. It is often the case that a young client is unable at first to express what she is feeling, let alone identify what others are feeling. The practitioner had better make sure that the young client has a good grasp of emotional concepts and is able to express them before proceeding.

A good way to increase emotional awareness is to have a young client list all the feelings she knows as a way of assessing her emotional vocabulary. The client can then be encouraged to express, both verbally and nonverbally, the different feelings she may have experienced in different situations and, if possible, to provide her thoughts and self-talk at these times. Waters (1982a) has suggested a number of techniques for expanding emotional insight. She suggests that flashcards with an emotion on each can be used in a variety of ways. "The therapist and child can play a guessing game where each in turn acts out the emotion on a chosen card and the other has to guess it, or each can take turns making up stories about each emotion. It is possible to go through the emotional flashcards and ask the child which emotions have been experienced that week" (p. 575). Waters also suggests that the young client can play an *emotional detective* and observe how different people handle different feelings.

For older children and adolescents who demonstrate sufficient levels of emotional awareness, it is possible to begin quite quickly to teach them, by employing a variety of strategies, methods, and techniques, the basic RET insight that thoughts, and not people or events, cause people to feel (and behave) as they do. Corollary principles and insights include that feelings come from thoughts, that different thoughts lead to different feelings, that pleasant/unpleasant thoughts lead to pleasant/unpleasant feelings, and that if you get too upset about something, it is very difficult to do anything to improve the situation.

In illustrating these basic RET principles, the practitioner may begin by asking the youngster a question. The practitioner may ask the youngster to think about why children of similar characteristics react so differently to the same situation. If a situation, event, or happening *causes* our emotions, then they should have the same feeling in the same situation. A concrete example would be if it snows some youngsters are happy, some are angry, and some are scared. "Why," the young client is asked, "do they feel differently?" Some youngsters come up with the answer that they must be thinking or imagining different things. "Correct!" you say (or you provide the answer if the youngster cannot), and you explain that the happy ones are probably thinking about missing school, the angry ones are thinking that their parents will force them to wear boots and gloves, and the ones who are worried are scared their school bus might slide off the road. Another way of illustrating this principle is to discuss how our feelings about something or someone can change if our thoughts change. Knaus (1974) provides the example of a youngster who gets angry when a stranger bumps or pushes her but who upon observing that the stranger was blind feels sad and guilty. The practitioner asks the young person to provide some of the thoughts that might lead to anger versus those that might lead to sadness or guilt. The practitioner provides these if the youngster has difficulty doing so. Children may require many concrete experiences and illustrations before they grasp the essentials of the ABC's. Finally, S. R. Harris (1976) provides the following illustration of how to teach groups of children that the same event occasions different feelings in different children:

> [We asked] children to rate on a continuum from –5 (very negative) to +5 (very positive) how they felt about such things as big dogs, eating spinach, and thunder and lightning. We found a wide variation in the emotional responses (point C) to the same event (point A). For example, one or two children had intense negative feelings about big dogs, some felt positive and others felt less intense or neutral. The children shared their thoughts about big dogs such as "I really like to see big dogs, I feel excited by them!" or "I don't like to see them, I'm scared of big dogs!" Through discussions we helped them understand that what they were thinking about affected how they felt about events in their lives. [p. 118]

In teaching the basis of the ABC model, it is often useful to use a chart to illustrate the relationship between activating events, thoughts (self-talk), and consequences. We frequently use a "happening–thoughts–feelings–behaviors" chart such as the one below to teach the basic RET insight that when (1) something happens to you, (2) you think about what happened, (3) the thoughts you have lead to a feeling, and (4) the feeling will affect how you react.

What happened	What were you thinking?	What were you feeling?	What did you do?

While it is generally believed that both the practitioner and client have to share "a similar cognitive view of psychological problems and speak in a common cognitively based language" (Sutton-Simon, 1981, p. 68), occasionally it is quite possible—especially when working with very young children—to assess and modify self-statements without discussing with the client the underlying rationale. For example, consider Richard, a boy in third grade, who was frequently seen crying after school when his mother was late in picking him up. After determining that there were no extenuating circumstances at home and that Richard had no major problems besides worrying from time to time about the standard of his work, it was decided that a limited RET contact might provide a solution. Richard was seen for two brief 10-minute sessions across a one-week period. During the first session, Richard was asked to describe his thoughts while he was waiting for his mother. He replied to the effect that "What if Mum forgets again, I'll be left all by myself, all alone." It seemed clear without probing for underlying beliefs that the self-statements concerning being forgotten and alone were greatly contributing to his feelings of worry. Richard was told that one way of feeling better was to say to himself while he was waiting for his mother, "It doesn't matter if I have to wait a little; I won't be forgotten for long, someone will pick me up; I can cope." Richard practiced saying this dialogue aloud to himself and was told to repeat it if he had to wait after school. During the following week, the several teachers on duty reported that Richard did not cry, even though his mother was late twice. Richard said he was less worried, and when asked why, he replied, "I said to myself, I can cope and that Mum will be here soon." Two months later, Richard was seen again and indicated that he was no longer worried about being left for a while after school. No attempt was made to teach Richard the relationship of thoughts and feelings. Children of Richard's age and younger are often quite as willing to learn to change their thoughts as they are willing to change their clothes for a class in physical education.

As a prerequisite to teaching young clients how to challenge and dispute irrational beliefs, it is sometimes necessary that the concepts of "rational" and "irrational" are formally taught. In working with younger clients and especially children, Waters (1982a) substitutes the term "helpful" and "hurtful" or "productive" and "unproductive" beliefs. Her explanation of these terms is as follows:

> Rational beliefs follow from reality, are self-enhancing, are apt to lead to achievement of goals, and result in appropriate emotions; whereas irrational beliefs do not follow from reality, are self-defeating, usually block one from achieving goals, and result in inappropriate feelings. [p. 572]

There are a number of instructional techniques we employ when teaching these concepts (see Bernard, 1975; Bernard, 1977). We usually present a definition of each concept (Knaus, 1974):

> Rational thought: A sensible and logical idea that seems to be true.
> Irrational thought: An unreasonable or absurd idea that seems to be false.

We then provide examples and nonexamples of rational and irrational thoughts. The youngster is provided with instructional worksheets where he is given practice examples to classify (see Table 21–1). Verbal prompts, explanations, and feedback are provided. When the youngster demonstrates that he can discriminate between rational and irrational thoughts, he is guided in applying these intellectual skills in analyzing the characteristics of his own thoughts.

In working with older children and adolescents, it is desirable to teach them a "disputation" or "challenging" strategy for deciding if their thoughts are rational or irrational. We define challenge as "To question yourself to see if your thought is rational or irrational" and teach that "To find out if a thought is rational or irrational, ask yourself 'Is there enough evidence for me to say the thought is

TABLE 21–1 Instructional Exercises for Teaching the Concepts *Rational* and *Irrational*

Directions: Place a mark (x) if you think the thought is rational or irrational. (Remember: Is the thought sensible and true, or is it absurd and false?)

	Rational	Irrational
1. Nobody in the world will ever be my friend.	_____	_____
2. I would be happier at school if I were better at my work.	_____	_____
3. I never do anything right.	_____	_____
4. If I am this bad at my work, I will never be good at anything.	_____	_____
5. Everybody hates me.	_____	_____
6. I wish I had more friends at school.	_____	_____
7. I can't stand doing homework.	_____	_____
8. I wish I could play football as well as John can.	_____	_____

true?' " If there is, the thought is rational, if not, the thought is irrational. This strategy is used in teaching the basics of empirical analysis and philosophical disputation. Waters (1982a) suggests that children can learn to challenge their irrational beliefs by asking themselves and answering the following series of questions:

1. Is this belief based on fact, opinion, inference or assumption? Where is the evidence that this is really so?
2. Is it really awful? Is it true I couldn't stand it? Is it the worst that it could be?
3. Is this belief getting me what I want?
4. Why shouldn't it be so? Do I always have to get what I want?
5. Where is the evidence that this makes me worthless? How can this make me worthless or less than human? [p. 576]

Once the young client has been taught the difference between rational and irrational, it is sometimes instructive to demonstrate through the use of examples from the practitioner's and the client's life the consequences of rational and irrational thinking. Waters (1982b) suggests the "What if" game to explore the consequences of "demandingness" and "awfulizing":

What if you were to demand that you should always get your way? (1) What would you feel? (2) What would you do? (3) How would others respond to you? (4) Would you be more likely to get your way than if you didn't make this demand? On the other hand, what would happen if you thought that you would like to get your way all the time, but couldn't stand it when you didn't get your way? (1) How would you feel? (2) What would you do? (3) How might others respond to you? [p. 20]

Emotional Problem Solving

In this section we detail a number of the basic cognitive change procedures used in RET.

Rational Self-statements. With younger children, the most common change procedure used to resolve emotional difficulties is rational self-instruction. This approach is a relatively straightforward one to employ. The practitioner (sometimes with the help of the young client) draws up a set of helpful self-statements that the client can substitute for the more upsetting self-talk used in a problematic situation. Waters (1982b) illustrates the elicitation of helpful and hurtful self-talk as a prelude to teaching a fourth-grade client the use of rational self-statements to combat her fear of sleeping over at a friend's house.

THERAPIST: Let's work on that right now. There are certain things you can say to yourself to create that scared feeling. Let's make a list of those hurtful thoughts that create that ache all over, that lump in your throat and that "crying" feeling. Once we identify those hurtful things then we can make a list of helpful things you can say to yourself, so you can comfort yourself and make yourself feel better. (Therapist gets out paper and pencil and writes down "Hurtful Thoughts.") Let's first make a list of the hurtful things you can say to yourself to create that scared feeling. If we can identify them then we can inoculate you against them. Let's suppose you are at your friend's house. What would some of those hurtful thoughts be?

CLIENT: Well, I usually feel worse if I've forgotten my stuffed animal, Snoopy, because he comforts me.

THERAPIST: So one might be: "It's awful, I forgot my Snoopy" (writing it down).

CLIENT: Yeah.

THERAPIST: It would be awful if everyone fell asleep before I did.

CLIENT: Yeah and it would be awful if my friend's parents went out and left me alone, or it would be awful if I call my mother to say goodnight and she wasn't home; and I can't think of anything else. Those are the main things.

THERAPIST: Now what we are going to do is come up with comforting, helpful things you can say to yourself to make yourself feel better when you are sleeping at your friend's. (Therapist writes "Helpful Thoughts" on paper.)

CLIENT: I guess I could hug my Snoopy and pretend he's comforting me.

THERAPIST: What would you pretend to have Snoopy say to you to comfort you?

CLIENT: Well, I'd probably have him say that I'm really safe and nothing scary can happen, and I'd probably fall asleep soon and feel better.

THERAPIST: What would be making you feel better?

CLIENT: My comforting thoughts I guess.

THERAPIST: Right. And now what I'd like to do is give you a chance to practice saying those helpful, comforting things to yourself, so when you are at a friend's house it will be easier for you to use what you've just learned to feel better.

CLIENT: I don't think I'm going to be able to do that unless I'm actually at a friend's house.

THERAPIST: You can practice ahead of time, and that way you'll be in a much better position to stop the hurtful thoughts and say the comforting thoughts when the time comes.

CLIENT: You know, I think I was thinking ahead too much and saying too many "what if's" to myself.

THERAPIST: Yes, "what if" is a good thing to ask yourself if you want to worry and scare yourself, because "what if's" create lots of uncertainty. An important thing to remember about "what if's" is that if you ask "what if" be sure you answer the question. For instance, if you ask, "What if she falls asleep first?" you can answer that by saying, "Well, if my friend falls asleep first that's too bad, I'll just try and relax and stay calm until I fall asleep too. So that's not so bad. [pp. 12–13]

The practitioner explains to the young client that by saying these new things when she starts to feel upset she will feel better and be happier. The "helpful self-talk" is typically modeled by the practitioner and then rehearsed aloud and silently by the young client, who is asked to imagine that they are in the troublesome situation. It is most important for the practitioner to reinforce the young client positively during the time the rational self-statements are being learned, as well as when the client in subsequent sessions reports that an attempt was made and/or success was achieved in employing the statements outside the practitioner's office. The young client is also encouraged to provide self-reinforcement in the form of an imaginary "pat on the back." A few examples will illustrate applications of rational self-statements.

Kanfer, Karoly, and Newman (1975) employed the following rational self-statements with six and seven year olds who were afraid of the dark:

Example A: "I am a brave boy (girl). I can take care of myself in the dark."
Example B: "The dark is a fun place to be. There are many good things in the dark."

They found that rational self-statements (Example A) that emphasize the child's competence to deal with the stress-inducing experience of exposure to the dark resulted in the longest tolerance times.

DiGiuseppe (1981) reported the use of self-instructional training with a six year old who was reported by her mother as deeply depressed about her parents' divorce:

Paula's father visited the child every Sunday. When the visits ended Paula cried about missing her dad. Also she cried frequently during the week, often giving the same reason. Coping statements were devised to help Paula ward off depression and crying. If she felt near tears Paula was instructed to say, "My daddy loves me and I'll see him next week." Using dolls and puppets the therapist played scenes where a father and daughter said goodbye and went away from each other. At each separation the child puppet used the coping statement and followed the appropriate behavior of no crying. Paula was then asked to take the role of the child character and use the coping statements in similar scenes. After only two sessions, Paula's crying after her father's visit stopped completely and had not re-occurred at the three-month follow up. [pp. 61–62]

In this case, it can be seen that while rational self-statements can work effectively to moderate emotional upset in a specific situation, one would not expect them to transfer across emotions or problem situations.

Bernard, Kratochwill, and Keefauver (1983), combined the use of rational self-instruction with philosophical disputation to bring about a reduction in the hair pulling of a 17-year-old girl. Disputational training aimed at changing beliefs was in the short run insufficient to totally eliminate hair pulling; moderate changes in the frequency of hair pulling occurred during weeks four through eight. At that point, the practitioner cognitively modeled a set of self-instructions that took the form of a problem-solving dialogue employed in self-instructional training. An example of the self-statements that the client progressively internalized is as follows:

PROBLEM DEFINITION:	"What am I supposed to do?"
PROBLEM APPROACH:	"I'm going to build a protective bubble around me so that nothing worries me until I get my homework done."
FOCUSING OF ATTENTION:	"I'd better pay attention to my assignment. What is the next thing I have to do?"
COPING STATEMENTS:	"Oh, I'm starting to get worried about school . . . and I just pulled out a hair. I know if I just relax and focus on my work that I won't worry."
SELF-REIN- FORCEMENT:	"Hey, that's great. I finished that bit of work. I didn't worry. And I didn't pull my hair. I knew I could do it!"

The introduction of these self-statements led to a rapid cessation of hair pulling. It was impossible to determine the relative effects of disputational training and self-instructional training in this study.

The following case study reported by DiGiuseppe and Bernard (1983) will indicate how RET in the form of rational self-statements can be used with very young and relatively unintelligent children:

Greg was a nine year old child who was referred by his parents for temper tantrums, pouting and non-cooperative behavior. Greg had a family history of extreme non-contingent reward. During most of his life, his parents had pampered him and he was allowed to do what he pleased. While this behavior was cute when he was younger, with maturity it became more unacceptable. Greg's parents attempted to have him follow rules and to behave appropriately. They punished him whenever Greg did not complete chores or age-appropriate behaviors. Greg believed that this meant a change in their affections and that they no longer cared for him. He also thought that it was terribly unfair that he should have to do such mundane things as clean his room and put his dirty clothes in the hamper. These things were just too difficult. Greg was a non-verbal child with low average intelligence and had difficulty following many of the disputing strategies. However, he was able to role play these situations with the therapist. During these role plays, the therapist modeled verbal self instructions such as "My parents care for me, they are only trying to do their job and help me grow up." "I don't have to feel upset about these things, I can do them." Through practicing these self statements and receiving reinforcement for appropriate behavior, Greg slowly learned to stop pouting and this provided the impetus for more mature, independent behaviors. [p. 74]

Empirical Analysis. A second, more complex solution for solving the emotional problems of young clients is achieved when the practitioner changes the inferences children make of their distortion of reality (DiGiuseppe & Bernard, 1983). While *not* tackling the client's irrational appraisals of distortions of reality, the empirical solution frequently results in a moderation of affect and an improvement in behavior, and is easier to teach young clients than is philosophical disputation. The practitioner is hereby warned, however, that empirical analysis taxes intellectual and creative resources. It is at first a difficult approach to master.

If one wishes to use this approach with children, it is most important that the young client is taught the basic concepts, such as (1) discriminating among facts, opinions, inferences, and assumptions and (2) the insight that what they are thinking and the ideas that they and others such as parents and teachers hold may not be true. DiGiuseppe (1981) provides some suggestions for teaching the child the importance of empirically testing ideas:

> This can be done by telling about ideas that people believed in the past but that we now know are different. For example, people once believed that the earth was flat and that the sun revolved around our planet, but through theory building and testing we know differently. [pp. 62–63]

The degree to which empirical analysis can be used depends partly on whether children can acquire these concepts and on the generalizability of the idea being empirically analyzed. The more concrete the idea, the easier it is to achieve an empirical solution. A case example will illustrate the use of empirical analysis. Craig, an extremely bright 13 year old (IQ 130+), was seen over an extended period to help him control his excessive worrying. In Craig's case, excessive worry led to Craig working too hard at school, getting tired, and eventually falling prey to periodic anxiety-related physical illnesses.

In spending many weekly sessions with Craig, it appeared that Craig held the idea that for him to achieve his goal at school of receiving very good grades, he must always put 100% effort in his homework. He seemed to accept this idea unquestioningly and interpreted all school assignments as requiring a total effort. Over weeks and weeks, little success was seen in getting Craig to cut some corners in his schoolwork when he found himself getting tired. Craig relentlessly pushed himself to the limit when objectively there was no reason why he had to push himself to the extreme. That is, it appeared highly probable that Craig could attain his goals with less of an effort. Rather than continuing to dispute with Craig his self-defined perfectionistic demand to be successful at his schoolwork, it was decided that an empirical analysis of Craig's untested ideas concerning the amount of effort required for success should be put to the test.

The cognitive-analytic question the therapist put to himself to set the stage for empirical analysis was, "What does Craig probably think about the importance of studying hard?" This was answered: "To achieve good grades in school, I must work as hard as I possibly can." Craig readily agreed that this was something "I probably do believe" although he had not considered it before. It was explained to Craig that it was quite possible that this belief (1) was what may be forcing him to work so hard, (2) may or may not be true, and (3) could be examined to see if it was true through conducting an experiment. Craig took up the challenge and agreed that if his idea was proved to be false he would restate it. The hypothesis that both the practitioner and Craig agreed to put to this test was, "I must put in high effort to obtain satisfactory grades." The experiment involved decreasing his effort in studying for a history exam. Craig agreed to review the material only once and not to overprepare. The hypothesis would be rejected if he obtained 85 or higher and rejected with a mark lower than 85. Two weeks later Craig reported he received a grade of 89 and was quite happy with the result. With no help from the practitioner, he concluded that he would put in less effort to get good grades and he would try to put his new idea into practice.

This episode was somewhat of a breakthrough in that up until that time Craig could not control the amount of time he worked, due to his fear of failure. When he realized that less work meant more fun and equally good grades, he was able to relax his approach to his studying.

DiGiuseppe (1981) described the case of Paul, a 10 year old who displayed a variety of antisocial behaviors such as temper tantrums and yelling at his parents. A behavioral analysis revealed that Paul generally argued whenever his parents disagreed on an issue, even if the difference of opinion did not result in a fight. A cognitive assessment indicated Paul endorsed two antiempirical ideas: (1) that disagreement leads to divorce; and (2) that he could not survive if his parents separated. DiGiuseppe elected to work on the first troublesome idea, as the second one is an exceedingly difficult one to dispute with children.

I asked Paul to set up an experiment to test his hypothesis that disagreement leads to divorce. He was willing to do so and we designed a questionnaire for this purpose. Paul polled his teacher and principal, several store-keepers, a police officer, and others about whether they decided to divorce every time they argued with their spouses. Paul found that disagreements were common in marriage and rarely resulted in divorce. His symptoms ceased. [p. 64]

Bard and Fisher (personal communication) demonstrate how the faulty inference of an adolescent, "Everything will turn out okay," can be corrected through the combined use of an empirical analysis and behavioral methods.

Dale T., for example, a 17 year old senior with high intelligence, had managed to con his parents and teachers, avoiding academic work and achieving marginal grades throughout high school. His mother blamed and nagged him. His father, a successful businessman, had given him various "incentives" to get better grades and the most recent was a car. Charming, pleasant, Dale had attended therapy sessions assuring the therapist that he would do much better academically, was much better motivated since his father gave him a car, could overcome his "laziness," etc. Obviously, everything would turn out O.K., except the work was not forthcoming and his academic achievement remained marginal. The parents were involved directly and committed themselves to the incentive program, stop nagging, resist being conned and to stick with this approach. The school counselor in turn worked with Dale's teachers to accept only conformity to rules, deadlines and assignments. Dale became less cheery and chatty, getting down to business with some distress and many complaints. He was directed to discuss goals and shown that his underachievement of the past three years was the direct result of his erroneously believing that everything would turn out O.K. whether or not he worked. He painfully started working and discovered that he was poorly prepared to enter college. He was able to define some academic and vocational goals meaningful to him, had been accepted into a college program and was able to minimize avoidance and manipulation, as his pleasure ticket through the remainder of his senior year. In giving up his belief that everything would turn out O.K. without work, he was able to see that with work, effort and planning many of his goals could be achieved.

In this example, we can see how faulty inferences about the relationship between effort and achievement lead an adolescent to interpret inaccurately the consequences of his behavior. It can be clearly seen in this example that faulty assumptions can lead to self-defeating behavior without the mediation of strong emotional arousal. While Dale in fact may experience low frustration tolerance because of his belief that "Life should be fun at all times," no doubt his other assumption that everything will be all right prevented him from even approaching school tasks that might occasion discomfort anxiety.

Another example by DiGiuseppe and Bernard (1983) will indicate how young children can be taught to change inferences concerning the meaning of events in their lives:

Sara was a nine year old girl who was particularly depressed because of the infrequency with which she saw her father. Her parents had been divorced for 6 years and her mother and father still continued to argue. Sara had a large number of siblings all of whom were much older than her and experienced a great deal of animosity towards the father. The father reacted by avoiding them. Our discussions revealed that Sara believed that since her father did not love or care for her mother or her siblings, he could not really care for her. Empirical disputing of this inference tested out quite the opposite. While the father made little attempt to see the siblings and continued to argue with the mother whenever he came to visit Sara, he came to visit Sara quite regularly. While dad was not the most demonstrative person, he was much more dedicated to this child than to any of his others and spent considerable amount of time visiting her, calling her, taking her places. Sara's upset was caused first by her inference that her father's behavior towards other members of the family indicated that he felt the same way towards her and the appraisal that if he did not care for her that would be catastrophic. Sara was quite unwilling even to discuss this last possibility. Challenging the idea that it wouldn't be terrible if a father didn't care for her led to silence and withdrawal. However, the empirical solution here got her quite interested in collecting data to verify her inferences. She was pleased with the results. This strategy was acceptable because of the therapist's inference that the father really did care for Sara. If the empirical disputing had not led in the direction it did, a more elegant approach would have been necessary. But here it was acceptable to limit ourselves with the empirical solution. [pp. 73–74]

A final word needs to be said concerning the use of empirical analysis. It is the case, as DiGiuseppe (1981) indicates, that children are sometimes faced with unchangeable, aversive events such as parents not caring. It would be a misdirected and inappropriate use of the strategy if a practitioner attempted to convince a child through "rigging" an experiment that a parent loved and cared for him when all evidence pointed to the contrary. As DiGiuseppe has insightfully observed, such "conning" teaches the child a warped sense of values and distorted meanings for the concepts of "love" and "caring" which might lead to negative and unintended interpersonal effects for the child later in life. When it appears that the young client is being brought up in an uncaring environment, a suggested course of action (apart from working directly with the parents where possible) is to teach the young child that he may be happy with the rest of his life, even though things at home may not be what he would desire them to be.

Disputation. The most widely used strategy for modifying irrational thinking is *disputation* (challenging). Challenging is used whenever and in whatever form possible to examine and change the variety of irrational concepts and beliefs that underlie emotional and behavioral problems of school-age children. Once the ABC's of RET have been taught, disputational techniques are employed to dissuade a young client from irrational thinking. Most of the work with young clients have employed cognitive methods for challenging irrationality, and it is to these we now turn.

There are a number of basic irrational concepts (e.g., "demandingness," "awfulizing," "self-downing") that interact to define the different irrational beliefs of the childhood period. These concepts operate in various combinations to produce different problems. The major role of disputation is to teach the client how to challenge these concepts and to reformulate them into rational counterparts. For older and more cognitively mature adolescents, it is possible to employ the RET preferential techniques of philosophical disputation of general and abstract irrational beliefs to bring about elegant solutions. With those young clients who are unable to handle the degree of abstraction required to achieve a preferential solution, it is suggested that the practitioner help the client examine the irrational concepts contained in their faulty appraisal of specific activating events about which they are upsetting themselves.

Howard Young (1974, 1983) has made significant contributions in demonstrating how philosophical disputation can be employed with adolescents. While his down-to-earth approach takes into account the difficulties of working with adolescents, he still manages to employ cognitive disputation effectively and relies heavily on "semantic clarity" to help teenagers rethink their problems.

Young (1983) indicates that, while he sometimes teaches adolescents the ABC model, introducing it verbally and using a cartoon drawing or illustration, he does not spend a great deal of time on presenting the formula. He prefers to tackle the irrational concepts that underlie adolescent thinking rather than having them understand the logic of RET theory. We now refer to Young's and others' methods and techniques for changing irrational thinking.

When the practitioner discovers evidence of "shoulds," "oughts," and "musts" together with the tendency for adolescents to treat their wants as desires ("I must have my way because it is deserved, earned, right, fair, just, etc."), Young (1983) suggests attempting to help his teenage clients to understand that using such absolutistic thinking results in both emotional and interpersonal difficulties. He suggests the following tactics:

1. Using "must" in place of "should." Teenagers use the word "should" so frequently and indiscriminately that sometimes just getting them to change the word to "must" gets the imperative quality across. Once this is established, they can begin to learn how to live without absolutes.
2. Using "gotta" in place of "should." "I should get an A" makes sense to a lot of teenagers, but "I gotta get an A" often encourages them to see the error of their ways.
3. Changing "should" to "no right." Another method of getting across the absolutistic meaning of "should," especially with angry teenagers, is to exchange "He shouldn't do that" for "He's got no right to do that." The irrationality of "He's got no right" is often easy for some teenagers to understand.
4. Using the want–need concept. Another way of getting teenagers to recognize and challenge absolutes is to teach them the difference between wanting and needing. I have found some of the most resistant and stubborn young people,

especially those involved in behavioral excesses, are capable of understanding the critical distinction between desires and necessities and of using this insight productively.

5. Teaching "should" equals unbreakable law. I sometimes get somewhere with young clients who have difficulty understanding the absolutistic meaning of "shoulds" and "musts" by suggesting they are upset because their self-proclaimed laws have been broken. "Debbie's Commandments have been violated," or "It was Tom's turn to be God, and he got upset because someone broke one of His rules," are examples of this approach. Once the adolescents understand what it means to be unrealistically demanding, I proceed to show them they do not run the universe, so they would better expect things to go wrong. [pp. 95–96]

In the following therapy concept, Walen et al. (1980, pp. 137–139) illustrate how to distinguish wants from needs. The client is a seven-year-old girl who is having trouble making friends at school.

THERAPIST: Do you need to play with them?
CLIENT: What does "need" mean?
THERAPIST: A need means this: what are some of the things that you need? You need water. What happens if you don't have water?
CLIENT: You die.
THERAPIST: That's right. What happens if you don't have food?
CLIENT: Die.
THERAPIST: That's right. Can we say that you need food?
CLIENT: Yeah.
THERAPIST: And water?
CLIENT: Yeah.
THERAPIST: And air?
CLIENT: Yeah.
THERAPIST: That's right. Do you *need* television?
CLIENT: No.
THERAPIST: But sometimes you say you need to watch TV, don't you?
CLIENT: Yeah, 'cause I like to.
THERAPIST: Yeah, you like to and you want to, but that's not a need is it?
CLIENT: No.
THERAPIST: No it's not. Do you need candy canes and ice cream?
CLIENT: No.
THERAPIST: You don't need them, but you want them, don't you?
CLIENT: Yeah.
THERAPIST: But you don't need them, do you?
CLIENT: No.
THERAPIST: Do you see the difference between a *want* and a *need*? What's the difference? You try to explain it to me.
CLIENT: A need is what you need to help you to live.
THERAPIST: A need is something you've got to have to live.

CLIENT: And a want is that you want to have it.

THERAPIST: That's right. You'd *like* to have it, it's enjoyable. Now what about: Lisa wants the kids in school to like her. Is that a want or a need?

CLIENT: A want.

THERAPIST: It's a want, right?

CLIENT: Right.

THERAPIST: So we talked a little bit about wants and needs. Now what happens if you tell yourself "Oh I *need* to have so-and-so play with me in school—I need to have her like me." How do you think you're going to feel if she doesn't like you?

CLIENT: Sad.

THERAPIST: Sad. Like sad a whole lot or sad a little bit?

CLIENT: A lot.

THERAPIST: A lot. How about if you said, "I need to have Kate like me and *need* to be her friend."

CLIENT: I *want* to be her friend.

THERAPIST: "I want to be her friend." Oh, but isn't there a difference? If you said, "I need to be her friend" and she wasn't, how would you feel?

CLIENT: And she wouldn't?

THERAPIST: And she wouldn't. And you said, "I gotta have her friendship—I need it to live—and she won't be my friend."

CLIENT: Sad.

THERAPIST: You'd be very sad. So what if you said to yourself instead, "I would like to have Kate like me. I want to be her friend, but if she's not gonna be my friend, I can live without it." Would you be sad a little bit or sad a lot?

CLIENT: Sad a little.

The second irrational concept that is subject to disputation is that of "awfulizing." The tendency to blow things out of proportion, to make mountains out of molehills, is characteristic of the thinking of people of all ages. In making adolescent clients aware that they are "awfulizing," and that more sensible and level-headed thinking is required, Young (1983) suggests the following:

1. Substituting the words disaster, catastrophe, or tragedy for awful, terrible, or horrible. The words awful, terrible, or horrible are so much a part of the average adolescent's working vocabulary that I have found it difficult to convince the adolescent that the meaning behind such words is the cause of his suffering. The emotionally distressed adolescent who insists his problem is awful is asked, "Was it a disaster?" or "Was it really a tragedy?" These words have a more precise meaning and can be subjected to question and reason more easily than "awful."

2. Using the phrase "end of the world" to show the client he or she is "awfulizing." Again I find that asking, "Would it be the end of the world?" usually elicits an eye-rolling "Of course not" from most adolescents and permits the next question "Then exactly what would it be?" The answer, almost always in the realm of realistic disadvantage, begins to persuade the client to correct his or her exaggerated evaluation of the problem.

3. Using the phrase "a fate worse than death." Once more the use of a familiar but obviously magnified term sometimes helps adolescents to begin to understand that their excessive, disturbing feelings come from exaggerated, unrealistic ideas in their minds.

4. Asking, "Could it be any worse?" Often young clients exaggerate, considering a situation totally bad. Encouraging them to conjure something that could make their problem even worse sometimes enables them to see that it is highly unlikely that any disadvantage (especially their own) is one-hundred-percent bad. This tactic can sometimes be used in a humorous way by adding all kinds of ridiculous dimensions to the problem situation. I find this approach helps clients realize that problems are not always as bad as they think they are; by viewing situations in less exaggerated and more realistic terms, they learn to feel much less distressed.

5. Asking, "What's the worst that could actually happen?" I show anxiety-ridden teenagers they are catastrophizing their complaints by encouraging them to focus on the most realistic but worst outcome they can imagine. This forces them to stay away from possibilities and to concentrate on actualities. In essence, they are learning to deal with the hassle and not the horror of the problem. [p. 95]

In working with young clients, it is frequently useful in helping them place a problem in perspective to employ a device called a catastrophe list developed by DiGiuseppe and Waters (in Walen et al., 1980). This technique, which can be employed with clients of all ages, has been described by Walen et al. (1980) as follows:

> On a blackboard or large sheet of paper, have the children list all the catastrophes they can think of (given the recent spate of catastrophic films and TV shows, this is easily accomplished). After listing towering infernos, tidal waves, invasions from outer space, earthquakes and atomic blasts, the therapist "remembers" one more, the child's complaint (e.g., "Tommy sat in my seat"). It will probably not be necessary to point out that one item does not belong on the list. [p. 126]

An irrational concept that is related to "awfulizing" and leads to a variety of behavioral effects (underachievement, drug addiction) associated with low frustration tolerance and discomfort anxiety is what we refer to as "I-can't-stand-it-itis." In working with adolescents who strongly believe that they cannot withstand any inconvenience or discomfort, Young (1983) recommends the following:

1. Substituting "unbearable" for "can't stand." Often I can help a young client realize how pernicious the "can't stand" concept is by equating it with the term "unbearable." Hearing things put this way, many teenagers conclude, "Well, it's not *that* bad. I mean I can *bear* it."

2. Explaining "difficult" versus "impossible." Often the "can't stand" concept can be better understood by investigating whether a particular problem situation is

impossible or is merely difficult to tolerate. Even some of the most resistant teenagers, grasping this point, can realize that just because something is a pain in the neck does not mean it cannot be lived with.

3. Substituting "won't" for "can't." Frequently, when I hear the word "can't," I quickly substitute "won't." This is an effective way of showing that the situation is governed by one's attitude, which is under the individual's control. It is the attitude, not the situation, that is overwhelming.

4. Suggesting to the client that he or she *is* tolerating the conflict in question. In spite of his complaints and protests, I remind him, he *is* enduring the problem. This tactic is especially useful with clients experiencing long-running problems with parents, teachers, or siblings. For example, the teenager who threatens to quit school in his senior year because he claims he can no longer stomach the bullshit is advised that he is, in fact, stomaching things. He may be miserable but he has, nevertheless, been putting up with school for twelve years, and this qualifies him as an outstanding stomacher of bullshit!

5. Explaining that a genuine "can't stand" situation would either end the client's life or render her unconscious. I frequently suggest that if her problem were truly impossible to bear, it would either cost her life or she would likely pass out from the overwhelming agony involved. Up to that point, I suggest, the client is standing the adversity or discomfort; she may not like it, but she is standing it. [p. 96–97]

Another major irrational concept underlying much child and adolescent irrational thinking that may be directly disputed is that of "self-downing" ("I'm bad if I make a mistake"; "I shouldn't make social mistakes"). This is an especially difficult concept to teach, as many children may not have achieved sufficient cognitive maturity to preserve a positive concept of self in the face of negative and contradictory evidence. Moreover, adolescents frequently judge themselves solely on the basis of peer opinion (Young, 1983). As low self-esteem may underly a variety of behavioral and emotional problems, it is most important that the RET practitioner spend when possible several sessions teaching the young clients the basic notion that it makes little sense to judge how "good" or "bad" they are on the basis of a small aspect of their behavior. Doing so can only lead to unhappiness and self-defeating behavior. RET practitioners go to great lengths to provide young clients with a multidimensional cognitive scheme for viewing their "selfs." Basic ideas we utilize in teaching the principle of "self-acceptance" are:

1. Every person is complex, not simple.
2. I am complex, not simple.
3. Every person is made up of many positive and negative qualities.
4. I am made up of many positive and negative qualities.
5. A person is not all good or bad because of some of her or his characteristics.
6. I am not all good or all bad.

7. When I only focus on the negative characteristics of a person, I feel worse about the person.
8. When I only focus on my negative qualities, I feel worse about myself.
9. Focusing *only* on my negative qualities is irrational. I have other positive qualities.
10. When I think negative, irrational thoughts about myself, I get more upset with myself than if I think negative rational thoughts.

The most elegant solution to self-downing is if the client accepts the basic RET principle that human beings are not rateable insofar as there is no commonly agreed-upon and exhaustive definition of "good" and "bad" people. We generally do not attempt this solution with younger clients, as its level of abstraction is too far removed from their life context and day-to-day concerns. Instead, we opt to teach youngsters not to use negative qualities that they and others perceive in themselves as sole criteria for deciding whether they are "okay" or "not okay." In as persuasive and forceful a way as possible we try to change their attitude toward and beliefs about their mistake making and imperfections and to get them to adopt a self-concept that incorporates the good as well as the bad. For example, we frequently use a *self-concept wheel* to illustrate a number of these basic ideas (Knaus, 1974). The client is invited to insert a range of their positive and negative personal characteristics, traits, and behaviors in the smaller circles that appear inside the self-concept wheel. The "positives" are used to dispute with the client the belief that he is bad because he may do things badly or breaks rules. Challenging feelings of inferiority is the central task in helping young clients overcome feelings of frustration, anger, guilt, and jealousy, as well as solving problems of procrastination, short-term behavior (sensation seeking), stealing, and physical violence.

Young (1983) demonstrates his creative application of RET by suggesting the following ways of combating "self-downing":

1. Using a visual aid. I draw a circle and label it "self." Next I draw a series of smaller circles inside the "self" circle. These represent the various traits, characteristics, and performances of the individual client. I try to demonstrate that rating one trait or feature as bad does not make all the other circles bad. In essence, I try to show adolescents they are a collection of qualities, some good and some bad, none of which equal the whole self.
2. Using an analogy. Although many examples can illustrate the illogicality of overgeneralizing from act to personhood, I have found that the flat tire example works best with teenagers. I ask if they would junk a whole car because it had a flat tire. The key word is junk. Once the client picks up on this word-image, I use it thereafter when they overgeneralize about mistakes or criticism. "There you go again," I tell them, "junking yourself because you did such and such."
3. Helping the client understand that although one is responsible for what one does, one is not the same as one does. This is sometimes tricky for adolescents

to understand. They frequently argue that if they do something bad, they too are bad. I counter by suggesting, "If you went around mooing like a cow, would that make you a cow?" I usually receive a negative answer. Then I say, "But you are the one doing it. How come it doesn't turn you into a cow?" A few more examples like this one, and clients usually begin to separate what they do from who they are.

4. Explaining the difference between a person-with-less and less-of-a-person. Young clients suffering from feelings of shame, embarrassment, or inferiority have usually fallen victim to downing or degrading themselves. To the client who gets criticized or makes mistakes I point out that such problems only prove he is a person with less of what he wants (success or approval) rather than less of a person. Sometimes I illustrate this principle by taking something from him (a shoe, a watch, etc.) and then asking, "What are you now? Are you less of a person or just a person with less of what you want?"

5. Showing that blaming oneself is like being punished twice for the same crime. With those adolescents who damn themselves and feel excessively guilty, I usually try to illustrate that mistakes and failings have built-in penalties. Whenever we err, I point out, we not only disappoint ourselves and fail to live up to our own standards, but we likely endure some kind of adverse consequence. Through examples I help clients to see that just living with the disappointments or consequences of their actions is punishment enough. Adding to it by damning oneself only adds insult to injury and makes matters worse than they need be. [pp. 97–98]

The following excerpt from a conversation with a 17-year-old girl illustrates how the girl's jealousy of her friend can be treated by teaching the client a more self-accepting view.

THERAPIST: You seem pretty upset. What are your feelings right now?

CLIENT: Well, I don't really know. It's not right, that's all.

THERAPIST: What do you mean, it's not right? What's not right?

CLIENT: Just because the others suck up to the teacher, they never get into trouble or have to repeat their homework. They get all the good things. The teacher likes them and I'm a nothing!

THERAPIST: Well, Jane, I can see there's some things there that are upsetting you. But as we've discussed previously, it is your thoughts about the situation that are causing this, that are making you feel worthless and jealous of your friends.

CLIENT: So what if I'm jealous? What does that change?

THERAPIST: It can change your feelings because it's your thoughts about the situation that control your emotions. Now, who said the teacher had to like you as much or more than the others? Is there anything that says a teacher isn't human and can't like some people more than others? Is it absolutely 100% "awful" that the teacher doesn't like you?

CLIENT: No, but . . .

THERAPIST: And even if your teacher doesn't think highly of you, and your friends are better off, that might not be fun, but it's not the end of the world. It

CLIENT: That's true, but it doesn't make things any easier for me.

THERAPIST: If you continue to think irrationally then it won't get any easier for you. If you're going to judge yourself on how much someone likes you and how much better off your friends are than you, then you'll waste so much energy being upset that you won't be able to do anything about changing your situation. Look at this objectively and you'll feel less upset.

CLIENT: I guess you're right. It's not so bad that this teacher doesn't like me. Other people like me. And my friends aren't always better off than me—and it wouldn't matter if they were!

THERAPIST: Why wouldn't it matter?

CLIENT: Because I'm not a worthless person just because somebody has more than me, or because somebody doesn't attend to me when I want them to.

THERAPIST: That's right. It doesn't matter how much attention and approval you get, it's not going to matter if you don't like yourself. And things aren't going to be the way you want at times, so you try to change them, or accept their existence.

CLIENT: Okay, I understand. Let me continue. It would be nice to do better, and if I try to get my homework done, I might have a more pleasant time in that class. And it would be better for me to concentrate on liking myself more instead of trying to get the teacher's attention. How's that for changing my irrational thoughts?

There are a number of irrational beliefs of school-age children that contain the component of mistake making (e.g., "I'm bad if I make a mistake"; "Adults should be perfect"; "I shouldn't make mistakes, especially social mistakes"). It is frequently the case that a young client believes that other people who are in positions of authority (parents, teachers) should never make mistakes (act unfairly). In getting the client to give up the demand for perfection in others, it is sometimes necessary to educate the client on the nature of and reasons underlying mistake making. Some of the ideas that we include in a mini-lecture are:

1. Everyone will always make mistakes.
2. No one is perfect.
3. Mistakes do not change a person's good qualities.
4. A person is not the same as his performance.
5. People are not bad because they make mistakes.
6. People who make mistakes do not deserve to be blamed and punished.
7. The reasons why people make mistakes are (a) lack of skill, (b) carelessness or poor judgment, (c) not having enough information, (d) unsound assumptions, (e) tired or ill, (f) different opinion, and (g) irrationality (adapted from Knaus, 1974).

The rational attitude that it is hoped will be adopted by the young client after discussion is that there is no point in overly upsetting oneself to the point where one's behavior compromises one's goals simply because someone is making a mistake such as not treating one fairly. Examples of rational self-statements that we have employed with a client who unduly upsets himself about his teacher's behavior are, "Oh well, there is my teacher acting stupidly again. I wish he was fairer. I'm irritated that he does not believe me when I tell him I've left my homework at home. He's probably having a bad day. No point in getting too angry."

For children and adolescents who put themselves down or get angry when they make mistakes, the following type of dialogue can be employed: "I can't quite get the hang of this. No point in getting too upset. I'll stay calm and try my best; mistakes are what learning is all about."

Another irrational concept that permeates childhood irrationality is that of fairness ("Parents should be fair"; "Schools and teachers should be fair at all times"). Fairness can be discussed at two levels. At the interpretation stage, it is often possible to have the young client examine his judgment of fairness to determine whether others would agree that his judgment of "unfairness" is an objective and sound one. For example, Robert, age 12, was referred for general aggressiveness and underachievement. During the period he was seen, he was suspended for three days because he refused to report to the principal's office after school to serve a detention he was given earlier in the day for fighting. Robert thought it was unfair that the principal gave him a detention when it really was not his fault that he got into the fight. The following discussion took place:

THERAPIST: What happened?

CLIENT: I got into trouble for fighting.

THERAPIST: Describe to me what went on.

CLIENT: I was wrestling with a friend. Had him in a headlock. Some other kid came up and was going to jump on my back. I swung around and hit him.

THERAPIST: And then what happened?

CLIENT: I was told to see the principal but I didn't go.

THERAPIST: Why not?

CLIENT: It wasn't my fault.

THERAPIST: How come?

CLIENT: He shouldn't have bothered us. We were playing by ourselves and he should have stayed away.

THERAPIST: But you struck the first blow?

CLIENT: (nods) If I didn't he would have jumped on me and hurt me.

THERAPIST: You sure?

CLIENT: Uh-huh.

THERAPIST: Look, Robert. I'm on your side, right?

CLIENT: Uh-huh.

THERAPIST: How do you know that?

CLIENT: You want to help me.

THERAPIST: That's right. Now I'm going to disagree with you that what happened was unfair, but remember, I'm on your side. O.K.?

CLIENT: Yes.

THERAPIST: Well, first of all, it sounds to me that you started it. You hit the other boy first?

CLIENT: Uh-huh.

THERAPIST: What is the school rule for fighting?

CLIENT: You're not supposed to.

THERAPIST: What happens if you get caught?

CLIENT: Probably put on the "D" [detention] list.

THERAPIST: Well then, was it fair for you to be given a detention by the principal?

CLIENT: No.

THERAPIST: Why?

CLIENT: Because I didn't start it.

THERAPIST: As the school rule is "no fighting" and it doesn't matter who starts it, I think it was fair that you were given a detention because you broke the law. Just imagine you're driving a car and exceeding the speed limit because you're thinking about something else and your mind isn't on the job. It's a bright sunny day and the road is free of much traffic. All of a sudden a police officer stops you and begins to give you a ticket for speeding. You say that it's not fair to get a ticket because you didn't mean to speed. The officer gives you one anyway. Who's fair in that situation?

CLIENT: The police officer.

THERAPIST: Why?

CLIENT: Because I was speeding.

THERAPIST: And what would happen if you didn't pay the ticket?

CLIENT: Go to jail?

THERAPIST: Well you might have to pay an even bigger fine, just like you had to serve a three-day suspension for not reporting for detention. Do you see that?

CLIENT: Yes.

THERAPIST: Now when you are in school, you have to obey the laws as well and you can't just say it's unfair because you didn't mean to. If you break a rule even if it wasn't totally your fault, it's fair to have to pay a ticket. Do you agree?

CLIENT: I guess.

THERAPIST: So in the future, try and think ahead and remember that if you break a rule, you'll have to pay the price.

The preferential solution, which was not attempted with Robert, was to work on the appraisal of "unfairness." The practitioner may use the previously described techniques for disputing "awfulizing" and "can't-stand-it-itis" in helping the client place the problem of unfairness on a continuum and in emphasizing that unfairness is a hassle and not a horror. In disputing the demandingness that often is an associated approach with ideas about fairness, the practitioner can simply teach that the world is an unfair place and that one had better not be surprised by or expect anything other than unfairness from time to time. Clients are encouraged to remain calm in the face of unfairness so that they are in a position to change things when possible and accept those things one cannot change. DiGiuseppe and Bernard (1983) illustrate how RET can be used to change a young client's appraisal of one particular unfair activating event:

Thomas was a 13 year old student with a history of behavioral and academic problems. Thomas reported that his teacher had a great dislike for him and she *had* become quite disgusted with him. As therapy progressed, Thomas made changes and behaved more appropriately in school. He became less angry, and less disruptive. However, empirical disputing of his thoughts that the teacher did not like him appeared to be accurate. Given the way he had been behaving it was hard to blame her. When Thomas would make some improvements or behaved well, she frequently did not acknowledge them or still accused him of behaving inappropriately. Thomas became angry at this point with the action potential of giving up and acting badly again. His irrational beliefs leading to this anger were somewhat along the lines that "people should be fair." My attempts to dispute this idea with Thomas got nowhere. He believed people should be fair. After all, how would the world survive if people couldn't be trusted. Fairness was necessary for social life, so he said. Rather than trying to convince him that unfairness was a fact of life, which it was, and that there were probably millions of unfair people out there, we focused on a more narrow set of beliefs. That is, that this particular teacher had to be fair. We discussed: particular reasons why she could be unfair; how we could not change her even though we thought most people should be fair; to have an ordered world we could not demand that she be fair and there is no way we could force her to be so. While Thomas was not willing to accept the fact that unfairness would survive in the universe, he was willing to concede that this particular individual would remain unfair and that he could tolerate that little degree of unfairness. Thus, while we did not reach an elegant solution in changing his appraisal to a wide span of stimuli, we did teach him to appraise this particular stimulus in a much different way. His anger was reduced and he continued to make behavioral gains throughout the school year. [p. 73]

There is one other irrational idea that we uncover daily in working with children and adolescents, which is that hard work and unpleasantness is something to be avoided at all times. The inability to tolerate the feelings associated with anxiety, frustration, anger, and the like is revealed across many irrational beliefs of the childhood period ("Things should come easily to me"; "I shouldn't have to wait for anything"; "Everything should be entertaining and/or enjoyable, with no unpleasantness whatsoever"). People appear to have different tolerance levels for dealing with frustration and stress, and these propensities underlie many different disorders. Low frustration tolerance is one of the most difficult tendencies to overcome. While it is relatively easy to dispute the irrational beliefs that underlie it, it is perhaps the most difficult area clients have in putting thoughts into action. The instinct for pleasure seeking and pain avoidance seems to far outweigh the pull of rationality.

In disputing ideas that underlie low frustration tolerance, it is most important that the practitioner combine cognitive and behavioral methods. A brief case examination will illustrate this approach. Darren, age 12, was seen over a three-month period for underachievement. Darren's main problem appeared to be an inability to settle down and start work and a tendency to tire and give up too quickly. A reasonably bright seventh grader, Darren's grades were generally in the C range. It became fairly apparent in talking with Darren that he had developed the bad habit of avoiding work whenever he began to think about doing his homework. Homework-related thoughts such as, "This is going to be hard work, I'll be missing out on my favorite television show; I really can't be bothered with all of this" led to mild feelings of discomfort anxiety, which Darren escalated into intense unpleasantness and arousal by labeling his initial anxiety as being extremely painful and intolerable. By this stage, Darren looked for any way out.

In helping Darren overcome his discomfort anxiety, the following rationale was used: "There is no question that hard work can be unpleasant. However, as you will probably agree, one of the hardest parts of hard work is getting started. Getting started is like getting over a hump, or a mental obstacle. Once you get over the obstacle, you'll be fine. Now, what we can do today and for the next weeks is to help you develop mental skills so you can get over your mental hump in the road with as little fuss as possible. There are two basic mental skills you will need to learn. First is to improve your concentration so you do not distract yourself with thoughts that divert you from your goal. Second, you will have to learn to accept that you will sometimes feel uncomfortable and that that's okay—a fact of life. What we hope to do is to get you into condition so that you will be less distracted and troubled by your feelings when you are preparing to study."

Stress inoculation and RET were combined to help Darren prepare for and deal with feelings of anxiety and to acquire a more rational way of looking at and describing different aspects of emotional reactions vis-à-vis the time he spent studying. Darren was also asked to monitor the amount of time he spent studying each night, which was graphed on a weekly basis and provided the basis for goal setting. He was shown how in his case it was better to start with easier subjects for homework rather than the more difficult ones, as his school study guide suggested. His teachers were informed of the program and agreed to make extra efforts to praise Darren's efforts. Overall, an attempt was made to get Darren to trade the immediate payoffs of work avoidance for the delayed satisfaction of teacher approval of improved grades. Without receiving any help or support at home from his mother (Darren's father had left home), Darren achieved a solid B performance for his final term's work, and the query as to whether Darren should repeat grade 7 was answered in the negative.

Rational–Emotive Imagery (REI). REI is a procedure for learning how to change emotions through changing cognitions. It has been described by Ellis as an "emotive disputational procedure," as its focus is initially more on emotional than cognitive change. Our experience with younger clients is that it is a procedure that is more effective and less threatening when employed after the client has achieved some intellectual insight into the ABC's of RET and, as a consequence, some coping skills. If early on in therapy a young client is asked to imagine a scene that evokes extremely painful sensations, the client may lose trust in the practitioner and, as has happened, terminate therapy. So it is important to make sure that the client is prepared for a potentially upsetting experience. Maultsby (1971) has indicated, and we agree, that REI is especially good for clients who seem to have accepted the RET viewpoint but who lack the emotional muscle to put it into practice.

We present a portion of Virginia Waters' (1982b) transcript to illustrate how REI can be combined with rational self-statements to produce emotional change in a young client.

THERAPIST: Now let's imagine a scene. First I'll play you and you can play the part of your friend. We'll pretend it's bedtime and I'll show you how you can say the comforting things to yourself to feel calmer. Then I'll give you a chance to practice.

CLIENT: OK.

THERAPIST: You begin and tell me it's time to go to bed and I'll take it from there.

CLIENT: Well, it's time to go to bed. Good night.

THERAPIST: Well, it's time to go to bed. I'm beginning to get that uncomfortable feeling, but it's not *too* uncomfortable. Now let's see what can I say to myself to make myself feel better. I'm very safe here. My friend is next to me and her parents are in the next room. I don't have to make myself feel uncomfortable by thinking those scarey thoughts and "what ifs" to myself. I'll have Snoopy talk to me and see what he has to say. I even feel comfortable lying here. I know I can see my mother tomorrow and she'll be fine and my father is fine and I feel pretty comfortable and I think I'm falling asleep. (snore)

CLIENT: (enthusiastically) And there's nothing to worry about if you sit down and think about it.

THERAPIST: That's right. There's absolutely nothing to worry about right now.

CLIENT: And I'm going to see my mother the next day. I'm only here for six hours, just for the night.

THERAPIST: That's right. Do you want to try it?

CLIENT: I don't think I could say all those things.

THERAPIST: That's OK. You don't have to do it just like I did. Just say what comes into your mind and then if you need some help we can write it down for you. OK?

CLIENT: Alright.

THERAPIST: Oh, it's time to go to bed!

CLIENT: Oh no! OK . . . Well, what do I have to worry about? Nothing! I have all my stuffed animals here. I have things to comfort me. I'm going to see my mother tomorrow. There's nothing to worry about. So I'll try and fall asleep before I say all those "what ifs" to myself. So I'll just try and fall asleep and if anything happens, my friend's parents are right there, and my friend is right next to me. So the worst thing would be if I woke her and that's not so bad. And I'm only here for a little while and for one night I can afford not to sleep at my own house. This is for real, not pretend. I feel better right now. Even if I were going to spend the night here tonight with you, I would feel alright.

THERAPIST: Did you notice a difference in how you felt, saying the comforting things to yourself?

CLIENT: Yes. Very much even now.

THERAPIST: Good, and if you practice thinking these comforting things, you'll be able to do it better and better each time. [pp. 17–19]

Practical Problem Solving

Practical problem solving can be employed both for practical and emotional problems, though it's primarily designed to resolve the former. Children frequently are in trouble, or are less than happy, because they do not have the skills to handle a situation. If someone teases them, they may not know of any other way to handle the situation than to fight. They may not be particularly upset at the time. Many children would like to have more friends but do not know how to get them. These socially withdrawn children may or may not experience debilitating levels of interpersonal anxiety that prevent them from meeting others. RET assesses deficits in the practical skills of young clients that may be of concern and creating some distress in the client and in others.

When emotional problems accompany practical ones, practical problem solving may function as a form of *behavioral disputation*. For example, a young client might say to herself, "I will never be able to complete all my homework; I'm hopeless," and feel depressed. By teaching her practical skills for thinking about how to be better organized and more efficient and by forcing her to force herself to actually complete various amounts of homework, her newly acquired behavioral skills provide evidence for rejecting her self-defeating belief and lead to a reduction in emotional stress.

In teaching practical skills, RET tries where possible to provide instruction in both how to *think about* a practical problem as well as how to go about solving it. While RET practitioners sometimes simply have to tell the client how best to handle a situation without going into what he should be thinking and saying, most practical problems involve the use of rational self-statements or more general cognition strategies (e.g., consequential and means–end thinking) combined with rehearsal of behavioral skills.

A number of RET practitioners (e.g., DiGiuseppe & Bernard, 1983; Waters, 1982a, 1982b) have arrived at a practical problem-solving format that can be readily employed, even with very young children, and includes the following steps (Waters, 1982a):

1. Define the problem in concrete, behavioral terms.
2. Generate as many alternative solutions as you can without evaluating them. Remember, quantity is more important than quality; the more solutions the better.
3. Go back and evaluate each alternative solution, giving both positive and negative consequences and eliminating absurd solutions.
4. Choose one or two of the best solutions and plan your procedures step by step.
5. Put your plan into action and evaluate results. [p. 576]

An illustration of the first two steps of this approach is contained in the following transcript from Waters (1982b):

THERAPIST: The other kind of problem people can have is a practical problem, and that has to do with wanting to change something in your life other than hurtful feelings, like . . .

CLIENT: I already did that.

THERAPIST: What did you do?

CLIENT: I changed my behavior and I listen more to my mother. That was a problem I changed.

THERAPIST: Good. Yes, I'll bet you have already solved some practical problems.

CLIENT: I did it and didn't know it.

THERAPIST: I'd like you to choose something else in your life which is a problem you would like to solve, and I'll show you a good way to go about solving it.

CLIENT: I'd like to change not seeing my friend P so much.

THERAPIST: OK, that's a really good problem to work on, but let me check something with you before we begin. How do you feel about not seeing P as much as you would like?

CLIENT: Not good. Sad, I guess. I'd like to see her more. I love her and want to see her more.

THERAPIST: Feeling sad is certainly unpleasant, but it is OK to feel sad if you aren't getting what you want. Do you ever feel angry and depressed about it?

CLIENT: Well, sometimes I used to but not now.

THERAPIST: Because when people feel hurtful feelings, like anger and depression, they create like an emotional or feeling fog, which clogs their brains and makes it very hard for them to see clearly and think clearly about how to solve the problem. I think that feeling sad is appropriate and won't get in the way of you solving this problem. What do you think?

CLIENT: I think if I was feeling really upset and crying over it, I'd be too hurt to think. I don't feel that way now.

THERAPIST: OK, let's begin. (Pulls out problem solving sheet, goes over instructions once.) The first step is to state the problem.

CLIENT: Not seeing P enough.

THERAPIST: OK. (Therapist records.) The second step is to come up with as many ideas as you can, as to how to see her more often. And while we're getting the ideas down, we aren't going to say whether they are good or bad, we're just going to get as many ideas as we can.

CLIENT: Well, my mother seeing P's mother more often. Can I write it? (Client records alternatives and then goes through the list, noting which are possible.)

> *1. My mother seeing P's mother more often.
> *2. I could join the Y with her.
> 3. Take other activities together.
> *4. Ask her mother to bring her over more often.
> *5. Ask my mother to bring me to her house more often.
> *6. Meet somewhere between our two houses.
> *7. Get a taxi to take us to each other's houses.
> 8. My grandfather could drive me over there.
> 9. Ride a bicycle over to P's house.
> *10. Go to the Beauty Parlour together.
> (* = Possible)

THERAPIST: Wow! There are seven possibilities here. That's quite good. We could probably go on like this, if we had time, and come up with even more alternatives.

CLIENT: Gee. There're a lot more things I could do than I realized. What's the next step?

THERAPIST: What the next step is, is to look at each of these possible alternatives and think of something positive and something negative that would happen for each one.

CLIENT: Like in the first one something positive would be that our mothers are friends and would like to see more of each other, which means my friend and I would see more of each other too, and something negative would be that they might not have the time to see more of each other.

THERAPIST: Right. That's good thinking. For homework you could take this list home and think about a positive and negative for each of the possibilities and we'll continue with this next week.

CLIENT: OK. I may write them down so I won't forget. [pp. 30–34]

In the next chapter we provide extensive illustration as to how cognitive procedures can be used to teach practical problem-solving skills.

PRACTICE AND APPLICATION

The final stage of RET involves helping the young client apply rational thinking skills outside the practitioner's office in real-life situations. While the task of teaching the basics of RET can usually be accomplished, it is quite another thing to see young clients spontaneously applying RET; therefore RET stresses "the importance of practicing the skills in a variety of settings and of specific homework assignments" (Waters, 1982a). Sounding a pessimistic note, Young (1983) indicates that

> problem solving, the basic goal of RET, is usually accomplished by persuading clients to put knowledge in therapy into practice in concrete situations. This usually requires conscious effort and hard work, traits that unfortunately are not high on the list of adolescent virtues. Young people are notoriously reluctant to apply themselves to any task that does not promise immediate results. It is important, therefore, not to harbour unrealistic expectations about counseling adolescents. Clinical experience has shown that teenagers usually do not undergo sweeping or dramatic personality changes, living happily ever after as a result of their therapy endeavours. Most come in for relatively few interviews; if these clients are handled skillfully along the lines I have suggested, they generally make moderate improvement. [p. 99]

The main way RET accomplishes the goals of the final stage of therapy is through *homework*. Once the young client accepts the possibility and desirability of change, the practitioner has sufficient leverage to "request" that the client "does one or two things between sessions." Here is an example of such a request: "That was good work today, Steven. You really did some good thinking. For next week, there are a few things I'd like you to practice that we discussed today. First, don't make mountains out of molehills. If something bad happens like your sisters refusing to play with you, remember to say to yourself the things we've written down to take home with you (e.g., It isn't that bad, I don't have to get angry). Second, on this piece of paper, I want you to keep track of how many times you get angry. Write down how angry you were on a scale of 1 to 10, what was happening, and what you did. And remember, pat yourself on the back when you control your temper."

Children and adolescents are used to being told by people at school to do certain things at home. While we avoid using the word "homework," we do communicate an attitude right from the beginning that it is expected that they will be doing work outside the sessions themselves. The homework phase is really the most taxing on the personal resources of the practitioner. It is at this time that some young clients begin to realize that the practitioner who up until then they had perceived as someone understanding and friendly is going to ask them to do things that they frequently do not want to do, oftentimes because whatever it is involves hard work. This puts the practitioner into the same role as the client's parents and teachers. The point at which the practitioner starts to request the youngster to change sometimes breaks the relationship. The client may quickly reinterpret the value he or she places on, and the trust placed in, the practitioner. By being aware of this, the practitioner may dispute with the young client the idea that "Because he is telling me to do something I don't want to do, he's no good" and that "It's unfair for him to ask me to do so."

Another point to keep in mind is that clients who tend to complete their school homework will tend to do what you ask them to do, while those who have a history of not handing in homework at school will tend not to follow through with you. Remember, the problems you face in getting a client cooperating with you will be the same as those faced by the young client's parents and teachers. Therefore, make sure you prepare both the client, parents, teachers, and yourself before you assign homework. If you know that the young client is not likely to do what you ask, either do not ask or make sure that the client is, because of the relationship she or he has developed with you, prepared to change past behavior. Not infrequently we set up a token reinforcement system with younger clients, to ensure appropriate levels of motivation. Communication and cooperation with parents is obviously essential.

There are numerous ways in which the young client may practice and apply skills acquired during sessions. Waters (1982a) indicates the following as typical homework assignments: (1) monitoring feelings; (2) making a list of personal demands; (3) REI; (4) practicing changing feelings and thoughts in a real situation; (5) taking a responsible risk; and (6) reinforcing self with positive self-talk.

Young (1983) recommends the following tactics to help teenagers learn what therapy is about, what to expect from their efforts, and how to put insight into action:

1. Explain psychological and emotional problems as habits. Sometimes I can encourage effort by adolescents through labeling their problems as habits. . . . What I usually do is ask in each session about progress. When a reported lack of improvement can be traced to a client's failure to put into practice what we have been discussing, I suggest that the client's problem, no matter how complicated or painful, is merely a habit. After some explaining and clarifying, I point out the client can expect improvement if he puts in the necessary work to change the habit. . . .
2. Checking out the client's expectations about therapy. Often adolescents have the wrong idea what to expect from counseling. Unless these misconceptions are corrected, clients will likely lose faith in therapy because it will not give them what they want. . . .
3. Writing out an ABC homework for them. Although I am frequently successful in helping adolescents understand why their thinking is irrational, I find it difficult to get them to practice challenging and correcting their irrational ideas outside of therapy sessions. . . . For this reason, I try to outline their problems on a blackboard or sheet of paper, using the ABC model. At each session, I try to take the client through the model, and I also suggest he take my writing efforts home with him and look at them if the problem comes up during the week. . . .
4. Sticking to accepted insights. Once a particular insight has been presented, understood, and accepted by a teenager, I strongly suggest that this information

be repeated without significant change. In other words, stick to what seems to impress the client as the cognitive source of his distress and use the same words, analogies, visual examples, and the like to reinforce the message. . . .

5. Tell the adolescent what to think. I have found, despite heroic efforts, some adolescents are not going to learn how to reason things out according to prescribed RET dogma. In such cases I simply give them the correct sentences to think. . . .

6. Arranging homework assignments. I usually try to design some kind of appropriate homework assignment for the client between sessions. . . . For instance, I might help a shy adolescent understand the cognitive sources of his shyness, but I also want to get him to do something assertive, such as going to a party, asking a girl out, or maybe saying no to someone he usually accommodates with a yes. I have found that young people are more likely to accept the ideas of rational thinking after they have tried them out in emotionally provoking experiences. [pp. 99–101]

We have found some of the following activities useful for reinforcing some of the RET ideas taught in sessions. We sometimes ask the young client to fill out a "happening–thought–feeling–behaving" diagram such as the one presented earlier in this chapter. The youngster is asked to write down the thoughts he has in a problematic situation, his feelings on a 1- to 10-point scale, his reactions, and whether his thought was rational or irrational. If the thought was irrational, there is space for a new rationally restated thought to be written, as well as for a rating of new feelings and a description of a new reaction. This information is then used as a focus of attention for the following session.

We also frequently design materials to emphasize certain RET concepts. Two examples are provided in Tables 21–2 and 21–3. In Table 21–2 a young client is asked to describe certain positive and negative qualities about himself in an effort to expand his self-concept. In Table 21–3 a young client is given practice in applying his knowledge about why people make mistakes. These types of tables are useful instructional devices for hard-to-teach material and are easy to develop.

It will be seen from these examples that much of RET homework emphasizes not only cognition but also the emotive and behavioral dimensions of human experience. It endeavors to link up cognitive with emotional and behavioral change through the use of experiential and imaginal exercises.

Another technique we have found valuable for promoting a thorough understanding and application of RET techniques is that of *rational role reversal* (Kassinove & DiGiuseppe, 1975). After the young client understands the rational ideas that underlie his problem, the practitioner assumes the role of the young client and the young client takes the role of the rational practitioner who explains to the young client the causes of his problem. "The therapist asks clarifying questions and raises cogent points that allow the client to forcefully rehearse rational thinking" (Grieger & Boyd, 1980, p. 180).

TABLE 21–2 My Characteristics

Positive Things about Me

Things I do:	1.
	2.
	3.
	4.
	5.

Things I do for other people:	1.
	2.
	3.
	4.
	5.

Things I feel:	1.
	2.
	3.
	4.
	5.

Personal things:	1.
	2.
	3.
	4.
	5.

Negative Things about Me
(Sometimes I. . . .)

Things I don't do:	1.
	2.
	3.
	4.
	5.

Things I don't do for other people:	1.
	2.
	3.
	4.
	5.

Things I feel:	1.
	2.
	3.
	4.
	5.

TABLE 21–3 Mistake Making

Causes of Mistakes	1. Lack of skill
	2. Carelessness or poor judgment
	3. Not studying or poor students
	4. Not having enough information, unsound assumption
	5. Tired or ill
	6. Different opinion

Directions: Fill in the chart

Mistake	Cause	Your Thoughts about Mistake Maker
1. A baby spills milk on the beautiful carpet		
2. Mr. Smith doesn't see a stop sign and crashes into another car. Both drivers are hurt.		
3. Ian fails an important exam.		
4. Mary thought Damian was an interesting boy. She went on a date with him and spent a boring evening.		
5. Mrs. Dow yells at Doug for not handing in his homework on time. Doug's father forgot to return it to Doug after he read it.		

A technique related to rational role reversal that an older child may employ successfully is called *rational proselytizing* (Bard, 1973). We have seen this technique employed by young clients who report to us that they have explained ideas to their parents in order to help them understand what they are doing in the sessions with the practitioner. This frequently helps speed up the rate at which the younger client acquires the basis of RET, and it can have the effect of improving the client's relationship with her family. Parents begin to see that their child is making an honest attempt to change.

Other cognitive and behavioral activities we employ as homework include

1. Practice of behaviors role played and rehearsed with the practitioner, such as verbal assertion and extinction.
2. Writing down upsetting thoughts young clients have during the week.
3. Trying out of alternatives generated during practical problem solving.
4. Asking other people to write down positive things about the young client. This is especially useful for negative clients.

The final stage of therapy is completed when the practitioner assesses that the goals of therapy have been achieved. Waters (1982a) suggests that RET practitioners ask the following questions:

Is this child able to resolve emotional upsets?
Is this child able to solve practical problems?
Does the child take responsibility for his own emotions?
Are the child and the parents satisfied with the progress? [p. 576]

We always inform parents and the child that, should they wish to resume treatment in the future, we are always available. Some practitioners send out follow-up forms to parents six to eight weeks after treatment sessions have been terminated.

MIDDLE INTERVIEW SESSIONS

The following is a brief listing of topics and content of intermediate interview sessions.

1. *Review and discuss presenting problems and problem analyses.* Parents and children frequently bring up different problems from those they presented in initial sessions. It is important for the practitioner to be aware of how clients are currently viewing their problems. If clients continuously change their problems each week, it may well be that they themselves are not fully aware of their problem. Value clarification as well as cognitive and emotive awareness exercises may have to be employed at these times.

2. *Discuss homework.* If clients have performed their homework activities, you know they are more likely to be with you and motivated to change. Data from homework concerning thoughts, feelings, and behaviors enable the practitioner to unravel more fully the dynamics of the problem. If homework is not completed, emphasis should be placed on the collaborative nature of the counseling relationship.

3. *Handling resistance to homework.* It is not unusual during the early days of therapy for clients to fail to carry out homework assignments. Practitioners

should not become overly discouraged, for, as Nina Woulff, an RET therapist, has pointed out, "it is this very resistance which is the royal road to the irrational beliefs which are perpetuating the cycle of interactions around the symptom" (1983, p. 379). Frequently it takes parents a number of sessions before they are fully compliant with directives to be, for example, firmer and stricter. This may be because of emotional difficulties (e.g., guilt) that are supported by irrational beliefs ("A child must love his parent all the time"). It is up to the practitioner to identify and challenge the irrational beliefs of parents and children that are interfering with progress.

4. *Decide upon form of treatment.* As therapy unfolds, it is up to the practitioner to decide whether a particular problem warrants all members of the family being seen together or separately. DiGiuseppe (1983) suggests that, if a child presents with manipulative behavior, parents and child should be seen separately. Some RET family practitioners employ a "mixed" form of treatment where the child is seen alone for the first part of the session, then the parents, and all members of the family are seen for the remainder of the session.

5. *Reinforce clients' progress.* Liberal praise for effort, as well as any progress, *however small,* is important. Praise behavior, not the client.

6. *Elicit new problems.* It is useful to question clients as to whether there are any new problems they wish to discuss. New problems help to define further the philosophy, beliefs, lifestyle, and goals of clients.

7. *Communicate summary interpretation of clients' problems.* Be sure to check out that your inferences concerning the ABC's of a problem relate with the clients'. If the clients do not accept your analysis, you've got to see whether you've missed important data or whether the clients are being resistant. In either case, the clients have to be won over to a cognitive viewpoint of their problems before RET can commence. (This is especially the case when cognitive disputational procedures are to be employed.)

8. *Select problem for session.* Younger clients, especially less verbal ones, will need to be guided in this selection process. Try to center your discussion around one problem instead of moving from one to another. Problems selected should be consistent with the different cognitive, emotive, and behavioral changes agreed to by the client (parents and/or child).

9. *Discuss RET goals and principles in terms of problem selected.* This step involves teaching basic insights and the ABC's of RET.

10. *Clients summarize in their own language what is to be changed and how it is to be changed.* Clients should have a pretty good idea of how their emotions, behaviors, and cognitions influence the attainment of their short- and long-term goals. With older children, adolescents, and parents the role of rational self-talk and disputational challenging should be recognized.

11. *Employ emotional and practical problem-solving procedures.* These procedures are geared to the developmental level of young clients and include those described in the skills-building section of this chapter.

12. *Repetition and rehearsal of procedures, including those required for homework.* As we have emphasized, the practice of rational thinking and other emotive and behavioral skills is crucial if clients are to maintain skills in real-life situations. Therefore, insure that sufficient time is provided during sessions for clients to practice basic cognitive change procedures. Also, it is very important that clients understand exactly what they need to do for homework (e.g., how to fill out a self-report form or carry out a behavioral assertiveness exercise).

13. *Schedule next appointment.* It is still a good idea to continue to see clients on a weekly basis (or more often if needed) to insure that progress is made by clients in solving their own emotional and practical problems.

LATER AND FINAL INTERVIEW SESSIONS

1. *Discuss homework and review previous weeks' progress and problems.* Homework becomes increasingly important as it reveals whether significant changes in clients are taking place. More and more time is spent in analyzing progress and setbacks in real-life situations. Clients are asked to recount significant success and failure experiences carefully. Such feedback enables the practitioner to design new experiences that tackle the idiosyncratic responsivity of clients.

2. *Repeat, modify, or employ new cognitive–emotive–behavioral procedures.* It may take many sessions for intractable problems to show improvement. For these problems, it is sometimes possible to introduce a number of different procedures across sessions (e.g., relaxation, assertiveness training, rational self-statements). In so doing, it becomes possible to determine which RET method works best and whether change takes place more quickly when cognitive, emotive, and/or behavioral changes are targeted.

3. *Assist clients to identify progress.* During later sessions, it is important to point out to both parents and children the different ways in which you see them improving. Praise for individual efforts to change may work to create improved self-esteem and internal locus of control. Sometimes parents are so enmeshed with the problems of their children that they fail to notice or appreciate significant changes that occur in their children. Children, too, overlook changes in their parents' behavior.

4. *Clients rehearse their approach to recurrence of problem.* One simple but effective way to prepare clients for a recurrence of problems is to prepare them for the eventuality. Indicating to clients that it is possible old problems may arise from time to time and they now have the skills to deal with them helps to insure that they are not caught unaware when problems arise and, as a consequence, are better able to handle them. Clients are asked to imagine problems reoccurring and to describe how they can rationally think their way out of them.

5. *Discuss ways of maintaining and generalizing progress.* As Ellis has

written and lectured about for many years, change requires *continuous* hard work and some people take almost a lifetime to break self-defeating thought patterns. Therefore, stress to clients that for therapeutic progress to be maintained, it is important to continue to practice the rational reformulation of irrational concepts and beliefs so that their overall belief system is permanently modified. It is extremely educative for the practitioner to ask clients how they would deal with novel situations that the practitioner can anticipate would be upsetting. The answers of clients indicate when they are likely to generalize the gains they have shown in dealing with specific problems. Other questions to ask could include (a) How do you explain the changes that have occurred? (b) How could you slip back into your old pattern? (c) Specifically, how would you have to think and react in order to get back into the old rut? (Woulff, 1983)

6. *Arrange for subsequent contact if required.* Our practice is to indicate to all clients that we are available in the future should they like to see us. This option enables some clients to face subsequent problems with more assurance, knowing they can be in contact with us if difficulties arise. We do not encourage a dependent relationship. Instead, we communicate an attitude of concern beyond the boundaries of counseling sessions.

CASE TRANSCRIPT

We end this chapter with an extended transcript of a final interview session with a 14-year-old boy, Craig. The major problem of concern both to him and his parents was his frequent illnesses (swollen glands, sore throat, fever, weakness) which occurred every month or so and kept him home three to five days. The outbreak of these bouts of illness appeared to be associated with stress of schooling and especially with homework and studying for tests. The client was extremely bright (IQ 130+). His main emotional difficulty was found to be "anxiety" associated with his "demandingness" and "perfectionistic" attitudes. In this last session, RET concepts were reviewed extensively so that the client could listen to them during the summer. (He tape recorded each session.) For this reason, the therapist tended to do a majority of the talking.

THERAPIST: What shall we talk about today? What sort of things are of concern that you would like to go over?

CLIENT: Uh, a relapse mainly. I need to concentrate more on not going overboard, so I don't keep studying too hard, too long, too much.

THERAPIST: Right. Well how do you know when you first of all might be studying too long, too hard? What's going to signal you to think positive thoughts? They are just not going to materialize all of a sudden; something has got to remind you to think positive thoughts and generally it's the problem as it starts to creep up, which in your case is what?

CLIENT: Um, I start feeling pretty worn out at say, 8:30, a quarter to nine, but because I still have a fair bit to go I keep going, because sometimes I usually don't get started till, say, 7:30.

THERAPIST: Uh-uh.

CLIENT: So.

THERAPIST: OK. Let's stop there just for a minute. Those are the body signals, we talked about those before.

CLIENT: Yes.

THERAPIST: Those are your signals to think first of all.

CLIENT: Yes.

THERAPIST: OK. Now you said positive thoughts and I would say yes, positive thoughts, but they are also signals for you to think about not pushing yourself too hard. That is the first message, when you feel yourself getting tired—you know—I'm getting tired, I'm likely to get sick, therefore I had better start to plan. Either plan times where I can have more rest or plan to go to bed at an earlier time and just forget about the work that I won't get done.

CLIENT: Yes.

THERAPIST: So your physical symptoms of tiredness, fatigue, and irritability, will be signals for you to start to think thoughts. OK, and for you those thoughts had better be I'd better think about relaxing and not pushing myself too hard, otherwise I am going to get sick. Does that make sense to you?

CLIENT: Yes.

THERAPIST: OK. Now I have a question for you. There are two ways to go about changing excessive worry, and I still think you tend to excessively worry about your school performance. One way is to lower your standards for yourself, and the other one is to keep the standards but expect, not expect less, but if you don't achieve those standards not to hammer yourself unmercifully. What's in the long run? Which one of these is a problem for you, and which one holds perhaps a partial solution for reducing your worry?

CLIENT: Um, I think the second one would be a better idea for me to think about, rather than having to lower my standards, because that really is what I don't want to do.

THERAPIST: Right. That second one is called—and it may now be an old friend of yours because I think it has come up before—*demandingness*. You demand that you achieve a high standard and when you don't you hammer yourself and that's what you worry about, you're worried about what happens if I don't live up to that high standard. This is what we talked about several weeks ago, and your worry was somehow your value . . . as a person would somehow be diminished and then you said, I think we agreed that that was irrational, that that wasn't a sensible thing, and you agreed to it although you said "It hasn't really sunken in."

CLIENT: Yes.

THERAPIST: So that would be something for you in the long run to practice thinking about. The fact is even if you don't get your A's in English it doesn't make you a worthless person; force yourself to believe that. You don't force yourself. You cling on to your old ideas while you give lip service to the new ones. To give up those old ideas you are going to have to force them out of your head. Every time you even think you might be thinking of them you must dispute them. You must say to yourself these are not true, Dr. Wise-one has told me this, I must believe him. So that's one idea that I think bears repetition and which in the long run will prevent relapses, because I think you probably still fight and push yourself too hard. The reason you do that is because you desperately need to get to that level and you are afraid not to get there. I am saying to you, over the long run, take some chances and if you don't get there see what the effects are going to be. You don't really give yourself a chance to see yet. Do you understand what I am saying? You don't allow yourself to fail. You struggle and you push yourself so hard so you won't fail, and what I am saying to you is when the opportunity comes up like middle year, take that chance and if it is a question of your health or the difference between a B+ or an A– I would think your health would want to come first; and also test your ego, test how strong a person you are to be able to sustain a less-than-perfect performance, because you are not going to be failing everything by and large, you just won't be doing as well as, because you set yourself a high standard don't you?

CLIENT: Yes, I do.

THERAPIST: OK. What does all that mean in your words? (laughs) Right, in 10 words or less.

CLIENT: (Laughs) Um, I shouldn't set myself the high standards and expect to reach them. I'll rephrase that. I shouldn't set myself high standards and work and work so I get there and then get sick.

THERAPIST: Right, that's a good point.

CLIENT: So, I either lower my standards or keep the high standards and realize that maybe I won't get there if I don't force myself to work as hard.

THERAPIST: What do we call it when you force yourself to reach that high standard? That's what you do with your friends when they don't achieve your standards for them, and the same thing you do with yourself. You demand, so we can change demands into preferences, so that when you feel that you are demanding of yourself the attainment of that high standard, you could dispute that demand by saying, "I'd like it. I'd prefer it, but I won't demand it." Because if you demand it you will push yourself too hard, so that would be called changing a demand into a preference or to liking or to a wish or, you know, it would be nice if that happened, but not I must, you know. Does that make sense?

CLIENT: Yes.

THERAPIST: You can see how you apply that to your friends.

CLIENT: Yes.

THERAPIST: Right. Now you said to me last week you weren't—because you do some of the things they do—you weren't going to demand that they be perfect. That's changing your standards, which is OK, but that's changing standards. Do you see that? You say I want . . . to be perfect. Because I realize I am imperfect, why should I expect that from them? There is no point in that. So, that is changing a standard, which is OK; but the other thing which I don't think you successfully dealt with with your friends is demanding, to stop demanding that they achieve any standard that you might set for them. You've lowered it, but what happens when they don't? We are all guilty of that, we feel very let down when people don't achieve minimal standards, right? I think we all could profit from just accepting people as they are and wishing they were different, but not demanding. Do you still think you've demanded a little in your own self?

CLIENT: Yes, probably.

THERAPIST: As you demanded of yourself?

CLIENT: Mm.

THERAPIST: I would think if there is one overriding belief and answer you hold about yourself and the world it is that of demandingness. You demand that you be perfect or almost totally successful in your work, and you demand that your friends be, live up to whatever your standards are. Now you have changed your standards, and that is half the solution. But why demand? What would be a healthier outlook toward friends, rather than demanding that they be the way you want them to be; what could you say to yourself?

CLIENT: So what, they're not doing what I expect of them, they are still good people.

THERAPIST: Right, but you do *care* that they are not living up to a certain standard, because you hold those as important, so rather than saying they *must* . . . they must what? Name something you value in your friends.

CLIENT: They must be generous.

THERAPIST: Right, and suppose you catch one being selfish in a moment where you think they should be generous, right? That's the point, that sort of problem. OK, then you could say rather, than they *must not* be selfish and he is a no-good-nik because he is, you could say I wish he wasn't as selfish at that moment as he is. I wish. Now what do you think the consequence of wishing he would be less selfish at that moment would be?

CLIENT: I wouldn't have the demand.

THERAPIST: Right. What would your emotions be then?

CLIENT: I wouldn't get worked up about it.

THERAPIST: As much.

CLIENT: As much.

THERAPIST: So, you would still be irritated, but you wouldn't be as worked up, and what happens when you get that worked up?

CLIENT: I get sick.

THERAPIST: Right. Well, how about with your friends? You would choose not to have them.

CLIENT: Yes.

THERAPIST: Remember you said you would like to have a few more friends, but because they'd let you down you get depressed a little bit. But if you adopted a more accepting attitude toward your friends and people you meet, then when they do let you down you can accept it and you don't get so emotionally upset that you feel so hurt, therefore you avoid those sorts of encounters. Do you see the quality of that demanding attitude and how it influences your emotions and behaviors toward others? That same attitude characterizes your relationship with yourself. Let's deal with it again in your world of work, your schoolwork. How does demanding relate to your feelings and your behavior, and what might you do to change the demandingness?

CLIENT: To change, I would say I wish that I could get an A– and B+ in these subjects, but I might not, so . . .

THERAPIST: Right.

CLIENT: It's not going to make me any worse a person, it just means that instead of getting an A– I got B+ and maybe because of that I won't get sick.

THERAPIST: Right, and how about your emotions relative to demanding? If you said I wish I could get an A– rather than a B+ but it is not the end of the world, what do you think your level of depression would be?

CLIENT: It wouldn't be as high.

THERAPIST: As it would be if what?

CLIENT: If I'm thinking I demand that I get A– rather than a B+.

THERAPIST: Right. So in terms of your question to prevent relapse in the long run, I still would argue that you could do more thinking homework by rechanging your thoughts. When you're overly stressed you will tend to get sick. Part of that stress is your very high expectation of yourself. Other people would be less stressed because they wouldn't demand perfection like you do. So part of your stress is brought about by what you bring to the situation. So you can have a friend of yours in a similar situation as you are in exams and wanting to do well, but because he doesn't demand perfection he is going to have less stress than you. Some of your friends are less demanding; I would guess all your friends would be less demanding of themselves than you are.

CLIENT: Yes.

THERAPIST: And they don't react the same way as you do. Your only problem is you have got this little Achilles heel for getting sick. Otherwise you would just be a worrier and you know that's unpleasant. Everyone lives with worry, but that worry is a stress reaction and that leads to you getting sick. I would say, in terms of preventing relapse, give some serious thought to being less demanding, and first apply it to your friends and see how that works. As I said, you have changed your attitudes about what you expect of them, but now try to change the demandingness and change your demands to preferences. Then force yourself to change your demands of yourself. If you can give up perfectionism and accept the fact that sometimes you will fail, then it doesn't mean you are worthless as you said, and that the world is going to come to an end. It doesn't you know. I know (laughs); I've failed enough times to prove it. There, then, you'll feel less stressed. It is only when you are scared of failing, scared of making a mistake, that everything is a stress, especially in school, which you value a lot. So if you accept the fact that even in your schoolwork it's OK to fail, that in the long run it doesn't matter, then you can relax a little bit more and you won't get as sick. Because I value my work, not as much as you do, but I think my standards for my work are probably almost as high as yours. If not, well, they couldn't be as crazy as yours (both laugh). I mean they are pretty high but I don't demand perfection. I have stress reactions. Do you have stress reactions? I have stress reactions but they are not as severe as yours, because I accept the fact that, first of all, if I fail I'll still live and others will accept me. That's a lesson that you'll learn, hopefully, through experience—that when you fail at things that you can accept yourself and others can accept you. Because you are likeable. There's nothing wrong with you, is there, that I know of? I find you reasonably pleasant and intelligent; so you'll have your friends, regardless if you fail once or twice. Remember, you said if you failed your music exam or something you would get laughed at by your friends, and you said that would cause you some embarrassment. They wouldn't hold that against you; that might show that you are human. So I still think you could do some more think work, but I certainly think you've also progressed a long way in your thinking from when I first talked with you—what would it be—six or eight weeks ago or something like that. Do you think you've had a chance to think through some of these ideas a bit further?

CLIENT: Yes.

THERAPIST: When I first saw you, you had the basics, didn't you? But I think now you have been hammered by me over and over so that it is starting to sink in.

CLIENT: Yes.

THERAPIST: Right. Now that you have recorded my wisdom, you can always take it with you. For next year—you'll be here next year?—I'm here for you, OK. So if you feel the urge to come in and repeat some of these things, rehearse them again, that would be OK, just to refresh your memory. . . . Well my speech is done for today, is there anything else you would like to bring up?

REFERENCES

Bard, J. A. Rational proselytizing. *Rational Living,* 1973, *8,* 13–15.

Bernard, M. E. The effects of advance organizers and within-text questions on the learning of a taxonomy of concepts. *Technical Report No. 357.* Wisconsin Research and Development Center for Cognitive Learning, 1975.

Bernard, M. E. The effects of advance organizer, sequence of instruction, and postorganizer on the learning and retention of a taxonomy of concepts. *The Australian Journal of Education,* 1977, *21,* 25–33.

Bernard, M. E., Kratochwill, T. R., & Keefauver, L. W. The effects of rational-emotive-therapy and self-instructional training on chronic hair-pulling. *Cognitive Therapy and Research,* 1983, *7,* 273–280.

De Voge, C. A behavioral approach to RET with children. *Rational Living,* 1974, *9,* 23–26.

DiGiuseppe, R. A. The use of behavioral modification to establish rational self-statements in children. *Rational Living,* 1975, *10,* 18–20.

DiGiuseppe, R. A. Cognitive therapy with children. In G. Emery, S. D. Hollon & R. C. Bedrosian (Eds.), *New directions in cognitive therapy.* New York: Guilford, 1981.

DiGiuseppe, R. A., & Bernard, M. E. Principles of assessment and methods of treatment with children. In A. Ellis & M. E. Bernard (Eds.), *Rational-emotive approaches to the problems of childhood*. New York: Plenum Press, 1983.

DiGiuseppe, R. A., & Kassinove, H. Effects of a rational-emotive school mental health program on children's emotional adjustment. *Journal of Community Psychology*, 1976, *4*, 382–387.

Ellis, A. Rejoinder: Elegant and inelegant RET. *The Counseling Psychologist*, 1977, *7*, 73–82.

Ellis, A., & Bernard, M. E. (Eds.), *Rational-emotive approaches to the problems of childhood*. New York: Plenum, 1983.

Grieger, R. M., & Boyd, J. D. *Rational-emotive therapy: A skills-based approach*. New York: Van Nostrand Reinhold, 1980.

Grieger, R. M., & Boyd, J. D. Childhood anxieties, fears and phobias: A cognitive-behavioral psychosituational approach. In A. Ellis & M. E. Bernard (Eds.), *Rational-emotive approaches to problems of childhood*. New York: Plenum, 1983.

Harris, S. R. Rational-emotive education and the human development program: A guidance study. *Elementary School Guidance and Counseling*, 1976, *11*, 113–123.

Kanfer, F. H., Karoly, P., & Newman, A. Reduction of children's fear of the dark by competence-related and situational thought-related verbal cues. *Journal of Consulting and Clinical Psychology*, 1975, *43*, 251–258.

Kassinove, H., & DiGiuseppe, R. A. Rational role reversal. *Rational Living*, 1975, *10*, 44–45.

Kendall, P. C., & Hollon, S. D. (Eds.), *Assessment strategies for cognitive-behavioral interventions*. New York: Academic Press, 1981.

Knaus, W. J. *Rational emotive education: A manual for elementary school teachers*. New York: Institute for Rational Living, 1974.

Spivack, G., & Shure, M. B. *Social adjustment of young children: A cognitive approach to solving real-life problems*. San Francisco, CA: Jossey-Bass, 1974.

Sutton-Simon, K. Assessing belief systems: Concepts and strategies. In P. C. Kendall and S. D. Hollon (Eds.), *Assessment strategies for cognitive-behavioral interventions*. New York: Academic Press, 1981.

Walen, S. R., DiGiuseppe, R., & Wessler, R. L. *A practitioner's guide to rational-emotive therapy*. New York: Oxford University Press, 1980.

Waters, V. The living school. *RETwork*, 1981, *1*, 1.

Waters, V. Therapies for children: Rational emotive therapy. In C. R. Reynolds & T. B. Gutkin (Eds.), *Handbook of school psychology*. New York: Wiley and Sons, 1982a.

Waters, V. RET with a child client. Unpublished manuscript, 1982b.

Woulff, N. Involving the family in the treatment of the child: A model for rational-emotive therapists. In A. Ellis & M. E. Bernard (Eds.), *Rational-emotive approaches to the problems of childhood*. New York: Plenum, 1983.

Young, H. S. A framework for working with adolescents. *Rational Living*, 1974, *9*, 2–7.

Young, H. S. Principles of assessment and methods of treatment with adolescents: Special considerations. In A. Ellis & M. E. Bernard (Eds.), *Rational-emotive approaches to the problems of childhood*. New York: Plenum Press, 1983.

22

RET and Women's Issues*

Janet Wolfe

Women have long been the primary consumers of psychotherapeutic services, outnumbering males at a ratio of two to one (Chesler, 1972; Worrell, 1980). The changing nature of male and female roles in the past 15 years, along with an emerging awareness on the part of the mental health community of the overrepresentation of women in certain emotional disorders, has pointed to a need for a therapy better geared to helping women with the practical and emotional problems they face as they attempt the exciting but difficult transition into more expanded roles. Rational-emotive therapy, combined with a critical examination of female sex-role socialization messages as a "primordial soup" in which irrational beliefs abound, is seen as a particularly effective approach for helping this population.

WOMEN'S ISSUES: AN UPDATE

Women, as we have stated, have traditionally been overrepresented in the therapy population (Rothblum, 1983). We know these women well. They come to therapy offices and clinics, most frequently with psychological disorders linked to powerlessness—feelings of inadequacy, chronic low self-esteem, guilt, passivity, depression, and anxiety. These symptoms are a natural byproduct of women's being steeped from childhood in the idea that their worth and happiness should derive from living for and through others (Heriot, 1983). Among the predominantly female disorders are depression (Weissman & Klerman, 1977), agoraphobia (Fodor, 1974), obesity (Fodor, 1982; Stuart, 1979), and anorexia

---

*This chapter was originally published in Albert Ellis and Michael Bernard (Eds.), *Applications of rational-emotive therapy* (New York: Plenum Press, 1985).

(Wooley & Wooley, 1980). Despite the significant overrepresentation of women in these disorders (e.g., anorexics are 75% to 85% women), few clinicians have attempted to try to understand the importance of sex-role learning when treating women with these types of disorders (Berzins, 1975).

In addition to dealing with these more "traditional" disorders, therapists are treating women clients whose conflicts are related to significant changes that have occurred in economic, political, and legal areas during the last 15 years. The women's movement, the changing composition of American families, and the 1979 Title IX Amendment of the Civil Rights Act are all sources of cultural change that have motivated individuals to alter their lifestyle activities, expectations, and value systems (Worell, 1980).

Women now are single parenting more frequently, marrying later, having fewer children, and are entering the ranks of the labor force at a very high rate (Block, 1979). Typical conflicts with which they are struggling include

"Do I have to be a superwoman?"
"Will I miss out on life if I don't have children?"
"How can I be happy and fulfilled if I don't have a relationship with a man?"
"How can I get my mate to share more responsibility at home?"
"How can I break into positions of power in my male-dominated field?"
"Where can I find a role model if I don't want to be like my mother or like a driven male executive?"
"Can I risk marriage without losing it all?"
"Can I really be myself with a man? Does he actually want an equal?"

CHANGING DIRECTIONS IN THERAPY FOR WOMEN

Society's discrimination against women is reflected in the way women's disturbances traditionally have been treated in therapy. In psychoanalytically oriented therapy, for example, strivings for autonomy or fulfillment outside the traditional roles of wife and mother have been interpreted as penis envy or masculine protest. Data from clients and therapists involved in nearly all types of therapy show that there is differential treatment of men and women. For example, when male and female neurotic depressives who are equally distressed are compared with regard to treatment length and prescription of medications, females are seen for more therapy sessions and given more potent medications than males (Stein, Del Gaudio, & Ansley, 1976). In studies comparing traditional and feminist therapists, most women thought of their nonfeminist therapist as manipulating them into the role of "proper" women and as being impersonal and paternalistic (Levine et al., 1974).

Stimulated by writings in the women's movement criticizing a traditional therapeutic treatment of women (Chesler, 1972; Wyckoff, 1977), there has been a growth in the therapeutic literature on the etiology of emotional stress in women and on potentially effective therapeutic procedures (Franks, 1979; Brodsky & Hare-Mustin, 1980; Robbins & Siegel, 1983). The importance of developing specialized skills and knowledge in treating women was underscored by an American Psychological Association Task Force, which recommended that mental health professionals develop greater sensitivity to women's mental sets and socioeconomic realities, and develop special psychological service delivery models tailored to them (APA, 1975, 1978).

Despite these recommendations, attention to sex-role issues appears to be restricted to a small group of mental health professionals (mainly women with a feminist orientation who typically make up 95% or more of the audiences at convention panels dealing with "women's issues.") Traditional clinical psychology training reinforces stereotyped views of women (Weisstein, 1971), and sexism continues to rear its head in the mental health community. For example, the findings of the "grandmother" of a number of studies on sex-role stereotypes and mental health problems demonstrate a double standard of mental health (Broverman et al., 1970). Clinicians rated healthy women as being more submissive, less independent, less competent, less adventurous, more easily influenced, less aggressive, less competitive, more excitable and emotional, and less objective than men. This negative assessment, which reflects sex-stereotyped societal standards of behavior, puts women in a double bind. If they adopt the healthier, more socially desirable behaviors of the "competent, mature adult," they risk censure for being unfeminine. If they adopt the less healthy and less socially desirable behaviors of a female, they are seen as "incompetent" and "immature" (Franks, 1982; Kelly et al., 1980).

Feminist recommendations for therapy with women are that therapists will abet mental health if they help both men and women to realize individual potential rather than adjustment to existing restrictive sex roles. This has been supported by a small but growing body of literature that supports the linkage between psychological androgyny (having a repertoire of both "masculine" and "feminine" behaviors) and positive mental health. Psychological androgyny has been found to be associated with greater maturity in our moral judgments (Block, 1973) and a higher level of self-esteem, while extreme femininity is correlated with high anxiety, high neuroticism, and low self-acceptance (Spence, Helmreich & Stapp, 1975). Bem and Lenney (1976) found that psychologically androgynous people felt comfortable in a broader range of activities, while masculine men and feminine women were uncomfortable when they engaged in activities that they perceived as "belonging" to the opposite sex.

Feminist therapists have emphasized the conflict between women's early training to become childlike, helpless, submissive, dutiful daughters, wives, and mothers, and their current hopes and expectations of becoming self-sufficient, autonomous, fully functioning, valued adult members of society (Robbins & Siegel, 1983). They point out that the active supporting of "deviance"—the freedom to rechoose alternative lifestyles—may be precisely what is needed to effect a more healthy behavioral pattern and social identity for today's woman (Rice & Rice, 1973; Barrett, Berg, Eaton, & Pomeroy, 1974).

HERSTORY

The last 12 years have seen the development at the Institute for Rational–Emotive Therapy in New York of one of the broadest-based therapy programs in the country addressed to women's issues (Wolfe, 1980). This includes six-session women's assertiveness, effectiveness, and sexuality groups; women's ongoing therapy groups; and workshops dealing with life cycle change and career entry, habit control (weight, stress management), and mother–daughter communications. Institute staff also have conducted workshops for professionals in sex-role issues in therapy and engaged in collaborative projects with various women's organizations, including the National Organization for Women (NOW) and a program to train minority women in the building trades. Leading rational–emotive therapists whose writing specializes in sex-role issues include Drs. Ingrid Zachary (1980), Penelope Russianoff (1982), Susan Walen (1983), Rose Oliver (1977), and Janet Wolfe (1975).

RAPPROCHEMENT BETWEEN RATIONAL–EMOTIVE THERAPY AND FEMINIST THERAPY

The therapy goal agreed upon by most feminist therapists is the development of autonomous individuals with personal strength, independence, and trust in self and in other women (Brodsky & Hare-Mustin, 1980; Loeffler & Fiedler, 1979). Feminist therapists also see the therapist as an agent of societal change, increasing the client's awareness of sociopolitical pressures and helping her to recognize her choices and change the context of her life (Hare-Mustin, 1983).

Rational–emotive therapy provides an effective and well-defined self-help system for facilitating personal growth and emotional well-being in women (Ellis, 1957, 1962, 1973, 1974, 1979; Ellis & Becker, 1982; Ellis & Harper, 1975). Those doing "feminist RET" do not support a standard of mental health for women that is different from that of men. They view RET as a humanistic, nonsexist vehicle for helping women work through their emotional and practical problems via a realistic, logical examination of their beliefs and philosophies (Ellis, 1974; Zachary, 1982). They teach a woman how to define her problems, identify the variables that influence her present feelings and actions, and alter both her behavior and her environment in positive ways.

More than any other school of therapy, RET seems to come closest to meeting the criteria for effective feminist therapy. First, it deals with the shoulds, musts, self-rating, and love-slobbism inherent in sex-role messages, and it provides a concrete method for disputing them. Second, it helps women to stop condemning themselves for their emotional disturbances and their ineffective behaviors. Third, it encourages autonomy through client involvement in goal setting and doing self-therapy and via its behavioral component, which teaches more effective behaviors. Fourth, it doesn't label assertiveness as masculine striving; and fifth, it shows women how to stop depressing themselves about the frustrations of a society that is not sex-fair, and of people who act in sexist ways, but to fight determinedly for "A-changes" (alterations in their environment). This last is essential, for, no matter how successfully women anti-awfulize or reduce self-downing, they still wind up with the short end of the stick unless they also work to improve their chances of increasing power, economic resources, and other elements involved in self-actualization (Wolfe, 1980).

ALL-WOMEN'S THERAPY GROUPS: RATIONALE

Being involved with others who endorse their therapeutic successes is especially important for women, who may receive considerable negative reinforcement for departures from "feminine" behaviors from such significant others as lovers, husbands, or parents (Krumboltz & Shapiro, 1979). Dependence on others' approval and poor self-acceptance may make it extremely difficult for women to accept themselves and persist in new behaviors in the face of heavy flak. Consequently, when a member of a women's group receives cheers from other members for moving toward autonomy, this provides an important transition from dependency on male validation to self-reinforcement.

Recognizing the environmental context of their problems is also facilitative of change. A woman who sees her helplessness and dependency as caused by some personal failure may tell herself, "I have no skills. I'm totally dependent on others. I'm a weak, sick person." But as she discovers the enculturated aspects of feminine helplessness, this same woman may make an entirely different set of self-statements: "These feelings of helplessness I have are very normal. I'm not a helpless person, but my society has taught me to play a helpless role" (Gornick & Moran, 1971; Krumboltz & Shapiro, 1979).

KEY INGREDIENTS IN RET WOMEN'S GROUPS

What is the more expanded RET approach to working with women at the Institute for Rational–Emotive Therapy? Whether done individually or in women's groups, the ingredients are essentially the same:

1. *Consciousness-raising.* Women discover, through discussion, how the culture has helped shape and maintain their faulty belief systems. To aid in this

process, members are from time to time assigned feminist literature on marriage, sexuality, and other topics.

2. *Goal setting.* As is commonly the case, RET women clients, collaborating with their therapist, learn to set their own goals. They thereby receive practice in counteracting passivity and dependency, in defining their own life plans instead of waiting for white knights to come along and plan for them. Women are asked to set up and review three-month plans and are encouraged to do time projections up to the age of 90.

3. *RET.* This involves "psyche-strengthening" work, namely, helping women change an "I'm helpless" belief system to one of optimism and self-acceptance. This phase also involves helping women develop better coping responses to the "real world" by teaching them to strengthen frustration tolerance and especially to handle their anxiety and rage.

4. *Therapist role modeling.* Because of the dearth of self-accepting and achieving female role models in women's lives, modeling and self-disclosure by the female therapist can provide an important coping model. For example, a client struggling to achieve greater autonomy and independence from her husband may benefit from a description of how the therapist and her spouse handle their finances.

5. *Participants as role models.* Additional role modeling is provided by encouraging group members to share how they achieved mastery of previous problem areas. This offers an additional source of effective role modeling and also helps the group members to give themselves credit for their successes as an antidote to their usual overfocusing on their flaws.

6. *Assertiveness training.* This constitutes a major remediation for women's passive and dependent behaviors. Cognitive and behavioral assignments are given to help women combat their fears of taking risks and of being disapproved of by others, to replace their habits of learned helplessness with those designed to increase personal effectiveness. An important part of assertiveness training is helping women to evaluate and cope with the possible negative consequences that may occur as a result of their assertions.

7. *Positive self-messages.* A large percentage of women have especially well-developed "flaw-detecting kits" and are practically addicted to self-downing (Russianoff, 1982). Women are regularly given assignments to write, or recite to their mirror, three positive traits or behaviors each day, or to "brag" aloud, first to the therapist and other group members and then to do so to others in their outside environment.

8. *Self-pleasuring assignments.* These are designed to combat cognitively and behaviorally the "put others first" and "I must not be selfish" sex-role messages. Homework assignments such as taking time for a long bubble bath, buying oneself flowers, getting a massage, or having caviar and cognac in front of a fire by oneself are useful means for reinforcing the idea that "I have the right to do

nice things for myself." At the same time, women's group members learn to give themselves the kinds of stroking often expected only from males.

9. *Encouragement of female friendships*. Women frequently use the term *relationship* as synonymous with heterosexual sex-love relationships (e.g., "I haven't had a relationship for years!"). In so doing, they negate or minimize the value and importance of female friendships. Friendships with women are encouraged as fine ways for women to get the loving, caring, sharing, support, intimacy, and nurturance they need in their lives, whether or not they are involved in a primary sex-love relationship.

10. *Focus on environmental resources and societal change*. RET women's groups go beyond the traditional boundaries of therapy and include all efforts and resources that we can muster to provide women with corrective socialization experiences and tools for environmental change. Unlocked from her paralyzing rage at discrimination on the job, for example, a woman may be encouraged to contact an organization that handles problems of sex discrimination. Extensive lists of resources, including battered women's shelters, women's professional organizations, and nonsexist gynecologists are kept by feminist rational–emotive therapists to help women work at changing some of the societal conditions they have successfully anti-awfulized about.

The remainder of this chapter will deal with two different clusters of problems for which rational–emotive/feminist therapy appears to provide help. The first is the high-prevalence disorders, which include the more apparent consequences of sex-role socialization: depression, phobias, and weight disorders. The second cluster is the relationship and work issues, including marriage, sexuality, mothering, and career. In both these areas, RET promotes emotional and behavioral competencies that help women transcend their early sex-role programming.

HIGH-PREVALENCE DISORDERS AS CONSEQUENCES OF SEX-ROLE SOCIALIZATION

Depression and Low Confidence

Women have twice as many depressive disorders as men (Weissman & Klerman, 1977). Seligman (1979) notes that the ratio between male and female depression may be as high as 1:10. Increasing numbers of researchers have found that depression is associated with the stress women experience from low social status, legal and economic discrimination, and learned helplessness (Guttentag & Salasin, 1976; Hare-Mustin, 1983).

NIMH statistics (Radloff, 1975) indicate that depression is higher in married women. In an attempt to account for the high depression rates, researchers have focused on the married woman's role (Franks, 1982). Homemakers are given considerable hard work but rarely recognized or rewarded for their work. When homemakers also work outside the home, they still wind up with few reinforcements in either area.

Although the cognitive process is the same for both depressed women and men, society especially tends to reinforce the negative messages that women tell themselves. Understanding the ecology of depression in terms of sex roles is important in treating depression (Franks, 1982). With their training to be submissive, dependent, and passive, women may indeed find that they have less control over their environment, so that the perception of the relationship between their efforts and any significant results in their lives could result in learned feelings of helplessness (Seligman, 1975). Believing themselves to be helpless, they fail to attempt the things that might help them achieve some success and mastery over their environment. They then feed themselves still more messages about their helplessness and worthlessness, thus perpetuating the vicious cycle (Ellis, 1962, 1974). These early themes of helplessness get expressed over and over in women clients' beliefs that they are stupid, helpless, inadequate, and incompetent, and in their limited ability to focus on what they *can* do because of their overfocus on what they *don't* do.

The rational–emotive therapist's goal is to help a woman riddled with hopeless/helpless cognitions and consequent self-downing to dispute them vigorously, albeit in a world where she has in fact a low status and where people who achieve more than she vigorously reinforce the idea of her helplessness and worthlessness. It is therefore especially helpful that the societal roots of women's role prescriptions be unearthed and analyzed. In helping a depressed single parent dispute her ideas that "I am a rotten mother" and "I am a reject because I don't have a mate," the therapist helps her challenge not only her own, but the societal view.

Training in environmental mastery becomes an important adjunct to RET in working with the depressed woman. The therapist may inform the client of community and other resources, including vocational training, women's business organizations, financial aid, and daycare centers (Grieger, 1982).

Phobias

Recent theoretical research and clinical writing have characterized clinical phobias as primarily female disorders (Brehony, 1983; Fodor, 1974). In spite of the preponderance of females in the phobia literature, there have been few attempts to explore the variables relevant to this sex difference.

Anxiety is a natural by product of people whose sense of worth is highly dependent on pleasing others (Ellis, 1962, 1974, 1979). Agoraphobia, generally the most incapacitating of the phobias, is characterized by extreme fearfulness and panic in open situations that require independent behavior. It usually leads to a housebound lifestyle, feelings of helplessness, and feelings of being trapped. Agoraphobia is far more common among females (Fodor, 1982); more than a million American women find their lives restricted by agoraphobic syndromes (Agras, Sylvester, & Oliveau, 1969). As Fodor (1974) suggests, female agoraphobics are often traditionally feminine and rigidly sex typed. With few goals of their own, they passively wait for others to take care of or direct them. Resentment, depression, restricted activity, nonassertiveness, and low self-esteem frequently follow (Jasin, 1983). These fearful behaviors are then reinforced by significant others in the woman's life (e.g., their husbands) as consonant with her sex role (Goldstein & Chambless, 1980).

Fear of the outside world makes sense when we realize that women have systematically been denied access (and have denied themselves access) to skills that would enable them to cope with common adult situations: traveling alone, buying a car, taking out a loan, or applying for a job (Heriot, 1983). They especially lack adequate assertiveness skills, a behavioral deficit that correlates with and is significantly included in agoraphobia.

Other phobias also tend to reflect women's tendency to see themselves as helpless and powerless. Their alleviation may mean the removal of important blocks to personal growth and educational or vocational achievement. Test anxiety, for example, is higher in women than in men. If testing is required to enter a profession, change careers, or rise to a higher level in a job, a woman's ambition may be undermined by fear. Public speaking anxiety has also been shown to be higher among women (Moulton, 1977) and may be one of the most important factors limiting women's vocational advancement.

Women also outnumber men in social phobias, which keep them from such goals as meeting new males, business networking, and meeting new women friends. Their task then becomes more difficult than that of their male counterparts. In addition to the usual fears of rejection, women confront the societal prejudice that a woman is defective or "hard up" if she initiates social contact with a man. In terms of business networking, it may be more difficult to approach a potential male contact because so much business dealing occurs mainly between men (the "old boy" network).

Weight Disorders

A billion-dollar medical, pharmaceutical, and publishing industry focused on weight reduction is supported by 20 million overweight women, or roughly one-quarter to one-third of the American female population (Fodor, 1982). Sex roles and sex-role stereotypes are correlated with weight problems (Stuart, 1979). In our culture, a woman's self-worth is seen as depending on her body image, and our media feature skinny, prepubescent girls as reflections of what is considered sexy. This is an ideal that is difficult for adult women to attain; it is biologically realistic for women to have more body fat than do men or teenage girls. The Victorian female's weight, including luxuriant bosom and full and voluptuous thighs, is far more in accordance with women's natural body build.

In contrast are the standards for men: The portly, cigar-smoking male is seen as attractive, or surely less stigmatized than a comparably built woman, despite the fact that being overweight is far riskier for males than for females.

So distorted do women's body images become that behavior therapists report as many as one-third of the applications for behavioral weight-control programs are by women of normal weight (Fodor, 1982). The cultural prescriptions for ideal weight have an obsessional nature that has encouraged many women to be miserable every time they pass a mirror, or to feel so embarrassed while having sex that they camouflage their thighs. Therapists had better try to understand the part played by sex-role stereotypes in the disturbance of anorexic or bulimic clients, who are extremely obsessed with food and staying slim and are confused about body image. The incidence of these disorders is appallingly high: Estimates of the rate of anorexia in teenage girls range from 0.4% to 4.0%. In a bulimia program conducted at Cornell University, an ad in the student paper drew 62 responses in two weeks (Boskind-White & White, 1983).

An effective rational–emotive program for working with women with weight disorders consists of helping clients to highlight some of the irrational cultural beliefs about being overweight and to recognize how they have made them into personal irrational beliefs (Fodor, 1982).

Cultural Message	Personal Irrational Belief
The ideal woman should look like Brooke Shields (teenage model).	If my body doesn't look like a model's, then I'm fat and disgusting. It is horrible to be fat.
Fat people are lazy and undisciplined.	I should be able to lose weight on my own, and if I don't, I'm a lazy, worthless person.
Thin women are more worthwhile.	I cannot possibly have a sex–love relationship, self-acceptance, or life enjoyment until I'm thin.

Many health professionals also hold society's prejudice against overweight women and set up behavioral and cognitive programs designed to shape the woman into the thin mold deified in our culture, rarely considering other alternatives. Such therapists would do well to challenge the assumptions that there is a standard weight for each person, that moderate overweight is unhealthy and deadly, that self-control is easy, and that women are unattractive and undesirable when moderately overweight. In doing consciousness raising with clients, the therapist can point out that the prejudices against overweight women can be viewed as "fatism" or "weightism," akin to sexism or racism. Clients can be encouraged to bring in their own examples, from magazines, TV, and shopping experiences, of societal messages relevant to thinness, sexual desirability, health, and self-control. Readings such as Orbach's *Fat Is a Feminist Issue* (1978) may be assigned. The focus is on helping clients to accept themselves unconditionally, no matter their body size.

Disputes include "Where is the evidence that I don't deserve to enjoy life as a fat person?" "Why can't fat people be happy?" Ultimately, clients begin to understand that "overweight" is not the problem; rather, it is their negative evaluations about it and themselves ("I can't stand to be overweight") or "I am a horrible person for being overweight"). These irrational beliefs perpetuate misery and preoccupation with dieting.

RELATIONSHIP AND WORK ISSUES FOR WOMEN

Marriage, Divorce, and Relationship Problems

Studies suggest that the social institution of marriage raises the risk of disorder for women but offers protection for men (Bernard, 1972). Married women who are not employed outside the home are at the highest risk for psychological disorder. They have the highest rates of entry into psychiatric treatment of any occupational group; they request (and receive) the greatest quantity of prescribed mood-modifying drugs (New York Narcotic Addiction Control Commission, 1971); and they report the highest incidence of psychogenic symptoms, such as nervousness, nightmares, dizziness, headaches, and related symptoms (Lief, 1975).

RET particularly specializes in helping women (and men) with marital and relationship problems (Ellis, 1957, 1977, 1979a, 1982; Ellis & Harper, 1961, 1975) by showing people their irrational beliefs about relating and how to dispute these beliefs. Typical irrational beliefs of women in marital conflict are "If the relationship ends, *I'm* to blame"; "I wasn't beautiful enough, interesting enough"; "I was too smart, too dumb, too demanding, inadequate, crazy, not sexy enough, too sexually demanding." The woman with marital problems damns herself if she does and damns herself if she doesn't, reflective of the societal rule that the woman is responsible for the success or failure of the relationship. It takes a good deal of rational restructuring to help her see that there are two people involved.

The following are some caveats RET therapists doing couples counseling should always keep in mind:

1. Beliefs about women's roles:
   a. Do you believe that a woman should stay home and take care of the children?
   b. Do you believe that working couples should equally divide the housework and other related tasks?

    c. In helping couples brainstorm options, would you bring up the possibility of the man becoming the homemaker while the woman goes back to school or advances her career?

2. General attitudes toward therapy:
   a. Do you tend to see the more overtly upset (usually the woman, since it's okay for women to cry) as being more disturbed than the calmer, quieter, and possibly emotionally constipated partner? Do you view emotional excess as a higher order of disturbance than emotional constipation?
   b. Are you colluding with the husband, either because you are more sympathetic to his views (e.g., that wives should do most of the housework) or because you may yourself have (or are) a "nagging" wife?
   c. Are you using extra energy to engage the male partner in an alliance, perhaps because you sense his reluctance to come in? Or because you accept the male partner as the person who holds the power in the relationship, and the power to keep the couple in therapy?
   d. Are you collaborating with the husband to cure the wife's passivity, neurosis, lack of assertiveness, and overdependence?
   e. Are you overemphasizing the woman's and overlooking the male's anger? It is common, especially for male therapists, to be reactive to female "bitchiness" in that they see the active female as angry and the active male as appropriately reacting to his wife's anger (Haan & Livson, 1973).

3. Attitudes of feminist therapists toward therapy:
   a. Are you colluding too much with the wife, perhaps sensing her passivity and wanting to help support her, and thereby reinforcing her passivity and dependency?
   b. Do you get angry with males and lose touch with your ability to be a sensitive reflector of what's happening when men become evasive and deny feelings?

Having some facts at your fingertips may often aid in consciousness raising and developing new options. A couple may be informed, for example, that men usually do one-third of the household tasks their wives do, whether the wives work or not (Baruch & Barnett, 1983), and that employed wives do nearly as much daily work around the house as homemakers do, while only 23% of the employed married men report a similar activity (Radloff, 1975).

Few areas are more poignant than the situation of a battered wife. Contemplating leaving after her fourth beating by her alcoholic husband, one client (who was actually the primary breadwinner) said, "If he treats me this way, I must be a terrible person. The kids need him, and so do I." This woman is a particularly sad example of the lack of self-confidence and problem-solving and goal-setting skills common in women who have resigned themselves to living out their marriages. Such a woman's thinking may be directly derivative of the confining stereotypes reinforced by our culture. She may be totally unable to imagine herself in another role (Martin, 1976). With her husband, she is battered and bruised, but coupled; without him, she sees herself as nothing.

The lot of the divorced or widowed woman is similarly grim. The woman contemplating divorce may suffer from an accumulation of disadvantages that severely limit the options she has for the rest of her life. Her earning capacity is usually much lower than her husband's. She has not had the same educational or vocational opportunities, and her career, if she has one, has generally been secondary and interrupted by family needs.

One of the biggest problems facing newly single women is that of raising children alone. The 1970 United States Census reports that more than 85% of single parents are women. Single mothers face loneliness, and insufficient funds, and legal issues, as well as the problems of developing new relationships, dependency, and autonomy.

The job of the rational–emotive therapist in such cases is a monumental one: (1) How can we counter self-blame in a society that teaches us that it is the woman who is primarily responsible for the success of her marriage and her children's mental health? (2) How can we build self-acceptance when everything that a woman tends to equate with being worthwhile (marriage, a happy home, vocational success) is not there? (3) How can we help her with the myriad tasks of supporting herself and reconstructing her life, when she has been fed messages of helplessness from early childhood onward?

Motherhood

To many women, regardless of their other interests, relationships, and accomplishments, mothering is the function that is central to their perceptions of themselves (Oliver, 1977). Yet in the process of undertaking this enormously difficult task of growing a child, they are frequently pinned between two difficult alternatives. If they have the economic means not to work outside the home, they potentially enter the ranks of the group with one of the highest rates of depression: women with young children who are full-time homemakers. However, the option of being a full-time homemaker and mother is a "privilege" available to fewer and fewer women. Today, 37% of women with children under five work, as compared with only 13% in 1948. Many working women must deal with prejudices from society and themselves, for example, that they are damaging their children permanently by working and that if they decide to work, they must be superwoman—hold down a job, attend to the physical and emotional needs of their children, and do all of these things perfectly, to the point of physical and psychological exhaustion (Zachary, 1980).

The option of remaining childless is also fraught with difficulties. There is still a stigma attached to the woman without children. She tends to be labeled deviant, infantile, or unwilling to accept the "feminine role."

The following is a list of caveats for therapists working with women on mothering issues:

1. In helping a woman dispute the irrational belief that she is a failure or rotten person if she imperfectly mothers, works at a job, or housecleans, have some additional facts handy to counter societal myths. For example, studies show that whether or not a mother is employed does not appear to be a determining factor in causing juvenile delinquency. It is the quality of a mother's care rather than the time consumed in such care that is of major significance (Women's Bureau, 1972).
2. Assign some women's liberation readings (e.g., chapters on marriage and motherhood) from the anthologies *Woman in Sexist Society* (Gornick & Moran, 1972) or *Sisterhood Is Powerful* (Morgan, 1970).
3. Place the client in a woman's therapy and/or support group, to help her see that she is not alone with her problems and for practical help in dealing with mothering problems.

Sexuality

Approximately 10% of American women never experience orgasm, and well over half of sexually active women do not regularly reach orgasm in their coital experiences (Kinsey, Pomeroy, Martin, & Gebhard, 1953); Hunt, 1974; Hite, 1976). Numerous women have problems of arousal and of low sexual interest.

It is widely agreed that feelings and beliefs are the cause of many sexual dysfunctions (Barbach, 1980; Lieblum, 1980). A good number of these beliefs are derivative of sex-role "shoulds." Woman grow up with highly conflicting messages about their sexuality. They are indoctrinated to save themselves for their one true love, yet at the same time to dress, walk, and talk seductively. Romanticism leads to an emphasis on beauty; sex becomes a means of barter; bodies are products to be improved for greatest marketability, with the emphasis on attraction and courtship, rather than consummation. Beauty and ability to lure become equated with sexuality, with many women only "feeling like a woman" when a man is around. The inability of some women to see themselves as having sexual feelings and desires other than those resulting from male initiation makes it difficult for them to become initiators or even active participants in the sex act.

Both sexes are victims of sexual ignorance, but in our culture it is the female who has been forbidden to accept herself as a sexual being. Too often, both arousal and nonarousal are viewed as "bad" or "wrong" and encourage anxiety.

In heterosexual relations, sex is frequently over before women even become aroused. By focusing on their appearance, comparing themselves to younger women, and worrying about pleasing their men, women lock themselves into a cycle of frustration that further exacerbates their inability to become aroused and to enjoy sex.

The following consciousness-raising exercise, "Nasty Names," is used both with women clients and in mixed sexuality groups, in order to illustrate sexual attitudes toward women. Clients are asked to call out all the names they can think of for sexually active women *(slut, whore, tramp);* for sexually selective women *(frigid, uptight, women's libber);* and for sexually active men *(swinger, Don Juan, playboy).* Finally, clients are asked to brainstorm the nastiest names that men can be called *(pussywhipped, henpecked, bastards, sons-of-bitches, faggots).* The exercise demonstrates dramatically (1) how women are globally labeled for their sexual behaviors: (2) how they are damned if they do and damned if they don't; (3) how there is a double standard for sexually active females and males; and (4) how we perpetuate a misogyny so pervasive that the worst thing a man can be called is something that derogates him by comparing him to a woman. Women tend to make themselves anxious over these words and behave in such a way as to avoid these "awful" labels. If not uncovered, these attitudes remain as schemata through which women perceive themselves and are perceived, interfering with among other things, with pleasurable sex.

A highly effective modality for treating women with sexual dysfunctions has been found to be all-women's groups (Barbach, 1980; Kuriansky, Sharpe, & O'Connor, 1976; Walen & Wolfe, 1983). In RET women's sexuality groups, the teaching of a general disturbance-combatting cognitive self-help approach often leads to a fairly rapid elimination of the target problem (90% to 100% learn to achieve orgasm after only six two-hour sessions). It also leads to generalization to other areas of the women's lives (Walen & Wolfe, 1983). In addition to sexual re-education and behavioral assignments, other cognitive foci in RET women's sexuality groups (and individual therapy) include unveiling and debunking erroneous sexual myths and sex-role programming that interfere with autonomy and self-determination in sexual and nonsexual areas (Walen & Wolfe, 1983). The following list illustrates these activities.

Cultural Messages	Personal Irrational Beliefs
Only Freud and men know how a woman's body works.	I should be able to orgasm through intercourse, and I'm a sexual failure if I can't.
Sexy = beautiful and young.	I must have a trim and firm body to enjoy sex. It would be awful if he saw my cellulite. Menopause and hysterectomy end my ability for sexual enjoyment.

Cultural Messages	Personal Irrational Beliefs
If you're in love, sex should automatically be terrific.	If he loves me, he should know what turns me on without my having to tell him. If I love him, I should want to have sex as much as he, enjoy swallowing his semen, etc.
Women are responsible for making relationships work.	If he's having trouble getting erections, I'm to blame. I must not hurt his feelings, make him feel emasculated. Sex is my obligation if I'm married.
It's wrong and selfish to put my interests first, or be sexually assertive.	I shouldn't take too long to come. It's selfish or unfeminine to ask for 20 minutes of clitoral stimulation; he must never feel uncomfortable or inconvenienced.
Liberated women should be sexually active and sexually assertive.	I should not say no to sex on the first date. I should initiate sex more, enjoy just about anything, and if I don't, I'm a prude. I should be having multiple orgasms.

Bibliotherapy for sexual problems includes the following: *Intelligent Woman's Guide to Dating and Mating* (Ellis, 1979); *The Great Orgasm Robbery* (Tepper, 1977); *Our Bodies, Ourselves* (Boston Women's Health Collective, 1976); *The Hite Report on Female Sexuality* (Hite, 1976); and *How to Be Sexually Assertive* (Wolfe, 1976).

Sexual Abuse: Harrassment, Incest, and Rape

Given that one out of every three females now alive in the United States will be raped at least once in her lifetime, and that one out of every four girls in the United States will be sexually abused in some way before she reaches the age of 18 (Weber, 1980), the topic of sexual assault is one of great urgency for anyone working with women or children.

The effects of sexual victimization may not become apparent until months or years after the event. At times the event itself may be suppressed; this is very common in incest. In other cases, there may be anger at the abuser or the judicial system, as well as guilt, shame, and sexual inhibition or dysfunction (Zachary, 1980). Because of the tremendous shame and secrecy surrounding the topic, professionals often fail to do the flushing-out required to open the topic with clients who do not pose it as a presenting complaint.

Better understanding of the cultural processes involved in sexual abuse may be achieved by viewing sexual assault as the extreme enactment of "male" and "female" roles as they are learned in this culture (Colao, 1983; O'Hare, 1983). For example, a rape victim is likely to focus on exaggerated perceptions of her inadequacy, powerlessness, and incompetence, and on thoughts such as "Being raped was my own fault," or "I am worthless now that I've been raped."

Professionals, as members of this society, may have internalized some of these myths and unconsciously perpetuate them in their work with clients. Some of these myths or irrational beliefs include the following:

1. Incest:
    a. It's usually a child's fantasy.
    b. It only happens among social outcasts or the psychiatrically disturbed.
    c. A bad mommy is responsible for the abuse.
    d. It may be okay because the child is at least getting sexual education at home and receiving affection.
2. Rape:
    a. Women provoke or incite attack (e.g., "I'm to blame for being in the wrong place or for wearing sexy clothes").
    b. Women never get raped by men they know.
    c. Women invent stories of rape to get men in trouble.
    d. Women secretly desire rape; they only say no because they're playing hard-to-get.
    e. "I'm devalued, soiled; it would be awful if people knew I was raped; I can't stand facing them."
    f. "I'll never be able to enjoy sex again."

RET is particularly well suited to the treatment of sexually abused clients. It shows them how to unconditionally accept themselves, no matter what transpired. It provides a coping method that they can use to control their feelings and actions and that can have a powerful therapeutic effect. The following are some caveats for therapists dealing with victims of sexual abuse:

1. In helping to dispute the client's anger cognitions, don't move in too quickly; empathize with her upset feelings first. If you don't, the client may continue to self-blame, or she may leave therapy.
2. Don't reinforce (even inadvertently) the idea that the abused woman did something to provoke the abuse.
3. Be aware of self-help groups in your community for incest and rape victims, as well as the addresses of any organizations dealing with sexual harrassment on the job.

Work Issues

We live in a time when 52% of the women in this country work outside the home, when one out of six families is being maintained by women, and when the bulk of young families depend on two workers to survive. In order to deal with women's feelings as they try to cope with new and often unfamiliar roles, let us look at society's attitudes toward working women and at the consequences of these attitudes on women's occupational patterns.

This is the coming of age of the woman worker, but what do women find? They find that the gap in income between men's and women's wages has actually increased in the last generation, and that women still earn 60¢ to every dollar that men earn (Reskin, 1984). They find that sex stereotyping in jobs is rampant and that women still work in a few familiar categories of jobs (clerical, service, and private household work), while men work in dozens. In 1958, 53% of all working women worked in these three female-dominated categories. By 1975, the figure was 58%. In 1958, 30% of all working women worked as clerks and secretaries. By 1975, this figure had increased to 35% (Norton, 1981).

Societal prejudices against the working woman abound. Competence in women is seen as a deviation from the social norms of the feminine stereotype. If women try to succeed or exercise power, everyone, including themselves, undervalues their accomplishments. The career oriented male is considered a go-getter, assertive, and on the ball. His female counterpart is called pushy, a ball-breaker, or a dyke and is frequently ignored or penalized for her assertive behavior. In the traditional hierarchical structure of most workplaces, women, in the lower ranks, rarely are given the right or the power to question, criticize, or suggest to the men who have authority over them.

The reality of a 40% divorce rate, which has amplified the fear of looking for security in marriage and ending up alone and desperate, has made many young women today, married and unmarried, seek security in careers. In so doing, they are expected to meet standards of performance in the workplace set in the past by and for men who had wives to take care of the details of living. At the same time, they are expected to perform as well at home and with children as women who are full-time homemakers and mothers. Their struggle to do so is exacerbated by a dearth of good dual-career role models; by magazine articles on superwomen who marvelously balance home, career, mothering, and social activities; by low sense of competence; by fears both of failure and success (Horner, 1969); and by a tendency to go for a series of jobs rather than a planned career.

The following are typical self-messages leading to low career aspirations:

"If I'm good, someone will come along and take care of me."
"I must not be too smart or assertive, lest I be seen as a castrating female."
"I must not speak too affirmatively of my abilities, lest I be thought 'un-feminine,' 'bragging.' "
"It's O.K. to make commitments to other people, but not to myself."

The following are typical self-messages leading to lack of assertiveness and minimal efforts at career advancement:

"There's no use in approaching my boss. Why bother—he's hopelessly sexist" (depression, anger).

"Things are unfair; they shouldn't be. I can't stand it" (low frustration tolerance).

"It's too late to change jobs, to get what I want, to be retrained" (depression, low frustration tolerance).

The following are typical negative self-messages of dual-career and career re-entry women:

"I must be young and beautiful (or more skilled) to get this job; and it's awful if I can't get it."

"I must be approved of by others (who criticize me for neglecting my kids), and if not, I'm a failure, a bad person."

"I shouldn't have to be starting at entry level; I should be beyond this stage already" (low frustration tolerance).

The following are typical negative self-statements perpetuated by occupationally successful women:

"I slipped into this job by a fluke. Any day they'll find out what an incompetent phony I am" (self-downing, catastrophizing).

"Even though I work 10 hours a day without even stopping for meals, I feel inadequate—I should be doing more" (perfectionism, self-downing).

The following is a list of suggestions for dealing with work issues in therapy with women:

1. Encourage women to:
   a. Look for good role models and possibly join a professional organization.
   b. Concentrate on the excitement (and not just the difficulties) of "pioneering".
   c. Develop a support network.
2. Encourage dual-career women to:
   a. Adopt different standards (e.g., less neatness for house and kids, less time with mate).
   b. See that kids may not be ruined, but rather may see their mother's being at work as a valuable educational experience and helpful in learning independence.
3. Have available a list of resources for helping women combat some of the inequities in the work world. Such a list could include Title VII of the Equal Employment Act of 1972, the names of agencies dealing with sex

discrimination, sources of nonstereotypic educational and vocational options, and names of professional women's organizations.

4. Be alert to the reduced expectations women have of themselves, and
    brainstorm other options than their stated goal of getting a $15-a-week raise
    on their secretarial job. For example, ask if they have thought of applying
    for managerial-level positions.
5. Do lots of assertiveness training to help change habits (e.g., failing to
    respond effectively to put-downs or sexual innuendos, or reticence to
    develop competitiveness). It is not uncommon for a $50,000-a-year execu-
    tive to break down in tears when her boss criticizes something she has
    done, or to act cute and seductive when her plan is rejected, or to sulk
    because she has been given a poor assignment. It is crucial that women
    learn how to ask for and get things without being manipulative or indirect.
6. Encourage covert and overt confidence building. Have clients log self-put-
    downs and replace them with comments like "I did that really well" and "I
    handled that criticism much better than I did last time." To boost confi-
    dence and help increase their self-marketing skills, ask clients to write a
    letter of recommendation about themselves.
7. Encourage women to develop skills they may have told themselves they
    "can't understand" (e.g., suggest they take a financial management
    course).

CASE STUDY

Nancy was a 28-year-old nurse whose presenting problems were depression, low
self-acceptance, and difficulties in her relationship with a married doctor. Therapy focused on helping her change her emotional overreactions, as well as on
ways to deal with a social system that made her daily work difficult and gave her
limited opportunities for career advancement (Table 22–1). Her problems at
work included dealing with other nurses who were in fierce competition for the
male doctors and coping with the sexist behavior of doctors. (During open-heart
surgery, for example, one surgeon kept backing up against her.)

CONCLUSION

American Psychological Association task forces (1975, 1978) have urged that
psychologists promote concepts of sexual equality as part of their practice and
have concluded that psychologists have a responsibility to examine their personal
roles in perpetuating the sex bias and sex-role stereotyping that can be so
destructive to the mental health of their women clients. RET, done within the

TABLE 22.1 RET and Adjunctive Therapy with Nancy

Problems	RET Work	Adjunctive Therapy and Resources
Anger and hurt at lover's inconsiderate behavior	Anti-awfulizing about his behavior	*Consciousness-raising/education:* Read articles on women in the workplace. Go to NOW (National Organization for Women) meeting. Record instances of sexism at work. Contact sexual harrassment organization for information on filing complaints.
Anger and hurt at nurses' backbiting	Anti-awfulizing about their behavior	*Skill building:* Take assertiveness training workshop. Read article on assertiveness for nurses (Herman, 1977). Practice assertiveness with friends. Do life-planning projection up to age 90.
Poor assertiveness skills with lover and people at work	Dispute idea that "I cannot effectively respond" and "I am a weak, wimpy person"	*Social support:* Look for new friends not preoccupied with men. Observe and talk to good female role models.
Low self-acceptance, helplessness, hopelessness, anger at herself for her financial dependence on lover	Dispute ideas that "I must be a worthless person if people treat me so badly"; "There is nothing I can do about my situation"; "I'm a bad person for having gotten myself into this situation." Give self 3 positive self-messages each day	*Economic support:* Investigate loan opportunities to replace financial dependence on lover. Consider part-time job. Consider possibility of training to become a nurse-anaesthesiologist.

417

framework of examining women's social context and the shoulds about social roles, offers a practical tool for helping women make broad cognitive and behavioral changes and develop their potential as full human beings.

REFERENCES

Agras, S., Sylvester, D., & Oliveau, D. (1969). The epidemiology of common fears and phobias. *Comprehensive Psychiatry, 10,* 151–156.

American Psychological Association Task Force. (1975). Report of the Task Force on Sex Bias and Sex Role Stereotyping in Psychotherapeutic Practice. *American Psychologist, 30,* 1169–1175.

American Psychological Association Task Force. (1978). Report of the Task Force on Sex Bias and Sex Role Stereotyping in Psychotherapeutic Practice: Guidelines for therapy with women. *American Psychologist, 33,* 1122–1133.

Barbach, L. G. (1980). *Women discover orgasm: A therapist's guide to a new treatment approach.* New York: Free Press/Macmillan.

Barrett, C. J., Berg, P. I., Eaton, E. M., & Pomeroy, E. L. (1974). Implications of women's liberation and the future of psychotherapy. *Psychotherapy: Theory, Research and Practice, 11*(1), 11–15.

Baruch, G., & Barnett, R. (1983). *Correlates of fathers' participation in family work: A technical report.* Wellesley, Mass.: Wellesley College Center for Research on Women.

Bem, S. L. & Lenney, E. (1976). Sex-typing and the avoidance of cross-sex behavior. *Journal of Personality and Social Psychology, 33,* 48–54.

Bernard, J. (1972). *The future of marriage.* New York: World.

Berzins, J. I. (1975, June). *Sex roles and psychotherapy: New directions for theory and research.* Paper presented at the 6th Annual Meeting, Society for Psychotherapy Research, Boston, Mass.

Block, J. (1973). Conceptions of sex role: Some cross-cultural and longitudinal perspectives. *American Psychologist, 28*(6), 512–526.

Block, J. (1979, March). *The changing American parent: Implications for child development.* Paper presented at meeting of the Society for Research in Child Development, San Francisco.

Boskind-White, M., & White, W. (1983). *Bulimarexia: The binge/purge cycle.* New York: Norton.

Boston Women's Health Collective. (1976). *Our bodies, ourselves.* New York: Simon and Schuster.

Brehony, K. (1983). Women and agoraphobia: A case for the etiological significance of the feminine sex-role stereotype. In V. Franks & E. Rothblum (Eds.), *Sex role stereotypes and women's mental health.* New York: Springer.

Brodsky, A. M., & Hare-Mustin, R. T. (Eds.), (1980a). *Women and psychotherapy: An assessment of research and practice.* New York: Guilford Press.

Brodsky, A. M., & Hare-Mustin, R. T. (1980b). Psychotherapy and women: Priorities for research. In A. Brodsky & R. Hare-Mustin (Eds.), *Women and psychotherapy: An assessment of research and practice.* New York: Guilford Press.

Broverman, C., Broverman, D., Clarkson, F., Rosenkrantz, P., & Vogel, S. (1970). Sex role stereotypes and clinical judgments of mental health. *Journal of Consulting and Clinical Psychology, 34,* 1–7.

Chesler, P. (1972). *Women and madness.* Garden City, N.Y.: Doubleday.

Colao, F. (1983). Therapists coping with sexual assault. In J. Robbins & R. Siegel (Eds.), *Women changing therapy.* New York: Haworth Press.

Ellis, A. (1957). *How to live with a "neurotic."* New York: Crown. [Rev. ed. (1975) North Hollywood, Calif.: Wilshire Books.]

Ellis, A. (1962). *Reason and emotion in psychotherapy.* Secaucus, N.J.: Citadel Press.

Ellis, A. (1973). *Humanistic psythotherapy: The rational–emotive approach.* New York: McGraw-Hill.

Ellis, A. (1974). Treatment of sex and love problems in women. In V. Franks & V. Burtle (Eds.), *Women in therapy.* New York: Brunner/Mazel.

Ellis, A. (1977). *How to live with—and without—anger.* Secaucus, N.J.: Citadel Press.

Ellis, A. (1979). *The intelligent woman's guide to dating and mating.* New York: Lyle Stuart.

Ellis, A. (1982). Rational–emotive family therapy. In A. M. Horne & M. H. Ohlsen (Eds.), *Family counseling and therapy*. Itasca, Ill.: Peacock.

Ellis, A., & Becker, I. (1982). *A guide to personal happiness*. North Hollywood, Calif.: Wilshire Books.

Ellis, A., & Harper, R. A. (1961). *A guide to successful marriage*. North Hollywood, Calif.: Wilshire Books.

Ellis, A., & Harper, R. A. (1975). *A new guide to rational living*. North Hollywood, Calif.: Wilshire Books.

Fodor, I. (1974). The phobic syndrome in women: Implications for treatment. In V. Franks & V. Burtle (Eds.), *Women in therapy*. New York: Brunner/Mazel.

Fodor, I. (1982). Toward an understanding of male/female differences in phobic anxiety disorders. In I. Al-Issa (Eds.), *Gender and psychopathology*. New York: Academic Press.

Fodor, I. (1983). Behavior therapy for the overweight woman. In M. Rosenbaum & C. Franks (Eds.), *Perspectives on behavior therapy in the eighties*. New York: Springer.

Franks, V. (1979). Gender and psychotherapy. In E. Gomberg & V. Franks (Eds.), *Gender and disordered behavior: Sex differences in psychopathology*. New York: Brunner/Mazel.

Franks, V. (1982, April). *Psychotherapy and women*. Letter No. 79. Belle Mead, N.J.: Carrier Foundation.

Glaser, K. (1976). Women's self-help groups as an alternative to therapy. *Psychotherapy: Theory, Research and Practice, 13*, 77–81.

Goldstein, A. J., & Chambless, D. L. (1980). The treatment of agoraphobia. In A. J. Goldstein and E. G. Foa (Eds.), *Handbook of behavioral interventions*. New York: John Wiley.

Gornick, V., & Moran, B. (1971). *Woman in sexist society*. New York: Basic Books.

Gornick, V., & Moran, B. (Eds.). (1972). *Woman in sexist society*. New York: Signet.

Grieger, I. Z. (1982). The cognitive basis of women's problems. In R. Grieger & I. Z. Grieger (Eds.), *Cognition and emotional disturbance*. New York: Human Sciences Press.

Guttentag, M., & Salasin, S. (1976). Women, men and mental health. In G. Cates, M. Scott, & R. Martyna (Eds.), *Women and men: Changing roles and perceptions*. Aspen, Colo.: Aspen Institute for Humanistic Studies.

Haan, N., & Livson, N. (1973). Sex differences in the eyes of expert personality assessors: Blind Spots? *Journal of Personality Assessment, 37*, 486–492.

Hare-Mustin, R. (1983). An appraisal of the relationship between women and psychotherapy: 80 years after the case of Dora. *American Psychologist, 38*, 593–602.

Heriot, J. (1983). The double bind: Healing the split. In J. Robbins & R. Siegel (Eds.), *Women changing therapy*. New York: Haworth Press.

Herman, S. (1977). Assertiveness: One answer to job dissatisfaction for nurses. In R. Alberti (Ed.), *Assertiveness: Innovations, applications, issues*. San Luis Obispo, CA: Impact.

Hite, S. (1976). *The Hite report*. New York: Macmillan.

Horner, M. (1969). Women's motive to avoid success. *Psychology Today, 62*, 36–38.

Hunt, M. *Sexual behavior in the 1970's*. (1974). Chicago: Playboy Press.

Jasin, S. (1983). Cognitive-behavioral treatment of agoraphobia in groups. In A. Freeman (Ed.), *Cognitive therapy in couples and groups*. New York: Plenum.

Kelly, J. A., Kern, J. M., Kirkley, B. G., Patterson, J. N., & Keane, F. M. (1980). Reactions to assertive versus nonassertive behavior: Differential effects for males and females, and implications for assertive training. *Behavior Therapy, 11*, 670–682.

Kinsey, A. C. Pomeroy, W. B., Martin, C. E., & Gebhard, P. H. (1953). *Sexual behavior in the human female*. New York: Simon & Schuster, Pocket Books.

Krumboltz, H. B., & Shapiro, J. (1979). Counseling women in behavioral self-direction. *Personnel & Guidance Journal, 4*, 415–418.

Kuriansky, J., Sharpe, L., & O'Connor, D. (1976, October). *Group treatment for women: The quest for orgasm*. Paper presented at the American Public Health Association of Washington, D.C.

Levine, S. V., Camin, L. E., & Levine, E. L. (1974). Sexism and psychiatry. *American Journal of Orthopsychiatry, 44*, 327–336.

Lieblum, S. (Speaker). (1980). *Sexual problems of women*. Cassette recording. New York: SMA Audio Cassettes.

Lief, H. (1975). Sexual counseling. In Romney, S., *The health care of women*. New York: McGraw-Hill.

Loeffler, D., & Fiedler, L. (1979) Woman—a sense of identity: A counseling intervention to facilitate personal growth in women. *Journal of Counseling Psychology, 26*(1), 51–57.

Martin, D. (1976). *Battered wives.* San Francisco: Glide.

Metropolitan Life Insurance Company. (1980). Mortality differentials favor women. *Statistical Bulletin, 61,* 2–3.

Morgan, R., (1970). *Sisterhood is powerful.* New York: Vintage.

Moulton, R. (1977). Some effects of the new feminism. *American Journal of Psychiatry, 134*(1), 3.

New York Narcotic Addiction Control Commission. (1971). *Differential drug use within New York State labor force: An assessment of drug use within the general population.* Albany, N.Y.: New York Narcotic Addiction Control Commission.

Norton, E. (1981). Remarks at First Annual Women in Crisis Conference. In P. Russianoff (Ed.), *Women in crisis.* New York: Human Sciences.

O'Hare, J., & Taylor, K. (1983). The reality of incest. In J. Robbins & R. Siegel (Eds.), *Women changing therapy.* New York: Haworth Press.

Oliver, R. (1977). The 'empty nest syndrome' as a focus of depression: A cognitive treatment model, based on rational–emotive therapy. *Psychotherapy: Theory, Research and Practice, 14*(1), 87–94.

Orbach, S. (1978). *Fat is a feminist issue.* New York and London: Paddington Press.

Radloff, L. (1975). Sex differences in depression: The effects of occupation and marital status. *Sex Roles, 1,* 249–265.

Reskin, B. (1984). Sex segregation in the work place. In *Gender at work: Perspectives on occupational segregation in comparable worth.* Washington, D.C.: Women's Research and Education Institute of the Congressional Caucus for Women's Issues.

Rice, J. K., & Rice, D. (1973). Implications of the women's liberation movement for psychotherapy. *American Journal of Psychiatry, 130,* 191–196.

Robbins, J. H., & Siegel, R. J. (Eds.). (1983). *Women changing therapy: New assessments, values and strategies in feminist therapy.* New York: Haworth Press.

Rothblum, E. (1983). Sex role stereotypes and depression in women. In V. Franks & E. Rothblum (Eds.), *Sex role stereotypes and women's mental health.* New York: Springer.

Russianoff, P. (1982). *Why do I think I'm nothing without a man?* New York: Bantam.

Seligman, M. (1975). *Helplessness.* San Francisco, Calif.: W. H. Freeman.

Seligman, M. (1979, October). Conference on learned helplessness. Charlottesville, Virginia.

Spence, J., Helmreich, R., & Stapp, J. (1975). Ratings of self and peers on sex-role attributes and their relation to self-esteem and conceptions of masculinity and femininity. *Journal of Personality and Social Psychology, 32,* 29–39.

Stein, L., DelGaudio, A., & Ansley, M. (1976). A comparison of male and female neurotic depressives. *Journal of Clinical Psychology, 32,* 19–21.

Stuart, R. B. (1979). Sex differences in obesity. In E. Bomberg & V. Franks (Eds.), *Gender and disordered behavior: Sex differences in psychopathology.* New York: Brunner/Mazel.

Tepper, S. (1977). *The great orgasm robbery.* Denver, Colo.: RMPP Publications.

Walen, S., & Wolfe, J. (1983). Sexual enhancement groups for women. In A. Freeman (Ed.), *Cognitive therapy with couples and groups.* New York: Plenum.

Weber, E. (1980, June). Sexual abuse begins at home. *Ms Magazine,* 122–131.

Weissman, M. M. & Klerman, G. L. (1977). Sex differences and the epidemiology of depression. *Archives of General Psychiatry, 34,* 98–111.

Weisstein, N. (1971). Psychology constructs the female, or the fantasy life of the male psychologist. In M. Garskof (Ed.), *Roles women play: Readings toward women's liberation.* Belmont, Calif.: Brooks-Cole.

Wisconsin Clearinghouse. (1980). *Shattering female sex-role stereotypes.* Madison, Wis.: Author.

Wolfe, J. (1975, September). *Rational–emotive therapy as an effective feminist therapy.* Paper presented at the American Psychological Association Convention, Chicago.

Wolfe, J. (1976). *How to be sexually assertive.* New York: Institute for Rational–Emotive Therapy.

Wolfe, J. (1980a, June). *Helping women change.* Paper presented at the 25th Anniversary Rational–Emotive Therapy Conference, New York.

Wolfe, J. (1980b, September). *Rational–emotive therapy women's groups: New model for an effective feminist therapy.* Paper presented at the American Psychological Association Annual Convention, Montreal, Canada.

Wooley, S., & Wooley, O. (1980). Eating disorders: Obesity and anorexia. In A. Brodsky & R. Hare-Mustin (Eds.), *Women and psychotherapy: An assessment of research and practice*. New York: Guilford Press.

Worell, J. (1980). New directions in counseling women. *Personnel and Guidance Journal, 58,* 477–484.

Wyckoff, H. (1977). *Solving women's problems*. New York: Grove Press.

Zachary, I. (1980). RET with women. Some special issues. In R. Grieger & J. Boyd (Eds.), *Rational–emotive therapy: A skills based approach*. New York: Van Nostrand Reinhold.

Appendixes

A

Professional Training Programs in Rational– Emotive Therapy

The Institute for Rational–Emotive Therapy in New York City and its several affiliates around the world offer official programs of study in RET. Only the parent institute in New York offers all four programs however, while the others offer some but not all programs, (see Appendix B for the names, addresses, and programs offered by each affiliate). The programs of study, all leading to certificates, are as follows.

PRIMARY CERTIFICATE PROGRAM

The mastery of RET theory and technique begins with the Primary Certificate Program. Participants study the fundamentals of RET, along with the application of its techniques.

Eligibility

The Primary Certificate Program is open to psychologists, counselors, social workers, physicians, nurses, and full-time graduate students. Minimum qualification for certificate candidacy is a master's degree in psychology or counseling, an M.S.W., M.D., or R.N.

Program Requirements

The Primary Certificate may be earned by completing one of the two following options. Candidates electing either option are required to complete assigned readings and written and oral examinations, as well as required to participate in all activities.

1. *Practicum Programs*. This option is a five-consecutive-day program that combines lecture, tape-recorded and videotaped demonstrations, and a variety of live individual and group experiences. In addition, participants receive approximately 14 hours of small-group supervision of their therapy sessions.
2. *Workshop Program*. In this option, the participant attends four one-day primary certificate workshops and receives five sessions of individual supervision.

Certificate

Candidates who fulfill all program requirements and whose RET skills are judged by the training faculty as meeting at least minimal standards of performance will receive a certificate. Admission to the Primary Certificate Program does not guarantee the awarding of a certificate.

INTERMEDIATE CERTIFICATE PROGRAM

The Intermediate Certificate Program provides training for Primary Certificate holders not eligible for or not wishing to participate in the Associate Fellowship Program. Candidates will further their knowledge of RET principles, theoretical foundations, and clinical applications during these training sessions. Featured in the program is RET supervision involving cases from the participants' professional caseloads.

Eligibility

Holders of the Primary Certificate Program are eligible for the Intermediate Certificate Program.

Program Requirements

Candidates are required to complete either (1) four one-day training workshops in addition to those required for the Primary Certificate and eight hours of individual supervision of therapy cases beyond supervision required for the Primary Certificate or (2) one five-day Associate Fellowship Practicum (see subsequent discussion).

Certificate

Candidates who fulfill all program requirements and whose RET skills are judged by the training faculty as meeting at least minimal standards of performance will be granted a certificate. Work completed as part of the Intermediate Program may be counted toward the requirements for the Associate Fellowship Certificate, provided the candidate meets eligibility requirements for that program. Admission to the Intermediate Certificate Program does not guarantee the awarding of a certificate.

ASSOCIATE FELLOWSHIP PROGRAM

This extensive program provides practitioners the opportunity to broaden their RET and other cognitive behavioral therapeutic techniques. Associate Fellow candidates receive supervision and seminars to increase their philosophical and empirical knowledge of RET.

Eligibility

A prerequisite for the Associate Fellowship Program is a Primary Certificate in RET. Beyond that, this program is open to certified psychologists (or those nearing completion of their doctorates), physicians, registered nurses, holders of the M.S.W., clergy with graduate training and counseling experience, and holders of master's degrees carrying caseloads of clients supervised in institutional settings.

Individuals who do not meet these requirements but who are working with clients (such as community workers, lawyers, vocational rehabilitation counselors) may enroll in the workshops but will be ineligible to receive the certificate.

Program Requirements

Candidates for the Associate Fellowship are required to complete the following:

1. Two five-day practica conducted 12 months apart must be done. Each practicum will consist of seminars and case supervision. In the seminars, the empirical and philosophical bases of rational–emotive therapy will be examined and their application to individual counseling and psychotherapy will be covered in depth. Areas for discussion will include psychological homework, rational–emotive imagery, and other intervention techniques. Group methods of RET also will be discussed. The seminars' aims are to help the practitioner develop a firm foundation for the application of rational–emotive principles to working with clients. *Case supervision* will involve peer counseling and cases in which the candidate is currently using RET approaches.
2. Twenty-four sessions of individual RET case supervision must be done

within a 12-month period. Candidates will arrange to hold these sessions by mail or in person with an institute-approved supervisor.

3. A tape-recorded RET therapy session must be submitted for evaluation by the International Training Standards and Review Committee (see Appendix C).

Certificate

Participants eligible for the Associate Fellowship who fulfill all program requirements and whose RET skills are judged by the training faculty as meeting at least minimal standards of performance will receive the Associate Fellowship. They then can enroll in training programs that can lead to training faculty status at the institute in New York. Admission to the Associate Fellowship Program does not guarantee the awarding of a certificate.

FELLOWSHIP PROGRAM

The Fellowship Program is the most comprehensive program of study offered. During this unique two-year course of study, participants receive in-depth training in rational–emotive and allied cognitive behavioral psychotherapeutic techniques. In operation 11 months per year, the clinical work can generally be met by working two evenings per week, with supervision on Wednesday afternoons from 1:00 to 5:00 PM. By special arrangement, persons on sabbatical leave or from out of town may complete the program in one year. Individuals admitted to the Fellowship Program receive a stipend of $3,600 per year, or, if they have a one-year program, $7,200.

Eligibility

Candidates for the Fellowship Program are required to hold a doctorate in psychology or counseling or an M.S.W. or M.D. degree. Candidates must be licensed or eligible for licensure in their professions. A limited number of predoctoral interns may be accepted into the Fellowship Program, provided they have signed dissertation proposals. Predoctoral interns pursue the same program as post-doctoral Fellows and receive the same stipend.

Program Requirements

The Fellowship Program offers highly diversified training, which includes the following:

1. *Clinical experience*. Fellowship candidates devote nine hours per week to clinical practice, coleading a therapy group with Albert Ellis and seeing approximately eight clients per week in the institute's moderate-cost clinic.
2. *Supervision*. Emphasis is placed on the personal as well as the professional aspects of the therapist's work. Medical and other consultants are brought in to provide a comprehensive training experience.
3. *Personal therapy experience*. In order to maximize their therapeutic potential, candidates are required to participate in a special therapy group made up only of Fellowship candidates.

Certificate

Candidates who fulfill all program requirements and whose RET skills are judged by the training faculty as meeting at least minimal standards of performance will be awarded a certificate and will become eligible for Fellowship membership in the institute. Opportunities are available for graduate Fellows to affiliate with the institute's treatment center as faculty or staff psychotherapists. Admission to the Fellowship Program does not guarantee the awarding of a certificate.

B

Rational–Emotive Therapy Affiliates

OFFERING PRIMARY CERTIFICATE AND ASSOCIATE FELLOWSHIP CERTIFICATE TRAINING

Mid-Atlantic Institute for Rational–Emotive Therapy
c/o Dr. Russell Grieger
2120 Ivy Rd., Suite B
Charlottesville, Va. 22903
(804) 296-0606, 973-3191

OFFERING PRIMARY CERTIFICATE TRAINING

Australian Institute for Rational–Emotive Therapy
c/o Dr. Michael E. Bernard
University of Melbourne, Dept. of Education
Parkville, Victoria 3052 Australia
(03) 341-6392

British Institute for Rational–Emotive Therapy
c/o Dr. Windy Dryden
209 Belchers Lane
Little Bromwich, Birmingham, England B9 5RT
(021) 772-7948

Cleveland Institute for Rational Living
c/o James A. Bard, Ph.D., & Harold R. Fisher, Ph.D.
3659 Green Rd.
Beachwood, Ohio 44122
(216) 464-1144

Denver Institute for Rational–Emotive Therapy
c/o Laura Knutson
2343 E. Evans Ave.
Denver, Colorado 80210
(303) 744-0025

Instituut voor Rationele Therapie
c/o Rene Diekstra, Ph.D.
St. Annastraat 61
6524 EH Nijmegen, Netherlands
080-23-24-36

Institute for Rational–Emotive Therapy—Italy
c/o Cesare de Silvestri, M.D., & Carola Schimmelpfenning, Dipl. Psych.
Via Prisciano 28
Rome, Italy 00136
(06) 345-1-482

Deutsches Institut fur Rational–Emotive Therapie
c/o Horst Zimmermann, Dipl. Psych., & Ursula Zimmermann, Dipl. Psych.
Kolner Str. 1, 4048 Grevenbroich 1, West Germany
02181/3027

Institute for Rational–Emotive Therapy
c/o Michael Broder, Ph.D.
1315 Walnut Street, Suite 1100
Philadelphia, Pa. 19107
(215) 545-7000

Mexican Institute for Rational–Emotive Therapy
c/o Dr. Patricia Leal
Taine 249, 2nd floor
Colonia Polanco, Mexico D.F.

OTHER AFFILIATES

Chicago Institute for Rational–Emotive Therapy
c/o Kenneth Peiser
2045 N. Larrabee, #7108
Chicago, Illinois 60614
(312) 649-9392

Institute for Rational Living (Clearwater)
c/o Robert H. Moore, Ph.D.
Belcher Executive Center
1437 S. Belcher Rd., Suite 118
Clearwater, Florida 33516
(813) 443-2096

Institute for Rational Living, N.W.
c/o John Williams, M.A.
3216 N.E. 45th Pl., #105
Seattle, Washington 98105
(206) 527-4884

C

Members of RET International Training Standards and Review Committee

Rene Diekstra, Ph.D.
Hooigracht 15
Leiden, Netherlands

Raymond DiGiuseppe, Ph.D.
230 Hilton Ave.
Hempstead, N.Y. 11550

Albert Ellis, Ph.D.
45 E. 65 St.
New York, N.Y. 10021

Harold Fisher, Ph.D.
3659 Green Rd.
Beachwood, Ohio 44122

Russell Grieger, Ph.D.
2120 Ivy Rd., Suite B
Charlottesville, Va. 22903

Howard Kassinove, Ph.D.
10 Ingold Dr.
Dix Hills, N.Y. 11746

Maxie Maultsby, Jr., M.D.
c/o Provident Hospital
Dept. of Psychiatry
3101 Towanda Ave.
Baltimore, Md. 21215

Ruth Wessler, Ph.D.
4408 Stanley Ave.
Downers Grove, Ill. 60515

Janet L. Wolfe, Ph.D.
45 E. 65 St.
New York, N.Y. 10021

Index